RELIGION AND REVOLUTION

Religion and Revolution

GUENTER LEWY

NEW YORK
OXFORD UNIVERSITY PRESS 1974

To Ilse, Barbara, and Peter

In truth, there never was any remarkable lawgiver amongst any people who did not resort to divine authority, as otherwise his laws would not have been accepted by the people; for there are many good laws, the importance of which is known to the sagacious lawgiver, but the reasons for which are not sufficiently evident to enable him to persuade others to submit to them; and therefore do wise men, for the purpose of removing this difficulty, resort to divine authority. (Book I, chapter xi)
It is therefore the duty of princes and heads of republics to uphold the foundations of the religion of their countries, for then it is easy to keep their people religious, and consequently well conducted and united. (Book I, chapter xii)
Machiavelli, Discourses on the First Ten Books of Titus Livius

It is not true that God wishes there to be rich men enjoying the good things of this world by exploiting the poor: it is not true that God wishes there to be poor people always wretched. Religion is not the opium of the people. Religion is a force that exalts the humble and casts down the mighty from their seats, that gives bread to the hungry and reduces to hunger the overeaters.

Christians and their pastors should know how to recognize the hand of the Almighty in those events that from time to time put down the mighty from their thrones and raise up the humble, send away the rich emptyhanded, and fill the hungry with good things.
Gospel and Revolution, *a pastoral letter by 16 Bishops of the Third World*

Do not despair, be not hesitant, and stop truckling to the godless villains. Begin to fight the battle for the Lord! Now is the time! Encourage your brethren not to offend God's testimony because, if they do, they will ruin everything. Everywhere in Germany, France, and neighboring foreign lands there is a great awakening; the Lord wants to start the game, and for the godless the time is up . . . . Even if there were only three of you, you would be able to fight one hundred thousand if you seek honor in God and in his name. Therefore, strike, strike, strike! This is the moment. These villains cower like dogs . . . . Have no concern for their misery; they will beg you, they will whine and cry like children. Do not show them any mercy. . . . Strike, strike, while the fire is hot . . . . Have no fear, God is on your side!
Thomas Müntzer's *call to battle during the German Peasants' War*

PREFACE

This study was begun almost ten years ago. Following the completion of *The Catholic Church and Nazi Germany*, a work that dealt with a political and social crisis in which the Catholic church had played a largely passive and accommodating role, my intention was to investigate the political posture of the church in other revolutionary upheavals of the past. However, I soon became dissatisfied with this framework of analysis, which struck me as too parochial, and I decided to examine the general relationship of religion and revolution on a larger, cross-cultural scale and from a comparative perspective. From here on the book grew and grew, until it reached its present dimensions. It is now a far bigger treatise than originally intended, but, I hope, also a more interesting work.

A word of introduction is in order about the organization of this book and ways to cope with its volume. The case material is divided into four sections, a division based upon types of revolutionary change rather than religions and one which in broad outline also corresponds to a chronological sequence. I begin by defining the problem to be investigated and provide a brief historical introduction to the political traditions of the major religions (Part I). I examine, next, a series of millenarian movements in which religion provides the inspiration for a messianic dream of terrestrial redemption (Part II). Millenarianism, the expectation of a lasting and final age of justice and bliss on earth, in the past has often been regarded as a totally irrational phenomenon, the preserve of crackpots and religious enthusiasts, and therefore of little interest to social scientists. I suggest that a belief that at times could embolden millions of people to attempt to overthrow the existing political and social order should not be dismissed in so cavalier a fashion, and, in Chapter 11, I therefore undertake a detailed analysis of the political significance of revolutionary millenarianism. This is followed by Part III, an exploration of contemporary religious nationalism in the context of anti-colonial strife. In Part IV, I turn to the encounter between the Catholic church and some modern revolutions of basically secular origins, and, in Part V, I conclude the case material with an examination of the role of religion in several countries of the Third World where religious ideas are enlisted to legitimate radical political and social change.

All of the case studies are self-contained and demand no more background than that provided in the Introduction. It is thus possible to read as few or as many of these chapters as a reader has inclination or leisure. Anyone interested primarily in the general conclusions of this study should concentrate on Chapters 2, 11, and 21–26. The brief references in these theoretical chapters to the historical episodes discussed and analyzed in Parts II–V may whet the reader's appetite for more detail and make him turn to the events, to me fascinating and exciting, that are described in these case studies of revolution. Indeed, a reader will probably find my conclusions more meaningful if he has previously gained some familiarity with the historical record on which these generalizations are based.

This is a work of systematic political and social theory, not of normative philosophy, anthropology, or history. I am not concerned here with the moral justification of either religion or revolution, and I have done neither field work nor have I discovered new historical data. I have sought to acquaint myself with as much of the original source material relating to my case studies as seemed necessary for an understanding of the controversies among specialists and for avoiding too facile use of their work, but in view of the scope of this study I have had to rely primarily upon secondary sources—the findings and observations of scholars with other interests in mind. I have poached upon the preserves of these specialists because the problems I was interested in cut across geographical boundaries, time periods, and disciplines, and because, in the final analysis, the only truly comparative and cross-disciplinary work is that which is carried on not by a group of cooperating specialists but within the mind of one individual investigator. The notes contain the more important sources utilized but no more than that. To cite all of the vast literature bearing on this subject would have converted the book from a work of interpretive scholarship into a bibliography. Every effort has been made to bring the case studies up to date, but revision to take account of the most recent scholarship is, of course, a process that can never be completed. I regret especially that I was unable to benefit from Bryan R. Wilson's new book, *Magic and the Millennium* (London, 1973), which arrived on my desk while I was reading proofs.

Seventeen case studies obviously do not exhaust the range of pertinent data, and specialists in various historical periods or areas will undoubtedly miss one of their favorite episodes. Such selectivity, however, is unavoidable. I set out to develop a framework of inquiry broad enough to allow a comparative analysis while still preserving a discussion of the cases in depth. The aim has been to steer a middle course between the book-length treatment each episode deserves and the fleeting illustrative and largely uninformative reference historical facts often receive in social science theorizing. I also have resisted the temptation to stray into allied problem areas. To probe the relationship of religion and revolution is necessarily to come upon other political manifestations of religion such as sacral kingship or the religious renunciation of and withdrawal from the world of politics. There are the questions posed by Max Weber about the significance of religion for modernization and economic development. All of these issues deserve and indeed have received full-length treatment in their own right, and I have here made only passing references to them for purposes of comparison and contrast.

The romanization of Chinese and the transliteration of Arabic titles of books and articles follow general usage, though I have omitted most diacritics as irritating to the non-specialist reader. Well-known names and terms are given in anglicized form.

I acknowledge with thanks several small awards from the Research Council of the University of Massachusetts/Amherst as well as a major grant from the Advanced Research Projects Agency, made under that agency's program in "Basic Research in Social Change." The latter support provided me with two leaves of absence from teaching duties and enabled me to engage several graduate students with such special language skills as Chinese, Arabic, and Portuguese as research assistants. During the tumultuous days of student protest in the late 1960's, I was criticized by radical students for serving the military establishment, and, at the same time, Senator J. W. Fulbright inserted into the *Congressional Record* summary descriptions of six of my case studies in order to demonstrate how the Department of Defense wasted the taxpayer's money on research without any utility to the military (*Congressional Record*, August 11, 1969, S9624–S9625). I leave it to my readers to evaluate these criticisms.

I also want to thank the Institute for Religion and Social Change, Honolulu, for the opportunity to attend the stimulating conference on Religion and Political Modernization held at the East-West Center in March of 1971. An early version of chapter 18 of this book was presented there as a conference paper and will be published by Yale University Press in the proceedings of the conference, *Religion and Political Modernization*, edited by Donald E. Smith.

In the collection of material for this study I have had the help of several research assistants to whom I want to record my indebtedness: Betsy Halpern Amaru, Carol Ann Childress, José Dória, Maria Teresa Chanco Goodrich, Hatem Ishaq Hussaini, Nathan Lai, Frederick A. Lazin, and Elizabeth Palter—all sometime students at the University of Massachusetts, Amherst; James Friguglietti and Mary Morgan, formerly at Harvard University and Smith College, respectively. The number of friends and colleagues who over the years have read and criticized chapters and sections of this study as it gradually took shape is large, and I express my gratitude to all of them. I am especially grateful to Stanley Rothman and Hans Speier whose critical reading of the theoretical chapters was most helpful. Needless to say, the conclusions reached in this book remain for better or for worse my own responsibility.

Two chapters and one section of another chapter have previously appeared in print; I acknowledge permission to republish in somewhat revised form as follows:

Preface

"Militant Buddhist Nationalism: The Case of Burma" is reprinted by permission from *Journal of Church and State* XIV (Winter 1972): 19–41.

An early version of Chapter 17 appeared under the title, "The Uses of Insurrection: The Church and Franco's War," in *Continuum* III (1965): 267–90 and is reprinted by permission of the editor, Justus George Lawler.

A section of Chapter 2 formed part of my essay, "Changing Conceptions of Political Legitimacy: Abandonment of Theocracy in the Islamic World," in David Spitz, ed., *Political Theory and Social Change* (New York, 1967) and is reprinted by permission of Aldine-Atherton Press.

A final word of gratitude is due my wife and my children for their forbearance.

G. L.

Northampton, Massachusetts
October 1973

CONTENTS

Contents

RELIGION AND REVOLUTION

Introduction

CHAPTER 1

Statement of the Problem

The political implications and consequences of the world's religions have been extremely varied. Religion has often been a force upholding the status quo, reinforcing the stability of society and enhancing political quietism. The Hindu doctrine of *karma*, for example, promising reincarnation into a higher caste as a reward for diligently fulfilling the obligations of one's station in this life, certainly discouraged social and political protest. Protestant Pentecostal sects in the United States, Latin America, and Africa downgrade deprivation here on earth and, by concentrating on communion with the Holy Spirit and the rewards of heaven, which are vouchsafed the faithful, help reconcile their members to a lowly social and economic status. Similar doctrines encouraging either meek acceptance of suffering or withdrawal from the tribulations of human society can be found in other religions. And yet, religion has also been an important force facilitating radical political and social change, providing the motivation, ideological justification, and social cohesion for rebellions and revolutions. Religiously inspired revolutionary movements have occurred throughout history; the search for the Millennium, often led by a messianic figure, has sparked numerous revolutionary movements many of which have produced significant political and social innovation. A series of basic questions, therefore, can be asked: Under what conditions does religion become a force for revolt rather than social integration? Can certain religious concepts and attitudes be singled out as promotive or inhibitive of revolutionary sentiments and activity? How relevant is the organizational structure of religion? How decisive is the role of charismatic prophet figures?

Before questions of such scope and magnitude can be considered, we must define certain concepts. Without a definition of key terms we lack a real subject; it is such a definition that designates and circumscribes the topic to be investigated.

A good definition should be precise in meaning and should clearly distinguish the phenomenon to be studied from others with which it might be confused if we rely on informal and nontechnical discourse. Thus a useful definition of religion should enable us to differentiate between religion and magic as well as, say, Judaism and ideologies like Marxism or fascism which often are called "secular religions." In our inquiry "religion" is defined as follows: *Religion is a cultural institution, a complex of symbols, articles of faith, and practices adhered to by a group of believers that are related to, and commonly invoke the aid of, superhuman powers and provide answers to questions of ultimate meaning.*

Religion, inasmuch as it involves man's intellectual and moral faculties, forms part of his culture. A particular religion constitutes an institution, for it is based on some kind of social organization, it continues to exist in a more or less stable form from generation to generation, and this existence generally does not depend upon new and creative acts of individuals. A philosophy of life like Marxism or communism can also become institutionalized, it can serve as the official ideology of a country's ruling party, as the basis of social values, and it can produce a pantheon of prophets. But whereas a visit to the embalmed body of Lenin in the Kremlin for some citizens of the Soviet Union may approach the quality of a religious experience, by and large ideologies lack what we consider the unique characteristic of religion, to wit, the belief in superhuman powers that assist or harm man. Such powers belong to the realm of the superhuman or, in intellectually more advanced societies, the realm of the supernatural, because they are more powerful than men or stand outside the regularities of nature by being invisible, immortal, and the like. Magic, too, invokes superhuman powers by utilizing religious means of communication such as prayer, meditation, and sacrifice, but, unlike religion, it does not provide answers to questions about man's nature, purpose, or fate. Magic serves as primitive man's technology; it enlists superhuman forces to control natural phenomena such as sickness or drought, but it does not speak to

man's quest for meaning or relate to what Paul Tillich has called
matters of "ultimate concern." [1]

Our research universe, therefore, will include Judaism, Christianity, Islam, Buddhism, Hinduism, Taoism, Confucianism, and
certain lesser known, often syncretic, cults of more limited distribution; it will exclude the so-called "secular religions" even
though the latter may also involve nonrational beliefs, quasi-apoc-
alyptic visions, the revered authority of prophets, or the satisfaction of certainty. In each case it will be necessary to focus on the
concrete manifestations of these systems of religious belief. The
category "religion," which is fairly clear in the Christian world,
for example, is much more problematical in countries like India
where religion and other elements of culture are intermixed. In
most peasant cultures we find a great tradition of the learned few
and the popular beliefs of the many which represent an amalgam
of different gods and spirits. The importance of distinguishing between religion as a system of ideas and the actual social institu-
tionalization of religious doctrines must therefore be borne in
mind at all times.[2]

It should be added that we will deal with religion solely as a
human activity and as a product of human consciousness. We
will not be concerned with the truth or falsity of religious beliefs;
our inquiry, limited to what is empirically available, is based on
what Peter Berger has fittingly described as "methodological
atheism." Such a perspective, unlike atheism, is essentially agnos-
tic, for while it views religion *sub specie temporis*, it leaves unanswered the question whether and how religion might also be
viewed *sub specie aeternitatis*. "In other words, to say that religion is a human projection does not logically preclude the possibility that the projected meanings may have an ultimate status independent of man." [3]

A useful definition of revolution, too, should delineate
recurring and important constitutive elements as well as reduce
terminological confusion.[4] Some writers insist that violence represents "an irreducible element of any revolution" [5]; others call revolution "any action, however bloodless, which transforms the political order to transform society." [6] In some countries—Burma,
Mexico, Egypt, and others—revolution is seen as the central
fact of a continuing social and political order, and "the Revolution" has become the symbol of national identity as well as legiti-

macy.[7] For our purposes we shall adopt the following definition of a "political revolution": *Revolution is an abrupt, though not necessarily violent, change in the political system, including the nature of rulership or constitution and the principles of legitimacy upon which these rest.*

This definition enables us to differentiate between revolution and rebellion, a distinction already made in antiquity. Aristotle in discussing the causes of sedition (*stasis*), among which he included the desire to bring the existing order in line with a different conception of justice, distinguished between the endeavor of a seditious party "to get the administration into the hands of its members" while continuing "to maintain the system of government" (rebellion) and sedition "directed against the existing constitution" with the intent "to change its nature" (revolution).[8] Some revolutions, like the French Revolution or the Russian Revolution of October 1917, introduced not only a new political constitution but a new social order. The American Revolution, on the other hand, only introduced a new political system.

A *coup d'état* is a rebellion; it changes the incumbents in office without challenging the authority of the office itself or changing the constitutional framework. Most rebellions lack an ideology that differs from the values prevailing in the society in question. The Twelve Articles of the German peasant uprising of 1525 with their limited demands for justice are a case in point (though most of the groups participating in this revolt soon went beyond this program of reform). It may not be possible to determine whether a particular revolutionary outbreak (a term we will use throughout in its broad and nontechnical sense) represents a rebellion or a revolution until we see what use the new masters make of their power.[9] The coup of the Free Officers in Egypt in 1952 at first appeared to be no more than the prelude to another shuffling of portfolios; it later turned into a revolution. Even a legal transfer of political power, like Hitler's appointment as German chancellor in January 1933, may usher in a revolution. Utilizing legal and illegal means, and violence as well as legislative processes, Hitler within several months succeeded in revolutionizing Germany's political, legal, and social reality. The Nazi Revolution was a revolution against modernity, but a revolution just the same.[10]

The difference between revolution and rebellion is thus clear in theory though often hard to apply in practice. As with the difference between revolution and reform, many cases will be borderline situations. Crane Brinton observes:

> The difference between a revolution and other kinds of changes in societies is, to judge from many past users of the term, logically nearer to that between a mountain and a hill than to that, say between the freezing point and the boiling point of a given substance. The physicist can measure boiling points exactly; the social scientist cannot measure change by any such exact thermometer, and say exactly when ordinary change boils over into revolutionary change.[11]

The phenomenon of revolution, the abrupt replacement of one political order by another, is as old as written history, and perhaps older, even though the term "revolution," borrowed from astronomy, has been in use only in modern times. The fact that many ancient visions of a new and better society involved a return to a Golden Age of the past, in our view, does not establish the unrevolutionary nature of these dreams. They must be judged by the existing situation, as the historican Lawrence Stone insisted, and then "it makes no difference whatever whether the idealized Golden Age is in the past or in the future. All that matters is the degree to which the vision differs from the reality of the present." [12] Moreover, many of these conceptions of a perfect age to come did involve a complete break with the past and conjured up a vision of something entirely new. For example, the "new heaven and new earth" predicted by the author of the New Testament Book of Revelation represented a dream of radical renewal, one that continued to have a powerful appeal to dissenters and sectarians in later centuries. To deny that mass movements such as the Bohemian Taborite movement of the fifteenth century, for instance, were genuinely revolutionary would appear to fly in the face of common sense, and if today we call many of these upheavals rebellions rather than revolutions this is due not so much to the alleged restricted scope of their goals and programs but rather to the fact that they were defeated or that they failed. Revolutionary mass movements inspired by eschatological religious visions can be found throughout the world.[13]

In our study we will deal for the most part with revolutions and revolutionary movements. Some of these involve revolts against foreign rule, whereas others are directed against a domestic elitist class. Some revolutionary outbreaks, such as the revolt of the Jews against Syrian rule under the Maccabees in 165 B.C., include elements of a struggle for national liberation as well as a struggle against domestic collaborators with foreign rulers. Millenarian movements like the cargo cults of Melanesia partake of elements of revolution, though they also exhibit traditional elements more in keeping with a rebellion. It will be part of our task to investigate whether religious variables contribute to the distinction between rebellion and revolution and whether they relate to the transformation of one into the other.

Our inquiry is not concerned with a systematic study of either religion or revolution per se, but rather with the interaction of these two phenomena—revolutionary upheavals in which religion is a causal variable. We explore their relationship through a detailed examination of seventeen case studies of revolution in which religion has played a significant role and by a concomitant study of ancillary evidence from other sources. The case study approach has been chosen in order to include material from a great variety of historical settings and because only a historical perspective can provide the dynamic view of social and, in particular, revolutionary change. Each case study, tracing the dissolution and overthrow of a particular political or social order, furnishes the opportunity to learn the causes—both underlying and precipitating—of a specific revolutionary upheaval while also contributing to an understanding of the general factors involved in revolutionary change. It is the careful analysis of such historical revolutions that makes possible an appreciation of the subtle relationship of ideas and events, religious beliefs and social life, and individuals and classes, as well as the vagaries of chance. History thus functions as the social theorist's laboratory and compensates him somewhat for the lack of experimental data.

The social theorist's use of history as a source of data upon which to base his hypotheses, as a panorama to stimulate his imagination, and as a testing ground for his conclusions is, of course, not new. The dependence of systematic political theory upon the comparative study of polities was first stressed by Aristotle; following him Machiavelli, Bodin, Montesquieu, Spencer, and many others have used historical data to discover similarities as well as differences in the development of political institutions or in what we today call political behavior. In the field of religion and politics Max Weber stands out as the most successful practitioner of the comparative method. Weber used data from societies widely separated from each other in time and space; his superiority over his distinguished predecessors, it has been suggested, was largely due to the availability of more reliable historical information.[14]

In our study of religion and revolution we will use comparative analysis. After examining in as complete a manner as the subject matter allows [15] the role of religion in particular revolutionary episodes, we will compare our conclusions to ascertain whether they resemble each other and whether they can lead to propositions that seem to hold true in a variety of societal and religious settings.[16] The comparative method facilitates the testing of conclusions and generalizations. One important way of making inferences about a cause is to determine the effects of the cause in other cases—to apply what John Stuart Mill called "the method of difference." The assumption, for example, that the attitude of the Spanish hierarchy toward Franco's rebellion was determined by traditional Catholic teaching on the legitimacy of resistance to constituted authority on its face is not unreasonable. Yet the adequacy of this assumption could be weakened by showing that the same body of doctrine in another set of analogous circumstances did not have the same results. The examination of deviant cases is important in view of the fact that one can find confirming evidence for most hypotheses, and, since, as Karl Popper has emphasized, it is disproof and not proof that enables us to strengthen hypotheses and establish causal relationships.[17]

The case study approach makes it possible to examine the role of the religious factor in concrete historical situations. This means, for example, that, instead of taking as one of our variables religious doctrine per se, we observe religious beliefs as actually interpreted and acted upon at certain times by individual men or groups of men. The intentions of the founders of the great religions—even if we could definitely ascertain how they lived and what their aims were—are for our purposes of secondary importance. Religious teachings never emerge or exist in a social vacuum, and we will raise the question why some men see or understand religious ideas differently from other men. In studying religious groups one must bear in mind that the political posture of these groups is influenced by nonreligious factors such as economic interests and political outlook of their members, leadership exerted by outstanding men, institutional concerns, and the like. Last, but not least, one must recognize the rich texture of human life which defies attempts to impose universal laws upon history; we must heed the warning of Marx, which that great theorist himself often forgot, against "using as one's master key a general historico-philosophical theory, the supreme virtue of which consists in being super-historical." [18] Social theory, if it is to yield meaningful insights and explanations rather than spectral categories or empyrean abstractions, must remain anchored in the real world of complexity and unexpected events. Its generalizations, as Robert Nisbet has insisted, must be derived from the empirical, the concrete, and the historical. "Whatever the demands of a social theory, the first demands to be served are those of the social reality we find alone in the historical record." [19]

The introductory survey in the following chapter is therefore historically oriented. We do not attempt to determine what Buddha, Jesus, or Mohammed really meant, but rather look at the way certain basic religious teachings have been perceived over time and what their political impact has been. For each of the great historical religions we have introduced as much detail as seemed necessary to provide a historical framework for our case studies.

CHAPTER 2

Religion and Revolution: The Major Traditions

HINDUISM

Hinduism, the dominant religion of India, is characterized by extraordinarily fluid doctrines and practices: it represents a highly "complex array of forms and myths and styles of life," a "farrago of beliefs and customs," [1] which has been used to justify political quietism, nonviolent resistance to foreign domination, and revolutionary terrorism.

The Vedic hymns, the earliest historical record of the Indo-Aryan invaders of northern India, were composed between 1500–1000 B.C.; they reveal an optimistic outlook on life and lack the ascetic temper so important in later Indian religious thought. The gods of the Aryans were hero-gods similar to those of Homeric times, and their kings were warrior-kings dependent upon the support of tribal assemblies. The acceptance of the king by his subjects cannot be understood in terms of modern elections, but, as one student of the period concludes, "the role of the people in the coronation ceremony, and their power to banish the king point to a degree of popular control in the Vedic age that was never equaled in later times." [2]

As the Aryan conquerors extended their domination over the darker aborigines, class lines hardened. The king became increasingly dependent upon rite and magic, and the power of the priest (*brahmana*) expanded. During this Brahmanic period of Indian history, which spanned the years 800–500 B.C., there emerged an increasingly rigid division of society into four classes—priests, warriors, peasants, and serfs—which, in modified form, has survived to this day. The origin of the Indian caste system is still

somewhat controversial, but its significance in the development of
the social order in later centuries is clear. Each class had its code
of divinely and socially approved conduct and duties (*dharma*),
and rank order was accepted as given and beyond challenge.
Birth into a particular class was the result of actions (*karma*) in
earlier existences, and only by diligently fulfilling the obligations
of his caste could an individual hope to be reborn into a higher
order. In this life there was no escape from the caste order. Such
a world view, as Max Weber observed, did not provide a basis
for social protest, there was no natural equality before God, "no
'natural' order of men and things in contrast to positive social
order. There was no sort of 'natural law.' " [3] Salvation meant
final emancipation from the cycle of rebirth, to be attained
through faithfully accepting the duties of one's class.

At the apex of the social pyramid stood the brahman, the authoritative interpretor of *dharma*, variously defined to include the
sacred Vedic tradition, custom, and the system of social duties.
The royal chaplain (*purohita*) was especially important. He pro-
cured victory through his prayer and sacrifice, he provided guidance, and, at times, he even served as the king's minister. Exalted
as the chief brahman's position was, in practice he did not challenge the secular authority. Unlike the Catholic priesthood in
medieval Europe, brahmans lacked a hierarchical church organization that could be used to build up temporal power. The separation of religious and secular spheres of authority was accepted,
and the system tended "to prevent irresponsible tyranny on the
one hand, and thoroughgoing theocracy on the other." [4]

The position of the brahmans was successfully challenged by
the rival systems of Jainism and Buddhism. Both arose during the
sixth century before the Christian era, that period of intellectual
ferment in the world that also gave rise to the Greek philosophers, the Hebrew prophets, Confucius, and Zarathustra. But
after about A.D. 200 both Jainism and Buddhism were gradually
displaced by the older creed which, embellished and modified by
heterodoxy, came to be known as Hinduism (the religion of the
Hindus—the Persian word for Indians). For reasons still only
partially understood, the earlier optimistic temper of Vedic
thought by now had been superseded by a wave of pessimism and
a desire to escape from the world. The universe was seen as
lodged in a period of decline and decay from which there was no

realistic hope of delivery. At the time of worst distress, according to one important school of Hindu cosmology, the universal god Vishnu would reappear as a messiah, judge the wicked, and restore the original age of plenty and happiness. But this incarnation of Vishnu under the name Kalki was not expected before the year 32,899 (on the Christian calendar).[5] The remoteness of the divine savior's appearance, and the fact that even he could not break the endlessly repeated cosmic cycle and bring lasting redemption, are important reasons why the idea of a messiah is not significant in Hinduism.[6]

Ancient and medieval Indian political thought considered man to be inherently evil and sinful, and kingship, instituted by divine decree, was the consequence of and remedy for man's imperfection. Only the ruler could preserve the social system and prevent total ruin.[7] Political thought emphasized order and cautioned against disturbing tradition and established institutions. It stressed the discharge of duties in a stratified social order, and it was centered around the concept of civil obligation. Still, as Drekmeier points out, "there always existed for the Hindu, as for the Western liberal, a criterion above the state by which its actions could be judged. It was not the idea of the sanctity of the individual personality or the association; it was sacred law and tradition." [8] The subject as such had no rights in the modern sense, but the ruler had duties and responsibilities under the sacred law from which privileges of the ruled could be inferred. Even the divine status that many Indian kings claimed did not confer arbitrary authority. At least in theory, only the king who fulfilled his duties could claim divine stature; divine right, as in medieval Europe, was "located in the institution of kingship and not in the king himself." [9] Moreover, divinity in the eyes of ancient India did not mean infallibility for even the gods could sin. Hence, the doctrine of royal divinity did not protect the king from possible challenge by his subjects.

The primary duty of the king was to protect his people and to promote their prosperity.[10] If he failed, he became subversive of *dharma* and most sources justified revolt against him. The *Mahabharata*, for example, the great epic of India, completed by about A.D. 400, says that "the subjects should arm themselves for killing that king who does not protect them, who simply plunders their riches, who confounds all distinctions." Such a king "should be killed by his subjects in a body like a dog that is affected with rabies and has become mad." [11] According to some traditions, the gods and not the people were to be relied upon to punish a ruler who had failed to fulfill the obligations of his office—a doctrine similar to the Chinese Mandate of Heaven concept [12]—but nearly all theorists are agreed that the king was subordinate to the sacred law and brought destruction upon himself by defying it. "Though there was no constitutional restraint on the Hindu king, the dharmic code itself must have served as a powerful check on his conduct in office. For the king, like the humblest of his subjects, could be reborn in a despised form." [13]

Of course, the moral justification of revolt against a tyrannical ruler does not amount to an acceptance of popular sovereignty as some recent writers have argued. Monarchy was the form of government commonly adhered to, and the history of pre-Muslim India knows many palace revolutions but not a single successful popular revolt.[14] The general spirit was one of acceptance of the stratified dharmic order, resignation to an imperfect world. The desire for a better life in the here and now was discouraged by the doctrine of *karma* and the general devaluation of earthly concerns. Freedom meant escape from the cycle of birth and rebirth; it related to the salvation of the soul rather than to the individual's status in society. Hence ancient India brought forth treatises on statecraft but no political philosophy in the Western sense. Political questions are answered through myths and legends, a fact that facilitated the emergence of divergent interpretations of India's political heritage by the awakening country's nationalist movement.

CONFUCIANISM

Traditional China has been called the land of three religions—Confucianism, Taoism, and Buddhism. Though this characterization is not inaccurate, it is inadequate in that it fails to take into account China's many syncretic sects and, especially, the indigenous religious system which left a deep and permanent imprint upon Chinese life. Since this religion developed and matured during the Shang, Chou, and Early Han dynasties, China's classical period, beginning about 1600 B.C., it is often called the classical religion.

Chinese classical religion had four main elements: Ancestor worship, the worship of Heaven and other native deities, divination, and sacrifice. Political and religious authority were combined, and the king served as high priest. He was called the "Son of Heaven" and was said to rule with the help of his divine ancestors. The welfare of the state and the fertility of the land and the people were seen as dependent upon the correct performance by the ruler-priest of certain state ceremonies, rituals, and sacrificial rites. Divination fortified political leadership, and political decisions thus became commands of the gods.[15]

The supreme god of the Shang period had been a powerful spirit called *Ti*, a god of vegetation. *Ti* was regarded as the founder of the Shang dynasty, and his royal descendants, therefore, ruled by right divine. When the leaders of the Chou tribe overthrew the Shang dynasty around 1028 B.C., they combined *Ti*, the ancestor spirit of the Shang, with their own cult of heaven (*T'ien*), in which the sun, the stars, and the earth were the objects of supreme worship. This merger helped the Chou kings legitimate their rebellion against the descendants of *Ti*, and it facilitated the transfer of the divine right to rule. The new supreme deity now was Heaven, an anthropomorphic power that directed the universe and took a personal interest in the well-being of the Chinese people. Moreover, this supreme god demanded righteousness and good government, and he deposed rulers who abused their office. The Shang dynasty, it was argued, had rebelled against Heaven, and it therefore had been rightfully overthrown; Heaven itself had conferred the right to rule upon the Chou.[16]

In the writings of the period the Duke of Chou appears as the author of this doctrine of the "Mandate of Heaven," an idea of far-reaching importance for Chinese political thought and practice. In a proclamation to the conquered Shang people the Duke, speaking in the name of his brother, King Wu, described the transfer of the favor of Heaven:

> . . . your ruler . . . was extremely dissolute, and despised the commands of Heaven . . . he was lazy and slothful, slighted the labours of government, and did not make pure sacrifices, so that Heaven sent down this ruin on him. . . .

Heaven then sought among your many regions . . . for one who
might be attentive to its commands, but there was none able to do
so. There was, however, our Chou king, who treated the multitudes well and was virtuous, and presided carefully over the sacrifices to the spirits and to Heaven. Heaven therefore instructed us
to avail ourselves of its favour; it chose us and gave us the decree
of Shang, to rule over your many regions.[17]

Confucius was born in 551 B.C. China by then had become an
unstable confederation of feudal principalities. The King of Chou
still used the title "Son of Heaven," but heads of states no longer
deferred to him. The teachings of Confucius, it appears, were
aimed at overcoming the political chaos of the day and at restoring peace; they were practical rather than metaphysical, and they
emphasized ethical conduct. The apotheosis of Confucius and his
elevation to the status of a divine sage, credited with moral infallibility, did not take place until centuries later. Confucius himself
went out of his way to disclaim any such attribute.[18]

This is not to say, as some modern interpreters have argued,
that Confucius was a pure humanist. He urged respect for the
spirits, emphasized the sacrificial ceremonies, and taught the importance of fate and of obedience and conformity to the way of
Heaven. Man fulfilled himself by acting in accordance with the
will of Heaven, the guiding divine providence. Though Confucius was sparing in his resort to supernatural sanctions for his
teachings, his deep personal piety and religiosity stand out
clearly. In this sense the original teachings of Confucius, which
stress man's dependence upon a supreme deity, lead logically to
the later doctrines of Confucianism, which must be considered a
religion and not simply an ethico-political philosophy.[19]

Confucius was a teacher who taught the virtues of a proper
member of the ruling feudal class, though he insisted that the distinction between the aristocracy and ordinary people be based
not upon birth but talent and virtue, a new idea. He stressed the
cultivation of character, the rules of conduct toward one's family
as well as society at large. The well-ordered, patriarchal family
was the prototype of state and society. At the same time, he had
broad ambitions to reform the ways of rulers in a more direct
manner. Confucius wanted them to return to the ways of their
ancestors when society had allegedly been fused into a well-
ordered whole, and the state had been headed by a sage-king cho-

sen for his individual merit. The early Chou period was pictured as such a utopia, and Confucius, albeit unsuccessfully, sought to find a savior-king who would, under his tutelage, bring back this ideal time of Chinese unity, peace, and justice.[20] The conception of history revealed here is regressive: the Golden Age of mankind lies in the past rather than in the future. "The movement of history since then has been one of progressive degeneration. Hence man's salvation consists not in the creation of something new, but in a return to what has already existed." [21] The human world, moreover, is part of the universal macrocosm and, like the latter, conforms to a pattern of cyclical rather than linear movement. History has neither beginning nor end, and the possibility of progress or of a final redemption of mankind, as we find it in Judaism, Christianity, and Islam, is denied.[22] The Confucian ethic held no idea of salvation. Though the world as it existed was not necessarily accepted "as given," and there was much criticism of the political order of the day, nevertheless, the best that mankind could expect under this theory of history was a return to the past when the *tao* (the governing principle and universal law of the cosmic and social order) was seen to have been in perfect operation. The fervor of a messianic movement seeking to usher in the Millennium, an age of new and unheard of perfection, was not likely to develop and, in fact, it never did emerge under the Confucian world view. As we shall see later, the messianic sects of China grew out of Taoism and Buddhism rather than Confucianism.

The doctrine of the Mandate of Heaven had been brought into being to legitimate the rebellion of the Chou, and it continued to serve as an instrument of social control, to command acceptance of political power. But just as the doctrine had justified the seizure of power by the Chou dynasty, it could be invoked by new aspirants after the supreme rulership for the mandate was not held in perpetuity. A ruler could antagonize Heaven which would then deprive him of the mandate and give it to another. The problem of how one could determine who was the rightful possessor of the Mandate of Heaven was solved by Mencius, Confucius' great pupil, born 390 BC., by the introduction of the criterion of public opinion, the acceptance of a ruler by the people. If a country was well administered, and the people were at peace with their king, this was an indication that Heaven approved of this ruler and that he enjoyed the heavenly mandate. On the other hand, if the people rallied to the cause of an insurgent who deposed the king this, too, was an expression of the will of Heaven and showed that the earlier ruler had lost his mandate. "Heaven," said Mencius, "does not express itself in words. Heaven indicates its wishes through the actions and service of others." [23]

Mencius went a step further than earlier proponents of the doctrine of the Mandate of Heaven and declared that when a ruler has lost Heaven's approval he may be resisted and even slain. The killing of Chou, the last king of the Shang dynasty, in his eyes was not regicide but the legitimate punishment of one who had forfeited the right to rule. To the question whether a subject may slay his prince, Mencius replied: "A man who despoils Humanity I call a robber; a man who despoils Justice, a ruffian. Robbers and ruffians are mere commoners. I was aware that the commoner Chou was slain, but unaware that a prince was slain." [24] As in Christian medieval thought the distinction between the office of kingship and the specific occupant of a royal throne enabled Christian writers to disobey the Pauline command not to resist those in power, so did Mencius here defend tyrannicide by invoking the Confucian moral duties of the ruler toward his subjects.

Mencius' emphasis on the role of the people, even if we assume that he meant only the educated elite, for very obvious reasons never became very popular with the rulers of China, though it never disappeared completely. In the later development of the doctrine of the Mandate of Heaven other indices of legitimacy took their place alongside that of public opinion. Strictly speaking, the Mandate of Heaven modified, if it did not rule out, the principle of hereditary succession, for each new Son of Heaven was chosen for his individual merit.[25] In practice, however, dynastic succession made an early appearance, and rulers attempted to legitimate their title by tracing their lineage to ancient emperors with gods as fathers. Needless to say, pretenders to the throne were no less adept at fabricating such genealogies to prove the divine origin of their families, and dynastic rivalries could not be prevented or settled geneologically.

Another way of strengthening or challenging legitimacy involved the appearance of portents and omens. Both emperors and rebels regularly resorted to such supernatural manifestations as evidence that they possessed the divine right. Known as the theory of the "interaction between Heaven and Man," it was first developed systematically by the Yin-Yang school of the third century B.C.; this theory postulated the close interdependency of the world of man and the world of nature. A disturbance in one sphere, it was asserted, would cause a disturbance in the other. Bad conduct on the part of the ruler, for example, could upset the harmony of the system and would lead to freakish occurrences in the natural world. An anthropomorphic Heaven would send warnings in the form of an eclipse of the sun on an unusual day such as New Year's, shooting stars, the birth of deformed animals or humans. If these warnings were disregarded Heaven could also impose punishments such as floods, earthquakes, and other natural disasters.[26]

The belief that freakish occurrences in the natural world could be explained in supernatural terms and had portentous significance undoubtedly was of ancient origin. During the Han dynasty (206 B.C.-A.D. 220) these beliefs were more explicitly linked to the political life of the country, and a corps of court astronomers was entrusted with interpreting the wishes of Heaven and peering into the secrets of Heaven's preordained plan for mankind. The government's monopoly on such interpretations was important because it prevented the use of unusual phenomena of nature by dissenting groups or individuals who might invoke them as signs of Heaven's displeasure with the ruler. Nevertheless, there is ample evidence to indicate that this control was never fully effective and that astronomy, astrology, and meteorology as well as outright magic and sorcery became political tools.[27]

The traditional Chinese monarch, unlike his counterpart in the Western tradition of divine right monarchy, was thus responsible not only to God but also to the people. His charisma depended upon his performance as ruler, and he was held accountable for his blunders. As Max Weber has correctly noted, Western monarchs reigning by divine right were *de facto* irresponsible, "but the Chinese emperor ruled in the genuine sense of charismatic authority. He had to prove himself as the 'Son of Heaven' and as the lord approved by Heaven insofar as the people fared well under him. If he failed, he simply lacked charisma. Thus, if the rivers broke the dikes, or if rain did not fall despite the sacrifices

made, it was evidence—such was expressly taught—that the
emperor did not have the charismatic qualities demanded by
Heaven." [28]

If the emperor was strong, and lucky, public penitence for his
sins would restore the luster of his throne and reestablish his charisma. But in many cases the discredited emperor would be overthrown or made to abdicate. The Confucian teachings of kindness
and moderation made the bloodless mode of political change the
preferred way, and Chinese history records many instances of
peaceful changes of dynasty. But with respect to the supernatural
sanctions involved in the transfer of the Mandate of Heaven,
there was no real difference between abdication and the forceful
seizure of the throne. Favorable omens were essential in both instances, and Confucian scholars usually stood ready with suitable
interpretations of portentous events.[29]

The short-lived Ch'in dynasty (221–207 B.C.) is credited with
the great achievement of unifying China and building a centralized state of great power. This vast empire was achieved through
conquest and extremely harsh political practices that followed the
ideas of the Legalist school of political thought. Instead of a government of virtue the Legalists emphasized the importance of a
strong ruler, wielding the sword of justice without undue humanitarian scruples. These repressive methods caused considerable
resentment, and when the Former Han dynasty assumed power
in 206 B.C. a new philosophical justification of the state took the
place of Legalism—Confucianism.

The Confucianism of the Han period was rather different from
the relatively sober and rational outlook of either Confucius or
Mencius. The Han emperors sought to fortify their imperial
power, "as the Chinese expression has it 'make a shield behind,'
and any god, demon, rite, or device of magic which served that
end was welcome to them." [30] As a result, and as we have had
occasion to note earlier, the court teamed with magicians, astrologers, and various other experts in the occult—many of them
Confucians—who interpreted omens and portents in the interests of the emperor and demonstrated his heavenly mandate
through elaborate rituals and ceremonies. In this new Confucianism, perhaps as a result of Legalist influence or simply for opportunistic reasons, the principle of hereditary monarchy was fully
accepted. Alongside the simple sayings of Confucius there devel-

oped an elaborate system of texts; disputes over the authenticity of these documents provided the occasion for endless quarrels. But Confucianism was not all superstition and magic. The Confucian scholars, the literati, were also increasingly the teachers and guardians of China's literary heritage, and their good will, therefore, was important beyond their role as diviners of fate. The final step in making Confucianism the official creed of the empire took place during the reign of Emperor Wu-ti (140–87 B.C.) whose acts can be compared to Constantine's adoption of Christianity. The learned Wu established five colleges in the capital for the study of the five Confucian Classics—the *Book of Change*, the *Book of History*, the *Book of Poetry*, the *Book of Rites*, and the *Spring and Autumn*. The authorship of these texts cannot be determined; they are collections of folk literature, legendary history, and magical observances. It is agreed today that most of them were written long before Confucius, though the Confucian school had preserved them. Han scholars attributed these works to the master and his disciples, and it was they who called them the "Confucian Classics." More importantly, these classics were made the basis of a system of competitive examinations for the civil service, and it was this action that truly marked the triumph of Confucianism. From that time on, and until the twentieth century, the Confucian scholar-officials functioned as the country's intellectual aristocracy and elite. The number of books in the sacred canon changed several times, and the examinations, too, were modified repeatedly, but until 1904 the system continued to channel the best minds into the service of the state. It provided the social order with a much needed stability and enabled it to survive the rise and fall of dynasties.

Some scholars have suggested that the Emperor Wu-ti granted Confucianism official recognition because its doctrines emphasized the subservience of subjects to their ruler and therefore would bolster his authority. Deference and complete subordination to elders and betters were indeed cardinal features of a social ethic that stressed the importance of maintaining the existing social hierarchy.[31] And yet, Confucianism also included a component of social criticism. The emphasis on family solidarity and filial piety not only inculcated obedience but also limited the authority of rulers. The state had to respect the institution of the family, and a king who failed to create conditions in which sons could maintain their parents in peace and comfort was seen to have forfeited his divine mandate. Moreover, though the subsidizing of scholarship by the government often made the Confucian literati subservient to the wishes of rulers, many times the scholars insisted upon the moral qualifications of kingship, and they used their position to criticize and restrain the exercise of absolute power.[32]

Confucianism from the time of Han was more than just a creed to be accepted or rejected; it became a part of China's ethos and shaped the thinking of its people as well as its rulers. But the state religion of traditional China did not consist only of adherence to the Confucian principles of morality. The Confucian Classics also contained the old doctrine of the supremacy of Heaven, which thus remained an important part of the Confucian orthodoxy. The emperor was regarded as the Son of Heaven, and he functioned as the high priest of the cult of Heaven. The temporal power in this way demonstrated its identification with divine providence, and an elaborate system of sacrifices and rituals, performed by the emperor upon the altars of the palace and in the ancestral temple of the imperial family in the capital, served to ensure Heaven's good will for the realm. Alongside the great deities of Heaven and Earth, the emperor also paid tribute to his deified ancestors, and he inaugurated the spring season with a ritual plowing.[33] The performance of these rites indicated possession of the Mandate of Heaven, and the worship of Heaven therefore was a jealously guarded prerogative of the monarch. The plea for Heaven's supernatural blessings was the exclusive preserve of the established ruler. Individuals and groups who engaged in private worship of Heaven therefore were suspected of seeking to enlist the sanction of Heaven in a political struggle for power and, as we shall see more fully below, they were vigorously persecuted.[34]

The cult of Heaven symbolized the bond between the supreme deity and the ruler, but it had no emotional appeal to the individual. The day-to-day religious needs of the Chinese from time immemorial had been met not only through ancestor worship but also by the worship of numerous deities and spirits. In the words of a student of Chinese religion:

In the villages and in other localities they have temples for the worship of mountains, streams, rocks, stones, and the like. Besides, the people worship in their temples all kinds of patron divinities whose origin it is often hardly possible, or quite impossible, to trace. They are generally thought to have lived as human beings. There are gods and goddesses, invoked for the cure of particular illnesses; goddesses for safety in childbearing; gods who impart riches, or, bestowing blessing on various professions, are patrons of the callings of life; in fine, a multitude of idols who bestow every possible grace and favor.[35]

After the emergence of Taoism and Buddhism, to which we will return, the popular religion was often enriched with accretions from these new religious systems until the origins of many of the magico-spiritual beliefs could no longer be determined. To the common people this blurring of religious doctrines hardly mattered. The majority of the Chinese, as the saying goes, have "worn a Confucian crown, a Taoist robe, and a pair of Buddhist sandals."[36] Whereas the literati regarded Confucianism, Taoism, and Buddhism mainly as systems of philosophy, the common people worshipped the founders of these systems—Confucius, Lao-tzu, and Buddha—as supernatural beings, often in the same local shrine. To obtain a male heir, a Chinese might pray in a Buddhist temple, whereas he might pray in a Taoist shrine, dedicated to the patron of medicine, for the return of his health.

The rulers of China disapproved of religious disputes that might lead to political disturbances, but they were otherwise indifferent to the eclectic approach to the search for divine blessings and spiritual salvation.[37] Except for some short-lived episodes of intolerance, the policy of the Chinese state resembled that of the Roman Empire at the time of the Antonines, and Gibbon's description of the resultant concord could well apply to traditional China: "The various modes of worship . . . were all considered by the people as equally true; by the philosopher as equally false; and by the magistrate as equally useful."[38] The unsystematic pluralism of cults that made up popular religion was incorporated into the state religion, and these cult gods became part of a hierarchy of deities at the apex of which stood Heaven. The worship of Heaven, as we have seen, was monopolized by the emperor, while officials at all levels fulfilled similar ritual obligations by regular sacrifices to lesser gods and spirits. Some local cults enjoyed official status, and sacrifices in cult temples were offered by the Confucian scholar class. Other shrines, including Taoist and Buddhist shrines, had their own priests, but were nevertheless considered, at least in the popular view, a part of the grand system of deities under the supremacy of Heaven.[39]

In China, therefore, no centralized priesthood emerged to challenge the state. The agents officiating in the sacrifices of the recognized cults were secular state officials. Buddhist and Taoist temples had priests, but both classes of shrines were characterized by a considerable diversity of gods and theological themes, and there existed no high priest with power to enforce orthodoxy or to rival the authority of the emperor and his Confucian scholar class.

The practice of honoring great men with temples and sacrifices throughout the country began with certain emperors at the beginning of the Han dynasty, and it eventually was extended to other important personages. Confucius who had made significant contributions to learning and morality was a fitting candidate for such honors, and from the middle of the first century A.D. on there developed a cult of Confucius with its own shrines and, later, temples. At first the cult was merely another instance of a professional group paying reverence to a patron god, and even later Confucius continued to be worshipped for the most part by the scholar class. Because this class was important in the administrative system of China, the state eventually adopted the cult of Confucius and encouraged it as a way of enhancing the prestige of the literati. It came to occupy a place in the state religion "between the cults of nature deities and the worship of ancestors, from both of which it borrowed." [40] Confucius now was not merely the patron saint of the scholars but of the state civil service, and the emperor would sacrifice to him whenever he visited the schools. Eventually some seventy of Confucius' disciples were added to the hierarchy of the cult, and sacrificial rites were performed before their tablets as well. With temples in every city, which were almost halls of fame for men of literary distinction, the cult of Confucius constituted an important part of the state religion and "added a religious element to the ideal of education." [41]

Confucianism as the state religion of traditional China thus had many different components, and one which was not necessarily the most important was the cult of Confucius. Central place was still occupied by the cult of Heaven which sanctified the office of the emperor. Despite the Confucian emphasis on public opinion as a barometer of divine favor, in the final analysis, the power of the throne was justified not by secular consent but by the power of the almighty Heaven.

The vastness of the imperial palace, the stately sacrifices to Heaven performed there by the emperor, the complex ceremonial rituals that surrounded the emperor's public appearances—all these contributed to the charisma of the emperor as the Son of Heaven and served as a "tangible reminder to the people that the power to govern was not an affair among men, but an arrangement between Heaven and the ruling group." [42] The Confucian stress on a sage monarch chosen on grounds of merit remained an ideal, defining the duties of a ruler, but it did not serve as a working principle to govern the succession. Confucianism accepted power as an accomplished fact, and, at least implicitly, it therefore went along with the historical adage, "The one who won [power] became a king; the one who lost [power] became a bandit." [43]

The various popular cults connected with the state religion similarly contributed to the maintenance of the moral and political order. They provided supernatural explanations for calamities and misfortune and thus directed blame away from the temporal authority. The importance of the cults to the political order was always recognized in the Confucian tradition. The *Book of Rites* (*Li Chi*), one of the Confucian Classics, stressed the importance of sacrifice as the surest way of "keeping men in good order," and the Confucian commentary on the mystic *Book of Change* puts it even more succinctly: "The sages devised guidance by the way of the gods, and the people in the empire became obedient." [44] Statements of this kind continued to be quoted down to recent times, testifying to the general recognition of the political role of the state religion.

BUDDHISM

Ancient Buddhism, as taught by its founder in the sixth century before the Christian era, showed little concern over the affairs of this world, and consequently it did not develop into a social or political philosophy. The Indian prince Siddartha Gotama, later called the Buddha (the Enlightened One), urged his followers to accept the Noble Eightfold Path of self-discipline and self-conquest; any transformation of society would be merely the incidental by-product of the religious transformation of the individual members making up the community.[45] Buddhism accepted earthly inequalities, including caste distinctions, as necessary outcomes of the law of *karma* (*kamma* in Pali) which rewarded or punished man according to his deeds in earlier existences. The revered Buddhist text, *The Questions of King Milinda*, explains the existence of human differences in the following way:

> The king said: "Why is it, Nagasena, that all men are not alike, but some are short-lived and some long-lived, . . . some without influence and some of great power, some poor and some wealthy, some low born and some high born, some stupid and some wise?" The Elder replied: "Why is it that all vegetables are not alike, but some are sour, and some salt, . . . and some astringent and some sweet?"
> "I fancy, Sir, it is because they come from different kinds of seeds."
> "And just so, great king, are the differences you have mentioned among men to be explained. For it has been said by the Blessed One: 'Beings, O brahmin, have each their own Karma, are inheritors of Karma. . . . It is Karma, that divides them into low and high and the like divisions.' "[46]

According to this teaching there was no point in changing the social order, for unfortunate social and political conditions, like the unhappy fate of individuals, were the results of bad *karma*, they were brought on by the evil actions in past incarnations of those who had now to endure these conditions. Suffering was inherent in the human condition, and it could be ended only by a complete transcendence of earthly life and its desires by the achievement of *nirvana* (*nibbana* in Pali) which would end the cycle of rebirth and usher in a life of perfect freedom—freedom from craving, resentment, pride, and fear. Society, then, was improved not through the redress of social grievances but through the improvement of the members of society who would exude their personal moral worth. The good society was a society in which the Buddhist holy man, the *arahat*, who had achieved *nirvana*, radiated virtue and moral integrity into the surrounding society of lay-believers.[47]

The teachings of the Buddha, preserved in the Pali Scriptures, do contain exhortations to rulers to practice piety and charity, but they include no prescription for social reform. Kingship is seen as an institution made necessary by man's greed and predilection for violence, and the legend describes the origin of monarchical rule as a contract between ruler and ruled.[48] But, unlike Western political thought, the Buddhist emphasis on justice and righteousness as the essence of kingship is not developed into an authoritative law to which an appeal could be made in case the king failed to live up to the moral qualifications declared desirable.[49] Though sovereignty theoretically emanated from the people, Buddhist tradition did not evolve a concrete theory of popular sovereignty or right of rebellion. The emergence of such a theory was discouraged, on one hand, by the devaluation of worldly concerns which we have already mentioned. Orthodox Buddhism knows no call for social revolution and no millenarian tradition, for all such social reformation was considered superficial at best "and in any case can be achieved only when a majority of people are inwardly reformed—which may not occur for ages to come, if ever."[50] On the other hand, Buddhist monarchs, in part in return for their support of the Buddhist religion, soon came to be granted semi-divine status, and this development further encouraged a spirit of passive obedience. The idea that a ruler could be considered a *bodhisattva*, a future Buddha (literally a "being of enlightenment"), is found in certain scriptures of Mahayana Buddhism, the school prevalent today in China, Tibet, and Japan; it also is found in the system of Theravada Buddhism, prevalent in Thailand, Cambodia, Laos, Burma, and Ceylon. Though all these countries at one time or another experienced political upheavals that were supported in the name of religion, Buddhism, in the main, did not formulate moral judgments concerning political or social issues which could have constituted a potential threat to autocratic rule. "More often than not," writes Kitagawa, "Buddhism accepted uncritically its assigned role, upholding the *status quo*, even serving as a spiritual tranquilizer for the oppressed peasantry by promising happiness in the world to come."[51]

The Buddhist ethic of withdrawal from all worldly concerns became institutionalized in the Sangha, the order of monks established by the Buddha. Their lives regulated by the *Vinaya*, the code of monastic discipline, the monks (*bhikkhus*) follow the founder's path to achieve the state of *nirvana* and to provide an example to the laity. On the popular level there is little hope of actually attaining the ultimate goal of Buddhism, and the laity, therefore, to

this day, concentrates on acquiring *pin* (merit) which may lead to
the tangible reward of superior rebirth entailing health, wealth,
prestige, and higher status. Merit theoretically can be achieved by
such observances as keeping the Five Precepts—refraining from
killing, stealing, sexual misconduct, bad speech, and drinking
liquor—though in the case of the typical villager adherence to
Buddhist teaching has always consisted more of certain ceremonial practices and almsgiving than of ethical conduct.[52] The
great difficulty of achieving ultimate salvation, which would end
the cycle of rebirth, according to a later doctrinal addition, could
be eased by the coming of Maitreya, the future Buddha, who will
bring peace and prosperity.[53] But the majority of Buddhists do
not expect this event in the foreseeable future, and the achievement of *nirvana* for them in any case is not a matter of urgency.
In the countries of Theravada Buddhism the messianic significance
of the Maitreya figure was further muted by the preemption of
this title by monarchs who claimed to be the *bodhisattva* Maitreya.[54]

According to the teaching of the Buddha, the monastic order
was bound by the vow of poverty, and the monks were expected
to live by alms. However, the obligation of the laity to provide
support for the monks gradually changed the character of the
order. Expecting to reap merit, monarchs and laymen dedicated
so much property to the Sangha that the monasteries gradually
accumulated considerable landed property which became vested
in the body of priests resident in a temple.[55] Royal patronage, in
particular, soon led to a close tie between the Sangha and the
state. The monks impressed upon the king the importance of protecting the Buddhist religion, and in return they helped legitimize
his rule, in effect becoming an "established church."

Buddhism became a creed with concrete implications for the
social order two centuries after the death of the Buddha under
the Indian monarch Asoka (Ashoka in Sanskrit) (274–236 B.C.)
whose conversion to Buddhism has been compared to the conversion of Emperor Constantine to Christianity. Asoka spread Buddhism by sending out missionaries, he supervised the purity of the
monastic order, and he attempted to make Buddhism more relevant to the life of the ordinary people, exhorting them to live
according to the commands of the *dhamma*, the way of righteousness. Perhaps Asoka's most original contribution to Buddhism was the ideal of a Buddhist "welfare state," in which the

government sought to promote such social conditions that would permit the leisure necessary for meditation. Asoka's social ethos was a welfare state "at least to the extent of guaranteeing the economic basis of leisure for meditation to everybody who wanted to withdraw from materially productive activities; nobody was to be excluded through a lack of monastery endowment; the whole people were to be enabled by the king to supply the monks with alms." [56] To this day Asoka's policy provides the model for the Buddhist ruler of the state, and it sets the norm for the relation of Buddhism to the social realm. The emphasis is still on personal morality, and there is no clear vision of an ideal Buddhist social order, but the propagation of the faith by the monarch and his commitment to welfare services established a pattern of dynamic interaction between state, religion, and society.

In recent times, members of the Sangha in South and Southeast Asia have indeed involved themselves in politics. Buddhism became a symbol of self-assertion against colonial rule. In Burma the title of the future Buddha was claimed by rebel leaders seeking to restore Buddhism to its former position of eminence. Buddhism, seemingly a specifically unpolitical religion teaching the renunciation of earthly life which Max Weber called a creed of "other-worldly mysticism" that leads to the "contemplative flight from the world," [57] has brought forth from the ranks of its monkhood important and prominent political leaders like U Ottama, Burma's first popular nationalist hero; Mapitigama Buddharakkhita, the one-time head of Ceylon's United Monks' Front, who was later sentenced to life imprisonment for instigating the murder of his country's prime minister in 1959; and Thich Tri Quang, who claimed to have helped overthrow three governments in South Vietnam. Organized groups of Buddhist monks, supposedly immersed in a cloistered life of meditation, in Burma, Vietnam, and Ceylon have taken to the streets, thus demonstrating their political influence. Their most successful interventions in politics, concludes Donald E. Smith, have been when a plausible enemy of Buddhism could be identified—a European imperialist government as in Burma, a Westernized indigenous elite as in Ceylon, a Catholic dictator as in Vietnam.[58]

* * *

The political manifestations of Buddhism in China followed a somewhat different path. Buddhism came to China in the first century of the Christian era. At first, during the rule of the Han dynasty, it was regarded as but another aspect of Taoism. There existed doctrinal similarities—the emphasis on concentration and meditation, abstinence from certain kinds of food, the control of the passions—and Buddhist missionaries exploited these resemblances in order to gain a foothold in China.[59] But gradually Buddhism developed a spirit of independence and during the period of political disunion that set in with the fall of the Han dynasty in A.D. 222, Buddhism advanced rapidly. Despite novel features like the practice of celibacy that opposed the Chinese stress on family life and numerous offspring, the spread of this foreign faith to all parts of China and among all classes of Chinese society was facilitated by the disunity of the country and the widespread suffering of its people. The orderliness of life that had characterized the Han period was gone, and in a time of social and political disintegration and recurring famines "a drowning humanity eagerly reached out for anything which suggested mental or material relief from their plight." [60]

The failure of Confucianism to satisfy the religious needs of the Chinese people has been mentioned, and this shortcoming proved particularly serious in times of instability and trouble. Buddhism offered succor just where Confucianism failed. It brought in a host of deities in the form of compassionate and merciful Buddhas, ready to help those in distress. The doctrine of *karma* provided a rational explanation of the woes of the period— suffering was in retribution for some demeritorious deeds of the past—while at the same time it buoyed up hopes by promising rebirth into a happier life in the future as a reward for meritorious conduct. The vision of rebirth into a hierarchy of heavens helped sustain people during the disappointments of their earthly lives.[61]

To the upper classes and the ruling groups, on the other hand, Buddhism commended itself through its magical aspects. Among the Buddhist monks in North China, in particular, there were many who were adept at interpreting omens, spells, and charms. They claimed the skill of predicting the outcome of battles, the loyalty of ministers and allies, and such services endeared them to the ruling houses who reciprocated by building temples and granting economic privileges to the monastic community.[62] To many of the alien dynasties ruling over China during this period of disunion, Buddhism, moreover, appealed as a religion that had been founded by a non-Chinese and that, unlike Confucianism, did not discriminate between Chinese and barbarians. In the great Toba empire of the fourth and fifth centuries, for example, Buddhism became in fact the state religion of these Turkish people. The emperor appointed a monk as head of the official church, and in return the monks accepted him as a reincarnation of the Buddha.[63] The acceptance of Buddhism was facilitated by the fact that it came to China in the form of the *Mahayana* (the Greater Vehicle) which offers salvation to all men and includes the belief in *bodhisattvas*, beings of enlightenment who postpone their own redemption in order to help others achieve *nirvana*. In the course of time the worship of *bodhisattvas* blended with the many local cults of traditional China, and Buddhist, Taoist, and Confucian elements combined into the popular religion we mentioned earlier. On the level of ideas, "the Mahayana Buddhist pity for all creatures and the hope of salvation for all humanity fused into the Confucian concept of universal benevolence and devotion to moral duties regardless of personal consequence."[64] This new ideological alignment, developing during the Sung dynasty (960–1279), is often called Neo-Confucianism.[65]

The Chinese ruling houses welcomed the fusion of diverse religious ideas in the popular religion; it satisfied the spiritual needs of the peasantry and helped promote political order and social stability. Buddhism, in particular, was appreciated as can be seen in these observations of a seventeenth-century official who explained his reasons for contributing to the repair of a local temple:

I have examined carefully into the methods of the ancient rulers. When the people are at peace, they are governed and live according to the proper rules of conduct (*Li*), but when troubles arise, punishments must be used. When these penalties are not sufficient to control the people, the sanctions of religion must be employed, for men are frightened by spiritual forces which they cannot see nor hear. We know that Buddha lived in ancient times, and we may employ his teaching, with that of Lao Tzi, even though we do not use their names, to reinforce the doctrines of Confucius. . . . Although the doctrines of the wheels of life (Karma and Salvation), of suffering and blessedness, were introduced to deceive the people, yet they were useful in frightening men, in awakening them to the necessity of right behavior, and in checking their sinful desires.[66]

Buddhism thus was useful as a means of social control, and many an emperor bestowed favors upon it for this utilitarian reason. But organized Buddhists also threatened important interests of the secular state, and this conflict explains the four great persecutions of Buddhists in 446, 574, 845, and 955. Commoners not infrequently sought refuge from conscription and taxation in the monasteries; noblemen and other officials often donated their lands to monasteries and entered the monkhood to evade taxes and other responsibilities. The state attempted to prevent the rise of such an economically nonproductive class by limiting the total number of Buddhist monks and by retaining the power to ordain and defrock monks.[67] Still, the resentment against this "state within the state" remained, and even under Buddhist emperors Buddhism was strictly controlled and supervised. Temples and monasteries had to stage festivals, not related to Buddhism, at the request of the court; temples were constructed and maintained by the state; monks were registered and subsidized by the imperial treasury; ordination involved examinations administered by the government. In these and many other ways the Confucian state guarded its prerogatives and interests, and Buddhism was able to exist only at the price of becoming "a sort of spiritual arm of the imperial government."[68] The fact that, as we shall see in Chapter 3, Buddhist ideas often inspired millenarian cults and rebellions reinforced the state's suspicions of Buddhism.

JUDAISM

From the beginning, Israel's religion was a religion of redemption. According to ancient belief, Yahweh had freed the Hebrews from the house of bondage, and he had made Israel his chosen people. The deliverance from Egypt, and the covenant relationship that followed this act of liberation, thus provided, as Charles puts it, the stay of Israel's "faith, the ground of its trust, and pledge of salvation in the dawn of evil days."[69] Characterized by confidence in the divine promises and the secure knowledge of being a people blessed by an all-powerful God, this notion of election created the foundation for Israel's future hope and eventually, after severe historical disappointment, became a fully developed eschatology.[70] Quite appropriately, the man who mediated the covenant at Mount Sinai, Moses, in Talmud and

Midrash is often called "the first redeemer," and he is compared
to the Messiah, "the last redeemer." [71]
Through Moses and the Exodus, Israel experienced Yahweh as
a God of action, a God who manifests his power through historical events, a God who has a purpose in world history. The enumeration of Yahweh's mighty deeds fills the pages of the Old
Testament, and the cultic commemoration of these deeds in Hebrew worship reinforced Israel's perception of history as a reflection of the divine will and plan. The Israelite idea of historical
events as divine manifestations has often been singled out as the
Hebrews' unique contribution toward a philosophy of history, a
break with the cyclical view of history widely followed by other
ancient religions and civilizations. Recent scholarship has suggested that this theme of divine purposeful action in history is
rather common in Mesopotamian and Hittite literature as well
and has questioned the uniqueness of the Israelite conception of
time and history.[72] Be that as it may, the central position of the
deity's saving acts in history in the cult of Israel does represent a
distinctive phenomenon. The strongly held conviction that in
human history God is working out his sovereign purpose for the
good of his chosen people has had an obvious and important impact on Israel's religion and on the idea of messianism, a central
feature of the Jewish creed and one with great significance for
the political ramifications of Judaism over the ages.

"Messiah" as a proper name or technical term for a personal
savior who is expected to act as an intermediary between God
and man, or head a universal Kingdom of God on earth, is not
used in the Old Testament or in the books of the Apocrypha. It
is used for the first time in the pseudepigraphic Book of Enoch,
which was probably composed between 94–64 B.C.[73] "Messiah,"
meaning the anointed, is used in I Samuel (2:10) and in other
parts of the Old Testament, but there it refers to actual or specific kings or priests, consecrated to their high office by the ceremony of pouring oil on their heads, rather than to a redeemer, a
"messiah," who is yet to come. The Messiah as an eschatological
figure, as a king of the final age, the glorious kingdom, is thus a
rather late development in the Jewish religion. It appears against
the background of the loss of Judean independence, in the apocalyptic writings popular during the days of Roman rule and oppression. Confronted with a reality that seemed to contradict

Yahweh's promises to his people, his people longed for a personal savior who would restore Israel to its former greatness and at the same time inaugurate a new age of happiness for the entire human race. "When faith rises up and overcomes the disappointment, the future hope of eschatology begins to be." [74]

But the lack of an idea of a personal messiah did not mean that there was no hope for a new age of earthly bliss. Such a general messianism was part of the very essence of the Jewish religion and its view of the role of God in the world. Specifically, it emerged from the idea of a covenant between Yahweh and the people of Israel, from the promises made to David of God's eternal rule in Zion, and from the hope of a realization of these promises under a descendant of David, an ideal ruler.

The relatively short period of an independent and unified monarchy in ancient Israel came to be seen by later generations as an age of unparalleled prosperity and justice, bestowed by God upon a righteous and God-fearing nation, and the house of David in particular was invested with superior qualities. Around 1000 B.C. David's political and military talents enabled him to unify the tribes of Israel and decisively defeat their enemies, thus making him the greatest of Israel's saviors and defenders. The idea that David had been called to power by divine designation, that Yahweh had chosen Zion as the earthly seat of his rule and had made a covenant with David to let his line rule forever and triumph over all its foes, became a dogma regularly reaffirmed in the cult. Through years when the promises were anything but realities, "the hope took root of an ideal Davidide to come, under whose just and triumphant rule the promises would be made actual. The cult was the seedbed from which sprang Israel's expectations of a Messiah." [75]

The connection between the Israelite ideal of kingship, the return of a true king who would put everything right, and the later idea of a coming messiah is clear. However, the related question of whether this conception of monarchy shared the Oriental view of the divine nature of kingship is one of great controversy. According to the so-called "Myth and Ritual School," the Davidic kings in Jerusalem were regarded as divine or semi-divine beings who followed a ritual pattern common to the entire ancient Near East. This cultic rite was that of the New Year festival in which the king as a dying and rising god of fertility reenacted the strug-

gle of creation and in thus assuring his country's well-being for
the following year in effect became a messiah.[76]
Critics have challenged the existence of such a single ritual pattern and a theory of divine kingship based thereon. They have
acknowledged that the custom of anointing the king to confer sacred status was taken over by the Israelites from the Canaanites
and that the Davidic kings, like the kings of many primitive peoples all over the world, were regarded as saviors, embodying and
ensuring the good estate and welfare of their subjects. All this
and more could be considered an adaptation of certain oriental
conceptions. At the same time, these critics emphasize that the Israelite king was seen as a man, endowed by Yahweh with some
superhuman qualities but always dependent upon him. There are
laudatory songs sung in honor of the king but no cult of worship
of him as a god. The Israelite king, it is stressed, is a bearer of
God's grace, the shepherd of God's chosen people, and therefore
not just a man like other men. But unlike the king in Egypt and
even Mesopotamia, the Hebrew monarch is neither a god on
earth nor a deified man; he performs the will of Yahweh and acts
as his vice-regent—no less and no more.[77] The often quoted
passage in Ps. 45:7 where the king seemingly is addressed as
"God," Martin Noth has argued, can be translated differently,
and, in any event, as a unique phrase in the Old Testament it can
hardly bear the burden of the thesis of divine kingship in Israel.[78]
    It is not for this writer to attempt to resolve a great debate
among learned specialists, but it can be said with some assurance
that the view of the critics of the Myth and Ritual School fits
better into the transcendentalism of the Hebrew religion and the
history of Jewish messianism than do other views. It is *the* basic
idea of the Israelite creed that Yahweh is not in nature; he is utterly distinct from the world and utterly supreme. Hence he can
have no rivals on earth, and even the acts of deliverance expected
of the descendants of David in the final analysis are his work.
The future Davidic ruler, unlike the later figure of the personal
messiah, was not seen as a redeemer per se. "The Lord is the redeemer," Klausner notes, "and the King-Messiah is only the head
of the redeemed people, its political and spiritual king."[79]
    The uniqueness and supremacy of Yahweh find expression also
in an anti-monarchical stream of thought most prominently associated with the warning by Samuel (I Sam. 8:11–18) against

deserting the rulership of Yahweh in favor of the rule of a human
being. Though this is probably the insertion of a later author, this
and similar passages highlight the strong hold of the theocratic
idea. Reinforced by the idea of chieftainship from the semi-nomadic period in Israel's history, which emphasized charismatic
leadership rather than dynastic descent, and strengthened by the
constant intrigues and usurpations that especially characterized
the monarchy in the northern kingdom, the anti-monarchical sentiment persisted and lent support to the popular view that Yahweh alone should be king in Israel. The political results of this
view during the Hellenistic and Roman periods will occupy us
later.

In the writings of the prophets we find sharp criticism of individual rulers but no attack upon the institution of kingship as
such. Their ideal of a future Kingdom of God was closely linked
to the expectation of a future David. Isaiah's messianic king is "a
shoot from the stump of Jesse" (11:1) who will sit upon the
throne of David and establish his kingdom "with justice and with
righteousness from this time forth and for evermore" (9:7). His
reign will be paradise regained; the idea of a Golden Age as an
era of past happiness is projected by the prophets into the future.
On the "Day of Yahweh," first mentioned in Amos 5:18–20,
God will execute judgment upon the wicked, whether in Israel
or among the surrounding nations, and the messianic era will become a fact. Certain great nations are here for the first time singled out as being instruments in God's hand to punish Israel and
do his will.

The prophets of doom predict the destruction of Israel (or
Judah), but as yet we find no eschatological message. The prophets are concerned with contemporary events; they speak of the
destruction of Israel and Judah as independent nations at the
hand of Assyria or Babylon by the direction of Yahweh, not of a
catastrophic destruction of the world.[80] Even Second Isaiah, writing after the fall of Jerusalem in 587 and during exile in Babylon,
concentrates upon the restoration of Israel, upon national and political deliverance, achieved through God's miraculous intervention. "In spite of his universal outlook," concludes Mowinckel,
"he is a Jew, affected by Jewish nationalism. The universal God
is the God of Israel and in spite of everything His kingdom is still
a kingdom of this world." [81]

The fall of Jerusalem and the destruction of the first Temple marked the end of Israel's existence as a nation. "Within the limits of what cultural and religious autonomy was left to them, the Jews formed a religious community, ruled by its own religious law under the government of their priests. It was a theocratic regime, and here again an ancient idea was reaffirmed and restated: Israel had God for king." [82] The centuries following the restoration of the Jews to Palestine are among the least well known in Jewish history, but strict adherence to tradition and law stands out as the basic feature of the post-exilic community, substituting for identity as a nation and statehood. For the Jews living under conditions of foreign rule, their country shrunk to the size of a small province around Jerusalem and their numbers decimated by deportation and emigration, political passivity became the appropriate mode of conduct and such quietism is indeed advocated in many biblical writings of the post-exilic period. Messianic ideas do not play an important role, and reliance upon God is stressed. "The Lord is good to those who wait for him, to the soul that seeks him," expounds the author of the Book of Lamentations. "It is good that one should wait quietly for the salvation of the Lord. It is good for a man that he bear the yoke in his youth." [83] After the unsuccessful uprisings of the Zealots and Bar Kochba and the severe suffering associated with the final failures to regain independence (Chapter 4) this philosophy of resignation was to become the dominant viewpoint in Judaism.

For a time there was still hope for national redemption, and, during the second century B.C., it began to emerge forcefully in apocalyptic and eschatological form. The apocalyptic writings go beyond the concept of the Day of Yahweh developed during the late Old Testament period. Their anonymous authors, using esoteric language which they place into the mouths of prophets long dead, seek to reveal the secrets of the last events thought to be imminent rather than far in an indefinite future; they share their visions of the mysteries of the cosmos, the sequence of generations and of ages to come. Indeed, disclosure of such secrets is the very essence of apocalypse which means "revelation." The eschatological element inheres in the idea of a catastrophic end of the present world order, the culmination of a cosmic struggle between God and the principle of evil. This dualistic view of the world, accompanied usually by a division of history into world

epochs leading to a final triumph of the forces of good, most
likely derived from Persian influences, from Zoroastrian eschatology.[84] But basically the flourishing of apocalypse, especially during the Hellenistic period, is the result of historical circumstances,
the desperate longing for national salvation in the midst of oppression. Jewish eschatology, therefore, was national. "The idea
of salvation for the individual was indissolubly linked with the
salvation of the people."[85] The intense religious character of
these longings and needs also helps explain why the role of Yahweh as king in many apocalyptic writings takes precedence over
the role of an earthly scion of David as a messiah. As Mowinckel
puts it succinctly: "It was for the presence of God himself in the
midst of His people that men longed."[86]

CHRISTIANITY

The historical Jesus, it appears, was a Jewish prophet during the
reign of the procurator Pontius Pilate, one among many, who
was crucified like other messianic pretenders before and after him,
probably in the year 30. He was condemned to death by the Romans as a political offender for having claimed to be the messianic
king of the Jews. "As seen by the Roman officials," writes a modern scholar, "the 'case of Jesus of Nazareth' belonged in the long
list of cases of Zealots, arrested for offenses against the Roman State in its Jewish provinces, who had to be rendered harmless."[87] Whether this judgment is regarded as an injustice (within
the Roman frame of reference) depends on an assessment of Jesus'
intentions, and such an assessment today, almost two thousand
years after the events in question, is a rather hopeless undertaking. Practically all our information about Jesus of Nazareth
comes to us from those who after his early death regarded him as
the founder of a new religion and did their best to dissociate him
from the political aims of Jewish nationalism.[88] Moreover, even
according to these Christian sources, compiled within a period of
less than one hundred years after Jesus' death, Jesus' teaching
about the imminent Kingdom of God, his attitude toward the use
of force, and perhaps even his pronouncement on the payment of
tribute are curiously equivocal. At least one of the disciples chosen by Jesus is said to have been a Zealot (Luke 6:15; Acts 1:13)
which fact could be seen to indicate that "the profession of

Zealot principles and aims was not incompatible with intimate participation in the mission of Jesus." [89] There is also the Slavonic version of Josephus' *Jewish War* that describes Jesus himself as a Zealot, and Robert Eisler has relied on this extensively. The quest for the historical Jesus, as countless scholars have come to realize, is thus made rather difficult. The experts undoubtedly will continue to disagree until and unless new reliable information about the Jew, Jesus of Nazareth, comes to light.

The teachings of Jesus of Nazareth about the coming Kingdom of God are obscure and ambivalent. They contain obvious links to the Jewish messianic tradition but also new, more spiritual, universal themes. According to the synoptic Gospels, Jesus himself expected his death, resurrection, and an early realization of the heavenly kingdom,[90] and it was this message of an imminent redemption which the first Christian preachers carried to their Jewish kinsmen as well as to the gentiles. Paul assured the Thessalonians that the Parousia, the Second Coming of Jesus the Christ, was near and that he and many of his fellow Christians would live to see the Day of the Lord.[91] Mark and the other synoptic writers similarly expected the speedy triumphant return of Jesus and the consummation of the messianic hope.

The expectation of an early end of this world was further encouraged by the persecution which many Christians experienced at the hands of the Roman authorities because they refused to acknowledge the divinity of the emperors. The Book of Revelation, probably written by a Palestinian exile named John during the last two decades of the first century, represents the best-known example of Christian apocalyptic thinking that emerged forcefully in response to and as an antidote for the sufferings of the persecuted.[92] Together with the Old Testament Book of Daniel, the Apocalypse of John has inspired countless poets and artists, and millenarian (or chiliastic) movements of various types have been based on it.

The author of Revelation holds out the promise of an impending advent of the Messiah: God has sent his angel to reveal "what must soon take place" (22:6). "The time is near" (22:10) when the returned Christ, defeating Satan (or the Antichrist as he is later called), will establish his messianic kingdom on earth, avenge the martyrs, and reign with them for 1000 years (20:4).[93] Following this millennial interregnum will come the Last Judgment and fi-

nally "a new heaven and a new earth" (21:1), as predicted by
Third Isaiah (65:17), when God will dwell with his people and
when "death shall be no more, neither shall there be mourning
nor crying nor pain" (21:4). As befits an apocalyptic work, this
prophecy of glorious tidings is clothed in an esoteric symbolism
with strange beasts and figures abounding.

Though the interpretation of many of these symbols has differed over the centuries, the overall impact of the Book of Revelation has been powerful. Its vision of a future golden age has
reinforced and supplemented with a concrete message of bliss the
original "good news" of Christianity, the egalitarian promise of
divine grace and salvation for a community in which "there is
neither Jew nor Greek, there is neither male nor female." [94]
Moreover, the Apocalypse of John presents in its most developed
and extreme form Christianity's dramatic conception of history,
leading toward the fulfillment of a definite goal, a philosophy of
history that stands in marked contrast to the Greek view of the
world in which everything reoccurs or the mystical conception
of most Eastern religions where all life is regarded as an endlessly
repeated cycle of death and regeneration.[95] It was this apocalyptic view of history, teleological and cataclysmic, as in its Jewish
antecedents, that has helped provide the ideological impulse for
numerous radical sects and revolutionary movements, for, as Norman Cohn has observed, "revolutionary chiliasm thrives best . . .
where history is imagined as having an inherent purpose which is
preordained to be realized on earth in a single, final consummation." [96] Such a conception of the temporal process is presupposed
also by certain secular religions of humanity, culminating in the
great totalitarian movements of our own age, and helps explain
their great self-assurance as well as ruthlessness.

During the first four centuries of the Christian church, belief in
the proximity of an eschatological climax was strong. Such eminent church fathers as Papias, Ignatius of Antioch, Irenaeus, Jus-
tin Martyr, Lactantius, and Tertullian expected an early realization of the millennial kingdom in which none would be hungry,
thirsty, or unhappy.[97] But as the years went by without the expected Parousia, and with the change in the political position of
the church, millenarian speculation declined. "The lapse of time
proved that the vivid expectancy of earlier days had not been justified, and the success of Christianity on the present earth lessened

the demand for an early catastrophic end of the world."⁹⁸ Christianity now was no longer a persecuted sect but the official religion of the Roman Empire, a powerful institution with a stake in the here-and-now. The growing influence of Greek ideas, especially Neoplatonism, also strengthened the view that salvation involved not a state of collective, quasi-terrestrial abundance in a millennial kingdom but a freeing of the self from all matter and the blessed abode of the individual soul in heaven.

The first real attempt to discredit millenarian speculations was undertaken by Origen in the third century, but it was the formulation of St. Augustine early in the fifth century, dismissing the Book of Revelation as a spiritual allegory, that finally became the new orthodoxy. The Millennium, the great theologian argued, was not something in the future; it was already here: "The Church even now is the kingdom of Christ, and the kingdom of heaven. Accordingly, even now His saints reign with Him."⁹⁹ A few years later, in the year 431, the Council of Ephesus denounced belief in a coming Millennium as a superstitious error, and millenarianism from then on was regarded as a heresy.

The tendency of many early Christians to reject the legitimacy of a pagan political order had led to the strong exhortations of St. Paul and St. Peter to obey the governing powers, and St. Augustine, too, had preached the same gospel of submissiveness. God appoints the kinds of rulers he judges the people worthy of, and, in view of his omnipotence and justice, tyrants must be considered God's retribution for the sins of the people. Both just kings and cruel tyrants reign by God's providence; none may be resisted.¹⁰⁰

Despite the seemingly unequivocal teachings of the New Testament and the early church fathers on the question of political obligation, Christianity, for most of its history, has not held a doctrinaire position on the subject of rebellion against constituted political authority. Along with the injunction of St. Paul in his "Letter to the Romans" to be subject to the powers that be and not to resist them (Rom. 13:1–2), Christianity has also always upheld the idea of a higher loyalty to its moral and religious principles which could require the Christian to "obey God rather than men" (Acts 5:29). Moreover, as the power of the church grew during the Middle Ages, and the papacy increasingly came into conflict with secular authority, political and institutional im-

peratives made the political teachings of the church more assertive. From the pontificate of Gregory VII in the eleventh century on, the papacy took it upon itself to sit in judgment upon
rulers, and, if necessary, to declare disobedient sons of the
church deposed and their subjects absolved of allegiance. A right
of resistance to tyranny emerged that drew additional strength
from basic medieval political ideas rooted in the political tradition
of the Germanic tribes, the Roman concept of popular sovereignty, and the mutuality of relations inherent in feudalism.[101]

For many centuries, the position of St. Thomas Aquinas on the
legitimacy of rebellion and tyrannicide was looked upon as authoritative. The great, thirteenth-century scholastic taught that a
tyrannical government was unjust and that "consequently the
overthrowing of such a government is not strictly sedition; except perhaps in the case that it is accompanied by such disorder
that the community suffered greater harm from the consequent
disturbances than it would from a continuance of the former
rule." [102] The tyrant himself, argued St. Thomas, was guilty of
sedition by spreading disorder among the people, and, in the case
of a usurper of political power, later interpreters held, he might
even be slain.[103] When the Council of Constance in 1415 condemned the doctrine of tyrannicide in a loosely worded decree
almost all theologians interpreted this ruling as prohibiting the
killing of legitimate rulers, who had degenerated into tyrants, but
not of usurpers.[104]

During the religious and political strife that accompanied the
Reformation and Counterreformation, Catholic theologians forcefully defended the right of resistance to tyrannical and/or heretical rulers. It was not until the eighteenth century, when the
forces of the Enlightenment and anticlericalism attacked the privileges of the church, that church doctrine abandoned these potentially revolutionary ideas in order to defend absolute monarchy
—the church's only source of protection. This alliance between
throne and altar in Europe lasted throughout the nineteenth century and in Latin America until very recent times. The
encyclical letters of Pope Gregory XVI (1831–46) and the Syl-
labus of Errors of Pius IX (1864) therefore resolutely condemned
any acts of rebellion, and even Leo XIII castigated revolutionary
violence, no matter how great the provocation:

And if at any time it happen that the power of the state is rashly and tyrannically wielded by Princes, the teaching of the Catholic Church does not allow an insurrection on private authority against them, lest public order be only the more disturbed, and lest society take greater hurt therefrom. And when affairs come to such a pass that there is no other hope of safety, she teaches that relief may be hastened by the merits of Christian patience and earnest prayers to God.[105]

But when in the twentieth century revolutionary movements appeared on the scene that were friendly to the church, Catholic teaching once more returned to an acceptance of resistance under certain circumstances. At the 1925 trial of Charles Maurras, the leader of the French right-wing movement Action Française, for having threatened the life of the French minister of the interior, Jacques Maritain, then a professor at the Catholic Institute of Paris, testified as a defense witness and argued the thesis "that Maurras' threat must be taken as the extreme measure of legitimate defense of social order." [106] The Mexican bishops in 1927, at least initially, supported the revolt of the Cristeros. And in 1937, against the background of the Spanish Civil War in which most members of the Spanish hierarchy sided with the rebel, General Franco, Pope Pius XI drew a distinction between just and unjust insurrections. He upheld "recourse to force" as an act of "self-defense" against those bringing a nation to ruin and merely insisted that the means used might not be intrinsically evil and "bring greater harm to the community than the harm they were intended to remedy." [107] More recently, Pope Paul VI affirmed a very similar position.

ISLAM

Mohammed organized his followers in a political community, which has been called variously a theocracy or nomocracy. It was a commonwealth at once religious and political in which God and his revealed word were the supreme authority, and where Mohammed, his apostle, was the Lord's vice-regent on earth. The Prophet's political power was derived from his religious mission; the primary purpose of government was the promotion and protection of the new religious faith. Even more than in other societies of the ancient Middle East, the Islamic community at Medina therefore knew no distinction between the spiritual and the temporal, between church and state. There existed no separation between man's obligation as a believer and his duties as a citizen. The temporal and the spiritual power were one and the same. The Islamic state was governed by God's law revealed to Mohammed, his messenger, who functioned both as religious prophet and temporal head of the community. Mohammed had founded what one observer had called a *"theocratie laique."* [108]

The Prophet died in A.D. 632 without designating a successor, and the Koran was similarly silent on the question of the appointment of a new ruler. It is likely that Mohammed refrained from picking a successor because he recognized the strength of Arab tribal tradition according to which the members of the tribe themselves chose a chieftain primarily on the basis of his qualities as a leader and his ability to inspire personal loyalty among his followers. In line with this principle, Omar, who later became the second caliph, proposed Abu Bakr, Mohammed's faithful friend, as the new leader; he proved acceptable and was called the successor (*caliph*) of the Prophet. Abu Bakr's political power was substantial, though he did not claim to be a divinely inspired prophet. The first caliph nominated his successor, Omar, and this nomination was accepted and confirmed by the community of Medina. The third and fourth caliphs were also elected in this way; however, violence now played a considerable role in the succession. Of the four caliphs following Mohammed, only the first died a natural death, the other three were murdered in office.

A somewhat greater measure of stability was reached with the fifth caliph, Mu'awiyah, who four years before his death nominated his son as his successor, thus founding a dynasty (the Umayyads) and formally introducing the hereditary principle. This principle was followed for the next 400 years. By the time the Abbasid dynasty in Baghdad replaced the Umayyads in the year 750, hereditary autocratic rule, a practice leaning heavily upon the ancient Persian concept of kingship by divine right, had become firmly established. "The prince, isolated from the uniform herd of his subjects, consecrated by divine designation for his office, legitimized by his descent from a long line of kings, guarded by an elaborate etiquette . . . this type of despot," notes von Grunebaum, "now merged successfully with the theocratic representative of Allah and much less successfully, with the Arab chieftain of olden days." [109] Whereas early tradition had considered the caliphate an elective office, the number of electors was eventually reduced to one, a change that amounted to an implicit acceptance of the hereditary principle with the predecessor appointing his successor. The myth of election survived, however, drawing strength from the oath of allegiance or *bay'a* paid to the new prince in the capital and throughout the growing Islamic empire.

Islamic constitutional doctrine developed gradually as a rationalization of the practice followed during the first two centuries of Islam. "The theory as embodied in the works of Mohammedan theologians and jurists was elaborated in order to suit already operating facts." [110] According to this theory, the ultimate source of political authority was God who had provided a ruler [*imam* (leader) or caliph] to be obeyed by the people in order to ensure peace and protect the faith. It was God who established princes and deprived them of power as he saw fit, though the representatives of the community chose the caliph, acting, as it were, in God's name. The candidate for the caliphate had to be of legal age, a freeman of the masculine sex, in the full possession of his physical and mental faculties, knowledgeable in the divine law as well as in the art of war, and, last but not least, a descendant of the *Quraysh*, the tribe to which the Prophet had belonged. The functions of the caliph were to govern the Muslim community as the successor of the Prophet and to protect and enforce the holy law. By accepting his office the caliph promised to exercise his powers within the limits of the law, and he validated this promise in a contract—confirmed by the *bay'a*—with the representatives of the community. If he violated this contract, the people were absolved of allegiance and theoretically could elect another caliph.

This was the theory as it evolved in its early form and for which theological sanction was found and read into the *Shari'a* —the Koran and the traditions. The Koran contained a number of injunctions to obey the messenger of God, Mohammed, and others set in authority over the community. [111] In the case of the traditions (*hadiths*), the sayings and usages ascribed to Mohammed, there is considerable evidence to indicate that some of

them were manipulated almost from the beginning. Inasmuch as
the doctrine of the contract between ruler and ruled made no
provision for removing a bad caliph short of revolution, the door
was opened to those who stressed the danger of chaos that would
follow from calling a ruler to account and who insisted on practically unquestioning obedience. This dread of anarchy was reinforced by the political instability, which was real enough. Disorder was fed by the uneasy coexistence of many different ethnic
and cultural groups in the same empire; by the continuing
strength shown by tribal kinship groups, undermining the loyalty
exacted by the central government; and by the existence of many
sons in the polygamous families of the ruling dynasty, encouraging rivalries and intrigues. In such a situation, characterized by
frequent assassinations and palace revolutions, many scholars emphasized the need for submissiveness to the ruling powers. Endeavoring to give this teaching theological grounding and to
work it into the mainstream of Islamic law, they produced sayings of the Prophet in defense of their tenets, "and as time went
on these became more and more categorical and detailed." The
tradition, Sir Hamilton Gibb concludes, "was being invaded by
forgeries on a vast scale, sometimes by editing and supplementing
genuine old traditions, more often by simple inventions." [112]
Ignaz Goldziher, the most outstanding critical student of the
Hadith, does not hesitate to speak of "pious fraud." [113]

The majority of the traditions relating to political conduct had
as their basic aim the buttressing of an uncompromising doctrine
of civic obedience. A few examples are cited—many of them
bear a striking resemblance to the teachings of early Christianity
which similarly aimed at shoring up civic order and stability:
"The Apostle of God said: Whoso obeys me, obeys God, and
whoso rebels against me, rebels against God; whoso obeys the
ruler, obeys me; and whoso rebels against the ruler, rebels against
me." [114] All earthly authority was seen as being of divine appointment, with a tyrant functioning as God's punishment for
man's sin: "The Prophet said: 'Do not abuse those who rule. If
they act uprightly, they shall have their reward, and your duty is
to show gratitude. If they do evil, they shall bear the burden, and
your duty is to endure patiently. They are a chastisement which
God inflicts upon those who he will; therefore accept the chastisement of God, not with indignation and wrath, but with hu-

mility and meekness.' " [115] The occasional tradition affirming the right and duty of Muslims to disobey and rebel against a ruler violating God's law was thus effectively checked by the introduction of those far more numerous sayings, that branded the creation of disorder without adequate justification a mortal sin. Reform movements and rebellions insisting on the religious orthodoxy of the ruling dynasty were suppressed—a subject to which we will return a little later.

The prestige and power of the early Abbasid caliphs was great. But the enormous Arab empire the first caliphs had built did not last. Spain broke away under an independent ruler in 756. By the year 909, Morocco, Tunisia, Egypt, and Syria had, in effect, become separate states, some with their own caliphate. Finally in the middle of the tenth century the caliph of Baghdad became a prisoner and pensioner of a military clique. Effective power was now wielded by the sultan, a military chieftain, whom the caliph was forced to invest with a show of legitimacy. The caliph still performed certain ceremonial functions, but essentially he had become a figurehead. A *de facto* separation between church and state had come about, and the jurists once again adjusted the theory to the new reality.

All but abandoning any attempt to defend and maintain the dignity of the caliph, the religious teachers (*ulama*) and jurists now taught that anyone in effective possession of political power had to be obeyed, no matter how irregular his assumption of power or how impious and barbarous his conduct. The Islamic community, no longer tied to any particular constitutional scheme, was held to be intact as long as the secular government formally recognized the *Shari'a*, consulted the *ulama*, and allowed individual Muslims to obey the holy law. The sultan's power was legitimized by the legal fiction of deriving his authority from that of the caliph; the new practice and the teaching of the theologians and jurists defending it were declared to be binding since the community accepted it. The saying credited to Mohammed, "My community will never agree upon an error" reinforced the hold of precedent. "Where the legists were forced to succumb to facts," notes a student of the sociology of Islam, "they called in aid the doctrine that *ijma'*, the agreement, actually the aquiescence of the community, justifies whatever happens in Islam." [116]

The fact that Islamic constitutional practice and theory had traveled a long way was frankly acknowledged by al-Ghazali (1064–1111), a scholar often acclaimed as the greatest Muslim after Mohammed. In his eyes the circumstances of the time required the acceptance of the ignominious position of the caliph and of the fact that government was by military power:

> The concessions made by us are not spontaneous, but necessity makes lawful what is forbidden. We know it is not allowed to feed on a dead animal: still, it would be worse to die of hunger. Of those that contend that the caliphate is dead forever and irreplaceable, we should like to ask: what is to be preferred, anarchy and the stoppage of social life for lack of a properly constituted authority, or acknowledgement of the existing order, whatever it be? Of these two alternatives, the jurist cannot but choose the latter.[117]

Actual power was in the hands of the sultan, al-Ghazali admitted, though the validity of his government depended upon the sultan's oath of allegiance to the caliph. However, since al-Ghazali accepted the practice of the day, according to which the caliph was appointed by the sultan, the function of the caliph was clearly reduced to being that of a symbol of unity, divine guidance, and historical continuity.[118]

When the fiction of the sultan's delegated authority became apparent, it was abandoned altogether. The legitimacy of the sultan was divorced from that of the caliph, success in assuming and maintaining the rulership being the only criterion. The Egyptian judge Ibn Jama'ah (1241–1332) realistically described this state of affairs:

> The sovereign has a right to govern until another and stronger one shall oust him from power and rule in his State. The latter will rule by the same title and will have to be acknowledged on the same grounds; for a government, however objectionable, is better than none at all; and between two evils we must choose the lesser.[119]

The above was written a few years after the Mongols had stormed Baghdad in 1258 and put the caliph to death. From that time on the institution of the caliphate was essentially extinct, a development noted by the famous, fourteenth-century Arab philosopher of history, Ibn-Khaldun. To be sure, the Mamluk rulers of Egypt for two and one-half centuries kept a descendant of the last Abbasid caliphs as a puppet, and the Turks, capturing Cairo in 1517, were said to have transferred the caliphate to the Ottoman line. But though the caliphate thus lived on in name until the twentieth century, its meaning had changed completely. In the late Ottoman period, the title, caliph, was increasingly assumed by sultans wanting to embellish their authority.

This, then, was the pattern of Islamic government that developed after the Baghdad caliphate was abolished. Any *de facto* ruler declaring his fealty to the *Shari'a* had a claim on the obedience of his Muslim subjects. The clerical class, the *ulama*, at times denounced the unrighteous ways of a sultan, but by and large they staunchly supported the government and warned against civil disorder. In practice as well as in theory, neither the *ulama* nor the individual were held to have rights as groups or individuals that could be asserted against the ruling authority. Inasmuch as Islam had not produced a separate religious establishment that could successfully challenge the state, no conflict developed between church and state as in medieval Christianity. Reinforced by the poverty soon to engulf many of the Muslim countries and their economic and social stagnation, the dominant trend was one of unrelieved political quietism, supported and encouraged by religious arguments. No matter how evil a ruler, the subject's duty was to obey, though the narrow scope of governmental action—usually limited to the defense of the realm and the creation of conditions under which Muslims could fulfill their religious obligations—minimized the ruler's demands upon his subjects. "The *civitas Dei*," writes von Grunebaum, "had failed and the Muslim community had accepted its failure." [120]

* * *

The development sketched out so far is that of the general body of orthodox Muslims known as *Sunnis*. But alongside this main stream, Islam has abounded in smaller tributaries—sects and heresies with their own theological views as well as different conceptions of political rule. In some instances, these sects were able to gain a hearing and eventually achieve a compromise with the majority Sunni position. In other instances, however, the challenge was sufficiently radical so as to make peaceful resolution of differences impossible. Such was the case with a movement that has been called the earliest sect of Islam, the so-called *Khawarij* or *Kharijites* (Seceders).

The early Khawarij were Bedouins who as nomads resented

the encroachment of the new Islamic state upon the freedoms of
their tribal society. This spirit of rebellion first burst out in open
revolt during the reign of the fourth caliph, Ali. Later, disturbed
over what they regarded as the irreligious and lax behavior of the
Umayyad caliphs, these "Puritans of Islam" continued to spread
terror among their opponents, often killing women and children
as well as male Muslims who disagreed with them. The Khawarij
considered themselves saints under moral obligation to revolt
against sinful government and its supporters. God alone in their
eyes was entitled to complete fealty. Applying the strict standards of the Prophet, they concluded that the Umayyad caliphs
were unbelievers, and therefore they had to be fought.

The doctrinal teaching of the Khawarij was far from unified,
with heresiologists listing as many as twenty-one subsects.[121]
Some of these, it appears, stressed the freedom of the human will
and opposed the concept of predestination. In a manner strikingly
similar to the teachings of the revolutionary Anabaptists of the
sixteenth century,[122] these Khawarij insisted that man was responsible for his own actions, that God wishes the good and not
the bad, and that it was, therefore, right and necessary to kill all
impious and tyrannical rulers and the people who followed
them.[123] Some orthodox theologians, in turn, did their best to
counter this view by embracing the necessity of believing in fate.
All acts, they said, must necessarily occur as decreed by God,
and this included the cruel deeds of tyrants, whom it was wrong,
therefore, to resist.[124] Abbasid theologians, strengthened by the
Persian tradition of divine right kingship, taught that any revolt,
no matter how extreme the provocation, was the most heinous of
crimes. This doctrine, writes Sir Gibb, "came to be consecrated
in the juristic maxim, 'Sixty years of tyranny are better than an
hour of civil strife.' "[125]

The Khawarij for a time had many followers. They benefited
from the social tensions that had built up among the Arab aristocracy, the individualistic Bedouins, and the non-Arab converts.
All upright Muslims, they taught, had the same rights in the Islamic community, whether rich or poor, freeman or slave, Arab
or non-Arab. The legitimacy of their leader, the *Imam*, depended
upon his personal merit, and if he erred his followers had the divine right to remove him. By the end of the eighth century the
Khawarij movement had been militarily crushed, though small

colonies of Khawarij survive to this day in Libya, Algeria, Oman, and Zanzibar.

Also benefiting from widespread social unrest during the first century of Islam was another, far more important, Islamic sect, the *Shi'a*. Shi'ism began as a legitimist political movement demanding that the caliphate be entrusted to the house of Ali, Mohammed's son-in-law and paternal first cousin. Soon, however, the Shi'ites attracted the support of the underprivileged classes, especially in garrison cities in lands conquered by the Arabs. These Muslims of non-Arabic descent, writes Bernard Lewis, rallied to a form of Islam "that challenged the legitimacy of the existing Arab aristocratic state. Their aspiration was for an order in which all Muslims would be equal and Arab birth would no longer carry privileges." [126]

In a situation where church and state were closely interdependent, such a challenge to the existing social system necessarily led to theological schism and the formation of sects. Practically all the Shi'ites attributed superhuman qualities to their chief, or Imam, a political and religious leader who, unlike the caliph of the orthodox Sunnis, could define and modify religious dogma and doctrine. The Imam of the Shi'a was appointed by his predecessor rather than elected; he was sinless and infallible and could not be deposed. Common to many of the Shi'ite sects was the belief in a divinely illuminated leader who would lead the oppressed out of their misery—a messianic figure or *Mahdi* (the rightly guided one).

The concept of a Mahdi is present neither in the Koran nor in the two great canonical collections of the Prophet's traditions, perhaps because in the orthodox creed Muslims are redeemed simply by virtue of their membership in the charismatic community of Islam. The concept first appeared within a generation of Mohammed's death, during a period of religious and dynastic turmoil. The belief in a redeemer who would restore the religious purity and glory of the Prophet's original creed was borrowed from Judaism and Christianity and probably was introduced by converted Jews and Christians.

The title "Mahdi" was first bestowed upon Mohammed, the son of Ali (Mohammed's son-in-law and the fourth caliph).[127] For the sects of the Shi'a this Mohammed became the first of a line of infallible leaders or Imams; the twelfth (or seventh) of these divinely appointed guides, taken up into heaven, is expected one day to return to earth as the Mahdi to establish an era of righteousness. Even though no important Sunni theologian committed himself to the idea of such a Mahdi, messianic traditions developed in Sunni Islam as well. Some of them embody the ancient mythological longing for an earthly paradise or Golden Age, a theme that predates both Judaism and Christianity. Thus one tradition states: "At the end of my Community, the Mahdi shall come forth. God shall send him abundant rain, and the earth shall bring forth her plants. He shall give wealth fairly; the cattle shall abound, and the Community shall be great." [128] Other traditions, such as the following, assign the Mahdi a more pronounced ethical mission: "He shall fill it [the earth] with justice and equity as it was filled with injustice and oppression. The heaven shall refuse nothing of its rain, nor shall the earth withhold anything of her plants." [129]

Whereas at first the Mahdi was seen merely as a just and rightful sovereign of the Prophet's kin who would displace those who had usurped and abused the caliphate, in time he became an eschatological figure connected with the approaching end of the world.[130] Many different and mutually discordant traditions gradually accumulated, and they were often put forth to bolster the political ambitions of particular claimants to the role of deliverer.[131] Famous theologians like Ibn Khaldun and al-Ghazali, therefore, were critical of the traditions concerning the coming of the Madhi.[132] Still, the popular desire for a redeemer who would usher in a reign of universal justice and well-being was too deeply ingrained, and the belief in the Mahdi eventually "established itself, not merely in Islamic folklore, but also in theology." [133] Mahdist movements have been numerous in such African countries penetrated by Islam as Senegal, Nigeria, and the Sudan, and in what today is Indonesia where the idea of the Mahdi merged with pre-Islamic concepts such as the appearance of a righteous prince.[134]

The most extreme of the early Shi'ite sects was one known as the *Isma'ilis*. Because of the secretive, quasi-masonic character of the movement, an amalgam of Shi'ite and Persian and Syrian gnostic sects, our knowledge of the movement's doctrines and activities is limited. It appears that the Isma'ilis found their main support among laborers, artisans, and other depressed classes.

Laws, they taught, were merely written and enacted to hold
down the masses and serve the interests of the ruling class. Those
who possessed access to the secret body of the knowledge of their
sect were not required to obey the law of the land. The Isma'ilis
exalted rebellion against the Sunni caliphs, and at the same time
they enforced the strictest obedience to their own Imam who was
endowed with supernatural powers.

A later branch of the Isma'ilis that flourished in the tenth and
eleventh centuries was the popular revolutionary movement of
the Carmathians, which was characterized by strongly eschatological views. "The time of manifestation is near," says one of the
few surviving original manifestos, from the year 1018, "the moment of the sword, the upheaval, the massacre of the impious and
their forcible annihilation, is approaching rapidly." [135] Another
offshoot, the "Assassins," staged frequently dramatic killings of
prominent opponents in mosques and in the court, one of their
most famous victims being the vizier and scholar, Nizam ul-
Mulk, who was assassinated in 1092. "By dying in the line of
duty," writes a student of the Assassins, "they were using their
bodies to purify their souls for the realms of light." [136] The modern successors of the Assassins, pacified and respectable, are the
Isma'ilis who follow the leadership of the Aga Khan.

The Carmathians, as noted, were especially successful among
the urban artisans, and they used the craft guilds to maintain
their influence long after their more ambitious military offensives
had been defeated. These guilds in time became the stronghold of
Islamic mysticism (*Sufism*) which fused Christian, Shi'ite, and
gnostic images and strongly appealed to the underprivileged
masses. Eventually the Sufi orders formally became Sunni and
lost much of their early revolutionary zeal. However, there were
occasional insurrections, led by guilds or Sufi preachers, like the
great revolt of the Ottoman dervishes in the early fifteenth century or the guild insurrections in seventeenth-century Istanbul.[137]

Throughout the first 1100 years of its existence Islam had its
share of political rebellions. The orthodox doctrine that stressed
the duty of practically unconditional obedience to those in
power was beset by heresies and sects that taught and practiced
the duty and rightfulness of revolt against impious or oppressive
authority. These two seemingly contradictory phenomena, of
course, are related. Muslim political doctrine and Islamic political

institutions failed to assure a peaceful resolution of differences over social and economic issues and an orderly succession, regional and tribal loyalties remained strong, and governments most of the time were incapable of inspiring the loyalty of their subjects by facing and solving the society's social problems in an equitable manner. In this situation, aggravated by geographical isolation and a poverty of resources, rebellions and military mutinies were frequent occurrences. In Algiers, for example, between 1671 and 1818, fourteen of the thirty rulers achieved power through military rebellion and the assassination of their predecessors.[138] These rivalries, internal wars, assassinations, and rebellions signaled the failure of Islamic political institutions while at the same time they assured the survival of Islam. "Traditional Islam," notes an astute observer, "survived for more than a millennium in a harsh and uncertain environment because it was capable of converting constant tension and conflict into a force for constant political renewal and social survival." [139] Rebellions, many of them inspired by religious motives, acted as a safety valve, attacked and undermined political authority but also often helped renovate it.

PART II

Millenarian Revolts

CHAPTER 3

Heterodoxy and Rebellion in Traditional China

TAOISM AND BUDDHISM

The unsatisfied religious needs that explain the popularity of China's many religious cults also contributed to the spread of the two great rivals of Confucianism—Taoism and Buddhism. Both arose during periods of political disorder and disunity when many people had lost faith in the official religion and sought new roads to salvation.

Taoism began as a philosophy rather than a religion. Practically nothing is known about its founder, Lao Tzu, who according to modern research is believed to have lived in the latter part of the fourth century; older scholars considered him a contemporary of Confucius, the sixth century B.C. We are in the same state of ignorance regarding Chuang Tzu, the great fourth-century poet of Taoism. The two classic works of this philosophic Taoism, the *Tao Te Ching* and *Chuang Tzu*, are ascribed by some scholars to Lao Tzu and Chuang Tzu, respectively; others regard them as composites of various teachings put together by a number of teachers. Both books are extremely vague and cryptic, and this has led to the most divergent interpretations of their meaning. When we open the translation of a Chinese classic like the *Tao Te Ching*, writes a recent student of Taoism, we therefore find "not a translation as we usually understand the word, but a spelling out in English of what is not spelled out in Chinese." [1]

Despite these ambiguities, several main themes can be noted. Like Confucius, Lao Tzu sought to bring man's life on earth into harmony with the law of the universe (*tao*). But instead of stressing a code of conduct, Lao Tzu advocated an almost mystic life of seclusion and withdrawal. Man's original nature was held to be kind; moral and legal codes degraded man by removing him from this original simplicity. Social and political ills, therefore, could not be cured by acts of the government; in fact such governmental intervention made things worse. The *Lao Tzu* declares: "The more restrictions and prohibitions there are in the world, the poorer the people will be. . . . The more laws are promulgated, the more thieves and bandits there will be." [2] In the same spirit Chuang Tzu taught a return to the ways of nature and indifference to life and death.

Taoism as a philosophy has continued to the present day, but, in terms of popularity, it was soon overtaken by the Taoist religion. In this religious variant the pursuit of immortality became the main goal; Lao Tzu eventually came to be worshipped as the creator of the world and the founder of a religion with its own temples, monasteries, priesthood, and liturgy.

Taoism as a religion may have begun with faith healers and magicians who were engaged in the search for immortality through magic, alchemy, and various hygienic techniques of respiration and special diets. During the early Han period these "specialists in immortality" often enjoyed imperial patronage, and they also attracted a growing following among the masses. The religious communities that emerged offered "hope and social stability under a hierarchy of religious leadership which made life once more tolerable and provided an avenue of status advancement for the ambitious and talented. The magical cults of Taoism raised confidence and morale and their organization reintroduced order to shattered lives." [3] The pantheon of Taoism came to be populated by numerous deities and spirits. Its ethical system, however, remained relatively undeveloped and borrowed extensively from both Confucianism and Buddhism. The main function of Taoist priests and monks was not moral leadership but rather the administration of an elaborate system of hygiene, mystic spells, divinations, fortune-telling, astrology, and other magical practices.

A religious and political reformer in the second century A.D., Chang Ling, was called the Heavenly Teacher by his followers, and he is often dubbed the first pope of the Taoist religion. His descendants continued to claim this title, but in actuality Taoism, as was the case with Buddhism, was not able to bring forth a central authority to which all its followers would submit. Parishes had their priests whose office often was hereditary, monasteries had their abbots. But beyond this basic hierarchy there was no unity, and Taoism was divided into many sects. "The Taoist church, like the Buddhist, was atomistic."[4]

In Taoism magic was cultivated to provide its followers with relief from various afflictions and misfortunes. By and large, Taoists accepted the existing institutions of society and had no plan for transforming the world, though the followers of dissenting subtraditions cultivated messianic hopes centered upon a perfect emperor who would realize the vision of the deified Lao Tzu. If such Taoist sects were often involved in political rebellions this was due not only to their doctrinal teaching but also to the spirit of group cohesion that characterized Taoist communities. Taoists stressed self-control, and the practice led to solidarity. In time of social unrest or political crisis these communities, often organized as secret societies, could easily be turned into a military force or a system of rebel cells.[5] However, this revolutionary role should not be exaggerated. As a rule Taoists lived in peace with the authorities, and their priests sought imperial patronage. In seeking the favor of those in power, Taoists were competing with Buddhists, and religious persecution often followed the triumph of one over the other.

The introduction and spread of Buddhism in China have been discussed earlier. The acceptance of Buddhism was enhanced by the fact that it was introduced in China in a modified form—the Mahayana. Unlike Theravada Buddhism, the Mahayana (the Greater Vehicle) offered salvation not only to the select few but to all. All men possessed the Buddha-nature and thus could attain Buddhahood, enlightenment, and salvation. To the common people this idea was a powerful magnet. The possibility of escaping military and labor services by joining a monastery further increased the attraction of Buddhism in an age of recurrent warfare.

In Mahayana Buddhism the promise of salvation for all is supported by the belief in *bodhisattvas*. Originally the term *bodhisattva* referred to the previous incarnations of the historical Buddha during which he had carried out mighty deeds of compassion that were celebrated in the highly popular *Jataka* or Birth

Stories. Later it came to be believed that many other Buddhas
were yet to appear and that the coming of Maitreya, the future
Buddha prophesied by Gotama Buddha, was being prepared for
by numerous *bodhisattvas*, working for the welfare of others and
making up the chain of being that would eventually lead to the
birth of Maitreya many thousands of years hence.[6] The *bodhisattvas*, though qualified to achieve salvation (*nirvana*), were said
to have chosen to remain in this world and practice self-sacrifice
in order to help others obtain enlightenment. Eventually it came
to be believed that these compassionate sublime beings facilitated
not only the achievement of salvation but the fulfillment of various earthly needs and desires. Numerous *bodhisattvas*, many of
them local gods adopted by Buddhism and unknown to the original creed, came to be worshipped by the simple people, and in
some Chinese Buddhist sects they were perceived as messianic figures who would relieve suffering and usher in a life of peace,
plenty, and happiness. It is easy to see how these beliefs could
change the generally world-renouncing character of Buddhist
teaching and introduce a dynamic and active concern for the reform of life on earth.

HETERODOXY AND REVOLT

Ever since the emergence of Taoism and Buddhism, and perhaps
even earlier, China had a multitude of religious sects and secret
societies. These groups flourished especially during periods of
economic or political crisis when a method of deliverance different from the prevailing orthodoxy had special appeal. Some of
these sects were direct offshoots of Buddhism and Taoism, others
were syncretic in character. Almost all of these groups were secret sects or societies not only or primarily because of special rituals, known only to the initiated, but because government persecution tended to drive them underground.[7] Religious movements
that did not win legal recognition therefore had to be prepared to
fight, and this is one important reason why so many peasant rebellions in Chinese history have had a religious ideology. "Se-
crecy and readiness to resist suppression," notes Yang, "were particularly necessary for religious sects that aimed at universal
salvation, as their doctrine usually claimed superior power for
their deities over the world order—a dogma that was obviously

offensive to the authoritarian temporal power, which would tolerate no superior doctrine other than the accepted orthodoxy." [8] Mere theological difference was usually not grounds for persecution, and we have seen how both Taoism and Buddhism were gradually absorbed into the state religion. The traditional and often ruthless suppression of heterodoxy had a political basis: the government feared fanatic uprisings by organized religious groups that had their own leaders and a mass following. Such movements, voluntary in character and based on conversion, clearly spelled the emergence of a competitive center of power should a leader acquire political ambitions.[9] For this reason the gathering of large numbers of people for a heterodox cause was always suspect, and any religious sect reaching sizable proportions would usually set the anti-heresy machinery in motion. Government edicts justifying these suppressions stressed the danger of unlicensed associations as can be seen from the following imperial decree of the year 1800 concerning measures taken against the White Lotus Society. Sectaries, the edict declared, will not be punished on account of their religious beliefs, "but they shall be punished if they hold meetings and violate the laws. . . . If they merely can keep quiet and obey the laws, their burning of incense and curing of the sick are not forbidden under the reign of this dynasty, as being at bottom works of benevolence prompted by commiseration. But when they take such works as a pretext for gathering people, for wielding arms, and gradually creating a thing of so high consequence as a rebellion, then the Sovereign's laws cannot tolerate them." [10] It is only fair to reiterate that the government's fear of certain kinds of sectarian movements and their consequent illegality often drove these movements to rebellion, thus creating a self-fulfilling prophecy about the relationship of heterodoxy and revolt.

Our information on specific sects and rebellions unfortunately is often scanty, but it is clear that many of them were millenarian or chiliastic in character. Following the increasingly accepted usage of anthropologists and historians, we employ these terms here and in the following chapters not in their literal and strictly historical sense, of the Kingdom of God of one thousand years' duration in the Judaic-Christian tradition (the Latin *millennium* and the Greek *chilias* mean a thousand years), but rather employ them figuratively and typologically, to denote the striving for an

age of eternal bliss, the searching for the end of human travail
once and for all. A brief examination of several such movements
in China will support this usage.

The revolt of the "Yellow Turbans" in A.D. 184 broke out after
many years of political corruption and a struggle for power
among the ruling groups. In 168 the eunuchs at the Han court
had seized power and killed many of the most prominent literati,
and this action resulted in a serious breakdown of the administrative machinery. A series of barbarian invasions and natural catas-
trophes contributed to unrest and insecurity. The population had
grown and economic conditions in the countryside probably
were bad, though there is no clear evidence that conditions had
become so unbearable as to drive people into rebellion.[11] It is
more likely that the weakening of the bureaucracy created an unusually favorable opportunity for a religious movement, led by an
ambitious man, to challenge the government. Exploitation and
poverty of the peasantry and repeated natural calamities like
floods, swarms of locusts, and pestilence appear to have been
some of the factors that prepared the ground for rebellion. The
more immediate cause probably was the demoralization of the
Han officialdom that shook the people's loyalty to the emperor
and fired the hopes of political opportunists.[12]

About the year 175 a certain Chang Chüeh founded a religious
movement which he called *T'ai P'ing Tao* (Way of Grand
Peace). Within ten years, intense missionary activity resulted in a
rapid spread of the sect in North China. Some writers have described the religious character of this movement as Taoist;[13]
others suggest that Chang Chüeh borrowed from both Taoism and
Buddhism but that he had his own doctrine.[14] Religious communities were organized with elaborate welfare schemes, and the
arrival of a happy world of supreme peace with a virtuous ruler
was prophesied. The sect made extensive use of confession and
faith healing.

We do not know at what point in his career Chang Chüeh laid
plans for a revolt. Once rebellion was decided upon, the religious
activity of the sect served as a political camouflage—a pattern
observable in many other Chinese peasant uprisings.[15] Nevertheless, in the winter of 184 a former disciple betrayed Chang
Chüeh, and it became necessary to start the rebellion sooner than
planned. Chang Chüeh assumed the title of Lord of Heaven Gen-

eral; his two brothers were made Lord of Earth General and Lord of Humanity General. In this way the three brothers presented themselves to the people as symbolic embodiments of heaven, earth, and man. The rebels wore yellow kerchiefs as a means of identification and therefore became known as the Yellow Turbans. Their number is given as 360,000.[16] After some initial setbacks the government forces rallied, and within a year the uprising had been suppressed with great ferocity. Chang Chüeh and his brothers were caught and executed. Meanwhile, in West China another religious group that was more directly Taoist rebelled. A levy of five bushels of rice was imposed upon the followers of this movement for faith healing, and the movement was therefore known as the "Five Bushels of Rice Movement." Certain similarities between the two communities led some scholars to regard them as related,[17] but there is no evidence of contact or fusion, and it appears to be mere accident that the Yellow Turbans and the Five Bushels of Rice rebelled in the same year.[18]

Despite the failure of both rebellions, many smaller outbreaks took place in the following years, and the downfall of the Han dynasty in 220 may have been due in part to the destruction and resulting discontent caused by these episodes of upheaval. Messianic speculations continued to be popular. A fifth-century Taoist text, composed during another period of political crisis, announced that "the empire will be abolished, but Heaven and Earth will be reestablished; then the Perfect Lord will manifest himself. . . . One sowing will yield nine crops. The human lifespan will increase; men will live up to three thousand years and then be transformed. Heaven and Earth will be in good order." [19] Even though Taoist priests later made the "Perfect Ruler" into an otherworldly god, Taoist messianism, with Lao Tzu deified as the master of the perfect emperor, continued to fuel dissenting movements.[20]

The Buddhist Maitreya sect is another religious movement involved in numerous rebellions. It began to make its appearance in the fourth century of the Christian era and spread rapidly especially during periods of unrest, turmoil, or corruption. Whereas in the orthodox tradition the coming of Maitreya was many thousands of years in the future, these Buddhist sectarians radically foreshortened the Maitreya expectation.[21] In times of hardship, the idea of the imminent descent of Maitreya from the Tushita heaven to deliver mankind from its state of wickedness and to bring peace and prosperity obviously had great appeal. A Buddhist writing describes what the world would be when Maitreya, a future Buddha, had actually become a Buddha in the world:

> All people will be kindhearted, doing the ten good deeds. Because they do good deeds, their lifespan will be long and filled with happiness and peace. Men and women will [cover the land] densely, cities and towns will border on one another, and chickens will fly from one to the other; in their farms, one planting will yield seven crops and plants will ripen of themselves without tilling or weeding.[22]

Ambitious rebel leaders claimed to be the incarnation of Maitreya himself or asserted that they were the just and virtuous rulers who would welcome the future Buddha upon his descent to earth.[23] Between 477 and 535, under the Northern Wei dynasty, there were no less than eight armed uprisings of peasants led by Buddhist monks.[24] A typical example is the monk Fa-ch'ing who rebelled in 515 with the slogan, "A new Buddha has appeared! Get rid of the old devils!" His followers destroyed Buddhist temples and killed many local officials before the uprising was brought under control.[25] Many such rebellions took place under the Sui, T'ang, and Sung dynasties, and the government reacted by vigorous suppression of the Maitreya cult. After the revolt of a certain Wang Tse in 1047 had been put down, government supervision became even more strict, and the Maitreya societies gradually disappeared. The basic theme of the Buddhist redeemer, however, lingered on in other Buddhist-inspired messianic movements, especially the White Lotus Society.

The White Lotus Society was founded during the early years of the Southern Sung dynasty (1127–1279) by a certain Mao Tzu-yüan. Its ideology was highly syncretic, and, though based on the Buddhist tradition, it showed Manichean and Taoist influences.[26] Despite the fact that the society had no concrete program to meet the practical needs of Chinese society, and, even though its advocacy of change was vague, it soon ran into the opposition of Confucianists and orthodox Buddhists alike and was banned repeatedly. In 1337 the first major rebellion attributable to the White Lotus Society took place. In 1351 a man named

Han Shan-t'ung led another uprising, rallying people with the slogan, "The country is in great confusion, and Maitreya is coming to be reborn." According to a contemporary commentator, because of great social inequalities many of the poor were "glad to join the rebellion." [27] Han Shan-t'ung's son, claiming to be an incarnation of Maitreya, gained control over a large part of North China, but in 1362 he was defeated by the Mongols. A member of a movement known as the Red Kerchief Bandits or the Red Army, the Buddhist monk Chu Yüan-chang, eventually succeeded in deposing the Yüan and in 1368 became the founder of the Ming dynasty. Chu, the son of a poor peasant, had fought under the slogan of an enlightened ruler appearing in the world, but one of the first things he did after ascending the throne was to ban all Maitreya and White Lotus Societies. He knew their insurrectionist tendencies and was unwilling to take chances.[28]

Surviving numerous persecutions, the White Lotus Society continued its clandestine existence, and it was involved in many uprisings under the Ming and Ch'ing (Manchu) dynasties. Animated by faith in the coming redeemer, Maitreya, who would bring deliverance from oppression and persecution, a rebellion broke out in 1566, and for a while the rebels controlled a large territory.[29] After the accession of the Ch'ing dynasty, the White Lotus Society added the nationalistic slogan: overthrow the alien Manchus. Its most formidable rebellion began in 1794, spread over nine provinces, and was not suppressed until the year 1805. Elements of White Lotus ideology appeared in several other revolts against the Manchus and could be found in the Boxer rebellion of 1900.[30] The Society has often been considered a political organization in religious guise,[31] but, given the dearth of reliable historical information on the sect, a determination of its true character in most cases is impossible.

The Yellow Turban, Maitreya, and the White Lotus Society rebellions are three prominent instances in what one scholar calls "an endless chain of religious rebellions that spread across the pages of Chinese history for two thousand years." [32] In a situation where more often than not the Confucian orthodoxy failed to meet not only the spiritual but also the basic material needs of the Chinese people, heterodox movements promising deliverance from both spiritual emptiness and everyday misery could never be completely suppressed. Led by men who as prophets claimed

the role of an intermediary between humanity and the gods, these
secret sects and societies time and again were able to attract a
mass following. In the words of Yang:

> As masses of troubled men scanned the horizon for an explanation
> of their plight and for deliverance from their suffering, prophecy
> answered them with momentous words of wisdom uttered not by
> men but by gods. When a traditional Chinese individual was in
> distress, he would go to the soothsayer, a diviner, or a fortune-
> teller to obtain an interpretation of his seemingly insoluble prob-
> lem and to receive some prediction of the outcome to guide his
> outlook and actions. When society was in distress, prophecy per-
> formed a similar function on a collective basis.[33]

These prophecies explained otherwise incomprehensible trage-
dies, and the cosmic laws they invoked restored a pattern of
order, if not hope, to men demoralized by events beyond their rational control or expectation. Promising redemption to believers
and extermination to the wicked who refused to embrace their
truth, sectarian movements attracted the downtrodden who
wished to be saved. Their leaders impressed the simple people by
predicting the coming of new calamities before the transition to
the next heavenly cycle could take place; an imperial edict of the
Ch'ing dynasty referred to this method of propaganda as
"frightening the people and alarming mankind with unfounded
heretic talk." [34] Since these prophecies were usually couched in
vague and obscure terms, and since life was indeed full of misfortune, the prophets rarely risked a refutation of their dire predictions.

Organized in small communities that often functioned as mu-
tual-aid brotherhoods, the sects and secret societies offered real
benefits in times of dislocation and crisis; they satisfied social
needs left unfulfilled by the Confucian system that did not extend
beyond kinship bonds. Sect leaders frequently fortified their authority through faith healing, utilizing spells and charms. Promising to enlist supernatural powers that would sweep aside all difficulties where ordinary human efforts had ended in failure and
despair, the heterodox movements stimulated hope.

And yet, it is important to note, traditional China's many rebellions, related or unrelated to religious heterodoxy, were
usually more revolutionary in rhetoric than in deed. The new
world of bliss and plenty remained a promise. "Peasant move-

ments in China," notes one of their students, "were not revolutionary movements; they were rebellions or revolts." [35] Chinese rebels shared with their antagonists basic cosmological and political assumptions such as the belief in Heaven as a spiritual force that conferred upon the virtuous the mandate to rule. The eyes of the rebels were fixed upon the past, and as soon as they triumphed they set about restoring and continuing the traditional socio-political order. "He who succeeds becomes Emperor, he who fails is a bandit," is an often-quoted Chinese proverb that takes note of this recurring pattern.[36] Rebel leaders, as we have discussed earlier, often tried to establish their legitimacy by claiming to be descendants of an emperor of a former dynasty. Rebels would kill hated local officials, but once in power they held examinations for a new corps of Confucian bureaucrats, and they worshipped Heaven to demonstrate that they had received the divine mandate to rule.

Chinese rebels inveighed against the privileges of the gentry or high taxes not so much as evils in themselves but as violations of Confucian principles. It is not until the ninth century that we encounter demands for remedying some social inequality and even these, for the most part, relied upon traditional Confucian concepts that opposed extremes in the distribution of land and wealth. Rebels showed sensitivity to the hardships of the people in their slogans, but, once successful, the rebels, except for such minor changes as lightening the tax burden or redistributing a few acres of land, maintained the traditional system of social stratification.[37]

The fact that religious sects have often rebelled against the Chinese state, and that peasant rebellions have usually been connected to heterodoxy, is generally accepted by students of traditional China. But given the paucity of reliable historical information the role of heresy is often difficult to assess. Did religious doctrines like those held by the Maitreya sect cause the masses to rebel or were these religious beliefs used as political camouflage by groups having essentially secular interests? Chinese Communist scholars, not surprisingly, generally downgrade the importance of religion. The main cause of peasant revolts, they argue, was the system of feudal exploitation. Religious doctrines, in their view, are controlled by the class struggle, and if some religious ideas were egalitarian in character this was so because they represented and reflected the revolutionary thought of peasants still

caught in religious consciousness. Communist writers are willing
to concede that religion functioned as an instrument of organization, mobilization, and propaganda, especially in the preparatory
stages of rebellions. Religious sects, they admit, provided unity
and mutual aid, and some religious ideas could be helpful to the
revolutionary cause, but by and large peasant revolts produced
their own revolutionary platforms and slogans.[38]

To most Western writers the picture appears more complicated. Thus, for example, if economic exploitation, with concomitant hardship, were one of the factors encouraging revolt this
was in good part the result of a religious interpretation of this
state of affairs that regarded economic misery as an indication
that the ruler had lost the Mandate of Heaven. Exploitation and
poverty in and by themselves have never and nowhere been
causes of rebellion. An ideological catalyst is needed to make people regard misery as unacceptable and unnecessary, and the religious concept of the Mandate of Heaven played just this role.
Famines due to crop failure or other national disasters, corrupt
governments that increased taxes and neglected public granaries,
irrigation, and water conservation [39]—these crises helped loosen
the traditional hold of the government on the people to drive
them to political opposition. But the willingness to engage in rebellion, to risk torture and death, required the sanction and encouragement of the gods. Writes Yang:

> It was in the name of an extraordinary god that a struggle was
> launched against a ruling power, which by abusing its office had
> forfeited its divine commission. Men needed assurance from a su-
> pernatural power, as proclaimed by the sectarian leaders, to over-
> come the awe they had for the established government. For an ex-
> traordinary action, men must have extraordinary justification
> beyond the finite world of secular and utilitarian reasoning. Reli-
> gion, with all its extraordinary supernatural claims, as illustrated in
> the contents of prophecy, helped to provide the necessary emo-
> tional support. With the gods' sanction, men not only felt justified
> in their unusual action but also felt sure they would win.[40]

Religion generated faith and confidence, if not fanaticism, and,
as we mentioned above, it also provided cohesion and discipline, a
prerequisite of collective action. Shared belief in a supernatural
power was a basis for a powerful social relationship and bond.
"The use of an oath and the burning of a written pledge with the
names of members on it were common parts of the initiation ritu-

als of many Chinese secret religious sects in order to impress the members with the fact that their membership was not only a contract between men but also a sacred tie confirmed by the gods and spirits."[41] In times of disorder this organization stood ready to act, and politically ambitious leaders had a ready-made organizational base from which to operate. The revolt of the Yellow Turbans led by Chang Chüeh probably was facilitated in this manner.

At times rebellions were the result of religious oppression and the necessity of defending a chosen way of religious life. Other times religious sects would turn to rebellion when a public crisis provided an opportune moment to satisfy political ambitions. An official comment on the Eight Diagram rebellion at the beginning of the nineteenth century noted that the sect was engaged in religious activities in normal times, but plotted for great political enterprise in times of famine and disorder.[42] Some sects and societies were predominantly political in character but used religion as a means of inducing group loyalty and solidarity. Not infrequently religious rituals also served as a front for purely political designs. The Buddhist practice of burning incense before the Buddha image appears to have functioned thus, and this fact may help explain why this and other Buddhist elements appear with such regularity among Chinese secret societies.[43]

Even though heterodox sects and societies drew most of their support from ordinary, uneducated people, especially the peasantry, they did not simply follow class lines. Some heterodox Taoist sects were rather numerous among the propertied classes.[44] Moreover, the leaders often came from the landowning or merchant class. Under pressure from government officials, these elements frequently made common cause with the peasantry. The rebellion of the Taoist Sun En in the year 399, for example, appears to have been a revolt of rich landowners against the government.[45] The Taoist-Manichean preachers Chung Hsiang and Yang Yao who rebelled in 1130 were wealthy and influential landlords who resented fiscal pressures from the government and used egalitarian slogans to rouse the peasantry and secure their support.[46] Confucianist literati who had passed the examinations but had failed to find employment and other disgruntled intellectuals also provided a reservoir of leadership for dissidents.[47] The crucial role of one such man in the nineteenth-century Taiping Rebellion will be examined in Chapter 7.

CHAPTER 4

Jewish Messianism: Eschatological Revolt and Divine Deliverance

THE MACCABEAN REVOLT

When Cyrus the Great captured Babylon in 539 B.C. the tolerant Persian monarch allowed the Jewish exiles to return to their homeland. The Jews remained subjects of the Persian empire, but the Persian overlords of Judea did not interfere with their religious beliefs and observances. The same pattern of toleration continued when, following an interlude of Egyptian rule, Palestine became part of the Seleucid empire. However, Hellenistic manners and customs then began to encroach upon Judea, but the process of Hellenization was not so much imposed upon the Jews by their foreign rulers as it was carried out by a section of the Jewish people, especially the upper classes and the educated. These Jewish Hellenizers sought to accommodate traditional Judaism to the spirit of the times and to free it from its isolation in a Greek world. Hence, they proceeded to "remove everything which smacked of separation, of the 'ghetto': Sabbath observance, beards, circumcision, and the namelessness of God which was otherwise to be met only among the most primitive peoples." [1] The leaders of this reform party were the high priests Jason and Menelaus, the heads of the Jewish community during the reign of Antiochus IV Epiphanes (176–163 B.C.).

Jewish tradition, following the books of the Maccabees, has ascribed the subsequent revolt against Antiochus Epiphanes to a despotic king's policy of religious persecution. Modern scholarship, on the other hand, considers the Maccabean revolt less as an uprising against foreign oppression, than as a civil war between the orthodox and reformist parties in the Jewish camp.[2] Indeed, some writers see the Hellenizers not only as the initiators of reform but also as the initiators of persecution. What is clear is that, from the beginning, the Hellenizing reforms encountered widespread opposition among broad sections of the Jerusalem public—craftsmen, laborers, and petty traders—as well as among the conservative-minded rural population. Leadership in the orthodox camp was provided by the class of scribes, the lay interpreters of the Torah, and among these, in particular, the sect of the Hasidim (the Pious). Inasmuch as the abolition of the ancestral laws by the high priests threatened to make these scribes superfluous, "the struggle of the Hasidim against the Hellenizers was not merely an ideological struggle for the maintenance of the commandments of the Law, but also the struggle of an entire class for its existence." [3]

Ferment among the Jerusalem population apparently reached the point of open rebellion as a result of the quartering of Syrian troops upon the Temple mount and the consequent desecration of the Temple by the introduction of pagan rites. It was this uprising, a recent historian has suggested, that precipitated the decrees of persecution by Antiochus and the fearful afflictions caused by them. If "devotion to the Mosaic Law was the watchword of the uprising, then that Law had to be extirpated if the rebellion was to be put down." [4] The infamous persecutory decrees, prohibiting the performance of the duties imposed by the ancestral tradition, now were necessary to weaken Jewish nationalism.

As is well known, and at this point we return to well-covered ground undisturbed by rival interpretations, Antiochus' policy had the opposite effect. The persecution fanned the nationalistic fervor and soon (167–166 B.C.) an open war broke out. Led at first by a priest named Mattathias of the Hasmonean family in the town of Modein, and after the death of Mattathias by his son, Judah, the rebels abandoned the earlier prohibition of self-defense on the Sabbath and generally took the offensive. Hellenizing Jews were slaughtered mercilessly, and several Syrian armies were routed. Judah, now known as the Maccabee (probably meaning the hammerer), captured Jerusalem, and in December 164 the purified Temple was consecrated anew.

The ground swell of patriotism and bravery in battle that enabled the Maccabean warriors to defeat armies several times their

size no doubt was strengthened by religious zeal, and Judah cultivated the religious feelings of his followers. Once again, as in pre-
prophetic times, religious and national enthusiasm went hand in
hand, and the struggle took on some of the characteristics of the
holy war of old. Desecrated Torah rolls and defiled priestly vest-
ments were exhibited to the troops, fasting and prayer preceded
battle, and God was called upon to save Israel.[5] While for the
Maccabees the desire for divine support and intervention did not
preclude a spirit of intense activism—God helps those who
help themselves could have been their motto—some of the Hasidim who supported or at least sympathized with their struggle
adopted a more negative attitude toward the efficacy of human
action. The Book of Daniel represents the thinking of this apocalyptic wing of the Hasidic sect; as fragments among the Dead Sea
Scrolls reveal, this work originally may have existed in many different versions representing the product of a school rather than of
one person.[6]

The Book of Daniel is the first great apocalyptic work of Judaism and its influence has been far-reaching, down to modern
times when it inspired the millenarian Fifth Monarchy Men during the Puritan Revolution. It was probably written after the first
successes of the Maccabean revolt but before the capture of Jerusalem, and it was addressed especially to the Hasidim whom it
sought to uplift and fortify. Using the name of a sixth-century
worthy named Daniel, the book tells how the tribulations of an
earlier age were overcome by the hero through his faith in God.
Even in the most hopeless situation, when the sage is cast into the
lion's den, God provides for miraculous deliverance by sending
angels who shut the mouths of the lions (6:22). All such suffering,
the pious author seeks to demonstrate, will come to an end; it is
part of a divine plan and fits into a historical scheme that inevitably leads to the ultimate goal of the Kingdom of God.

In Daniel's famous dream (Chapter 7) the reader is told of four
successive kingdoms or monarchies that are symbolized by four
beasts. It is the last of these mythological creatures, standing for
the ferocious reign of Antiochus Epiphanes, that is described as
"terrible and dreadful and exceedingly strong" (7:7), yet it is destined to be slain and thus paves the way for the fifth kingdom.
This empire, through God's judgment, will be given to "the
saints of the Most High," to Israel personified as a "son of man"

(7:13); [7] "their kingdom shall be an everlasting Kingdom" and all other peoples and nations "shall serve and obey them" (7:27). The enduring messianic Kingdom of God is thus conceived as an earthly universal state, administered by the Jewish saints. By a complicated calculation in "weeks of years" the Hasidic author seeks to show that this final stage of history is at hand. At the moment of deliverance, those who have been martyred during the days of persecution or fallen in defense of the true faith, will be resurrected "to everlasting life" while the Hellenizers and apostates will awake "to shame and everlasting contempt" (12:2). In this way the author not only encouraged the expectation of imminent redemption for the whole nation but also offered a personal reward for those who went forth to death in martyrdom or battle.[8] The ideas of the resurrection of the dead, taken over from Hellenism, and of reward and punishment for each individual were thus introduced into Judaism from which eventually they passed into Christianity and Islam.[9]

The great transformation predicted by the apocalyptic visionary is not brought about by a messiah. The "son of man" to whom God gives dominion and glory is a symbolic representation of the whole people Israel, though later writers tended to see this son of man as the Messiah. The author of the Book of Daniel is convinced that Israel will be delivered by God himself. He who had dared to "rise up against the Prince of princes" will be brought down by a spiritual divine intervention but "by no human hand" (8:25). The Hasid Daniel considers the military action of the Maccabees as "little help" (11:34), whereas he praises those who patiently suffer martyrdom; they are the "wise who shall make many understand, though they shall fall by sword or flame" (11:33). "It is fortitude under persecution that he encourages," concludes a student of the Book of Daniel, "rather than revolt against oppression, and in this he is the forerunner of other apocalyptics." [10] The notion that divine deliverance will come at the moment of greatest need (12:1), originally in Ezekiel, foreshadows the idea of the "messianic woes" or the "birth pangs of the Messiah," another frequent theme in Jewish apocalyptic.[11]

The Book of Daniel thus involves all the different strands of Jewish messianism, both quietistic and revolutionary. Incorporating ancient mythological material, Jewish eschatology emerged in a period of extreme affliction at a time when earlier messianic

hopes no longer offered spiritual solace. The Book of Daniel now
became the prototype of the so-called pseudepigraphic books
that, in order to receive a hearing, were published under the
name of some great personality in Israel's past (the Book of
Enoch, the Book of Baruch, The Fourth Book of Ezra, etc.), for
the Law was considered supreme, prophecy dead, and the canon
closed.[12] As we have mentioned earlier, Daniel is also, of course, an
example of apocalyptic writing, revealing glimpses of the future.
The entire class of pseudepigrapha, and especially apocalyptic
writing, found little favor among the official spokesmen of later
Judaism, and they excluded most of them from the canon. These
mysterious messianic portrayals and calculations, if was feared by
many of the rabbis, "would inflame overmuch the imagination of
the masses and incite them to revolt." [13] Whereas the authors of
Jewish apocalypse frequently deprecated human assertiveness—
the Book of Daniel is a case in point—such writings, nevertheless,
found eager acceptance particularly in days of tribulation and at
times did indeed inflame the passions to the point of rebellion.

A difference of opinion over the question of whether to win a
national victory by force of arms or trustingly to wait for the intervention of God was one of the causes of the split that soon developed between Judah and many of his fellow-warriors on one
side and the quietistic and apocalyptic Hasidim on the other. We
do not know how many of the Hasidim ever actively participated
in the Maccabean military struggle. The First Book of Maccabees
relates that a group of Hasidim joined the fight under Mattathias
and they are called "mighty warriors of Israel" (2:42), but we do
not know how large this warlike wing of the Hasidim was. In
any event, the alliance did not last. Demetrius Soter, who in 162
had seized the throne of Syria, sought to end the rebellion by offering the Jews religious freedom, and at this point the Hasidim
withdrew their support from Judah and recognized the high
priest Alcimus, an appointee of the Syrians. Satisfied with the assurance of freedom of worship and the right to observe the Jewish law, the Hasidim made their peace with the Hellenizers, while
Judah insisted on continuing the struggle until complete national
independence had been achieved. The Hasidim were unwilling to
fight for such a secular goal, and from this point on (the peace of
162 B.C.) they begin to disappear from the map of history. Their
spiritual offspring, it has been pointed out, are the Pharisees and

Essenes who perpetuated the Hasidims' legalism and quietism, respectively. The possibility of a link to the Zadokite sect and to other groups behind the Dead Sea Scrolls has also been suggested.[14]

The revolt of the Maccabees now assumed the character of a political struggle for national freedom. In 161 Judah entered into an alliance with the Romans but Demetrius at this point resolved to end the annoying problem once and for all; he massed a large army and in the spring of 160 decisively defeated the Jews. Judah himself fell in the battle. That the Maccabean party was finally able to drive out the Hellenizers and achieve independence after all was due primarily to the internal dissensions in the Syrian empire and its consequent decline of power. For some one hundred years the Hasmonean family ruled in relative security, and the nation expanded beyond the narrow frontiers of Judea over the whole of Palestine.

The attainment of a strong Jewish state, covering practically the entire territory of the old Israelite tribes, kindled an aggressive national spirit, and some enthusiasts saw in these events the fulfillment of ancient messianic prophecies. The author of the First Book of Maccabees, writing in the last quarter of the second century B.C., described the rule of the Hasmonean high priest Simon (142–134) in language which reads like a paraphrase of the messianic glories predicted by earlier biblical texts.[15] Simon's son, John Hyrcanus, apparently also sought to be considered the Messiah, and, in 104 B.C., Aristobulus assumed the name king. The change from commonwealth to monarchy came at a time when the Hasmonean dynasty had evolved into an autocratic and widely despised ruling house—"at a remote extreme from the ideal of the ruler in the golden age as he is figured in such prophecies as Isa. 11:1–5." [16] When Judea in 63 B.C. became a vassal princedom of the Romans, once again subdued by an alien and pagan power, the representatives of the nation begged Pompey to abolish the royal form of government and Judea reverted to the old constitution under a high priesthood. Popular imagination now returned to the weaving of legends about a redeeming messianic king, a true shoot of David rather than a man belonging to a dynasty of usurpers. "With the end of the Hasmoneans," concludes Bickermann, "the messianic period of Jewish history begins." [17]

ESCHATOLOGICAL WAR AGAINST ROME: THE ZEALOTS

The Pharisees, the most influential force in the Jewish community during the first one hundred years of Roman overlordship, believed in the eventual coming of the Messiah, but they did not interpret this belief as a call to action. God would send the Messiah in his good time. In the tradition of the Hasidim, the Pharisees emphasized the importance of religious observance—they may have been called "pharisees" (literally "separatists") because of their insistence upon separation from impurity and defilement —but they did not meddle in politics. The fact that the Jewish high priest now was a Roman vassal in their eyes was not important as long as the Jews possessed religious liberty. In realistic recognition of the overwhelming strength of the Romans, the Pharisees made the Jewish religion the line of defense of the Jewish people. "They were not a dynastic or nationalist party, and were content with the freedom they enjoyed to pursue their religious studies and practices and to labor with their countrymen for a better observance of the divine law." [18]

The messianic expectation was stronger among the "popular prophets," the authors of pseudepigraphic apocalyptic writings, who provided "food for the marvel-seeking imagination of the common people" [19] as well as inspiration for the slowly growing resistance movement against foreign rule. The fostering of a spirit of rebellion was an indirect result, for most of these apocalyptic works did not advocate the use of force. As in the Book of Daniel at the time of the Maccabean revolt, the new apocalyptic writers predicted that the approaching messianic deliverance of Israel from the Romans would take place through God's direct intervention or through the action of a messiah sent by him. The pious author of the Psalms of Solomon, probably writing soon after Pompey's death in 48 B.C., called the current distress a punishment from God which one had to endure patiently. Such patience would find its reward in the life to come: "We hope in God, our deliverer" (17:3). The enemies of Israel will be destroyed, it was proclaimed, "The Lord Himself is our king for ever and ever" (17:51).[20] Similarly, the Assumption of Moses, composed most likely during the first quarter of the Christian era, advocated the martyrdom of the innocent as a means of promoting divine vengeance and hurrying the eschatological delivery.[21]

In the Apocalypse of Baruch of the latter half of the first century
of the Christian era it is the Messiah "who will summon all the
nations, and some of them he will spare and some of them he will
slay" (LXXII:2).[22]

Yet these apocalyptic works, despite their often pronouncedly
quietistic teaching, did of course encourage the belief in an early
liberation and inflamed the desires of those prepared to force the
hand of God by direct action. Such a group emerged during the
years following the death of Herod the Great (4 B.C.) when Judea
had become a Roman province. The immediate occasion for the
emergence of a radical anti-Roman movement was the census ordered in the year 6 of the Christian era by the Roman legate
prior to the imposition of a system of tribute. Among the masses
of the people, impoverished by the high taxes exacted during the
extravagant reign of Herod, this measure caused great unrest, and
an offshoot of the Pharisees, under the leadership of a certain
Judah of Galilee and assisted by a Pharisee named Zadok, now
began to channel this unrest into organized resistance. Flavius Josephus later named this party "the Fourth Philosophy" for he discussed it after the Sadducees, Pharisees, and Essenes; others called
them the Galileans (Luke 13:1) or Zealots. It is the latter name,
referring to their religious zeal, that is most appropriate, for it
touches the core of their teaching, the theological legitimation of
their program of rebellion.[23]

The followers of Judah the Galilean were inspired by Phineas,
the grandson of Aaron the priest. According to biblical tradition
(Numbers 25:7–11), at a time of apostasy and intermarriage
with foreign peoples, Phineas had served his God with zeal by
killing an Israelite guilty of demonstratively taking a pagan
woman. In gratitude for this passionate loyalty, the story continued, God had taken his punishment, the plague, from the people
of Israel. In a similar way the Zealots now hoped to turn away
God's new wrath that had resulted in subjection to a foreign
ruler. In their eyes, this oppression was a punishment for the
Jews' failure to recognize God's sovereignty and for not con-
forming fully to his law. By seizing the sword like Phineas and
zealously proceeding against the Romans and their collaborators,
these Jewish patriots sought to demonstrate their complete loyalty to God and to bring about his redeeming intervention. During the Seleucid persecution, remembrance of the zeal of Phineas

had inspired Mattathias the Hasmonean to kill a Jew about to sacrifice upon a pagan altar, and in the wake of this charismatic deed all those "zealous for the law" (I Macc. 2:27) had taken up arms in defense of the holy covenant. The Zealots' resort to violence quite consciously followed this old tradition. Their nationalism, too, was "motivated by a dynamic theology of zeal for the Torah." [24]

Like the Pharisees, the Zealots wanted to make Israel a holy nation, but unlike their more pacifistic brethren they insisted that this goal could be achieved only by refusing obedience to any king but God. As Josephus reports, they held God to be their only lord and master; their leader Judah regarded the payment of tribute a recognition of Roman rule and thus a violation of the absolute sovereignty of Yahweh. Disappointed by the selfish and hellenized reign of the later Hasmoneans and Herod, the Zealots returned to the old Israelite ideal of theocracy. Disenchanted with human rulers, some of whom had or continued to commit the sacrilege of claiming divine status, they sought to realize the kingship of God, perhaps with a godly high priest as his vice-regent on earth.[25] The Zealots believed it to be their religious duty to actively resist the alien power that had seized the land promised Israel by the God of Abraham, Isaac, and Jacob in a holy covenant.

The Zealots shared with the apocalyptics the certainty of early redemption by God. They were willing to do battle with the powerful Romans because they trusted God to come to their aid just as in earlier days he had delivered their ancestors from slavery in Egypt. "The history of their people, recorded in a holy scripture, was a veritable *Heilsgeschichte*, abounding with thrilling accounts of how Yahweh had saved those who faithfully and courageously had withstood the impious heathen—from Joshua to Judas Maccabaeus, long and inspiring was the roll of Israel's heroes whose faith and daring had been so signally rewarded by their God." [26] It is likely that the Zealots regarded the current tribulations as the messianic woes, the last days before the coming of the Kingdom of God. The age was rife with messianic expectations; popular chronologies expected the coming of the Messiah around the second quarter of the first Christian century, and numerous pretenders appeared to predict an imminent divine manifestation.[27]

There was one all-important difference, however, between the apocalyptics and the Zealots. Whereas the former, as we have seen, by and large maintained that freedom from the yoke of Rome would be brought about by supernatural power, the latter believed that God would usher in the new age only if the pious zealously participated in the realization of the divine plan. Josephus describes the Zealots' libertarian activism in these words: "The Deity does not co-operate in restoring liberty otherwise than by influencing man's decision, and God will be much more ready to assist us if we do not shirk the toil entailed by the great cause which we have at heart." [28] Seeing the need for cooperation with God, the Zealots called for eschatological war against Rome; the so-called War Scroll of the Dead Sea documents, to be discussed below, best fits this program. Later Jewish tradition, under the impact of several disastrous defeats in fighting such holy wars, rejected this audacious assertiveness as an illegitimate "pressing for the end" of the world.[29]

Our knowledge of the history of the Zealots during the next sixty years is limited. It appears that the uprising organized by Judah the Galilean against the census failed and that Judah himself was killed.[30] But the movement he had founded did not disappear, and with three of Judah's sons taking a leading part it continued to gather strength. The Zealots gained supporters especially among the poorer segments of the Jewish population—landless peasants and the inferior orders of the priesthood. Judah himself is described by Josephus as a "sophist," and there can be little doubt that the patriotic movement included many sophists or rabbis who provided ideological inspiration. Not every Zealot, of course, was imbued only with such lofty religious ideals. As economic conditions in a badly administered country went from bad to worse, lawless and desperate characters were attracted to the guerilla movement which often became indistinguishable from plain banditry, preying upon Romans and Jews alike. The Jewish renegade Josephus, who did his best to portray all of the freedom fighters as criminals, called the Zealots "brigands" or "robbers," but this characterization would seem to apply only to some of their supporters. A movement that eventually was able to win over broad masses of the Jewish people and lead them into war against Rome could not have been motivated primarily by a desire for private gain.[31]

Under the procurator Felix (A.D. 52–60) rebellion became widespread and constant. Unable as yet to prevail in open battle, the Zealots added a new tactic to their expanding activities. Some of their men armed themselves with a small dagger (*sica*), and, thus made inconspicuous, they singled out for assassination in particular Jews known for their pro-Roman sympathies. The well-known Jewish historian, Graetz, calls these *Sicarii* the "scum of the Zealot party,"[32] though this harsh judgment would seem to rely too much on Josephus' highly prejudicial account. Among those who fell victim to the dagger of the *Sicarii* was the high priest Jonathan, a man of moderate sentiments. Meanwhile, bands of Zealots increasingly controlled the countryside and the Romans reacted with cruel repression. Josephus reports that "the number of the robbers whom he [Felix] caused to be crucified was incalculable, as also that of the citizens whom he arrested and punished as having been in league with them."[33]

The spread of the Zealot movement and the increase in stepped-up Roman persecution were accompanied by the growth of messianic fervor and the appearance of enthusiastic prophets and messianic pretenders. During the reign of the procurator Cuspius Fadus (A.D. 44–?), a prophet named Theudas led a large group of followers to the Jordan where he sought to prove his divine mission in the fight against Rome with the claim that he could part the stream by a mere word. The Roman ruler sent a troop of horsemen against Theudas and many in the group, including the would-be Messiah, were killed.[34] Josephus tells of other "deceivers and impostors" who led credulous multitudes into the desert where God would perform miracles of deliverance. Under the procurator Felix, an Egyptian Jew with a following of 4000 (Acts 21:38) or 30,000 (according to Josephus) promised like a second Joshua that at his word the walls of Jerusalem would come tumbling down and that this miracle would signal the rout of the Roman garrison. Again, the procurator sent troops and scattered the rebellious Jews. The Egyptian himself escaped.[35]

The appearance of John the Baptist and Jesus of Nazareth fits into this setting of heightened messianic expectations albeit at a time when the Zealot movement had not yet reached its zenith. Josephus describes John as a good and pious man, and it is possible that Herod Antipas had him imprisoned and put to death in

A.D. 29 simply to prevent the mischief that a prophetic figure of great popularity might cause in an unsettled time.[36] Robert Eisler, on the other hand, thinks that "Jesus attributed to the Baptist the authorship of the Zealotic activist movement for independence" and he links John to the "men of violence" who take the Kingdom of Heaven "by force" (Matthew 11:11–12; Luke 16:16).[37] A resolution of these rival interpretations is out of place here as is an evaluation of Jesus' much disputed political role, the subject of a vast literature. The Jewish position on Jesus' messiahship is summed up succinctly by the medieval philosopher Maimonides, who concludes, without mentioning Jesus by name, in a passage later expurgated: "But if he does not meet with full success, or is slain, it is obvious that he is not the Messiah promised in the Torah."[38]

The documents discovered at Qumran, the so-called Dead Sea Scrolls, throw important additional light on the various Jewish sects and parties existing in the decades before and during the Great Jewish Revolt.[39] Again, the literature on the Qumran documents is enormous, and we will have to limit ourselves here to certain basic points.

The Dead Sea Scrolls reveal the existence of a Jewish monastic community on the shore of the Dead Sea, a religious and military order bound by a rigid discipline, adhering to a unique calendar, and composing and copying an extensive literature. The origins of this religious sect are disputed. A link to the Zadokites, a party defending the Zadokite lineage of the priesthood, is possible. The monastic style of life of the Qumran community has lent plausibility to the suggestion that the Dead Sea covenanters were Essenes, an order of pious Jews who withdrew into small rural communities where they practiced a life of strict religious observance and detachment from politics. The Essenes, our sources indicate, were pacifists and pietists who taught acceptance of the ruling powers, but at least some of the documents found at Qumran indicate a rather different political posture that suggests a close affinity, if not identity, with the Zealots.[40]

The scroll of *The War of the Sons of Light with the Sons of Darkness*, in particular, stands out as an intensely militant, anti-Roman document. The covenanters here are summoned to battle against the forces of evil, a call is issued for the final struggle that will bring the deliverance of Israel and the destruction of the

pagan nations. It is of significance that this eschatological war is
won not only through divine intervention, the action of "a great
and terrible God, to despoil all our enemies before us" (col. x),
but also as a result of the valiant efforts of his holy warriors—
"volunteers for war, blameless in spirit and flesh, and ready for
the day of venegance" (col. vi.).[41] This idea of cooperation of
man with God in the achievement of "peace and blessing" and
"eternal light," as we have seen earlier, is a characteristic Zealot
doctrine, and its presence forces us to regard this scroll as more
than just another piece of Jewish eschatological writing. Cecil
Roth calls it "an extraordinary admixture of reality, military
awareness, and apocalyptic expectation," [42] and, relying upon the
nature of the *War* scroll and other evidence, he argues that the
men of Qumran, after the year A.D. 6, were Zealots. The monastic
settlement, founded by Essenes, was taken over by the followers
of Judah the Galilean during their revolt against the census, Roth
suggests, and became the Zealots' religious focus, the center of
their leader's activity and teaching.[43] Even those authorities who
have taken the position that the Dead Sea covenanters were Essenes have had to admit the influence of Zealot thinking upon
them. De Vaux calls the *War* scroll "possibly . . . inspired by the
fanaticism of [the] Zealots." [44] Hengel notes that it reveals "a
zealotic radicalization of the Essenes," [45] and Burrows thinks that
"possibly some members of the community joined the Zealots in
the last decades before the destruction of the temple." [46] We will
return to this topic a little later.

Relations between the Romans and the Jews went from bad to
worse under the procurator Gessius Florus who assumed office in
A.D. 64. The wealthy classes, too, now were subjected to oppressive taxation and even the Temple treasure was plundered. After
a bloody clash in the streets of Jerusalem, a young priest, Eleazar,
persuaded his colleagues in the Temple to stop the daily sacrifice
for the emperor (spring A.D. 66). This step was tantamount to a
repudiation of Roman rule and was indeed interpreted as such by
Jews and Romans alike. At the same time, an army of Zealots
under Menahem, the last surviving son of Judah the Galilean,
seized the fortress Masada on the Dead Sea coast; the period of
guerilla warfare had given way to full-scale war. In vain did the
upper clergy, the Sadduccees, and other men of rank and position
in Jerusalem warn their fellow citizens against such a final test of
strength.

The conservative posture of the upper classes probably was reinforced by the fear of losing their property, for the Zealots sought to enforce social justice as well as a puritanical Judaism. Josephus reports that at the outbreak of the rebellion they burned the public archives in order to destroy the money-lenders' bonds and make the collection of debts impossible. It was probably during the first days of the Great Revolt that Hananiah, the suffragan high priest, predicted that the repudiation of allegiance to Rome would lead to anarchy: "Pray for the peace of the kingdom, since but for fear thereof we had swallowed up each his neighbour alive." [47] Hananiah's saying was preserved in the Talmud and often commented upon. Johanan ben Zakkai, the most prominent leader of the Pharisees, also opposed the rebellion, but his peace party lost ground rapidly.

The battle for Jerusalem was decided by the arrival of Menahem and his army, well equipped from the armory of Masada. Josephus writes that the Zealot leader entered Jerusalem "like a veritable king," and this report, supported by Talmudic evidence, would seem to indicate that he was greeted as the Messiah.[48] This claim for exalted leadership appears to have been one of the reasons for a break between Menahem and the rebel-priest Eleazar that ended with the murder of Menahem. In the *Commentary on Habakkuk*, one of the Dead Sea scrolls, we read of the murder of the "Teacher of Righteousness" by a "wicked priest" and this account may refer to the killing of Menahem by his rival in Jerusalem.[49] The identity of the Zealot leader, Menahem, with the teacher of righteousness, would, if it were ever substantiated, also prove the Zealot character of the Dead Sea covenanters. Writers holding to the latter view surmise that most of the followers of Menahem left Jerusalem after their leader's death and withdrew sullenly to their strongholds on the Dead Sea coast, Qumran and Masada. The literature of the covenanters indeed is full of denunciations of a priestly faction whom it regarded as the covert enemy of God. Hostility to those in control of the Holy City may explain why the Zealots, entrenched at Masada, later did not engage in any diversionary action against the Romans laying siege to Jerusalem. In their eyes, as Roth suggests, the powers of darkness, who had murdered the teacher of righteousness stood in the way of divine support. "Only when they had been swept away, and the people had turned to perfect social justice on the one hand, to correct observance of all religious prescriptions on the other, would God return to comfort the remnant of His people and give them victory." [50]

The messianic and eschatological fervor that remained strong among the defenders of Jerusalem even after the departure of some of the Zealots also in good part exlains the internecine strife that developed in the winter of 67–68. To the soldiers of a holy war, convinced that God was on their side, the suppression of all error and the achievement of the reign of virtue were the indispensable condition of divine intervention leading to the rout of God's enemies. Josephus describes the tripartite warfare in the Jewish camp among the factions of Simon bar Giora, John of Gishcala, and Eleazar ben Simon as mainly the outcome of personal ambition, but it appears to have also been a struggle among the adherents of rival social and religious programs. "Indeed," Cecil Roth observes, "the conviction that God would grant victory only when his will was meticulously obeyed made these struggles logically necessary: for only thus could the divine favour be ensured." [51] Josephus' writings provide many indications of such messianic excitement. Among the causes of the revolt he names "an ambiguous oracle" found in the Jewish sacred writings which the Jews interpreted to mean that "at that time from their country one should rule the world." [52]

In return for their zealous fight for the cause of God, the Jewish defenders of Jerusalem expected God's saving intervention, and this reliance upon God became all the stronger as the military situation deteriorated. They remembered the saying of Daniel that God's people will be delivered at "a time of trouble, such as never has been since there was a nation" (12:1). Setbacks in the struggle thus did not discourage the Jews but were seen as signs of the messianic woes preceding the moment of delivery.[53] The deliberate burning of the granaries in the beleaguered city must be explained by the same apocalyptic logic: by destroying the food supply the fanatic defenders not only demonstrated their complete trust in God but also brought the city nearer to the last extremity and thus hastened the moment when God would manifest himself to save his people.[54] As is discussed elsewhere in this study, a similar destruction of property is common among modern African messianic movements and the Melanesian cargo cults.

Recognition of the eschatologial character of the war enables us to understand the heroic fight put up by the Jews in the face of overwhelming Roman superiority, the disdain for death which the Romans regarded as madness and which made Tacitus describe the Jewish war as the greatest war of all times. The growing number of victims was seen by the Jews as a seed of the coming Kingdom of God, an invitation to God to avenge the blood of his martyrs. The fervor with which the Zealots "accepted and bore suffering" solicited even the grudging admiration of Josephus.[55] Confidence in God's forthcoming miraculous aid remained strong until the last moment. With the Temple aflame, a prophet appeared announcing that the Messiah was at hand, and the Romans storming the Temple on the tenth of Ab of the year 70 found in the outer court a crowd of 6000 assembled in anticipation of just such a messianic deliverer.[56]

The fall of Jerusalem to the army of Titus for all practical purposes meant the end of the Great Revolt. The fortresses Herodium and Macaerus probably fell during the following year. Masada, the last stronghold of the Zealots, was protected by a mountainous terrain that made the utilization of siege machinery extremely difficult. The defenders of this fortress perched on a high rock, probably still expecting divine deliverance at the worst moment of the fight, were able to hold out until April 73. The recent finding at Masada of fragments of a scroll containing the peculiar liturgy of the Dead Sea covenanters has strengthened the case of those who have argued for the identity of the men of Qumran with the Zealots though others have seen this discovery as evidence that "a considerable number of Essenes also joined the rebellion." [57] When further resistance had become hopeless, a descendant of Judah the Galilean, according to Josephus' account, persuaded his companions to slay their own families and then put one another to death. Thus when the Romans finally entered the fortress they found only the dead bodies of the defenders and their wives and children. The argument of Solomon Zeitlin that the *Sicarii* holed up in Masada committed suicide without defending the fortress [58] and the suggestion of Trude Weiss-Rosmarin that the story of the mass suicide represents a conscious fabrication of Josephus [59] have not been given much credence.

The destruction of the Second Temple in Jerusalem brought to an end an epoch in Jewish history. In the eyes of many Jews revolutionary messianism had discredited itself—it was to raise its head but once more in the following century—and a trend that was to make Judaism entirely "Torah-centered rather than land-centered" began.[60] Much of the credit for this transformation is generally given to Johanan ben Zakkai, the leader of the Phari-sees, who escaped from besieged Jerusalem in the year 68, surren-dered to Vespasian, and obtained from the Roman general per-mission to open a new academy in the town of Javneh, a center of pro-Roman loyalists. To Johanan "messianism was useful as a consolatory doctrine; it was pernicious as a guide to practical policy." [61] In the tradition of the Pharisees, he argued that undis-turbed religious practice and in particular the study of the Torah were decisively more important than the achievement or mainte-nance of political independence. For many generations to come this view of Judaism was normative. The desperate courage of the defenders of Masada, fortified by an eschatological messian-ism, was remembered as an act of martyrdom rather than as the expression of a heroic and assertive nationalism. Masada as a sym-bol of defiance was revived in modern Israel. The elite of the res-urrected Jewish state's defense forces climb to the summit of this desolate rock in order to swear there the oath of allegiance: "Ma-sada shall not fall again."

THE REBELLION OF BAR KOCHBA

The Jewish war against Rome did not cause widespread destruc-tion. Many towns had opened their gates to the Romans without a fight, and the victors neither engaged in large-scale deportations nor did they institute religious persecutions. Very soon the Jews were able to reconstitute a measure of self-government in which the assembly of scholars (the rabbis) at Javneh took the place of the Sanhedrin of Jerusalem. Judaism had reached the form it was to keep for a thousand years, a sophocracy or government by sages.[62]

Still, with Jerusalem turned into a Roman garrison town and the Temple in ruins, a disaster of major proportions had overtaken the Jews, and an explanation was required. The Pharisees blamed the sins of Israel and as before counseled submission to the ruling power. Johanan ben Zakkai discouraged messianic expectations: "If you have a sapling in your hand, and it is said to you, Behold, there is the Messiah—go on with your planting, and afterwards go out and receive him." [63] But apocalyptic writings that promised an early redemption nevertheless made their appearance and probably found a ready echo. A typical work is the Fourth Book of Ezra, compiled and published about the year 120 from sources dating back as far as the reign of Domitian (A.D. 81–96). In the so-called Eagle-vision the author identifies Daniel's wicked fourth kingdom with the Roman empire and predicts its destruction by the Lion of Judah, the Messiah springing from the seed of David (12:32). Those who survive the messianic woes will participate in a world-wide deliverance in which the earth will be freed from violence, and they will "hope for the judgment and mercy of him that made her" (11:46).[64] The political element is very pronounced here, though it is linked to an eschatological sequel, a general resurrection, and a Last Judgment ushering in a new era of the world.

The emperors Vespasian, Domitian, and Trajan ordered searches for and the execution of all scions of the house of David which may indicate the continuation of rebellious ferment.[65] During the last years of the reign of Trajan (A.D. 115–117), who was involved in a campaign against the Parthians, revolts broke out in Egypt, Cyreneika, and Cyprus in which the Jews, eager to settle old scores, attacked their Greek fellow citizens as well as the Romans. In Africa they were led by a messiah-king, Andrew of Lycia. The unrest spread to Palestine itself and is remembered as the "war of Quietus," the name of the Moorish general appointed governor of the troublesome province. In Babylonia, too, a fierce insurrection erupted. The fact that many of these uprisings took place in different Jewish centers simultaneously would seem to point to an overall plan to shake off Roman rule. Unfortunately, no Tacitus or Josephus has left us a report on this revolt, which was only suppressed after two years of fighting; the revolt was not quite extinguished when Hadrian became emperor in A.D. 117.

In Palestine underground activity continued and gradually increased in scope and intensity. By the year 125 open war was in progress, and it was in response to this revolt that Hadrian issued decrees forbidding on pain of death the practice of circumcision and the recitation of the *Shema* at public services.[66] The former decree, derived from an older prohibition of castration, was not directed against Judaism alone, though it meant a grave attack upon Jewish belief. The second order, on the other hand, had obvious political connotations. The first verse of this important prayer reads: "God is our Lord, God is one." At a time of nationalistic unrest this Jewish acclamation, recalling the Zealot slogan of the absolute sovereignty of God, indeed had a revolutionary meaning. "Hadrian may have seen in it a protest against his ambitions, a watchword to defy his divine authority." [67]

The Jewish community was divided in its reactions to these decrees. Some of the militant nationalists argued that Judaism needed soldiers not martyrs, and they therefore recommended submission to any commandment when faced with the threat of death. Others defended the obligation of martyrdom, while still another faction maintained that since the most important element in Judaism was study of the Torah, Jews could yield to any restrictions on the observance of the Law provided their schools were not closed. The conclave of the rabbis, assembled at Lydda, at a date that cannot be firmly established, finally decided upon a national policy. Study is all important, the rabbis concluded, for it alone can lead to observance. It was, therefore, permissible in certain situations of great risk to forego the observance of the Law in order to preserve the academies required for the education of future generations. However, certain commandments—involving the existence of one God, the sanctity of life, and the purity of the home—were so basic that their violation could not be countenanced under any circumstances. A rule, proposed by the esteemed Akiba, was therefore adopted: "While most of the commandments may be violated to save one's life, three groups of laws must be preserved at all costs and at all times. They are those which forbid idol-worship, murder and the infringement of chastity." [68] Moreover, once a public breach of even lesser laws is demanded martyrdom must be accepted.[69] This decision of Lydda became the fundamental policy of the Jews in the centuries that followed, and we will have occasion to return to it.

The precipitating cause of the outbreak of yet another desperate war against Rome was the decision of Hadrian in the year 130 to restore Jerusalem as a fortress against the Parthians. The Jews apparently thought that this plan would involve also a rebuilding of the Temple for which they had petitioned for a long time,[70] but it soon became evident that the Emperor intended to erect on that holy site of the Jews a pagan temple, where he himself was to be worshipped as the personification of Jupiter. Under the im-

pact of this cruel blow, the messianic frenzy broke out with renewed furor: "A new Antiochus ruled the world, ready to
stretch forth his thrice defiled hand against the sacred shrine itself. Surely now God would awaken to the needs of His people,
and reveal Himself through them as He had through the Maccabees three centuries earlier." [71]

Our sources of information about the revolt that ensued (A.D.
132) are meager, though its messianic character appears to be well
established. The leader of the rebellion, a certain Simon ben (or
bar) Kozebah of unknown origin, soon after its outbreak, was acclaimed by Rabbi Akiba, perhaps the most notable scholar of the
day, as the Messiah and the Jewish masses followed his lead.
Upon first seeing Bar Kozebah, Akiba is supposed to have said,
"This is the messianic king" and, seeing in him the "star out of
Jacob" of Balaam's prophecy (Numbers 24:17), he henceforth
called him "Bar Kochba"—the "star man"—a name preserved in Christian sources. [72]

We know next to nothing about Bar Kochba the man. What
appear to be fifteen letters written by Bar Kochba were found in
1960 in a cave at Nahal Hever in the Judean desert, but the
light they throw on the life and personality of the writer is very
limited. [73] The fragments of two letters found in another cave, in
Wadi Murabba'at, are even less revealing. [74] The chapter dealing
with Bar Kochba's personal life in the only modern book-length
study of the movement consequently is a mere five-and-one-half
pages long. [75] We do know that he was not of the house of
David, and Akiba recognized him as the Messiah apparently
solely by his spirit of heroism; his early victories seemed to prove
that God was supporting his cause. The fact that Bar Kochba
was able to regain Jerusalem where he probably started rebuilding the Temple may also have contributed to his messianic stature. [76] One of the tasks of a Jewish messiah is to induce his people
to obey the Law, and Bar Kochba forcefully fulfilled this assignment, including the carrying out of compulsory circumcision.
The Jewish Christians in particular, who were at that time still a
part of the Jewish people, were persecuted severely. Two rival
messianic claims here collided head on. The Jewish Christians
could not deny their own messiah, and they therefore had to refuse to recognize and follow Bar Kochba. For this constancy of
faith they suffered greatly. [77]

Not all the rabbis shared Akiba's euphoria. The Palestinian

Talmud reports that when the great scholar acclaimed Bar Kochba as the Messiah his colleague Johanan ben Torta replied: Akiba, "the grass will grow on your cheeks before the son of David comes." [78] According to the Babylonian Talmud, Rabbi Jose ben Kisma argued that defying the government was not allowed even for the sake of religion, and he warned that opposition to the Romans was inviting doom. Once in conversation with Rabbi Hanina ben Teradion, later to suffer martyrdom, Jose asked his friend, "Knoweth thou not that it is Heaven that has ordained this [Roman] nation to reign? For though she has set waste His House, burnt His Temple and caused His best to perish, still is she firmly established!" When Hanina expressed his absolute reliance upon God's will, Jose replied: "I am telling thee plain facts, and thou sayest 'Heaven will show mercy.' " [79] However, most of the rabbis apparently forsook their traditional caution and sided with Bar Kochba. Had this not been the case, suggests one prominent historian of the period, the war could hardly have lasted three and one-half years and enlisted the eager participation of tens of thousands of Jews from inside and outside Palestine, for the rabbis enjoyed unchallenged authority as the teachers of their people.[80]

That Bar Kochba was able to arouse wild enthusiasm among the masses cannot be doubted, and Jews from remote places came to fight under the banners of the new messianic king. Bar Kochba and his men succeeded in driving the Romans out of Judea, and possibly other parts of Palestine as well, and the regaining of national independence was announced by the striking of coins containing such propagandistic legends as "For the Freedom of Jerusalem," the year of "the Redemption of Zion," or "the Freedom of Israel." Bar Kochba thus signified that his movement was in the tradition of the Maccabees and Zealots who had struck very similar coins proclaiming their battle for the glory of the Temple, Holy Zion, and Israel. National freedom and religious salvation once again were judged to be one and indivisible.

Though Bar Kochba's followers could derive comfort and inspiration from the example of the Maccabees, who had won victory against equally overwhelming odds, in the long run they were not able to prevail over the well-equipped Roman legions led by Hadrian's best generals. Rome, unlike the Seleucid empire in 165 B.C., was now at the pinnacle of its military and political grandeur, and the unequal struggle, despite great heroism on the part of the Jews, had to end in defeat. The last stronghold of Bar Kochba, the mountain fortress of Beth-ther near Jerusalem, fell after a long and stubborn defense in the year 135; Bar Kochba himself probably lost his life fighting. The war, according to the Roman historian Dio Cassius, cost the Jews 580,000 killed in action. Tens of thousands were sold into slavery, and countless others died of hunger, disease, or in fires. Judea became almost a desert. These figures, concludes Salo Baron, are doubtless exaggerated, "but they give us an idea of the tremendous impression made on contemporaries by the staggering Jewish losses." [81] Moreover, the Romans now carried out their plan to paganize the Holy City and the Jews remaining in what came to be called Philistinian Syria (or briefly Palestine) were subjected to the most cruel religious persecution that led to the martyrdom of numerous Jewish sages, including the famous Akiba. In view of the disastrous results of Bar Kochba's audacious undertaking, it is small wonder that later Talmudic and Midrashic literature refers to him not as Bar Kochba (the "star man") but only as Bar Kozebah. Because of the miserable collapse of what turned out to be the desperate venture of a pseudo-messiah, a few writers even call him Simon the liar or deceiver, a possible though somewhat strained rendering of the name "Kozebah." [82]

ABANDONMENT OF THE HEROIC PATH

Convinced of Yahweh's special providence on their behalf, the Jews had risen against Roman rule three times within one hundred years, and the results had been catastrophic. The messianic hope and the expectation of God's miraculous intervention had proved a delusion; Palestinian Jewry and the great Jewish centers of Egypt and Cyprus never recovered from the ravages of these wars and the disillusionment coming in their wake. The Jews now became a nonpolitical nation spread over an ever larger territory, a "society held together not by political power but by religious belief." [83]

Despite the loss of political independence and the dispersion of the Jewish people, the true home of the Jews remained Jerusalem and the land of Israel; the idea of an eventual return from the four corners of the earth was never abandoned. Hope for the ful-

fillment of the covenant promises and the ultimate regathering of
the exiles in the messianic age remained alive in the prayers of the
synagogue. Short-lived messianic movements and uprisings continued to emerge in all parts of the Diaspora. But this sectarian
messianism received little, if any, support from the rabbinical authorities.[84] For the rabbis in both Palestine and Babylon the messianic idea no longer was predominantly political. The messianic
hope was transformed from an activist and militant program of
fighting against foreign pagan enemies into one of passive and patient waiting, the expectation of a redemption that lay in the indefinite future and could not and should not be hurried.[85]

The new messianism had several characteristics anticipated in
the political quietism of the Pharisees, especially that of Johanan
ben Zakkai. Indeed, notes Baron, "continuity of outlook and
mode of living was so well maintained that many rabbinic teachings, if handed down anonymously, cannot be confidently dated
before or after 135 on internal evidence alone." [86] The redemption of Israel lay entirely in God's hands, the rabbinic teachers of
the second and third centuries emphasized, and this became the
accepted view of "normative Judaism." According to the Palestinian sage, Johanan ben Nappaha (A.D. 190–297), all past attempts at redeeming Israel had been failures since human agencies
had been employed. Moses had redeemed Israel from Egypt but
she was soon enslaved by Babylon. Redemption from the rule of
Babylon by Daniel and his followers was followed by enslave-
ment by Greece and Rome. True redemption had to differ from
these temporary victories. Said Johanan: "We have grown weary
of being enslaved and redeemed in order to be enslaved again.
We no longer wish to be redeemed by flesh and blood; our redeemer is the Lord of hosts." [87]

The deliverance of Israel would be God's doing; it was not for
men to take His work into their hands or to prescribe or even
calculate the timing of the fulfillment of God's plan. Prophetic,
apocalyptic, and eschatological writings were more than ever discouraged, and attempts to compute the date of the messianic redemption were censured. "May the curse of heaven fall upon
those who calculate the date of the advent of the messiah and
thus create political and social unrest among the people." [88] Altogether, the messianic age lost much of the luster it had possessed
in the apocalyptic literature, and final redemption was postponed

to "the world to come," the glories of which were known to
God alone. Seeking to dampen enthusiastic and extravagant messianic hopes, the celebrated third-century Mar Samuel in Babylon
insisted (and Maimonides in the twelfth century quoted his teaching with approval): "The sole difference between the present and
the messianic days is delivery from servitude to foreign powers." [89]
From the third century on and right through the Middle Ages,
Jews were convinced that they would be freed and redeemed in
only one way—by a life of concentration on the Torah that
would make them worthy of God and recover the divine favor.
Simon the Just, the high priest at the time of Alexander the
Great, was supposed to have said, "The world rests on three
things: the Torah, worship and loving-kindness," and medieval
Jewry took on the task of realizing this old saying. Study of the
Torah and fulfillment of its commandments came to be seen as
the prerequisites of redemption, as the seed of the messianic age.
According to Simon ben Johai, a pupil of Akiba, Israel would be
delivered forthwith after keeping two Sabbaths according to rule,
and the third-century Rabbi Levi, going it one better, was convinced that the Messiah would surely come if Israel would keep
only a single Sabbath as it was prescribed.[90]

As intellectual leadership passed gradually from Palestinian to
Babylonian Judaism, and more and more Jews lived away from
their native land, the expectation of political and national redemption weakened and the person of the Messiah became increasingly spiritual. The enigmatic figure of the Messiah ben Joseph, a hero who fights and dies for his people, provides a
short-lived exception to this trend; Moore calls him a "curious
aberration." [91] The decline of the political aspect of the messianic
idea finds another expression in the many Talmudic warnings
against rebellion that seeks to force God's hand and hurry the
end.

The Talmudic and Midrashic materials that reproduce the rabbinic sayings in question are not free of contradiction; rather than
systematic doctrine they represent the hoarded intellectual labor
of centuries. Nevertheless, we can find in both Talmud and Midrash certain constant themes. Influenced, no doubt, by the bitter
experience of several abortive messianic revolts, the rabbis taught
acceptance of government, and this teaching again became Judaism's norm for many centuries to come. The third-century Pales-

tinian, Rabbi Levi, admonished his countrymen to accept Roman rule and suggested that Israel's suffering was caused by her repeated desire to go to war against tyrannical nations. Those who stand up against the wave, he argued, will be swept away, but those who do not offer resistance will remain in place.[92] A little later, Jose ben Haninah similarly counseled moderation, citing two oaths, "one addressed to Israel and one to the other nations. God adjured Israel not to rebel against the yoke of the Governments, and He adjured the Governments not to make their yoke too heavy on Israel, for by making their yoke too heavy on Israel they would cause the end to come before it was due."[93]

Jeremiah had advised the Jews taken to Babylon to seek the welfare of that city, "to pray to the Lord on its behalf, for in its welfare you will find welfare" (29:7), and at the outbreak of the great war against Rome, as we have seen, the suffragan high priest had appealed to this saying in arguing against the Zealot-led revolt. Several later rabbis similarly praised the Roman government for imposing law upon men and preserving public security.[94] During the Middle Ages, when the Jews depended upon the protection of the ruling powers—imperial, royal, episcopal, or municipal—the injunction to pray for the welfare of the state was practiced literally, and Jews prayed for the well-being of their rulers.[95] The active messianism that had motivated the rebellion of the Zealots and the followers of Bar Kochba had yielded to a spirit of resignation to foreign tutelage.

The formula that provided the final break with the slogan of the Zealots, "No Lord but God," was proclaimed by the revered Mar Samuel, head of the third-century school of Nehardea in Babylonia. "The law of the Government is law" (*dina de-malkhuta dina*), Samuel ruled[96]; the law of the country in which Jews resided was binding even if such law conflicted with Jewish law on the subject. This dictum of Samuel was repeatedly quoted all through the Middle Ages and made it possible for Jews to live in foreign countries. The rule was self-imposed, and authoritative Jewish teachers had to apply it to specific state regulations and decrees, but, in principle, at least, the subjection to gentile sovereigns and their law was thus justified.[97]

Whereas Samuel's formula, *dina de-malkhuta dina*, was frequently appealed to, especially in civil affairs, it was always understood that the law of the gentile government should not take precedence over Jewish religious institutions or beliefs. The supremacy of God's law is affirmed in the Midrash. In an exposition of Numbers, the Jew is told to obey the king's command, but he is also reminded that if the king's decree violates "the words of the Omnipresent" he "must reject the will of a mortal for the will of God." [98] In another Midrash the believer is warned not to rebel against the government even if it imposes harsh decrees but not to obey it if it requires the annulment of Torah and its commandments.[99] This rule was modified, as we have seen, during the Hadrianic persecution to allow, under threat of death, the transgression of all commandments except those where idolatry, chastity, and murder were at stake. To justify this far-reaching concession the rabbis cited Leviticus 18:5 where God asks that his statutes and ordinances be kept "by doing which a man shall live." This was taken to mean that God's commandments were to be means of life and not death. At the same time, the Talmud explained that this exception to the supremacy of the Torah could be invoked only "when in private, but not in public." [100] "In public" was defined to mean an act which is beheld by at least ten Jews.[101]

The teachings of the rabbis on the duty and limits of obedience were tested again during the severe persecutions that followed in the wake of the crusades. Seeking life rather than martyrdom, the Jews employed every conceivable means to save themselves. They applied for or purchased the protection of the authorities, they sought refuge with benevolent neighbors and rulers, they tried to bribe the leaders of the crusaders. In some cases they fortified their quarters and fought back as best they could, though decrees forbidding the Jews to bear arms set definite limits to this mode of survival.[102] When all else failed there remained conversion or martyrdom. Entire communities, it appears, were forcibly converted while others were slaughtered or practiced preventive self-immolation in order to avoid the temptation of saving their lives through an abandonment of the ancestral faith. "It is impossible," writes Baron, "even remotely to estimate the ratio of such converts, voluntary or involuntary, to the number of the dead. The Hebrew chroniclers underplay the number of weak-kneed, and stress only the acts of heroism on the part of the resisters." [103] The impression created by these chronicles that except for a few individuals all the Jews of Germany "sanctified the Name" (practiced *Kiddush Hashem*), another careful scholar concludes, is most certainly incorrect.[104]

Mass suicide had been committed also by the last defenders of Judean independence in the great revolt against Rome of the first Christian century. In the case of the Zealots, as we have indicated earlier, such an action often represented a last desperate attempt to spur God into an act of miraculous deliverance of his faithful people. For the medieval elders and rabbis, on the other hand, self-immolation or the martyr's death at the hand of rioters and pogromists had the character of a religious sacrifice, of a sure passport to heaven. Not the Maccabean or Zealot warriors, but the Hasmonean and later martyrs such as Rabbi Akiba were extolled as inspiring examples to be imitated. Reinforced by the disdain felt for the later Hasmonean dynasty, as well as by the negative view taken by the rabbis of activist religious zeal, the apocryphal story of Hannah and her seven sons, who were martyred rather than violate God's law (2 Macc.7), outperformed in the memory of men the warlike exploits of Mattathias and his sons.[105]

The ethos of resignation of medieval Jewry is borne out by another significant fact. Despite the upheaval caused by the crusades and the savage persecutions that resulted in the complete destruction of many Jewish communities in Europe and Palestine, we find little messianic agitation. "Not a single apocalypse was written during that period," writes Gershom G. Scholem.[106] The leaders of the so-called "devout of Germany," the German Hasidim, stressed imperviousness to the scorn, shame, and humiliation visited upon them by their persecutors, while they radically opposed all messianic speculations and especially all attempts at "computing the end." The famous Jehudah the Hasid (c. 1140–1217) equated prophecies about the coming of the Messiah with witchcraft, sorcery, and intercourse with demons. This vigorous opposition, surmises Baron, was based at least in part on apprehensions "lest the ensuing disappointment cause much despair among the masses and ultimately lead weaker souls to abandon their faith." [107]

Medieval Jewish thinking accepted the Jews' suffering as punishment for past sins or as purification. "Sufferings ennoble man's nature and bring man nearer to God." [108] The martyrs could face death with fortitude for they were convinced of the future life of blessedness and happiness that would be the reward of their steadfastness. The Jew no longer made history, Nahum Glatzer has noted appropriately, he suffered and endured it. Israel led an extra-historical existence characterized by passivity and disregard of the political world.[109]

During the seventeenth century, the messianic hope was revived in its old fervor for the last time. The resurrection of messianism followed a series of catastrophic events for European Jewry—the expulsion from Spain and Portugal and a wave of unprecedented massacres at the hand of Chmelnitski and his hordes in Poland and the Ukraine in 1648 and 1658 that resulted in the death of well over 100,000 Jews. Against the background of the Spanish exodus, seen as the woes preceding the messianic era, there developed a new school of Jewish mysticism in Safed, Palestine, in which apocalyptic and messianic elements merged with the traditional aspects of Kabbalism. The old mysticism had concentrated on unraveling the mysteries of the beginning of time; the new Kabbalah focused upon the final stages of the cosmological process and the end to Israel's suffering and degradation. The revival of Jewish eschatology was encouraged by the spirit of religious excitement caused by the Reformation and the preoccupation with eschatology in the Christian camp. In this situation, aggravated by the hardships of the Thirty Years' War, the appearance of Sabbatai Zevi and Nathan of Gaza precipitated a most vigorous outburst of messianism "by liberating the latent energies and potentialities which had gradually accumulated during the generations immediately preceding them. The eruption of the volcano, when it came, was terrific." [110]

Sabbatai Zevi announced his messiahship in Smyrna in 1665, and the Jewish masses of Europe responded with a frenzy that knew no bounds. In many places all normal activity came to a standstill for Jews expected an imminent move to the Holy Land. Even the apostasy of the would-be messiah did not end the ferment for a long time. Several new messianic pretenders followed Sabbatai in short order, and the messianic spirit remained strong until well into the eighteenth century. Messianism eventually yielded to the new currents of nationalism, liberalism, and demands for emancipation. Orthodox Jews, particularly in Eastern Europe, were thoroughly disillusioned and "took up an attitude which clearly said: we shall not be taken again." [111]

Once more, then, the hope for delivery became focused upon God. Reliance upon divine intervention, as we have seen in the case of the Zealots, need not deprive the individual of the will and capacity to act; indeed it can be a spur to forceful human assertion. But this idea of cooperation between man and God in the achievement of messianic bliss did not survive the calamitous defeats of the Jewish uprisings against Rome, and later Jewish thinking insisted that the deliverance of Israel would be God's doing exclusively. God would send the Messiah when the Jews proved their loyalty to the Torah. The notion that pious Jewish warriors, imbued with zeal for the Law, could induce God to redeem his people had discredited itself just as life in the Diaspora and ghetto made such a posture completely irrelevant.

The Jews' abandonment of the heroic path undoubtedly is one—though clearly only one element among many others— in the much discussed paucity of Jewish resistance to the Nazi onslaught. During the two millennia of the dispersion, the Jews, like other oppressed minorities, had come to rely for their survival upon compromise, guile, and appeasement of and submission to those in power. This heritage,[112] which had enabled the Jewish community to live through the intermittent pogroms and expulsions of earlier days, served them ill when it came face to face with an enemy whose persecution was not intermittent but systematic and continuous, and who was bent upon achieving "the final solution of the Jewish question." The life of medieval Jews had obliged them to unlearn the practice of resisting their foes. In the words of one survivor:

> The Ghetto Jews were not warriors. For more than two thousand years the Word had been more highly respected than the Sword. We were the descendants of that people who has created the image of the lion and wolf lying down with the lamb, of swords being beaten into plough shares. The history of the Jews in the Diaspora was a history of being driven from place to place, too often locked up in Ghettos, subjected to periodic persecution and pogrom and it was not conducive to the development of the military virtues. Heroic armed exploits by Jews in the Diaspora had been the exception, not the rule.[113]

To the absence, over many generations, of a tradition of militant assertiveness we must add the stout belief and reliance upon God's redeeming aid in the hour of need. For a people with a long history of persecution and survival, who had outlasted the evil deeds of a Pharaoh, a Haman, and a Torquemada, it was difficult to believe that God would fail them during this new affliction. Among the orthodox Jews—and at least in Eastern Europe they constituted the majority—"the belief that God would redeem his people by himself remained strong." [114] The Bible was full of stories showing how the Lord had fought for the Israelites—it was a God "majestic in holiness, terrible in glorious deeds" (Exodus 15:11)—and devout faith in these accounts, while giving confidence, "deprived many Jews of the capacity for active resistance." [115]

Confidence in the coming of the Messiah appears to have been widespread during those days of impending doom. The song "Ani Maamin" ("I believe with perfect faith in the coming of the Messiah") was very popular in the Warsaw ghetto, and, in the view of one knowledgeable observer, it illustrated the mood and feelings "not only of the Orthodox Jews." [116] The attitude expressed in this song, "and though he tarry, none the less do I believe," showed moral strength and an unbroken spirit, but it may also have reinforced the disinclination to actively fight the Nazis. Chaim Kaplan records in his diary that people were busily calculating the date of the onset of the messianic age and kept on doing so despite repeated disappointments. Dashed hopes, Kaplan noted years before the development of the psychological theory of cognitive dissonance, "will not prevent people from finding more proofs [that redemption is imminent], nor other people from believing them." [117]

During the Middle Ages, the tradition of *Kiddush Hashem* was an assertion of human dignity. The Jew who had the choice of submitting to the idolatry of baptism or death and who opted for "santifying the name" and martyrdom thereby demonstrated a strength of faith and spiritual courage. But the quiet acceptance of their fate on the part of so many Jews during World War II, though seemingly in the same tradition, was different precisely because these people were deprived of the choice between life and death. As Leon Poliakov has correctly noted, "By leaving them with no other alternative than to die . . . the Nazi juggernaut robbed the Jewish martyrdom of its positive significance." [118] Convinced of the utter senselessness of meekly submitting to death at the hand of the Nazi murder squads and of regarding such death as a sign of nearing national redemption, the Jewish underground in Wilno in January 1942 pleadingly called upon the Jews of Wilno not to "go like sheep to the slaughter" [119] and instead to struggle against the Germans in every conceivable way for there was nothing to lose. A surviving leader of this same underground group, Abba Kovner, recalled the courage of those who had fallen fighting but he went on to deny the meaningfulness of the death of those many others who had failed to retaliate. "We shall not bestow the title 'hero' on those who were exterminated in the slaughter pit. We, unlike others, shall not reserve a place for them in the Temple of Heroism. We dare not even say that they died a martyr's death. . . . The community of Israel was not consciously martyred. . . . Our people as a whole went to death like a flock of sheep." [120]

Kovner may have been unduly harsh in his judgment. The difficulty of obtaining arms, the hostility of much of the local population in the East toward the Jews, and many other hardships made it unlikely that more than a relatively small number of men and women of outstanding courage would choose the path of armed struggle. The fear of endangering through revolt those who might perhaps otherwise save themselves further discouraged those who might have resisted. But the fact remains that the possibility of such resistance was further handicapped by the absence of a heroic tradition, by rabbis who quoted Mar Samuel's dictum "The law of the government is law" and banned revolt,[121] by rabbis who preached "God has given life and God will take it away" and counseled compliance.[122] Not all rabbis counseled compliance, and not all orthodox Jews accepted this counsel. Among the fighters of the Warsaw Ghetto were a number of religious Jews, but in general the nonorthodox segments of the Jewish community predominated among those prepared to resist. A religious legacy that enabled men, women, and children to confront their murderers with poise and dignity should not be scorned or equated with cowardice, but neither should it be ignored as a legacy that led to submissiveness to the point of unresisting death.

In modern times, a Jewish historian has suggested, Judaism's messianic vision of history reappeared in secular form in revolutionary socialism where it encouraged an apocalyptic view of the future "Day of Judgment, after which justice and peace would

reign supreme and history really begin as it were with all conflicts and contradictions resolved." [123] More recently, political
Zionism and eventually joy over the successful establishment of a
new Jewish state for many Jews have merged with and absorbed
the 2000-year-old messianic hope for deliverance, termination of
the Diaspora, and the reconstitution of the independence of Israel.

CHAPTER 5

Revolutionary Millenarianism during the German Reformation

MEDIEVAL ROOTS

Early in the fifth century St. Augustine dismissed the Book of Revelation as a spiritual allegory, and this teaching became the new orthodoxy. St. Augustine had seemingly succeeded in laying the ghost of millenarian expectation, but the idea was too attractive to disappear completely. All through the Middle Ages it led an underground existence intermittently bursting forth, especially at times of general uncertainty, to challenge the official teaching of the church. The notion of a forthcoming redemption appealed "to the minds of the unprivileged, the oppressed, the disoriented and the unbalanced" [1] as well as to spiritually minded individuals dissatisfied with an increasingly institutionalized religion and eager to regain the original eschatological outlook of the teachings of Jesus and the early church. To the eschatology of the Book of Revelation was now joined another body of apocalyptic writings, known as the medieval Sibylline Oracles, that proclaimed the Roman emperor a messianic king who would usher in the Golden Age. Reedited and reinterpreted many times, these oracles had enormous influence. Both the returned Christ and the savior of the Sibylline tradition, it was believed, would defeat the archenemy of God, the demonic Antichrist, whose evil deeds stood in the way of righteousness while at the same time they heralded the approaching end of the world. In the words of Norman Cohn:

> Generation after generation lived in constant expectation of the all-destroying demon whose reign was indeed to be lawless chaos, an age given over to robbery and rapine, torture and massacre, but

was also to be the prelude to the longed-for consummation, the Second Coming and the Kingdom of the Saints. People were always on the watch for the "signs" which, according to the prophetic tradition, were to herald and accompany the final "time of troubles"; and since the "signs" included bad rulers, civil discord, war, drought, famine, plague, comets, sudden deaths of prominent persons and an increase in general sinfulness, there was never any difficulty about finding them. Invasion or the threat of invasion by Huns, Magyars, Mongols, Saracens or Turks always stirred memories of those hordes of Antichrist, the peoples of Gog and Magog. Above all, any ruler who could be regarded as a tyrant was apt to take on the features of Antichrist; in which case hostile chroniclers would give him the title of *rex iniquus*. When such a monarch died, leaving the prophecies unfulfilled, he would be degraded, just like the *rex justus*, to the rank of "precursor"; and the waiting would be resumed.[2]

The approach of the year 1000 gave rise to new hopes of the Second Coming [3] and so did the recurring crusades of the common people, in search of the heavenly Jerusalem described in the Book of Revelation. But the most influential single force encouraging a revival of millenarian prophecy, was the Calabrian abbot, Joachim of Fiore (1145–1202). Toward the end of his life, this deeply religious man described a new scheme of history, based on the idea of the holy trinity, that divided the story of mankind into three phases. The first age was that of God the Father, the second the age of the Son and the New Testament, and the third was the age of the Holy Spirit and of the "eternal gospel" foretold in Revelation 14:6. This last age, which Joachim expected in the very near future, would be one of love and freedom. In contrast to the corruption of the present age, including the church, men in the age of the eternal gospel would live in voluntary poverty bent only upon the worship of God. Despite the obvious tension between the Joachimite vision and the accepted Augustinian doctrine, Joachim's reputation for holiness and learning as well as the somewhat vague nature of the predicted consummation probably spared him a charge of heresy.[4]

Joachim's historical scheme contained no appeal for action; the third age would come without man's help. On the other hand, Joachim's more zealous followers transformed the speculations of a quiet hermit into an activist, messianic creed. The Calabrian monk's praise of voluntary poverty appealed especially to the radical wing of the Franciscan order, the Spiritual Franciscans or Fraticelli, and they seized upon and extended his teachings. In 1254 there appeared in Paris a book entitled *Introduction to the Eternal Gospel* that was an immediate sensation, and it soon became more famous than Joachim's own writings. Apparently written by one of the leaders of the Fraticelli, the *Introduction* predicted the onset of the age of the Holy Spirit for the year 1260. This would be brought about by the Spiritual Franciscans to whom the eternal gospel was entrusted as a special gift. The apocalyptic manifesto also prophesied the downfall of the papacy before the new age of love and liberty could begin.[5]

The appearance of the *Introduction* coincided with a wave of eschatological sentiment encouraged by events like the eclipse of the sun in 1239, the failure of St. Louis' first crusade in 1249, the famine of 1258, the pestilence of 1259, and the first outbreak of the Flagellants in 1260. Despite the condemnation of Joachimite doctrine by the church, prophecies foretelling the imminent coming of the Antichrist and the destruction of the world continued to appear, and the Joachimite faith left its strong imprint upon the following centuries down to the Reformation, to provide the ideological base for a multitude of millenarian expectations and movements.[6] "The sense of impending doom," notes a historian of heterodoxy, "was not confined to persecuted sects, but permeated much of the outlook of the later middle ages, affecting some of its most prominent figures, like the line of Czech reformers . . . , later the Hussites, as well as ecclesiastics like Pierre d'Ailly, John Gerson and of course Wyclif." [7]

Marxist scholars, like the medievalist Ernst Werner, for example, have interpreted medieval millenarian movements as rudimentary or groping forms of the class struggle. In their view, situations of social and economic tension produce both millenarian movements and their leaders.[8] Non-Marxist students, too, have often adopted a similar explanation. Thus, H. Richard Niebuhr writes:

> Intellectual naïveté and practical need combine to create a marked propensity toward millenarianism, with its promise of tangible goods and of the reversal of all present social systems of rank. From the first century onward, apocalypticism has always been most at home among the disinherited. The same combination of need and social experience brings forth in these classes a deeper ap-

preciation of the radical character of the ethics of the gospel and greater resistance to the tendency to compromise with the morality of power than is found among their more fortunate brethren.[9]

Speaking of sectarianism generally, Werner Stark argues: "All through history, the lowest ranks of society have been the prime recruiting ground of heresies and schisms. Marxists are, by and large, within their rights when they claim that sect movements are phenomena of an ongoing class struggle in societies within which the class conflict has not yet become conscious." [10]

The evidence put at our disposal by medieval chroniclers, inquisitorial tribunals, and other sources fails to support the Marxist thesis. As concerns heterodoxy generally, most scholars agree with the conclusion of Gordon Leff that medieval heresy in all its diversity should be treated as genuine religious dissent rather than purely as a manifestation of the class struggle.[11] "It is obvious," writes Austin P. Evans, a medievalist sympathetic to interpretations of Christian heresy in terms of social roots, "that the primary motivation of speculative heresy in the Middle Ages was religious." [12] Following a careful discussion, J. B. Russell concludes, the "evidence reveals nothing that would allow us to ascribe a class basis for early medieval dissent." [13] The downtrodden and disinherited of medieval Europe, contrary to Niebuhr's ostensibly plausible suggestion, do not in fact form the backbone of religious dissenters. Peasants—whether serfs, petty freemen, or something else, the sources generally do not tell us—appear prominently among dissidents from the eighth to the eleventh centuries, Russell finds, but since serfs and freemen in those days made up well over seventy per cent of the population, a preponderance of peasants is only to be expected.[14] A new upsurge of popular heresy in the twelfth century followed the increased and deepened piety produced by the reform program sponsored by the papacy in the preceding century, by the vigor and energy of the crusades, and, especially, by the appeal to the example of the apostles made by church reformers. Piety produced heretics as well as saints. The incapacity of many of the clergy to give spiritual guidance either by teaching or example led to anticlericalism if not antisacerdotalism and often encouraged the repudiation of other institutions and doctrines of the church.[15]

In the case of millenarian sentiments and movements, the Marxist thesis is similarly unsupported. "If poverty, hardships and an often oppressive dependence could by themselves generate it," Norman Cohn writes, "revolutionary chiliasm would have run strong amongst the peasantry of medieval Europe. In point of fact it was seldom to be found at all . . . it was only very rarely that settled peasants could be induced to embark on the pursuit of the Millennium." [16] The millenarianism of the Spiritual Franciscans was not a protest of poor peasants against a rich and exploiting church. The Fraticelli were drawn mainly from the more privileged social strata, "notably from the mixture of noble and merchant families which formed the dominant class in the Italian towns. Far from belonging to the poor peasantry, many of them had renounced great wealth in order to become poorer than any beggar. And when they condemned the wealth and worldliness of papacy and church they were protesting not against economic exploitation but against a defection of spiritual authority." [17] The worldly papacy and church in their eyes had lost their legitimacy. Far from seeking to improve social and economic conditions, the Fraticelli, as the Cathari before them, opposed the growing wealth of their society and sought a return to the apostolic purity of pristine Christianity. Their ideal was holy poverty, the enhancement of the purity of the individual Christian rather than the search for a worldly utopia of material plenty.[18]

Other noneconomic factors contributed to the emergence and spread of millenarian movements. Some followers of the heresy of the Free Spirit, which flourished from the thirteenth century on, were Joachimites; they advocated a third age in which the true believers, in possession of Christian liberty, were free of all moral restraint. It would seem that not all reports of sexual orgies and other violations of existing mores can be dismissed as the invention of hostile critics.[19] The heresy of the Free Spirit, spread by wandering prophets, appears to have had a special appeal to unmarried women and widows in the upper strata of urban society who found themselves idle and neglected and therefore were receptive to special experiments in religious experience. "The Millennium of the Free Spirit was an invisible empire, held together by the emotional bonds—which of course were often erotic bonds—between men and women." [20]

The inspired confessors and preachers disseminating the heretical doctrine often were former monks and priests, another typical finding for such millenarian groups. They were led not by members of the working classes but by intellectuals or semi-intellectuals, often from the lower middle class. Not blessed with an outstanding intellect, many of these men made a virtue of necessity and argued for the importance of enthusiastic and quasi-mystical experiences as against the dry and uninspiring philosophizing of orthodox scholasticism.[21] The search for a sense of community and an emotionally satisfying experience, we can note in passing, plays a similarly important role in contemporary messianic movements in Africa just as it appears to be a factor in the political radicalism of today's students who in the majority are not economically disadvantaged. It is interesting to register here yet another parallel: Just as the contemporary New Left has made no headway whatever among the working class, whose interests it seeks to defend, and indeed often have encountered an outright hostile reception, so medieval heretics in many instances drew the enmity of "the people" who lynched defendants before ecclesiastical tribunals to satisfy their offended religious sentiments.[22]

The rejection of a narrowly conceived Marxist interpretation of medieval millenarianism does not mean, of course, that the social milieu in which such movements began and spread is not important. Norman Cohn has suggested that millenarian groups, led by a prophet obsessed with apocalyptic fantasies, usually emerged in the midst of a great ongoing revolt whose more limited and realistic aims the enthusiasts sought to exploit, appropriate, and transform into a cataclysmic struggle for a radically new world. This appears to have been the pattern in the case of John Ball and the English peasant revolt of 1381, the ultraradical Taborites in the Hussite uprising in Bohemia in the fifteenth century, Thomas Müntzer in the German peasants' revolt of 1525, and also the militant Anabaptists at Münster. In each instance we see a relatively small group struggling to master a mass movement different in outlook, strategy, and social composition. As noted, the goals of the mass movement were usually quite narrow. "On the other hand," writes Cohn, "the aims of the millenarian group in each case corresponded not to the objective social situation and the possibilities it offered but to the salvationist fantasies of a handful of freelance preachers; and they were accordingly boundless."[23] The religious enthusiast, hitherto passively expecting an early end of the world, was thus afforded the opportunity to realize his personal visions. The coming of the Millennium no longer depended exclusively upon the Parousia but could be brought about by concerted human action and by exterminating the godless who stood in the way of the divine redemption. The spread of such a millenarian movement, therefore, was due as much to the persuasiveness and charisma of the revolutionary prophet as to the frustrations and gullability of the masses whose language and longings the leader understood and whom he succeeded in galvanizing into a desperate struggle for a totally new and better world.

A pattern of "revolution in the revolution" can indeed be found in the Bohemian Taborite uprising, an outgrowth of the Czech reform movement started by John Hus (1369–1415). The Hussite movement, which has been called "the birth of the Protestant Reformation," [24] sought a number of religious reforms as well as the achievement of a national church free of Roman (and German) control. But within this reform movement there soon developed a more radical sectarian group who preached a return to the simplicity of the original apostolic church and the approaching end of the world. The availability of the text of the Bible in the Czech vernacular, spread through the translations and sermons of Hus and his followers, contributed to the conviction that the age was an extraordinary age in which the very sources of Christianity had been rediscovered and to which Christ would finally return. The building of a true church of simple believers had been the key tenet of the Waldensian heresy, and Bohemian followers of this "self-constituted church within a church" [25] may well have inspired the Hussite sectarians. A number of former Catholic priests, led by one Martinek Hauska, now added to the basically pacifist creed of the Waldensians the millenarian prophecy of the imminent advent of Christ which, in part as a reaction to persecution, eventually turned into a program of militant and ruthless chiliasm. Joachim of Fiore's idea of a radically new age, inaugurated by the Holy Spirit, here merged with the vision of an earthly paradise brought about by the efforts of God's elect. The Taborite movement can be considered the first truly revolutionary mass movement of modern times.[26]

The radical Hussites organized new congregations in several South Bohemian cities, old centers of popular heresy, in which all

lived together as brothers and feudal bonds and dues were abolished. The center became a new settlement which the radical
priests named "Mount Tabor." In February 1420, the Taborite
leaders predicted, a terrible catastrophe would overtake all other
towns and villages and only those on "the mountains" would escape the divine wrath. The Taborite brethren, it was said, were
the body of Christ who had returned secretly and was working
through them; they had the mission of purifying the earth by destroying the godless. This ideology of chiliastic, total war was the
most striking innovation of the Taborites. The present time was a
time of vengeance and punishment, argued the Taborite priest
John Capek whose tracts, we are told by a contemporary, were
"more full of blood than a fish-pond is of water." Quoting for
support the Old Testament doctrine of holy war, Capek urged
the Taborites to exterminate all those who refused to join the
brethren in promoting their chiliastic program, "the liberation of
every truth, the increase of the praise of God, the securing of
human salvation, and the destruction of sins." The faithful were
encouraged to plunge their swords into the enemies of Christ and
to wash their hands in their victims' blood. The punishment of
the sinners was "according to the will of the Holy Spirit." [27]
After the conclusion of this struggle, the messianic woes, Christ
would openly rule over the millennial kingdom, a new age in
which there would be no kings, princes, or prelates and all property would be owned in common.[28]

Led by a very able commander, John Ziska, and benefiting
from the heightened religious intensity created by the Hussite reform, for a time the Taborites attracted considerable support.
Their egalitarian program appealed especially to the poor in the
towns as well as to parts of the peasantry though the movement
was by no means restricted to the lower classes.[29] But the exigencies of the military campaigns as well as the excesses of the more
extreme wing within the Taborite camp soon led to an abandonment of the advanced social experiments. The doctrine of chiliastic, total war, too, was given up, and by about 1422 the main
Taborite movement had rejected the earlier blood-and-thunder
preaching. After the final defeat of the Taborite army at the battle of Lipan in 1434 a strong reaction set in against any use of
force; the intellectual descendants of the Taborites, the Bohemian
or Moravian Brethren, were pacifists and preached nonviolence as a

sacred principle.[30] The revolutionary chiliasm of the early Taborites reemerged about one hundred years later in Germany during another period of eschatological excitement that coincided with a major religious and social upheaval.

THOMAS MÜNTZER AND THE GERMAN PEASANTS' WAR

The early years of the Protestant Reformation were a period of renewed millennial hope, though many of the forces creating this mood were not new. As in the preceding centuries "amid all nations and social groups there flourished a host of irrational forces: a preoccupation with diabolic agencies, witchcraft and sortilege, a curious blend of eschatological expectancy with a dread of universal dissolution. Disease, insecurity and the shortness of life not only urged men to thoughts of salvation but made them listen eagerly to apocalyptic teachings and yearn for sudden changes which would usher in an age of gold." This is the bizarre world shown by Hieronymus Bosch (c. 1450–1516) and by Dürer in "Four Horsemen of the Apocalypse." [31] Into this fertile soil fell the seed of Lutheran reform. The spirit of religious renewal and excitement, the scriptural purism and biblicism, the suffering incurred by many of the reformed believers, and Luther's own portrayal of the papacy as the Antichrist foretold for the last days, all combined now to produce a climate of widespread eschatological expectation.[32] The conviction that the end prophesied in the Bible was at hand and "a new heaven and a new earth" imminent was especially strong among those independent spirits whom today we call the Radical or Left Wing of the Reformation. The commitment to revolutionary chiliasm, the establishment by God's elect of the reign of Christ on earth in a millennial kingdom, indeed represents the most important element common to both Thomas Müntzer and the revolutionary wing of the Anabaptists. In each case, forceful and charismatic leaders, alleging inspiration by the Holy Spirit as their credentials, were able to link their personal apocalyptic visions with an ongoing mass movement and to capture it long enough to leave their special mark upon history.

Born in Thuringia in 1488 or 1489 into a middle-class family, Thomas Müntzer's life reveals a restless search for religious certainty. He was a priest, well-versed in Scripture, a man with deep roots in the mystic tradition of doubt, self-denial, and Christian discipleship, on the one hand, and Joachimite spiritualism on the other. An early sympathizer of Luther, Müntzer nevertheless downgraded the Bible, considering it subordinate to the tormenting experience of the inner word, the spirit. It was in response to the urging of the spirit, communicated through visions and dreams, that Müntzer eventually came to consider himself called to help realize the Kingdom of God on earth, to transform the world as proclaimed by apocalyptic Judaism and early Christianity.[33]

In 1520 Müntzer accepted a ministry in Zwickau, and it was in this important industrial center near the Bohemian border that he came under the influence of a weaver named Niklas Storch who taught the Taborite doctrine of the war of the elect against the godless that would usher in the Millennium. The association of weaver and heretic, found all through the Middle Ages, has given rise to the suggestion that this type of work, performed in a sitting position to the monotonous droning of the loom, tended to produce a semi-hypnotic state favorable to mystical speculations and sectarian types of religious thought.[34] There is strong evidence, on the other hand, that many heretics, in southern France and elsewhere, chose the occupation of weaver since they wanted to live on the fruits of their hands and because this trade, always in need of occasional labor, especially suited wandering preachers. Thus it was not weavers who became heretics but heretics who became weavers.[35] And yet, since weavers were far more vulnerable than most medieval craftsmen to periodic change in the supply of raw materials and the sale of the finished product in the export trade, their dependent and precarious position may well have produced anxieties and frustrations that could often find an outlet in religious heresy. In early sixteenth-century Zwickau, at any rate, there existed a large population of poor weavers, suffering from unemployment and rapidly rising prices, who eagerly absorbed the apocalyptic teachings of Storch and his newest convert to chiliasm, Thomas Müntzer.[36]

The rising tension in the town, fed by the preaching of the temperamental and passionate Müntzer, in April 1521 culminated in an uprising that was suppressed, and Müntzer fled to Prague where he probably hoped to find the remaining Taborites. In his

"Prague Manifesto," published in four versions,[37] Müntzer proclaimed the approaching victory of the elect and threatened the
Czechs with God's judgment in the form of a Turkish invasion if
they failed to support the millenarian cause. But the Bohemians, it
appears, were no longer receptive to this revolutionary gospel,
and the disappointed Müntzer left Prague. For the next two years
he wandered from place to place until, in 1523, he settled down
as minister in the small Thuringian town of Allstedt where he
married and soon established a reputation as a highly effective
preacher. The moment was propitious. The approach of an unusual stellar configuration in early 1524 had caused widespread
excitement and fear; Müntzer's apocalyptic message found a favorable reception among the artisans of Allstedt and among the
peasants from the surrounding countryside and the miners from
the nearby copper mines at Mansfeld. It was from among these
followers that in March 1524 Müntzer organized a clandestine
military organization, the "League of the Elect." Membership in
the League was open to all who acknowledged the call of the
spirit. As opposed to Luther, Müntzer believed in the salvation of
all believers and he rejected the idea of reprobation.[38] Given his
strong desire to build the Kingdom of God on earth, Müntzer
could not afford to tolerate doubts about the ability of man's will
to realize the good and achieve salvation by personal effort.[39]
The body of the elect, therefore, welcomed all prepared to join
in the task of wielding the sword against the godless and cleansing the world of evil.

  Müntzer still harbored hopes that the worldly authorities
would support his mission. When in July of 1524 he was asked to
preach before the two princes of Saxony, Duke John (brother of
Frederic the Wise, the protector of Luther) and his son, John
Frederic, he chose as his text the second chapter of Daniel. "The
Spirit of God," he told his noble listeners, "is revealing to many
elect, pious persons a decisive, inevitable, imminent reformation
. . . and the process of ending the fifth monarchy of the world is
in full swing." [40] The princes should listen to the "new Daniel"
who had arisen, the not overly modest Müntzer declared, and use
their sword against the wicked. "Get them out of the way and
eliminate them, unless you want to be minister of the devil rather
than of God, as Paul calls you." [41] The task of true Christian authority was not merely to maintain order but also actively to as-

sist in the transformation of the world. "Therefore let not the evildoers live longer who make us turn away from God (Deut. 13:5). For the godless person has no right to live when he is in the way of the pious." [42] The enemies of the gospel should be offered a chance to abandon their evil role, but if they persist, "may they be slain without any mercy. . . . The weeds must be plucked out of the vineyard of God in the time of harvest. Then the beautiful red wheat will acquire substantial rootage and come up properly." [43] The fiery sermon ended with Müntzer's exhortation to his distinguished audience to implement the wisdom of Daniel and to kill all "godless rulers . . . especially the priests and monks who revile the gospel as heresy for us and wish to be considered at the same time as the best Christians." Once more he reminded his listeners: "The godless have no right to live except as the elect wish to grant it to them." [44]

When the princes failed to assume the role Müntzer had assigned them, of becoming the executors of God's wrath against the godless, to function as the vanguard of the revolutionary saints, the prophet's thought became further radicalized. Worldly authority, he now argued, was made unnecessary by true belief and the fear of God; the time had come to do away with all tyrants. In two pamphlets written soon after the sermon before the princes, and directed in part against Luther, Müntzer now focused upon the common people, the poor, who were exploited by the rich and powerful. And yet, his concern for social justice was not an end in itself. Only the Christian freed from external extremities, the pressure of oppressive taxes and dues, Müntzer felt, would be able to know the needed inner distress, the fear of God. Most of Müntzer's Marxist admirers have depicted the chiliastic prophet as a social revolutionary, the harbinger of modern communism,[45] but their interpretation of Müntzer's message appears highly strained if not impossible. Müntzer did not primarily seek social justice but rather hoped for social conditions that would enable Christians to have true faith. Müntzer was preoccupied not with better days on earth, but with the end of all days, the last things.[46] Even during the high point of his involvement with the rebelling peasants, a more perceptive Marxist scholar noted that Müntzer's indifference toward material goals remained a basic element of his ethical system.[47]

The authorities at Allstedt took an increasingly dim view of

Müntzer's inflammatory preaching, and in August 1524 the war-
rior-priest fled the town to try his luck at nearby Mühlhausen.
He allied himself with a town minister of similar views, Heinrich
Pfeiffer, but their plan to take over Mühlhausen failed, and
within a month both men were driven out. In early 1525, after a
period of wandering in southern Germany, Müntzer returned to
Mühlhausen, where the political climate had changed. Here the
final part of the prophet's life drama, his involvement with the
German peasant war, was acted out.

Unrest among the German peasantry, on the increase since the
latter part of the fifteenth century, had reached alarming proportions during the years 1513–17. Whereas earlier the peasants for
the most part had limited their demands to the rectification of
local grievances and the observance of old custom and feudal
law, the peasant movement now assumed more organized, prov-
ince-wide proportions, and the far more ambitious goals were justified in the name of divine justice and divine law, the Gospel.
Probably as the result of Hussite influence, many of the peasants
no longer merely demanded a return to the good old law, undermined by the breakup of feudalism and the introduction of
Roman law, but envisaged a new social and political order in
which the old authorities would be overthrown, and serfdom and
all taxes, tithes, and other dues would be abolished. This was the
revolutionary program of the peasants united under the emblem
of the peasant clog, the *Bundschuh*, and it was this movement
that received further encouragement from Luther's successful
challenge to established authority and his appeal to Scripture and
Christian liberty.[48]

The libertarian impulse provided by the Protestant Reformation can be seen in *The Twelve Articles*, formulated by the rebelling Swabian peasants in late February 1525, a program that
called for "Christian freedom" and relied extensively upon the
Bible. The struggle for the old and the divine law, hitherto
fought out in separate camps, merged under cover of the Gospel.[49] Still, *The Twelve Articles*, with its strictly agrarian demands, was not a radical document, and the peasant uprising that
now spread through southern Germany and Thuringia was not a
millenarian movement. As in the English Peasants' Revolt of
1381, the rebelling peasants were not starving men. They were
better off than ever before, and, notes Cohn, "particularly the

peasants who everywhere took the initiative in the insurrection, so far from being driven on by sheer misery and desperation, belonged to a rising and self-confident class. They were people whose position was improving both socially and economically and who for that very reason were impatient of the obstacles which stood in the way of further advance." [50] The leaders of the revolt were the rich and important men of the village who often forced the poorer peasants to join them.[51]

The rebelling peasants, expecting Luther's support, sent him a copy of *The Twelve Articles*, but the Reformer of Wittenberg disowned their movement. The demand for an end to serfdom, bolstered by Scripture, Luther replied in April 1525, meant "to interpret Christian freedom in an entirely material sense. . . . This article would make all men equal and so change the spiritual Kingdom of Christ into an external worldly one." The Christian way of dealing with misfortune is "to suffer in patience and call upon God for help. Because you do not do this and depend upon your own strength, there comes it that God does not help you." [52] For Müntzer, on the other hand, the uprising of the peasants was proof that the last days were approaching, and he threw himself wholeheartedly into the struggle. On April 26 Müntzer addressed a letter to the Mansfeld miners, the strong supporters of his "League of the Elect," calling on them to join the battle:

> Do not despair, be not hesitant, and stop truckling to the godless villains. Begin to fight the battle for the Lord! Now is the time! Encourage your brethren not to offend God's testimony because, if they do, they will ruin everything. Everywhere in Germany, France, and neighboring foreign lands there is a great awakening; the Lord wants to start the game, and for the godless the time is up. . . . Even if there were only three of you, you would be able to fight one hundred thousand if you seek honor in God and in his name. Therefore, strike, strike, strike! This is the moment. These villains cower like dogs. . . . Have no concern for their misery; they will beg you, they will whine and cry like children. Do not show them any mercy. . . . Strike, strike, while the fire is hot. . . . Have no fear, God is on your side! [53]

The letter was signed "Thomas Müntzer, a servant of God against the Godless," and it was in his role as chiliastic prophet that Müntzer now assumed command of the Thuringian peasant revolt. There was no other real leadership. At his orders, flags were made with a rainbow, symbolic of the new covenant, and the inscription, "The Word of God endures forever." Money was collected, recruits were trained, weapons and ammunition were stockpiled. Several hundred men from Allstedt had responded to Müntzer's appeal for help, and at the head of this group of devoted followers Müntzer on May 7, 1525 set out from Mühlhausen to join a peasants' army encamped near Frankenhausen. The forces of the princes had ample artillery and a sizable troop of cavalry; the peasants, though numerically stronger, were poorly armed. Yet, Müntzer was able to shore up their courage with the assurance that God would assist them as he had helped David in his fight with Goliath. A rainbow appearing on the day of the battle over the camp of the princes was seen as a sign of divine favor. But the beginning of an artillery barrage, laid on the peasants while they were still singing Müntzer's hymn, "Come, Holy Spirit, our Lord," restored them to reality. The peasants fled in panic toward Frankenhausen, the army of the princes on their heels; some 5000 peasants lost their lives in the unequal contest.[54]

Müntzer had hidden in a cellar in Frankenhausen, but he was recognized and seized. Under torture he repudiated his militant program and admonished the peasants "to obey their masters." It is possible that this retraction [55] was not only due to physical pain. Müntzer undoubtedly knew the words of Jeremiah that genuine prophecy is recognized through fulfillment: through the coming to pass of a prophecy "it will be known that the Lord has truly sent the prophet" (28:9). The failure of his cause may have convinced Müntzer that his apocalyptic message had been based on self-deception.[56] On May 27, 1525 Müntzer, along with Pfeiffer, was beheaded.

THE MILLENARIAN KINGDOM OF THE ANABAPTISTS AT MÜNSTER

The question of a link, direct or indirect, between the revolutionary millenarianism of Thomas Müntzer and radical Anabaptism has long been the subject of controversy. Luther and other contemporaries of the early Anabaptists, seeking to discredit their pious opponents, lumped all Anabaptists with Thomas Müntzer, a confusion facilitated by the external similarity of the names

Müntzer and Münster, the seat of the Anabaptist Millennium. Modern Mennonites, on the other hand, the spiritual descendants of the sixteenth-century Anabaptists, by and large have tried to dissociate their predecessors and themselves from Müntzer. They have pointed out that there was no adult baptism in either Zwickau or Mühlhausen, that Müntzer basically rejected the external rite of baptism, and they therefore conclude that "Müntzer was in no sense an Anabaptist." [57]

This conclusion would seem to be open to challenge. In a strictly chronological sense Müntzer's life, of course, predates Anabaptism, and records of the only direct contact between one of the Swiss Brethren, Conrad Grebel, and Müntzer reveal profound disagreements.[58] At the same time, it is clear that some important aspects of Müntzer's teachings reappeared in radical Anabaptism, and this is hardly a coincidence. Both the Thuringian prophet of revolutionary chiliasm and the radical Anabaptists were possessed by an intense eschatological mood, and this expectation of an early Second Coming could lead quite logically, just as it did with Müntzer, in part as a reaction to persecution, to the use of force to help usher in the Kingdom of Christ and punish its godless opponents. The Mennonite scholar, Robert Friedman, indeed admits that Müntzer's ideas were "in the neighborhood of the kingdom of Münster of 1534–1535" [59] without giving due recognition to the fact that the Münsterites after all were Anabaptists. Three of Müntzer's closest followers and helpers, Hans Hut, Hans Römer, and Melchior Rinck, eventually became Anabaptists, and two of these men, as we will see soon, continued to teach a variation of Müntzer's revolutionary creed for quite a while. In the case of Bernhard Rothmann, the theologian of the heavenly Jerusalem of Münster, the similarities in doctrine are pronounced. It would be going too far to call Müntzer the father of the Anabaptist movement as Heinrich Bullinger and some later Lutheran historians have done, but neither should one ignore the ideological closeness between at least some wings of Anabaptism and the Turingian visionary.[60]

Anabaptism simultaneously emerged in Switzerland and South Germany. On January 21, 1525, the first known rebaptism of modern times took place when the layman Conrad Grebel of Zurich rebaptized a former priest. On the very same day, "the birthday of Anabaptism," [61] Hans Denck was banished from Nuremberg

because of his proto-Anabaptist views. In both cases, we are dealing with the beginnings of a religious movement that opposed the
creation of yet another church, whether of the Lutheran or
Zwinglian persuasion; instead, as a reformation of the Reformation, they set out to realize the ethic of the Sermon on the Mount
in a "true church" based on the pattern of the apostolic community.[62] In the language of Ernst Troeltsch, the Anabaptists represented a sect, a religious group "resolute in their determination
to confess Christ before men and to leave the world to its fate." [63]

Despite the fact that Anabaptism never was a homogeneous
movement and that it was characterized by an ideological incoherence due to the sect's emphasis on Christian living and its neglect of systematic theology, we can note a few basic beliefs. As
indicated by their name, the Anabaptists rejected the validity of
infant baptism and insisted on baptizing or rebaptizing those old
enough to understand the necessity for repentance and faith.
Adult baptism derived not only from a literalist interpretation of
Scripture—a strict adherence to the prescribed sequence of
events outlined in Mark 16:16: "He who believes and is baptized
will be saved"—but also from the Anabaptists' overriding aim
which was to return to the life of the early church. "Their
objective," notes Littell, "was not to introduce something new
but to restore something old." [64] But since this religious primitiv-
ism was but an aspect of their profound misgivings about the age
in which they lived, it led to eschatology. The return to the pure
and inspired faith of the founders of the Christian faith for the
Anabaptists meant not only the recapitulation of past virtue but
also the beginning of greater things to come. The fellowship of
the believers, the brotherhood of the reborn, marked the beginning of the end of history; the Kingdom of God was being set up
here and now and the end of days was close at hand.

The social teachings of the Anabaptists, too, emanated from a
radical biblical literalism and from the endeavor to recapture the
spirit of brotherhood in the early church. Mutual aid and a sharing of goods were taught and practiced not to overcome social
injustice but to realize a life of true discipleship and to demonstrate love, helpfulness, and good will to all men. A minority
group of the Anabaptists, the Hutterites, developed a philosophy
of full economic equality that led to the establishment of communal living. But most Anabaptists continued to live their regular

individual lives, with property being "regarded as a sacred trust, existing not only for the possessor, but also for the benefit of his fellowmen." [65]

Though the willingness to share goods with those in need often enough drew charges of subversion, it was the Anabaptists' attitude to public authority that more than anything else aroused the ire of their opponents and brought down upon the group the accusation of sedition, with severe persecution. Committed to an ethic of love, most Anabaptists opposed the assumption of public office as well as participation in warfare. Both the office of the magistrate and military service required the use of force and, therefore, were forbidden to the true Christian. The fact that the Anabaptists affirmed the obligation of obeying the civil authorities as long as the prior claims of God were not violated did not matter much. In an age in which the state was seen as a Christian state, the existence of a sect of people who denied the Christian character of public authority and in fact often cursed the latter as un-Christian could not but create an image of disrespect if not rebelliousness.[66] The doctrine of the duty of rebellion against godless authority taught by Thomas Müntzer and later by a few revolutionary Anabaptists alarmed both Protestants and Catholics.

The teachings of the Anabaptists reveal obvious parallels to the fourth-century Donatists, the original Anabaptists, as well as to medieval heretic sects, in particular, the Waldensians. The influence of the ideas of Joachim of Fiore and of the Taborites is also apparent. Does the indebtedness to the latter movement explain the emergence of Anabaptist militant chiliasm at Münster? How can we account for the creation of this theocracy, accompanied by an attitude of bloodthirsty ferocity, by a pacifist sect like the Anabaptists?

According to most Marxist writers, the Anabaptists, like the followers of Thomas Müntzer earlier, were members of the exploited and oppressed lower classes, and the explosion at Münster for them, therefore, is but the culmination of an ongoing class struggle fought out in religious guise. The information available on the social composition of the sect does not sustain this thesis. In Switzerland Anabaptism began in the urban centers where it spread among all classes. Conrad Grebel, the moving spirit of the Swiss Brethren, was a member of a wealthy, patrician family, a well-educated humanist, and so were many of his early co-work-

ers and converts. Only after the suppression of the movement in
the cities did Anabaptism spread to towns and villages, and after
1527 it was largely confined to the peasantry. At no time can a
special appeal to the downtrodden be detected,[67] and the same
pattern emerges from a detailed investigation of the Anabaptists
in the South German state of Würtemberg. Here, too, the movement at first took root in the larger cities and their surroundings
and, after vigorous persecution there, turned into a predominantly rural sect. The urban artisans who became Anabaptists
were of various income levels—we find rich masters as well as
penniless apprentices—and the same distribution prevailed
among Anabaptist peasants. "The social composition of the Anabaptist congregations by and large reflects the social structure of
the Würtemberg villages." [68]

This is not to deny that many of the ordinary people everywhere reacted to Anabaptism with sympathy. The sect's opposition to war, to the death penalty, and to force in general, as well
as the fact that most of the itinerant Anabaptist preachers were
workingmen, easily able to establish rapport with the village population, undoubtedly helped swell its ranks. The radical biblicism
and the simplicity of the Anabaptist message also appealed to the
peasantry. Last, the persecuted Anabaptists were a closely knit
community and this, too, enhanced the sect's attractiveness. For
some people religion is a matter of belonging and feeling; the Anabaptist emphasis on the spirit and a direct conversion experience,
often expressing itself in dancing, acting like children, and speaking in tongues,[69] furnished the ordinary man of the sixteenth
century, as at other times, with "a psychologically effective escape from the drudgeries of an unromantic, unaesthetic life." [70]

Still, it is significant that many of the poorest sections of Würtemberg remained completely untouched by Anabaptism, while
in other sections familial and personal factors more than anything
else were decisive in the sect's spread. Indeed, the most common
personal motive for joining the Anabaptists appears to have been
a deep conviction of sin and a longing for forgiveness.[71] All of
this is hardly in accord with the Marxist thesis of Anabaptism as
a manifestation of a primitive class struggle. A student of Anabaptist economic thinking writes: "The notion that the discontented,
destitute, and disinherited flocked to the movement in hope of
getting easy material gain bears neither historical scrutiny

nor logical evaluation, for Anabaptism stressed giving, not receiving." [72]

The change from an ethic of nonviolence and suffering, from the pacifism that always was embraced by the majority of Anabaptists, to militant chiliasm as we find it in Münster must thus be explained by other than economic factors. One should first note that movements with a strong eschatological emphasis tend easily to move into a revolutionary path or at least to join the revolutions of others. As we have seen, this is what happened with the radical Taborites in fifteenth-century Bohemia and again with Thomas Müntzer. In the dynamics of social upheaval the willingness to incur voluntary poverty can swiftly turn into the attempt to force poverty upon the rich,[73] just as the passive expectation of the coming of the Millennium can quickly give way to the attempt to bring about the Kingdom of Heaven by resorting to force. Moreover, and more specifically, the ruthless persecution to which the Anabaptists were subjected at first appears to have had a radicalizing effect. "It was not only that the Anabaptists were confirmed in their hostility to the state and the established order," writes Cohn, "they interpreted their suffering in apocalyptic terms, as the last great onslaught of Satan and Antichrist against the Saints, as those 'messianic woes' which were to usher in the Millennium. Many Anabaptists became obsessed by imaginings of a day of reckoning when they themselves would arise to overthrow the mighty and, under a Christ who had returned at last, establish a Millennium on earth." [74] Finally, the Anabaptist encouragement of an inner religious experience and of prophecy necessarily left the sect at the mercy of divergent revelations and inspirations from the spirit. The appearance and acceptance as prophets of men who had lost patience with waiting for the Second Coming and who claimed a divine mandate for hurrying the end, therefore, cannot come as a surprise. The fact that most Anabaptists remained peaceful and submissive shows that this transition to militant chiliasm was not inevitable, whereas the fact that it did take place reveals the potential violence of the sect's eschatological beliefs.[75]

The activities of two disciples of Thomas Müntzer, who had become Anabaptists, foreshadow the later events at Münster. Hans Hut, a Thuringian bookbinder and salesman, went on teaching the imminent coming of Christ and the punishment of the godless even after the defeat of the peasants at Frankenhausen. In May 1526 he was rebaptized by Hans Denck, yet his eschatological message changed but little. God, not man, he now argued, had to give the sign for the final struggle. Hut regarded the Turks as the instruments of God's wrath who would help usher in the Millennium, which was to take place in 1528. Hut was arrested and tortured, and he died in his cell at Augsburg in early December 1527, but his chiliastic prophecies continued to circulate widely in central and southern Germany.[76] Hans Römer, another battlefield comrade of Müntzer, went one step further. He not only predicted the return of Christ within eleven months but planned the seizure of the city of Erfurt in preparation for the impending day of judgment. The plot was discovered and Römer had to flee,[77] yet such an undertaking by an Anabaptist is significant.

The preoccupation with predicting the date of the end of the world was relatively rare in South German and Swiss Anabaptism. An eschatological emphasis, on the other hand, was characteristic of most Dutch Anabaptists, and this development was due largely to the influence of Melchior Hoffmann, the energetic itinerant lay preacher who spread Anabaptism in Northwest Germany (East Friesland) and Holland. Hoffmann declared the city of Strassburg to be the New Jerusalem from which the 144,-000 heralds mentioned in Revelation 14:1 would go forth to regenerate the world. His preaching was full of chiliastic expectations, and even though, as Williams observes correctly, Hoffmann "did not countenance a resort to violence to advance the cosmic calendar nor social revolution to accelerate the divine 'breakthrough,'"[78] he must nevertheless be regarded as a harbinger of the Münster episode. We find in his doctrine both the reliance upon prophecy—Hoffmann and a co-worker apparently considered themselves as the prophets Enoch and Elijah, precursors of the Millennium—as well as the burning interest in a visible reign of Christ on earth. A recent historian calls Hoffmann "the evil genius of Anabaptism,"[79] though, one should add, that he was hardly the only, or even the most important enthusiast. The Dutch Anabaptists John Matthys and John Bockelson (known as John of Leyden), two of the central characters in the drama of Münster, can certainly be given this title with equal, if not greater, ease.

The followers of Melchior Hoffmann in Holland were called Melchiorites. The spiritual ground for the spread of Anabaptism in the Low Countries had been prepared by the late medieval sacramentarians, who had sought to spiritualize the meaning of the sacraments of the mass and baptism. Moreover, while in most other European countries Anabaptism developed out of dissatisfaction with what is often called the Magisterial Reformation, in Holland Anabaptism represented the first attack of Reformed thinking upon Catholicism. It therefore became "the earliest bearer of religiously oriented Dutch-Flemish national self-consciousness" [80] and quickly assumed the character of a mass movement reaching all strata of the population.[81] Unusually hard times, due to a combination of unfavorable political and economic developments as well as a natural catastrophe, are said to have made many of the poorer people receptive to the chiliastic message of the Melchiorite preachers,[82] but the fact that the movement's "predominant constituency was of the lower class" [83] in itself does not establish this point. "On the whole," another writer concludes, "Anabaptism in the Netherlands did not draw its strength from any particular class or profession. . . . There was no such thing as the class appeal of Anabaptism." [84]

Whether as a result of economic distress or of severe persecution, Dutch Anabaptism retained the pronounced chiliastic emphasis introduced by Hoffmann. During the years 1533–35 there emerged a group within the Melchiorite camp that announced the end of the time of suffering and called upon the saints to help establish the Millennium. The most prominent leader of this group was the baker John Matthys of Amsterdam who claimed divine inspiration as a prophet, sent out apostles to spread his revolutionary message, and soon built up a large following. In early 1534 Matthys took refuge in Münster where he found a hospitable climate and quickly assumed control of the local Anabaptist movement.

The city of Münster, with a bishop as its temporal as well as spiritual ruler, had gradually developed a Protestant community. Support for the Reformed creed was especially strong among the merchants, opposed to the economic policies of their bishop-sovereign, and it was among this class as well as the artisans, that Anabaptism found many adherents. The most effective Protestant preacher had been a young chaplain, Bernhard Rothmann, and

from about 1533 on Rothmann emerged as the leader of the local
Anabaptists as well. The bishop was now on the defensive; Münster became a haven for dissenters, and large numbers of persecuted Anabaptists from North Germany and Holland flocked to
the town. The economic situation in Northwest Germany during
these years had deteriorated. Typhus, cholera, crop failures, inflation, a recession in the Netherlands, and heavy taxes had taken
their toll.[85] Within the city of Münster the antagonism between
the bishop and the merchants had grown, and the charismatic
Matthys was able to capitalize on this tense situation.

By January 1534 about one-quarter of the population of Münster were Anabaptists, and their influence grew rapidly as Catholics and Lutherans, expecting an armed intervention on the part
of the bishop, left the city. In the elections for the town council
held on February 23 the Anabaptists scored an overwhelming
victory and Matthys now proclaimed Münster the New Jerusalem that would survive the cataclysmic end to befall the rest of
the world before Easter. The siege of the town by the bishop at
this time was regarded by the prophet as a sign of the messianic
woes. In order to purify the city of the elect of all uncleanness
Matthys proposed to execute all remaining Catholics and Lutherans, but Bernd Knipperdollinck, an influential young merchant
and one of the two newly elected Anabaptist mayors, was able to
change the order to expulsion. In the midst of winter and a severe
snowstorm "the godless" were driven from the city while all
wanting to remain were rebaptized in a mass ceremony that
lasted three days. By early March Münster was free of unbelievers, and the children of God who remained addressed one another as "brother" and "sister." Their ranks were now swollen by
several thousand Anabaptists from Holland and North Germany
who had made their way to the city of the saints.

Even though the formal structure of the city government was not
changed at first, de facto power lay in the hands of Matthys. Invoking divine revelation, the Dutch prophet ruled as charismatic
leader. All books but the Bible were banned and burned and
Matthys' interpretation of Scripture became the authoritative
word that was not to be challenged. His rule of Münster lasted
less than six weeks but it was long enough to result in some far-
reaching changes such as the confiscation of the property of the
exiles and the abolition of private ownership of money, food, and

real property. These measures, advocated by Rothmann for some time before the onset of the siege, can be considered "an outgrowth of military exigency reinforcing a desire inherent in Anabaptism everywhere to restore the communal life of the primitive church." [86]

On Easter Sunday, April 4, 1534, John Matthys, invoking a special divine command, led a sortie of two hundred hymn-singers against the episcopal forces. The prophet apparently was convinced that God would help him lift the siege practically single-handedly, but instead he and his companions were slaughtered. Matthys' place was taken by his ambitious young disciple, John Bockelson, or John of Leyden, who had been waiting in the wings. Born out of wedlock, Bockelson had learned the trade of tailor but had gone bankrupt in 1533. After rebaptism by Matthys, he had been chosen as one of the first apostles and in January 1534 Bockelson had appeared in Münster to preach the revelations of his master. He was then a young man of twenty-five, endowed with unusually good looks and great eloquence, and filled with ambition to promote the glory of God. Cohn calls him "a megalomaniac, whose behavior cannot be adequately interpreted either simply as sincere fanaticism or simply as calculating hypocrisy." [87] The judgment of another writer who refers to Bockelson as the "incarnation of absolute evil," a man for whom religion meant little,[88] probably is simplistic.

Bockelson introduced a new phase of the New Jerusalem. He dismissed the mayors and the council elected in February and instead established himself and twelve elders as the governing body of the city. A new, far stricter code of laws was issued and enforced with extreme harshness. Sin became a crime and the death penalty was imposed for offenses such as blasphemy, scolding one's parents, adultery, spreading scandal, and complaining.[89] The Old Testament was now followed literally; Münster had become a city of warrior-saints.

The strict regulation of sexual behavior came to an end when Bockelson decided to introduce polygamy. Insisting on the literal fulfillment of the Old Testament command, "Be fruitful and multiply" (Gen. 1:28), Bockelson himself led the way by marrying the beautiful widow of Matthys and building up a harem of fifteen wives. Many of the men who had left the city had not taken their wives and maids along; casualties among the male population also had been heavy so that Münster now had about 5000 women and only 2000 men. By forcing all women below a certain age to marry or remarry and making the husbands responsible for their wives, Bockelson also was able to obtain a measure of supervision over the female population, whose participation in disturbances had been frequent.[90] When despite harsh penalties and executions marital discord got out of control, divorce was permitted, and the end result of Bockelson's marriage reform was something not very different from free love. "Even if much in the hostile accounts which we possess is discounted as exaggeration, it seems certain," concludes Cohn, "that norms of sexual behavior in the Kingdom of the Saints traversed the whole arc from a rigorous puritanism to sheer promiscuity." [91]

In early September 1534, following the successful repulsion of a major attack upon the city, Bockelson had himself annointed and crowned "King of the New Zion." A luxurious court was set up, the sumptuous life of which contrasted sharply with the shortages increasingly afflicting the rest of the saints. But a brutal system of terror held the masses in check; the messianic king arbitrarily chose victims himself and personally carried out public beheadings. "In his mingled shyness and ruthlessness, religious fanaticism and maniacal wickedness," writes Williams, "he made life wretched for his subjects, and also for his wives." [92]

Bockelson realized that his own troops alone would be unable to defeat the forces of the bishop who enjoyed the help of Protestant rulers. He, therefore, sent out apostles to the Netherlands calling upon the Dutch Anabaptists to form an army for the relief of Münster and by joining the New Jerusalem to be among the 144,000 who would escape annihilation on the Day of Judgment. The task of providing the ideological support for this call to action fell upon the chief court theologian, Bernhard Rothmann. In four pamphlets, published between October 1534 and June 1535, Rothmann obligingly fulfilled this commission, though, as one critic notes correctly, "the transparent propagandistic purpose of these pamphlets should not blind us to the fact that they contain a generally consistent body of ideas and offer us direct access to Münsterite self-understanding." [93]

Rothmann's chief task was to convince the Dutch Melchiorites that it was unnecessary, if not outright wrong, to meekly go on accepting suffering and that the hour to resist and defeat the godless had now arrived. Dividing the history of mankind into three periods, Rothmann argued that the "Restitution" of the true faith at Münster marked the end of the second age. The coming of the third age, a new heaven and new earth and the temporal reign of the returned Christ, were imminent and the vengeance of the saints on the godless was a necessary prelude to the Second Coming.

> Now, dear brothers, the time of vengeance is here. God has raised the promised David and armed him for vengeance and punishment over Babylon and its people. Therefore, dear brothers, arm for battle, not only with the apostles' humble weapon of suffering, but also with vengeance, the magnificent armor of David, to stamp out the entire Babylonian power and the entire godless establishment with the power and help of God. Think that you can do to them everything they have done to you; indeed, they shall receive in the same measure with which they have measured out. . . . Let God, the Lord of Lords, who has determined and through his prophets predicted this from the beginning of the world, awaken your heart with the power of his spirit and arm you and his whole Israel. . . .[94]

The belief of many that God and his angels would come down from heaven to take vengeance on the godless was erroneous, Rothmann maintained. We, the saints, God's servants, must ourselves carry out this glorious revenge, we must be God's tool and subdue the enemies of Christ. The nonresistance of the early church had been appropriate only for an earlier age. Now, as predicted by the prophet Joel, plowshares and hoes had to be made into swords and spears (Jl. 3:10). Only after the throne of David had been raised anew—a step already taken in Münster through the coming of John of Leyden—and after the frightful dominion of Antichrist had been fully abolished, only then could the Second Coming take place. "Then the peaceful Solomon, the eternal king and annointed God, Christ, will enter and possess the throne of his father, David, and his Kingdom shall have no end." [95]

Rothmann's revolutionary chiliasm is very close to that of Thomas Müntzer, and it is therefore not at all surprising that Luther and his contemporaries regarded the prophet of Mühlhausen as the first of the radical enthusiasts and Anabaptists. In terms of ultimate outcome, the New Jerusalem at Münster ended as disas-

trously as that of Müntzer. Bockelson's prophecies of an approaching relief force were time and again proved wrong, and
after February 1535 the town was completely surrounded by besieging forces. By April starvation was raging in Münster, and the
inhabitants were reduced to eating rats, old shoes, and, eventually, the bodies of the dead. The end came in June when two
men betrayed one of the gates to the episcopal forces. During the
night of June 24, 1535 the besiegers were able to enter the town
and a frightful massacre ensued in which practically all the male
defenders were slaughtered. Rothmann apparently died fighting.
Bockelson and two other leading Anabaptists were captured and
taken on a tour of exhibition throughout North Germany. Only
the ex-king made a partial recantation and accused others in the
hope of saving his life. Perhaps, comments one writer, the former
tailor from Leyden really was nothing but an "adroit, power-
hungry charlatan." [96] On January 22, 1536 in Münster the three
prize captives were publicly tortured to death with red-hot irons
and their bodies, put into cages, were suspended from a centrally
located church tower where they remained until World War II.

The debacle of Münster led to the rapid decline of militant
Anabaptist chiliasm. A group of Dutch Melchiorites, led by
John of Batenburg, for a time continued to adhere to the militant
eschatology of the Münsterites: they killed their opponents,
plundered churches, and continued to practice polygamy and the
community of goods.[97] Thirty years after the capture of Batenburg, in 1567, a cobbler named John Willemsen proclaimed himself the Messiah and tried to set up another New Jerusalem in
Westphalia.[98] But these were short-lived episodes running
counter to the mainstream of Anabaptism that returned to the
pacifism and quietism of the founders. In the Netherlands, Menno
Simons and the brothers Dirk and Obbe Philips did their best to
dissociate themselves and the movement from the disaster of
Münster. Eschatological thinking persisted, but the coming Kingdom of God in the main was again conceived of as a spiritual entity providing hope for the covenant of sufferers. "The eschatological hope loomed large in their thinking because of its value in
fortifying them against the rigorous persecution which they faced
on every side, from the state and the Church, from Roman
Catholics and Protestants alike." [99]

For many years to come, the "horrors of Münster" indeed

could not but increase the severity of suppression. The debauchery and violence that had accompanied the attempt to set up the reign of the Anabaptist saints confirmed the worst fears of the persecutors and strengthened their conviction that suppression was right and proper. In the Netherlands it was not until 1577 that the Mennonites, as they are now called, were granted civil and religious freedom,[100] and in other countries it was even later. Offshoots of Anabaptism survive to this day as sectarian organizations of mutual aid and brotherhood who have withdrawn from a world they failed to convert to their ways.

CHAPTER 6

The Kingdom of the Saints
in the Puritan Revolution:
The Fifth Monarchy Men

A PROPITIOUS SETTING

The appearance of millenarian agitation in the Puritan Revolution should not come as a surprise. "Religion was not the thing at first contested for," Oliver Cromwell recalled in his speech before the first Protectorate Parliament on January 22, 1654.[1] The Great Rebellion, indeed, had many underlying political, social, and economic causes, but the religious issue soon came to play a major role. "It is as safe as any generalization of history can be," writes Lawrence Stone, "to say that without the ideas, the organization and the leadership supplied by Puritanism there would have geen no revolution at all."[2] For Cromwell, the Puritan chaplains, and many of the rank and file of the New Model Army, the Civil War quickly assumed the character of a religious struggle. These men believed that they were fighting for God's cause, and a truly religious reformation, that their victories were the victories of Armageddon, and that the establishment of Christ's kingdom on earth was not far off. The millenarian Fifth Monarchy movement arose out of this intensely spiritual mood and the atmosphere of religious excitement pervading the Civil War period.

Millenarian speculation, of course, was neither limited to army circles nor did it just begin in the 1640's. The religious tensions created by the Reformation in the sixteenth century and the political chaos following in its wake encouraged the belief in an imminent dissolution of all things secular on the continent as well as in England. Biblical exegesis had long attracted the most brilliant minds, and numerous learned authors had undertaken studies of the numerical calculations in the biblical prophecies, including the date of the Second Coming of Christ and the end of the world. A mathematical genius like John Napier of Merchiston, the inventor of logarithms, in 1593 published his *Plaine Discovery of the Whole Revelation of St. John* in which he explained, in precise mathematical terms, the prophetic phrases of the Apocalypse and predicted that the Day of Judgment would fall between the years 1688 and 1700. Puritan divines were particularly drawn to this enterprise. In Calvinist theology the world was a battleground between Christ and Antichrist; God's elect, the saints assisted by the Holy Spirit, had the task of progressively subduing Antichrist by perfecting and sanctifying the church and society. This theocratic conception often had strong eschatological overtones. "In fact," notes a recent student of Puritanism, "the distinction between millenarian and Calvinist theocratic patterns often broke down at this point, for at times it was by no means uncommon for orthodox Calvinists to feel that for the sake of the elect God was foreshortening the period in which his Church must prepare the world and was hastening the descent of the New Jerusalem." Another writer speaks of an "implicit millenarianism" that pervaded the thinking of English Protestants in the first half of the seventeenth century.[3]

Thomas Brightman's *Apocalypsis Apocalypseos*, published in 1609, and Joseph Mede's *Clavis Apocalyptica*, 1627, were among the more important works calculating and predicting the early advent of the millenarian Kingdom of Christ, and more popular versions began to appear after the gathering of the Long Parliament in 1640. In the following year, John Archer, an Independent preacher, published his pamphlet, *The Personal Reign of Christ upon Earth*, in which he undertook a careful exposition and comparison of the mysteries set forth in Daniel and Revelation and fixed the date for the coming of Christ for the year 1700.[4] Also in 1641, a pamphlet entitled *A Glimpse of Sion's Glory*, probably written by Hanserd Knollys, predicted the onset of Christ's kingdom for 1650. The writer, like other Puritan divines, voiced his appreciation of God's special providence for England—a country elected to play a leading role in the divine plan. "It is through our wretched wickedness if his [God's] kingly power be not fully set up amongst us in all his ordinances. And that we should have an opportunity to set up his kingly

power amongst us here, while it is so much opposed and so little
known in the world, it is a great mercy." [5]

With the coming of the Civil War the number of millenarian
tracts multiplied rapidly. According to Grotius, eighty such
tracts had appeared in England by 1649.[6] The victories of Cromwell's Ironsides were seen widely as the fulfillment of divine
prophecy: God was with his saints, and the establishment of his
kingdom on English soil was in the making. Ecstasies and prophecies, and preachers and groups of religious enthusiasts of the most
varied sorts, multiplied enormously; millenarian hopes permeated
all strata of the population. Great and unprecedented times had
arrived in which God was shaking the old order and pouring out
his spirit among his chosen people. England, the only major Protestant state, was an elect nation destined to play a crucial role in
the destruction of Rome and the hastening of the end of the
world.[7]

English Puritanism, having neither an infallible earthly authority nor an Erastian power that could ensure a consistent interpretation of the Bible, was highly susceptible to fission.[8] The encouragement of an immediate, personal, religious experience militated
against the emergence of any systematic theology; this also characterized the religious ideas of the army chaplains among whom
millenarian currents ran strongly. Some, like John Saltmarsh, held
to a highly spiritualized view of the approaching Millennium in
which any external manifestation of the eschatological hope was
rejected. The Kingdom of Christ, he argued, would be ushered in
through the progressive revelation of God in the Spirit to individual believers and without the need for human exertion.[9] Others, like Hugh Peters, in the terminology of Reinhold Niebuhr,
were "fighting" saints and ready for direct action. The work of
God will go on even if we all sat still, Peters declared in the debates among the officers at Whitehall on December 14, 1648, yet
"I am not in the mind we should put our hands in our pockets
and wait what will come." [10] Thomas Collier, in a sermon
preached in September 1647 on the text, "Behold, I create new
heavens, and a new earth" (Isa. 65:17), disagreed with those who
thought "that Christ shall come and reign personally, subduing
his enemies and exalting his people, and that this is the new
heaven and the new earth." At the same time, he affirmed that in
the approaching Kingdom of God the power of ruling would be

in the hands of those "who are acquainted with, and have an interest in, the righteous God. . . . The nations shall become the nations of Christ, and the government shall be in the hands of the Saints."[11] Reliance upon the elect—upon good men rather than upon a good constitution or duly elected representative institutions—was one of the few constant themes in the political thought of the millenarian army preachers. From this defense of rule by the saintly few it was but a small step to a general attack upon the monarchy, a position to which not only the army chaplains but the leaders of the army, too, were moving steadily.

THE RISE OF THE FIFTH MONARCHY MEN

The slogan "No king but Jesus" gained in popularity after the execution of King Charles in January 1649. The millenarians benefited from the acute insecurity pervading the country in the wake of the overthrow of the throne. The loss of the king, one historian notes, "was more than could easily be assimilated: religious men, even when in sympathy with the regicides, abhorred the vacuum created. The demise of the monarchy could be only in order to open the way for the kingship of Christ. The crown must be laid at the feet of Jesus, for the government would be upon his shoulders."[12] In the eyes of religious enthusiasts Charles I was the little horn of the beast spoken of in Daniel, and his execution adumbrated the approach of the Fifth Monarchy, the reign of Christ.

The first collective effort to establish the Fifth Monarchy and the emergence of the millenarians as an organized group or party took the form of a petition from Norfolk, presented to the leaders of the army in February 1649. The authors of *Certain Queries Humbly Presented in Way of Petition by many Christian People Dispersed Abroad throughout the County of Norfolk* declared that they expected "new heavens and a new earth" and they warned against patching up "the old worldly government" of the ungodly. Instead, a visible Kingdom of Christ and the saints was to be erected though it would come into being not "by human power and authority" but by mandate of God and Christ. The saints and people of God were called upon to lay aside all differences and divisions, "to associate together into several church-societies and corporations (according to the Congregational way) till being increased and multiplied, they may combine into general assemblies or church-parliaments (according to the Presbyterian way); and then shall God give them authority and rule over the nations and kingdoms of the world." Rule by such elected or delegated bodies was to continue "till Christ come in person." The advent of this Fifth Monarchy was "to be expected about this time we live in." [13]

The petition from Norfolk was unsigned, and we know neither the number of people connected with it nor their religious affiliation. The first appearance of the movement in London dates from the end of 1651 when meetings were reported at the church of All Hallows the Great and later in the parish of St. Anne's, Blackfriars. The preachers at these meetings were practically all Baptists, whereas the rank and file appear to have been Independents as well as Baptists. Even though the English Baptists, like the Dutch Mennonites who had shaped their theology, had long since disowned John of Leyden's attempt at Münster to establish the Millennium by force, the public still associated them with the chiliastic Anabaptists. The fact that the Fifth Monarchy Men were often called Baptists or Anabaptists, therefore, was in part due to the desire of their opponents to discredit the new millenarian movement.[14]

We know very little about the social composition of the Fifth Monarchy Men. We do know that millenarian ideas in those days of religious excitement appealed to all levels of society, though the particular revolutionary millenarianism typified by the Fifth Monarchy movement apparently especially attracted men and women from the lower classes and was to be found mainly in the towns. Literacy there was higher, and this facilitated the spread of ideas. As Capp notes, "the preoccupation of the Fifth Monarchists with political power probably also contributed to the movement's urban character." [15]

Another important source of recruits was the army, where, as in the towns, traditional social patterns had weakened. Here the Fifth Monarchy party found some of its most active leaders; several officers with the rank of colonel or above belonged to the party, and many others sympathized with it.[16] Indeed the idea of rule by the saintly few, as we shall soon see, appealed to Cromwell himself. It is, therefore, quite inappropriate to consider the Fifth Monarchy Men a movement of social protest whose spokes-

men were inspired by "acute social consciousness." [17] Though
some of these men decried oppression by the rich or corruption
of lawyers, at bottom they cared not so much for the material rewards of this world as for the spiritual enrichment provided for
the elect by the Holy Spirit. They were religious enthusiasts who
sought not to promote the rights of the downtrodden masses but
government by an elite of saints. In this sense, the Fifth Monarchy Men carried to an extreme a tendency inherent in Puritanism. In the words of Michael Walzer, they were "revolutionaries"
striving to transform "all society and all men in the image of their
own salvation." From such men, narrow and fanatical, one does
not expect or receive freedom. "Their great achievement is what
is known in the sociology of revolution as the *terror*, the effort to
create a holy commonwealth and to force man to be godly." [18]
Like the Taborites and revolutionary Anabaptists before them,
and the Jacobins and Bolsheviks after them, the Fifth Monarchy
Men were part of a wide spectrum of revolutionary chiliasm and
closer to the modern phenomenon of totalitarianism than to a
genuine movement of popular liberation or democracy.

Relations between the Fifth Monarchy Men and Cromwell at
first were good. Like the millenarian enthusiasts, the strongman of
England was greatly dissatisfied with the intractable and do-noth-
ing Rump Parliament, and he listened sympathetically to the
ideas of Major-General Thomas Harrison, a member of the Council of Officers and an active Fifth Monarchy Man. The daring
Harrison, an Independent of whom Hugh Peters spoke as "that
godly and gallant gentleman," [19] had distinguished himself during
the Civil War and his advocacy of rule by the saints appealed to
Cromwell; it was said that Cromwell had a genuine liking for
"godly" men.[20] Hearing that members of the Rump Parliament
were preparing to vote themselves a term of office of indefinite
duration, Cromwell, on April 20, 1653, told Parliament that "the
Lord had done with them, and had chosen other instruments for
the carrying on his work, that were more worthy," [21] and dissolved it. A troop of soldiers cleared the House, while Harrison
pulled the Speaker from his seat which he had refused to leave
voluntarily.

Most of the Fifth Monarchy Men were jubilant at this turn of
events and hailed Cromwell as the new Moses destined by God to
lead England into the new order. Advice on how to set up the

government of the saints was freely given. One suggestion was that the government of saints, according to biblical precedent, be chosen by lot. Others proposed that the saints come from the ranks of the army. John Rogers, the preacher at St. Thomas Apostle and a vocal if somewhat erratic spokesman of the Fifth Monarchy party, suggested that the government be put into the hands of a Sanhedrin of seventy godly men chosen by Cromwell, "the great Deliverer of his people (through God's grace) out of the house of Egypt." [22] Harrison, too, favored a Sanhedrin, and the new form of government finally decided upon by the officers incorporated several features favored by the millenarians. The executive power was lodged in the Council of State composed of Cromwell and twelve others; the Fifth Monarchy Man, Colonel Okey, had proposed a council of thirteen members, a number representing Christ and the twelve Apostles.[23] The legislature was to consist of 140 faithful and God-fearing men, to be chosen by Cromwell and the army officers from nominees suggested by the Independent (sectarian) congregations all over the country. However, only fifteen persons were proposed by the churches, and the Council of Officers picked whom it pleased.[24]

On July 4, 1653, Cromwell addressed the members of the new Nominated or Little Parliament, later derisively called Barebone's Parliament (from Praise-God Barebone, a Baptist and leather merchant and one of its more prominent members). Cromwell's speech reflected the millenarian mood of Parliament. He began by reviewing the course of the revolution and its tribulations, "invasions, secret Designs, open and public Attempts, all quashed in so short a time, and this by the very signal appearance of God Himself." [25] In fervent and enthusiastic language Cromwell then proceeded to hail the godly men:

> Truly you are called by God, "as Judah was" to "rule with Him," and for Him. And you are called to be faithful with the Saints who have been instrumental to your call. . . . I confess I never looked to see such a Day as this . . . when Jesus Christ should be so owned as He is, this day, in this Work. . . . And why should we be afraid to say or think, That *this* may be the door to usher-in the Things that God has promised. . . . Indeed I do think somewhat is at the door; we are at the threshhold;—and therefore it becomes us to lift-up our heads, and encourage ourselves in the Lord. And we have thought, some of us, That it is our duties to *endeavour* this way; not merely to *look* at that Prophecy in Daniel, "And the

Kingdom shall not be delivered to another people," "and passively wait." Truly God hath brought this your hands; by the owning of your call; blessing the Military Power. . . . Truly seeing things are ʾthus, that you are at the edge of the Promises and Prophecies.[26]

For the next five months the Nominated Parliament addressed itself to the task of implementing this lofty mandate given them by Cromwell, but it soon became apparent that the assembly was divided between a minority of radical reformers and a majority of more moderate members. The former faction was composed of no more than sixty of the members and the members fully identified with the Fifth Monarchy Men numbered less than twenty.[27] Still, the radicals made up their lack in numbers by regularity of attendance and zeal and thus often commanded a majority. The fact that seats had been given to men like Fairfax, without sectarian church connections, had disappointed the religious enthusiasts; relations between Cromwell and Harrison are said to have cooled somewhat after this. Nevertheless, by and large, expectations were high. The *Faithful Scout* of July 8, authored by Daniel Border, a Baptist with strong Fifth Monarchy sympathies, greeted the Nominated Parliament of the saints with a reference to "these Overturning, Overturning, Overturning dayes," and expressed the hope that it would "endeavor the directing of the Kingdom of Jesus Christ to the uttermost parts of the Earth." [28] In a declaration adopted July 12, the saints themselves stated that they wanted to be instruments of God's work by promoting the gospel, breaking yokes, and removing burdens.[29]

One of the first reform measures involved the problem of tithes. In the matter of a religious settlement Cromwell had been rather dilatory, church and state were still not fully separated, as demanded by the Independents and other sectarians over a period of time, and maintenance by tithes was not interfered with. "The effect was a wobbly State Church with Independents, baptists, presbyterians and other denominations being selected by some authority or other as fit and proper ministers." [30] A proposal that no tithes be paid after November 3, 1653 was now made, but the moderates, anxious to devise first some other mode of payment for ministers, succeeded in having the measure referred to a committee. However, on two other issues, the abolition of the Court of Chancery and the establishment of civil marriage, more radical sentiments prevailed. Also passed without much controversy was an act providing for the relief of poor prisoners and lunatics.[31]

The fears of the moderates were raised when a committee was appointed to study law reform. The Fifth Monarchy Men were known to favor the abolition of the existing laws of England and the substitution for them of the biblical law of God. Some legal reform was favored by all, but the radical proposal of the millenarians clearly went beyond what the moderates were willing to support. When the committee on tithes brought in its report, which included a provision for state commissioners to eject unqualified ministers, the moderates, in defeating the proposal, were able to muster no more than a majority of two. Afraid that they would not be able to stop the Fifth Monarchy Men and their radical schemes, they now decided to end the assembly and resign their powers into the hands of Cromwell. They arranged to meet early on the morning of December 12, 1653, and a motion dissolving the assembly carried before some of the radicals had arrived. A minority of twenty-seven members objecting to this move were ejected from the chamber by force. Thus ended the Nominated Parliament of the Saints.

Cromwell, who had watched the proceedings of the Nominated Parliament with growing concern, was happy about its dissolution. He shared the desire of the Fifth Monarchy Men to see the Kingdom of Christ on earth, but he also was a political realist who wanted orderly government, and he was deeply suspicious of the fanaticism of the millenarians. Harrison, Cromwell is said to have once remarked, "is an honest man, and aims at good things, yet from the impatience of his spirit will not wait the Lord's leisure, but hurries me on to that which he and all honest men will have cause to repent." [32]

To the Fifth Monarchy Men the dissolution of Barebone's Parliament came as a great blow, and at numerous meetings they sharply criticized the new Instrument of Government of December 16, 1653 making Cromwell Lord Protector of England. Leading this harsh verbal onslaught upon Cromwell were two preachers, Christopher Feake and Vavasor Powell. On December 18, while preaching at Christ Church, Newgate Street, both men called him "the dissemblingest perjured villain in the world," and they prophesied that his reign would be short.[33] On the following evening, the day of Cromwell's proclamation as Lord Protector, Powell intimated in a sermon at St. Anne, Blackfriars, that

Cromwell was the vile or contemptible person to whom, according to Daniel 11:21 "royal majesty has not been given" but who would "obtain the kingdom by flatterers." "Lord," he cried, "have our army men all apostatised from their principles. What has become of all their declarations, protestations, and professions? Are they choked with lands, parks and manors? Let us go home and pray, and say, 'Lord, wilt Thou have Oliver Cromwell or Jesus Christ to reign over us?' " [34] At the same service, Feake hinted pointedly that not the late King Charles but Cromwell was the "Little Horn" of Daniel's prophecy who would make war upon the saints and who the saints would destroy upon inheriting the Fifth Monarchy. Both men were arrested the following day though they gained their release a few days later. Together with John Simpson, a noted Fifth Monarchy preacher, Feake was arrested again on January 28 under a new ordinance that made any attack upon the legitimacy of the existing government a treasonable offense. Powell escaped to the mountains of his native Wales.

John Rogers, who at first had not participated in the millenarians' condemnation of Cromwell, soon joined the chorus. He criticized the "ridiculous pomp and vanity" displayed by the Lord Protector and the Council of State and he prayed for the day "when all absolute power shall be devolved into the hand of Christ; when we shall have no Lord Protector but our Lord Jesus." [35] Rogers, too, was arrested in July 1654; Harrison was banished to the country.

Reports were circulating meanwhile of an impending uprising by the Fifth Monarchy Men. The Baptists, always suspected of subversive designs, at a meeting of representatives from all parts of the country found it necessary to issue a formal statement affirming their loyalty to the government. They denied that they knew "any ground for the saints, as such, to expect that the Rule and Government of the World should be put into their hands, until that day in which the Lord Jesus shall visibly descend from heaven." [36] Many individual Baptists, nevertheless, were said to be making common cause with the millenarians; secret enlistments of military saints were reported from Wales where Vavasor Powell had been at work preaching and stirring up opposition since his escape from London at the beginning of the year.

On September 3, 1654, the new Parliament met and Cromwell

in his opening address castigated the millenarian visionaries. The
new assembly was predominantly Presbyterian; the excesses of
the Nominated Parliament had discredited the radicals' cause, and
only four of them had won reelection. The Lord Protector
bluntly warned against an error fallen into by many sincere people, the mistaken notion of the Fifth Monarchy:

> A thing pretending more spirituality than anything else. A notion I
> hope we all honour, and wait, and hope for "the fulfillment of":
> That Jesus Christ *will* have a time to set up His Reign in our
> hearts; by subduing those corruptions and lusts and evils that are
> there; which now reign more in the world than, I hope, in due
> time they shall do. And when more fulness of the Spirit is poured
> forth to subdue iniquity, and bring-in everlasting righteousness,
> then will the approach of that glory be. . . . The carnal divisions
> and contentions among Christians, so common, are not the symp-
> toms of that Kingdom!—But for men, on this principle, to betitle
> themselves, that they are the only men to rule kingdoms, govern
> nations, and give laws to people, and determine of property and
> liberty and everything else,—upon such a pretension as this is:
> —truly they had need to give clear manifestations of God's pres-
> ence with them, before wise men will receive or submit to their
> conclusions! [37]

The Fifth Monarchy Men, not intimidated, continued to attack
the new government. During the week of Parliament's convening
they issued a manifesto entitled, *A Declaration of several of the
Churches of Christ, and Godly people in and about the City of
London, concerning the Kingly Interest of Christ, and the present sufferings of his Cause and Saints in England.* The millenarians disowned any participation in "carnal plots" but otherwise
sharply attacked the army for abandoning its old principles.[38] On
September 22 a less restrained sermon by Thomas Goodwin was
published:

A
Sermon
of the
Fifth Monarchy,
Proving by Invincible Arguments
That the Saints shall have a Kingdom
here on Earth
Which is yet to come, after the Fourth
Monarchy is destroy'd by the Sword of
the Saints, the followers of the Lamb.[39]

In the face of these repeated threats and provocations Cromwell conducted himself with considerable restraint which can be explained only by his personal sympathies with the cause of the millenarians. He found it difficult to deal harshly with men who did but exaggerate his own Puritanism. On several occasions Cromwell engaged in debate with the leading figures of the Fifth Monarchy party in which he promised them full freedom to teach the word of God if only they would desist from sedition. This they refused to do. Four lay leaders of the millenarians, including Harrison, told the Lord Protector in February 1655, that his government was "a government set up against the will of God, and in opposition to the Kingdom of Christ, and was anti-Christian and Babylonish, and they did expect that God would pour his wrath upon it." Such a political authority was illegitimate, it need not be obeyed, and "arms may be taken up against it." Their great objection to the present constitution was that "it had a parliament in it, whereby power is derived from the people, whereas all power belongs to Christ." [40] The four self-avowed revolutionaries thereupon were imprisoned.

Convinced of the early advent of the Millennium in which Christ would govern with his saints and provide for all needs, the Fifth Monarchy Men by and large neglected the issues of practical politics. Their political and social ideas, therefore, were rather nebulous and shallow. The primary inspiration was, of course, the Book of Revelation and the Book of Daniel, though the millenarians differed in their "scriptural arithmetic." Some expected the onset of the Fifth Monarchy almost momentarily, others arrived at a date as remote as 1701.[41] The rule of the saints would begin in England but should spread from there to the rest of the world. The Fifth Monarchy Men, therefore, repeatedly called upon Cromwell to prosecute vigorously the war against Holland so as to gain a foothold on the continent. John Spittlehouse, in a pamphlet published in 1653, *The First Addresses to His Excellencie the Lord General . . . containing Certain Rules and Directions How to advance the Kingdom of Jesus Christ over the Face of the whole Earth*, urged Cromwell not to rest content with his doings at home but to "persevere in the work of the Lord in forraign parts, and not make peace with the Gibeonites or any other Nation which the Lord hath a controverse withal, and who are designed to destruction." [42] In his pamphlet, *Sagrir, or Doomesday drawing nigh* (1653), Rogers predicted that by 1660 the Fifth

Monarchy would be as far as Rome and by 1666 it would be "visible in all the earth." [43]

The mathematician John Pell, a trusted advisor of Cromwell, wrote to Thurloe in March 1655: "Men variously impoverished by the long troubles, full of discontents, and tired by long expectation of amendment, must needs have great propensions to hearken to those that proclaim times of refreshing—a golden age —at hand, . . . glad tidings under the name of the kingdom of Christ and of the saints; especially when so many prophecies are cited and applied to these times." [44] The message of the approaching Millennium at times indeed had special appeal to the poor. After the dissolution of the Rump Parliament, Vavasor Powell announced from the pulpit at Whitehall that in the new government of the saints "law should stream down like a river freely, as for twenty shillings what formerly cost twenty pounds, impartially as the saints please, and it should run as rivers do, close to the doors." [45] A programmatic statement of 1657, *A Standard Set Up*, promised that in the coming rule of the saints no person would be exempt from the law and none would be imprisoned without a legal cause. Excise, customs, and tithes would be abolished: "All oppressions and grievances in the tenure of lands" such as fines and rents would be "abrogated and clean removed." The Supreme Council or Sanhedrin would make changes in the state's foundations of freedom only according to "the good of the people." [46] Small wonder that the rank and file Fifth Monarchy Men were apparently mostly artisans, journeymen, and apprentices who at least in part were motivated by "considerations of vengeance on their social superiors, the end of all taxation, and a generalized vision of future bliss." [47]

The political and social ideas of the Fifth Monarchy Men revealed some affinity to the thinking of the Levellers whom Cromwell had succeeded in destroying as an effective political force by the spring of 1649 but whose ideas, nevertheless, had had considerable impact. We find here, writes one historian, "the same humaneness, and the same indignation against social wrong." [48] Of course, no more than the Levellers did the Fifth Monarchy Men, in attacking certain abuses in the society of their day, seek to bring about a general "leveling." John Spittlehouse, for example, had high praise for "the ranks and orders of men, whereby England hath been known for hundreds of years; as a Nobleman, a Gentleman, a Yeoman, (that being a good interest of the Nation, and a great one:)." [49] Indeed, as we have noted before, the elitism of the Fifth Monarchy Men was pronounced, and this clearly distinguished them from the Levellers who had aimed at full political equality for all Englishmen. The millenarians gave rights only to the self-proclaimed saints who were to exercise, as one of their spokesmen put it, the "supremacy of power" and were to function as "the Lamb's Military Officers." [50]

Most Fifth Monarchy Men were vocal in their denunciation of the civil law of England which, as Rogers wrote, amounted to "slavery and tyranny"; as the Jews had been robbed and spoiled by the Romans "so we by the Normans [were] robbed of all our rights." He, therefore, proposed to "set up the laws of God in the stead of men's," [51] to make Scripture, especially the Old Testament, the only law of the land. But whether their motive was biblical literalism or a preoccupation with human wickedness or a desire to sanctify the world and struggle against sin, the net effect of this projected reintroduction of the Mosaic law and its enforcement by the saints could only have been a thoroughly repressive regime and a declaration of war against ordinary humanity. The manifesto of the Fifth Monarchy Men of 1660, *A Door of Hope*, expressed the desire "to take off all yoaks and oppressions both of a civil and spiritual nature from the necks of the poor people," but then went on to categorize as "the greatest sins" offenses such as "swearing, drunkenness, sabbath-breaking, whoredome, pride, lasciviousness, stage plays, blasphemy, popery, superstition, idolatry" which should be severely punished.[52] Aspinwall denounced the English law's imposition of the death penalty for theft, pointing out that the Bible demanded only double restitution, but using the same standard of judgment he rejected the institution of the jury since there was no mention of it in the Scriptures. His criminal code prescribed capital punishment for twelve offenses including adultery, wilfully profaning the Sabbath, and "cursing the Rulers of the people." Any appeal against a judgment of the saints was ruled out "because that would be a dishonour to Christ." [53] Surely Cromwell was right when he told the leaders of the millenarians at one of his meetings with them, "Why, I tell you there be Anabaptists and they would cut the throats of them that are not under their forms . . . and so would you Fifth-Monarchy-Men. It is fit to keep all these forms out of power." [54]

From the beginning the Fifth Monarchy Men were in disagree-

ment on whether forceful action was necessary in order to hasten
the coming of the Kingdom of Christ. It appears that many of the
millenarians, perhaps a majority, rejected violence; in the two attempts made by the radical faction, which was chiefly concentrated in London, to establish the rule of the saints by force the
pacific millenarians refused to participate. There also were those,
of course, who, while not rejecting bloodshed in principle, deemed
the hour not ripe for such an undertaking. In fact, men like John
Simpson and William Erbury moved from one position to the
other in response to circumstances. Most of the Fifth Monarchy
Men denied the legitimacy of the protectorate government and
did their best to discredit Cromwell's rule by means of vitupera-
tive sermons and pamphlets.

For the moderate millenarians the advent of the Fifth Monarchy could not be hastened. The saints were quietly to await the
arrival of the Millennium and meanwhile be subject to civil authority. The Fifth Monarchy Men, declared Aspinwall in the
summer of 1656, are "the best and truest friends unto Government, and count it their duty to be faithful unto their trust, be
the Rulers what they may, or the form of government what it
will. Only they take themselves bound in Conscience to rebuke
sin, and bear witness against unrighteousness, in any person, of
what quality soever, and in any form of Government
whatsoever."[55] The saints could remove stumbling blocks from
the way of the Lord by reminding rulers of their duty and per-
suading them to set up the laws of God, but the final great transformation would not be realized by material weapons; it would
be accomplished "not by power, nor by might but by my Spirit,
saith the Lord, Zech., 4, 6."[56]

The more militant Fifth Monarchy Men agreed that the time
of the coming Millennium was divinely predetermined and could
not be changed by men, but they, nevertheless, assigned an active
role to the saints, God's instruments. It was the duty of God's
elect to read and understand Scripture, to listen to the divine call,
and then to act out the role assigned to them: the carrying out of
the glorious work of deliverance. Christ's injunction to his followers not to resist evil and to love one's enemies, insisted Mary
Cary, applied only to the private sphere. In public life, the sword
rather than love was the instrument of salvation.[57] In the coming
battle against the beast's government, Rogers wrote in a pamphlet

published in 1657, the slain of the Lord shall be many—"the
blood of the vintage will be up unto the horses' bridles (Rev.
XIV. 20)." But their cause could not fail because we are "heirs of
the promise." "Therefore, Up, O ye Saints, to take the Kingdom
(Dan. VII. 18) and to possess it for ever. . . . Be valiant, like
David's worthies." [58] Similar calls to battle against Christ's enemies
were found in the sermons of Vavasor Powell and in William Erbury's *Lord of Hosts* of 1648.

Cromwell's government was not unaware of these calls for rebellion. "'Tis certain," wrote Thurloe to Henry Cromwell in
1655, "that the Fifth Monarchy Men, some of them I mean, have
designs of putting us unto blood." [59] The notorious agitator,
Powell, was still traveling around his native Wales stirring up
trouble; in June 1656 he presided over a meeting of more than
four hundred people who had come together out of seven or eight
counties.[60] Equally disquieting were reports of a new drawing together of Fifth Monarchy Men and Baptists. Government inform-
ers reported a growing excitement at meetings of young men
held at All Hallows and Swan Alley in London. The government
was denounced as oppressing the saints of God and its fall was
predicted. "It was said that the time of their deliverance was approaching and that the sword of the Lord was whetted and going
forth against the enemies of His People." [61] The actual number of
Fifth Monarchy Men at that time is difficult to establish with any
precision. The highest estimate was made in 1655 by one of their
preachers, Feake, who gave the figure of 40,000 members. It
seems probable that their number never exceeded 10,000.[62] In
1656 the strength of the movement was said to be diminishing
through desertions to the Quakers and Baptists, but ferment
among the diehards was increasing.

PLOTS AND DEFEATS

Concrete plans to overthrow Cromwell's government began to be
laid in July 1656. At a meeting of Fifth Monarchy Men in London it was decided that the time for pulling down Babylon and
its adherents had arrived and that the saints had to do it by the
sword. The zealots divided themselves into five groups of about
twenty-five members each with a leader to keep an eye on the
gathering of arms and money. The leaders of the groups were to

keep in touch with each other. Contact was also made with the Commonwealth Men, a group of republicans favoring a democratically elected parliament in the tradition of the defunct Levellers. At these negotiations for an alliance against the Protectorate, the chief spokesman for the Fifth Monarchy Men was the wine-cooper, Thomas Venner; a recently written tract by Sir Henry Vane, a man with sympathies for both the millenarians and the Commonwealth Men, entitled *A Healing Question Propounded and Resolved*, formed the basis of the discussions. But though both parties were anxious to depose Cromwell's government they could not come to an understanding. The Commonwealth Men insisted on settling the composition and method of election of the proposed new government, while the Fifth Monarchy Men were preoccupied with the divine mandate of the saints and felt that all details should be left to the providence of God. Harrison and Colonel Rich were invited to mediate the differences between the realists and visionaries, but they refused to have anything to do with the plotters.[63]

In September 1656 the financially pressed Cromwell had to convene a new Parliament. The exclusion of about one hundred members as potential troublemakers increased the bitterness of the Fifth Monarchy Men who gave vent to their feelings in a pamphlet entitled *The Banner of Truth Displayed . . . Being the Substance of several Consultations . . . kept by a Certain Number of Christians, who are waiting for the visible appearance of Christ's Kingdome*. The anonymous authors castigated the government as "beast-like powers" and traitors and called for the exclusive rule of "the Saints of the Most High." The Fourth Monarchy would have to be totally destroyed and in order to set up the Fifth Monarchy the saints should appear "in a military Posture for Christ" and "do smiting work." The hour for the call to action was near. Similarly wild denunciations of Cromwell and his government could be heard in the sermons of Feake and Rogers, both recently released from prison.[64]

By January 1657 Venner and his associates were preparing the details of their insurrection, though a plot in the same month to assassinate Cromwell appears not to have been connected with the wine-cooper's little band. In an account of the uprising prepared later by the secretary of the Council of State, John Thurloe, Venner's men were described as "mean fellows of noe note, but such as had blowne up one another by a weekly meeting they had at a place called Swan Alley in Coleman Street." He described the plot as "a designe of a very strange nature, and built upon very extraordinary pretences." [65] This characterization was accurate. The organizers of the uprising were all obscure men; the leading figures of the Fifth Monarchy Men for one reason or another had declined to participate.

In order to justify and publicize the revolt the plotters drew up a manifesto entitled *A Standard Set Up* from which we have already quoted the call for the abolition of all oppressive taxes. Reviewing the events since the Parliament of Saints, the declaration called the resignation of that body's authority invalid and Cromwell's assumption of power an act of usurpation. The Lord Protector's actions exceeded the treason of the late king; "he hath sinned against the Lord Jesus Christ and His people." The existing government, the manifesto continued, must be "broken and removed" in order to make way for "the kingdom of Christ." In the new state the Supreme legislative power would be in the Lord Jesus Christ and the Scriptures, his "revealed will and rule," the only law. A Sanhedrin representing "the whole Body of the Saints" would govern according to the biblical percepts; it would be elected yearly "by the Lord's Freemen—those who have a right with Christ in and according to the new Covenant." The manifesto closed with an appeal to all the brethren to unite for the cause of Christ's kingdom and to enlist under the banner of the Lord Jesus. Even though few in number the conspirators comforted themselves with biblical texts such as these passages from Isaiah: "A little one shall become a thousand, and a small one a strong nation" and "a thousand shall flee at the rebuke of one"; these two verses were quoted under the title of the manifesto.[66]

As the moment for action drew near dissension developed over the question whether the appointed moment for deliverance had truly arrived. Some of the brethren argued that according to the arithmetic of the Book of Revelation the reign of the Beast had another two months to run and argued to postpone the rising. Venner, however, pressed on with the preparations: horses, pistols, and ammunition were bought, and the day for taking up arms was fixed for midnight April 9. Organized as much as possible along biblical lines, and with officers chosen by lot, the small band of insurgents numbering no more than eighty men arranged to meet at a rendezvous at Mile End Green. Here the revolt was to be proclaimed, their standard bearing a lion unfurled. Venner, living in his world of chiliastic dreams, apparently expected that at that historic moment thousands would flock to the cause of Christ and join in the destruction of Babylon.[67]

Before these plans could be executed, reality caught up with the visionaries. Government spies had infiltrated the plot, and, in the early evening of April 9, Venner and twenty-three of his men were arrested as they were praying, booted and spurred, for the success of the enterprise at a house in Shoreditch. Several other depots were also raided, and considerable stores of arms and ammunition, as well as copies of the manifesto, were seized. The other plotters managed to escape and attempted to stage the now leaderless revolt at the end of April. They, too, were eventually captured.

The reaction of the government was surprisingly mild. Venner was brought before Cromwell and the Council of State where the Lord Protector, still harboring some sympathy for the millenarians, spoke to him in a friendly manner. But the wine-cooper replied insolently, and he and his associates were sent to the Tower. The decision not to put the plotters on trial in itself amounted to a grant of clemency. Harrison and several veteran leaders of the Fifth Monarchy Men were also arrested and interrogated, but in the absence of conclusive evidence they were soon released. The uprising had involved a tiny band of religious fanatics, but contemporary observers, nevertheless, took a serious view of it. At a time of general insecurity and royalist as well as republican plots the outbreak could well have led to bigger things. Henry Cromwell used the opportunity to urge his father to accept the crown and to reestablish the monarchy in order to bring back public peace: "These wild notions concerning the right of saints to reign, and the imaginary immediate government of Christ upon earth, must needs call aloud for some settlement of the government." [68]

Opposition to the restoration of the monarchy was strong in army circles, and Cromwell, after some hesitation, decided to decline the crown urged upon him. Instability and unrest meanwhile increased as both royalists and republicans stepped up their hostile acts. In February 1658 John Rogers and several other

Fifth Monarchy Men who had been distributing pamphlets among the soldiers urging them to "destroy the Beast with his supporters" [69] were arrested. When Cromwell, worn out by personal tragedy and the strains of his long years in public office, died in September, rumors of another impending coup by the millenarians followed each other in quick succession. The reestablishment of the Commonwealth, without a Lord Protector, in May 1659 pacified the Fifth Monarchy Men for a while. Several of their leaders were given public office, and when a royalist insurrection in Cheshire threatened the new regime many of the millenarians joined the hastily formed volunteer regiments commanded by Sir Henry Vane. But the short honeymoon did not last, for the restored Rump Parliament proved no more willing than earlier bodies to adopt the millenarian proposals of the Fifth Monarchy Men. The latters' expressions of dissatisfaction and threats of violence now added to the prevailing uncertainty, and in April 1660 a newly convened Parliament, fearing a decline into anarchy, voted to offer the crown to Charles II.

Two prominent Fifth Monarchy Men, Major-General Harrison and John Carew, were among the regicides put on trial for their part in the execution of Charles I. Harrison defended himself by challenging the right of the court to try and judge an action carried out in the name and with the authority of Parliament and by pointing to his religious mandate: "I followed not my own judgment; I did what I did, as out of conscience to the Lord . . . desiring to make the revealed will of God in his Holy Scriptures as a guide for me." [70] Addressing the crowd assembled for his execution from the gallows, Harrison again affirmed his conviction that he had done no wrong: "I have again and again besought the Lord with tears to make known his will and mind to me concerning it; and to this day he hath rather confirmed me in the justice of it." [71] John Carew, too, was found guilty of high treason and was hanged two days after Harrison. Both men went to their death with dignity and courage.

The sensational finale of the Fifth Monarchy Men was still to come. Venner and his fellow insurrectionists had been released from jail in February 1659, and the restoration of the monarchy found them busily plotting another uprising. As in 1657, a tract was prepared setting forth the aims of the millenarians. It was entitled *A Door of Hope or A Call and Declaration for the gath-*

ering together of the first ripe Fruits unto the Standard of our Lord King Jesus. Charles II was called "a professed enemy, a rebel and traitor to Christ," and the saints were asked to "become soldiers in the Lamb's Army, abhorring mercenary principles and interests" and to drive the Lord's enemies from the country. With this accomplished, the not overly modest plotters then proposed "to go on to France, Spain, Germany and Rome, to destroy the beast and whore, to burn her flesh with fire, to throw her down with violence as a millstone into the sea . . . to bring not only these, but all the nations to the subjection of Christ." [72] The saints were called to do God's work, the tract pronounced, their "hearts broken with the love of Christ and boiling over, and having tasted through choice distinguishing grace, the preciousness, power, and love of a soul-endearing Jesus." The time for this glorious undertaking was now; "the sweet harmony and agreement of the prophecies . . . the undeniable signs of the times," all pointed to it and made the saints "mightily awakened and stirred up." [73]

The day of the desperate venture was fixed for January 6, 1661, the Feast of the Epiphany. Venner's band this time consisted of no more than fifty men, but fighting with furious fanaticism and bravery they managed to throw London into turmoil for almost three days. When it was all over, twenty-two of the insurgents were dead and twenty, including the badly wounded Venner, had been taken prisoner. The forces of the government also lost twenty-two men. Retribution this time was swift and merciless. Condemned on charges of murder and high treason, Venner and one of his chief lieutenants were hanged and quartered on January 19; fifteen others were executed a few days later.[74]

Thus ended the second grotesque attempt to inaugurate the reign of the saints by force. Rumors of new plans for revolt continued to be heard for some time to come,[75] and in June 1662 the government found it necessary to display a show of firmness by bringing to trial Sir Henry Vane, in custody since July 1660. Vane was a friend of the Fifth Monarchy Men but otherwise was innocent of any plotting. He, too, was found guilty of high treason and executed. "The coming of Christ," he declared on the scaffold, "in order to a sudden and revival of his cause, and spreading his kingdom over the face of the whole earth, is most clear to the eye of my faith, even that faith in which I die."[76]

But despite occasional reports of renewed Fifth Monarchy activity the movement by now had spent itself and many former activists drifted into the camp of the Quakers. Some of the congregations ministered to by Vavasor Powell, the fiercest defender of millenarianism in Wales, now became the chief source of strength of the groups of Friends in Mid-Wales.[77] The Quakers, too, had millenarian leanings, but their chiliasm was spiritualized, and they had abandoned any attempt or desire to rush the coming of the Millennium by forceful human action.[78] Discouraged and defeated by the Restoration and two instances of failed prophecy most of the sectarians now turned toward spiritual religion and the inner life.[79] Repeated defeat led to deradicalization.

POSTSCRIPT

The defeats and ultimate decline of the Fifth Monarchy movement, despite the generally propitious setting provided by the Puritan Revolution and its atmosphere of religious excitement, require an explanation. Among the factors involved in this record of failure one should mention, first of all, the absence of forceful leadership. The movement lacked a charismatic prophet figure who could dominate it. Some of the more prominent men, like John Rogers, showed signs of mental unbalance; others, like Thomas Harrison, were ambivalent on the question of resorting to violence. Those who finally took the helm in the work of actual plotting were undistinguished little men like Thomas Venner. The movement attracted no theologians, and the saints' lack of academic ability is manifest in their pamphlets.[80]

The forces of the establishment, on the other hand, had as their leader a man of great political skill and charisma. It was not only that Oliver Cromwell regarded himself as a ruler in the Davidic sense, a servant of the Lord who combined the spiritual authority of the prophet with the exercise of secular power, but many of the English people for a long time accepted this flattering image. They therefore were ill inclined to abandon their military hero's leadership in favor of some wild-eyed, fanatic visionaries. The various sectarians themselves had contributed not a little to the strength of Cromwell's charisma. Gerrard Winstanley, the leader of the Diggers, a community of religious mystics who sought to

introduce a primitivist Millennium without private property and
coercive government, in 1652 dedicated his *Law of Freedom* to
Cromwell, and he seems seriously to have hoped that this man of
providence would put his ideas into effect.[81] The Fifth Monarchy
Men, at the time of the convening of the Parliament of Saints in
1653, celebrated the Lord General as God's "choice instrument"
to execute the biblical judgment on the Little Horn, Charles I.
When the militant millenarians later shifted gears and in a radical
about-face began to vilify the Lord Protector as the beast of
Daniel's prophecy, the man in the street turned away from them.
The claims of the self-selected saints to rulership became the
foundation of Cromwell's power and a strong line of defense.

Last, the agitation of the Fifth Monarchy Men took place at a
time of improving economic conditions and amidst a desire for
stability. The Civil War of the 1640's had cost the lives of some
100,000 Englishmen, about ten per cent of the adult male population.[82] Many others had been maimed, or their homes had been
burned or looted. The destruction of growing crops, the seizure
of livestock and goods, the exactions of armies in cash and kind
had caused much acute distress.[83] But the physical destruction of
the war was quickly made good, and the early part of the Protectorate was marked by an increase in confidence and business and
a revival of trade and industry. The country benefited from the
strengthening of England's position among the nations as a result
of Cromwell's forceful foreign policy. The extreme suffering of
the war years was over, and, though reliable data are sparse, there
is some evidence that pauperism declined between 1650 and 1660.
Real wages during this period were said to have been higher than
during any previous period in the century.[84] The Fifth Monarchy prophecy of impending doom thus was somewhat out of
tune with prevailing conditions and sentiments.

The last years of the Protectorate, on the other hand, especially
after the death of Cromwell, were a time of growing political and
economic instability, and discontent was rife. But the country
was no longer in a mood to engage in new political or social experiments. "The Restoration," writes one historian, "was the act
of men of all kinds sick of the slaughter, violence, repression, fanaticism and (let us not forget) the extortionate public finance
that had marked the previous twenty years." [85] Englishmen had
fought and suffered for ideas and ideals, but now they had had

enough. Idealism gave way to an intensely pragmatic and utilitarian outlook in which the zealousness of the Fifth Monarchy Men constituted a curious anachronism.

Lack of strong leadership, the rival charisma of Cromwell, and the conditions in England in the years 1649 to 1661 thus combined to bring about the demise of the Fifth Monarchy movement. In the decades to come millenarian sentiments declined into insignificance. Enthusiasm and passion now yielded to calmer modes of religious interest and activity. During the eighteenth century, an age of reason, growing scepticism, and internal stability, millenarianism all but died out. In the years of uncertainty and conflict during the French Revolution and the rise of Napoleon, as well as in the time of social unrest after 1815, only a few village messiahs proclaimed the Second Coming and "henceforth millenarianism became a harmless hobby for cranky country parsons." [86] These harsh words of a Marxist historian may not do full justice to modern millenarian sects like the Shakers, the Irvingites, the Darbyites, the Mormons, the Second Adventists, or Jehovah's Witnesses, but all of these groups have indeed abandoned the activist fervor of earlier movements and have withdrawn into resigned expectation and an apolitical quietism. The radical chiliastic impulse, on the other hand, has reemerged in secular form in such diverse revolutionary movements as the Jacobins, Utopian socialism, Marxism, and bolshevism.

CHAPTER 7

The Taiping Rebellion

ORIGINS AND EARLY FORTUNES

In the middle of the nineteenth century China experienced a revolutionary upheaval of major proportions that has been called the "world's most disastrous civil war" [1] and "the greatest pre-modern mass movement in history." [2] In the wake of this fourteen-year conflict (1850–64), whole provinces were in ruins, and at least ten million and perhaps as many as forty million people were dead. Western history calls this upheaval the Taiping Rebellion and we will follow this usage, whereas most modern Chinese historians, seeking to call attention to its constructive results, call it the Taiping Revolution.

There can be little doubt that the Taiping Rebellion differed in important ways from earlier Chinese rebel movements. Ever since the Ch'in dynasty (221–207 B.C.) had unified the country and established a centralized form of government, China had seen countless rebellions but no real revolution. "Of all nations that have attained a certain degree of civilization," a nineteenth-century English writer observed, "the Chinese are the least revolutionary and the most rebellious." [3] As we have seen in Chapter 3, Chinese rebels basically accepted the Confucian world view, and even Taoist- and Buddhist-inspired messianic movements for the most part operated within cosmological assumptions that could and usually soon did accommodate themselves to the Confucian state religion. The Taiping Rebellion, on the other hand, was truly a revolution, albeit an abortive one, against Chinese civilization. This extraordinary movement sought not only to destroy the ruling Manchu dynasty, but it also attacked the Chinese politi-

cal and social system and its ideology, Confucianism. The Taipings set out to build a heavenly commonwealth on earth which
they called the *T'ai-p'ing t'ien-kuo* (Heavenly Kingdom of Great
Peace). The titular leader of the rebellion, Hung Hsiu-ch'üan,
claimed to be God's son sent down to earth to redeem the
Chinese people and establish a new ideal world of righteousness
and well-being.

Conditions for a rebellion against the Manchu dynasty were favorable in mid-nineteenth-century China.[4] A severe agrarian crisis had been created by an unprecedented increase in population
quite out of proportion to the increase in the amount of land
under cultivation. According to one estimate, between 1772 and
1812 the population of the country had grown by 190 per cent
while land under cultivation had increased by only 35 per cent.[5]
The pressure of a rapidly growing population on limited agricultural resources was aggravated by a series of particularly devastating natural calamities. Drought, floods, earthquakes, sand-
storms, hail, and the failure of crops followed each other in
dreadful succession and caused repeated famines. A Roman Catholic missionary in Kiangsi reported in 1833 that the general desti-
tution of the province was such that people were selling their
wives and children, and many were living on the bark of trees.[6]
Conditions in many other provinces were no better, and thousands died of starvation.

The lot of the impoverished peasant was made worse by usurious money-lenders and by oppressive taxation. Tax abuse was
particularly severe in the Yangtse provinces where "the people
often had to pay several times the legal amount of taxes." [7] The
economic situation of the villages also was adversely affected by
the Western trade that had greatly increased since the turn of the
century. This trade brought with it not only a flooding of the
Chinese market with foreign goods, thus undermining the village
home industry, but it also created a serious imbalance of exports
and imports and a consequent currency problem. The growing
import of opium, in particular, had led to a great outflow of silver which in turn led to a devaluation of copper, the currency
used in local buying and selling. "This greatly aggravated the financial problems of the Chinese farming population, whose tax and
rent payments were calculated in silver but whose income was
based on devaluated copper." [8]

The recurring economic crises of the first half of the nineteenth century resulted in a great increase in the number of homeless migrants roaming the countryside and in banditry with which the corrupt and inefficient Ch'ing government was unable to cope. China's defeat in the Opium War (1839–42) had demonstrated the inability of the professional army to defend the country against outside attack, and the government forces were similarly unable to deal with internal unrest. This situation provided the ideal setting for the activity of secret societies, which contributed to local unrest, but which often also functioned as local defense organizations.

A formidable uprising of the White Lotus Society had finally been suppressed in 1805, but branches and remnants of this sectarian brotherhood continued to be active especially in the southern provinces. As seen throughout Chinese history, these groups provided aid and protection for their members, and therefore they had a special appeal during times of disorder and economic stress. Their underground pattern of organization could easily be transformed into a political and military structure engaged in rebellion. Government reports in the period before the Taiping Rebellion record many such outbreaks. "The Taiping revolt," notes Yang, "was but the climax of a half-century of widespread political action by religious societies that blanketed every part of the Ch'ing empire at a time when dynastic strength was on the decline." [9]

In the southern provinces of Kwangtung and Kwangsi, where the Taiping Rebellion originated, China's socioeconomic and political problems were aggravated by ethnic conflicts between the Punti, Hakka, and Yao peoples which resulted in small-scale warfare between villages. Local unrest in these provinces was constant and created a climate of instability and lawlessness. Insecure, oppressed, and often enough in the state of starvation the peasant population of this area reacted sympathetically to the Taiping ideal of the brotherhood of man and a coming state of harmony. [10]

The elements of unrest sketched out so far—corruption in government, natural disasters, overtaxation, general insecurity, and banditry—had, of course, characterized many rebellious uprisings in China's past. When these rebellions had been successful on a large scale, they had sometimes led to the establishment of a new dynasty. In order to understand why the Taiping Rebellion developed into a revolutionary movement that went beyond the limited aims of earlier revolts, and why it sought to destroy the traditional political and social order and its Confucian ethic, we must take into account a novel ideological element—Christianity. We must also recognize the important role played by the charismatic leadership of Hung Hsiu-ch'üan, an unusually perceptive though mentally disturbed person, who transmitted the new religious teaching and assumed a messianic function.

Hung Hsiu-ch'üan was born in 1814, the son of a peasant family in Kwangtung province. He was a gifted child, with an extraordinarily good memory, and, after several years attendance in the village school, he had acquired a good knowledge of the Confucian Classics.[11] His parents had high hopes that their able son would acquire the learning and degrees of a Confucian scholar, in traditional China the road to a life of material comfort, power, and fame both for the aspirant himself and his family. Hung presented himself for the first of the official examinations at the age of fifteen, but after passing the preliminary examination he failed in the main examination given at Canton that would have admitted him to gentry status. Like many disappointed candidates he later tried several times to pass this crucial test but never succeeded. In the intervals between the examinations he supported himself by teaching in village schools. Not surprisingly he became increasingly embittered and frustrated. As an unsuccessful scholar he was part of that "marginal group from which in periods of crisis the leaders or supporters of rebellious movements often came." [12]

During the provincial examination at Canton in 1836 the twenty-four-year-old Hung had his first contact with Christianity when he met two Protestant missionaries in the streets. He received from them a tract entitled *Good Words for Exhorting the Age*, written by a convert named Liang A-fa, the first Chinese Protestant pastor. At the time Hung looked over this pamphlet very superficially, but it was to have decisive influence on him later.

In 1837 Hung took the first degree examination for the second time and failed again. This time the disappointed young man became seriously ill. He had to be carried home from Canton, was confined to his bed, and was delirious for days on end. Moods of severe depression and melancholia alternated with outbursts of aggression and violent gestures. His family feared for his life and regarded his fits of rage as signs of madness. According to Hung's own account, the entire illness lasted forty days, though some authors regard this number a later embellishment added so as to make his sickness resemble the forty days of Jesus' fasting.[13] It was six years later that Hung told of a series of visions which he said he had experienced during his repeated episodes of trance or stupor. We will return to these hallucinatory experiences later.

After his recovery Hung again taught in village schools. His personality and behavior, it is reported, were changed. He was more assertive, took an active interest in politics, had delusions of grandeur, and expressed vague ambitions of becoming a ruler of the land. In 1843 Hung for the third and last time took the examination and again failed. He returned home full of anger and swore to get even with those who stood in the way of his social advancement. Shortly thereafter his cousin, Lien Ching-fang, discovered in Hung's box of books the Protestant pamphlet, which the young candidate had picked up in Canton in 1836. After the cousin had read the tract and told Hung of its unusual religious doctrine, the latter, too, now read it carefully and was greatly impressed. The Christian message of redemption, communicated to man through Jesus the savior of mankind, appealed to Hung who had himself nurtured the idea of becoming the redeemer of his downtrodden people. The story of the dying and resurrected Jesus also lent itself to an explanation of his own illness, which must have been embarrassing to him.

The *Good Words for Exhorting the Age* was a collection of nine tracts. Long selections from the Old and New Testaments, from a clumsy and poor translation by the Scottish Presbyterian missionary, Robert Morrison, were followed by interpretive essays, similar to sermons, by Liang A-fa. The first Chinese pastor was not a well-read, accomplished theologian, and his essays presented a rather simplistic Christian doctrine that was mingled with elements of Buddhism, Taoism, Confucianism, and all sorts of folk beliefs. There was no systematic scheme, covering the entire spectrum of Christian theology and rituals, and the overall orientation reflected the fundamentalism of Liang A-fa's mentor, Robert Morrison. Hung derived most of his limited knowledge of Christianity from Liang A-fa's work, and many of the peculiarities of Taiping ideology and practice can be traced to this source.

The God of Liang A-fa, and later of Hung, was the creator and almighty ruler of heaven and earth who tolerated no rivals and demanded the destruction of all idols. "This doctrine of the absolute power of God," notes Teng, "made a deep impression on Hung Hsiu-ch'üan, who saw himself as a deputy of God and established his rule along equally despotic lines." [14] The role of God as the loving and kind father was not developed, and the discussion of Christian ethics was similarly weak. The virtues of humility and love were underplayed. Liang A-fa held that the people should worship this jealous and stern God, obey his commands, and then "they would permanently enjoy the good fortune of great peace (t'ai-p'ing)." This idea of a classical Golden Age of great peace had often inspired the Chinese people, especially in times of turmoil and civil war, and ". . . this pervasive longing of their countrymen for peace evidently influenced the Taiping leaders in their selection of the title 'T'ai-p'ing t'ien-kuo' " [15] (Heavenly Kingdom of Great Peace).

Liang A-fa's book had talked about the need of purifying body and soul and becoming a new man, but the details of the rite of baptism were not discussed. Hung and Lien Ching-fang, therefore, baptized themselves by jumping into a river and washing the whole body. Among Hung's first converts was another cousin, Hung Jen-kan, who later played an important role in the Taiping regime. It was to Hung Jen-kan that Hung now told the story of his visions during his serious illness in 1837; in time this story was to substantiate his claim of a mission to realize God's rule on earth. In 1852 Hung Jen-kan, who in his childhood had witnessed his cousin's strange illness, related Hung's account of this vision to the Reverend Theodore Hamberg in Hong Kong with whom he studied Christian doctrine. Hamberg asked Hung Jen-kan to put the story in writing and two years later published the bizarre account as a book.[16] In 1860, Hung Hsiu-ch'üan ordered his two older brothers to write a report of what they had seen, but this official document of the Taiping court, entitled "Gospel Jointly Witnessed and Heard by the Imperial Eldest and Second Eldest Brothers," was considerably embellished to fit special political purposes.[17] The story told to and published by the Reverend Hamberg, on the other hand, is generally considered reliable.

According to Hung Hsiu-ch'üan's recollection, as told to his

cousin in 1843, while lying ill in his bed he had been transported
to a beautiful place where after a cleansing ceremony a venerable
old man complained to him about the depravity of the human
race. Thereupon the old man gave him a sword and commanded
him to exterminate all demons and evil spirits. In later visions
Hung also met a man of middle age, whom he called his older
brother, who had instructed him how to act in his appointed
task. The old man also had reproved Confucius for failing to ex-
pound the true doctrine. All through the forty days of his illness
he had fought with the demons, and the wild behavior witnessed
by his family had been the outward manifestation of this battle.
Now, reading Liang A-fa's *Good Words for Exhorting the Age*,
Hung told his cousin, he finally understood the meaning of his
visions. The venerable old man had been God, the heavenly father; the middle-aged man was Jesus, the savior, and he himself
was another son of God called upon to eradicate evil from the
earth.

Hung Hsiu-ch'üan had now found a religious sanction for his
mission. The historical record is unambiguous about this basic
fact, though there are differing opinions over the question
whether the story of the ascent to heaven represented a new belief of Hung originating in 1843 or whether Hung really experienced these hallucinations during his illness in 1837. A modern
Chinese scholar, subscribing to the latter view, regards these hallucinations as the beginning of a long process of religious conversion that was stimulated perhaps by Hung's contact with the
Christian missionaries in Canton in 1836, reached a climax during
his illness, and was completed in 1843 upon his reading the *Good
Words for Exhorting the Age*.[18] Another Chinese expert on the
Taiping Rebellion is content to say that Hung "professed to have
had visions," [19] and Franz Michael, too, quoted above, believes
that the Christian teachings taken from the work of Liang A-fa
were used by Hung to dress his earlier illness in religious garb
and provided "the framework for the delusions of grandeur created by his illness." [20] There is general agreement that Hung in
1837 had passed through an acute psychotic episode and that his
subsequent megalomanic convictions, overbearing manner, outbursts of anger, and paranoiac behavior suggest a continuing and
gradually worsening mental illness, the precise nature of which is
difficult to determine.[21]

Among Hung's early converts was his friend and fellow teacher Feng Yün-shan. Because of their opposition to the worship of idols both men soon ran into the hostility of the villagers and eventually lost their jobs. They became wandering preachers and in the following two years converted several hundred peasants in the Kwangtung and Kwangsi provinces. For a month or so in 1847 Hung studied Bible in Canton with an American missionary, I. J. Roberts, a Southern Baptist, but this brief episode of learning did not contribute much to Hung's always limited knowledge of Christian doctrine. At Thistle Mountain, a strategic mountain area in southern Kwangsi, his friend Feng, meanwhile, had succeeded in setting up a formal organization called the Association or Society of God Worshippers. Most of the first few thousand members, like Hung himself, were Hakkas, a group of settlers from North China who had migrated south and, because of their different customs and traditions, often clashed with the Punti majority. The Hakkas were a hardy people who had a reputation for courage and a tendency to take extreme and unadaptable positions on all issues.[22]

Famine, banditry, and the hostility of their neighbors contributed to the spread of the new gospel among the Hakka peoples. The God Worshippers had many characteristics of the traditional Chinese secret societies except that their religious faith in a personal God and the promise of salvation in a life after death differed markedly from the vague Buddhist, Taoist, and Confucian ideas usually found in these societies. Hung joined Feng in August 1847, and, under the joint leadership of Hung and Feng, the growing community of the God Worshippers gradually assumed a more militant and rebellious character. It soon served not only the purpose of protection against the Punti but also provided an outlet for Hung's political ambitions and his hostility to the Manchu dynasty. The term Taiping was already in use, and Hung called himself the *Chüng Wang* or Noble King.[23] Alongside Hung and Feng there now emerged two new leaders, the one-time government clerk Yang Hsiu-ch'ing and the peasant Hsia Ch'ao-kuei. Both of these ambitious men established their credentials as leaders through repeated trances and seizures in which they claimed to represent the Holy Spirit and Jesus who through them provided instructions to the God Worshippers. Franz Michael believes that "while Hung must have been genuinely con-

vinced of his own ascent to Heaven and of his divine mission,
Yang's actions seem to indicate that he was playing a part." [24] It
should also be noted that the Hakkas were ardent believers in sorcery and spirit worship. Operating in the midst of such a climate
it is, therefore, not surprising that Yang and Hsia used this
method to control their followers.[25]

By the middle of 1850 Hung and Feng had made definite plans
for an uprising. The original Hakka elements were now joined by
some Punti and people of other tribal groups who, probably because of severe economic hardships, had decided to make common cause with the God Worshippers, and accepted their teachings. Several bandit units had also attached themselves to the
Taipings who now had a military camp at Chin-t'ien and numbered in excess of 10,000 people. Another concentration developed at Hua-chou in the neighboring district of P'ing-nan. Both
Taiping forces soon found themselves under attack by government troops, and for a time their situation was precarious. In January 1851 the two groups finally combined forces and won a decisive victory over the government troops. At Chin-t'ien on
January 11, 1851, Hung's thirty-eighth birthday, the latter now
proclaimed the formation of a new dynasty, the *T'ai-p'ing t'ien-
kuo*, the Heavenly Kingdom of Great Peace. Yang, as commander of the central corps, emerged as the most important military leader of the movement, and Hung assumed the title of
T'ien Wang or Heavenly King and began to issue orders under
this title.[26]

Their morale bolstered by victory, the Taipings gradually became a highly disciplined military force. Their army followed the
model of the classical *Chou-li* system, an organizational scheme
that combined the military and civilian aspects of government.[27]
Men and women were kept in different units and camps, and
contact between them was strictly forbidden. This measure, of
great utility for the maintenance of discipline in a mobile force,
was justified by religious ideas about the sacred character of chastity, though the promise was made that after the defeat of the demons and the conquest of the empire families would be reunited.
The Taiping leaders considered themselves exempt from the ban
on sexual relations and soon established a personal harem. They
also enjoyed other privileges. Whereas the rank and file were required to hand over their belongings to a common treasury, from

which they received their daily needs, the leaders' control over this treasury permitted them to use a greater share for themselves and eventually enabled them to live a life of pompous luxury. The Taipings were regarded as a large family of brothers and sisters and all property was seen belonging to the head of the family, the Heavenly Father, whose representative on earth was the *T'ien Wang*, the younger brother of Jesus.[28] Five other secondary leaders were also described as brothers of Jesus.

From September 1851 to April 1852 the Taipings occupied the hill town of Yung-an where they reorganized their forces and indoctrinated their many new followers. Under a new and more formal hierarchical scheme adopted at Yung-an, Hung, the Heavenly King, now invested each of his "brothers" with the title of *wang* or king. In addition to the East King, West King, South King, and North King, there was an Assistant King, and every king was granted his own administrative staff. The *T'ien Wang* himself was to be addressed as the "Sovereign" and remained the head of the movement. Yang, the East King, was placed in control of the administration, and, as the commander of all the armies, his central position was formally confirmed. In order to give their government the aura of a traditional Chinese dynasty the Taiping leaders issued their first special calendar.[29]

On April 5, 1852 the Taiping forces broke through the lines of the poorly trained, besieging government forces, inflicting heavy losses. There now began the advance north through Kwangsi and Hunan into the Yangtze valley, which, within less than one year, was to lead to the capture of Nanking. All along their route the Taipings issued proclamations to spread their ideas and to gain popular support. Those who surrendered were treated well, but all who resisted were branded demons and slaughtered. Within the Taiping army the strictest discipline was maintained through an elaborate system of rules and punishments. The army's fighting spirit was strengthened by the promise of ascent to heaven, immortality for soldiers fallen in battle, and the lavish enjoyment of the fruits of victory for those who would live to see the establishment of a capital for the Heavenly Kingdom on earth.

During the march on Nanking the ranks of the Taipings grew to over a million people. Not all members of this vast movement joined the Taiping family voluntarily; some were impressed into newly created military units. But many came of their own will, attracted by features of Taiping life and propaganda involving a common treasury that would provide for one's daily needs, tax relief, the condemnation of the gentry landlords; the often-repeated promise to "free the common people from their miseries" [30] proved a powerful magnet especially for the destitute peasantry. In a time of chaos the ideal of peace also had a strong appeal. Last, the Taipings attacked the Manchus as foreign barbarians, who had usurped the throne contrary to the will of Heaven, and thus they were able to capitalize on Chinese traditional and nationalistic sentiments. The empire, the Taipings declared in a typical proclamation issued by Yang, the East King, in 1852, belongs to the Chinese and not to the Tartars. The latter have "robbed them of their food and clothing, as well as oppressed and ravished their sons and daughters." Yang promised "to revenge the insult offered to God in deceiving Heaven, and below to deliver China from its inverted position, thus sternly sweeping away every vestige of Tartar influence and unitedly enjoying the happiness of the Taiping dynasty." [31]

The politics of the Taiping propaganda attracted followers of the anti-Manchu societies who were not inclined to accept the Taipings' novel religious teachings.[32] At the same time it is clear that it was precisely the sense of religious purpose—the faith in a powerful personal God and membership in a great family of brothers and sisters—that held together the various elements in the Taiping movement and explained their extraordinary discipline and heroism in battle.[33] This spirit of fellowship proved itself in the Taipings' rapid advance through the Yangtze valley. On March 19, 1853 they occupied the city of Nanking which became the capital of their Heavenly Kingdom.

THE TAIPING STATE AND ITS IDEOLOGY

Seen theologically, Taiping society was a community of brothers and sisters whose father was God and who were led in God's ways by God's representatives on earth, the Heavenly King and his brothers. As a matter of political reality, however, the Taiping state was a centralized regime in which all aspects of life—the family, food, clothing, education—were under the strict control of the self-appointed Taiping leaders who enforced a rigid discipline by means of rewards—titles of nobility, fine houses, etc.—and harsh punishment. The leaders' exalted status, which was unquestioned, was based on their claim to be interpreters of the divine will, and not surprisingly this sharing of charismatic authority soon led to a merciless struggle for power.

From the beginning of his career Yang, the East King, had sought a position of preeminence, and after the conquest of Nanking this ambitious man finally succeeded in making the Heavenly King a near figurehead, while he himself assumed the leading role in the political hierarchy. Trances, divine visitations, and revelations served to legitimate his superior standing, but the prophet's ruthlessness, high-handed behavior, and dissolute personal life soon created serious discontent. When the military situation in 1856 looked opportune, a conspiracy against the East King was hatched, and on September 2, 1856 Wei Ch'ang-hui, the North King, assassinated Yang and killed his family and followers in a bloody slaughter that is said to have claimed the lives of twenty thousand men and women.[34] When Shih Ta-k'aim the Assistant King, reproached Wei for this mayhem the North King turned against him as well and murdered all of the Assistant King's family and court in the capital; Shih himself escaped and led his troops against Nanking to take revenge. At this point, it appears, Hung, the Heavenly King, finally asserted himself and killed the North King and his family.

The details of this vast power struggle are not completely clear, but that it left the Taipings without effective leadership is beyond dispute. Despite his cruelties Yang had been an able organizer and administrator; the sick Hung was unable to fill the void created by Yang's murder. Among the East King's most important edicts had been the "Land System of the Heavenly Dynasty," [35] a law issued early in 1854 that established not only the regulation of agriculture but the basic political structure of the Taiping state as well. Under this revolutionary measure the population was organized into military units of twenty-five families, each under the command of a sergeant who was in charge of education and religious ceremonies as well as work. Four such units were under the command of a lieutenant, and so forth, up to the largest administrative unit, an army corps. In this way the entire population, writes Michael, "was under the discipline and administration of military commanders who were at the same time military officers, administrators, and doctrinal and religious

leaders of their units, a system of total control of all life by the
state which had no parallel in Chinese history." [36] The leader of
the basic unit determined how much of the crop the people
could keep for their own food and how much seed should be
kept for the planting of new crops. The remainder was deposited
in the common treasury. In the language of the law: "When all
the people in the empire will not take anything as their own but
submit all things to the Supreme Lord, then the Lord will make
use of them, and in the universal family of the empire, every
place will be equal and every individual well fed and clothed." [37]

The law provided that land be classified into different grades
and redistributed in accordance with the number and age of the
members of the family. However, this basic and perhaps most
revolutionary aspect of the legislation was never implemented.[38]
Though initially the land law with its promise of land distribution and the common sharing of all goods and crops had great
appeal to the peasantry, in practice the peasants neither owned
the land nor enjoyed the fruit of their labor. In some cases the
Taipings at first freed tenants from the payment of rent to the
landlords, but in most instances they left the existing social structure intact and collected as much tax and grain as they could get
for shipment to Nanking. The lot of the peasantry, therefore, depended concretely on the attitudes and needs of local commanders and the Taipings' military fortunes. As the latter deteriorated, and the discipline of the Taiping armies weakened, the
treatment of the peasant population worsened. In the words of
Michael: "When, therefore, the original attraction of an opportunity to escape from local misery by joining a military force out
to conquer the empire was past, when the Taipings had to settle
down to govern the population of the rich Yangtze delta, they
could control by military force but could not draw to their side a
population whose loyalty would not be captured by religious
promises or by a new form of all-inclusive tax for a 'sacred treasury' had it been applied." [39]

The Taiping land law, if implemented, would have amounted
to a social revolution. As it worked out its effect was more limited. It did establish a new system of administration, patterned on
military discipline, in which political, economic, and religious authority were combined. Every officer reported on the people
under his command. Rewards meant promotion to higher office;

punishment consisted of demotion or death. The lowest level to which one could be demoted was that of husbandman, the worker in the field. The humble status assigned to the peasant shows that the Taiping state cannot be considered the creation of a peasant rebellion working for the interests of the peasants. Even under those provisions of the land law that remained unimplemented, the land belonged to the Heavenly King though it was allotted to the people for cultivation. The practice of the law simply amounted to a new system of taxation. The common treasury prevailed in the army, where no plunder or loot was to be kept by an individual, and in the capital where everybody was organized on a military basis. It enabled the Heavenly King to lead a life of luxury and imperial grandeur. His train of attendants exceeded 1600 men, among them 100 celestial grooms, 300 celestial musicians, 30 men in charge of celestial robes, and so on.[40]

I will not discuss the military ventures of the Taipings here in any detail. Some Taiping leaders were able strategists who innovated military techniques, which has prompted the Chinese Communists to make special studies of them. Like other rebellions fueled by religious beliefs, the Taipings made use of magic to render the bodies of their soldiers invulnerable to bullets, and the fighting spirit of their armies, helped along by liquor, by and large was excellent.[41] Still, after a year at Nanking, the main force of the Taipings' expeditionary drives—against Peking in the north and up the Yangtze river into western China—had spent itself, and the contest with the troops of the emperor developed into a seesaw battle. This gave the government time to build up new armies and under the leadership of the able Tseng Kuo-fan these forces, calling on all Chinese to defend the traditional Confucian order, eventually triumphed over the Taipings.

After the murder of the East and North Kings in 1856 the Taipings lacked political leadership, and their military commanders in the field were essentially on their own. As the Heavenly King's capacity to think rationally deteriorated, he withdrew more and more from all government affairs. His condition is reflected in the "Poems by the Heavenly Father," addressed to the 200 wives and many more concubines in Hung's harem, issued in 1857. These verses exhibit Hung's confused state of mind, his fantastic egotism, and self-indulgence.[42] In the following years

Hung's delusions of grandeur increased. In some of his edicts issued after 1860 he now declared himself equal to God. Contemporary observers as well as all later students agree that toward the
end of his career Hung displayed all the symptoms of a
disordered mind.[43]

For a while after the great purge of 1856 Hung's older brothers
managed the affairs of state at Nanking, but badly. In April 1859
the cousin of the Heavenly King and one of his earliest followers,
Hung Jen-kan, arrived in Nanking. The Heavenly King welcomed him with obvious relief, elevated him to the position of
Kan Wang (Shield King) and chief of staff, and for a time the
cause of the Taipings again enjoyed effective leadership. Hung
Jen-kan was an able man, imbued with a strong and rational religious faith. His efforts to reestablish a system of central government were successful in part, he devised a system of examinations
to create an educated elite, and he sought to improve relations
between the Taipings and the foreigners.[44]

For a short time the efforts of the *Kan Wang* succeeded in re-
versing the trend of defeat. The military fortunes of the Taipings
were helped by the fact that, since 1853, the Manchu government
had had to fight also the Nien rebellion, a local uprising in the
Huai Valley northeast of Nanking organized by a secret society
probably descended from the White Lotus Society.[45] In the years
1857 to 1859 Taiping and Nien forces engaged in several joint
military operations, but this cooperation did not continue. The
Kan Wang's efforts to establish an overall strategy and to assert
control over the largely autonomous local military commanders
failed, and in the spring of 1861 he seems to have lost his battle
for a reorganized government in Nanking as well. The downfall
of the *Kan Wang*, who had been the last hope of the Taipings, led
to a final defeat in 1864.

There remains the important task of examining and analyzing
the Taiping ideology which contributed so much to the elan of
the movement. First, we note the millenarian element embodied
in the very title of the newly created regime—Heavenly Kingdom of Great Peace. The polysyllable *T'ai-p'ing* or great peace
was a term of great antiquity; it was the name of the last and
most utopian of the famous three ages mentioned in the *Spring
and Autumn*, one of the five Confucian Classics.[46] Many earlier
heterodox movements in Chinese history, like the revolt of the

Yellow Turbans in the second century A.D., had used this millenarian concept. The Taipings taught that God had sent the Heavenly King to earth to "give peace to the ten thousand nations, so that everyone might share the true happiness." [47] The first (in Chinese, the second) part of the name of the Taiping dynasty, on the other hand, lacked Chinese antecedents and probably was derived from the New Testament concept, "Kingdom of Heaven." The word *T'ien-kuo* or Heavenly Kingdom is found in Liang A-fa's *Good Words for Exhorting the Age* from which Hung may have taken it.

Once established at Nanking the Taipings printed large editions of the Old and New Testaments. The annotations made by the Heavenly King on the margins of different books of the Taiping Bible reveal Hung's millenarian interpretation of Christianity. The Kingdom of Heaven for him meant not only the place to which Christians ascend to enjoy the eternal blessings but also the heavenly kingdom he had established on earth with Nanking the heavenly capital. Commenting on John's vision of "a new heaven and a new earth" in Chapter 21 of the Book of Revelation, Hung wrote: "The New Jerusalem, the Heavenly Capital, is where God and Christ descended into the world, bringing both myself and the young Monarch [Hung's son] to be the sovereigns, establishing the heaven of the Heavenly Court. God's heaven now exists among men. It is fulfilled. Respect this." [48] The Taiping religion thus promised not only otherworldly salvation but the realization of heaven on earth as well. The Chinese were seen as God's chosen people who would rule China, the Kingdom of Heaven, and eventually the whole universe. The Heavenly King was called "the true Sovereign of all nations in the world." [49]

The Taipings' crude millenarianism was one of the reasons why Christian missionaries visiting the Taipings at Nanking came away calling the Taiping faith blasphemous. Yet the Christian component in the complex of ideas making up the Taiping ideology undoubtedly is the most important. The most crucial and novel element in the Taiping movement, its monotheism, was of Christian origin. The multiplicity of gods that had characterized Confucianism and Chinese popular religion was vehemently repudiated, and instead Hung taught the belief in one omnipotent and omniscient God who was the creator of the world but who also continued to take an active interest in human affairs and could be reached through prayer without the intermediary service of a priest. The image of the Taiping God owed much to the Old Testament. He not only was the God of battles, who intervened personally at critical moments in the military progress of the movement, but he also was an extremely jealous and stern god who resented and severely punished disobedience to his commands.[50] Hung, the Heavenly King, saw himself as imitating God's righteous anger, and he consequently enforced a strict code of moral conduct. "Christianity," writes Michael, "to Hung was a battle between God and the devil, and this battle was in Hung's mind a very personal one. It was his mission to fight for God and to kill the demons or send them to hell." It was his task to bring the people back to the worship of the true God and to follow His will as interpreted by Hung and other mediums. "This simplified righteousness was a very suitable ideology for a rebellious movement." [51]

Other Christian ideas reappeared in more garbled form. Jesus remained God's son but not his only son for Hung was Jesus' younger brother who shared Christ's mission of redeeming mankind. The doctrine of the Trinity the Taipings did not understand at all, and the aggressive Yang could successfully pass himself off as the Holy Ghost. Even though the Taipings made much of the idea of brotherhood their practice of a common treasury did not invoke biblical precedent. One writer notes that the number of principles and illustrations taken from the Bible remained relatively small because of "the small portion of the Bible which the Taiping Chinese could really understand." [52] Thus concepts like heaven, hell, eternal life, etc., were readily accepted because they fitted into the religious setting of Chinese society. Many of the more spiritual and ethical elements of Christianity, on the other hand, did not enter Taiping religion. Boardman concludes that even though the Christian part of the Taiping ideology overshadowed all others, "Taiping religion still was not Christianity." [53]

The Taipings borrowed the concept of *T'ien* or Heaven from traditional Confucian sources, and it became one of the many Chinese terms used by them for God. As we have seen earlier, the idea that the ruler was the Son of Heaven was very old and had often been used to prove the divine origin of the emperor's authority. The Confucian Classics repeatedly referred to Heaven's appointment of the people's ruler, and the Mandate of Heaven provided both legitimacy of rule as well as support of the right of rebellion. The Taipings linked the rightfulness of their new dynasty to the same source; their writings speak of Hung as receiving God's mandate and being sent to earth by the Heavenly Father to rule the world. "August Heaven," an edict of the year 1853 declared, "has lost patience and has commanded our Heavenly King to display respectfully the grandeur of Heaven to raise the banner of righteousness . . . in order to wreak the vengeance of God on high on those who have deceived Heaven." [54]

Even though the Taipings' concept of *T'ien* as the father of mankind was innovatively literal—God had a human physique and even a wife—the Taipings insisted that their worship of God was the true original religion of China, and they quoted passages from Mencius and the Confucian Classics to show the identity of their god and Heaven. An edict issued by Hung's son in 1861 declared: "The true doctrine of my Father (God) and of my adopted Father (Christ), is the religion of Heaven." [55] Hung called himself the "truly appointed Son of Heaven," using "a term which raised hope and inspiration in the hearts of the Chinese and had for them a consoling power like that of *Messiah* for the Jews." [56] Moreover, by insisting that God, as the universal father of man, should be worshipped by all they made the traditional cult of Heaven, previously the exclusive preserve of the Emperor, a more satisfying emotional experience for the masses of the people.

The Taipings made other attempts to appear as traditional and Chinese as possible, adding such Confucian virtues as benevolence, filial piety, and loyalty to their ethical system. In Hung's famous dream Confucius was criticized for having misled the people, and in their campaign against polytheism the Taipings destroyed the Confucian temples and tablets. Still, they permitted the study of the Confucian classical texts in a revised edition; the Taipings' funeral services and their system of examinations also showed many parallels to Confucian usage and custom.[57]

Among the untraditional elements of Taiping ideology was the furious proscription of all forms of idolatry—ancestor worship was forbidden and Buddhist temples, images, and even libraries were destroyed. Buddhist and Taoist monks and nuns, too, were persecuted as part of the Taipings' battle against demons and heresy. Still, terms of Buddhist, Taoist, and Mohist origin abound in their ideology which one interpreter has called "a nondescript body of ideas for which there is no adequate term." [58] It appears that Hung and his chief lieutenants adopted whatever concepts served their political purpose with the result that Taiping ideology is a conglomeration of Christian, Confucian, and other ideas. There are layers of different conceptual schemes all held together by the practical aims of the movement itself. Hung sought to overthrow the Manchus, and Taiping ideology, as fashioned by him, became an instrument to legitimize this enterprise in his own eyes as well as in those of his followers. Taiping religion conferred religious sanction upon a political movement and transformed a rebellion of starving and dislocated peasants into a revolutionary attack upon the traditional Confucian order.

The importance of Taiping ideology in the impressive victories of the movement is difficult to ascertain. Hung's early followers appear to have been greatly affected by the new millenarian and egalitarian faith.[59] On the other hand, many of those who lived in the conquered territories, some distance from the heavenly capital, probably had only a rudimentary acquaintance with Taiping religion.

DECLINE AND FALL

Much of the credit for the defeat of the Taiping forces must go to Tseng Kuo-fan, a man of great administrative and military talents, who has been called the "George Washington of the Far East." [60] It was under his leadership that the Manchu armies were finally able to halt the advance of the Taipings. Foreign aid, like the "Ever Victorious Army" led by Captain Gordon, was secondary. The beginning of the end came with the recapture of Anking in 1861. Soochow fell in late 1863 and Changchow early in 1864. With much of the Yangtze valley lost, Nanking was threatened, and the heavenly capital of the Taiping regime fell on July 19, 1864. The capture of Nanking led to a terrible massacre of the defenders who refused to surrender. The fanaticism of the Taipings and the policy of Tseng Kuo-fan, whose goal was the extermination of the whole movement,[61] made the slaughter inevitable.

Hung Hsiu-ch'üan, the Heavenly King, did not live to see the end of his dream. He died on June 1, 1864, possibly as a result of taking poison.[62] Hung's son replaced him as the new Heavenly King, but the fall of the capital killed the spirit of the movement. The remaining Taiping armies were defeated one by one, and their leaders were executed after writing their traditional confessions—important sources of our knowledge of the Taiping movement.

There were several reasons for the failure of the Taiping Rebellion. Except in the early years, the Taipings never really had the support of the peasantry. Their egalitarian land system was never implemented, whereas the imperial forces carried out a concerted program of tax relief.[63] Moreover, the iconoclasm of the Taiping religion, expressed in the destruction of Confucian and Buddhist temples and of the images of local deities and in the prohibition of ancestor worship, alienated most of the Chinese people who were not ready for such a radical break with their traditional beliefs. The strong Christian component of the Taiping ideology created the image of an alien creed, and, as a result of the widespread bitterness toward foreigners, and especially the English because of the first Anglo-Chinese war, the Taipings bore the stigma of being unpatriotic. This undermined the nationalistic appeal of the movement. Even the Manchus, whom the Taipings attacked as Tartars, could claim to be better Chinese for they respected and observed the traditional Chinese culture and religion.[64] Thus, the Taipings' "faith that had been a pillar of strength to the internal structure became for them a stumbling-block in their relations with possible allies and with the Chinese people as a whole." [65]

The Taipings' assault upon the Confucian system antagonized the intelligentsia and gentry especially, and the failure of these social groups to make common cause with the rebels was another important reason for the defeat of Taiping. The educated class was repelled by the incoherence and uncouthness of the Taiping doctrine and by the attack upon the traditional social order, while the system of civil service with examinations based upon the Taiping literature did not offset this loss of administrative talent. Toward the end of their regime the Taipings tried to modify the anti-Confucian elements of their teaching, but the damage had been done. Tseng Kuo-fan meanwhile had been able to rally

the gentry to save Confucian civilization, and it was the determined resistance of the newly formed armies, fighting under gentry leadership and imbued with the desire to avenge Confucius
and Mencius, that finally defeated the Taipings.[66]

The concentration of talent and leadership on the imperial side
stood in sharp contrast to the political corruption and the divisive
struggles for power in the Taiping camp—still another factor
in their eventual defeat. The Heavenly King and his chief lieutenants lived a life of luxury and licence which could not but
weaken the morale and discipline of their armies. Hung Hsiu-
ch'üan, one historian has concluded, "was no Chinese Lenin." [67]
His failure to provide strong leadership and his gradual withdrawal from state affairs opened the door to destructive internal
strife. Thus the peculiar cast of mind which earlier had made him
organize the Taiping rebellion and provide it with its special ideology later led to his downfall. "His weakness as well as his
strength as a leader were both determined in an intimate manner
by his illness." [68]

Chinese Communist writers for a long time considered the
Taiping Rebellion a revolutionary movement for political, economic, and racial equality; Hung Hsiu-ch'üan was praised as a
forerunner of the nineteenth-century nationalistic movement.
Since the late 1950's mainland historians, probably to preserve the
uniqueness of their own revolution led by their Communist
party, have stressed the inevitable failure of the Taipings due to
the lack of leadership by the industrial proletariat.[69] Western
writers, too, have had difficulty in assessing the chief characteristics and significance of the Taiping Rebellion. Most of them emphasize the roots of the movement in agrarian discontent, but
they also see it as a dynastic revolt against the Manchus and as a
political revolution against the traditional political and social system, a revolt for which the millenarian Taiping religion provided
the ideological legitimation.[70] Taking note of these different elements in uneasy coexistence, one recent student of the Taipings
has concluded: "It was a confused and complex movement, half
backward, half forward looking, which fits neatly into no single
category of description, whether Confucian, Christian or Marxist.
. . . Its very magnitude and strangeness, a complex mixture of old
and modern, Western and Chinese, rational and absurd, makes
any attempt at final judgement upon it hazardous at best." [71]

The effects of the Taiping Rebellion are somewhat clearer. In defeating the Taipings the traditional order reasserted itself once more. All through the campaign the emperor had called upon the gods to help defeat the rebels against Heaven, and when at last Nanking, the rebel capital, was captured "there was a burst of religious activities including the impressive imperial sacrifice to Heaven and Earth, the supplication to the spirits of the imperial ancestors, and the numerous sacrifices to local deities by officials in the provincial communities, all offering thanks for divine assistance in the great achievement." [72] And yet, this victory in many ways was hollow and left the Manchu regime exhausted and rent by countrywide insurrections. The throne had been saved, but the imperial government found itself unable to control the military-political organizations formed by the gentry against the Taipings which now posed a formidable challenge to the political authority of the dynasty.[73] The very fact that so many Chinese could abandon their traditional beliefs and embrace such a radically new doctrine as the Taiping religion pointed up the weakness of the old order. The Taiping Rebellion thus marks the beginning of the end of Confucian China.

According to refugees from Communist China in Hong Kong, when the peasants of Kwangtung province were being forced into cooperatives in the 1950's, they looked for the magical return of the Taiping king, Hung Hsiu-ch'üan, to lead the resistance against this attempt to take away dominion over their land.[74] Other than that the Taiping Rebellion appears to have left no trace. Like other millenarian revolts in China and elsewhere this particular challenge to the traditional system failed, and the modernization of China took place under secular auspices.

Much of what the Taipings attempted to do, notes Teng, "embodied in such slogans as 'land to the tillers,' 'down with the Manchu devils,' equality between men and women, national independence, language simplification" was carried on by Sun Yat-sen and the republican regime established by him in the 1911 revolution.[75] This regime, in turn, was overthrown by the Communists who, like the Taipings, were able to capitalize on agrarian discontent. Thus in place of the transient, quasi-totalitarian order of the Taipings China today is subject to a truly totalitarian system that despite recurrent crises of leadership appears to have staying power and durability.

CHAPTER 8

The Mahdia in the Sudan

BACKGROUND

The millenarian tradition in Islam, known as Mahdism, is old. It found its earliest full development in the sects of the heretical *Shi'a*, but messianic expectations soon spread among orthodox *Sunni* Muslims also. Throughout the history of Islam numerous religious and political reformers have claimed to be the promised deliverers of their people; the messianic kingdom of the Sudanese mystic Mohammed Ahmed in the late nineteenth century, the subject of this chapter, represents probably the best known but by no means the only such historical episode.

Mahdis have been especially frequent in Africa. According to one knowledgeable student of Islam in Africa, its "Arab-Negroid and Arab-Hamite peoples form very susceptible material to mass suggestion, with their innate anthropolatry saving the would-be Mahdi the laborious work of gaining adherents." [1] Tensions between Muslim communities and their pagan overlords and neighbors also contributed to the spread of Mahdist ideas. The *jihads* (holy wars) fought under the leadership of Shehu Usuman dan Fodio in the Niger-Chad region between 1804 and 1817, for example, encouraged Mahdism and beliefs in the approaching end of time. The Shehu's successful military exploits were seen as the vanguard of the soon-to-follow appearance of the Mahdi, and classical books of Islamic eschatology continued to be extensively read and quoted by his successors. Given the traffic between the Fulani empire and the Sudan it is likely that this Mahdist literature current in the Niger-Chad area had found its way to the Sudan. [2]

The popularity of Sufism or Islamic mysticism in the Sudan was another factor promoting the spread of Mahdist and eschatological beliefs there. Because the people were desperately poor, and the God of orthodox Islam was exalted and unapproachable, the cult of saints who would act as Allah's intermediaries was widespread. In the eighteenth and nineteenth centuries these Sufi fraternities or religious orders acquired new vigor as a result of the great religious revival undertaken by the Wahhabis in the Arabian peninsula and the Sanusiya order in what is now Libya. After the armies of Mohammed Ali had conquered the Sudan in 1820–22, the new Egyptian rulers tried to promote orthodox Islam, though, because of the great emotional appeal of Sufism, this endeavor had only very limited success. They introduced a system of religious courts, built mosques, and staffed them with religious teachers trained in orthodox theology. The imposition of this *ulama* class antagonized the leadership of the Sufi orders for it threatened their social and political power.[3] The fact that the Egyptian officials were exploitative, brutal, corrupt, and often immoral gave rise to feelings of religious revulsion and contempt among the Sudanese and further encouraged anti-Egyptian sentiments.

The most important cause of Sudanese discontent, however, was the attempt of the Egyptian government to suppress the slave trade, a profitable economic activity that involved all classes of society and every part of the country. Prodded by his European creditors and the British government, the Khedive Isma'il (1863–79) in particular made a prolonged and concerted effort to abolish the slave trade, a drive that soon began to show positive results. The moving force was a British officer, Charles George Gordon, whom the Khedive first appointed governor of Equatoria and who in 1877 became governor-general of the entire Sudan. The violent methods employed by Gordon against the slave traders did much to disrupt the economy of the country and antagonized most of the tribal leaders of the Sudan.[4]

In June 1879 the Khedive Isma'il was deposed by the Sultan of Turkey, the formal overlord of Egypt, who was however subservient to the European powers and especially to Britain and France. Gordon, who had come to the Sudan at the personal request of Ismail, resented the shameful treatment to which Ismail had been subjected and thereupon resigned his office. Ismail's successor, Tawfiq, was a weak ruler and during his reign the slave trade revived somewhat. Still, dislike of Egyptian rule remained strong. In 1881 "the right man and the right conditions combined to ensure a successful revolt." [5]

THE RISE OF THE MAHDI

Mohammed Ahmed was born in 1844 or 1845, the fourth son of a humble Sudanese builder of boats who claimed descent from the Prophet. From an early age the young man showed a strong interest in religion, and at the age of sixteen he joined a Sufi order called Sammaniya. After seven years of apprenticeship, during which he gained a reputation for asceticism and humility toward his master, Mohammed Sharif, Mohammed Ahmed was licensed as a *shaykh* (local head and religious leader) of his order and was sent out as a religious missionary. In 1870 he established his headquarters on Aba Island in the White Nile, some two hundred miles south of Khartoum, and he soon developed a large following among the local tribes. Around 1878, in part perhaps because of the growing popularity of the younger *shaykh*, a break took place between Shaykh Mohammed Sharif and Mohammed Ahmed, and the latter attached himself to a rival head of the Sammaniya order, Shaykh al-Qurashi. Upon the death of this old *shaykh* some two years later, Mohammed Ahmed was recognized as the new master, and he became one of the leaders of the Sammaniya order.

As we have mentioned earlier, Mahdist expectations were current in the Sudan at this time—due in part to social and political discontent with Egyptian rule and in part to "a genuine religious revulsion from the low morality of the Egyptian administrators, when judged by the standards of primitive Islam." [6] According to tradition the coming of the Mahdi was to take place at the end of a century, and, since the thirteenth Muslim century was now drawing to a close, another felicitous omen was seen. Early in 1881 a certain Abdullahi ben Mohammed, a member of a pious family from Darfur in the western Sudan, came to Mohammed Ahmed and requested admission to the Sammaniya order. According to popular tradition, the new convert twice swooned at the sight of the master and then greeted him as the expected Mahdi. It is a historical fact that Mohammed Ahmed declared himself the Mahdi shortly after his meeting with Abdullahi. The latter's family had originated in the Niger-Chad region [7] where Mahdist ideas were widespread, and Abdullahi had been seeking a Mahdi for some time. His influence on Mohammed Ahmed appears to have been strong from the first moment—he quickly became the Mahdi's right-hand man—though Mohammed Ahmed's own inner convictions and his awareness of the popular Mahdist expectations also undoubtedly had an important share in his assumption of the Mahdiship.[8]

In March 1881 Mohammed Ahmed revealed the secret of his divine election first to Abdullahi and then to his other disciples. On a visit to El Obeid in the province of Kordofan he declared his Mahdiship to the educated religious men as well as to the common people who were deeply impressed by his preaching. Back on Aba Island finally, on June 29, 1881, he openly proclaimed himself the Mahdi of Islam, and he sent out letters to various notables asking them to join him.

The essence of the Mahdi's message at this point was purely religious. He preached complete trust in God, a renunciation of earthly vanities, and the happiness of the world to come for true believers. Yet this call for the establishment of a community following the primitive Muslim model also constituted a threat to the Egyptian administration of the Sudan. It meant the repudiation of the changes in the *Shari'a*, the revealed law of God, introduced by the Turks and Egyptians in order to come to terms with the Western world of the nineteenth century. Moreover, there soon emerged a close connection between the basic motive of religious reform—the enforcement of a pure Islam—and local political and social grievances as can be seen in the following proclamation of the Mahdi:

> Verily these Turks . . . thought that theirs was the kingdom and the command was in their hands. They transgressed the command of [God's] apostles and of His prophets and of him who commanded them to imitate them. They judged by other than God's revelation [i.e. the Qur'an] and altered the *Shari'a* of Our Lord Muhammad, the Apostle of God, and corrupted the Faith of God and placed poll-tax [*al-jizya*] on your necks together with the rest of the Muslims. . . . Verily the Turks would drag away your men in chains, imprison them in fetters, take captive your women and your children and slay unrighteously the soul under God's protection, and all this was because of the poll-tax, which neither God

nor His Apostle had commanded. Moreover, they had no mercy upon the small among you nor respect for the great among you.[9]

Thus the Mahdi was, from the beginning, thrust into the role of a Sudanese nationalist though the fight against the "Turks" —the generic name given to anyone with light skin whether Egyptian, European, or genuinely Turkish—always retained its religious orientation, it was a *jihad*, a holy war. Those not accepting the Mahdiship of Mohammed Ahmed were stigmatized as infidels. In a message sent to Governor-General Mohammed Ra'uf Pasha, the Mahdi openly threatened hostilities against unbelievers in his mission: "The warnings are clear and the sword purifies him who does not believe. Let it be known that . . . there came to me a sword and I was informed that none should be victorious over me while I had it. The Prophet informed me that God would take whoever comes against me as an enemy, either by weakness or by drowning." [10]

The Mahdi here was thinking of resisting an attack upon Aba Island which indeed was quick in coming. After a deputation of *ulama* had failed to convince Mohammed Ahmed of the falsity of his claims, the governor-general dispatched two companies of troops to arrest the Mahdi. On August 12, 1881 the badly led attackers were ambushed by a band of 350 Mahdists armed with sticks, swords, and spears and fled back to their steamer. The Mahdi had scored his first victory.[11]

Despite this easy victory the Mahdi realized how vulnerable his position on Aba Island was, and, on the next day, accompanied by his following, he set out for the safety of the Nuba Mountains in southeastern Kordofan. This retreat, far from demoralizing the Mahdists, served as an inspiration, for the Mahdi described it as a reenactment of the flight (*hijra*) of the Prophet from Mecca to Medina. Using another parallel with the Prophet, the Mahdi called his followers *Ansar* (helpers), the name originally given to the supporters of Mohammed at Medina. After arriving at their new refuge, located at the border of Kordofan and Fashoda provinces, the *Ansar* were attacked by a large force under the command of the governor of Fashoda. The Mahdi again set an ambush, on December 9 the attackers were routed, and the governor himself was killed. A large quantity of arms and other booty fell into the hands of the Mahdi who was hailed for his second mirac-

ulous victory. According to an old legend the Mahdi was to
come from Mount Massa in Morocco. Without much ado Mohammed Ahmed declared that Jabal Qadir in the Nuba Mountains was the fabled Mount Massa.[12]

The Mahdi's prestige meanwhile continued to grow, and he
gained many new followers. He benefited from the weak and virtually bankrupt position of the young Khedive Tawfiq in Cairo
whose army had mutinied. No reinforcements, therefore, could be
sent to the Sudan, and the leaders of the expedition that set out
against the Mahdi in the spring of 1882 badly miscalculated the
strength and resolution of the *Ansar*. On May 30, 1882 the
Mahdists attacked and won their third decisive victory. Again, a
large quantity of booty was taken and the Mahdi's reputation
soared, while the reputation of the Egyptian administration sank.

During the following months the Mahdi extended his influence
to include the semi-nomadic tribes of Kordofan who had been hit
hard by Gordon's anti-slavery campaign and who were receptive
to an anti-Egyptian appeal. The government forces had superior
artillery and firearms, but the *Ansar* made up in number and fanaticism what they lacked in equipment. Moreover, the Mahdi by
now had captured large quantities of rifles and some of his troops,
largely recruited from captured government soldiers, were
equipped with modern weapons. In September 1882 the forces of
the Mahdi began a siege of El Obeid, the capital of Kordofan,
and on January 19, 1883 the city surrendered to the *Ansar*. This
great victory appears to have confirmed the Mahdi's belief in the
universality of his divinely inspired mission. In a pronouncement
to his followers, the scope of his *jihad* was described thus:

> The Apostle of God gave me good tidings in the prophetic vision,
> and said to me, "As thou hast prayed in El Obeid, thou shalt pray
> in Khartoum, then thou shalt pray in the mosque of Berber, then
> thou shalt pray at the Sacred House of God [the Ka'ba of Mecca],
> then thou shalt pray in the mosque of Yathrib [Medina], then thou
> shalt pray in the mosque of Egypt, then thou shalt pray at the
> Holy House [Jerusalem], then thou shalt pray in the mosque of
> al-'Iraq, then thou shalt pray in the mosque of al-Kufa." [13]

The Mahdi's followers were linked to their supreme commander by the traditional oath of allegiance (*bay'a*) which in its
later form was clearly modeled upon the pledge given by the
early *Ansar* of the Prophet:

We have sworn allegiance to God and His Apostle, and we have
sworn allegiance to you, in asserting the unity of God, that we will
not associate anyone with Him, we will not steal, we will not commit adultery, we will not bring false accusations and we will not
disobey you in what is lawful. We have sworn allegiance to you in
renouncing this world and abandoning it, and being content with
what is with God, desiring what is with God and the world to
come, and we will not flee from the *jihad*.[14]

    This oath summarized some of the most important elements of
the Mahdi's teachings. The central message was eschatological
—the *Ansar* were living in the last days and were fighting to
bring about the rule of God on earth through His representative,
the Mahdi. Trusting in God the *Ansar* were to destroy this
world and to construct the world to come. In practice this
meant revolutionizing the Sudanese way of life. The *Ansar* were
to renounce all earthly vanities and to forego doing all the things
the hated "Turks" were doing. They dressed in a simple and
rough cotton shirt or *jibba* which, as it became old, was patched
and repatched. Women were to be veiled and had to forego their
gold and silver ornaments; bad language, intoxicants, tobacco,
amulets, music, dancing, and marriage feasts and circumcision
feasts were strongly forbidden.

    To the poor and disadvantaged the Mahdi's message of asceti-
cism was a source of comfort: "Their poverty, hunger and dreary
toil were no longer things to regret, but cause for pride and joy,
because they prepared the way to ease and happiness hereafter."
The corrupt and licentious "Turks," on the other hand, were
branded infidels. The Mahdi's teachings thus gave his followers
"pride not only in themselves, but contempt for their rulers." [15]
His proclamations were delivered with eloquence; he was a man
renowned for his sanctity and mysterious powers. External signs
such as descent from the Prophet and a mole on his right cheek
confirmed his Mahdiship; visions and invincibility on the battlefield gave testimony to his divine commission.

    The conquest of Kordofan and the fall of El Obeid in particu-
lar brought the *Ansar* a large amount of booty in the form of
goods, money, slaves, beasts, and arms. Not surprisingly, this
great accession of wealth jeopardized the Mahdi's preaching of
asceticism and called for strict punishment for violators as well as
rebukes such as the following: "You have preferred earthly life to

the world to come and loved to gather booty and wealth and deserted with it. . . . I have warned you in this my letter out of mercy towards you . . . so that you may restore the booty you have taken." [16] The Mahdi decreed that all booty was to be divided in accordance with the rule of the *Shari'a*—one-fifth went to the leader and the rest became the property of the community as a whole, to be deposited in a central treasury (*Bayt al-Mal*) and to be distributed according to need. Justice was administered in accordance with the sacred law of Islam; the divinely inspired Mahdi, assisted by his deputies and a *Qadi al-Islam* (judge of Islam), provided guidance on particular problems and thus gradually built up a body of legislation for the new Mahdist state in the making.

Of course, while the *jihad* was in progress there was no time to establish an orderly administration. The Mahdi, as supreme commander, was aided by three assistants who carried the title *Khalifa*, meaning successor or deputy, and who corresponded to the four companions and successors of the Prophet. However, only one of these three men, the trusted Abdullahi, could claim to be the Mahdi's successor. From the beginning, the "Khalifa of the Mahdi" was thus a *primus inter pares*.[17] Each of the three caliphs was also in charge of one of the three divisions of the Mahdist army, known by the color of the flag around which they mustered on parade or in battle. As the Mahdi's state grew, subordinate commanders (*emirs*) on campaign away from the main body of the Mahdist army became in effect military commanders of the regions under their control.[18] The Mahdi's offer in May 1883 to make Sayyid al-Mahdi, the head of the powerful Lybian Sanusiya order, one of his four caliphs was scornfully ignored by this man whom his own followers regarded as the Mahdi.[19]

The puritanism that governed the Mahdi's code of behavior was to be found also in his view of Islam. Religion had become too complicated; the *ulama* had written too many books dealing with obscure and trivial points of doctrine. The Mahdi demonstrated his scorn for formal theology by burning many of the books written by theologians and by compiling his own book of prayer.[20] The *ulama*, whose *raison d'être* was thus challenged, responded by branding Mohammed Ahmed a dangerous heretic and challenging his credentials as the Mahdi. But such sober theological refutations were no match for the Mahdi's charisma.

Mohammed Ahmed's self-confidence can be seen in a letter sent to the *mufti* (canon lawyer) of the eastern Egyptian Sudan in July 1882 that confirms his claims with an apocalyptic vision:

> [The Prophet] unveiled to me the Day of Resurrection. The Turks whom I had killed complained to God, and said, "O our God, O Lord, the Imam, the Mahdi slew us without warning." I said, "O Lord, I gave them warning and information. They would not accept my words, but followed the words of the *'ulama'*, and attacked me." The Prophet was present as a witness to that, and said to them, "Your sin is upon you. The Imam, the Mahdi gave you information and warning, and you did not accept it of him, but listened to the words of your *'ulama'*." [21]

The Mahdi owed his success and growing power to the strength of his personality, to the weakness of his opponents, and to the support given him by three elements or groups who opposed the Egyptian administration for quite different reasons. There were, first, the ascetic pietists who, like Mohammed Ahmed himself and his original disciples, desired a purification of Islam and a radical reform of social customs. To these puritans the rule of the "Turks" had lost legitimacy because the Islamic principles had been abandoned. Second, there were the malcontents who opposed the Egyptian administration primarily because of the attempted suppression of the slave trade which threatened their livelihood. Third, probably the largest group of supporters were the mass of tribesmen, especially the nomads of the western Sudan. To these men, the *jihad* was attractive not because it was a passport to heaven but because of the excitement of fighting and the lure of booty. The promise of an end to taxation and of sharing of goods strongly appealed to the generally poor and exploited tribesmen, though many of them feared the loss of their autonomy through military rule. These hesitations gradually yielded to fear of the Mahdi's ruthless tactics against his opponents. The tribesmen remained a fickle element in the Mahdi's camp and often abandoned the *jihad* when their material desires had been satisfied.[22]

The Mahdi's early victories against far better equipped and disciplined military forces contributed to his growing appeal and enabled him to hold together these three different elements who had little more in common than the desire to be rid of the

"Turks." In time the success of the *jihad* created its own mystique. In the battle with Shallali Pasha in May 1882, the bullets of the "Turks" were said to have turned to water; it was believed that the blessings of the Mahdi would prevent any true believer from harm in battle.[23] The Egyptian authorities meanwhile continued to underestimate the strength of the Mahdist rebellion, and this poor judgment was shared by the British who in July 1882 landed troops in Alexandria and put the Khedive under British tutelage. In the autumn of that year it was decided to send a large expeditionary force against the Mahdi.

In September 1883 an Egyptian army of 10,000 men set out from Khartoum in the direction of Kordofan, but disaster beset the expedition from the start. Most of the soldiers were inadequately trained, the country and climate were harsh, provisions soon ran short, friction developed between the Egyptian officers and Hicks Pasha, a veteran British officer, and his staff. The Mahdi's men harassed the attacking force daily, while his propaganda sought to undermine the troops' will to fight. On November 5, 1883 the Mahdi dealt the weary, thirsty, and demoralized Egyptian army the final blow. Attacking with a confident force of over 20,000 men he easily succeeded in breaking through the Egyptians' defenses, and a general slaughter ensued. No more than some 250 men survived; Hicks Pasha and his officers fell fighting to the last round. A week later the victorious Mahdi made a triumphant entry into El Obeid.

The entire western Sudan was now in the hands of Mohammed Ahmed. On December 23, Slatin Pasha, the Austrian-born governor of Darfur province, surrendered and became a prisoner of the Mahdi. His captivity was to last twelve years.[24] The Mahdi received acclaim and recognition from far and wide. The British advised abandonment of the Sudan, and the Egyptian government asked for the dispatch of a qualified British officer to supervise the retreat of the remaining Egyptian forces.

The man who was chosen for this task was Charles George Gordon. In January 1884 he set out for Egypt and upon arrival he was reappointed governor-general of the Sudan. The nature of his undertaking was thus confused from the beginning. The British government had had in mind a mission of information-gathering and advice; the Khedive and Sir Evelyn Baring, the British consul-general in Cairo, wanted him to act as an executive as well. This contributed to the disastrous outcome of Gordon's mission.

Gordon was supremely confident as well as deeply religious. He had helped defeat the Taiping Rebellion in China in 1863, and in his new task he once again considered himself the instrument of God's will. Just before leaving Cairo he wrote his sister, "If God is with me, who can or will be hurtful to me?" [25] Gordon obviously grossly underestimated the power and influence of the Mahdi who by now was the religious leader and political master of half of the Sudan. Hoping to establish a peaceful relationship with the Mahdi, Gordon sent him a letter appointing him sultan of Kordofan. Mohammed Ahmed's reply was arrogant and scornful: "Know that I am the Expected Mahdi, the Successor of the Apostle of God. Thus I have no need of the sultanate, nor of the kingdom of Kordofan or elsewhere, nor of the wealth of this world and its vanity. I am but the slave of God, guiding unto God and to what is with Him. . . ." [26]

On February 18, 1884 Gordon arrived in Khartoum where he was received with great enthusiasm. He announced that no more taxes would be collected for two years, that there would be no attempts to suppress the slave trade, and that rule over the Sudan would be returned to its former sultans. But these belated measures failed to weaken the Mahdi's hold over the Sudan, and Gordon soon found himself under siege in Khartoum. On March 12 the telegraph line to the north was cut, and communications with Cairo now became irregular and extremely slow. The original plan to evacuate the Egyptian forces from the Sudan thus became impossible to execute; the British government, anxious not to become involved, refused to send a relief force. It was not until August that the pressure of public opinion in Britain forced the government to agree to the dispatch of such an expedition. By then Gordon's position had seriously deteriorated.

The story of the siege of Khartoum has been told many times and does not require repetition here. On January 26, 1885 the city fell to the forces of the Mahdi. Sixty hours later two steamers carrying an advance party of the main relief force, still many miles away, arrived before the walls of Khartoum. By that time the city had been sacked, and Gordon's head had been delivered to the Mahdi.

On January 30 the Mahdi made his triumphant entry into the

capital of the Sudan. At first he seems to have wanted to make his headquarters in Khartoum, but he soon changed his mind and gave orders to build a new capital on the plain north of Fort Omdurman, just west of Khartoum. From here preparations were made for a further extension of the *jihad*. King John IV of Abyssinia was asked to accept Islam, and in June the Mahdi addressed a letter to the Khedive in Cairo threatening him with an invasion of Egypt. He urged the Egyptian ruler to "free himself from being a captive of the enemies of God" and to submit to the divinely appointed Mahdi so that "we shall all be one force to establish the Faith, to expel the enemies of God from the land of the Muslims, to exterminate and extirpate them to the last one, if they do not turn to God and submit." The Mahdi claimed to have been informed by the Prophet that the victory of the Mahdia was assured and that he would possess the whole earth.[27]

A few days after the dispatch of this confident letter, on June 22, 1885, the Mahdi suddenly died. In the months since his great victory over Gordon he was said to have taken up a life of luxury and unbridled sensuality—his harem allegedly consisted of some one hundred wives and concubines[28]—and rumor had it that he had been poisoned by one of his concubines.[29] It is more likely that he died of natural causes; his captive, Slatin, ascribed the Mahdi's death to typhus.[30]

THE REIGN OF THE KHALIFA

The Mahdi's unexpected death left his followers stupefied. According to some accounts, the Mahdi on his deathbed had nominated the Khalifa Abdullahi as his successor.[31] Be that as it may, Abdullahi had always been Mohammed Ahmed's right-hand man, and no serious challenge to his succession appears to have arisen. After the burial of the Mahdi the remaining two Khalifas, other important figures in the regime, and the rank and file of the armies in Omdurman swore their allegiance to Abdullahi. Abdullahi's explanation of the premature death of the Mahdi can be seen from a letter which he addressed to the people of Egypt:

> Do not trouble yourself over the cessation of that divine assistance with the passing of the Mahdi, for between the Mahdi and his ancestor, the elect Prophet, is a close similarity. When the Prophet passed away, the assistance remained with his noble Companions

until the Faith of God was confirmed and its compass extended as
you know. The passing of the Mahdi to the world to come before
the conquests of Mecca, Constantinople, and other cities . . . does
not impugn his being the Mahdi of the end of the age, of whose
manifestation the Prophet gave the Muslim community good Tidings.[32]

The momentum given the Mahdist movement by its founder
was also maintained by other, less religious factors. Many of the
Sudanese tribes who had assisted the Mahdi in the fight against
the Egyptians were not easily persuaded to serve the Khalifa, and
only a renewal of the *jihad* enabled Abdullahi to create for his
rule the legitimating sanctions of Mahdism. The Anglo-Egyptian
relief force for Gordon had withdrawn, but the idea of invading
Egypt was not abandoned. After defeating several tribal chal-
lengers and conducting a successful campaign against Abyssinia,
the Khalifa assembled a strong expeditionary force. In a letter to
the Khedive dispatched in April 1887 the Khalifa restated his
messianic goal: "Were my aim in this affair the possession of the
transient world and its passing glory, which brings no advantage,
there would be enough in the Sudan and its adjoining regions, as
you know, because of their extent and the variety of their fruits.
But as God knows, my aim is only the revival of the Muhamma-
dan *Sunna* and the path of the Prophet among the generality of
mankind." The Khedive was once again asked to submit, and he
was urged to join the Mahdist forces fighting the infidels.[33]

The difficulty of provisioning and holding together a large
army delayed the attack until 1889. The commander of this force,
al-Nujumi, was very able, but his line of advance led through the
barren Nubian desert, and the Egyptians did not rally to the side
of the Mahdists as they had been expected to. On August 3, 1889,
near the village of Tushki, the battle was finally joined. The
Mahdist army, inferior in number, fire power, and discipline, was
thoroughly defeated by a combined Egyptian-British force. Some
4000 were taken prisoner; among those killed was the courageous
al-Nujumi.[34]

The defeat of the invasion of Egypt marked the end of the ex-
pansionistic phase of Mahdism. "Henceforward," writes Holt,
"although the old apocalyptic language continued to be used and
the old religious sanctions to be invoked, the Mahdist state lost its
wider theological connotations and was reduced to a Sudanese

sultanate which embodied in its administration much of the personnel and practice of its Egyptian predecessor." [35]

The Mahdi had only barely begun to organize his millenarian
theocracy, and the task of building a workable state amid the
jealousies of the tribal leaders proved no mean undertaking. The
Khalifa accomplished this difficult assignment through a combination of ruthlessness and administrative ability. His European
captives have pictured him as a ferocious tyrant, a blood-thirsty
monster. He undoubtedly was a vain, distrustful, and ambition-
driven man who loved power; occasionally he acted with cruelty
and vengefulness toward tribes and individuals who opposed him.
But though he was a brutal ruler in a brutal world he was no
monster. He could show patience and restraint, and during his
thirteen-year rule not a single European captive was put to
death.[36] His quick intelligence, strength of will, and resoluteness
in decision made him an able administrator who through force of
character made up for his lack of the magnetism that had characterized the personality of the Mahdi. The Khalifa's private life remained simple, and, though the religious character of the Mahdia
declined during his reign, he was not a hypocrite who used religion only to maintain his dictatorial rule. "The reality," concludes
Holt, "was less simple. In Abdallahi religious enthusiasm, administrative talent, and personal ambition combined and competed
for mastery." [37]

Overthrowing traditional hereditary tribal chiefs, transferring
tribes of doubtful loyalty to Omdurman, and exploiting old rivalries, the Khalifa managed to control his unstable realm. In each
province there was a governor responsible directly to him; the
Khalifa was assisted by a staff he had for the most part appointed.
There was the *Qadi al-Islam* who presided over the high court
and reviewed all important cases decided by the provincial
judges. Justice was dispensed according to Muslim law and punishment was severe. The penalty for theft was the loss of the
right hand; for highway robbery, the loss of the right hand and
left foot. Serious crimes also involved the confiscation of property
for the benefit of the central treasury. The controller of this *Bayt
al-Mal*—a combination storehouse, auction market, and treasury
—was the most important civil official in the state.[38]

Despite this imposing structure of absolute power the Khalifa's
regime soon began to show signs of serious trouble. The numer-

ous military campaigns accompanied by severe losses and the transfers of population had led to the neglect of agriculture. In 1888 the rains failed and in the following year the entire Sudan suffered from a severe famine. In 1890 locusts destroyed large parts of the yearly crop and widespread suffering again resulted. During the following years the Khalifa's armies experienced a series of defeats. In the south he lost control over most of Equatoria and all of Bahr al-Ghazal province. In the east the entire Red Sea littoral had to be abandoned. Most importantly, by 1895 the threat of invasion by an Egyptian-British army from the north was imminent.

Since the loss of Khartoum intensive training by the British had turned the Egyptian army into an efficient military force. The reconquest of the Sudan thus became again an attainable goal and by 1896 British opinion, too, had turned in this direction. The desire to settle scores with the Mahdists and to avenge the death of Gordon remained strong. The gruesome stories told by Europeans who had escaped the clutches of the Khalifa were convincing proof that the Sudanese were suffering under a horrible tyranny from which they would welcome being liberated. And finally, the designs of the French on the southwestern Sudan brought about the decision to help Egypt reconquer the Sudan.

The Khalifa's army still was no more than a tribal *levée en masse* that had to compensate through number and sheer courage for its inferiority in equipment, discipline, and organization. The main problems for the Anglo-Egyptian expedition, commanded by Sir Herbert Kitchener, therefore, were mainly to force their opponents into an open battle and to move and supply the expedition over hundreds of miles of inhospitable territory. The crucial challenge of transport was solved by building a railroad through the Nubian desert; at the end of 1897 some 300 miles of the Nile, including the cities of Abu Hamed and Berber, had been reconquered without any heavy fighting. The decisive engagement took place in the following year. On September 9, 1898 the main Mahdist forces, numbering nearly 60,000 men, met Kitchener's army of 25,800 men in open battle outside the Mahdist capital of Omdurman and despite fanatical ardor and courage they were badly routed. "The slaughter," writes one historian, "was the most spectacular triumph yet achieved in war by weapons of precision over the spear, the sword and the old-fashioned

musket." The Mahdist army suffered 10,800 killed and an estimated 16,000 wounded, of the Anglo-Egyptian army 48 were
killed and 382 wounded.[39] The Khalifa and several thousand of his
followers escaped to the south.

The end had come for the Mahdi's cause. On January 19, 1899
the British and Egyptian governments signed an agreement establishing a condominium (joint) government over the Sudan. In
March 1899 the French agreed to relinquish all territorial claims
to southern Sudan. On November 24, 1899 the last engagement of
the Mahdia was fought in which once again the machine gun
won the day. After the battle, the Khalifa of the Mahdi and his
chief lieutenants were found among the dead.

EPILOGUE

The Mahdia had ended, but Mahdist expectations continued to
exist in the Sudan. Nourished by the belief that after the Mahdi
the *nabi* Isa (the Prophet Jesus) would come and deliver the
faithful, Mahdist risings, albeit of primarily local character, took
place at least once yearly for well over twenty years.[40] The most
serious of these revolts was the Katfiyya rising of 1908 in which
an old Mahdist, 'Abd al-Qadir, preached the *jihad*.[41] In the first
thirty years of the condominium more than 170 military expedi-
tions were sent out to quell disturbances, most of which were
messianic in nature.[42]

The eventual defeat of the Mahdia could not blot out the
memory of the early great victories of the Mahdi, and these
triumphs encouraged many others outside the Sudan proper to
declare themselves Mahdis. In Nigeria, as a result of heavy taxes
and moves to abolish slavery, numerous Mahdis made their
appearance—from 1900 to 1905 there were twelve in the province of Sokoto alone.[43] In Somaliland Mohammed ibn 'Abd Allah
in 1899 proclaimed himself the Mahdi and rose in open rebellion
against the British. Expedition after expedition was sent out, but
the rising could not be crushed until 1920 when its leader, called
by the British "the mad Mullah," died of influenza.[44]

In the Sudan, meanwhile, the Mahdist movement gradually
changed into a religious sect, known as the neo-Mahdia (or simply the *Ansar*). Led by a son of the Mahdi, 'Abd ar-Rahman al-
Mahdi Pasha, a man of great wealth who had been knighted by

the British, the neo-Mahdia became respectable and supported the nationalist movement for self-government and independence. 'Abd ar-Rahman's aspirations were primarily secular, but he also made use of the prestige he had inherited as a son of the Mahdi, the latter still being revered by most Sudanese as a saint and great national hero. For many of his followers 'Abd ar-Rahman was the *nabi* Isa who would drive out the British and usher in the Millennium.[45]

'Abd ar-Rahman died in 1959, three years after the Sudan achieved independence. The *Ansar*, led by a grandson of the Mahdi, Imam al-Hadi Ahmed al-Mahdi, now dominated a section of the Umma party, one of the Sudan's two main political forces. In May 1969 left-wing officers seized power and aligned the country with Nasser's Egypt. On May 30, 1970, the Mahdists staged an insurrection against the military regime, with bloody fighting in the streets of Khartoum and Omdurman. The rising failed and on April 1 the government announced that Imam al-Hadi Ahmed al-Mahdi and a group of his supporters had been killed by a Sudanese border patrol while trying to escape to Ethiopia.[46] It remains to be seen whether the *Ansar* will be able to recover from this blow that removed the last surviving descendant of the Mahdi.

Another outcome of the Mahdia must be mentioned. Neither the Mahdi nor the Khalifa had ever succeeded in establishing their hegemony over the Negroid tribesmen of the southern Sudan. Their repeated raids seeking ivory, supplies, and slaves had upset the traditional pattern of tribal life without, however, converting the animists to Islam. The only lasting effect has been the southerner's hatred and fear of the northern Sudanese.[47] During the following decades Christian missionaries converted about one-tenth of the southern population, today numbering about four million; the rest still belonged to the various indigenous religions. Both segments deeply resented the hegemony of the Muslim North, and in 1955 a secessionist military revolt broke out in Equatoria province, which was to last seventeen years, claiming an estimated half a million lives.

The rebels called themselves the Anyanya which is the name of the deadly poison of the mamba, a large snake inhabiting the African river banks which serves as their emblem. By 1968 some 5000 guerrillas were fighting the Muslim government in Khartoum; the cruelty practiced during this civil war forced large numbers of southerners to flee to the neighboring countries of Uganda, the Congo, and the Central African Republic.[48] The leftist government of Gafaar al-Nimeiry, which came to power in the military *coup d'état* of 1969, offered regional autonomy to the three southern provinces of Bahr al-Ghazal, the Upper Nile, and Equatoria; a national charter drawn up by this government in early 1971 described the Sudan as an integral part of both the African and Arab revolutions,[49] but despite these concessions the struggle for independence continued. Finally on February 27, 1972, an agreement ending the civil war was signed in Addis Ababa which granted the South self-government within the framework of a new Sudanese constitution.[50]

The very existence of the southern separatist movement, meanwhile, had created an ambivalent attitude on the part of the Sudanese government to the projected Arab federation with the United Arab Republic, Libya, and Syria, for it was feared that any move in the direction of a pan-Arab or pan-Islamic union would further aggravate the civil war in the South. It is surely paradoxical that one consequence of the Mahdia, a movement for the union of all true Muslims, today puts obstacles in the path of Arab and Islamic unity.

CHAPTER 9

Messianism and Rebellion in Twentieth-Century Africa

RELIGIOUS SEPARATISM

The spread of Christianity in Africa has been rapid. Whereas in 1900 Christians constituted a mere 3 per cent of the population, by 1970 28 per cent of all Africans were Christians (97 million). The annual growth rate of the entire Christian community in 1965 was about 5.2 per cent, more than twice the average population increase for the continent which was 2.5 per cent.[1] Several reasons can be given for this extremely fast growth of African Christianity, much of it taking place under the auspices of missions. First, since in traditional African thinking the world of the spirits was seen as controlling human fortunes, it was logical for Africans to assume that the secret of the white man's power was to be found in his religion. Again in the same vein, Christianity was identified with the material plenty of European civilization, and the acceptance of the white man's religion therefore seemed a sure way of sharing in his riches.[2] Last, Christianity offered liberation from sorcery, the primitive man's devil and the source of his misery. The washing away of sin through baptism and the promise of salvation were seen as ways of achieving lasting security against the ever-present threat of misfortune, disease, and death all of which were attributed to witchcraft and sorcery.[3]

The promise of protection against witchcraft and sorcery continues to be one of the attractions of the Christian religion, but the other expected benefits of Christianity largely failed to materialize. Behind the missionaries came colonial administrators and instead of becoming wealthy Africans were subjected to often cruel exploitation. Their resultant frustrations led to considerable disenchantment with missionary Christianity and to the emergence of the phenomenon of religious separatism.

The first secession from a mission church took place in 1872 in Basutoland, where the first tribal church was organized in 1884 by a native Wesleyan minister of the Tembu tribe in South Africa, and the first so-called "Ethiopian church" was founded on the Witwatersrand in 1892. By 1913 there were 30 separatist churches in South Africa, by 1948 the figure had risen to 800, and by 1960 there were 2000.[4] Looking at the African continent as a whole, David B. Barrett in 1967 counted some 5000 distinct ecclesiastical and religious bodies in 34 African nations, arising either by separation from foreign mission churches or, in a few cases, by the initiative of Africans working outside the missions. These independent churches drew members from 290 different tribes and had some seven million nominal adherents; this number was growing at the rate of 300,000 to 400,000 a year. In addition, for every successful attempt to form a separatist body there had been several that failed to reach the point of schism, another 5000 that were launched but collapsed, and a large number that continued to exist within established churches.[5]

Many of the early separatist churches called themselves "Ethiopian," for this name expressed their desire to escape humiliation in the white man's places of worship and their striving to achieve independence and emancipation. Their leaders had heard the missionaries refer in their sermons to the 68th Psalm where God is called upon to scatter the people who delight in war, to give strength and power to *his* people, and it is written: "Princes shall come out of Egypt; Ethiopia shall soon stretch out her hands unto God." [6] Nationalistic-minded African ministers interpreted this to presage the self-government of the African church under African leaders and this identification of Ethiopia with liberated Africa was facilitated by the defeat of the Italians at the battle of Adowa in 1896. The kingdom of Ethiopia now assumed new stature and importance as an African nation that had been able to triumph over a European colonial power. The fact that this African state possessed a national Christian church with an ancient tradition and its own liturgical language and sacred literature further increased its prestige.[7]

Initially the Ethiopian churches were movements of protest: against the domination of the white missions, against the South

African Natives Land Act of 1913 that restricted the right of Africans to purchase or rent land except in designated areas, against the disrupting impact of European culture upon native patterns of life. Ethiopian preachers participated in the Zulu Rebellion of 1906 promising ascendancy over the Europeans; in many instances the act of secession from the parent church was accompanied by apocalyptic preaching by leaders who predicted that the end of the world was at hand and that only God's elect, the sons of Cush, would be privileged to enter a dreamland—Ethiopia— a place of peace, justice, and plenty. After 1945, the element of protest weakens and a tendency toward accommodation emerges. Millenarian movements that fail to live up to the highly unrealistic expectations they created in their followers become churches characterized by an ambivalent attitude toward the white churches. The slogan "Africa for Africans" continues to be heard in the independent churches, but in their organization and theology churches of the Ethiopian type largely follow the pattern of the mission churches from which they seceded. Their leaders, who started out as prophets and fiery orators, if not revolutionaries, tend to assume many of the traditional functions of tribal chiefs or kings as the churches grow. The life of the church copies many features of the world of the whites; in South Africa, where these churches are most prevalent, they fit well into the pattern of apartheid.

Bishop Sundkler in a pioneering study describes another type of independent church as Zionist. Despite the fact that these two types rarely exist in a perfectly pure state—there are many cases of Ethiopian churches with marked Zionist features [8]— certain important differences can be noted. Whereas the Ethiopian churches are largely orthodox in their religious teachings, the Zionist groups are characterized by a far more syncretistic theology. They exhibit Christian revivalist elements in the tradition of the American Pentecostal churches, from which the African Zionists often borrow their names. In particular, missionaries of the Christian Catholic Apostolic Church in Zion, founded in Chicago in 1896, were instrumental in encouraging the first African Zionist churches. More importantly, alongside Christian components we find food taboos, purification rites, sorcery, faith healing, and witch-finding derived from the religious heritage of old Africa. Many of them are cults with only precarious links to

Christianity. Some Zionist groups, notes Sundkler, are "deliber-ately nativistic, and churches of this kind in the end become the bridge over which Africans are brought back to the old heathen-ism from whence they once came." [9]

The leader of a Zionist church is a prophet and healer with faith healing one of his major activities. He is usually surrounded by a large number of leaders and subleaders, a situation that often leads to more secessions. Most of the Zionist churches are not na-tionalistic or politically oriented. Isaiah Shembe's Nazarite Church in South Africa, for example, desires peace between the races and seems to regard white supremacy as an expression of God's will.[10] The most important activity of these churches is the promise of deliverance from the powers of evil, especially witchcraft and sickness. A recent study of Zionist churches in Rhodesia found recruitment of new members to be largely the result of faith-heal-ing activities.[11] In western Nigeria this type of independent church is known as "aladura," that is, the praying people. Else-where in West Africa, they are often called "spiritual churches," because they channel God's spiritual power to help men in their fears and problems.[12]

Many different hypotheses have been offered to explain the phenomenon of the independent churches—whether orthodox or nativistic. Sundkler and Balandier have stressed the importance of racial discrimination and economic exploitation. The former draws attention to the impact of the Natives Land Act of 1913 in South Africa that left one million Europeans holding a larger share of the land than approximately five million Africans who were restricted to the so-called reserves. Even where white set-tlers bought land fairly such purchases often violated the African belief that tribal land was ultimately under the control of the ancestors and therefore inalienable. Since missionaries, too, settled on tribal land the growing sense of grievance over the alienation of land inevitably affected the native attitude to them and created tension between the mission churches and their African pa-rishioners. Sundkler notes that "the increase in the number of Bantu independent churches could be shown on a diagram as a parallel to the tightening squeeze of the Natives through land legislation." [13]

The enactment of the color bar for skilled labor in the South African mining industry in 1926 that led to considerable unemployment among African skilled artisans and craftsmen, and a consequent deterioration of race relations, is cited by Sundkler as another important factor. In a similar vein, Balandier correlates the emergence of black churches and the presence of rapid social change accompanied by racial discrimination as created by the mining industry in South Africa and the Congo.[14] Sundkler finds that a considerable number of independent church leaders are unemployed skilled workmen; he furthermore stresses the impact of the color bar in other spheres of South African life, "the 'Separatist' church is, on the part of the African, his logical reply to the Whites' policy of segregation and separation." [15]

Other writers, while not denying the impact of economic and social factors, stress the importance of more spiritual elements. In Nigeria, Parrinder finds, the color bar is less prominent and secessions came primarily because of a reaction against the spiritual dryness and stern moralism that characterized the mission churches.[16] For Africans newly arrived in the cities and deprived of the social ties and festive occasions they had enjoyed in their traditional tribal life, the mission churches are not sufficiently inspirational. The new African churches, on the other hand, supply a sense of fellowship and belonging and a new earthly and spiritual home in the midst of a chaotic world of rapid social change. A familiar atmosphere is created by drums, dancing, singing, hand-clapping, and other ceremonial practices, and this also meets the need for an emotional experience.[17] It is interesting that breakaway churches in both Europe and America have often catered to the same spiritual needs. The emotionalism of early Methodism, it has been suggested, provided "a psychologically effective escape from the drudgeries of an unromantic, unaesthetic life," just as the emotionalism of Negro sects in the United States was in part "a reaction against the monotony and misery of laborious days on the plantation or in the factory." [18] The Methodist chapel in eighteenth-century England brought a sense of belonging to the uprooted of the Industrial Revolution in a way that was very similar to the way the African separatist churches satisfy the search for community among Africans living in the squalor of shanty towns.[19]

The same unfulfilled needs exist in many African rural areas and on the reserves among women in particular. Their problem is aggravated by the periodic absence of large numbers of men who

have left for the cities to work or to search for work. In addition
to the fact that the independent churches claim to meet such un-
resolved problems of women as barrenness and domestic difficulties, "independency seems to release much feminine religious zeal
hitherto latent." [20] The preponderance of women in the independent churches is also explained by the missionary attack on
the traditional African family, an issue felt more keenly by
women than by men. The missionaries' stricture against polygamy, ancestral and fertility cults and other tribal institutions, and
certain customs and practices linking religion and family life is
regarded as an illegitimate interference with African ways. The
black churches, many of which sanction polygamy, are seen as
the defenders of the traditional culture and of the ethnic group
threatened by the inroads of alien mores.[21]

The clash of cultures, of which the assault on the fundamental
unit of African traditional society, the family, is only one manifestation, is probably one of the basic causes of independency.
Just as in the United States the secession of Negroes from mixed
churches was largely a movement of self-assertion, representing a
way of escaping the white man's overbearing attitude toward colored Christians,[22] so independency in Africa fed on the lack of
sensitivity and the paternalism often displayed by the missionaries. Africans educated in the mission schools came to resent the
failure of white Christianity to understand African ways and to
treat Africans as equals. The grossly unequal treatment, in contrast with the teachings of the Christian Scriptures, antagonized
in particular those individuals with the talent or ambition to be
leaders. In America, according to a student of the Negro church,
the barring of Negroes from the political life of the community
made the church the arena of their political activities. "It was the
area of social life where ambitious individuals could achieve distinction and the symbol of status. The church was the arena in
which the struggle for power and the thirst for power could be
satisfied." [23] Similarly, in Africa, the founding of an independent
church provides the opportunity to satisfy ambition and talent, it
functions as a safety valve [24] for frustrations.

That racial tension and discrimination are not the only factors
contributing to the creation of independent churches is demonstrated by the continuing secession of one African leader after another. The desire for prestige and power leads to the formation of

new splinter groups and churches, and even in the newly independent countries of Africa the trend toward independency has
not stopped. By 1967, it was estimated, over one hundred new religious bodies had come into existence each year, many of them
in the free nations of the continent. About sixty new secessions
have taken place in Kenya since independence in 1963, nearly
two hundred in Ghana since 1957. "The removal of colonialism
from the scene," writes Barrett, "has therefore solved nothing as
far as the needs of independents are concerned; the movements
continue and even proliferate." [25] Millenarian movements, it has
been observed by many writers, are particularly prone to fission
because of the fundamentalist reliance upon direct inspiration,
which can be claimed by anyone, and because they attack authority and probably attract rebellious and contentious people.[26]
The same factor appears to be at work in the independent African churches even if their millenarian teaching is not at all pronounced.

The proliferation of new secessions, by and large, takes place
among nominally Protestant groups. The eight hundred independent Bantu churches in South Africa, Sundkler writes, "are, as it
were, the arithmetical progression of sectarian divisions in the
West" [27]—divisions that since the Reformation have not afflicted the Roman Catholic church to any degree. This raises the
question of whether the phenomenon of independent churches
arises out of a specifically Protestant background and, if so, what
in Protestantism produces separatism.

In a few instances independent churches or prophet movements
have appeared in a Catholic setting. In the Congo, in the early
eighteenth century, there was a prophetess, Kimpa Vita or Donna
Beatrice, who claimed to be St. Antony; she preached against the
foreign Catholic priests and predicted an early day of judgment
that would usher in a Golden Age for the people of the Congo.[28]
Several other prophets with Catholic backgrounds can be found,
and individual Catholics have joined secessionist movements, the
largest and best known of these being the *Legio Maria* (Legion of
Mary Church) in Kenya which began at the time of independence
in 1963 and, despite splits, is said to have 100,000 members. Yet,
in the vast majority of cases independent churches have developed in areas of Protestant missionary activity. Barrett found a
definite correlation between secessions and the ratio of Protestant

missionaries to total population, and he concludes that separatism indeed emerges out of a Protestant climate.[29] He furthermore showed a marked correlation between independency and the existence of vernacular Scriptures. In tribes having no Bible available in the vernacular, the probability of separation is 23 per cent; with readings from the Bible only, it is 56 per cent; with the new Testaments, it is 67 per cent; and with complete Bibles, it is 81 per cent.[30] Since until very recent times translations of the Bible were made available to the natives only by Protestant missions, these figures help explain why the great majority of separatist churches appear in Protestant missionary territory. The above statistics also help explain the correlation of separatism with high literacy and relatively high *per capita* income.[31] A reading of the Scriptures presupposes literacy; and since Bibles, even with the subsidy provided by the United Bible Societies, are expensive, they will be purchased more frequently among the more prosperous tribes. That the independent churches indeed are not primarily movements of economic protest we will have occasion to demonstrate in more detail below.

Further analysis of these factors enables us to go beyond a statistical correlation. A causal relationship between separatism and the existence of vernacular Scriptures can be inferred by noting that the translations in most cases appeared well before the onset of independency. Also, it is possible to show that "in the minds of numerous separatists, it was the scriptures which initially started them thinking and which later provided them with the necessary motivation and legitimation." Barrett concludes therefore "that vernacular scriptures have been a major causative factor in the spread of independency in Africa, though not of course the only one." [32]

The power of religious writings to generate religious movements is, of course, most fully demonstrated by the European Reformation of the sixteenth century. The same pattern was and continues to be at work in Africa. The printed Scriptures thrust into the popular consciousness a powerful religious dynamic and helped African Christians articulate their grievances at the contrast they were beginning to perceive between mission and biblical Christianity.[33] By 1965 readings from the Bible had appeared in 395 different vernacular translations, New Testaments in 181 sub-Saharan languages, and complete Bibles in 74 languages.[34]

The availability of these vernacular Scriptures enabled African Christians to detect such historical facts as the lack of biblical support for monogamy, the polygamous practice of the Patriarchs, the vital importance of family and land, and the emphasis upon sacrifice, fertility, and sexuality in the Old Testament. In short, the vernacular Scriptures could be used to demonstrate the differences between the teachings of the missions, often hostile to traditional African customs, and the Bible itself. A student of the rise of Ethiopianism in Nigeria from 1875–90 writes: "Unrestricted access to the Bible, with its notions of equality, justice and non-racialism provided the early converts with a valid weapon which they were not reluctant to employ against the missionaries who brushed these ideals aside in Church administration and in their relations with the converts." [35] In many cases, as we shall see below, the teachings of the Bible eventually became arguments not only against the missionaries but against the entire colonial society that professed to practice Christianity.

The connection between Protestantism and the rise of independent churches is now clearer. As one author explains it: "Separatism, or 'Ethiopianism,' it might then be argued, represents the restatement, in terms appropriate to twentieth-century Africa, of certain basic Protestant principles: the appeal from Authority to the Scriptures; the emphasis on the right of individual interpretation; the protest against rigidity in moral and social theory; the demand for a national Church and a national hierarchy." [36] Looking at the same problem in a different way, one can explain the smaller number of separatist movements arising from Roman Catholicism by its greater attractiveness to and compatibility with the African temperament. The African reverence for ancestors finds satisfaction in the importance attributed by Catholics to their saints as mediators between God and man, while emotional and spiritual needs can find expression in Catholic sacraments and ceremonials.[37] Last, the more centralized structure and the denial of salvation to anyone leaving the Catholic church further inhibit secession.[38]

The majority of African independent churches then, in effect, have functioned as forerunners, if not rudimentary forms, of political nationalist organizations. A sentiment of protest and independence has been channeled into a spiritual and ecclesiastical area, while this religious radicalism in many cases has cast doubts on the legitimacy of the entire colonial order. Whether the separatist group tends toward quietism and withdrawal from political contest or becomes involved in active conflict with the authorities appears to depend in part on the reaction of the authorities. "Some movements have been primarily religious in their original concerns and activities, but have been forced into political action or revolt when colonial authorities have misinterpreted them as centres of subversion, insofar as any new independent African activity and organization was regarded as politically dangerous." [39] Opposition from a newly independent regime can have the same politicizing effect. Last, but of equal importance, the political posture of an independent church will be determined by the character of its leadership. Whereas the development of independent churches is related to the presence and interaction of a number of different historical, sociological, and religious factors, the necessary and indispensable condition for the emergence of such a group is the appearance of a charismatic leader, a founder-prophet, with a compelling innovation. The presence of such a visionary and prophet is particularly important in the creation of messianic and millenarian movements which we will now discuss.

MILLENARIAN MOVEMENTS

The five religious movements discussed in this section all had a charismatic leader and all were involved in clashes with political authority, albeit to varying degrees. The messianic character of these movements differed from movement to movement, and in at least one instance the violent outburst was directed not against a colonial regime but against a newly independent African government. Still, it would appear that all of these movements derive from similar causes and also share many forms of activity.

Ennoch Mgijima's Israelites and the Bullhoek Incident of 1921

Ennoch Mgijima was born in 1858. He made a living as a lot-holder in the Bullhoek location near Queenstown, South Africa. Originally a Methodist, Ennoch from about 1910 led the life of a wandering preacher who prophesied the approaching end of the world and asked for repentance in anticipation of the Last Judgment. Around September 1912, Ennoch left the Methodist church, joined an American Negro church, the Church of God

and Saints of Christ, and established his own tabernacle. Ennoch
continued to call his growing group by the above name even
after it had been expelled from the Church of God and Saints of
Christ in 1918, apparently because of its anti-white sentiments.[40]

Ennoch's followers called themselves "Israelites." The group
accepted the Jewish calendar, kept the Sabbath, celebrated the
annual festival of Passover, and rejected the New Testament as a
fiction of the white man. The Israelites were seen as God's elect
whom Jehovah would deliver from bondage as earlier He had delivered His children out of Egypt. The identification with the
Jews was conscious and deliberate, a phenomenon found also
among the Maoris of New Zealand and some aborigines in Poly-
nesia. In the eyes of these natives, seeking self-determination and
liberation from their oppressive masters, the Jews represented an
unparalled example of a people able to overcome all manner of
persecution, they projected an image of anguish and successful
survival that had an obvious appeal.[41]

Ennoch was a forceful orator and personality. He first claimed
the titles "Bishop" and "Watchman" (following Ezekiel 3:17).
From about 1920 on he also called himself "Prophet," a title
which he reinforced by reports of visions and divine messages.
His followers regarded him as a mediator between God and man.
The title "King of Israel" also appeared on some documents.[42]
The messianic character of the sect was pronounced.

In 1920 a group of Ennoch's followers sold their possessions
and erected some 300 huts on Crown land at Ntabelanga to wait
for the end of the world. They regarded this location holy soil
and refused to abandon it. The Israelites declined to pay taxes;
births and deaths were no longer registered. Ennoch reported the
vision of a forthcoming holy war directed by God. The time of
Jehovah, he announced, had come. The Israelites taunted the police and engaged in military drills, some with spears, others with
rifles.[43]

The government, which until then had handled the group with
considerable patience, finally dispatched a military force. On May
24, 1921, some 500 fanatic Israelites, assured by Ennoch that the
bullets of the white man would turn to water, hurled themselves
against the machine guns of the police. Within minutes 163 Israelites were dead and 129 wounded. Ennoch himself was taken
captive and the huts of the settlement were destroyed. In Decem-

ber 1921 the prophet and two of his lieutenants were sentenced
to six years of hard labor, but Ennoch was released in 1923. He
died in 1928. The sect continues to exist, although it has lost its
militant character.

The success of Ennoch in building his sect of devoted followers has been attributed to many factors: resentment against a
white mission that had benefited from a redistribution of land,
Ennoch's impressive personality and his apocalyptic, anti-European teaching that fell on fertile soil, a permissive code of behavior (including, according to some accounts, the acceptance of polygamy), the holding of dances accompanied by fanatic and
weird chants.[44]

Kimbanguism in the Lower Congo

Kimbanguism probably represents Africa's best-known messianic
movement. Swedish accounts often speak of it as Ngunzism, a
term derived from the word *Ngunza*, meaning an emissary
from the divine world, preacher, or prophet. Most writers call
the movement Kimbanguism, from the name of its founder, Kimbangu.[45]

Simon Kimbangu was born around 1889 in Nkamba in the
Lower Congo, a stronghold of Protestantism. He is described by
one source as a fanatical Protestant, very familiar with the Bible
and especially the Old Testament. His mother is said to have
cured the sick by means of herbs and leaves chosen according to
instructions received in visions. Her son, too, was given to visions, tremors, rolling of the eyes, and an ability to fall into a
trance-like state. Andersson calls him a "natural mystic." [46]

In the early part of April 1921, after a sequence of dreams and
visions that occurred over an appreciable length of time, Kimbangu emerged as a healer and prophet. His fame increased
quickly. "Rumour, spreading like wildfire all over the country,
declared him to be a great miracle-worker. The blind it was said,
regained their sight, the deaf their hearing, and the crippled the
use of their limbs. None went away from him without being
helped. He was even supposed to have resurrected the dead." [47]
Despite independent reports by medical men and missionaries that
failed to confirm a single case of faith healing, Kimbangu's reputation soared, and large numbers of people flocked to Nkamba to
be healed. Because so few Africans had professional medical ser-

vices available to them, Kimbangu, like many other leaders of African independent churches and sects, became important primarily because of his alleged healing ability.

But Kimbangu was a preacher as well as a healer. The Bible was always in his hands, and his meetings included hymns, prayers, and sermons. Though Kimbangu undoubtedly was influenced by pre-Christian ideas and practices in the realm of ritual, his teachings were Christian. As a result, attendance at the Protestant missions in the area greatly increased, as did the demand for Bibles and hymnbooks. The fact that a black person had become a great prophet, perhaps a savior, greatly impressed the Africans and gave rise to native pride, but Kimbangu's teachings themselves were devoid of anti-white sentiments.[48]

As the movement grew, Kimbangu could no longer handle the large crowds alone, and he chose prophets from among his followers who, like the master, engaged in preaching and healing. Soon even these assistants, commissioned by Kimbangu, proved insufficient, and a large number of prophets appeared, many of whom the leader had never even seen. It appears that some of these men used the movement to spread anti-European ideas. Propaganda for the establishment of a black church was disseminated and well received, and some agitators urged the natives not to pay taxes. The movement now appeared to be out of Kimbangu's control, and the Belgian administration began to be concerned about a possible breakdown of law and order.

In June 1921 a warrant was issued for Kimbangu's arrest; he was seized but escaped. His followers spoke of a miracle and Kimbangu's prestige rose even higher. Some preachers in the movement now began to announce that the Second Coming of Christ was imminent, they predicted the liberation of Africa and the expulsion of the whites by a black messiah and described Kimbangu as the future ruler of Africa. These ideas were widely disseminated by word of mouth as well as in songs.[49] Still, no attempts were made to bring about this longed-for state of affairs by force. Most of Kimbangu's followers were convinced that God would intervene and they waited for this apocalyptic event. "In relation to law and order, this meant that the prophet movement was much more a safety-valve for tension, than a combustion chamber for explosion."[50]

On September 10, for reasons that are not at all clear, Kimbangu returned to Nkamba. Emulating the example of Jesus, he apparently had decided to surrender to the authorities. On September 14, 1921 he was arrested for the second time, and, with a large number of his followers, taken to Thysville where he was brought to trial. When questioned by the military tribunal, Kimbangu acknowledged that he was a prophet and claimed to have resurrected the dead through God's inspiration. On October 16 the court handed down its judgment. Kimbangu was found guilty of having spread false religious ideas among the natives and unleashing the forces of fanaticism against the established authorities that resulted in seditious songs and isolated acts of rebellion.[51] He was sentenced to death, and eleven of his lieutenants were sentenced to life imprisonment. Local colonists pleaded for his immediate execution, but upon intervention of Protestant missionaries and of the colonial government his sentence was remitted to life imprisonment. He was incarcerated in a jail in Elizabethville where he stayed until his death some thirty years later.

Kimbangu had been at liberty as a prophet for a period of less than six months, he now was entirely out of touch with his followers, yet the movement he had inspired did not die. "Indeed it may be surmised," writes Andersson, "that the aura of martyrdom which now accrued to the Prophet gave added weight and urgency to the ideas propagated by him." [52] From this time on, the nationalistic and anti-white tendencies emerged more and more forcefully. The leaders of the "Black National Clan," as the new Congo church was called, were to isolate themselves from all contact with Europeans, no taxes were to be paid, the children of members were to be sent to schools organized by the cult in which hatred for whites and the slogan "Africa for the Africans" would be propagated. The people in the villages were instructed to adopt an attitude of apparent meekness but be ready for the day when the yoke of servitude would be broken.[53]

The Belgian authorities, after a short period of tolerating the cult's schools and churches, declared Kimbanguism a potential danger to the state and sought to suppress it. No one was to be allowed to preach in the villages without a certificate from a mission. Under the impact of these and other repressive measures, the movement became still more revolutionary. Hopes for the future were sustained by "news" that American Negroes would come to the aid of their suffering brethren in the Congo and deliver them from bondage and that "God would send firearms from Heaven, so that the foreigners might be annihilated." [54] In January 1924 several thousand Africans demonstrated in Thysville against the imprisonment of Kimbanguist followers.[55] Their antagonism toward the missionaries led to various forms of sabotage such as arson.

By 1930 the movement had spread beyond the boundaries of the Belgian Congo, and Kimbanguism was to be found in Portuguese Angola and the French (or Middle) Congo. Pagan elements now made their appearance alongside Christian ideas of a coming holy war led by Jehovah that would usher in the new kingdom. Simon Kimbangu and all those imprisoned, it was prophesied repeatedly, were about to return to their country. There was more talk of the reestablishment of the national kingdom by Kimbangu, the people's Messiah, than of Christ, the savior from sin. A text circulated among the villagers in 1930 asked them to be ready for the war that was approaching and told them that Kimbangu was about to come back.[56]

Kimbanguism was given a new uplift by the arrival of the Salvation Army in the Congo in 1935. The red letter "S" on the collar of the Salvation Army missionaries was believed to stand for "Simon"; the Salvation Army was regarded as Simon Kimbangu reincarnated in European form so that the whites could not again prevent him from doing his work. Large numbers of Kimbanguists flocked to Salvation Army meetings. The music, drums, and flags at the services appealed to the Africans. For reasons that are not clear the idea now spread that anyone who shook hands with a Salvation Army officer was thereby proved innocent of witchcraft; large crowds attended the activities of the Salvation Army apparently because of anxieties about witchcraft.[57]

Kimbanguism continued to exist as a decentralized underground cult throughout the 1940's. After the Second World War, the leader of one of these groups, Joseph Diangienda, Kimbangu's third son, began to organize a church on more orthodox Protestant lines. By 1956 it was known as "The Church of Jesus Christ on Earth by Simon Kimbangu" (EJCSK), and by the end of 1958 some 60,000 people were estimated to belong to this illegal organization.[58] The founder, Kimbangu, was seen as Christ's messenger and comforter of the blacks, and his eventual return was expected. In general, however, the element of political protest had been abandoned, and in December 1959, less than six months before the granting of independence, the Belgian authorities lifted the ban on the movement which became a legally recognized body. In April 1960 Kimbangu's remains were brought back to the Lower Congo and enshrined in a mausoleum in his native village, Nkamba, which has become the spiritual center of the EJCSK.[59]

Since independence in 1960 the EJCSK has continued to grow. Two prominent Kimbanguists have occupied significant political posts—Emmanuel Bamba, minister of finance from May 1962 until June 1964, and Charles Kisolokele, oldest son of Kimbangu, who served as labor minister in 1961–62.[60] In 1966 the EJCSK applied for membership in the World Council of Churches. It then claimed some 200,000 adult members.[61] Today the EJCSK is the leading indigenous church of the Republic of Zaïre. But having become a church, the EJCSK now experienced the phenomenon of separatism when the "Prophetic Church of Mayumbe" broke away from the parent body charging it with "giving way to the temptations of worldly action." Soon the Prophetic Church of Mayumbe in turn was plagued by secession, and there now exist several Kimbanguist churches.[62]

National independence for the Congo had been achieved by secular associations arising in the 1950's in the urban population, but the contribution of Kimbanguism toward the attainment of this goal should not be minimized. Kimbanguism helped develop a sense of ethnic unity and identity while at the same time, by providing a channel for the expression of radical hostility to the colonial regime, it "created a pre-disposition toward subsequent diffusion of explicitly nationalist ideas." [63] What began as a demand for religious and cultural independence thus eventually awakened a demand for political self-determination.

The Black Messiah André Matswa

André Matswa was born around 1899, a member of the Sundi-Ladi tribe in the French Congo not far from Brazzaville. He attended a Catholic mission school in his native village, and during the First World War he served in the French Army and became a non-commissioned officer. After the war he went to Paris where he met members of various left-wing movements as well as other Africans. It is generally conceded that Matswa's Paris experiences did more to shape his thinking than did his youthful religious impressions from the mission.[64] The movement which he organized in 1926, "L'Association Amicale des Originaires de l'Afrique Equatoriale Française," known as Amicalism, at that time certainly had purely secular aims—to provide financial aid for needy natives from French Equatorial Africa in Paris. Money was raised in Paris as well as in the villages of French Equatorial Africa.[65]

The collection of money appears to have been accompanied by the propagation of pan-African ideas, and the French authorities, therefore, soon withdrew their support. In 1928 the premises of the organization in Brazzaville and Paris were searched, money and documents were seized, and finally Matswa himself was arrested and sent to Brazzaville for trial. Matswa was tried for alleged irregularities, together with three of his lieutenants in April 1930; all four were sentenced to three years' imprisonment and ten years' exile. Attempts on the part of their supporters to free the defendants by force failed though the disturbances were serious enough to require the intervention of troops.[66]

The imprisoned and banished Matswa quickly became a hero in the minds of his fellow tribesmen, and, following his death in captivity in 1942, Matswa came to be regarded as a messiah. Many of Matswa's countrymen refused to believe that he was dead, and they expected him to return to them. They spoke of him in messianic terminology as, for example: "The Whites may perhaps have killed him but he has risen again, and one day he shall return in power and majesty and drive away the Whites and their Black troops." [67] In 1947 Matswa's name was put up for election to the legislative assembly, and the dead man received an absolute majority.[68]

The secular leader had thus been transformed into "Jesus Matswa" and the mutual aid society into the messianic cult "Nzambi ya Minda" (the Religion of the Candle). In this religious movement, the figure of Christ was replaced by that of André Matswa to whom prayers were directed as follows: "Father Matswa, deliver the Congo." In one description of a prayer house, a chest was used as an altar screen before which was placed a picture of Matswa, surrounded by flowers and lighted candles.[69] Like Kimbangu earlier, Matswa was frequently called "King of the

Congo." Religious songs expressed the yearning for his helping hand as in this example popular in Brazzaville:

> *We others who have no support,*
> *We others who have no defender;*
> *God, all-powerful father, watch over us*
> *Father Congo, father, who will remember us?*
> *We others, who will remember us?*
> *Matswa, all-powerful father, watch over us.*
> *Matswa, all-powerful father, send us a defender.*[70]

Once again, then, Christianity had spurred emancipation. As summed up by Balandier: "It has provided the example of a Messiah who, sacrificed by the public powers as a common criminal, triumphs over the authorities to the infinite joy of the believers. It has brought all the revolutionary force it possessed at the time of its origins, together with the expectation inherited from Jewish messianism." [71] The martyrdom of Matswa served as the basis for the growth of a black church that aroused enthusiasm, a revolutionary spirit, and renewed self-confidence. Matswa became a symbol of unity transcending clan and social status, a national hero, and the man chosen by God to liberate the Congo. It is interesting to note that in the former French Congo the same spirit of rebelliousness has continued even after the attainment of independence and has led to arrests and prison terms for members of the cult of Matswa who refused to submit to the census and pay taxes.[72]

Kitawala

The Kitawala movement is an outgrowth of the American Watchtower Society. The millenarian ideas of the American founder, Pastor Charles T. Russell, were introduced into Nyasaland, about 1908, by Elliott Kamwana, a young Tonga, who had learned of the creed from Joseph Booth, an English Baptist missionary in Cape Town. Kamwana preached to receptive Africans Russell's prophecy that in October 1914 Christ's Second Advent would take place. He added that a new order would then come into being in which the country would be free of the whites and be governed by the natives and that there would be no more taxation. Within less than a year some 10,000 Africans around the

Scottish Livingstonia mission were baptized into the new millenarian faith.[73] The teachings of the Watchtower movement that
both existing churches and states are creatures of Satan and
would be destroyed after cosmic cataclysms had an obvious appeal to Africans unhappy under colonial rule and their missionary adjuncts. The possibility of baptism without learning a catechism, the somewhat laxer discipline prevailing in Kamwana's
church, and the promise of material aid from the rich American
Watchtower Society were other factors in the appeal of the
movement.[74]

During the 1920's, this African offshoot of the Watchtower
movement spread from Nyasaland to Rhodesia, the Belgian
Congo, and Portuguese Africa. In Rhodesia it became known as
"Chitawala" and in the Congo as "Kitawala"—*tawala* being
an African rendering of "tower." [75] By 1930, the Kitawala movement was entrenched in the Congo in the urban centers of Ka-
tanga province and spread from there into the rural areas. In 1936
Kitawala was a factor in rioting in the Mweru-Luapula district,
and in 1944 it was implicated in an insurrection among the Bak-
umu in Orientale and Kivu provinces.[76] The Belgian administration responded by dissolving the sect successively in all the provinces. Kitawala appealed especially to the young and more
prosperous members of the native working class in the mines to
whom the movement, despite its egalitarianism, offered new opportunities for social advancement and status.[77] Another observer
stresses the integrative role of the movement in a situation of severe social disequilibrium and psychical dislocation caused by the
inroads of Western culture.[78]

In Northern Rhodesia, where, after a brief period of suppression, Kitawala was tolerated, the movement has been more of an
Ethiopian church, largely without radical tendencies. It functions
as a closely knit brotherhood with a comforting sense of group
membership that looks forward to a glorious future.[79]

The beliefs and practices of the Kitawala sect—and the
movement is almost entirely without direction from the parent
Watchtower organization, it should be added—varies in different parts of Central Africa, but certain common elements stand
out. Kitawala is definitely anti-white and rejects any idea of a
rapprochement between the black and white races. Armageddon, the final and conclusive struggle between the forces of good

and evil, is also the decisive battle between blacks and whites. In the golden age to follow the possessions of the killed or vanquished whites will become the property of the Kitawalas.[80] The prophecy is one of an ideal theocratic world order in which blacks will be free from the terrors of sorcery and will enjoy abundance, liberty, and happiness.

In some places it was believed that in the coming Kingdom of God blacks would be turned into whites and would thus be able to enjoy all the riches hitherto reserved to whites.[81] The Europeans were accused of having distorted Christianity and of having hidden its true significance. Still, the teachings of Kitawala, for the most part, involved strong elements of an apocalyptic dream rather than a nationalist program of action. A historian of Northern Rhodesia writes of the movement in that country: "They left their party programme to the Almighty and when Jehovah failed to intervene much of their enthusiasm evaporated. . . ." [82] As a rule, Kitawala has discouraged violence.[83] Its teaching, by and large, appears to have had a quietistic effect, satisfying certain deeply felt psychological needs for reassurance and explanation while at the same time deprecating the significance of earthly misery. In the words of a Rhodesian observer:

> The doctrine that men were now living in times of unequalled woe seemed reasonable enough to poverty stricken villagers, shaken out of their old ways by new ideas and impositions; it was even more comforting to be told that these times of woe were themselves a sure sign of salvation at hand. The District Commissioner, Ndola, for instance, felt convinced that the Watch Tower faith had helped people through the misery of moving to the reserves, to the loss of valued village sites, and made them indifferent to the tax and the slump. For what was the use of worrying too much about these things? The day of judgment was at hand, and then the just would gain their reward whatever happened! [84]

In the post-independence period the Kitawala sect has often run into trouble with the new African authorities. In October 1967 it was banned in Malawi (formerly Nyasaland), and, following widespread attacks by members of the youth wing of the ruling Malawi Congress party in late September 1972, some 10,000 of the Witnesses fled into neighboring Zambia.[85] It appears that a religious group oriented toward heaven is looked upon with suspicion "in newly emergent nations where national identity, common purpose and allegiance to the state are all in need of reinforcement." [86] The same conflict has led to the demise of the Lumpa church in Zambia.

The Lumpa Church of Alice Lenshina

Alice Lenshina received her early religious instruction from the Church of Scotland Mission in Northern Rhodesia. In 1953 she had a vision of being carried by angels before Jesus and being charged to become his witness and the bearer of a purifying message. Within two years Lenshina was leading a separatist movement, and by 1956 up to 1000 pilgrims a week were visiting her at Kasomo to be baptized and confess their sins. [87] The strength and vitality of the new church undoubtedly was derived from Lenshina's religious experience, and the illiterate prophet's belief in her own death, rebirth, and personal confrontation with the deity. To a people with traditional reverence for persons possessed of spirits, Lenshina's vision had great appeal. [88]

During 1956 small grass-roofed huts, serving as churches, were springing up in Northern and Southern Rhodesia, the Copper Belt, and as far away as Tanganyika and Nyasaland. By 1958 the break with the mission church was complete. The name "Lumpa church" began to be used which, Lenshina explained, meant "in a hurry": "The churches promise you salvation tomorrow. I offer you salvation today." [89] Many local Europeans, on the other hand, believed that Lumpa meant "for black people only." Several of Lenshina's more prominent followers were known as active nationalists, including her husband, Petros Robert Kaunda, the brother of Kenneth Kaunda, future prime minister of Zambia. Some of these men had been dismissed from government or mission employment. A song beginning "The white men are your enemies" was popular in the Lumpa church. New converts abandoned their European names, and Lenshina began to baptize them with new African names.

Lenshina herself disclaimed any interest in politics or in the propagation of anti-European sentiments. She insisted on being a good Christian who accepted the brotherhood of all men. Her teachings were puritanical and prohibited drinking, smoking, adultery, polygamy, anger, and rudeness. At the same time, these strict moral standards led to an intolerant self-righteousness on the part of her followers and resulted in clashes with other Christians. Africans unwilling to make the pilgrimage to Lenshina were accused of being unwilling to give up witchcraft, and African mission priests were assaulted.[90]

Militancy was reinforced by the apocalyptic nature of many of Lenshina's sermons and hymns. The following is an example of the eschatological imagery employed:

> *You fool, run, the fire is coming near.*
> *Now remember Sodom and Gomorrah.*
> *Jesus made the fire fall down;*
> *all were burnt!*
>
> *The sign of the enemies,*
> *the sign of the enemies.*
> *If you are a sinner, you shall suffer.*
> *You shall suffer as Satan suffered.*[91]

Rumors told of the expected coming of Christ on a black cloud, and, when the great church at Kasomo was opened with elaborate ceremony in November 1958, many of Lenshina's followers assembled for the occasion apparently expected Christ's appearance at that moment. A special pillar was said to have been built on which he could alight. Following the disappointment of this millenarian expectancy it is possible that many of the worshippers returned to their homes with their faith in Lenshina considerably shaken.[92]

In December 1962 the first African-dominated government was formed in Northern Rhodesia and Kaunda's United National Independence party (U.N.I.P.) was beginning to emerge as the strongest African political force. Friction now was developing between the U.N.I.P. and the Lumpa church, which was estimated to have close to 60,000 members. The African nationalists, who were for the most part non-religious, resented the time spent by religious-minded Africans in devotions and other church activities. They showed "considerable impatience with Lumpa theological and liturgical preoccupations, particularly the concern with witchcraft and its exorcism." [93] Incidents between U.N.I.P. members and Lumpa zealots, reported as early as 1959, became more frequent and violent as the U.N.I.P. began to make inroads upon Lumpa membership and after Lenshina in 1963 had forbidden her followers participation in any type of political activity which she branded a kind of terrestrial witchcraft. Lenshina's other-worldly tendencies had always been strong, but the timing of this pronouncement—coming at the moment when nationalist and political fervor, in anticipation of full independence, was high—could not but generate conflict. Lumpa members now saw themselves as God's elect, persecuted by the forces of evil. The stage for a holy war was being set.

Under increasing pressure from nationalist militants to join the U.N.I.P., members of the Lumpa church during 1963–64 had built and congregated in fortified villages. Kaunda's government finally ordered the Lumpa members to lay down their arms and to leave these villages. July 20, 1964 was set as the deadline for the fulfillment of this order. On July 24 a clash between armed Lumpas and police resulted in more than 30 Lumpa deaths. Violence now mounted, and the government sent troops against the Lumpa stockades with orders to disperse and resettle the inhabitants in their original villages. They encountered fanatical resistance which, within three weeks of violent fighting, left more than 600 dead.[94] The Lumpa church now was banned; Lenshina and her husband were detained.

According to some observers, the direction of Lumpa affairs had fallen, in 1960, into the hands of her husband and a group of deacons who were more concerned with wealth, prestige, and power than spiritual matters. If correct, this might account for the violence of July–August 1964 which ill accords with the restrained personality of Alice Lenshina; all visitors described her as pious, simple, and matronly.[95] At the same time, the ferocious resistance of the Lumpas, wildly and hopelessly assaulting troops equipped with modern weapons, undoubtedly can also be traced to their self-righteous sense of group salvation and their eschatological religious ideas which encouraged fanaticism.

The popularity of Lenshina's movement, as of many independent churches, had been due in part to the sense of community which her group had provided. For another, Lenshina was highly successful in relieving the fears of witchcraft of her followers. She promised protection against witchcraft as well as solace for life's tribulations and encouragement generally. "Her role in some ways resembled that of the Western psychiatrist. Kasomo also became a kind of Rhodesian Lourdes with crowds of sick and worried Africans waiting to speak to her and hear her advice. Many seemed to gain comfort and confidence from her help." [96]

The Lumpa church emerged in colonial times and for a while provided an outlet for nationalistic sentiments. The continued existence of the Lumpa sect, albeit with diminished popularity, under African rule demonstrates that anti-colonial factors provide only a partial explanation for this kind of religious organization. Spiritual needs, which remain unsatisfied even after independence, clearly are another important factor in the flourishing of such movements. When the very existence of such a sect is directly threatened, as the Lumpa church was in Northern Rhodesia in 1964, the forces of fanaticism will become unleashed and the same ferocious fighting that in other settings was directed against the white opponents of the movement will be directed against the new African authorities. A millenarian movement has a momentum of its own, and it is neither fully accounted for by colonial oppression nor can it easily be stopped by the attainment of political independence. That is one of the important lessons of the Lumpa uprising of 1964.

CONCLUSION

African millenarianism can be characterized as syncretic as well as post-Christian. It contains tribal and traditional elements like belief in the return of ancestral heroes and other mythical beings. These beliefs have provided a link with religious concerns of the past and have helped Africans assimilate the Christian ideas of a messiah and of a radical transformation of this world—the concept of eschatology. The orientation of most African peoples, it should be remembered, is toward the past and does not include the idea of a future Millennium. Spirits bring benefits and provide help in cases of misfortune, but they do not usher in a messianic age.[97] "Man looks back whence he came," writes a student of African myths and language, "and man is certain that nothing will bring this world to a conclusion. The universe is endless. There is nothing to suggest that the rhythm of days, months, seasons and years will ever come to a halt, just as there is no end to the rhythm of birth, marriage, procreation and death."[98] This world view, typical of most simple societies, has been challenged by the Christian message of a radically new world of bliss that lies in the future, involving a totally different way of looking at man, time, and history. Small wonder that most Africans have understood this new heaven in basically materialistic terms, a way of thinking facilitated no doubt by the fact that the African's traditional hereafter, too, is seen as something physical and materialistic. This post-Christian element can be seen in the fact that the African messiah is not the harbinger of a spiritual kingdom but rather a prophet of political liberation and social justice here on earth. The admonition of Matthew 6:31 to have trust in God who will supply food, drink, and clothing is taken quite literally and so is verse 33: "But seek first his kingdom and his righteousness, and all these things shall be yours as well," in which primary importance is attached to the assurance that the heavenly Father knows of the need for "all these things" (verse 32) and will indeed provide food and clothing for his needy children.[99]

Moreover, the black savior, like the Jewish messiah earlier, is the liberator of a particular group; universalistic Christianity is given a particularist reinterpretation. Jesus himself often is now of limited importance—he is *one* of the benefactors of his people —while the crucial role is played by a prophet figure arising among the blacks themselves, a Kimbangu or Matswa.[100] The fact that many of these men were relatively undistinguished figures if measured by conventional standards would seem to indicate the great yearning for and the need of prophets. "The important thing about these leaders seems not to be what they were but what they symbolized." [101]

Like most other millenarian movements, African millenarianism arises in a period of transition. African civilizations before the coming of the white man experienced prophetic movements even though our knowledge of them is rather limited.[102] But the real flourishing of millenarian aspirations set in as a result of the social dislocations caused by colonial rule and the inroads of Western culture. Narrow tribal horizons were shattered, while modernization achieved only partial results. Millenarianism is thus a "halfway" phenomenon; "it occurs mainly during the intermediate, 'neither here nor there' stages of modernization." [103] Its doctrine represents a mixture of myth and ideology, it often reveals a kind of "sacred nationalism" [104]—a mode of political expression appropriate for a society in which the distinction between politics and religion is still largely unperceived.

This does not mean that all of these movements are politically radical. The millenarian sect of Mumboism among the Gusii people of Kenya, for example, which came into being just before the First World War and after the decisive defeat of two military revolts, advocated a withdrawal from the world of action and limited itself to prophecies, dreams, and rituals. It predicted the early coming of a great cataclysm in which the colonial order would be utterly destroyed, and the poor Africans would become rich and powerful, but beyond this symbolic rejection of the hated British and some passive resistance there was no call for the implementation of the millenarian dream.[105] Similarly, the millenarianism of the Kitawala by and large encouraged a pattern of quietism and many of the followers of Kimbangu, too, waited for God's intervention and the movement, therefore, acted in part as a safety valve for tension. The Ethiopian churches of South Africa, it has been noted, enhance the apartheid policy of the white-dominated government of that country.[106] Not all millenarian movements can be considered agents of political modernization. A movement like Kimbanguism indeed promoted ethnic unity and identity, but many other movements are essentially tribal rather than pan-tribal in their political aspirations. After the development of secular politics and the emergence of a secular nationalism, movements like the Lumpa church of Zambia can hinder national integration.

Whereas until recently most modern African millenarian movements arose in a setting of forced acculturation and racial discrimination, it would be a mistake to see them exclusively as primitive expressions of political and social protest.[107] As we have seen, such new cults emerge even after independence has been attained; at times the founding of a new sect is merely a means of asserting the autonomy of a tribal group vis-à-vis its African neighbor, or it serves to satisfy the leadership aspirations of an ambitious African who can find no other outlet or who deems purely political activity uncongenial to his religious temperament.[108] A prophetic movement that is successful in attracting a large following and becoming a church will often experience the secession of purists who want to maintain the original nonconformist impulse. Even during the colonial period one cannot ignore the strictly spiritual aspects of these movements—the desire for a more sincere or satisfying religious experience than missionary Christianity had to offer and the search for community in the midst of the breakdown of the old tribal order. In the impersonal wilderness of a modern society they "can give to men a sense of being at home." [109] Last, there is what one writer has called "the entertainment value in the social and ritual life of these movements. They almost all act to replace the village boredom and deprivation with the satisfaction of sociability and religious adventure." [110] It would be rash to assume that the attainment of nationalist goals will also at the same time bring immediate satisfaction to the spiritual and communal strivings of African villagers. One can therefore expect that new millenarian movements will continue to emerge and develop in independent Africa.

CHAPTER 10

The Cargo Cults of Melanesia

ORIGINS AND CENTRAL FEATURES

During the last eighty years or so, but particularly since the two world wars, a series of strange religious cults have made their appearance in a little known part of the world known as Melanesia. Northeast of Australia, Melanesia contains New Guinea, after Greenland, the world's largest island, as well as groups of smaller islands like the New Hebrides, New Caledonia, the Fiji Islands, and the Solomon Islands. All of these areas, until very recently at least, were administered by colonial powers; their populations, varying in size from about three million on New Guinea to a few hundred people on some of the tiny coral atolls, for the most part lived a stone-age type existence in small and isolated social units and had only recently been reached by European or Australian traders, administrators, and Christian missionaries.

All of the reported cults are in some way related to the presence of the white man, though it is not impossible that similar movements could have existed earlier. They are recognizable as doctrinal offshoots of some branch of Christianity and bear the hallmarks of a millenarian movement. A prophet usually announces the early advent of an age of bliss and plenty to be inaugurated by the return of dead ancestors who will bring with them European goods of all kinds which the white man had diverted from their rightful owners. The natives prepare themselves for this great event by staging various rites, ceremonies, songs, and dances; they also build landing and unloading facilities for the ships, vans, or airplanes in which the goods are expected to arrive. Meanwhile regular economic activities often are suspended, no food is grown, and existing stores are sometimes destroyed. When the date predicted for the arrival of the goods passes without the fulfillment of the prophecy the prophet is usually discredited but not the prophecy itself. A slightly modified form of the cult, led by a new prophet, will often emerge some time later. Because the central feature in all the cults, differing as they may in various other details, is the arrival of goods, they are known as cargo cults.[1]

One of the first such cults to be described in some detail is the so-called Vailala Madness which developed in the Gulf Division of Papua, the southeastern part of New Guinea administered by Australia since 1906. The movement was first reported in 1919 and was said to have involved a large number of coastal villages, one of them being that of Vailala. An old man named Evara was prophesing the coming of a steamer that would carry the spirits of dead ancestors and "cargo" such as flour, rice, and tobacco. The whites would be driven out, and the cargo would be distributed to the villagers, the rightful owners. Others reported visions of heaven in which houses were built of solid stone and where food, including the white man's oranges, watermelons, bananas, and sheep, was plentiful.

Traditional religious rituals were abandoned and in their place came three new features of obviously European origin. First, tables and benches were set up and ritually decorated with flowers and food. Here relatives of dead men, seated in European style and dressed in their best cloth, held feasts instead of working in their gardens or following their regular trade. Second, the villagers erected special temples, which resembled mission churches, usually in the center of the villages. Sitting on the verandas of their houses, cult leaders claimed to be communicating with the spirits of the dead or with God. Third, flagpoles, perhaps in imitation of the telegraph, were used to "establish contact" with the dead or with the steamer that was under way bearing the cargo. A leader would stand at the foot of the pole, a message would enter him and come out of his mouth in the form of a meaningless song that was taken up by the people around him. Altogether, the cult was characterized by much quasi-hysterical behavior—swaying and tottering movements, rolling eyes, and instances of ecstatic possession. At the same time, discipline was

strictly enforced and members were enjoined to abandon stealing
and adultery and to observe the Christian Sabbath.²

The beginning of the cult was related to a sermon on the resurrection preached by a white missionary. The area involved was
one of vigorous evangelism by Roman Catholic, Methodist, and
Anglican missionaries. The majority of the more active adherents
of the Vailala Madness were said to be former indentured laborers, returned from work in faraway plantations and oil fields.
There was considerable hostility toward the white man, expressed
in the slogan "Papua for the Papuans." Still, the ancestors figur-
ing so prominently in the cult were described as whites. The significance of this and other features will occupy us later.

By 1923 the movement had spread considerably, partly by informal visiting as well as by the organized evangelism of a few
leaders. Strong opposition from the government and the missions
finally succeeded in halting the cult. Several leaders were arrested
and fined, others were exposed as rank impostors. Many natives
by then had suffered malnutrition for food was running low due
to the abandonment of gardening and to the continuous feasting.
By 1935 the cult had collapsed, though a similar movement developed in this part of Papua at the end of the Second World War.

In Dutch New Guinea, the western part of the island now a
part of Indonesia and known as West Irian, millenarian manifestations had been reported for a very long time. As early as 1855 a
native had proclaimed himself a *konor*, a herald of a redeemer
who would usher in the Millennium. The redeemer himself,
known as Mansren, figured in a large number of native myths.
Upon his arrival a Golden Age of plenty would begin: the old
would become young and the sick well, the dead would return,
there would be an abundance of women, food, and ornaments.
Work would no longer be necessary, and taxation would cease.³
In 1886 the first prophecy of the coming of a ship full of goods
was reported, and the rapid spread of Christianity during the following decades introduced many new Christian elements into the
Mansren myth. Apocalyptic passages from the Scriptures were favored. Jesus was said to have been a Papuan, a fact the whites
had hidden by tearing out the first page of the Bible. Variations
of the myth made their appearance at increasingly frequent intervals and some of these episodes led to violence between the

Dutch administration and the natives. The most significant of
these movements began just before the Second World War and
continued into the time of Japanese rule.[4]

In 1939 an old woman named Angganita, a baptized Christian
living on a small islet in the Schouten Islands north of Geelvink
Bay, began to have visions and to prophesy. Angganita had five
times miraculously recovered from serious illness, and she was
said to have the gift of eternal life. She retold the stories of earlier
konors and prophesied the coming of ships bearing ancestors and
cargo. Because of her anti-Dutch posture the prophetess was arrested, but her following increased rapidly despite her absence.
Hundreds of men and women engaged in ecstatic dancing and
prayers to the ancestors; Mansren's early arrival on a huge ship
laden with cargo was predicted, and rafts were built to unload
the goods. Strangers were excluded from these ceremonies and
the cult gradually assumed militant features.

The Japanese, arriving in 1942, at first were greeted as libera-
tors, but these illusions were soon dispelled, and the rapidly
spreading movement found itself in open conflict with the new
conquerors. Local groups were organized in military fashion;
members armed themselves with knives and wooden rifles that
were expected to turn into real weapons at the coming of the
Millennium. A holy drink promising invulnerability was dispensed which, when coupled with the observance of certain taboos, would turn bullets into water. Similar beliefs, it is worth
noting, have been found in other millenarian movements many
thousands of miles away and at widely differing times.[5]

Armed struggle against the Japanese became widespread, but
they crushed the native bands one by one. Whole villages were
deported, and forced labor was imposed upon men, women, and
children. When in 1944 the Americans attacked Biak, the largest
of the Schouten Islands, the natives welcomed them enthusiasti-
cally. The arrival of numerous ships and landing craft, from
which large quantities of war material and other supplies were
unloaded, seemed the fulfillment of prophecy: the cargo had finally come. Only gradually did this image of the Americans as the
true deliverers die out. Though the natives at first were given
food they slowly began to understand that the cargo was not
meant for them. The Millennium was not about to be realized.

Another typical cargo cult developed in the Madang district of New Guinea. The area involved, located in the northern portion of the eastern half of the island, was administered as a mandate on behalf of the League of Nations by Australia until 1945, and since then it has become a trusteeship territory. The Madang district had had a very active Roman Catholic mission and the prophet of the cult under discussion, Mambu, was himself a baptized Roman Catholic. In December 1937, shortly after his return from a term of contract labor, Mambu started to preach an anti-white doctrine compounded of Christian and pagan elements. His base of operations became the Suaru Bay area, a region in which the mission had not been overly successful. The people there built Mambu a special house and a number of temples, and from there the movement spread rapidly with only the most remote villages remaining unaffected.

Mambu told his followers that they should no longer submit to the exploitation of white men, whether they be missionaries, administrators, planters, or traders, for a new order was about to be born. The ancestors would come with ships and cargo for all; the riches would be unloaded in a huge harbor in front of Mambu's house. Even now, the prophet maintained, the ancestors inside a volcano of Manam Island and in the lands of the white man were manufacturing and dispatching goods for their descendants, but the perfidious white men, entrusted with the transport, changed the labels and seized the cargo for themselves. All this thievery would now come to an end. At the right moment all work in the gardens should stop, and pigs and gardens should be destroyed. Otherwise, the ancestors would withhold their cargo of plenty for all.[6]

Until the arrival of the ancestors, Mambu insisted, the villagers should refuse to pay taxes to the government and instead make payments to him, "The Black King." They should refuse to work for the government and stay away from the mission churches and schools. Those who disobeyed this injunction would not partake of the glories of the coming Millennium and anyone who happened to be in such a church or school at the moment of delivery would be burned and consumed in a holocaust. A series of rites were instituted, and prayers were offered at the ancestral graves. Traditional clothing was abandoned and ceremoniously buried;

only loincloths and the long female dresses introduced by the Europeans were worn. In this way the natives' claim to European goods and power was symbolically asserted.[7]

Mambu's teaching was eagerly accepted by old people and women. Paradoxically, the younger migrant laborers, most affected by European rule and exploitation and by no means well disposed toward the whites, were not so eager to abstain from contact with the white man and his goods. As Worsley notes, these men "refused to forgo present prospects of obtaining limited wealth for apocalyptic visions of ultimate luxury." [8]

After both European merchants and missionaries had become worried about the spread of Mambu's influence, the government acted in March 1938. Mambu was arrested, exiled, and sentenced to six months' imprisonment. However, his followers remained unshaken, and waves of new cult activity continued to break out from time to time.

In 1939–40 the Madang district of New Guinea saw the spread of the Letub movement, a cargo cult built around a traditional dance. The missions were abandoned and prayers were made to the ancestors at village cemeteries asking them to send cargo. In some places, gardens, pigs, and other forms of property were destroyed or discarded to demonstrate the natives' poverty and need and to shame the ancestors into honoring their obligations to the living. Prophets claiming the power of healing sprang up; one man declared himself to be the Apostle Paul. The villagers insisted that they were Christians and that the cult was the true way of worshipping God.[9]

During the Japanese occupation of Madang, from 1943 to 1944, cargo cults continued to flourish. After the liberation, a movement led by a former police-boy, Kaum, prepared to drive the whites out by force. The natives set up camps in which military exercises with dummy rifles took up the mornings; late afternoon and evenings were spent in prayers and religious instruction. An airstrip and storehouses were built in the bush, for this time the ancestors would bring the cargo traveling in airplanes so that the Europeans could not steal the goods *en route*. Neither the failure of a rebellion led by Kaum in the Bagasin area in November 1944 nor his subsequent imprisonment weakened the movement. As soon as the prophet was back from jail, the fanatical Kaum revived the cult. He claimed that while imprisoned he had been killed and gone to Heaven where God had named him Konsel (Council?) and he had seen the ancestors make cargo. A special ritual, held at night, was now started to maintain contact with the dead. Food and tobacco were set out as offerings to the ancestors on a small table and after Kaum had eaten a meal prepared for him by his attendants, the people would assemble and pray to the prophet: "O Father Konsel, you are sorry for us. You can help us. We have nothing—no aircraft, no ships, no jeeps, nothing at all. The Europeans steal our cargo. You will be sorry for us and see that we get something." Kaum would then relay this prayer to God, and during the night he was said to have dreams in which he was in contact with heaven and the ancestors.[10]

A revival of the Letub cult in 1946 brought to the fore the most outstanding of all cargo leaders, the famous Yali. During the war Yali had served with distinction in the Australian army, reaching the rank of Sergeant-Major. With peace returned, Yali became an official of the new administration, but for the natives, embittered over the Europeans' failure to share their wealth, he quickly became the new messiah who would help bring the cargo. Yali at first resisted the overtures of the Letub men, but eventually he accepted the leadership of the cult and converted it into a violent anti-mission movement. Disillusioned with Christianity, the natives went back to worship the traditional deities as the source of cargo. Offerings to the deities were made to persuade them to hand over cargo to the ancestors who would deliver the goods to their descendants. The cargo was to include rifles, ammunition, and other military equipment to drive out the Europeans. The old pagan rituals and the taboos associated with them were revived.[11]

Going from village to village, the dynamic Yali and his lieutenants were able to build the cult into a mass movement. Special Yali-houses replaced the mission churches as social and religious centers in the villages. Missionaries were threatened with violence, and illegal taxes were levied. In 1950 Yali was arrested and charged with incitement to rape and extortion of money. He was sentenced to six and one-half years imprisonment, and, with the disappearance of their charismatic leader, the movement lost momentum and eventually was suppressed. By the mid-sixties Yali had become president of the local government council and denounced adherence to cargo cults as a retrograde aberration.[12]

Little would be gained from multiplying examples of cargo cults. Whether on New Guinea or the Solomon Islands or the New Hebrides the phenomenon is strikingly similar. As a recent student of the cargo cults notes, "When one reads a description of a new cult one always has the impression that he has read it all before. A good description of one of the cults fits almost exactly any other even though it has arisen hundreds of miles away." [13] Some of this similarity, of course, may be due to diffusion. We know that news of the cults spread from island to island—by radio, traders, missionaries, prisoners, etc. But as the comparative study of millenarian movements clearly shows, instances of independent and often concurrent origins of specific manifestations of messianism should not be ruled out. The prediction that the opponents' bullets will turn to water, mentioned earlier, or the injunction to neglect normal economic activities have cropped up in other widely separated parts of the world.[14] In any case, even if one were to attribute the similarity of features entirely to diffusion, one would still face the task of explaining why these diffused ideas about cargo cults were so readily accepted by different Melanesian societies. We turn next, then, to this problem.

EXPLANATION

It has been suggested that cargo cults have arisen under such varied conditions that it is impossible to give a general explanation of their occurrence. The common and peculiar factors that can be found, argues Judy Inglis, are too trivial to provide sufficient ground for an explanation, and we are therefore "led back to the particular and the essentially unpredictable." [15] This argument, it would seem, is unnecessarily self-defeating. It may well be that we are unable to predict the occurrence of new cargo cults, but this does not mean that we cannot provide explanations for many of these phenomena—we can point out the conditions under which these cults occur without knowing what is sufficient to produce them. This state of affairs, quite common in the social sciences, is not a cause for despair. After all, as one critic of Inglis' argument notes, "the aim of science is to explain, not to predict; prediction is a subordinate aim to be used to test explanatory theories. It is subordinate because retrodiction can function in the same way as a test." [16]

By thus "predicting" the past, i.e., by checking our explanation against past events, we can rule out some explanations. For example, the theory that cargo cults have as one cause the presence of Christian missionaries, and especially Protestant missionaries, can be eliminated by such retrodiction. It is no doubt true that the teachings of missionaries about the coming Kingdom of God and the resurrection of the dead have contributed certain Christian features to many of the cargo cults, but the fact remains that the same message has been preached by Christian missionaries in other parts of the world without giving rise to cargo cults. Thus, in Africa we find millenarian movements, evoked in part by Christian teachings, but no cargo cults. The motif of the ship bringing salvation has occurred there in a few instances, but it is not tied in with other features that are characteristic of the Melanesian cargo cults.[17]

Some other explanations can be rejected as being too general. Most of the cargo cults, as we have seen, are accompanied by widespread hysterical behavior—twitching, gesticulation, use of gibberish, trances, fantasies, wild dancing, and so forth. It is probable that such hysterical phenomena, spreading through a community as if by contagion, are caused by strong feelings of deprivation and frustration; the dancing manias of medieval Europe, one investigator found, were especially common after the dreadful miseries of the Black Death.[18] Catharsis and relief from great strain are gained by this kind of motor behavior, though we should bear in mind that in simple societies, where inhibitions on emotional expressions have not been imposed by a system of polite conventions, religion will often express itself in highly emotional terms and with great fervor.[19] But in any event, while this kind of psychopathological explanation can account for mass hysteria in general, it does not explain the phenomenon of cargo cults in particular. The "explanation fails because it is too general and the crucial step in the argument from psychological universals to cargo cult particulars is never taken." [20]

The key element in the cargo cult phenomenon, setting it apart from other forms of millenarianism, is the preoccupation with material goods; our explanation, therefore, should begin with this element. As we might expect, this recurring theme is related to a fundamental tenet of life in Melanesia. "The ethnography of Melanesia," writes one observer, "creates an impression of peoples moved by an intense desire for material wealth, its symbols, and the benefits of possession." [21] A penetrating examination of Tangu society, in the Madang district of New Guinea, revealed that "the great majority of dreams concern food: success in the hunt, or a large harvest followed by a feast." [22] Melanesian religion, too, is characterized by a preoccupation with material welfare. It is not concerned with spiritual values—problems of moral good and evil or questions of the ultimate meaning of life and death—but rather, according to one anthropologist, it is regarded "as a 'technology,' by means of which man could guarantee his own well-being. With the aid of ritual made effective by the observance of taboos (which had no ethical significance in themselves), he maintained proper relationships with gods and spirits, and so ensured that they conferred material benefits on him." [23] The native religion, thus, is anthropocentric: the gods and spirits are all part of the ordinary physical environment, they live on earth and can be manipulated for the benefit of man. The categories of the "natural" and "supernatural," therefore, are hardly applicable to the religions of these simple people. Gods and spirits, while more powerful than man, are definitely part of the order of nature.

Another important and equally relevant tenet of the native religion is the worship of the dead ancestors and the belief in their annual return during the festival of the New Year seeking food with which to sustain themselves. By offering food to the dead the natives believe they can overcome the burden of sin that is created by tilling the soil and disturbing the earth in which the dead are buried. By extending the spirits of the dead special ritual honors such as dances and the playing of music, they can be induced to promote the interests of their living descendants by bringing them game, protecting their crops, and watching over them in warfare. Also traditional and of obvious importance for the cargo cults are the idea of a legendary hero, who becomes embodied in a prophet, and the belief that the spirit of every deceased person is transported on a ship to the final dwelling place of the dead which is an island across the sea. [24]

Given the all-pervasive interest of Melanesian society in production, trade, and feasting, the sudden appearance of the white Europeans, who looked different from anything the natives in their closed world had ever seen and who were able to produce foodstuffs and artifacts of practically infinite variety and in vast quantities, created a tremendous cultural shock as well as a problem demanding an answer. The natives explained this phenomenon in magico-religious terms, the only type of explanation for the unknown or unintelligible available to them. Hence in some cases, members of exploring parties, handing out presents to smooth their paths, were welcomed with great emotion as returning ancestors. This reception of the Europeans was facilitated by the fact that in Melanesia ghosts are white (clay-white is the color with which widows paint themselves during mourning).[25] In turn, Christianity, the religion of the powerful and wealthy Europeans, came to be interpreted and recast in the same materialistic and anthropocentric mold characteristic of the native religion. In the words of the anthropologist, Peter Lawrence:

> The central theme was that God should look towards man and advance his worldly interests. Thus all the main teachings of the new religion—The Creation, The Fall of Man, The Great Flood, and even the Resurrection and Second Coming—were stripped of their spirituality and given a thoroughly pragmatic meaning. They became a new origin myth of the cargo, while Christian faith, worship, and morality were understood as the effective means of obtaining it: the *rot bilong kako* (Pidgin English), the road along which the cargo would come.[26]

In the early stages of European penetration the natives, therefore, often eagerly embraced Christianity. Wild hopes were entertained about the golden and happy future that lay in store for Christian converts—the kingdom to come was one of bliss and material wealth. The fact that the missionaries by the standards of the natives lived in conditions of luxury, handing out goods as rewards for conversion and religious zeal, further encouraged this interpretation of Christianity as a new "technology" for obtaining wealth.[27] But when the expected worldly benefits failed to materialize, the natives developed in many cases a new syncretic body of belief, the cargo myth, a mixture of native, traditional elements and certain aspects of Christianity as they understood it. The missionaries who had been preaching about the coming renewal of the world, the imminent arrival of Christ, and the resurrection of the dead—doctrines that found a ready echo in the natives' own religion—in practice did not take seriously these millenarian and eschatological beliefs about the early advent of paradise. The natives, therefore, gradually became convinced that the missionaries were hiding something from them. As one of them told a Lutheran missionary in 1933:

> How is it we cannot obtain the origin of wealth? You hide this secret from us. What is ours is only rubbish, you keep the truth for yourselves. We know that all that is the white man's work is forbidden to us. We would like to progress, but the white man wants to keep us in our state of Kanakas [Pidgin English for native]. The Mission, it is true, has given us the word of God, but it does not help us black men. The white men hide from us the secret of the Cargo. . . .[28]

This, then, was the situation in which cargo cults emerged: the white man enjoyed a seemingly endless supply of riches that arrived in mysterious fashion from beyond the horizon. Since these strangers did practically no work the natives, ignorant of anything but the simple ways of their own society, concluded that some secret magical power was the key to the wealth of the Europeans or Australians, that the cargo came from a deity helped by the ancestors and under human direction. The simple celebrations which the isolated Europeans staged upon the arrival of a ship or airplane bearing essential supplies fitted well into this explanation. "They assembled for a few drinks and to renew friendships with the master or pilot. The whole gathering could easily give the impression—especially to those already conditioned to see it in that light—of marking the successful culmination of a ritual undertaking." [29]

The immediate cause for the emergence of a cargo cult, its catalyst, is the prophet, a leader who claims to have fathomed the white man's magic and who promises the natives access to the coveted cargo. There are no cults without prophets and the prophet's role, therefore, is crucial. Most prophets have been well-traveled men (only one female leader is recorded) who have had prolonged contact with the white man's world. Many of them have been mission teachers. As we would expect, these are men of distinctive personality and better than average intelligence, though often eccentric and known to deviate from customary ways.[30] They are charismatic individuals without formal status who "came up from the ranks" which means that the existence of a chieftainship with strong political authority tends to inhibit the development of cargo cults even when other facilitating conditions are present.[31] Most of the prophets appear to be genuinely inspired visionaries, but cases are reported of charlatans who exploited the credulity of their followers for personal ends. The cargo motif is a means of achieving social distinction and "the hierarchy of assistants required to maintain the cult provides further openings for men of ability who would otherwise be condemned to obscurity. Some of them have subsequently become leaders in their own right."[32] As in the case of African millenarian movements, the lack of outlets for energetic and ambitious men, whose aspirations have been awakened and blocked at the same time, helps explain the fissiparous nature of the cults.[33]

The teachings of the prophets often involve the destruction of hitherto treasured material objects. Following orders, the villagers will often slaughter their precious pigs or destroy their crops as if to prove to themselves and to the spirits their complete confidence in the prophet and in the imminent redemption. The Millennium cannot arrive, it is believed, until the old ways have been abolished. The pattern here is strikingly similar to the slaughter of several hundred thousands heads of cattle ordered by Zulu prophets in South Africa in 1850 and again in 1856. Only if the people had killed what was dearest to them, their cattle, could the new realm of happiness proclaimed by the prophets come into being.[34] The desire to break radically with the past also expresses itself in the iconoclastic violation of old taboos. Traditional objects of worship are smashed, women sometimes are instructed to cede free sexual rights. Thus a new morality is asserted and the members of the cult, who in order to flout the old values had to summon up great sources of energy and resolution, are bound together in mutual guilt and mutual support.[35] Here, too, are numerous parallels to other millenarian movements. The leaders of such groups will often test and strengthen their charismatic authority by making their followers spurn the ancient ideology and in this way tie them to their leadership.[36] It also is possible that such self-aggression and self-destruction represents an instance of frustration and aggression turned inward because of a lack of another outlet.[37]

The prophets often claim to be in direct communication with the ancestors, but the real test of a leader's divine mandate is his mastery of ritual which is to guarantee an eventual "delivery of

the goods." When a prophecy fails to come true, several explanations lie at hand—evil forces intervened, the rituals were not
performed correctly, etc. Finally, the prophet may be discredited,
but the cargo cult as such is rarely held refuted. As one observer
notes: Either, therefore, the activities and rites of a cargo cult satisfy the yearnings both of individuals and the community concerned, "independent of a success in terms of actually obtaining
cargo, or the participants are being faced with repeated frustrations. On going to the evidence we find something of both." [38]
The desire for a cargo cult experience sometimes is so intense that
any white man can precipitate a cult; the anthropologist, Peter
Lawrence, once found himself the center of rumors that could
have developed into a full-fledged movement.

All of the cults contain anti-European elements. The Europeans are seen as standing in the way of the returning ancestors
or having stolen the cargo on the way or withholding the secret
of obtaining cargo, etc. At the same time, the natives seek to be
like whites, i.e., to enjoy riches and status as do the Europeans. In
an indigenous society where wealth is a crucial measurement of
the importance of a man, the obtaining of cargo is not only a
matter of satisfying economic wants, it also becomes a matter of
enhancing self-respect. The natives want to create a new man
who can hold his own in the new colonial society, a competent
and responsible individual who is no longer relegated to a position of inferiority and contempt.[39]

The main elements of the cargo cult should now be accounted
for. The cults arise in a situation where new desires and wants
have been generated, but adequate means to satisfy them are not
available. Confronted with the rich and powerful Europeans, the
natives feel deprived, and they seek to overcome this deprivation
in the only way known to them—by creating a system of magico-religious beliefs and rituals that promise to bring them precious cargo. The natives respond to the pressures created by contact with the Europeans in terms of their traditional values, for
secular and scientific solutions to problems are still beyond them.
Their small and primitive society having been disturbed, the natives seek to reestablish certainty by assimilating the new to the
old. The cargo cults, as Lawrence points out, are essentially conservative rather than revolutionary. They are "attributable to too
little rather than too much change. Although the people may

have thought at times that they were creating a different way of life, it was old attitudes and concepts that primarily directed their actions." [40]

THE FUTURE OF CARGO CULTS

Because of their anti-European features the cargo cults have been called rudimentary forms of nationalism. Previously hostile and separate peoples have been welded together by the cults; at times a new centralized leadership has emerged that organized and led an anti-colonial movement. And yet, as we have seen, the cults are also oriented toward the past and thus may delay rather than promote the emergence of a militant nationalism. It is no accident that the cargo cults have flourished in the villages rather than in the towns of Melanesia. As the natives become more familiar with the ways of the white man and better educated, cargo movements yield to secular forms of political organization.

The transition to modernity is, of course, a gradual process. Cargo cults still occur from time to time, and cargo beliefs are often used by local politicians who for the natives function not as representatives but as saviors. In the elections to Papua-New Guinea's first territorial legislature, the House of Assembly, held in 1964, several cult leaders were among the 38 indigenous members chosen.[41] Not surprisingly, a real understanding of the workings of government and of the political process is still confined to the sophisticated few.

Despite the fact that cargo cult activity is technically a penal offense, the Australian administration, over the objections of some native politicians, in recent years has preferred to turn a blind eye. In 1971 the case of one such cult, in New Guinea's jungled East Sepik district, attracted international attention when Matthias Yaliwan, a sometime policeman and Catholic mission employee, led some 4000 of his cult followers to the top of fog-shrouded Mount Turu. At the summit, a sacred place for the natives, he ceremoniously removed two survey markers that had been planted there by a United States Air Force team in 1962. Yaliwan promised that pulling up the markers would unlock a vast treasure deposited there by ancestral spirits, crops would grow profusely, and game would be plentiful in the bush. Despite the failure of this prophecy Yaliwan's popularity was apparently undiminished; in the elections to the House of Assembly held in the spring of the following year, Yaliwan polled 7200 votes to 435 for his nearest rival.[42]

In some cases cargo cults lose their activist drive. "The Day of the millennium is pushed farther back into the remote future: The Kingdom of the Lord is to come, not on this earth, but in the next world; and the faithful are to gain entrance to it not by fighting for it in the here-and-now with their strong right arms but by leading quiet, virtuous lives." [43] This transformation is due to repeated defeat as well as to the expression of political aspirations through new channels, including political parties. At such a stage of development, solutions involving the intervention of spirits play an increasingly smaller role and the cargo cult declines to the status of folklore.[44] This, indeed, appears to be the pattern.

Revolutionary Millenarianism: Theoretical Analysis

CHARACTERISTICS

The phenomenon of revolutionary millenarianism, which we have examined in the preceding chapters in eight different manifestations, summarily described, involves religiously inspired mass movements that seek imminent, total, ultimate, this-worldly, collective salvation, to be achieved not only through human action but through the help of a supernatural or superhuman agency.[1] The salvation sought is imminent for it is to come soon if not immediately; it is total for it will radically and completely transform human life and usher in perfection itself; it is ultimate since it will bring the last and final redemption; it is this-worldly for it is to be realized here on earth rather than in some other-worldly heaven; it is collective for it is to redeem not just chosen individuals but an organized group of faithful if not humanity itself. Last, this terrestrial salvation will come to pass as a result of human desire or effort, but it will also require intervention by supernatural or superhuman forces.

Certain mass movements of modern times, such as revolutionary Marxism and bolshevism, share many of the characteristics of revolutionary millenarianism, and they, therefore, have often been called secular religions or secularized millenarian movements. However, there is one all-important difference. Missing from these political movements with millenarian overtones is the supernatural element; the Marxist conception of history involves determinism, but, despite certain metaphysical qualities, it rests ultimately on a rationalistic conception of human nature and the worth of human action. Revolutionary millenarianism must also be distin-

guished from Christian millenarian sects like the various branches
of the adventist movement or Jehovah's Witnesses. The members
of these religious bodies believe in the early Second Coming of
Christ and the establishment of a millenarian kingdom on earth,
but this expectation for them is a matter of passive waiting and
does not lead to specific actions.[2] They are religious sects, not social movements; they view human society as corrupt and evil, but
they do not actively seek to change the social or political order.
The seventeenth-century Jewish Sabbatean movement, too, was
nonpolitical and nonrevolutionary. Sometimes a millenarian
movement is essentially quietistic and nonpolitical at the beginning and becomes radicalized later. The opposite path of development, i.e., deradicalization, can also be observed. We will return
to this pattern of change, which often involves rather fluid dividing lines, below.

   Apart from these basic features—the search for imminent,
total, ultimate, this-worldly, collective salvation requiring both
human action and supernatural intervention—the goals and
characteristics of revolutionary millenarian movements exhibit
a considerable diversity, thus reflecting their origin in different
cultural settings. They all look forward to a radically new and
perfect age to come, but their vision of this future age of eternal
happiness varies according to which traditional ideas are embraced. Different answers are given to such questions as how
soon the perfect age will begin, what combination of human action and divine intervention is necessary for the Millennium to
occur, whether violence should be used to bring it about, what
role will be played by prophets or messianic figures. In this
chapter we will look at some of the recurring themes and traits
that transcend specific cultural and historic conditions.

Charismatic Leadership

Leadership in millenarian movements in practically all cases is
charismatic. The authority of the charismatic leader, as Max
Weber explained in his well-known elucidation of the term, is accepted because of his followers' "belief in the extraordinary quality of the specific *person*."[3] Because of the way the leader's personality is perceived and valued by his followers, this person "is
set apart from ordinary men and treated as endowed with supernatural, superhuman, or at least specifically exceptional powers or

qualities. These are such as are not accessible to the ordinary person, but are regarded as of divine origin or as exemplary, and on the basis of them the individual concerned is treated as a leader."[4]

Given the radical aims of revolutionary millenarian movements, which seek a complete change in the organization of society, and, in view of the intense and total commitment required of their members, it is, of course, not surprising that most of these social movements have charismatic leaders. The receptivity of most people for what is wholly new is limited; for an extraordinary action men must have extraordinary justification. Hence in a religious milieu—the typical setting of millenarianism—mobilization for drastically new goals requires supernatural sanction and the charismatic leader provides just that. He is the link between God (or the gods or spirits) and man, he provides the legitimation for the radical attack upon the existing order, his mandate reassures his followers and enables him to pronounce: "It is written—but I say unto you . . . ."

The messianic message of Jesus of Nazareth and his prophecy of the coming of the Kingdom of God are ambivalent, but most leaders of millenarian movements have made unambiguous messianic claims. The leader of the Jewish revolt against Rome in the second century of the Christian era, Bar Kochba; numerous Chinese rebels appearing as Maitreya, the returned Buddha; the king of the Anabaptist saints in Münster, John of Leyden; the Sudanese Mahdi; the Heavenly King of the Taiping Rebellion in the nineteenth century—these and many other millenarian leaders were seen as human-divine saviors of their people or of God's elect. In some instances, as in the case of the black messiah André Matswa in the French Congo, the messianic title was bestowed upon the leader posthumously, whereas the prophets of other millenarian movements acted as precursors of the messiah or messiahs (as in the Melanesian cargo cults where the spirits of the dead ancestors often function as multiple messiahs). The figure of the leader of the movement and the figure of the messiah may be entirely distinct, and in a few cases messiahs play no role whatever. In some of the cargo cults Japanese or American soldiers were thought to be the agents of liberation, and even mechanical devices like flying saucers can be expected to trigger off the age of bliss. Thus, though the great majority of movements are both

millenarian and messianic, there is no necessary connection between the two.[5]

The leader of the millenarian movement need not be a messianic figure, but he practically always is charismatic. This charisma can take many different forms. In the case of Jewish,
Christian, Islamic, or Buddhist messiahs or God-ordained redeem-
ers, the supernatural mandate, focused upon one person, is most
pronounced and so is the element of charisma. In primitive societies a similar role is played by spirits of ancestors or culture heroes who are expected to return and introduce an age of plenty.
All of these messianic types are outstanding figures with great
achievements or special gifts. On the other hand, some millenarian leaders are not particularly distinguished individuals. "In
some regions," notes Yonina Talmon, "millenarianism is an endemic force, and when it reaches a flash-point it may seize upon
any available figure. The initiative in such cases comes primarily
from believers who sometimes almost impose the leadership position on their leader. Some of the leaders are in fact pale and in-
significant. Their elevation to such a position seems to be
accidental—they happen to be there and fulfilled the urgent
need for a prophet." [6] This pattern of leadership being bestowed
rather than emerging as a result of self-selection confirmed by a
following is especially frequent in the Melanesian cargo cults.
Another difference between messianic figures and prophets can
be seen in the fact that whereas the messiah usually is a mediator
between the human and the divine, with close kinship ties to the
deity, the prophet announces the good tidings by virtue of a mission he claims to have received from God or the gods.[7] He himself remains a mere human.

Whether a messianic figure or prophet, the charismatic leader
of a revolutionary millenarian movement offers the vision of a
new society and leads his followers toward this goal. Social psy-
chologists and sociologists studying the phenomenon of leadership have been unable to find personality traits common to all
leaders, and instead, taking a "situational" approach, they see the
leader as one who fits the needs of a particular group in a specific
situation.[8] Charismatic leadership, in particular, depends upon the
attitudes and perceptions of those who will be followers, and
since these followers will differ in different societies (and in the
same society at different times) it should be apparent that there

can be no universal charismatic type.[9] Still, we can note certain characteristics that are commonly seen as basic to a charismatic relationship. The charismatic leader very often is a person with a high energy level and considerable vitality, he exhibits coolness in the face of danger or crisis, he has fanatical faith in his cause, and he is able to evoke devotion, enthusiasm, and self-sacrifice from his followers. The charismatic leader is usually an effective orator, and his charismatic appeal often is further enhanced by the dramatic solution of a major crisis or by the performance of miraculous acts like healing the sick. As part of their personal magnetism many charismatic leaders are said to have extraordinary eyes.[10]

The charismatic leader of a revolutionary millenarian movement proposes to transform his society, he looks toward the future. Yet, to find a following, he must also communicate a sense of continuity between himself and the values, myths, and heroes of the past. His message must be appropriate to the social climate in which he operates, and his acceptance as a charismatic leader depends decisively upon the reactions of his would-be followers. As Max Weber emphasized, a leader's charisma depends on and is validated by the perceptions of the people he leads. It is not so much what a leader is but how he is regarded by those subject to his authority that determines the extent of his charisma.[11] Once a leader's charisma has been established even failure and death will not easily shake his followers' faith in him. Indeed, martyrdom often serves to enhance charisma. The African prophets Simon Kimbangu and André Matswa, for example, became more rather than less popular after their imprisonment and death.

Conceptions of Time, History, and Conflict

Members of revolutionary millenarian movements look forward to a radically new social order on earth which will represent the consummation of history. They seek not an amelioration of the human condition but an end to history as such. Humanity will be freed from pain and unhappiness, and an age of eternal bliss will begin. In many cases it is believed that such a redemption will be preceded by a great catastrophe. The world as we know it will be destroyed to prepare for the new and perfect order. Even if this apocalyptic view does not include a cosmic eschatological event, there is often the belief that the time just before the moment of redemption will be one of special stress and great suffering. God's people, the Jewish Book of Daniel prophesied, will be delivered at the moment of greatest need, and similar expectations of "messianic woes"—unprecedented upheavals and calamities as signs of the beginning of the end—can be found in other millenarian movements. Seen psychologically, as Mühlmann notes, the situation is, of course, exactly reversed. Because the present is felt to be a time of terrible and unbearable afflictions, millenarianism creates the escapist view of a terrestrial state of perfection to come. The conception of the messianic woes reflects a feeling of extreme alienation from life as it is and the need to escape from history.[12]

Salvation on earth, the millenarians believe, cannot come to pass without divine intervention. Yet, in practically all movements we also find a definite commitment to human action. The believers must employ certain measures such as prayer and cleansing to ensure their preparedness for the great event, and, more importantly, they must act to hasten the moment of redemption. Indeed, the main difference between members of millenarian sects and members of revolutionary millenarian movements is precisely the latters' resolve to revolt against their rulers to end the present state of corruption. Embued with the conviction that the end of human travail is near and that the elect are working in accordance with the divine plan of salvation, these millenarian groups possess a spirit of heroic action and extreme dedication. Believers pit themselves against the forces of evil and in one final and catastrophic struggle expect to usher in the new and yet timeless age of perfection. We have observed such an ideology of holy and total war among the Zealots in their fight against Rome, the Bohemian Taborites, the German peasants in their uprising led by Thomas Müntzer, the radical Anabaptists, the Fifth Monarchy Men in the Puritan Revolution, the Taipings in nineteenth-century China, the Sudanese Mahdia, and some of the Melanesian cargo cult and African messianic movement members.

The essence of a millenarian movement, the unwillingness to participate in ordinary human affairs and the rejection of earthly authority, results in conflict with the surrounding world and many times provoke rulers into a violent reaction; frequently a pattern of hostility is thus created without any deliberate plan on the part of the millenarians. In other cases, the willingness to use violence in order to bring about the age of nonviolence and peace is there from the very beginning. Whether a millenarian movement will be reluctantly violent or violent by design appears to depend on the religious and cultural setting in which it develops, on the chances for victory in a violent conflict, and on the nature of the leadership—all factors to which we will return at a later point in our discussion.

Millenarian groups consider themselves a religious elite, they often compensate for their lowly status in this world by claiming that they are God's elect who can do no wrong. This elitism and the accompanying sense of mission account for much of the ruthlessness and brutality seen in millenarian revolts. The enthusiasm of these groups, the spirit of total dedication to a cause of overriding importance, the conviction of doing God's will, often lead to a dehumanization of the opponent who is conceived as all evil and all depraved. The Manichean logic of sharply dividing the world into forces of good and evil was carried to its extreme by the Taipings who called their enemies outright demons. Originally noble impulses can thus be transformed into a reality of hatred and violence.[13]

The same logic of religious enthusiasm also explains the frequent occurrence of internal strife. The bitter factional disputes among the defenders of Jerusalem in the Jewish war against Rome, for example, can be traced in part to the desire of men engaged in a holy war to institute a reign of virtue and to obey God's will meticulously—the indispensable condition to obtain the divine intervention that would lead to the rout of God's enemies. Since human beings usually develop different readings of God's will, the insistence of the true believer on divine inspiration and ideological unity almost necessarily leads to splits and conflicts in the movement. The charismatic leader cannot tolerate diversity; any divergence from his view of truth is heresy that must be extirpated. The attraction that millenarian movements, in rebellion against authority, probably hold for non-conformist and contentious people may further increase divisions within such groups.[14]

Millenarianism is distinctly future oriented. The messianic redemption expected by the Jewish prophets and apocalyptic writers, notes Gershom Scholem, is utopian, it "does not repeat anything that has ever been, but presents something new."[15] Even where the idea of a return to an earlier state of affairs plays an important role, as with the followers of the medieval prophet, Joachim of Fiore, who admired the primitive purity of the Apostles of Christ, the dynamic strength derived from the millenarian creed springs from the conviction that the future will transcend the past. Speaking of the later Joachimites, Marjorie Reeves writes: "Their reading of past history enabled them to complete the pattern of things to come in the Last Age and to find their own cosmic role within this pattern. Their models might be drawn from the past, but their belief was that the life of the future would far exceed that of the past. It was not so much a recapturing of the life of the first Apostles that they expected as the creating of the life of new apostles." [16] It was in part this confident faith in a radically new future, and the inference that the coming Third Age would mean a perfection greater even than that of Christ and his Apostles, that brought on the Joachimites the charge of heresy.

The strong commitment to a decisively new future often leads to a rejection of traditional norms and religious symbols. This antinomianism and iconoclasm sometimes is a result of the conscious desire to emphasize the distinctiveness of the millenarian group. The Taipings, for example, destroyed Taoist, Buddhist, and Confucian temples and statues, in part to establish the radically new character of their religion. The wish to break completely with the past can also lead to the ritualized violation of old taboos, especially sexual conventions. In this way a new morality is asserted, the members of the group are bound together in common guilt, and internal cohesion and solidarity are strengthened. In Melanesia and South Africa, it would appear, millenarians sought to prove to themselves and to the spirits complete confidence in their charismatic leaders and in the imminence of redemption, and they therefore engaged in the wholesale destruction of pigs, cows, crops, and other treasured material objects. In the siege of Jerusalem by the Romans in the Great Jewish War the defenders may have burned the granaries for the same reason—to demonstrate their complete trust in God and in his imminent saving intervention.

Some millenarian movements are characterized by highly emotional displays of trances, mass possession, and motor phenomena such as shaking, twitching, and convulsions. These phenomena are especially widespread in Africa and among the Melanesian cargo cults where they may be tied to prevailing mores. "It would be a grievous error," writes a psychiatrist interested in comparative study, "to suppose that if a certain form of behaviour in some culture or other resembles insane behaviour it is necessarily abnormal." [17] On the other hand, more general factors may also account for these outbursts of ecstasy. Hysterical phenomena can be caused by strong feelings of deprivation, frustration, and strain for which certain kinds of motor behavior may provide relief. Also, as noted by H. Richard Niebuhr, emotional fervor is a common mark of the religion of the untutored and less privileged. "Where the power of abstract thought has not been highly developed and where inhibitions on emotional expression have not been set up by a system of polite conventions, religion must and will express itself in emotional terms." [18] The informality and spontaneity of religious expression may also give the faithful a taste of the complete liberation that is vouchsafed them in the millenarian era.[19]

Revolutionary millenarianism frequently has a special appeal to the downtrodden, the victims of political or social distress, but in many millenarian movements class does not satisfactorily explain participation in such movements. Whole communities or societies have at times been caught up in the millenarian dream. Students of German Anabaptism in the sixteenth century and of the Fifth Monarchy Men during the Puritan Revolution consider family background one of the more significant variables explaining membership. Also, women often outnumber men in these emotion-charged sectarian groups. The data at our disposal unfortunately are usually too spotty to allow a rigorous determination of the characteristics of individual participants.

Despite the pronounced forward-looking tendency of millenarian movements their vision of the future usually contains traditional elements. Indeed, as Yonina Talmon has emphasized, "it is precisely this combination of a radical revolutionary position with traditionalism which accounts for the widespread appeal of these movements." [20] Thus, for example, much of the attraction of the Taiping Rebellion can be traced to its promise of an imminent heavenly kingdom of peace, a concept that adroitly combined traditional and innovative goals. The emphasis on restoring a former condition of bliss is usually strongest during cultural disruption as when people subjected to the foreign customs of a colonial power seek to revive certain features of their traditional culture. Anthropologists call such movements "restorative" or "nativistic." [21] Basically, however, all millenarian movements partake of both restorative and innovative elements, they are oriented to the past and the future at the same time.

CAUSES

Most fundamentally, millenarian movements simply express man's dissatisfaction with the human condition, the yearning for a happier existence than is possible on earth. Since no society throughout history has been able to provide a life free of hardships and sorrows it is hardly surprising that the dream of escaping history and of reaching an age of perfection, a land without evil, or of regaining the lost paradise, has been so widespread among men at almost all times.

And yet, universal as are the difficulties of human life, millenarianism has not been the only response of man to adversity. Whole societies have suffered dumbly, others have sought to change their lot by means of reform or political or social revolution. The question, therefore, arises what specifically causes the millenarian variant of revolutionary movements. Why do some people at certain times engage in the pursuit of the millenarian dream, the search for total and ultimate redemption on earth? We suggest that such millenarian movements develop (1) in situations of distress or disorientation the roots of which are not clearly understood or which are seen as not solvable by ordinary and available remedies, (2) when a society or group is deeply attached to religious ways of thinking about the world and when the religion of that society attaches importance to millenarian ideas, (3) when a man (or men) obsessed with salvationist phantasies succeeds in establishing his charismatic leadership over a social movement.

It should be borne in mind that all these factors must be present, and indeed they usually are interrelated. The causative factor "distress," for example, as we will see in more detail later, does not represent an objective fact, corresponding to a specific empirical reality, but depends very decisively on how individuals or groups of men *perceive* reality. Leaders, and especially charismatic ones, through their teachings may often produce in their followers a strong sense of dissatisfaction and deprivation that may not have otherwise developed. Conversely, a certain kind of person will be accepted as a charismatic leader only in very specific stressful situations. Many religious ideas, too, are ambiguous and will be interpreted differently at different times and places, depending on the social setting and the political leanings of believers and leaders. The Christian idea of the "Kingdom of God" or the Confucian "Mandate of Heaven" are obvious cases in point. Last, there remains the element of historical accident that further complicates any causal analysis. If Hung Hsiu-ch'üan had passed his examinations or if Oliver Cromwell had followed his inclination in the early 1630's to emigrate to America, the course of two revolutionary millenarian movements might have taken a completely different route or they might never have begun. The most that we are able to say, therefore, is that in certain situations, given the appearance of certain ideas and men, the emergence of revolutionary millenarianism is likely.

Distress, Deprivation, and Disorientation

Dissatisfaction with the prevailing social, economic, religious, or political order that is strong enough to drive people into revolutionary action can be produced by factors external or internal to the society in question. Resentment following the loss of national independence to a foreign conqueror is an example of such an externally caused dissatisfaction; severe hardships resulting from a natural catastrophe or from oppression by a native ruling class are internally caused. In either case the hope for deliverance by revolutionary millenarianism can develop when the sense of distress is very acute and ordinary remedies are not forthcoming.

Subjection to a foreign power will be felt as especially humiliating when the people who have lost their independence considered themselves to be divinely favored or when a dethroned ruler was also a religious leader. The ancient Israelites saw themselves as God's chosen people who had been vouchsafed victory over all of their enemies through a special covenant. The destruction of the First Temple and the loss of independence successively to the Persians, Syrians, and Romans, therefore, were particularly devastating blows for which the Jews were ill prepared and which they considered preludes to the inevitable appearance of the messianic deliverer who would make God's promises of re-

demption come to pass. Similarly, following the British conquest
of Burma in 1885–86, the Buddhist people of this subjugated
country lost not only their native king but the traditional head
and protector of their religion. The resultant sense of bitterness
and distress eventually exploded in the millenarian Saya San rebellion of 1930–31 which promised the liberation of Burma
from the heathen English and the inauguration of a Golden Age
under an ideal Buddhist ruler.

A millenarian response to foreign rule is also likely when the
alien power seeks to suppress or seriously interfere with the religion of the colonized people. The decrees of the Roman emperor
Hadrian forbidding the practice of circumcision, the recitation at
public services of the most important Jewish prayer, the *Shema*,
and his decision in A.D. 130 to erect a pagan temple in the holy
city of Jerusalem, probably precipitated the messianic rebellion
against Roman rule led by Bar Kochba. In the nineteenth-century
Sudan the Mahdi's cause profited not only from the attempts of
the Egyptian rulers to stamp out the economically profitable
slave trade but also from their insistence on promoting a more orthodox form of Islam. In twentieth-century Africa, too, revolutionary millenarian movements have been encouraged by simultaneous political, cultural, and religious distress. African messianism
has arisen in a setting of colonial rule, racial discrimination, and
forced acculturation which has interfered with political and social as well as religious activities. Millenarianism there at times has
functioned as a kind of "sacred nationalism," a struggle to overcome the inferior status imposed by both colonial administrators
and missionaries.

Internally caused distress leading to revolutionary millenarianism has also been frequent. In late-medieval Europe
millenarian movements arose in areas where social change was
swift, where trade and industry were developing, where the population was increasing rapidly, and where traditional group ties
were dissolving. "Revolutionary millenarianism," writes Norman
Cohn, "drew its strength from a population living on the margin
of society—peasants without land or with too little land even
for subsistence; journeymen and unskilled workers living under
the continuous threat of unemployment; beggars and vagabonds
—in fact from the amorphous mass of people who were not simply poor but who could find no assured and recognized place in

society at all. These people lacked the material and emotional support afforded by traditional social groups; their kinship-groups had disintegrated and they were not effectively organized in village communities or in guilds; for them there existed no regular, institutionalized methods of voicing their grievances or pressing their claims." [22] For such groups of the oppressed and disinherited the idea of Christ's return to earth to establish a reign of perfect justice and well-being had an obvious appeal. Often the precipitating events for such movements were plagues, long droughts, devastating fires, and similar calamities which drastically aggravated endemic deprivation and were seen as signs of the beginning of the end.

Economic and social distress, it should be added, are not the only sources of millenarianism. During the Reformation the spirit of religious renewal, excitement, and biblicism produced a climate of widespread eschatological expectations in which hope for the Second Coming of Christ was strong. These expectations were reinforced by the discovery of the New World, for it was believed that the conversion of the remaining heathen races of mankind foreshadowed the approaching end predicted in the Book of Revelation when multitudes "from every nation, from all tribes and peoples and tongues" (7:9) would stand before the throne of God.[23] The suffering of the early Reformed believers contributed to the eschatological fervor. Many of the Anabaptists, in particular, severely persecuted by both Catholics and Protestants, interpreted their tribulations in apocalyptic terms, the messianic woes, and as a prelude to the day of reckoning when they would overthrow the godless and help establish the Kingdom of God on earth. For these radical sectarians both the pope, whom Luther himself had called the Antichrist, and the major reformers had lost all spiritual authority and legitimacy; the search for more immediate and authentic methods of redemption than the hierarchical churches were able to offer eventually led them into the path of revolutionary millenarianism. Resentment of the worldliness of the clergy and doubt about the ability of ostentatiously living prelates to help man attain salvation had had a similar effect in medieval times. Thus religious deprivation, too, can be a cause of millenarian revolt, and its impact will be especially strong when it is combined with other sources of distress. The fact that the economic situation in Holland and northwest Germany during the early 1530's had badly deteriorated facilitated the rise of the millenarian prophet John Matthys of Amsterdam and helped him establish the New Jerusalem at Münster.

A subjective awareness of distress shared by a group or society is crucial in all these types of severe dissatisfaction. As students of mass movements have recognized for some time, it is not so much the severity of deprivation that motivates revolutionaries as the discrepancy between legitimate expectations and the means for their satisfaction, a subjective state known as "relative deprivation." Such a discrepancy can be created either by a drastic worsening of conditions or by new and expanded horizons or by a combination of both.[24] Thus revolutionary millenarianism in medieval Europe developed during a time of rapid social change when poverty and hardship were no longer taken for granted, when new wants had been created amidst a widening gap between rich and poor. A militant Jewish messianism, as we have noted earlier, emerged as a result of severely disappointed hope, the contrast between the promises made by God to his chosen people and the harsh reality of foreign rule and oppression. In the colonized countries of Asia and Africa, too, relative deprivation was the key to anti-European agitation. Since the time of the First World War, in particular, people under colonial rule had become increasingly aware of the economic and social gap between their own condition and that of their European colonizers. The resultant severe resentment, when more direct political remedies were out of reach, led to millenarian agitation. The fact that frustrated expectation, rather than actual suffering, causes such movements of protest can be seen in some of the cargo cults in the east central highlands of New Guinea. Here the white man had not yet entered the secluded habitat of these people, and their material or social condition had not changed, when, because these aborigines had heard tales of the riches of the white man, they developed an intense desire for the white man's goods. Such changed expectations and the acute frustration that followed the inability to satisfy these new wants eventually led to the emergence of a cargo cult.[25]

The development of new expectations that have remained unfulfilled has also been an important factor in the rise of African messianic movements. As a result of reading the Bible, which had been translated into their own languages, and exposure to the biblical ideals of equality, justice, and fairness, African Christian converts began to perceive the discrepancy between biblical Christianity and the discriminatory and patronizing ways of the European missionaries and colonial rulers. These religious writings and the prophetic strain contained in them thrust into the popular consciousness a powerful revolutionary dynamic, creating a strong sense of religious and eventually political deprivation which helped generate revolutionary millenarian movements.

In many cases it is not so much economic deprivation on the part of the lower classes in a stratified society but the experience by an entire colonized people of disorientation and anomie that causes millenarian movements. The impact of a powerful and totally different culture, the transition from a relatively stable village community to a fast-changing and impersonal urban life—all these aspects of the modernization process can have a highly unsettling effect and create considerable anxiety and existential dread. In such a situation, a crisis comparable to the identity crisis of the individual may occur in an entire community,[26] and a new religious cult that allays these anxieties and creates a secure sense of identity may arise. The emergence of several thousand separatist churches in twentieth-century Africa can be traced in part to this phenomenon; many of these independent churches have developed into revolutionary millenarian movements.

Distress, deprivation, and disorientation create preconditions for revolutionary unrest, but this unrest will take the form of millenarianism only in certain cultural and religious settings. An examination of the nature of such settings is our next task.

Millenarian Beliefs

Revolutionary millenarian movements have arisen only in countries or among groups in which religion determines and dominates the total world outlook, in periods when the political and religious aspects of society were still largely undifferentiated.[27] In such a milieu any challenge to the prevailing value system must be couched in religious language, and leadership tends to be charismatic. This was often the situation in medieval Europe, and it is the situation in many of the developing nations where education is limited, and the nature of the problems confronting these societies is often not clearly perceived. In most countries of Europe and the Americas, however, intellectual modernization, beginning with the skeptical mentality and the scientific discoveries of the sixteenth and seventeenth centuries, has created a situation in which traditional religious ideas no longer permeate the ethos of society. Social problems can now be attacked frontally, and revolutionary movements follow a more secular model; they emphasize political action rather than reliance upon supernatural assistance. In such a setting we can still find millenarian sects, attracting individuals of fundamentalist religious temperament, but most of those seeking a remedy for severe economic, political, or social distress will support secular revolutionary movements.

Messianic ideas can be found in most cultures and religions. They were present in Egypt in the seventeenth century B.C. and perhaps earlier; they were also to be found in Babylon at about the same time.[28] A strong millenarian tradition developed for the first time in Persian Zoroastrianism, linked to the eschatological myth of an end of the world by fire. This event, from which the good would escape unharmed, it was believed, would bring "a new world, free from old age, death, decomposition and corruption" and "the world shall be perfectly renewed."[29] From Persia this new conception of time and history, breaking with the view of practically all traditional societies that man's existence is caught in an infinite repetition of cosmic cycles and promising him an end to suffering, probably found its way into Judaism and from there into Christianity and Islam.[30] The Book of Daniel, written at the height of the Maccabean revolt, about 165 B.C., is the first great apocalyptic work of Judaism, and it has been the prototype of all later works of eschatology. Written at a time of terrible hardships for the Jewish people suffering under Syrian rule, the Book of Daniel has most of the elements of millenarian hope—deliverance by God at the moment of greatest need, the imminent coming of an everlasting Kingdom of God to be the final stage of history, the resurrection of the dead. Many other such apocalyptic works were written during the time of Roman lordship over Palestine, and early Christianity, too, despite the ambivalent teachings of Jesus of Nazareth himself about the coming Kingdom of God, had a pronounced millenarian character. The Apocalypse of John (or the Book of Revelation), which was probably written during a time of severe persecution in the last two decades of the first Christian century, is the most famous Christian apocalyptic work. Its prophecy of a return of Christ to establish his messianic kingdom on earth for 1000 years, an inter-regnum to be followed by "a new heaven and a new earth" (21:1) where there will be neither death nor pain, has had a powerful influence upon later millenarian movements.

Both Judaism and Christianity, and later Islam, have a teleological philosophy of history, that God's plan will be fulfilled and that mankind will finally be redeemed in a state of universal happiness. Not surprisingly it has been this linear view of history that has provided the most probable setting for a variety of millenarian traditions and movements. Revolutionary chiliasm, Norman Cohn has observed, thrives best "where history is imagined as having an inherent purpose which is preordained to be realized on earth in a single, final consummation." [31] It is more difficult to construct a millenarian belief system when the world is seen as caught in an endlessly repeated cycle of death and regeneration, and the majority of millenarian movements are indeed linked to the Judaic-Christian tradition. Because of its world-wide missionary activity Christianity, in particular, has most frequently been the basis of millenarianism. Despite the fact that orthodox Christianity has repudiated the idea of a terrestrial kingdom of abundance and happiness and instead, following St. Augustine, has stressed the promise of the spiritual delivery of the individual soul in heaven, the millenarian tradition has always retained a foothold in Christianity. Indeed, wherever Christian missionaries have gone to work, the millenarian promise of an eternal earthly paradise has had a strong appeal for new converts.

In modern times it has been Protestantism with its tradition of individual interpretation of Scripture and, especially, millenarian branches like the Seventh Day Adventists and the Watchtower movement that have spread millenarian ideas. In a few instances millenarian movements have appeared in a Catholic setting. The sect of the Antonians in the Congo of the early eighteenth century, the Lazzaretti movement in Italy in 1870, a revival of the medieval Joachimite heresy, or the millenarianism of the Brazilian messiah, Antonio Conselheiro, in the late nineteenth century, are cases in point.[32] The leaders of several Melanesian cargo cults have been baptized Roman Catholics. But the hierarchical organization of the Catholic church by and large has succeeded in discouraging millenarian tendencies, just as the hierarchy has managed to institutionalize and co-opt the apocalyptic visions of the

church's mystics and seers.[33] Such visions could threaten not
only long-held doctrinal positions but also more tangible political
interests of the church. A decree of the Sacred Congregation of
the Holy Office issued on July 21, 1944 once again reaffirmed the
inadmissibility of teaching the millenarian doctrine of the return
of Jesus Christ to preside over a visible terrestrial kingdom.[34] In
modern Africa the great majority of millenarian movements have
emerged in a Protestant climate, especially as the result of an unrestricted access to the Bible and the prophetic message contained
therein. In some cases we can even trace the influence of specific
millenarian elements. The favorite book in the Bible of Te Va,
the leader of the Hauhau movement among the Maori people of
New Zealand in 1862, was the Book of Revelation.[35] The Exodus
story of the miraculous deliverance of the Jews from slavery in
Egypt has been another inspiration to revolt—in Africa as well
as among black slaves in North America.[36]

Whereas the linear conception of history of the Judaic-Chris-
tian-Islamic tradition has been conducive to the development of
millenarian ideas, the great religions of Asia—Hinduism, Buddhism, Taoism—have not entirely lacked such tendencies. In
Hinduism the reappearance of Vishnu as Kalki will usher in an
age of abundance; in Buddhism the coming of Maitreya, the future Buddha, will introduce a life of peace and plenty; in Taoism
a perfect ruler will appear to transform life on earth and guarantee man's immortality. However, these messianic ideas have not
always led to millenarian movements. In India, for example, the
millenarian myth of Kalki has not caught the popular imagination. This may have been due to the enormous lengths of the
eternally recurring cycles of Hindu chronology which puts the
coming of the redeemer so far in the future as to take away all
hope of relief in any humanly foreseeable time. Moreover, since
Hinduism knows no end of history, and the coming of Kalki was
believed to repeat itself at the end of each of these huge time periods, the figure of the savior lacked the unique status of the Messiah in the Judaic-Christian tradition. The help offered by the
Hindu redeemer is not final, he cannot create a new heaven and
earth or arise above the perpetual flux of history.[37] There is no
promise of an ultimate triumph of the good or the vindication of
the righteous. Last, the conception in Hinduism of human history
as part of a cyclical cosmic process moving according to inexora-

ble laws leaves little if any room for man's history-making ability; [38] the other-worldly orientation of Hinduism with its devaluation of earthly success, the absence of egalitarian ideas, the acceptance of the rigid caste system, and the fact that Hindu religion has brought forth only what Max Weber called "exemplary prophets," men who provided a model for a way of life of personal virtue,[39] seem further to have discouraged the spread of millenarian ideas. The few reported cases of Indian millenarian movements, such as the Birsaites among the Munda tribe of Bihar in the years 1874 to 1901, are predominantly Christian both in inspiration and idiom.[40]

In the case of Theravada Buddhism dominant in Ceylon, Burma, Thailand, and India, the cyclical conception of history with its immense stretches of time and the absence of either a beginning or an end of the world also appears to have discouraged hope for the final salvation of mankind. The Theravada, the "teaching of the elders," knows the idea of Maitreya, the future Buddha, but this messianic figure by and large has not inspired revolutionary millenarianism. His coming is not expected in the foreseeable future, and his role then is limited mainly to that of helping man achieve spiritual liberation, the removal of ignorance. The belief in Maitreya in Ceylon involves the notion of a god granting favors to his devotees rather than that of a savior.[41] The fact that kings, many of whom were anything but benefactors of their people, often claimed the title of the future Buddha further weakened the revolutionary significance of such a messiah. During the numerous armed clashes that preceded the conquest and pacification of Burma by the British in the nineteenth and early twentieth centuries the titles of Universal Monarch and Maitreya were claimed by rebel leaders, some of them monks, seeking to restore Buddhism to its former position of eminence. Even after independence was achieved the coming of such a righteous king continued to be expected by what one observer has called a "messianic Buddhist association." [42] An uprising in Thailand around the turn of the century is said to have begun with the prophecy of the coming of a "noble righteous ruler" with great merit who would rule the world.[43] But these appear to be phenomena arising in special circumstances, exceptions to the rule. Theravada Buddhism generally has not produced millenarianism. In Burma the so-called messianic associations have remained "semi-subterranean personalized cults without impact on Buddhism or on the majority of its followers." [44]

Mahayana Buddhism, on the other hand, recognizes *bodhisatt-vas* (literally "beings of enlightenment"), who are believed to have stayed in this world to help others reach enlightenment, and some Chinese Buddhist sects worshipped these saviors as messianic figures who would relieve suffering and bring happiness and prosperity. Usually a minority religion, Chinese Buddhism conse-quently has frequently played a revolutionary role. Almost from the time Buddhism was introduced in China in the first century of the Christian era, various Buddhist sects and secret societies have led millenarian revolts of the peasantry, promising delivery from turmoil and poverty. Various subsects of Taoism similarly were occasionally involved in rebellion. Messianic hope here cen-tered on a perfect emperor who would realize the vision of the deified Lao Tzu. In a situation where the Confucian orthodoxy often failed to meet both the spiritual and material needs of the Chinese people, heterodox movements promising relief from spiri-tual emptiness and everyday misery were never completely elimi-nated. Thus despite the fact that orthodox Chinese Buddhism and Taoism have few elements conducive to messianism, unorthodox branches of both religions have often been involved in millenarian movements. The fact that, once they were successful, these rebel movements restored and continued the traditional socio-political order rather than introducing basic changes does not change the revolutionary appeal of these heterodox sects.

Messianic, eschatological, and millenarian ideas and movements can also be found outside the major world religions, in primitive societies not in contact with Christianity or any other developed religious system. Many preliterate societies know the concept of a returning hero or god. One such redeemer, known as Mansren, who was expected to inaugurate an age of plenty and resurrect the dead, figured prominently in several New Guinean myths which later fused with the Western-inspired cargo cults. A re-cent movement among the Khmu of Laos involved the myth of a culture hero immured in a cave who will distribute his great store of goods after the proper ritual acts have been performed.[45] The case of the Guarani Indians of Amazonian Brazil is another exam-ple of a millenarian movement that apparently arose in an en-tirely independent fashion and without contact with other cultures. Expecting an end of the world, these Indians engaged in periodic migrations to the sea from where they hoped to reach the "land without evil" and escape the coming cosmic catastrophe. As much as we can tell, these migrations, involving fights against hostile Indians and whites on the way, were not prompted by population pressure, famine, or war, nor by contact with the Portuguese conquerors. To escape from the Europeans the Guaranis could have moved into the next valley in the vast underpopulated regions of the Amazonian interior. It would indeed appear that we are here dealing with a messianic movement motivated entirely by religion and perhaps rooted in existential dread—a projection of fears of the death of the human body.[46] That the desire to live in a pure and beautiful world may have been intensified by the shock of the Portuguese conquest cannot be ruled out, though it seems clear that the idea of the "land without evil" itself predates the coming of the Europeans.[47]

Revolutionary millenarianism, we can conclude, can be motivated by a great variety of messianic beliefs. Judaic-Christian messianism is undoubtedly the most widespread of these beliefs, but it is not the only one. It is "fatuously and absurdly ethnocentric to suppose," writes an American student of these phenomena, "that every native messiah is necessarily patterned on a European Christ. The fact is not so much that all native messiahs derive historically from the only genuine messiah, as that Christ himself is one example of a culturally very common type." [48] Certain religious belief systems more than others are conducive to the emergence of messianic ideas, but sometimes millenarian movements can develop even in the framework of a cyclical, world-renouncing cosmology.

Prophets

Social movements require leadership, but the leader is not necessarily one of the causes of such movements. In the case of revolutionary millenarianism, on the other hand, leaders usually are just that. They are impelled by motives that combine sincere altruism, selfish aims, and religiosity and they are often mad or emotionally disturbed; they act to help bring a millenarian movement into being.

The leader of a revolutionary millenarian movement is the bearer of the chiliastic prophecy. Unlike the mystic, the prophet actively seeks a following for his ethical and political message; [49] he is a charismatic individual whose inspiration usually derives from some special episode or experience in his life history. Sometimes the future prophet has hallucinatory and salvationist phantasies for months if not years without finding a following, without becoming the leader of a group. In other instances the prophet's personal religious experience and the birth of a movement are almost simultaneous. In either case the charismatic prophet is not just a "reflection" of certain social processes. As Max Weber has argued, the bearer of charisma often acts as an innovative force to change the course of history. There was nothing inevitable about the emergence of prophet figures like Mohammed Ahmed, the mystic leader of the Mahdia of the Sudan, or Hung Hsiu-ch'üan, the crazed heavenly king of the Taiping Rebellion. Each man left his special imprint upon the fate of his people. Their prophecy, even though based in part on their cultural heritage, sprang from their own, very personal religious experience and became an important factor in a powerful social movement. Even where messianic expectations are rampant, as in the time of Jesus of Nazareth, the objective situation that may encourage the emergence of a charismatic leader does not determine the nature of the prophetic message. The charismatic millenarian leader, therefore, is always an initiator; his vision creates the new ideology of a movement.[50]

Leadership by the charismatic prophet has been termed the catalyst of the millenarian movement; the leader's function is "to make a latent conflict conscious, to give form to a pre-existing movement, to impart direction to its energies, and to help it focus on definite ends." As in the case of a substance introduced to catalyze a chemical reaction, the effect of the leader is said to be determined by the situation in which he acts, "without the right substances and setting his intervention would be entirely without avail." [51] The analogy of chemical catalysis stresses dynamic interaction here of certain social conditions and a charismatic leader. As we have argued earlier, there can be no millenarian movement without distress or disorientation being perceived. But the charismatic leader does not merely reflect distress or precipitate and activate ideas already in existence; he does not only champion felt needs. A leader, no matter how gifted, cannot conjure a social movement out of a void, but the charismatic leader may create or increase the expectations and dissatisfactions which lead to a revolutionary situation.[52]

The millenarian prophecy carried and spread by the charismatic leader often functions as the source of revolutionary sentiments and ideas. A common pattern here is the simultaneous appearance of an individual with extraordinary leadership ability and apocalyptic fantasies and an ongoing social upheaval. The prophecy of total redemption injected by Thomas Müntzer into the German peasant movement, by John of Leyden into the attempts of the merchants and artisans of Münster to oppose the economic policies of their bishop-sovereign, by Hung Hsiuchu'üan into the search of the bandit-ridden peasants of Kwangsi province in nineteenth-century China for security, transformed each of these limited movements into a revolutionary attack upon the political and social order. It was the millenarian prophecy pronounced by the charismatic figure that created a revolutionary mass movement where previously there had existed only a demand for the reform of certain concrete grievances. On the strength of supernatural revelation the conflict was described as a cataclysm that would transform the world once and for all. The ideology of these revolutionary millenarian movements, as Norman Cohn speaking of European medieval examples emphasizes, "in each case corresponded not to the objective social situation and the possibilities it offered but to the salvationist fantasies of a handful of freelance preachers; and they were accordingly boundless." [53] That, too, of course, is one of the main reasons why all of these movements failed.

By pointing out the connection between overreaching aims and failure we do not want to suggest a pattern of historical inevitability. Though millenarian movements have so far always been unsuccessful in their great design—the new world of peace and perfection has eluded them—in many instances these movements have scored impressive victories and achieved many of their goals before they were finally defeated at great cost. To be sure, in the process of consolidating earthly successes a millenarian movement often loses much of its apocalyptic fervor. The victorious Mahdist regime in the Sudan, for example, gradually took on the features of a traditional sultanate, and the building of a workable state by the Khalifa, the successor of the Mahdi, necessitated abandoning the principles of millenarian theocracy. But

to the extent that a revolutionary millenarian movement thus becomes more "realistic" its chances of success grow and it is at this
point that able leadership can make the difference between victory and defeat. Thus an ambitious Chinese Buddhist monk
leading a rebellion of the millenarian Maitreya sect in 1368 succeeded in deposing the Yuan and became the founder of the
Ming dynasty. The Fifth Monarchy Men during the Puritan
Revolution, on the other hand, were handicapped by their lack of
forceful and sufficiently charismatic leaders, and their grand designs, therefore, were probably doomed from the very start. Even
in a situation of intense millenarian excitement as in the Puritan
Revolution the quality of leadership is crucial.

   Do charismatic leaders emerge in certain social settings more
often than in others? Basically, of course, the culture of a society
must sanction the kind of leader-follower relationship that is involved in the phenomenon of charismatic leadership. Several leading figures of the Taiping Rebellion were able to establish their
credentials as charismatic leaders through the practice of sorcery,
a commonly accepted activity among the Hakka people in southern China where the Taipings originated. Such a validation of
charisma would seem out of place in an atheistic society like
Communist China or in an essentially secular society committed
to rationality like the United States today. Some segments of the
counterculture in the United States, disillusioned with science
and technology, may find solace in magic and the rituals of satan-
ism but these are obviously marginal phenomena.[54]

   It has also been suggested by many writers, including Max
Weber, that charismatic individuals will be the natural leaders "in
times of psychic, physical, economic, ethical, religious, political
distress."[55] The fact that in such a milieu of perceived deprivation charismatic leadership is often easily transferred from one
person to another—the succession of John Matthys by John
Bockelson as prophet-king of the Anabaptist New Jerusalem in
Münster is a good example—indicates how persistent the demand for charisma is in certain circumstances.[56] The Protestant
Reformation, generally, was undoubtedly a strong stimulus to the
spirit of prophecy. "The abolition of mediators, the stress on the
individual conscience," observes Christopher Hill, "left God
speaking direct to his elect. It was incumbent on them to make
public his message."[57]

In stressing the importance of a milieu favorable to charisma, we must bear in mind that, as indicated earlier, the prophet himself is often the active revolutionary agent whose message crystallizes the crisis that demanded charismatic leadership. Stated succinctly: "The point to be made is that the actions of the leader may help define the situation that is stipulated as a prerequisite or precondition of his emergence." [58] The prophet not only reflects an objective situation, the world as it is, but his ambitious and challenging vision of what the world ought to be decisively shapes the environment in which he operates. As a student of medieval millenarian prophecy has pointed out, the prophet's ideas, stimulating the imagination, give his followers hope and thus move them to action. "A prophet foretells the future; he can also create it." [59] There exists a pattern of dynamic interaction between leader and situation in which the message of the prophet is more than just a response to collective needs in a time of trouble. He, too, is a cause.

The finding that prophetic figures are seen most frequently in times of crisis and disorder may also help us understand the process of religious conversion that often precedes the emergence of such a prophet. Many of the great religious prophets of mankind as well as many of the charismatic leaders of millenarian movements have been described as men suffering from various mental disorders. St. Paul, Mohammed, and most of the Jewish prophets like Hosea, Isaiah, and Jeremiah are said to have exhibited signs of psychotic behavior—visions, hallucinatory experiences, ecstatic states, and trances. The ecstacy of the pre-exile prophets, writes Max Weber, "was accompanied or preceded by a variety of pathological states and acts." [60] Similar behavior patterns have been reported for many of the minor prophets who led millenarian revolts. Indeed, several of these men were obviously deranged. Hung Hsiu-ch'üan, John of Leyden, Sabbatai Zevi, Mohammed ibn 'Abd Allah (known as the mad Mullah), Antonio Conselheiro are some of the better known millenarian leaders about whose mental illness there can be little doubt. However, all these men were able to function as charismatic leaders of social movements, they turned their abnormal mental behavior into a special asset, and in many cases their experience of religious conversion functioned as a therapeutic process, facilitating a constructive use of internal conflicts.

The great majority of reported cases of religious conversion involve adolescents.[61] For such young people, as William James observed, conversion may be a perfectly normal phenomenon, "incidental to the passage from the child's small universe to the wider intellectual and spiritual life of maturity."[62] A study of the youthful members of a Swedish revivalist church revealed that almost all of them had been brought up in religious homes and their conversion was merely "a detail in a larger socialization process."[63] On the other hand, the experience of religious conversion by adult prophetic figures usually has pathological roots, it represents a way of overcoming severe mental stress, and such religious conversion is therefore often only a pseudosolution of personal problems.[64]

Mental strain can be caused by severe traumatic experiences. The repeated failure of Hung Hsiu-ch'üan to pass his civil service examinations is a good example of how frustrated ambition and humiliation can lead to mental disturbance. A state of serious social and religious disorganization, interfering with the normal processes of maturation and a secure sense of personal identity, may also produce mental stress. In seventeenth-century England, it has been suggested, large numbers of men, facing the terror of sin and damnation without the Catholic confession and absolution, and having been taken out of the certainties of the medieval village, became Puritan "saints" in order to escape social disorder and personal anxiety.[65] Whatever the source of mental stress, religious conversion may relieve it.

Practically all reported cases of adult religious conversion include a history of suffering. "Whether it be the experience of illness, mutilation, imprisonment, or hunger, or some domestic misfortune, or moral perturbation," notes one student of this psychological phenomenon, "it is indisputable that every true conversion has suffering for its antecedent."[66] There is helplessness, anxiety, and a sense of oppression and nervousness.[67] Prior to the conversion experience many persons are inactive and depressed, with an extreme sense of guilt. The actual experience of religious conversion is usually an acute hallucinatory episode of brief duration which results in an observable change in behavior. Stress and tension are reduced if not alleviated, feelings of escape from sin and of happiness and exaltation are expressed, and a new sense of identity emerges. A fresh psychic systematization, a "reintegration of the ego," [68] has taken place as a result of which the convert is said to be "twice-born."

The precise physiological mechanisms of this dramatic therapeutic experience are not clear. The anthropologist A.F.C. Wallace has described religious conversion as "mazeway synthesis," a reorganization of the brain's codified archive of perceptions of the external world and its values. At a critical point of mazeway disorder, Wallace argues, a convulsive effort takes place to overcome the severe stress experienced, a new value system is created that is linked to the existence of supernatural beings, and internal biopsychic equilibrium is restored. As an example of such prophetic revelation and religious inspiration Wallace uses the conversion of an Indian named Handsome Lake among the Seneca tribe of New York state in 1799 which led to the creation of a new Indian religion.[69] Needless to say, this explanation of the physiology of religious conversion remains highly speculative.

Some men who have gone through the experience of religious conversion become strong personalities and leaders, capable of inspiring enthusiasm and devotion to a cause.[70] Social support, in turn, tends to have a stabilizing impact on the personality of the prophet. The eccentricities of George Fox, the founder of Quakerism, are said to have become less marked as large numbers of people responded to his message.[71] For other men, however, the therapeutic value of conversion is incomplete. If ego strength is insufficient to handle the "combined unconscious and conscious conflicts," a psychiatrist studying religious conversion has observed, a loss of reality testing and the development of a delusional system may result.[72] Behavior may then be marked by irrational, hysterical, and destructive actions. Many of the wonder-working saviors of medieval Europe are described by Norman Cohn as such paranoid megalomaniacs who "saw themselves as incarnate gods or at least as vessels of divinity, they really believed that through their coming all things would be made new."[73] Clinicians are well familiar with this disorder called "reformatory or religious paranoia." Patients afflicted with this disease feel "called upon to reform society and bring about a new state of paradise on earth, or preach a new gospel."[74] In situations of social distress such a messianic conviction can easily communicate itself to a multitude of followers, and if the environment is one where eccentric and extravagant behavior is readily accepted it will be difficult to distinguish the godly from the mentally ill.[75] Indeed, sometimes the yearning for such deliverers is so great that crude imposters manage to pass themselves off as saviors of their people. Given our limited knowledge of human motivation and beliefs the question of whether someone is a sincere fanatic or an imposter or a mixture of both is usually difficult to answer. That many such men, whatever their precise psychic make-up, have had a tremendous influence in history is clear.

OUTCOMES

All revolutionary millenarian movements in history have failed to accomplish their central objective—the attainment of heaven on earth. The Millennium has not come, and, as one would expect, this failure of the prophecy of redemption has usually created serious problems for such movements. Most of them have indeed been relatively short-lived. The promise of imminent and total delivery at first is a source of strength, attracting followers eager to participate in the final struggle for justice and plenty, but, when setbacks occur and divine assistance fails to materialize, the movement commonly fails to survive this disappointment and disintegrates.

Millenarians have reacted to defeats and dashed hopes in several different ways. For some of them a cushioning effect to initial failure was provided by the concept of the "messianic woes." According to this idea, first found in the Book of Daniel, God will redeem his people at the moment of greatest need and only after a prolonged period of intense suffering. It was reliance upon this prophecy that hardened the resistance of the Jews defending Jerusalem against the Romans in the Great Jewish War and inspired them to fight on ferociously until the very end of the long siege. Altogether it is probably true that the promise of final redemption and divine assistance makes people accept with great willingness supreme sacrifices and acts as a counterforce to the rational calculation of the chances of success.

In the case of some Christian millenarian sects when the Second Coming of Christ does not occur as prophesied, there follows not an immediate dispersion of the disappointed members but instead increased proselytizing. Thus the American Second

Adventists or Millerites, for example, tried to resolve the cognitive dissonance induced by the failure of Jesus to appear in the year 1840, as predicted, by stepping up their missionary activity. Similar reactions have been reported about a more recent flying saucer cult. In the words of the investigators of this seemingly paradoxical phenomenon: "If more and more people can be persuaded that the system of belief is correct, then clearly it must, after all, be correct." [76] They add that there is a limit, however, beyond which belief cannot withstand disconfirmation. The Millerites survived several disappointments, but after another date set for the return of Christ, October 22, 1844, had proven incorrect the sect finally collapsed. In the case of revolutionary millenarian movements the impact of disappointed hope is greatly magnified by the heavy casualties which a suppressed revolt usually entails. Few movements, therefore, have been able to maintain their enthusiasm for any length of time after a number of serious defeats.

A more typical response to repeated rout is the adjustment of the doctrine that originally provided the impulse for the revolutionary movement. Jewish messianism, after three catastrophic defeats at the hands of the Romans, was transformed from a militant creed of eschatological war against pagan enemies into a doctrine of passive waiting for delivery by God, a redemption that would take place in the indefinite future and that should not be hurried. A similar change in doctrine can be observed in the case of Jehovah's Witnesses. After prophetic failures in 1878, 1881, and 1914, explained retrospectively as a result of the fallibility of human judgment, the sect for some years refrained from any dated prophecy of the Second Coming of Christ, while at the same time it asserted that certain supernatural "events," constituting symbolic proof of the millenarian prophecy and not open to disconfirmation, had actually transpired. The more recently heard predictions tied to the middle of the 1970's are couched in sufficiently vague language to minimize the danger of falsification by empirical counterevidence.[77]

The substitution of a diffuse and spongy prophecy for a specific one, involving a precise date, time, and place, represents a possible course of action for millenarian sects committed to passive waiting for God's saving action. It probably is less useful to a revolutionary millenarian movement which cannot so easily manipulate the zeal and enthusiasm of its supporters who are anxious to play their part in the cosmic drama. In the case of the latter, therefore, decisive defeat has usually led to radical change in the character and ideology of the movement. Thus after the Taborites had finally been crushed at the battle of Lipan in 1434, the doctrine of chiliastic total war gave way to nonviolence preached as a sacred principle. The intellectual descendants of the bloodthirsty Taborites, the Bohemian or Moravian Brethren, were dedicated pacifists. Similarly, following the disaster of Münster, the Anabaptists returned to the political quietism of the founders of the sect. Known as Mennonites, the Dutch Anabaptists again conceived of the coming Kingdom of God as an entirely spiritual entity. Various offshoots of Anbaptism survive to this day as communities of mutual aid and brotherhood who have withdrawn from a world they failed to convert to their ways.

Sometimes when the chance of scoring a military upset over the oppressors appears completely unrealistic a millenarian movement may make a commitment to nonviolence from the very beginning. Thus in the late 1880's, after the end of the Indian wars, the prophets of the Ghost Dance religion among the North American Plains Indians predicted that after a series of disastrous earthquakes, storms, and floods a happy Millennium would follow in which the Indians would enjoy boundless prairies covered with wild grass and filled with great herds of buffalo and other game. Generally the prophets of this rapidly spreading cult warned against fighting and preached amity with the white man. The battle of Wounded Knee on December 29, 1890 was the result of an unfortunate incident and certainly was not planned by the Sioux who suffered so horribly in the resulting massacre.[78] Similarly, the millenarian sect of Mumboism among the Gusii people of Kenya, which came into being just before the First World War after two decisive military defeats, advocated a withdrawal from the world of action. The sect limited itself to rituals and prophecies of the coming of a great cataclysm in which British colonial rule would be utterly destroyed and the Africans would become rich and powerful.[79]

The fact that Russian society, though often charged with apocalyptic expectations, failed to bring forth revolutionary millenarian movements as found in the West may also be due in large measure to the hopelessness of armed rebellion, the result of the oppressive institution of serfdom and the heavy hand of the

Tsars. Under these circumstances, the Old Believers (or *Raskol-niki*) in the second half of the seventeenth century, as one of their historians notes, "found flight from Antichrist's power a more attractive alternative than open revolt." [80] Thousands of others burned themselves to death rather than submit to the liturgical reforms of Patriarch Nikon. Flight from an ostensibly Christian world in order to preserve the true faith and martyrdom or self-mutilation appear to have been traditional responses to persecution in the Russian church. The sect of the Skoptsy, which first appeared around 1770, expected the coming of the Millennium when their number reached 144,000, the symbol of completeness foretold in the Book of Revelation (7:4), but they made no effort to hurry the end and were generally law abiding.[81] Indeed the Skoptsys' rejection of the world, from the early days of the sect expressed most dramatically in the practice of voluntary castration, found numerous adherents among the upper classes.[82] Russian sectarianism, undoubtedly, has often provided a rallying point for the discontented and oppressed, but the example of the Old Believers and the Skoptsy makes untenable the assertion of the sociologist Stark that this religious dissent was "above all a vehicle for the revolutionary feelings of a downtrodden class." [83]

If decisive military defeat usually spells the end of a revolutionary millenarian movement so does success. Deradicalization caused by the emergence of a large organizational structure, a mass constituency, and a recognized place in society is, of course, a phenomenon well known from observation of various modern radical political movements [84] as well as religious movements. The histories of Zoroastrianism, Christianity, Islam, and the Bahai faith provide examples of the transformation of a millenarian creed into an institutionalized religion.[85] The natural process, with the passage of time, often leads to changes in structure and doctrine. By its very nature, H. Richard Niebuhr has argued, the sectarian type of organization has difficulty surviving the arrival of children born to the members of the first generation. The sect must then "take on the character of an educational and disciplinary institution, with the purpose of bringing the new generation into conformity with the ideals and customs which have become traditional. Rarely does a second generation hold the convictions it has inherited with a fervor equal to that of its fathers, who fashioned these convictions in the heat of conflict and at the risk of martyrdom. As generation succeeds generation, the isolation of the community from the world becomes more difficult." [86] Changes in the basic character of a religion or movement are usually the result of mutually reinforcing factors. Thus the fact that the illegal Kimbanguist cult in the Congo after the Second World War had gradually abandoned political protest probably was one of the reasons for its rapid expansion. The deradicalization of the former militant, anti-white movement led the Belgian authorities to grant legal recognition to "The Church of Jesus Christ on Earth by Simon Kimbangu," and this legalization in turn contributed to the rapid growth of the church and furthered the trend of deradicalization. The relationship between success and deradicalization is thus one of dynamic interaction.

A similar pattern of unintended consequences is at work when a sect thrives economically as a result of religious discipline. H. Richard Niebuhr observed in his study of the origins of denominationalism that "wealth frequently increases when the sect subjects itself to the discipline of asceticism in work and expenditure," [87] and such worldly success contributes to the attenuation of the revolutionary impulse. Thus the peasant members of the erstwhile revolutionary millenarian sect of the Lazzarettiani today are more than averagely well-off and contain many men of substance.[88] Needless to say, a movement that has prospered will find it difficult to maintain its original sense of alienation from the world, it "acquires a stake in the stability of the order in which this success has been won." [89]

Another frequent trend, especially in many developing nations, is the transformation of revolutionary millenarianism into secular political radicalism and nationalism. For this reason many students consider revolutionary millenarianism in primitive societies an essentially pre-political phenomenon that occurs mainly in periods of transition. Millenarianism, suggests Yonina Talmon, generally "does not appear in areas largely untouched by modernization, and it appears only rarely in areas in which modernization has reached an advanced stage. It occurs mainly during the intermediate, 'neither here nor there' stages of modernization." [90] Millenarian movements often play a unifying role here, bringing together previously isolated or even hostile groups in a new unity transcending kinship and provincial loyalties. Millenarianism thus is a precursor of political awakening, and functions as a "rudimentary nationalism"[91] which sooner or later is "followed by movements of a more rational kind."[92]

Both in Africa and Melanesia millenarian movements have indeed served as a kind of preparatory school for nationalists and revolutionaries. As the natives of Melanesia become more familiar with the ways of the white man and better educated their cargo cults often yield to secular forms of political organization. In Africa, millenarianism has functioned as a kind of "sacred nationalism." And yet, many of these movements are tribal rather than pan-tribal in their political aspirations, and the preoccupation with religious concerns often can lead to quietism and thus delay the development of secular politics. After the achievement of independence, movements like the Lumpa church of Zambia can become a real hindrance to national integration; new regimes, demanding an exclusive and direct relationship with their citizens, distrust the millenarians' organizational capacity, and conflict ensues.[93] Last, but equally important, we must beware of a mechanical, evolutionary interpretation of millenarianism. Whereas the most frequent sequence of development in these emerging nations indeed is from religion to politics the opposite trend can also be observed. In the case of André Matswa in the former French Congo, for example, a political movement with purely secular aims changed into a messianic cult,[94] albeit with pronounced political content, and a similar change occurred in the Hauhau movement of the Maori people of New Zealand in 1862.[95]

In the advanced societies of the West millenarianism has largely become the preserve of fundamentalist sects, and revolutionary impulses have found secular outlets. This is probably due, on the one hand, to the fact that these societies are no longer dominated by a religious ethos and, on the other hand, to the slim chance of success of a rebellion led by a small group of militants. For the same reason, secular insurrectionist movements like the Blanquists and revolutionary Anarchists have been superseded by class parties emphasizing political organization and political action. In such a setting millenarian sects like Jehovah's Witnesses or the Adventists are non-political and pacifist. As Worsley notes, these sects "blame the world's evils not on the rulers of society, on a dominant Church or on a foreign government, but on the people themselves as worldly sinners. Their sins are the root of evil; salvation can come only by recognition of guilt and by self-purification, not by war against the ungodly Establishment." [96] The saints are still expected to inherit the earth, but their triumph depends on God not on human action. Our knowledge of the social composition of these sects is rather limited, but it would seem that they appeal primarily not to the very poor but to the lonely, to people with limited education or in the backwaters of a society overwhelmingly committed to rationality, science, and progress.[97] Many of the converts to the millenarian Doomsday Cult studied by John Lofland had been raised in small towns and rural communities, and all of them had "retained a general propensity to impose religious meaning on events." [98] As a student of Pentecostalism has pointed out, even with the alleviation of the worst poverty, modern society still has many underprivileged—men and women who are or consider themselves disadvantaged and rejected for reasons of appearance, education, temperament, etc.[99]

The United States of America, being a largely Protestant country, has always provided a fertile setting for sectarians of all kinds, including millenarians. During the colonial period many preachers regarded the Indians as the ten lost tribes of Israel, and their conversion was seen to herald the imminence of the Millennium.[100] Adventist speculation became especially rife in the nineteenth century. "In the uncertain conditions of a new country, literal biblicism was a substitute for the standards of order that had been imposed in England by a settled church, monarchy, aristocracy, gentry and the magistracy and government. Needing, as had the Puritans before them, a model for social organization, they, too, identified themselves as a convenant people. With the Bible as the basis for interpreting their destiny they were, in troubled times, easily led to millennial speculation." [101] Within the framework of an open and pluralistic society, and in a cultural setting stressing optimism and growth, these millenarian sects were not likely to start a revolution; it was in part a reflection of the strength of the democratic ethos in America that even underprivileged racial minorities like the Indians and the blacks did not subscribe to revolutionary millenarianism.

In recent years, the explosive mixture of increasing status, rising expectations, and continuing discriminatory practices, experienced primarily by northern urban blacks, has somewhat changed this situation. Black militancy today openly challenges peaceful change, gradualism, and integration, yet though we find religious bodies like the Black Muslims emphasizing racial pride and black identity there are still no revolutionary millenarian movements. In a situation where radical political action, including the resort to violence, has produced results innovative black Christian theologians like Albert B. Cleage, the pastor of the Shrine of the Black Madonna in Detroit, explicitly warn against religious escapism and reliance upon divine intervention. Black Christians suffering oppression in a white man's land, he argues, must recapture the spirit of the Old Testament prophets and of Jesus who is pictured as "a revolutionary black leader." Black Christians must repudiate "the individualistic and other-worldly doctrines of Paul and the white man," they must come together as black people and reinterpret the Christian message "in terms of the needs of the Black Revolution." [102] In the spirit of a kind of black "theology of revolution" Cleage writes:

> We no longer feel helpless as black people. We do not feel that we must sit and wait for God to intervene and settle our problems for us. We waited for four houndred years and he didn't do much of anything, so for the next four hundred years we're going to be fighting to change conditions for ourselves. ... We have come to understand how God works in the world. Now we know that God is going to give us strength for our struggle. As black preachers we must tell our people that we are God's chosen people and that God is fighting with us as we fight. When we march, when we take it to the streets in open conflict, we must understand that in the stamping feet and the thunder of violence we can hear the voice of God.[103]

The fact that the radical religious impulse here finds an outlet in the political demand for black power rather than in the idea of a black Millennium would seem to support the point made earlier that millenarian movements develop primarily in situations of deprivation where no ordinary remedies seem available. In the contemporary United States political action and even playing at revolution are usable tactics, and this tends to undercut the attraction of revolutionary millenarianism.

In Latin America, too, despite much social distress, revolutionary millenarianism is not a viable option. Growing numbers of men and women from the lower classes are attracted to the Pentecostal sects where the message is not the Second Coming of

Christ but "the far more appealing prospect of an immediate coming of the deity. The repentant believer may expect this descent of the Holy Spirit *here and now* rather than in a distant future." [104] The jump to an emotional communion with Jesus is smaller and easier than the commitment to armed struggle and, moreover, brings more immediate rewards. The charismatic leaders of Pentecostalism offer salvation from sickness; the social evils from which the underprivileged suffer are downgraded and offset by the emphasis on the community of the saved where the faithful are the elite. The Pentecostal groups, like many Protestant sects generally, thus "substitute religious status for social status," [105] the sense of belonging to a chosen group is a source of emotional support and enhances self-respect.

Revolutionary millenarian movements have largely disappeared from the advanced societies of Europe and America, but this does not mean the eclipse of millenarianism. Indeed it can be argued that starting with the Enlightenment in the eighteenth century, millenarianism has simply been secularized and, thus refashioned, has reappeared in certain types of radical political revolutionism. The point of transition in this secularization of an old religious doctrine, as E. L. Tuveson has convincingly demonstrated, was the eighteenth-century idea of progress—"the notion of history as a process generally moving upwards by a series of majestic stages, culminating *inevitably* in some great, transforming event which is to solve the dilemmas of society." [106] As a result of the merger of the concept of providence with that of natural law there was born a new secular version of millenarianism, human progress had become a kind of secularized salvation. We find it institutionalized in the worship of liberty and the cult of reason in the Year II of the French Revolution. In the nineteenth and twentieth centuries nationalism, too, associated with the idea of progress, has often been expressed in messianic form: the whole nation, because of extraordinary attributes and divine favor, is seen destined to bring about "a new order of things and to raise humanity to new ethical standards." [107] The special mission of the United States of America has often been seen in terms of such a secular salvation.

The millenarian theme can be clearly seen in the revolutionary thought of Marx and Engels.[108] History, replacing God, now becomes the force that moves mankind to the inevitable day of judgment when the mighty are cast down and the lowly exalted, when the expropriators are expropriated. Because of its long suffering the proletariat is destined to become the collective savior and redeemer of humanity; a social class rather than a particular nation now forms the community of the elect and functions as the agent of historical change. There follows the reign of the saints, the dictatorship of the proletariat, and then the kingdom of heaven—the egalitarian classless and stateless society, the realm of love and trust, free of conflict and compulsion. Only then, Marx and Engels believed, would man fully become man. Human history truly begins at the moment when the laws governing all previous history have finally been overcome and transcended. The escape from history is then complete.

According to Marxism, the great transformation, the victory of the proletarian revolution holding promise of eternal salvation, will come about necessarily as a result of severe contradictions in bourgeois society, but not without human effort. "The consummation of time is guaranteed by history," writes an astute observer, "but history is not justified by faith alone, but by works." It is the rigor of Marxism's deterministic creed that "arouses in the believers the most resolute and patient action and thus their acts confirm the faith, and the faith the acts." [109] The same synthesis of determinism and revolutionary assertion, a secular apocalyptic activism, can be found in anarchism. The dying world of the bourgeoisie has had its day, declared the Russian anarchist Sergei Nechaev: "Its end is inevitable, we must act to hasten that end." [110]

In the case of Leninist communism and Maoism, often called secular religions, an element of prophecy has been added: the promise of necessary delivery is vouchsafed by a line of prophets who are invoked as authoritative figures and cited as the Bible was in earlier times. The founders of the creed, Marx and Engels, have been joined by the great interpreters—Lenin, Stalin, Mao. The exalted status of these men has been downgraded by the current unpopularity of the cult of the personality in the Soviet Union, though the personal adulation rendered Chairman Mao in Communist China hardly knows bounds and at times approaches true deification.

Apocalyptic elements are also strong in the contemporary New Left. Maurice Cranston, in a volume of essays about some of the

New Left's leading theorists such as Sartre, Marcuse, Fanon, and Guevara, suggests that the ideas of these men can perhaps be understood only in categories drawn from religion and that they should be seen as "prophets and preachers, breathing fire and brimstone in the wilderness of an irreligious age." [111] A sociologist studying the New Left calls its enthusiastic members, endowed with the zeal of the true believer, the "Anabaptists of the Welfare State." [112] It may be that in a situation where improving social conditions are outpaced by rapidly rising expectations a restless iconoclasm and apocalypticism are somehow endemic to the affluent and bored intelligentsia, searching for a political and social role.[113] The millenarian motif, it would appear, has yet to run its course.

PART III

Religion and Anti-Colonial Strife

CHAPTER 12

Militant Hindu Nationalism:
The Early Phase

THE RISE OF INDIAN NATIONALISM

Before the British conquest India had known episodic political
dominions that included almost all of the vast country, but most
of the time the subcontinent had been divided into warring states
with no sense of national consciousness and unity. It was the impact of a foreign conqueror that laid the groundwork for the
emergence of a national movement which eventually succeeded
in ousting the foreigner. Under British rule and through a fairly
efficient administration India achieved political unification, a national economy, and a modern system of communications. Most
importantly, the introduction of English education created a new
elite with Western ideas of freedom and democracy. Modern education brought forth a class of intellectuals that could transcend
the boundaries of caste and province and the multitude of
tongues. It was this Western-educated, native intelligentsia that
eventually supplied the leadership in India's nationalist movement.[1]

The first result of European culture was a period of intellectual
anarchy created by the collision of Western skepticism and scientific thought and Hindu traditions. Westernism then became the
fashion of the day, and everything Eastern was denounced as
backward and superstitious.[2] But gradually this worship of all
things Western gave way to a new pride in India's native heritage. As the nineteenth century progressed, educated Hindus became interested in their ancient literature and religion. The revival of Hinduism was helped along by the writings of European
scholars like Max Müller, England's foremost Sanskritist, and by

the enthusiasm of the Theosophical Society (led in India by Mrs. Annie Besant) for the values of Indian civilization. By about 1870 the pressure of Western cultural penetration and Christian missionary activity had led to the emergence of a Hindu cultural nationalism.

The exponents of Hindu revivalism argued that Western materialistic civilization was destructive of Indian culture, and they preached the historic superiority of the Aryan tradition. With the aid of its ancient wisdom Hindu India could regain its old strength, the revival of the old culture would restore India's past greatness. The ancestral faith was to be rejuvenated and a new patriotism built and cultivated. Indian unity was linked to Hinduism for large numbers of Hindus were found in every region of India. The Muslims and other native minorities were ignored.

The revival of Hinduism was accompanied by reform movements which sought to remove from Hindu life such customs as child marriage, sutteeism,* and caste restrictions which by Western standards were degenerate and reactionary. Some of these movements endeavoring to foster an enlightened practice of Hinduism, such as the Brahma Samaj founded in 1828 by Raja Rammohan Roy, developed before the emergence of Indian nationalism though the national movement later considered itself indebted to them.[3] Others, like the Arya Samaj, started in 1875 by Swami Dayananda Saraswati, were frankly nationalistic from the very beginning. Using the rallying cry "Back to the Vedas," the Arya Samaj advocated the formation of a new national character and sought to inspire nationalists "with pride in the past and hope in the future." [4] Similarly, the Ramakrishna Mission, founded in 1892 by Swami Vivekananda to further the spiritual work of the Bengali mystic Ramakrishna, called for the building of an Indian nation based on the Hindu religion. Vivekananda argued that liberty required freedom from all bondage—physical and mental, as well as political—and he thus incorporated the Western idea of political and social liberty into the classical Indian conception of freedom as spiritual salvation.[5]

Another important figure engaged in fusing national and religious ideas was the Bengali novelist Bankim Chandra Chatterjee

---

* The cremation of a widow on the funeral pyre of her late husband.

whom his admirers have compared to Sir Walter Scott, particularly because of the strongly patriotic character of his writings.
In his most famous novel, *Ananda Math* (The Abbey of Bliss),
published in 1882, Bankim combined country and divinity into
the concept "the mother," and the poem *Bande Mataram* (Hail to
the Mother) soon became the *Marseillaise* of the nationalist movement. "The concept of the divine Motherland," notes one critic,
"equating as it did love of country with love of God, made an in-
stinctive appeal to the devout Hindu peasantry, for whom the
secular reformism and Westernized nationalism of the Moderate
leaders [of the Indian National Congress] remained beyond
comprehension." [6]

There was a quickening of nationalistic sentiment during the
last quarter of the nineteenth century, especially in the politically
more advanced province of Bengal. Surendranath Banerjea, a professor in Calcutta, organized secret societies which spread the nationalist and revolutionary ideas of George Washington, Kossuth,
Garibaldi, and Mazzini. New political journals like the *Tribune*
in Lahore and *The Voice of India* in Bombay furthered nationalist aims. The year 1885 saw the founding of the Indian National
Congress, though the early years of this organization were
marked by a very moderate and non-revolutionary outlook. The
separation of India from Great Britain was not yet envisaged, and
India's progress was thought to depend upon British help. "Protests against government policies consisted of thoughtfully
worded petitions calculated to appeal to the sense of reason and
fair play of officials." [7] The Western-educated professional people
dominating the Congress took pains to emphasize that religious
affiliation was irrelevant to membership in an organization devoted to public secular affairs, but in practice the membership
during the first meetings was predominantly Hindu. For most of
these men Indian nationalism was synonymous with Hindu nationalism.

The early nationalist movement was a movement of urban intellectuals who spoke a common language and had common
grievances. The overwhelming majority of the population was
not touched as can be seen from the fact that as late as 1930 only
2 per cent of all Indians could speak English [8]—for many years
the tongue of the national movement. What gave the nationalists
the beginning of a mass base was the upheaval resulting from the

decision of the British government in December 1903 to partition
Bengal, the largest and most populous province of British India.
This move was strongly attacked by the nationalists from the
very beginning as an attempt to create a split between Muslims
and Hindus and thus undermine Bengali nationalism; mass agitation really got underway after the announcement of partition on
July 19, 1905. A resolution to use only Indian-made articles led
to the so-called Swadeshi movement (*Swadeshi*, one's own country). Weapons included the boycott of British goods and a program of national education which involved the establishment of
schools combining Western education and Indian culture. The
anti-partition movement began in Bengal as an expression of Bengali nationalism, but it quickly spread to other parts of India.
Later Indian writers have called it "India's first Freedom's battle,"
and they have suggested that "it holds the same significant place
in our national annals as does the French Revolution in the awakening of modern Europe." [9] Indeed, the Swadeshi movement soon
assumed a clearly political character that increasingly promoted
the idea of *swaraj* (self-government) to be achieved through organized passive resistance.

The Congress formally endorsed the Swadeshi movement at its
Calcutta meeting in 1906, but being a moderate body it showed
no great enthusiasm for the boycott and other more radical tactics. It was the failure of the Congress majority to provide energetic leadership for the growing nationalist movement that in
1907 led to a split in its ranks and to the formation of a "New
Party." Those in favor of constitutional methods of agitation became known as the Moderates; the radicals were called Nationalists or Extremists. The origins of the latter group reach back into
the last years of the nineteenth century, and their ideas, centering
around a militant Hindu nationalism, continue to influence contemporary Indian politics.

THE THEORY AND PRACTICE OF MILITANT
HINDU NATIONALISM

The leaders of the "New Party" had been veteran activists in the
Indian national movement for many years. Bal Gangadhar Tilak
—teacher, Sanskrit scholar, and editor of two newspapers in Maharashtra province—had been advocating a radical nationalist

course since 1894. At that time he had organized two annual festivals in honor of the Hindu God Ganpati and the Maratha leader Shivaji (who had led his people against their Muslim rulers); both festivals were used to build up Hindu solidarity and anti-British sentiment. After his first imprisonment in the nationalist cause in 1897 Tilak acquired the title *Lokamanya* (literally, revered by the people) and to this day he is most commonly spoken of as "The Lokamanya." [10] In a book published at the height of anti-British agitation in 1910 the well-known British journalist, Valentine Chirol, suggested that "if any one can claim to be truly the father of Indian unrest, it is Bal Gangadhar Tilak." [11] Nehru called Tilak "the father of Indian nationalism," and in 1920, on hearing of Tilak's death, Gandhi is said to have exclaimed, "My strongest bulwark is gone." [12]

No less distinguished and admired was Aurobindo Ghose, a Bengali who had received a thoroughly Western education in England; he was soon attracted to the national movement and spent the last forty years of his life in seclusion as a Hindu philosopher-saint. As early as 1893 Aurobindo had attacked the Congress "as a middle-class organ, selfish and disingenious in its public action and hollow in its professions of a large and disinterested patriotism." [13] During the years 1906–08 he edited the *Bande Mataram*, first a daily and later also a weekly newspaper in Calcutta, which until its suppression by the British bureaucracy was one of the main organs of the Swadeshi movement. A Western scholar has called Aurobindo "probably the outstanding intellectual associated with the revolutionary philosophy in Bengal." [14]

Where Aurobindo appealed to his countrymen through the sheer power of his writings, the third leader of the Extremists, Bipin Chandra Pal, excelled through his eloquence as a speaker. An author and educator in Bengal, Pal in 1901 began to publish the English weekly *New India*, another organ of militant Indian nationalism. During the anti-partition agitation he traveled extensively through all parts of the huge country; a report of the British Intelligence Branch referred to him as "the chief of the itinerant demagogues," a man "who did more to influence the minds of the masses against the Government than any one else." [15]

The fourth leader of the Extremists, Lala Lajpat Rai, was a leading member of the bar in Lahore, capital of the Punjab. Indian writers include him in the radical triumvirate of Lal, Bal,

and Pal. Lajpat Rai was one of the leaders of the Arya Samaj, of
which he authored a history, and he quickly became the nationalist leader of northwest India. His death in 1928 was precipitated
by a beating by police during a political demonstration.

The leaders of the extremist bloc did not think alike on all issues, and they revealed certain differences of temperament. "The
writings of Pal and Aurobindo," notes one critic, "are characterized by an exalted, inspired and fervid emotionalism. . . . Tilak
on the other hand had a strong sense of the real and the concrete
. . . and there is far less emphasis on the vision of the spiritualized society and the gnostic community." [16] Still, all of them
shared certain important ideas and ways of thinking.

The Extremists were strongly influenced by the Hindu revivalism that had come to the fore during the last quarter of the nineteenth century. Ancient India, Aurobindo wrote in *Bande Mataram* in 1907, had once been "the fountain of human light, the
apex of human civilization, the exemplar of courage and humanity, the perfection of good government and settled society, the
mother of all religions, the teacher of all wisdom and
philosophy." [17] Since those glorious days the country had suffered much and its pride had been trampled into the dust. Hunger, misery, and despair had triumphed. But God had not forsaken his chosen people. Through a revival of the Hindu religion
India could regain the exalted position it had once held.
Hinduism provided the common tie that could overcome differences of caste, language, and custom and re-establish unity and
greatness. If we lay stress on the ancient tradition and heritage,
Tilak wrote in an appeal to his countrymen, and forget "all the
minor differences that exist between different sects, then by the
grace of providence we shall ere long be able to consolidate all
the different sects into a mighty Hindu nation. This ought to be
the ambition of every Hindu." [18]

Aurobindo in Bengal and Tilak in the Deccan at first worked
to arouse local patriotism, but this soon gave way to a deeply religious nationalism that encompassed all of India. "This movement in Bengal," declared Aurobindo, "this movement of nationalism is not guided by any self-interest. . . . It is a religion which
we are trying to live. It is a religion by which we are trying to
realize God in the nation, in our fellow-countrymen." [19] The
new nationalism, Pal argued, represented not a mere civic or eco-

nomic or political ideal. "It is a religion." [20] Religion, suggested
Tilak, not only provided a tie between man and God but also between man and man. It, therefore, was "an element in
nationality." [21] A religion of patriotism had been born, a faith
that had its martyrs, a creed that held up before its converts a
mighty ideal.

Central in this new religious patriotism was the love and worship of the divine motherland, a concept first developed by Chatterjee and further enriched and brought to life through the poetic
language of Aurobindo:

> The feeling of almost physical delight in the touch of the mother-
> soil, of the winds that blow from Indian seas, of the rivers that
> stream from Indian hills, in the hearing of Indian speech, music,
> poetry, in the familiar sights, sounds, habits, dress, manners of our
> Indian life, this is the physical root of that love. The pride in our
> past, the pain of our present, the passion for the future are its
> trunk and branches. Self-sacrifice and self-forgetfulness, great ser-
> vice, high endurance for the country are its fruit. And the sap
> which keeps it alive is the realization of the Motherhood of God in
> the country, the vision of the Mother, the knowledge of the
> Mother, the perpetual contemplation, adoration and service of the
> Mother. [22]

God revealed himself in the history and greatness of the Indian
nation. It was God who was behind Indian nationalism and saw
to it that it would attain its goal. In his famous Uttarpara speech
of 1909 Aurobindo described how Sri Krishna (one of the most
important Hindu deities) had visited him in jail and had assured
him of his help and guidance in these words: "I am in the nation
and its uprising and . . . what I will, shall be, not what others
will. What I choose to bring about, no human power can
stay." [23] God manifested himself in the national movement as well
as in those who opposed it. "I am working in everybody and
whatever men may think or do, they can do nothing but help in
my purpose." [24] The repression of the English bureaucracy was
the hammer of God that was beating India into shape so that it
could be molded into a mighty nation and become an instrument for God's work in the world.

The belief in the messianic greatness and mission of India drew
strength from the newly found sense of national pride and
uniqueness. The movement for the national liberation of India

sought political emancipation not as an end in itself but as a precondition for the fulfillment of India's spiritual destiny. India was
rising, said Aurobindo, "to shed the eternal light entrusted to her
over the world." [25] It sought to develop Hindu spirituality, the
essential keynote of which was the unity of God and man. "It
seeks to bring the Kingdom of Heaven on earth, in a sense not realized by Christian consciousness in Europe or America. It seeks
to establish a New Jerusalem in this world." [26] Even the less spiritual leaders in the extremist group emphasized the importance of
the tie between India and the world. Patriotism, maintained Pal,
"is good, excellent, divine only when it furthers the ends of universal humanity. Nationality divorced from humanity is a source
of weakness and evil, and not of strength and good." [27]

The Extremists invoked God's help but warned against passive
reliance upon divine delivery. They therefore worked hard to
cultivate strength and determination in their followers. "Our actual enemy," Aurobindo wrote in 1893, "is not any force exterior
to ourselves, but our own crying weaknesses, our cowardice, our
selfishness, our hypocrisy, our purblind sentimentalism." [28] Nothing could be gained by begging and meek appeals to the good
will of the foreign rulers—the way of the Moderates dominating the Congress. "The Indian people," Tilak urged in the *Kesari*,
"must adopt the way of resistance to achieve the complete rights
of *svarajya*." [29] India's liberation will be achieved by the grace of
God, but it will not do to sit idle. "There is a very old principle
that God helps them who help themselves. The principle occurs
in the *Rigveda*. God becomes incarnate. When? . . . God does
not become incarnate for idle people. He becomes incarnate for
industrious people. Therefore begin work." [30] People once awakened cannot be put down like dogs and slaves, Lajpat Rai told
the 21st meeting of the Congress in 1905. "Why be loyal? Once
the policy of Boycott be adopted prepare for the consequences.
Do not behave like cowards." [31] The old idea, declared Pal, was
to get political rights by petitioning the government. "The new
hope is to help the people to grow into these by their own internal strength and evolution. The spirit that is abroad in India
today is the spirit of self-assertion and self-reliance." [32]

In order to encourage action and to overcome the Indian tradition of renunciation and escapism from the turmoil of this world,
the Extremists, especially Tilak and Aurobindo, appealed to the

authority of the *Bhagavad Gita* (The Song of the Lord)—
India's most popular book of devotion. The *Gita* is part of the
Mahabharata, the over-1500-year-old, great Hindu epic, and for
centuries it has been India's principal source of religious inspiration. Because of its popularity as well as its content this "New
Testament of Hinduism" was ideally suited to provide religious
sanction for the spirit of activist nationalism the Extremists
sought to enhance.

During the winter of 1910–11, while he was held in a British
jail in Mandalay, Tilak undertook a systematic and scholarly analysis of the *Gita* in order to derive from it the duty of all citizens
to act for the liberation of the nation. The result was a book entitled *Srimad Bhagavadgita Rahasya* (The Secret Meaning of the
Gita) that was published in 1915 and translated into several Indian languages as well as into English. Tilak took issue with a
widely accepted interpretation according to which the *Gita* expounded the renunciation of action as the highest duty. This philosophy, he suggested, had been spread by Jainism and Buddhism,
and it had weakened India's defenses against foreign conquerors.
The true spirit of the *Gita* required not the giving up of worldly
life but the remaining in it. The *Gita*, Tilak maintained, taught
the obligation of fulfilling the duties of one's station in life "with
a pure mind and without an eye to the fruit." [33] In order to
achieve salvation and gain release from the cycle of rebirth one
should not be passive, an imperative which in any event could
not be realized, but rather one should act unselfishly and disinter-
estedly. Thus the warrior should not retreat from battle but fight
without hate for the good of the country. "The Gita neither ad-
vises nor intends that when one becomes non-inimical, one should
also become non-retaliatory." [34] Going one step further Tilak
argued that the duty of acting for the public welfare was not
only a caste duty but "the duty of all citizens when the nation is
threatened by internal decay or external oppression." [35]

Tilak believed that unlike previous interpreters of the *Gita*,
whose interpretations reflected their special interests, he had succeeded in discovering the famous book's true meaning. This claim
is probably too ambitious. An outstanding American student of
the *Gita* has noted the widely differing readings of its fundamental philosophy and concluded: "Like many another religious
book, it is taken to prove almost anything." [36] Tilak's interpreta-

tion in his view was "neither better nor worse than scores of others." [37] Be that as it may, the fact remains that Tilak's work had the effect of strengthening the vigor of the Indian nationalist movement. The "Father of Indian Unrest" was assisted in this endeavor by Aurobindo who also preached the importance of forceful assertion. "Politics," Aurobindo wrote in 1907, "is concerned with masses of mankind and not with individuals. To ask masses of mankind to act as saints, to rise to the height of divine love and practice it in relation to their adversaries or oppressors is to ignore human nature. It is to set a premium on injustice and violence by paralysing the hand of the deliverer when raised to strike. The Gita is the best answer to those who shrink from battle as a sin, and [from] aggression as a lowering of morality." [38]

Both Tilak and Aurobindo thus were able to derive the legitimacy of righteous violence from the *Gita*, and their followers were quick to translate this doctrine into deeds. Even though the leaders of the extremist faction were careful in their writings not to seem to be instigating violence, they always made it clear that the question of the means to be used in India's struggle was one of tactics and not principle. Writing in 1907 Aurobindo described three methods of resistance to oppression: (1) passive resistance; (2) assassinations, riots, strikes, and agrarian risings; and (3) armed revolt. Aurobindo opted for the first of these methods but not, as he emphasized, because of moral objections to the use of force. "The choice by a subject nation of the means it will use for vindicating its liberty is best determined by the circumstances of its servitude. The present circumstances in India seem to point to passive resistance as our most natural and suitable weapon. We would not for a moment be understood to base this conclusion upon any condemnation of other methods as in all circumstances criminal and unjustifiable." [39] The nationalist movement will adhere to passive resistance and respect the law, Pal declared in the same year, as long as the law respects the Indians' rights to life and property. Other means, such as those employed by the French, American, and Russian revolutionists, may "suggest themselves with the gradual unfolding of events." [40] And Tilak explained, "The time is surely not yet for lawlessness, for we have not yet exhausted all the possibilities of what may be claimed as legitimate and lawful action." [41]

Active resistance and the use of force thus would be necessary if the oppression of the English bureaucracy were to make the legal struggle for liberty impossible, if the foreign ruler were to use force to prevent orderly meetings. The right of self-defense then would justify retaliation. In the words of Aurobindo:

> Under certain circumstances, a civil struggle becomes in reality a battle and the morality of war is different from the morality of peace. To shrink from bloodshed and violence under such circumstances is a weakness deserving as severe a rebuke as Sri Krishna addressed to Arjuna when he shrank from the colossal civil slaughter on the field of Kurukshetra. Liberty is the life-breath of a nation; and when the life is attacked, when it is sought to suppress all chance of breathing by violent pressure, any and every means of self-preservation becomes right and justifiable,—just as it is lawful for a man who is being strangled to rid himself of the pressure on this throat by any means in his power.[42]

The example of France showed that the progress of a country toward freedom will not always take the form of a "decent and orderly expansion" but may require "purification by blood and fire." [43] No method of action, Aurobindo insisted, is good or bad in itself "except as it truly helps or hinders our progress toward national emancipation." [44] Unrest, in the eyes of Lajpat Rai, was an essential harbinger of progress, and India's release from political slavery necessitated her going through a "hell of unrest." [45]

In reply to those who denied the legitimacy of rebellion against established authority the Extremists invoked the right of revolt against tyranny. The duties of a king and his people were reciprocal, Tilak explained in 1907. Even though the king or sovereign was part and parcel of the Godhead, according to ancient scriptures and lawbooks, this principle of divinity did not allow him absolute and arbitrary powers or require that his tyranny be quietly borne. "The divine king as soon as he ceases to be just ceases also to be divine. He becomes an *asura* [demon] and this depreciated divinity is forthwith replaced by a deity, the divinity of which is not so alloyed." [46] Thus even if the divinity of kingship were to be accepted, Tilak argued, oppression and injustice could not be justified, and India's struggle against the tyranny of the British crown was legitimate.

Although all the Extremists were scornful of the "mendicant" tactics of the Moderates, they differed on the meaning of *swaraj*. For Tilak it meant home rule under British sovereignty. He fought for a self-governing India within the empire. For the others the ideal of self-government ruled out retaining any ties whatsoever to Britain. "Our ideal is freedom," declared Pal in 1906, "which means absence of all foreign control." [47] Aurobindo, similarly, demanded complete independence: "The entire removal of foreign control in order to make way for perfect national liberty." [48]

The emergence of the "New Party" in 1907 came at a time when the Swadeshi movement had begun to awaken India's illiterate masses, and the Extremists made great efforts to build up mass support for the nationalist cause. Wherever possible they abandoned English and resorted to the local languages of the common people. As a result the nationalist movement ceased to be the exclusive concern of the English-educated intellectual elite and began to assume the character of a mass movement. Under conditions of severe repression by the British bureaucracy this also meant, however, that the extremist leaders were unable to retain full control over their followers in the vast country. Some of the latter were not content with relying on passive resistance and went over to deeds of violence and individual terror.

Terrorism first showed its face in 1897 when the brothers Chapekar killed two government officers in Poona (Deccan). The two brothers, orthodox Brahmins, had formed a society for physical and military training which they called the "Society for the Removal of Obstacles to the Hindu Religion." [49] The close tie between orthodox Hinduism and political terrorism first demonstrated here was to continue to characterize the revolutionary movement for many years.

Violence manifested itself next in Bengal. In 1902 Barindra Ghose, the younger brother of Sri Aurobindo, began to organize Bengali schools of physical training to counteract the slur of unmanliness and to prepare young Bengalis for revolutionary action. His militancy became more popular after the announcement of the proposed partition of Bengal; a further stimulus was provided by the Japanese victories in Manchuria over Russia in 1904—widely heralded as the triumph of an Asian nation over a European power. The first revolutionary secret society, the Anushilan Samiti, was formed at this time in Calcutta, and soon branch societies sprang up in other parts of Bengal. Difficulties of communication prevented central direction of these groups, but their plan of action was identical. They manufactured explosives, collected firearms, trained in the use of firearms, and engaged in acts of terror against British officials as well as against Indians refusing to provide financial support. "Barindra spoke of political murder as a means of educating the people for facing death and daring anything for their country's sake. He believed there was a constant demand for political murders, in order to embolden the people and satisfy their desire for vengeance." [50]

From Bengal the terrorist movement spread to the Punjab, and occasional acts of violence cropped up in other provinces as well. From 1906 to 1918 the British counted 210 "revolutionary outrages" in Bengal which killed 82 and wounded 121 persons.[51] The viceroy, Lord Minto, narrowly escaped death; four attempts were made upon the life of the lieutenant governor of Bengal. In 1908, at Muzafferpur in Bengal, a bomb intended for a district magistrate killed two English ladies named Kennedy. In 1912 a bomb was thrown at Lord Hardinge, the successor to Minto, upon his state entry into Delhi seriously wounding him and killing or injuring several of his attendants. Terrorist activities continued through World War I, though the heavy hand of government repression combined with the promise of reform gradually brought about a slackening of violence.[52]

The revolutionary movement drew upon the ideas of Garibaldi, Mazzini, and the Russian anarchists and nihilists, but Hindu religious inspiration always occupied a key place. The *Gita*, in particular, was studied extensively and interpreted as a call to all Indians to struggle boldly and fearlessly against evildoers, to be willing to face death if necessary. The goddess Kali or Durga, symbolizing conflict, became the favorite deity of the revolutionaries, and the ceremony of initiation required the new member to take a vow before the goddess with a sword and a copy of the *Gita* placed upon his head. A clandestine leaflet called upon the youth of India to pledge themselves to the task of destroying the hated foreigner, and the necessary physical and spiritual strength was to be gained by relying upon the Hindu religion.[53] The newspaper *Jugantar* (New Era), founded in March 1906 by Barindra Ghose and several other revolutionaries, soon became amazingly popular by expounding the doctrines of militant Hinduism. A typical article suggested that firm resolution could bring an end to English rule within a single day for the number of Englishmen was strictly limited. "Lay down your life, but first take a life. The worship of the goddess will not be consummated if you sacrifice your lives at the shrine of independence without shedding blood." [54] An article in another vernacular paper, entitled "The Potency of Vedic Prayers," reminded the reader of the duty of retaliation against alien oppressors: "Brahmans should take up arms and protect religion. When one is face to face with such people they should be slaughtered without hesitation. Not the slightest blame attaches to the slayer." [55]

The attitude of the Indian people to this cult of violence was ambivalent. In 1907 the Moderates in the Congress went on record as emphatically condemning "the detestable outrages and deeds of violence which have been committed recently in some parts of the country, and which are abhorrent to the loyal, humane and peace-loving nature of His Majesty's Indian subjects of every denomination." [56] In the same year the Arya Samaj, too, declared that it was dedicated to peace and order and condemned "revolutions, bloodshed, disorder, clannish malevolence and racial hatred" as fatal to the spread of the true Vedic religion.[57] But the people in general did not share these sentiments. "When a bomb is thrown," noted Lajpat Rai, "the people genuinely condemn the bomb thrower, are sincere in their detestation, but when he is hanged or transported exiled, they are sorry for him. Their original abhorrence changes into sympathy and then into love. They are martyrs of the national cause. They may be misguided, even mad, but they are martyrs all the same." [58] Many in the educated community, if they did not approve of the bomb outrages, thought at least that the government deserved it.[59]

Those dedicated to the philosophy of the bomb considered themselves pupils of Tilak, Aurobindo, and Pal, and they drew much of the inspiration for their deeds from the eloquent writings and speeches of these men. The emphasis of the Extremists on the necessity of resolution and sacrifice to achieve the goal of political emancipation imparted a spirit of revolution to the nationalist struggle. But the exact relationship of the leaders of the extremist party to the terroristic movement is somewhat difficult to reconstruct. It is clear that none of the extremist leaders were ever directly involved in terrorist activities, though Tilak and Aurobindo especially provided a philosophical and religious rationale for violence and at the very least condoned resort to it.

In June 1897, at a time when the strong measures taken by the British government to prevent the spread of the plague in Poona had created considerable unrest and resentment, Tilak held the second of his Shivaji festivals. Several speakers celebrated Shivaji, the man who in 1659 had killed the Muslim general Afzal Khan and freed Maharashtra, and they held him up as an example to be followed in the struggle for independence. Tilak himself defended Shivaji's killing of the alien Muslim conqueror as the act of a great man that could not be judged by the canons of ordinary morality. He told the festive audience:

> Did Shivaji commit a sin in killing Afzal Khan? The answer to this question can be found in the Mahabharata itself. Shrimat Krishna preached in the *Gita* that we have a right even to kill our own *guru* and our kinsmen. No blame attaches to any person if he is doing deeds without being actuated by a desire to reap the fruits of his deeds. . . . If thieves enter our house and we have not strength enough in our fists to drive them out, we should without hesitation lock them up and burn them alive. God has not conferred upon the foreigners the grant inscribed on a copper plate to the Kingdom of Hindustan.[60]

About a week later the brothers Chapekar assassinated Walter Charles Rand, who was in charge of the fight against the plague, and another British officer. Tilak knew the assassins and helped them elude the police though he probably was not privy to the plot itself. One scholar, after careful review of the evidence, concludes that Tilak certainly approved of Rand's assassination, "that he tried his best to aid and protect the Chapekars after he knew of their crime, that he may have helped inspire their action, and at any rate provided ethical justification for it was based on the scripture they most revered." [61] In 1908, after the killing of the Kennedy ladies, Tilak denied that such an action could be regarded as an ordinary murder "owing to the supposition on the part of the perpetrators that they were doing a sort of beneficent act." [62] Tilak could not explicitly condone the killing, but his readers certainly knew what he meant. There is no doubt that Tilak accepted violence in a righteous cause, including assassinations, as justifiable and free of the stain of sin.

Aurobindo held very similar views. "Aggression," he wrote in 1907, "is unjust only when unprovoked; violence, unrighteous when used wantonly or for unrighteous ends." [63] At about the same time Aurobindo wrote a little book entitled *Bhavani Mandir* (Temple of Bhavani), in which he outlined the founding of an order of young ascetics who would consecrate themselves to the liberation of the motherland. The scheme envisaged a temple dedicated to the goddess Bhavani, a manifestation of Kali, hidden in a secret place where the members of the order would acquire strength in preparation for the armed struggle for independence. The pamphlet quickly became a kind of handbook for the revolutionary groups of Bengal.[64] There is evidence to indicate that Aurobindo was in close contact with the group around the *Jugantar* weekly and that he maintained this active liaison until his withdrawal from politics in 1910.[65] In a work published posthumously Aurobindo himself admitted that he had been actively engaged in organizing revolutionary activities.[66] Lieutenant-Governor Baker, in a letter to the viceroy, characterized Aurobindo as "an active generator of revolutionary sentiment. He is imbued with a semi-religious fanaticism which is a powerful factor in attracting adherents to his cause: and I attribute the spread of seditious doctrines to him personally in a greater degree than to any other single individual in Bengal, or possibly in India." [67] This appraisal does not appear to be exaggerated.

THE HERITAGE OF HINDU MILITANCY

Unable to overcome the political apathy of the illiterate peasantry and lacking the necessary strength to score meaningful victories against the British, the revolutionary movement in Bengal and the rest of India gradually weakened. By 1910 the revolutionaries had lost the guidance or inspiration of most of the extremist leaders. Tilak was imprisoned in Burma, Pal and Lajpat Rai were in voluntary exile in Britain, Aurobindo had abandoned politics and was devoting himself to spiritual pursuits. In the years that followed both Tilak and Pal condemned the cult of the bomb and stressed the need of working along constitutional paths. The rescinding of the partition of Bengal in 1911 and the mood of conciliation created by the outbreak of World War I paved the way for the return of the former Extremists to the Congress. By 1916 the old quarrel between Moderates and Extremists was essentially patched up; the Congress was committed to the attainment of home rule by constitutional means. Tilak died in 1920, and leadership in the nationalist movement passed to Gandhi.

The achievement of Indian independence is usually attributed to Gandhi's nonviolent resistance movement, but the contribution of the Extremists to the successful outcome of the nationalist struggle cannot be ignored. Indeed, some students of early Indian nationalism actually assign greater importance to the militants. "In assessing the overall contribution of the moderates and the extremists towards the attainment of India's independence," writes Argov, "the militant agitation of the extremists rather than the constitutional methods of the moderates was chiefly responsible for the transfer of power in 1947." [68] The very idea of passive resistance was first applied in India not by Gandhi but by the anti-partition movement in Bengal in which the Extremists played a leading role. Though the violent methods pursued by the revolutionary movement, fathered and partly encouraged by the Extremists, did not lead to tangible results and actually increased British repression, the heavy hand of the bureaucracy reacting to the campaign of terror increased anti-British feeling and indirectly strengthened the general appeal of Indian nationalism. Most importantly, the Extremists by appealing to religion and using religious symbolism were able to broaden the base of the nationalist movement. Joining religious and political ideals they in effect created Hindu nationalism and awoke the Indian masses. They gave the people a form of political consciousness, a desire for independence, a feeling of patriotism, and a motive to participate in the liberation of their country. "They showed for the first time how it was possible to arouse a poor, tradition-bound, politically unconscious mass of people to political action through the use of cultural techniques of appeal that were understandable to them." [69] In a country where the great majority of the people were Hindus and where religion was closely entwined with the development of Indian civilization, the cultivation of such a religious nationalism was probably the only way to build a mass movement.[70] Gandhi, while differing from the Extremists on several basic issues, continued to make his appeal to the people in traditional, religious terms.

Several historical and sociological factors contributed to the dominantly religious and revivalistic character of Indian nationalism. These elements were absent from the development of European nationalism though in varying degrees they are present in other new nations that have recently emerged from Western tutelage. First, the hold of the Hindu religion over the Indian masses and the exalted position of the scriptures of ancient India had never been effectively challenged by either rationalism or modern science. The educated had gone through a period of Westernism, but this had soon been superseded by a powerful Hindu renaissance. As we have seen, this religious revivalism assumed definitely messianic overtones to provide the basis for the emergence of Indian nationalism. Second, the presence of a Muslim minority, with its separatist aspirations encouraged by the British, intensified Hindu consciousness and strengthened the ethnic and religious element in Indian nationalism. Thus while the latter exhibited many of the same features as European nationalism—romanticism, encouragement of and pride in vernacular literature and native art, glorification of the past [71]—it also was characterized by a distinctly religious style that had no European parallel. Indian nationalism was an indirect result of British rule and Western education. At the same time, national feeling was decisively shaped and molded by traditional ideas without which Indian nationalism would hardly have attained its eventual powerful momentum.[72]

If the combination of religion and politics in the form of Hindu nationalism was crucial in the birth and growth of Indian national consciousness, it also exacted a heavy price which continues to be paid to this day. Hindu nationalism almost certainly delayed much needed social reform. Unlike earlier Hindu reformers, many of the militant nationalists in the late nineteenth and early twentieth century resolutely opposed all reforms of the status of widows, the age of marriage, or the caste system. "We have fumbled through the nineteenth century," wrote Aurobindo in 1907, "prattling of enlightenment and national regeneration; and the result has been not national progress, but national confusion and weakness . . . political freedom is the life-breath of a nation; to attempt social reform, educational reform, industrial expansion, the moral improvement of the race without aiming first and foremost at political freedom, is the very height of ignorance and futility." [73] Tilak was even more vehement in denouncing such reforms as destructive interfering by foreigners in the religious life of the Hindu people. It may well be, as noted by a recent student of Tilak's life, that the latter was not really so much convinced of the harmfulness of social reform as "he appears to have been supremely aware of the fact that a potent method of achieving swift popularity was by criticizing unpopular innovations." [74] The end result was, nevertheless, that Tilak and his followers lent their prestige to the defense of practices and superstitions that contributed to India's misery and poverty. Distrust if not outright opposition to social reform by orthodox Hindus has remained a serious problem in the modernization of India.

Another serious liability of Hindu nationalism has been its impact on relations between Muslims and Hindus. To be sure, all of the militant nationalist leaders stressed the importance of national unity in the struggle against the foreign oppressor, and the Congress repeatedly went on record as desiring the harmonious cooperation of the various communities of the country. But in point of fact the emphasis on Hinduism in Indian nationalism could not but exacerbate the latent hostility between Hindus and Muslims. Tilak's writings and activities, notes Louis Dumont, were directed against the British, but "necessarily bred communalism in the simultaneously antagonized Muslim partner." [75] Significantly, the Muslim League was founded in 1906 during the period of Extremist ascendancy in the Congress.[76] It is thus not farfetched to suggest that the Extremists bear a share of the responsibility for the communal riots that intermittently plagued the country in the 1920's and 1930's and for the partition of India and the disastrous bloodshed following in its wake.

Militant Hindu nationalism has provided much of the direct inspiration for India's Hindu communal parties. A young admirer and follower of Tilak, V. D. Savarkar, became the leader of the Hindu Mahasabha, the first of the Hindu communal organizations on the Indian political scene. K. B. Hedgewar, the founder in 1925 of the militant Rashtriya Swayamsevak Sangh (RSS; usually translated as National Volunteer Corps) was similarly a disciple of the early Tilak and in the period of 1910–15 Hedgewar was in contact with Pal and terrorist groups in Calcutta.[77] The assassin of Gandhi in 1948 was a fanatical Hindu communalist who had had past associations with both the Hindu Mahasabha and the RSS, a fact leading to the temporary ban of the RSS. More recently the Bharatiya Jana Sangh, founded in 1951, has scored impressive gains.[78] The Jana Sangh rejects the communalist label opponents have attempted to attach to it, but in fact its program is hardly distinguishable from that of its predecessors; it includes a ban on cow slaughter, the repeal of the Hindu Marriage Act and other "anti-Hindu" laws, and a tough policy toward Pakistan.

The leaders of the Congress have always stressed their unalterable opposition to communalist politics. On April 3, 1948, Nehru declared in the Constituent Assembly that "the alliance of religion and politics in the shape of communalism is a most dangerous alliance, and it yields the most abnormal kind of illegitimate brood." Again in December 1955 Nehru warned against the communalist trend. "It is a separatist trend. It is a disruptive trend. It is a trend full of hatred. It is a trend that is bad for India today." [79] But words will not eradicate communalism. The transition to modernity in a traditional society creates stresses and strains on which fundamentalism and communalism thrive. In a situation where industrialization and secularization cause serious social and psychological dislocations, communalism appears as a form of protest. Appealing to both patriotic and religious sentiments, India's "communalist parties play up the solidarities, the securities, the privileged access to scarce resources which social structures like caste, religion and ethnolinguistic community have always afforded Indians and whose survival depends upon the retention of salient features of the traditional culture pattern." [80]

Communalism will continue to pose a challenge to political stability and social progress until India's secular statesmen have solved the problems of population control and economic development and have provided stable leadership. Millions are voting for the Congress party because it is the party of Gandhi and Nehru, both of whom were, and continue even after their deaths to be, the objects of deep personal devotion and reverence. It remains to be seen whether the Indian people will be able to develop a similar sense of loyalty to the ideal of secular democracy. Should this transfer of allegiance fail to take place, the blame will fall in part upon the Extremists, who created Hindu nationalism, and upon their successors, who keep cultivating the "marriage of religion and politics" at a time when this union has ceased playing a constructive and progressive role.

CHAPTER 13

Gandhi, Nonviolence, and the Struggle for Indian Independence

THE DOCTRINE OF SATYAGRAHA

Gandhi never issued a definitive statement of his philosophy. He was primarily an activist rather than a man of theory, and most of his extensive body of writing consists of short articles written to solve immediate political problems. Compiled over a period of some thirty years, and covering a variety of situations, Gandhi's writings abound in contradictions and represent what one Western student has called an "unsystematized and often inconsistent jungle." [1] Still certain main themes stand out, and these make it possible to formulate an over-all view of the Gandhian approach to politics.

Gandhi was not the first to teach or practice nonviolent resistance to British rule in India. Most of the so-called Extremists at the turn of the century and the Swadeshi movement of 1905 had expounded on the necessity of passive resistance. But whereas this earlier commitment to nonviolence had been dictated by circumstances and never amounted to more than a tactical choice to be abandoned under changed conditions, the Gandhian doctrine of satyagraha rested upon ethical principles and did not depend upon tactical considerations.

The term "satyagraha" was coined during Gandhi's stay in South Africa where he led a series of campaigns aimed at defending the rights of Indian immigrants. Gandhi first called the movement "passive resistance," but he soon was dissatisfied with this label and announced a competition with a prize for a better and more suitable name. One competitor came forth with the word "sadagraha" (firmness in a good cause). Gandhi relates his reaction:

> I liked the word, but it did not fully represent the whole idea I
> wished it to connote. I therefore corrected it to "Satyagraha."
> Truth (Satya) implies love and firmness (Agraha) engenders and
> therefore serves as a synonym for force. I thus began to call the In-
> dian movement "Satyagraha," that is to say, the Force which is
> born of Truth and Love or non-violence.[2]

Passive resistance, in Gandhi's view, had a negative connotation;
it was a weapon of the weak who had no other recourse and
therefore chose nonviolence. Satyagraha, on the other hand, was
a more active state than physical resistance or violence, it represented a method of determination and positive action that required resolution and a strong character. "I am not pleading for
India to practice non-violence, because she is weak," Gandhi
wrote in 1920. "I want her to practice non-violence being conscious of her strength and power."[3] Those fearful of resisting the
British were not wanted in the satyagraha movement and cowardice was regarded as demoralizing to such an exent that it was
seen as worse than violence. "I do believe," Gandhi insisted, "that
where there is only a choice between cowardice and violence, I
would advise violence."[4]

Satyagraha involved the striving for truth. Relative truth was
what the voice within told you, that which you believed to be
true at this moment. God alone represented Absolute Truth, and
the search for Him was long and arduous. Gandhi called the story
of his life "The Story of My Experiments with Truth," and he
always insisted that all he had done, and this included his political activities, was to aim to find God. "What I want to achieve,—
what I have been striving and pining to achieve these thirty
years,—is self-realization, to see God face to face, to attain
Moksha [literally freedom from birth and death; the nearest English equivalent is salvation]."[5]

The search for truth and self-realization had deep roots in the
Indian tradition but Gandhi gave it a new meaning. For him it
not only represented an ideal of individual spiritual salvation but
required positive social service for nation and mankind.

> To see the universal and all-pervading Spirit of Truth face to face
> one must be able to love the meanest of creation as oneself. And a

man who aspires after that cannot afford to keep out of any field of life. That is why my devotion to Truth has drawn me into the field of politics; and I can say without the slightest hesitation, and yet in all humility, that those who say that religion has nothing to do with politics do not know what religion means.[6]

All of man's activities represented an indivisible whole, and they could not be separated into watertight compartments. Hence there was no religion apart from practical affairs; one could not lead a religious life without identifying with mankind and its problems. Among these unsolved problems the unjust subjugation of India ranked high. "I live for India's freedom and would die for it, because it is part of Truth. Only a free India can worship the true God." [7]

The means and basis for discovering truth was *ahimsa* or non-violence. Here again an old Hindu virtue was given a new dynamic interpretation. Since what appeared to be truth to one could appear to be error to another, and, since none could rightfully claim a monopoly upon the truth, one's opponent had to be weaned from error by patience and sympathy rather than coerced or punished. However, nonviolence was not synonymous with inaction. "I accept the interpretation of Ahimsa," Gandhi wrote in 1921, "namely that it is not merely a negative state of harmlessness but it is a positive state of love, of doing good even to the evil-doer. But it does not mean helping the evil-doer to continue the wrong or tolerating it by passive acquiescence. On the contrary, love, the active state of Ahimsa, requires you to resist the wrong-doer by dissociating yourself from him even though it may offend him or injure him physically." [8] Hence *ahimsa* was perfectly consistent with disobedience to unjust laws. A law repugnant to conscience should not be obeyed, and nonviolent disobedience to such a statute was obligatory upon him who sought to disassociate himself from evil. "Disobedience is a right that belongs to every human being and it becomes a sacred duty when it springs from civility or, which is the same thing, love." [9]

Though satyagraha was to be followed to bring about social or political change, this goal was to be achieved not by coercion or force but by effecting a change in the minds of men. Satyagraha excluded "every form of violence, direct or indirect, veiled or unveiled, and whether in thought, word or deed. . . . Satyagraha is gentle, it never wounds. It must not be the result of anger or mal-ice. It is never fussy, never impatient, never vociferous. It is the direct opposite of compulsion. It was conceived as a complete substitute for violence." [10] The aim was to convert the wrong-doer. Hence he was neither to be coerced nor embarrassed or hu-miliated. Instead, the object of satyagraha was to awaken in the other party through love the innate sense of justice possessed even by the worst tyrant.

One all-important way of attaining the moral persuasion of a wrongdoer was through the willingness of the satyagraha to incur suffering. By submitting to violence without retaliation one could make the opponent spend his anger, compel him to ponder over his actions, and soften his heart. Conscious suffering also ex-pressed the unwavering commitment to nonviolence even under conditions of provocation and duress.

> Suffering injury in one's own person is . . . of the essence of non-violence and is the chosen substitute for violence to others. It is not because I value life low that I can countenance with joy thousands voluntarily losing their lives for Satyagraha, but because I know that it results in the long run in the least loss of life, and, what is more, it ennobles those who lose their lives and morally enriches the world for their sacrifice. [11]

Gandhi declared himself an uncompromising opponent of violent methods even to serve the noblest of causes; the moral purity of the means had to be preserved even if it meant forsaking the goal of liberating India. "My interest in India's freedom will cease," Gandhi stated in 1924, "if she adopts violent means, for their fruit will not be freedom but slavery in disguise." [12]

Gandhi downgraded the achievement of Indian independence for another reason. He preferred to speak of *swaraj* (self-rule), and for him this term had the same meaning it had had in the ear-lier Indian tradition: One who rules himself, one who is spiri-tually free. [13] Political freedom for India was a means to a higher end, namely spiritual freedom. Real *swaraj*, Gandhi insisted, "will come not by the acquisition of authority by a few but by the ac-quisition of the capacity by all to resist authority when abused. In other words, *swaraj* is to be attained by educating the masses to a sense of their capacity to regulate and control authority. Mere withdrawal of the English is not independence." [14] The Indian people were in a state of moral corruption and could not govern themselves. "The millions will be just as badly off as they are today, if some one made it possible to kill off every Englishman to-morrow. The responsibility is more ours than that of the English for the present state of things. The English will be powerless to do evil if we will but do good. Hence my incessant emphasis on reform from within." [15] Only those who could rule themselves by being humble and controlling their passions could be expected to rule themselves politically. Gandhi's insistence on his personal asceticism as well as on the moral purification of his followers was derived from this emphasis on self-control—a point to which we will return.

The spirit of satyagraha required contrition and humility. "Non-violence means reliance on God, the Rock of Ages. If we would seek His aid, we must approach Him with a humble and contrite heart." [16] Satyagraha presupposed faith in the living presence of God in whose hands and under whose guidance the movement stood. "The leader depends not on his own strength but on that of God." [17] Hence Gandhi believed that satyagraha could overcome any obstacle. Satyagraha in adverse circumstances would succeed through the intervention of God. "The non-violent technique does not depend for its success on the good-will of the dictators," Gandhi told an English visitor in the 1930's. "For a non-violent resistor depends upon the unfailing assistance of God, which sustains him throughout difficulties which would otherwise be considered insurmountable. His faith makes him indomitable." [18]

Though Gandhi's commitment to nonviolence was seemingly absolute, it did admit of exceptions. Given a choice between cowardice and violence, as has been mentioned, Gandhi opted for violence. "I would rather have India resort to arms in order to defend her honour," he wrote in 1920, "than that she should in a cowardly manner become or remain a helpless witness to her own dishonour." [19] Gandhi also accepted the necessity of taking life for food, killing vermin and carnivorous beasts like tigers that threatened villages, and mercy-killing of mortally sick, suffering animals and humans. Even manslaughter was deemed necessary in certain cases. "Suppose a man runs amuck and goes furiously about sword in hand, and killing any one that comes his way, and no one dares to capture him alive. . . . From the point of view of *ahimsa* it is the plain duty of every one to kill such a man."[20] According to Louis Fisher, Gandhi in 1947 approved of India's action in sending troops to Kashmir to repel the tribal invaders encouraged by the Pakistani government.[21] On the other hand, not until 1942 did he sanction the use of force against the Axis powers during World War II, and there were other inconsistencies.

Gandhi was not a builder of systems but, as he called himself, a practical idealist, and despite his attempted strict adherence to certain principles, his action often defied logic and baffled his followers. The leader of satyagraha, Gandhi maintained, depended upon the guidance of God. "He acts as the Voice within guides him. Very often, therefore, what are practical politics so-called are unrealities to him, though in the end his prove to be the most practical politics."[22] Many times, Gandhi would defer a decision because the "inner light" was not clear, and for the same reason he would refrain from devising plans of action. "It may be," he wrote in 1939, "as has happened throughout my life, that I shall know the next step only after the first has been taken. I have faith that when the time for action has arrived, the plan will be found ready."[23] Gandhi's colleagues, as we shall see, were often exasperated by the mystic's reliance upon divine guidance.

Gandhi derived the inspiration for his doctrine of satyagraha from several different sources. Born in 1869, he grew up in a highly religious home—his parents were staunch adherents of Vaishnavism (or Vishnuism), one of the two major theistic sects of Hinduism that comes closest to a conception of monotheism. Early in life he thus came to regard God as a Supreme Being endowed with auspicious qualities; he also learned maxims like "There is nothing higher than Truth" and that *ahimsa* was the highest virtue. The emphasis on nonviolence was also taught by the Jains who had many adherents in Gujarat, the home region of the Gandhi family.

Gandhi's father was friendly with many people who were Muslims and Zoroastrians, and young Gandhi was exposed to discussions about the merits of different religious faiths.[24] While studying law in England he also delved into the Old and New Testaments. The Sermon on the Mount, in particular, impressed him, and he saw in it similarities to the *Gita*, which, as he later shamefully admitted, he read for the first time in London at the age of twenty. It was during his stay of twenty-one years in South Africa that his philosophy of life crystallized. There he came into closer contact with Christians, Muslims, and Theosophists; he read Tolstoy, Thoreau, and Ruskin. Tolstoy's spiritual interpretation of Christianity, his emphasis on overcoming hatred by love and nonresistance, especially appealed to Gandhi, and these ideas seemed to him closely related to Buddhist and Jainist teaching of *ahimsa*.[25] The influence of Western thinkers upon Gandhi's developing outlook was thus great, but it is also clear that none of these fundamentally affected his deepest convictions. In each case he was attracted to these writers because they reflected his own thinking—"the influence was that of corroboration of an already accepted ethical precept, a crystallization of basic moral predisposition, or the formulation, for purposes of specific application, of a nucleus principle."[26]

The dominant force in Gandhi's life was Hinduism. It is the Hindu religion, Gandhi said in 1920, "which I certainly prize above all other religions."[27] The main elements making up the doctrine of satyagraha had deep roots in the Hindu tradition. Aphorisms extolling the greatness of truth and *ahimsa* are known in every Indian village; stories from the Hindu, Buddhist, and Jain classics illustrate the duty of nonviolence. The call for self-suffering, too, fell upon fertile soil in a country where asceticism had long been part of religion. Old and long-accepted forms of resistance without overt violence like *dharna* (sitting at the door of an opponent until the alleged wrong is redressed), fasting, and *hartal* (the demonstration of extreme dissatisfaction with a governmental measure by ceasing work and closing shops) facilitated the acceptance of the Gandhian technique of nonviolent resistance by the Indian people.[28]

But Gandhi was more than a traditionalist. He used the familiar to promote the novel. Gandhi introduced Western humanist concepts into the Indian tradition, and his identification with Hinduism, to the chagrin of many of his followers, was far from uncritical. The conception of religion he finally came to accept was highly eclectic and syncretic. It gave Hinduism a universal attire and included Christianity, Islam, Buddhism, and indeed all religions within the fold of truth. Religion for him meant ethics rather than theology or metaphysics.

Gandhi spoke of God as ultimate reality, and satyagraha for

him was a means of reaching God, a means of self-realization. This was good Hindu doctrine. But Gandhi's stress on service to humanity rather than aloofness from this world was somewhat unorthodox. "If I found myself entirely absorbed in the service of the community," Gandhi recalled, "the reason behind it was my desire for self-realization, I had made the religion of service my own, as I felt that God could be realized only through service. And service for me was the service of India. . . ." [29] "God to me," Gandhi explained, "is Truth and Love; God is ethics and morality; God is fearlessness." [30]

In 1903 Gandhi joined a group of Christians and Theosophists in South Africa to study the *Gita,* and this "New Testament of Hinduism" quickly became for him the book *par excellence* for the knowledge of Truth. The *Gita* "became an infallible guide to conduct. It became my dictionary of daily reference. . . . I turned to this dictionary of conduct for a ready solution of all my troubles and trials." [31] Again, however, Gandhi's interpretation broke with orthodoxy. The entire *Mahabharata,* according to him, was fiction. The battle setting for the *Gita* was not an historical battle but rather an allegory. It related to the struggle in man's heart between his passions and selfishness on one hand and his spiritual nature on the other. The war described in the *Gita* was a war for the performance of one's duty irrespective of the consequences. Gandhi agreed with Tilak and other interpreters of the *Gita* that the epic poem taught the virtue of selfless action as against renunciation. But where Tilak had argued for the legitimacy of righteous violence, Gandhi insisted that the *Gita* forbade violence even for good causes. Resort to force would always involve anger and hatred, would always lead to attachment to the fruits of action, the prohibition of which represented the central teaching of the *Gita.* Salvation was attained by the unselfish performance of good deeds and this path, Gandhi felt, led necessarily to *ahimsa.*

> Let it be granted, that according to the letter of the Gita it is possible to say that warfare is consistent with renunciation of fruit. But after 40 years unremitting endeavor fully to enforce the teaching of the Gita in my own life, I have, in all humility, felt that perfect renunciation is impossible without perfect observance of *ahimsa* in every shape and form.[32]

There were many who disagreed with Gandhi's interpretation of the *Gita* and of the political principles derived therefrom. Gandhi replied to them that while he appreciated their position he would continue to adhere to his reading. "My belief in the Hindu Scriptures," he declared in 1920, "does not require me to accept every word and every verse as divinely inspired. . . . I decline to be bound by any interpretation, however learned it may be, if it is repugnant to reason or moral sense." [33] Gandhi's commitment to nonviolence and satyagraha outranked any scriptural authority.

THE PRACTICE OF SATYAGRAHA: THE MYSTIC IN POLITICS

In 1915 Gandhi returned from South Africa to India, and within a few years he had become the undisputed leader of the Indian National Congress. He caught the imagination of the Indian masses as had no other Indian public figure in modern times. What explains this rapid rise to the top? Why did India follow Gandhi? Was it because of his personal saintliness or his political skills?

"Gandhi," Nehru noted, "was essentially a man of religion, a Hindu to the innermost of his being." [34] There can be little doubt that Gandhi's tremendous appeal to the people of India rested in good part upon his qualities as a prophet endowed with spiritual powers. He was the embodiment of a Hindu holy man—practicing renunciation, self-control, fasting, and penance—and the masses of Indian humanity accepted him as a man of God. The Indian tradition had always emphasized that personal virtue had public consequences and that a man's claim to wisdom as a statesman was proportional to his capacity for self-restraint. Gandhi voluntarily took on a life of celibacy because he shared this belief in the importance of asceticism, and many of his followers believed that his political potency depended on it. "Gandhi's political effectiveness," an astute American observer has remarked, "rested on the fact, among other things, that those who observed his career believed that his self-control would indeed endow him with extraordinary powers to compel the environment." [35] Nehru wrote in the middle thirties:

Perhaps in every other country he would be out of place today, but India still seems to understand, or at least appreciate, the prophetic-religious type of man, talking of sin and salvation and nonviolence. Indian mythology is full of stories of great ascetics, who, by the rigor of their sacrifices and self-imposed penance, built up a "mountain of merit" which threatened the dominion of some of the lesser gods and upset the established order. These myths have often come to my mind when I have watched the amazing energy and inner power of Gandhiji, coming out of some inexhaustible spiritual reservoir.[36]

The Indian villagers called Gandhi a *mahatma* (a great soul), and throngs of simple people consistently demanded his blessing. Gandhi himself resolutely opposed the cult developing around his figure. "I lay claim to nothing exclusively divine in me. I do not claim prophetship," he wrote in 1924. "I am but a struggling, erring humble servant of India and therefore of humanity. There is already enough superstition in our country. No effort should be spared to resist further addition in the shape of Gandhi worship."[37] Still, the reverence persisted, and his very style of leadership encouraged it. His use of religious terminology, his simple dress, the staff in his hand, the seating posture he took up, like Buddha, when making speeches—all this evoked the image of a man of God.

Gandhi thus enjoyed what Max Weber called charismatic authority. Charisma, according to Weber, stood for "a certain quality of an individual personality by virtue of which he is set apart from ordinary men and treated as endowed with supernatural, superhuman, or at least specifically exceptional powers or qualities. These are such as are not accessible to the ordinary person, but are regarded as of divine origin or as exemplary, and on the basis of them the individual concerned is treated as a leader."[38] Gandhi fitted this model of leadership, and it provides an important key to the loyalty and reverence which he enjoyed to such an extraordinary degree.

Gandhi, through his simple mode of speech, clothing, and food, consciously identified himself with the starving masses of India, and this was another source of his success and acceptance as a popular leader. "Gandhi," concluded Nehru, "does represent the peasant masses of India . . . he is the idealized personification of those vast millions. Of course, he is not the average peasant. A

man of the keenest intellect, of fine feeling and good taste . . . all
this so utterly unlike and beyond a peasant. And yet withal he is
the greatest peasant, with a peasant's outlook on affairs. . . ." [39]
Gandhi tried to live like a peasant and speak like a peasant, and
the common man responded to him and hailed him as his spokesman. In 1931 Winston Churchill attempted to ridicule Gandhi by
calling him a half-naked fakir, but it was just this appearance that
contributed to his great hold over the Indian people.

Gandhi appealed to the illiterate millions of India's countryside, but he also attracted the intellectuals. Nehru recalls how
Gandhi impressed a meeting of Muslim leaders in 1920: "He
spoke well in his best dictatorial vein. He was humble but also
clear-cut, and hard as a diamond, pleasant and soft-spoken but inflexible and terribly earnest. His eyes were mild and deep, yet out
of them blazed a fierce energy and determination." [40] It was the
utter sincerity of the man, his self-confidence, and the impression
of a tremendous inner reserve of power that drew people to Gandhi even though they often disagreed with him. He was "the
symbol of India's independence and militant nationalism, the un-
yielding opponent of all those who sought to enslave her," and
when the struggle was on, Nehru noted, "that symbol became
all-important and everything else was secondary." [41]

The fact that the Gandhian program of nonviolent action
seemed the only realistic one under the circumstances also enhanced his standing among the intelligentsia. The slow constitutional path as well as the path of terrorism had failed to bring results; the socialists were still weak, and they frightened the
upper-class members of the Congress. Hence Gandhi's call for
nonviolent mass resistance rallied the nationalist movement behind him, and, where the idea itself failed to persuade, Gandhi
helped matters along by his great skill in neutralizing and disarm-
ing opposition. Many of his colleagues agree that Gandhi had a
dictatorial strain in him and often acted like an autocrat. Gandhi
thought that he knew best, and most of the time he was able to
get the other leaders of the Congress to follow him. "Always we
had the feeling," Nehru writes, "that, while we might be more
logical, Gandhiji knew India far better than we did, and a man
who could command such tremendous devotion and loyalty must
have something in him that corresponds to the needs and aspirations of the masses." [42]

Gandhi dominated the Congress even though his goals were far from clear and even though he often bewildered his colleagues by his inconsistencies and frequent twists and turns. "What, after all, was he aiming at?" Nehru asked himself in 1934. "In spite of the closest association with him for many years, I am not clear in my own mind about his objective. I doubt if he is clear himself." [43] Gandhi's speech was often nebulous, and he went along improvising his method of action without much forethought of the overall objective. During the years of the struggle for independence Gandhi's political eccentricities were often ignored, and he benefited from the charisma of his personality. It is only in the years since his death that the record of Gandhi's leadership has been subjected to a more critical examination and the findings are not all positive. The judgment of one of India's most distinguished historians, Dr. R. C. Majumdar, is typical of those who have undertaken the difficult task of stripping away the halo of infallibility cast around Gandhi during his lifetime:

A historian must uphold the great ideal of truth which was so dear to Gandhi himself, and if we delineate the political life of Gandhi with strict adherence to truth, the whole truth and nothing but the truth, it will, I believe, be patent to all that Gandhi was lacking in both political wisdom and political strategy—as we commonly understand these terms—and far from being infallible, committed serious blunders, one after another, in pursuit of some Utopian ideals and methods which had no basis in reality.[44]

Other Indians have used even stronger language. "Whether we like it or not," another man of stature has written, "Mahatma Gandhi was a dismal political failure, as he was bound to be in the circumstances. . . . Religion and politics are basically incompatible disciplines. One is concerned with eternal life and the other with temporal values. They cannot be reconciled; and in any attempt to do so, as Gandhi tried to, both are bound to suffer." [45] William James, discussing the political role of the saint, claimed that saintly methods like nonresistance generate irresistible creative energies and constitute practical proof that in the case of holy men "worldly wisdom may be safely transcended." [46] The part played by Gandhi—a man who sought to be both a religious man and a politician—in the Indian independence movement would seem to cast doubt upon this proposition. The tension between Gandhi's role as a prophetic figure, following what he considered to be the voice of God within him, and his function as a national leader, attending to political realities, is writ large over the last thirty years of Gandhi's life. At times this conflict led to his temporary withdrawal from active leadership and even from membership in the Congress, though he always returned to its fold. Gandhi's position as "permanent super-president," as Nehru called him, accounts for many of the mistakes committed by the Congress.

Gandhi entered the Indian freedom movement at a time of comparative quiet. The Extremists had been deprived of their leadership, and by 1916 the quarrel between them and the more moderate elements of the Congress had been settled. In 1915 Mrs. Annie Besant had formed a Home-Rule League that had quickly become a rallying point for activist sentiment. With the exception of a few revolutionaries who sought the help of Germany, India cooperated with Britain in World War I and expected substantial political concessions in return. These hopes were disappointed. In March 1919 the Indian government enacted the Rowlatt Act extending the strict wartime controls, a law which the Indian nationalists interpreted as a slap in the face. Gandhi appealed to his countrymen to observe a *hartal*—work was to cease and all places of business were to close for one day—to prepare for a satyagraha campaign against the repressive legislation. The *hartal* was observed, but violence soon broke out too. In Delhi troops fired on rioters, and in the Punjab a week of unrest and violence culminated in the Amritsar massacre of April 13 which left 379 Indians dead and 1137 wounded. Five days later Gandhi, shocked at the bloodshed, suspended satyagraha. To undertake the campaign without adequate prior education in nonviolence, he declared in a speech, had been a "Himalayan miscalculation." [47]

In December 1919 Parliament adopted the Government of India Act that implemented a reform scheme known as the Montague-Chelmsford Report. The Act provided for a system of dyarchy with Indians in control of certain departments in the provincial governments, while other departments were "reserved" and kept under the exclusive control of a British governor. When the Report was announced in July 1918 it split the Nationalist movement. Tilak and Mrs. Besant considered the proposed reforms a sham, while others regarded them as a substantial advance toward self-government. When the Congress met shortly after the enactment of the scheme in December 1919, Gandhi argued in favor of giving the reforms a fair trial. But six months later Gandhi had completed a radical about-face and demanded a mass movement against the government which he called "satanic." A new era in Indian politics was to begin.

Gandhi's decisive change has been variously explained. It has been argued that the rising tide of mass unrest forced Gandhi and the Congress to abandon the earlier line of cooperation.[48] Gandhi himself stressed his own complete disillusionment with the sincerity of the British government as a result of the whitewashing of the culprits of the Amritsar atrocity and the injustice inflicted upon the Indian Muslims by the terms of the Treaty of Sèvres. This instrument imposed a severe peace upon Turkey; it dismembered the Ottoman Empire, the ruler of which was the caliph or spiritual head of Islam and revered as such by millions of Indian Muslims. The Treaty of Sèvres consequently was interpreted as an attack upon the Muslim religion, and the Khilafat (or caliphate) issue quickly developed into an anti-British movement of considerable momentum. Gandhi, sensing an opportunity of uniting all Indians in a common struggle against Britain, forcefully supported the Khilafat movement, and he was able to convince the Congress of follow suit. At a special session held at Calcutta in September 1920 the Congress decided to launch a program of nonviolent non-cooperation in support of the Khilafat movement to force the British government to grant India *swaraj* (self-rule). Indians were to boycott the courts, withdraw from the schools and colleges, and refuse to cooperate with the new political reforms.

The decisions taken at Calcutta represented a decisive event in India's history. "This special session at Calcutta," Nehru wrote, "began the Gandhi era in Congress politics. . . . The whole look of the Congress changed; European clothes vanished, and soon only *khadi* [homespun cotton cloth] was to be seen; a new class of delegate, chiefly drawn from the lower middle classes became the type of Congressman; the language used became increasingly Hindustanic, or sometimes the language of the province where the session was held. . . ."[49] On August 1 Tilak died, and Gandhi became the unchallenged master of the Congress. Under Gan-

dhi's leadership the Congress abandoned the aim of self-government to be attained by gradual constitutional progress in favor of
the new goal of *swaraj* to be achieved by means of peaceful and
nonviolent action. According to one interpretation giving up
constitutional politics was a grave mistake. "The disjunction that
took place, under Gandhian leadership, between constitutionalism
and mass action, the essential sanction for all successful political
activity, unnecessarily delayed Indian freedom, and by delaying
it, created or aggravated other problems which earlier freedom
would have obviated or at any rate mitigated." [50] Mass action agitation, instead of being used as a lever for political reforms and a
constitutional settlement, became welded to all-or-nothing demands, the acceptance of which could not realistically be expected.

The non-cooperation movement was started in 1921 and was
widely supported all over the country. As during the Swadeshi
movement, goods of foreign manufacture were boycotted; the
symbolic burning of foreign cloth attracted huge crowds. Parts
of India's college and secondary educational systems were seriously disrupted. The combination of a rising cost of living, misery in the countryside, and growing discontent with the government resulted in a mass upsurge as had not been experienced
since the Great Mutiny of 1857. Large numbers of Congress
workers and leaders were arrested. "Nineteen-twenty-one,"
Nehru recalled, "was an extraordinary year for us. There was a
strange mixture of nationalism and politics and religion and mysticism and fanaticism. Behind all this was agrarian trouble and, in
the big cities, a rising working-class movement." [51] Gandhi believed that victory was near: "I invite even the sceptics to follow
the programme of Non-co-operation as a trial, and I promise that
there will be Swaraj in India during the year, if the programme is
carried out in its fulness." [52]

Despite Gandhi's exhortations to practice *ahimsa*, the unfolding
movement increasingly assumed a violent character. Strikes, riots,
and attacks upon property were widespread. On February 1,
1922 Gandhi addressed an ultimatum to the viceroy threatening a
campaign of mass civil disobedience in the district of Bardoli in
Gujarat unless the demands of the Congress were met. But on
February 5 a mob of Congress workers attacked a police station
at Chauri Chaura in the United Provinces, set it afire, and burned

twenty-one policemen to death. A few days later Gandhi and his
Congress Working Committee meeting in Bardoli suspended the
entire program of non-cooperation and civil disobedience. On
March 10 Gandhi was arrested, tried, and sentenced to six year's
imprisonment.

The Bardoli decision hit the Congress like a bombshell. The
principal lieutenants of Gandhi, who were in prison, were angry
and sent letters of protest to him. The movement had been halted
and paralyzed from within just when it appeared to be succeeding. To the young Nehru Gandhi's action called into question
the entire philosophy of satyagraha:

> Chauri Chaura may have been and was a deplorable occurrence
> and wholly opposed to the spirit of the nonviolent movement; but
> were a remote village and a mob of excited peasants in an out-of-
> of-the-way place going to put an end, for some time at least, to our
> national struggle for freedom? If this was the inevitable conse-
> quence of a sporadic act of violence, then surely there was some-
> thing lacking in the philosophy and technique of a nonviolent
> struggle. For it seemed to us to be impossible to guarantee against
> the occurrence of some such untoward incident. Must we train the
> three hundred and odd millions of India in the theory and practice
> of nonviolent action before we could go forward? And, even so,
> how many of us could say that under the extreme provocation
> from the police we would be able to a remain perfectly peaceful.[53]

There appears to have been another reason for Gandhi's decision to end the campaign. The resolution of Bardoli, in addition
to condemning violence, also declared that the Congress opposed
the nonpayment of taxes and rent payments, and it reaffirmed the
legal rights of the landlords. "The middle-class leaders of the nationalist movement," writes an American historian, "including
wealthy landowners and industrialists, were fearful of a genuine
popular movement that might become an attack on all property,
privilege, and power—Indian as well as British." [54] The Congress derived much of its financial support from Indian capitalists
and landowners and it was, in part, to reassure these interests that
the non-cooperation movement was halted.

The satyagraha campaign that was to have ushered in India's
freedom thus failed, and the national movement was left demoralized. Gandhi's standing within the Congress was seriously diminished. Ardent nationalists like Mrs. Besant, C. R. Das, and Tagore

attacked the method of direct action as being purely negative and pleaded to take up the political fight inside the legislatures. Out of this sentiment was born the Swaraj party, led by the elder Nehru and Das, which held the center of the political stage until the death of Das in 1925.

The hope of achieving Hindu-Muslim unity was also shattered. The Khilafat movement had fired religious fanaticism and had led to a mass exodus of Indian Muslims to Afghanistan as well as to serious communal riots. Between 1923 and 1927 communal outbreaks took a toll of five hundred dead and five thousand injured.[55] In Madras province the Moplahs, a Muslim people, rose in rebellion and attacked their Hindu neighbors. Hundreds of Hindus lost their lives, and more than two thousand Moplahs were killed by the troops restoring order.[56] As a result of this clash the All-India Muslim League withdrew from the Congress-led campaign of non-cooperation, and, after the Khilafat agitation had been broken by the Turkish Republic's abolition of both the sultanate and caliphate, the former Khilaphatists became the bitterest enemies of the Congress.

The failure to find an easy solution to the Hindu-Muslim problem should not have come as a surprise. A side issue like the caliphate question could hardly have been expected to overcome long-standing differences that separated the two communities. Moreover, as an Indian historian has pointed out, "Gandhi failed to realize that the pan-Islamic movement in India, which he chose to lead, cut at the very root of Indian nationality. By his own admission that the Khilafat question was a vital one for Indian Muslims, even more vital than Home Rule for India, Gandhi himself, put a seal of approval to the oft-repeated claim of Indian Muslims that they formed a separate nation, they were in India but not of India."[57] Last, but of great importance, though Gandhi no doubt sincerely desired Hindu-Muslim unity, his own personal conduct and the way he conducted the freedom movement could not but antagonize the Muslims. "Civil disobedience involved an appeal to the masses," one observer writes, "and an appeal to the masses by an organization headed and symbolized by Gandhi was necessarily an emotional, semi-religious appeal to the Hindu masses and not to the Muslims; for Gandhi with all his fads and fastings, his goats's milk, mud baths, days of silence and fetish of non-violence was pre-eminently a Hindu. He himself claimed to be 'a

Muslim, a Hindu, a Buddhist, a Christian, a Jew, a Parsee.' But this claim did not cut much ice; indeed who but a Hindu could entertain such a preposterous hope of being all things to all men?" [58]

Gandhi rejected the goal of a secular state sought by most of the other leaders of the Congress, and under his influence the movement, in Nehru's words, "took on a revivalist character so far as the masses were concerned." [59] Small wonder that a Muslim writer, looking back upon the years of Gandhi's domination of the Congress, could conclude that the Mahatma was "entirely devoted to the cause of Hinduism. Nationalism and non-violence were points of strategy only to achieve his objective, namely Hindu ascendency." [60] Such an appraisal is hardly fair, but it is easy to see how it could have been made. As long as the Congress was led by men speaking the language of Western liberalism and constitutionalism Muslim intellectuals could feel at home in it. But during the Gandhian era the movement increasingly took on a Hindu complexion and that alienated its Muslim members. A man like Mohammed Ali Jinnah, who in 1917 had been a keen supporter of the Congress and who at that time had described the threat of Hindu domination as a bogy, by 1928 had departed from the Congress and soon became the main spokesman for the idea of Pakistan—a separate Muslim state.[61]

Gandhi was released from prison early in 1924, and, by the end of the decade, he had recaptured his position of leadership in the Congress. A new generation of young, more radical nationalists like Jawaharlal Nehru and Subhas Chandras Bose had emerged, and it was Gandhi who was chosen as the natural mediator between the various nationalist factions. At the Calcutta meeting of the Congress in December 1928 a resolution, sponsored by Gandhi, was adopted that satisfied both moderates and radicals: By January 1, 1930 Britain was to be asked to agree to grant India complete home rule, with independence or under dominion status; a round-table conference was to be convened to work out a suitable constitution. Unless these demands were met a new campaign of nonviolent non-cooperation would be started. When the British government responded by agreeing to a round-table conference but without making a commitment to immediate dominion status the stage was set for another round of direct action.

On March 12, 1930 civil disobedience began with a pilgrimage by Gandhi and 79 disciples to the sea to defy the salt tax. The 170-mile march made headlines all over the world and ended on April 6 when salt water was placed on a fire in a symbolic act of defiance of the government's monopoly on the manufacture of salt.[62] Gandhi was imprisoned on May 5, but the movement went on without him in spite of the mass arrests of satyagrahas. Officials resigned; liquor shops and places of foreign business were boycotted. The campaign was supported by the destitute workers and peasants as well as by Indian businessmen who welcomed the opportunity of hurting their British and Japanese competitors. Once again outbreaks of violence marred the movement. Rioting occurred in many of the big cities, and many government officials were murdered.

The first round-table conference convened in London in November 1930. It was attended by delegates representing all parties except the Congress. At the end of the conference an amnesty was proclaimed for all political prisoners in India, and on January 26, 1931 Gandhi and the other Congress leaders were released. A little over two months later an agreement, known as the Delhi or Gandhi-Irwin Pact, between Gandhi and the viceroy was signed. The civil disobedience campaign was suspended, and the Congress agreed to attend the second session of the round-table conference. The British government made a few minor concessions, but basically the pact did not secure a single aim of the Congress, not even the repeal of the salt tax. After a lengthy and painful struggle the Congress had gained nothing in its fight for self-government.[63]

Gandhi attended the second round of the round-table conference in the fall of 1931 as the sole representative of the Congress, but he followed a line of obstruction and the conference adjourned without results. While it was in session new violence broke out in India, and the government responded by a series of repressive ordinances. Returned from London, Gandhi renewed the civil disobedience campaign, and he and many other Congress leaders were once again arrested and imprisoned without trial. After Prime Minister MacDonald announced a scheme for solving the communal problem according to which the electorate was to be divided into twelve separate constituencies, including one for the untouchables, Gandhi on September 20, 1932, began a "fast unto death." Nehru later recalled: "Again I

watched the emotional upheaval of the country during the fast,
and I wondered more and more if this was the right method in
politics. It seemed to be sheer revivalism, and clear thinking had
not a ghost of a chance against it." [64] Six days later Gandhi
ended his fast in return for a compromise that gave the untouchables reserved seats but no separate electorate. The civil disobedience movement, meanwhile, was slowly collapsing. In May 1934
the Congress formally suspended mass civil disobedience; only
Gandhi was to continue satyagraha. The movement had come to
an end without accomplishing anything.

The defeat of the second direct action campaign again affected
Gandhi's popularity. Though the Mahatma's saintly life and sacrifices had inspired the masses as never before, his failure as a politician was equally plain. The imprisoned Nehru was especially
upset over the statement Gandhi had issued when withdrawing
civil disobedience. At the beginning of this second campaign the
Mahatma had made it clear that he would not abandon civil disobedience because of sporadic violence, but the reason Gandhi
gave now for ending the mass movement was hardly more logical: He had decided to be the sole representative of civil resistance in action because a valued companion of long standing had
been reluctant to perform his prison tasks, thus acting counter to
the rules of satyagraha. "Was a vast national movement involving
scores of thousands directly and millions indirectly to be thrown
out of gear because an individual had erred?" Nehru asked bit-
terly. "This seemed to me a monstrous proposition and an immoral one." Nehru conceded that the civil resistance movement had
had to be suspended. "But the reason he had given seemed to me
an insult to intelligence and an amazing performance for a leader
of a national movement." Gandhi had advised the members of the
Congress to learn the art and beauty of self-denial and voluntary
poverty, to engage in hand-spinning, and, generally, to cultivate
personal purity. "This was the political program that we were to
follow. A vast distance seemed to separate him from me. With a
stab of pain I felt that the cords of allegiance that had bound me
to him for many years had snapped." [65]

During the next five years Gandhi retired from politics and occupied himself with social reform. In the spring of 1936 the Congress decided to contest the elections to be held under the new
constitution enacted by Parliament a year earlier, and in 1937

Congress won a sweeping victory, gaining about 70 per cent of the votes cast. The fact that Congress failed to invite the Muslim League, with which it had concluded an electoral pact, to form a coalition government in some of the Hindu-majority provinces has been held to have been a fatal error—a major factor that eventually led to the creation of Pakistan. Both Nehru and Gandhi indulged in the self-deception that the Congress could and did represent all Indians, including the Muslims, and they regarded the League leaders as relics of an outworn feudalism who would soon be disowned by the Muslim masses.[66] Gandhi, in particular, made a fetish of close contact with the masses at the village level, and he had no interest in political or legal arrangements that would allay Muslim fears of Hindu domination. The Muslim League leaders, in turn, rejected the suggestion that they should dissolve their own organization as the price for sharing political power, and the two communities drifted apart. In October 1937, Jinnah declared that Muslims could not expect fair play under Congress government.[67]

On September 3, 1939 Great Britain declared war upon Nazi Germany, and on the same day the British viceroy in India proclaimed that India as well was at war with Germany. The Congress, while deploring Nazi aggression against Poland, declared that the wishes of the Indian people had been deliberately ignored, and when its demand for immediate self-government was turned down, the eight provincial Congress governments resigned. Gandhi declared that as a pacifist he could not support the war, he praised France's surrender in 1940, and he advised the English people to let Hitler occupy the British Isles and then fight the Nazis with the methods of nonviolence.[68]

The moderate elements of the Congress took a more serious and realistic view of Britain's predicament. In July 1940 the All-India Congress Committee repudiated Gandhi's policy of nonviolence and offered to support the war effort if Britain would proclaim India's independence and form a provisional national government. The British government responded that dominion status was indeed its objective for India but that full weight should be given to the views of the minorities and that fundamental constitutional changes in the midst of the war were impossible. The Congress felt rebuffed and turned again to Gandhi. In October 1940 a new campaign of individual satyagraha was

launched. Members of Congress were selected to give anti-war
speeches and to allow themselves to be arrested. The speeches
included the slogan: "It is wrong to help the British war effort
with men or money; the only worthy effort is to resist all war with
non-violent resistance." [69] One year from October 1940, 23,223
persons had been jailed.[70]

By the end of 1941 the civil disobedience campaign had slack-
ened. On December 3 the British government, fearful of the rapid
advances made by Japan in the Pacific, and seeking to conciliate
India, released most political prisoners. After Pearl Harbor and
the American and British declarations of war on Japan, the
Working Committee of the Congress for the second time during
the war broke with Gandhi and announced that it was ready to
cooperate in the defense of India against Japan. On March 11,
1942, against the background of Japanese victories in Malaya and
Burma, Churchill announced that he was sending Sir Stafford
Cripps, leader of the House of Commons and a long-time champion of Indian independence, to India to settle the constitutional
problem. But the Cripps mission failed to resolve the deadlock between Congress and the British government. Gandhi, who earlier,
because of his fear of violence, had been very reluctant to launch
a mass movement, now began to think in terms of an organized
mass effort against the British. With the Japanese knocking at India's door, he seems to have felt, the British would quickly come
to terms. After the easy defeat of British forces in Singapore and
Burma, Gandhi may also have thought that the days of Britain in
India were numbered. As usual he had no precise plan of action.
"When I pressed him to tell us what exactly would be the program of resistance," recalls a one-time president of the Congress,
"he had no clear idea. The only thing he mentioned during our
discussions was that, unlike previous occasions, this time the people would not court imprisonment voluntarily." [71]

On August 8, 1942 the All-India Congress Committee adopted
the so-called "Quit India Resolution." Britain was asked to grant
India immediate independence in return for which a free India
would throw all her great resources into the struggle for freedom
against Nazi, Fascist, and Imperialist aggression. This endorsement of armed resistance represented a retreat from pacifism in
which even Gandhi most reluctantly concurred. On the other
hand, over-all leadership of the new campaign was put into Gan-

dhi's hands. Should Britain refuse to free India forthwith, "a mass struggle on non-violent lines on the widest possible scale" was to begin. "Such a struggle must inevitably be under the leadership of Gandhiji and the Committee requests him to take the lead and guide the nation in the steps to be taken." The Indian people were asked to "remember that non-violence is the basis of the movement." [72]

Gandhi had intended to enter into immediate negotiations with the viceroy, but the British government was not willing to take any chances. It arrested all leaders of the Congress, including Gandhi, and outlawed the organization. The serious disorder and violence that followed lasted several weeks; English writers have called it the "Congress Rebellion." Actually, and at least initially, this was "a revolt without leaders and without any definite program of action." [73] Crowds attacked the symbols of British authority and power—police stations, post offices, and railway stations. Government buildings were set on fire, and British officials were assaulted. As the mass movement subsided a revolutionary leadership emerged that distributed pamphlets inciting the people to form guerilla bands and adopted such slogans as "We shall do or die." [74] The policy of nonviolence went under, though, perhaps as a result of more than twenty years of the teaching of *ahimsa*, only about 100 persons were killed by mobs in the course of the disturbances. [75] Official estimates of the number of people who lost their lives or were injured as the result of police or military firings were given as 1,028 killed and 3,200 wounded; unofficial figures of the number of deaths vary from 10,000 to 40,000. [76]

The violent "Quit India" movement, just as the earlier civil disobedience campaigns, thus ended in failure. The country's administrative machinery and police by and large had remained loyal to their masters. Still, it became increasingly clear to everyone that British rule in India was soon to come to an end. The tide of nationalism, encouraged and supported either by the Japanese as an anti-Allied weapon or by the Allies as a resistance movement against the Japanese, was rising all over Asia. [77] The formation of the Indian National Army under Subhas Chandra Bose, which attacked India in 1944, the refusal of the Royal Air Force in India to obey orders in January 1946, and the mutiny of the naval officers in Bombay in February of that year all indicated that the British could no longer take the loyalty of the Armed Forces for granted. Also, on July 1, 1945, the British Labor party ousted Winston Churchill, long considered hostile to India's aspirations for independence; Britain was war-weary, and sentiment ran strongly against retaining India against her will.[78] Prolonged negotiations among the British government, the Congress, and the Muslim League finally ended in an agreement to partition India. On July 18, 1947 the Indian Independence Bill providing for the transfer of power to two dominions, the Union of India and Pakistan, became law. Independence came at midnight, August 14, 1947.

Gandhi, to whom the constituent assembly in New Delhi paid special tribute as an architect of India's freedom, had had practically no role in the final decisions leading to independence. To the last he expressed opposition to the creation of Pakistan, but he was overruled by the other leaders of Congress.[79] On January 30, 1948 he was shot to death by a Hindu fanatic. Thus came to an end the life of a man who had been both prophet and leading statesman of a struggling India for nearly three decades.

GANDHI'S CONTRIBUTION TO INDIAN INDEPENDENCE

According to a popular notion India achieved her freedom under the leadership of Gandhi by means of a nonviolent struggle that proves the power of love in a world ostensibly committed to force. Considered in the light of all available data it would appear that this view represents a simplification if not a misreading of history.

One can begin by raising the question whether satyagraha as conceived by Gandhi was ever really tried in India. It is generally conceded that the great majority of the people involved in Gandhi's various campaigns did not understand the principles of satyagraha and did not see in it a spiritual effort to overcome evil. Gandhi himself admitted in 1940: "We in India have never given non-violence the trial it deserves. The marvel is that we have attained so much even with our mixed non-violence." [80] Even his most trusted lieutenants did not really believe in nonviolence as a creed but accepted passive resistance as a political expedient implicit in the situation; they saw in it a useful way of mobilizing large masses for political action. For the Congress, Nehru writes, "the non-violent method was not, and could not be, a religion or an unchallengeable creed or dogma. It could only be a policy and a method promising certain results. . . ." [81] Whereas for Gandhi nonviolence ranked higher than even India's freedom, the other leaders of the Congress, though they admired the Gandhian doctrine, never paid absolute allegiance to it. Several resolutions condemning political murder passed by narrow majorities only. The pressure for resort to violence was often great, and if the Congress never decided to use force it was not because its leaders believed in not embarrassing the enemy or sought to effect in him a change of heart but because the failure of violence was a foregone conclusion.

In point of fact, violence did play a considerable role in the ultimate achievement of political independence. By itself, of course, no matter how heroic its exponents, it could never have brought decisive results. But the recurring episodes of individual terror and outbreaks of mass riots weakened the morale of the colonial regime, while at the same time they hardened the will of the people. Lajpat Rai observed in 1914: "There are those who blame the Extremists for having injured the cause by making the British rulers alert and by forcing them by their impatience, their extremism, their madness to adopt a policy of repression. These people forget that under foreign rule peace unalloyed by repression would be fatal. The political consciousness created by the Extremists in a decade could not have been created by the moderates in half a century." [82]

The Indian nationalist movement, even during the period of Gandhi's leadership, was a mixture of violence and nonviolence. It was hardly ever pure *ahimsa* as demanded by Gandhi's teaching. Hence satyagraha as such, R. C. Majumdar has argued convincingly, was never really put to the test, and it therefore cannot be credited with the attainment of independence.[83] The British left India because of a number of circumstances that have been mentioned but not because their hearts had been touched by the suffering they were causing India. The outcome most likely would have been the same even if Gandhi had never appeared on the scene. The gradual awakening of the Indian masses and the emergence of a nationalist leadership were the result of developments not limited to India. "The people," writes Nehru, "were the principal actors, and behind them, pushing them on, were great historical urges which prepared them and made them ready to listen to their leader's piping. But for that historical setting and political and social urges, no leaders or agitators could have inspired them to action." [84]

All this is not meant to deny Gandhi's important role or contribution to the Indian freedom movement. It was under his leadership that the Congress became a mass organization; it was Gandhi's dynamism that inspired the timid and demoralized millions to overcome their lethargy, "repairing wounds in self-esteem inflicted by generations of imperial subjection, restoring courage and potency." [85] As Nehru observed in 1944:

> To the vast majority of India's people he is the symbol of India determined to be free, of militant nationalism, of a refusal to submit to arrogant might, of never agreeing to anything involving national dishonor. Though many people in India may disagree with him on a hundred matters, though they may criticize him or even part company from him on some particular issues, at a time of action and struggle when India's freedom is at stake, they flock to him again and look up to him as their inevitable leader.[86]

But if Gandhi thus was the foremost and most outstanding of India's leaders this was not due to his espousal of nonviolence and still less to his archaic social and economic theories. Gandhi, despite his work for the abolition of untouchability, always remained a staunch believer in the traditional Hindu social order —the division into four hereditary castes. He was opposed to modern technology which alone can overcome an underdeveloped country's grinding misery, and he praised poverty and suffering. The Western-oriented and secular-minded leaders of Congress put up with these utopian ideas of Gandhi knowing full well that a free India could and would not go back to primitiveness. They accepted Gandhi as he was, though many of them at times were troubled by his objectives and choice of tactics.

One can also wonder or, perhaps better, speculate whether India could not have achieved her freedom earlier and less painfully by following constitutional methods—by accepting the reforms offered by Britain and by carrying on mass agitation for more until the goal of full dominion status or independence was attained. Gandhi resorted to the sanction of mass action but did not utilize it for a clearly defined constitutional purpose.[87] A gradual transfer of power achieved under a secular leadership, paying heed to Muslim sensitivities, might have undercut Hindu-Muslim antagonism and thus conceivably might have prevented the partition of India and the tremendous human suffering that came in its wake. Britain undoubtedly made its own share of mistakes and was unnecessarily slow in accepting the inevitable. But, as an American historian has remarked in connection with the constitution of 1935, "the Congress made an equal error in magnifying only the rights and powers that were withheld without investigating and appreciating the political rights and opportunities conferred." [88]

Last, it is necessary to note that whatever limited success passive resistance and Gandhi's practice of fasts and self-suffering may have had was probably due to the fact that India's antagonist was democratic Britain. It is doubtful that the same results could have been achieved against a government or a people free from the fetters of liberalism and the rule of law. A truly terrorist state would have silenced a Gandhi so quickly and thoroughly that neither the people of the vast subcontinent of India nor the rest of the world would ever have heard of him.[89] A totalitarian regime would hardly tolerate the mobilization of public opinion which Gandhi always considered crucial for the success of satyagraha. This point should be borne in mind because of the often extravagant claims made for the efficacy of the Gandhian technique. Wherever nonviolent resistance has scored some positive results—whether it be against the British in India or the Germans in Norway during World War II or against segregationists in the American South—these results have been due to the impact of concerted mass agitation rather than to a conversion of the oppressors. A holy man like Gandhi could enlist the devotion extended to a spiritual guru for political purposes. More generally, such a man, through the example of his saintly life, as William James observed, can be "a leaven of righteousness in the world" [90]—no more and no less.

CHAPTER 14

Militant Buddhist Nationalism: The Case of Burma

RELIGION AND GOVERNMENT IN TRADITIONAL BURMA

The close tie between Buddhism and the Burmese sense of national identity and culture that proved crucial in the emergence of Burmese nationalism can be traced back almost 1000 years. According to tradition, Buddhism was brought to the Mons, one of the leading ethnic groups of Burma, during the Buddha's lifetime. But it was not until the reign of King Anawrahta, who united Burma into a single kingdom and founded the first Burmese empire in the year 1044, that Theravada Buddhism became the dominant religion of the country. At a time when Buddhism had all but disappeared from its original home, India, Burma thus emerged as the main center of what has always been regarded as the orthodox school of Buddhism, and its people believed that they were destined to preserve the purity of the Buddha's gospel.

Political authority in old Burma and until the final loss of independence in 1885 was buttressed by several religious sanctions. The first consisted of elaborate and dazzling Hindu court ceremonies performed by Brahman priests from India. These masters of sacred ritual were active especially at coronations, royal weddings, and audiences. Being learned in astrology they also were consulted on the selection of auspicious locations for the capital and lucky dates for the inauguration of important undertakings. The prominent role of Brahmins at the court of kings who took pride in defending and promoting the Buddhist faith reveals the importance of the impact of Hinduism on Burmese culture.[1]

A second religious sanction of government was similarly borrowed from India. The king was not only expected to follow the lore of lucky and unlucky days, and thus bring his activities in harmony with the universe, he also was seen as residing at the very center of the macrocosmos which Hindu and Buddhist cosmology located at mythical Mount Meru. The king's capital and his palace were identified with this celestial mountain, the abode of the guardian gods of the world, and in this way the ruler himself attained divine status. He was the representative of Indra, the Hindu god of rain, and his exalted status was assured as long as he controlled the royal palace and owned a white elephant, the magical symbol and guarantee of fertility and rainfall.[2]

The doctrine of *karma*, taught by both Hinduism and Buddhism, was the third sanction supporting royal authority. The king's vast power and riches were regarded as outstanding examples of merit and reward accumulated in previous existences. As long as the ruler continued to accumulate additional merit by supporting the Buddhist monkhood, building pagodas, and promoting the welfare of his subjects, the guilt of evil deeds like bloodshed was offset, and his title was secure even if it were acquired through rebellion and murder. On the other hand, it was believed that if the *karma* of the king's past good deeds were not sufficiently replenished, or if it were outdone by the demerit of subsequent evil actions, he would perish. Hence some of the most ruthless and tyrannical Burmese rulers were at the same time the most lavish patrons of Buddhism and the most generous providers of social welfare.[3]

The king's role as defender and supporter of the Buddhist faith was the most important factor in ensuring the allegiance of his subjects. Starting with King Anawrahta in the eleventh century, who attempted to suppress the indigenous animistic religion involving the worship of *nats* (spirits), all Burmese rulers took great pride in promoting Buddhism, and their subjects praised these efforts. "Despite the manifold abuses of power arising from royal despotism," notes a historian of Burma, "which led Burmans traditionally to identify the government itself with such basic scourges as fire, flood, famine, and evil enemies, kingship merited popular appreciation because of its dedication to religious ends." [4] Patronage of Buddhism thus buttressed the king's legitimacy and enhanced the loyalty and support of the various ethnic peoples of Burma—the Burmans, Mons, Shans, and Arakanese—for whom the most important bond of unity was their common religious faith.

The king, in addition to promoting Buddhism by taking care of the monks and building shrines and temples, also acted to safeguard the purity of the faith by appointing the head of the Sangha hierarchy, suppressing heresy, and enforcing discipline within the order. The chief agency of royal control was the *thathanabaing* (possessor of discipline and instruction), a kind of archbishop, who was appointed by the king. The primate was assisted by a commission of eight monks (*pongyis*); under him were district "bishops" called *gainggyoks*. This organization enforced monastic discipline, settled controversies within the order, organized the holding of annual examinations, and generally supervised monastic training. Routine discipline, however, was normally maintained locally, and the court-created hierarchy was often a loose affair.[5]

Though the king invested the primate, who served at his pleasure, the *thathanabaing*'s authority in matters of ecclesiastical organization and discipline was great, and interference by the king in sacerdotal affairs was rare. The monarch needed the Sangha for it strengthened the royal authority in numerous ways, especially in its function as the country's teaching profession. Every village had its monastery or temple with one or more monks in residence, and here the local boys learned reading and writing and the basic principles of Buddhism. In a country whose political structure was unstable at the center and often ineffectual outside of the capital, the Sangha performed an important function of social control by teaching the virtues of meekness and humility. "Along with the headman, the monks kept watch over the manners and morals of the village and admonished the people to obey the laws and to pay their taxes."[6] The villagers revered the wearers of the yellow robe, and the prestige of the king was enhanced by his support of the Sangha.

In some instances monks were sent on diplomatic missions, and they occasionally interceded to save the lives of persons wantonly condemned. But by and large the Sangha did not interfere in politics, and it largely failed to mitigate the brutality of Burmese kingship. For example, the monks were not strong enough to challenge the established practice of new kings of killing their brothers and other kinsmen whose presence might challenge the stability of their rule. "Neither the personal influence of the *thathānabaing* nor the humanitarian principles of the Buddhist faith seem to have moderated appreciably the unrestrained violence which characterized most of the reigns."[7] Monks sometimes led revolts, but such participation in rebellions was rare, and Buddhism generally functioned as a stabilizing force.

The cause of kingship was also furthered by the claims of certain rulers, convinced of their extraordinary religious merits, to be a *bodhisattva*, a future Buddha. According to the canon, a monarch successfully championing the cosmic moral law of the Buddha was a Universal Monarch (*Cakravartin* in Sanskrit or *Setkya-Min* in the Burmese adaptation—literally a "Wheel-turning King," i.e. one who upholds the most basic teachings of Buddhism stated in the Buddha's first sermon, the "Sermon of the Turning of the Wheel of the Law"). Such an ideal Buddhist ruler was seen as preparing the way for the descent of the Buddha as Maitreya (Metteya in Pali) who would usher in an age of plenty, universal love, and compassion. Several Burmese kings asserted or believed themselves to be this Buddhist redeemer. King Bodawpaya (1782–1819) made the claim to be Maitreya though he failed to convince the Sangha. In other cases, it appears, the people accepted the assertion, and the charisma of kingship was appropriately enhanced.[8]

Great as was the Burmese kings' power, it was not unlimited. In the coronation vows the monarch swore not only to respect the laws of Buddha, but he also promised to watch over the people as though they were his sons and daughters. Kingship traditionally was seen as based on a contract between ruler and subjects, and the king was expected to live up to the people's trust. The way in which individual monarchs responded to this old convention varied a good deal though almost all of them sought to win at least the approval of the Sangha—the representatives of the public conscience.[9] The peace and prosperity of the realm were regarded as dependent upon the moral behavior of the king, and misfortune would be blamed upon his injustice and misuse of power. The literature of Buddhism told of kings who had come to a sad end because of their arbitrary rule; the monarch's fear of rebellion was expected to restrain would-be tyrants. In practice, however, this expectation did not materialize. In fact, it appears that the fear of rebellion provided further incentive for oppressive rule: kings became increasingly autocratic at the first sign of opposition in order to discourage resistance.[10] In a few instances Burmese monarchs did not even hesitate to massacre monks suspected of subversive designs. In 1540 King Thohanbwa is said to have killed 360 monks and plundered monastic property. According to the chronicles, King Alaungpaya (1752–60) threw 3000 monks to the elephants who trampled them to death as punishment for having opposed his will.[11] Uprisings that did succeed rarely improved the lot of the people; the latter therefore by and large willingly obeyed their rulers, no matter how autocratic, for they preferred the maintenance of law and order to the confusion and unrest of frequent rebellions.

THE ORIGINS OF MODERN BUDDHIST NATIONALISM

The loss of Burmese independence to Great Britain was a gradual process that lasted one hundred years. Friction between Burma and British India began to develop after 1784, and it culminated in the first Anglo-Burman War of 1824–25. The second war (1852) resulted in the British conquest of Lower Burma. The final collapse came during the reign of King Thibaw—in the third and final Anglo-Burman War of 1885–86. On November 28, 1885 Mandalay fell to the British, and the king and his two principal queens were sent into exile. On February 26, 1886 Burma formally became a province of British India.

The defeat of the king and the seizure of the capital had been a relatively easy affair, but the pacification of the countryside required four years. Disbanded soldiers were joined by peasants. Even monks participated in the guerilla fighting, and in many places the leadership of the rebellion was in their hands. As in earlier outbreaks of resistance to the British, religion was one of the most important factors. The abolition of the monarchy, a national and religious symbol, had created a serious institutional and psychological void. A British administrator observed in 1887:

> The Burman cannot conceive of a religion without a Defender of the Faith—a king who appoints and rules the Buddhist hierarchy. The extinction of the monarchy left the nation, according to the people's notions, without a religion. We have overthrown the king and destroyed all traces of kingly rule. Naturally they look upon this as the destruction of their nationality.[12]

After the second Anglo-Burmese War large numbers of monks, unwilling to live under an alien government, had migrated from Lower to Upper Burma. Those who stayed behind felt abandoned and often became corrupt. The British government had refused to assume the traditional patronage of Buddhism or to appoint a primate to enforce discipline. The same state of affairs now threatened the rest of the country. The British authorities not only abolished the court and traditional local self-government, they did away with the ecclesiastical commissions that enforced the decrees of the *thathanabaing*. The latter's juridical functions were severely curtailed when civil courts were vested with exclusive jurisdiction over all disputes of a civil nature, and ecclesiastical authority was all but destroyed when a secular judge overruled a disciplinary decision of the Sangha in 1891.[13] When the last *thathanabaing* appointed by the king died in 1895, no successor was named. Gradually the entire machinery for regulating admission to the Sangha and disciplining its members broke down, and monastic standards deteriorated.

Coinciding with the decline of the monastic order and its loss of prestige was a general weakening of the social order. In Lower Burma, in particular, capital and labor from India introduced a new type of commercial rice cultivation. A footloose Burmese peasant proletariat came eventually to populate much of this area; the cultivators were debt-ridden and lacked a permanent domicile in a stable community.[14] Lawlessness spread and defied police controls. Sporadic outbreaks of anti-British violence plagued the country. Some of the leaders were again monks who claimed to be future Buddhas, harbingers of a Golden Age that would dawn with the freeing of Buddhist Burma from British rule.[15]

Some writers have characterized this early anti-British agitation as "xenophobic reactions to foreign rule" and have called it a traditionalist-oriented "pre-nationalism."[16] It is no doubt true that these periodic outbursts against foreign domination had as their goal the restoration of the old order rather than the establishment of a modern nation along the Western model. Still, the people of Burma could look back upon 800 years of Burmese history in one country, and they were possessed by a strong sense of national pride. "In fact," writes a Burmese scholar, "hemmed in by the teeming millions of China on one side and of India on the other, the Burmese were able to survive as an independent people,

mainly because of their strong sense of nationalism." [17] The traditional order that the anti-British rebels were trying to resurrect
thus had many attributes of a nation-state, and it would seem
quite appropriate to call these outbursts manifestations of a traditional Burmese nationalism rather than mere anomic disturbances.[18] Moreover, these poorly organized outbursts were very
soon to merge with a more modern type of nationalist movement.

   Throughout the history of Burma Buddhism had functioned as
the crucial integrative force in society and culture. At the turn of
the century the traditional religion once again began to assume
the role of a unifying factor, and it provided the basis for the
emergence of an increasingly aggressive nationalist movement.
The Sangha resented the competition of government and missionary schools and the consequent loss of their former hold over education. The monks were disturbed by the breakdown of their
religious hierarchy and the colonial government's pampering of
religious minorities. Widespread resentment of the foreigner
brought about a new flourishing of interest and pride in the
Buddhist religion. Europeans might be richer and stronger, many
Burmese seemed to say to themselves, but all this was as nothing
since they did not possess the jewel of true faith.[19] Buddhism became a symbol of self-assertion against the colonial regime.

   With the Sangha in a state of stagnation the revival of Buddhism was centered mainly in lay circles and among Anglicized
urban intellectuals. Buddhist associations with educational and social ideals were formed in the 1890's; in 1902 the first "Young
Men's Buddhist Association" (YMBA) came into being. Of the
221 books published in Burma during the year 1908, 83 were devoted to religion. In 1909 two Buddhist newspapers and a peri-
odical made their appearance under YMBA sponsorship, and in
the following year the Burma Research Society was launched. In
the countryside a growing number of itinerant monks were preaching the Buddhist gospel.[20]

   The YMBA at the beginning was almost exclusively urban.
The movement was led by young lawyers and undergraduates;
the members were students, clerks, and junior officials of the colonial government who had been educated in English schools.[21]
At first the organization was more social and educational in nature than political; its purpose was to effect a renaissance of Burmese and Buddhist values, and its members sought to adjust the

country's traditional culture to that of the West. As time went on the YMBA became more politically oriented, and gradually it became a training ground for Burma's future nationalist statesmen. As in India and the East generally, nationalistic sentiment was encouraged by Japan's victory over Russia in 1905—the triumph of an Asian country over a Western power. The independence of the neighboring Buddhist kingdom of Siam reminded the Burmese of the glories of their own past. Revolutionary ideas seeped in from India and China; their impact was heightened by the emphasis on the ideas of democracy and self-determination current in the First World War.[22]

In 1916 the YMBA for the first time became actively involved in political agitation. At issue was the refusal of Europeans to remove their shoes on pagoda premises. This wanton disregard of Buddhist custom had aroused opposition as early as 1901; under the leadership of U Thein Maung, a barrister, a movement now got under way to put an end to this manifestation of disrespect to the Buddhist religion and Sangha, and nationalist sentiment quickly rallied. Most YMBA branch associations actively supported the agitation which became an outlet for anti-British sentiment. The organization by now had spread into the villages, though the unrest was largely confined to Rangoon. The government finally granted to each local *pongyi* the right to regulate the matter of footwear for his pagoda as he chose, but it refused to issue a general decree as demanded by the Buddhists. This ostensibly religious issue thus had become the first important anti-British skirmish involving the educated and often Westernized urban intelligentsia. "The primary role played by religious considerations in the emergence of naissant Burmese nationalism," concludes Cady, "can be attributed to the fact that religion afforded the only universally acceptable symbol to represent an accumulation of grievances, economic, social, and psychological, which were as yet for the most part inarticulate and incapable of direct political exploitation." [23]

Proposals for Indian constitutional reform discussed during and after the First World War had not included Burma; it was alleged that the country was politically immature. The most that Britain seemed ready to grant was a scheme of self-government on the district level. A series of mass meetings sponsored by the YMBA in 1919 protested this decision, and a delegation was sent to Lon-

don to plead the Burmese case for more self-rule. After considerable delay the British government in late 1920 finally agreed to
include Burma within the dyarchy system of India, but by that
time the Burmese nationalists had increased their demands. Violent revolutionary protest was in the air; political agitation had
ceased to be the exclusive concern of the Burmese, Western-oriented intelligentsia. "The popular revolution for political freedom
had begun." [24]

THE UNRULY 1920's: THE HEYDAY OF THE
POLITICAL MONKS

The *pongyis* were brought into the burgeoning nationalist agitation through the movement for national schools which followed
the student strike against the new University of Rangoon in 1920.
The students objected to the high standards announced for the
proposed university, which they interpreted as a move to limit
the number of Burmans in attendance. They also protested the
meager representation of Burmans on the governing bodies of the
university. On December 4, 1920, two days before the dedication
ceremonies, a boycott was started which soon was 100 per cent
effective. Under the influence of Indian agitators, who sought
support and endorsement of the policy of non-cooperation
adopted by the Indian National Congress led by Gandhi, the student movement broadened its demands to include complete home
rule for Burma and a rejection of the dyarchy reforms—a
two-part division of executive authority with most powers "reserved" to the British governor—just secured in London. From
Rangoon the strike spread to all government schools as well as to
a few American missionary schools. Editors and monks joined the
strike movement and demanded a system of national schools entirely free from British support and control. Seeking to enlist
non-Buddhist support, the Central Council of the Young Men's
Buddhist Associations leading the strike now changed its name to
"General Council of Burmese Associations" (GCBA).[25]

The strike held up fairly well during the year 1921. In many
localities Buddhist monks acted as teachers in the improvised national schools. But discipline was lacking, and the monks, who
were almost totally unequipped to handle modern learning, were
poor substitutes for the trained teachers. By the end of 1922 the

experiment had essentially collapsed. Still, the political effects of the university strike and national school movement were great. In the words of Cady: "They marked the birth of revolutionary nationalism in Burma. December 4, 'National Day,' was eventually designated a holiday. The educational agitation brought the teaching *pongyis* into the national movement as never before, and a fateful pattern was developed for using the university and the schools as instruments of political opposition." [26]

A further and far more decisive impetus for the emergence of the monks as the grass-roots leaders of the nationalist cause was provided by the activities of the *pongyi* U Ottama whose name is indissolubly linked to the phenomenon of political monks of Burma. U Ottama had spent several years in India where he had become acquainted with the aims and methods of agitation of the Indian National Congress. He also had studied in Japan and was said to have learned to appreciate the Japanese characteristics of discipline and perseverance. Upon his return to Burma in 1921 he quickly became the acknowledged leader of the politically active monks. During the interwar period Burma had approximately 100,000 *pongyis*,[27] though this figure cannot be regarded as exact because of the often temporary nature of Sangha membership—many Burmans don the yellow robe temporarily in order to escape from the stress of the world or, occasionally, to escape the reach of the law. Probably only a minority of the monks took an active role in the nationalist movement, but most of them were in sympathy with the nationalist cause, and their backing proved a crucial factor in the development of Burmese nationalism into a popular movement. The *pongyis* had good reasons for opposing alien rule which rapidly eroded the status and prestige of the monk. "There was no place for him in the new Western-oriented social hierarchy, his educational functions were assumed by other agencies, an unknown foreign language prevented him from understanding what was going on, and westernized Burmese laymen increasingly regarded him as irrelevant to modern life." [28] Small wonder that the *pongyis* emerged as the most aggressively nationalistic force on the scene—a fertile soil for U Ottama's preaching.

U Ottama toured the country and in his speeches called for nonpayment of taxes and non-cooperation with the British administration. He demanded home rule and promised that France

and America would come to Burma's aid. His emphasis varied
with the nature of his audience and circumstances. Many of his
speeches were religiously colored to give the struggle for independence a Buddhist meaning so as to convince the traditionalist
rural masses. *Nirvana*, deliverance from universal suffering, U Ottama told the villagers, could not be obtained without prior deliverance from political bondage. "*Pongyis* pray for Nirvana but
slaves can never obtain it, therefore they must pray for release
from slavery in this life." [29] This modernistic interpretation of
Buddhism successfully merged with popular prophecies of a perfect Buddhist society headed by an ideal Buddhist ruler who
would humble all foreign conquerors and unbelievers. [30]

In the days of the Burmese kings, according to U Ottama, the
Burmese people's religion and culture had prospered, whereas
British rule degraded and corrupted their morals. The monks
therefore had to fight to prevent the total destruction of the national religion. The struggle for independence was to be nonviolent, but resort to force was not rejected in principle. Violent
incidents, in fact, became a fairly common occurrence, and
monks often were the instigators or perpetrators. When a Burmese theatrical group performed for the visiting Prince of Wales
in 1922, ignoring a boycott of the royal visitor declared by the
GCBA and the political monks, it was later attacked by a group
of *pongyis* armed with knives, stones, and sticks, and several of
the actors were seriously wounded. [31] Two months earlier a
pitched battle between several hundred monks and police had
taken place in Rangoon. In the countryside crops were destroyed,
cattle maimed, and arson and murder committed. Many of these
deeds were committed by lay political agitators or ordinary criminals who had sought the shelter of the yellow robe. With the
breakdown of social controls it became more and more difficult
to distinguish between the opportunistic criminal and the violent
nationalist. [32]

The political involvement of the monks was facilitated by several factors. The *pongyis* in the cities and towns lived in monasteries of several hundred members, and it was easy to mobilize
them for meetings or demonstrations. Every village had at least
one monk, and, by virtue of this fact, the Sangha had a ready-
made political network no political party could match. The government, for its part, found it difficult to initiate proceedings

against the political monks. The *pongyis* enjoyed the admiration and reverence of the Burmese masses, and any attempt to arrest, prosecute, and convict monks for violations of the law inevitably triggered popular indignation and charges of persecution of the sacred Sangha. Last, the British had earlier practiced a policy of neutrality and non-interference in religious matters, and for several years the Sangha had been without a *thathanabaing*. The colonial administration had feared that a strong Buddhist primate might become a threat to British rule. In 1903 a new *thathanabaing* had been recognized, but his authority was strictly limited, and this weakness of the Sangha hierarchy freed the monks from the traditional restraints, and they could thus carry on their nationalistic activities. In vain did the government now strengthen the primate's authority. A conservative *thathanabaing* in 1921 forbade monks to participate in any form of political agitation, but by this time discipline had become so weak that the political monks could simply disregard this order.[33]

The principal coordinator of the monks' political activities was the General Council of Sangha Sametggi (GCSS) organized in 1922. The influence of this politicized faction of the Sangha was strongest in the villages. The British had forbidden the headmen, who were officials and presumably allies of the government, to participate in politics and the political monks stepped in to fill this vacuum of leadership. Very soon they gained control of many of the village *athins*—political associations set up by the GCBA in 1921–22. The *pongyi* radicals also worked in close cooperation with the leaders of the so-called Bu athins, conspiratorial secret organizations that appeared in the villages in 1922 and that fought for home rule by violence and intimidation.[34] The Bu athins were declared illegal in August 1923, but their appeal could not be ended by edict. Tension between the government and the rural population was increased by an agricultural crisis. The land was slowly but steadily passing into the hands of money-lending landlords. At the time of the census of 1921 only 50 per cent of the agriculturists in Lower Burma owned their own land; 27 per cent were landless laborers and 22 per cent tenants.[35] The loss of land and growing agrarian distress undermined communal life and fed the fires of discontent.

The political monks used prophecies, magic, and other more modern forms of agitation to turn the villagers against the foreign government and its agents—the police, the courts, the tax collector, and the village headman. They pleaded for a boycott of foreign goods, the establishment of national schools, boycott of the civil courts, and abstinence from liquor and other intoxicants. The ultimate goal of the *pongyis* was home rule, a term borrowed from India; it meant for most of them a restoration of the old order in which a king and the Sangha would rule cooperatively, and the monks once again would be the moral leaders.[36]

The political monks' distrust of Western political ideas and institutions found expression in their call for a boycott of the elections to the legislative council under the Burma Reforms Act of June 1922. The *pongyis* excelled in direct agitation on the village level; a shift of focus of the nationalist movement toward a political struggle within an elected legislative chamber could only diminish their influence.[37] A majority of the lay GCBA, committed to home rule and opposed to the dyarchy scheme, similarly decided to boycott the elections and as a result the inauguration of dyarchy on January 1, 1923, representing a considerable advance in self government, met hardly any popular acclaim.

Relations between the different factions of the GCBA and the monks' GCSS during the following years were not always smooth. U Ottama advocated a line of revolutionary action, including a campaign for the nonpayment of taxes, whereas many members of the GCBA favored a more moderate course and gradually came to resent *pongyi* attempts at leadership. Still, the westernized intelligentsia could not dispense with the political monks and the massive political ground swell generated by them. In the words of Cady: "In contrast with the situation in India, where the Congress Party found its main support among the middle class and business and professional people, Burma had no such indigenous middle class. If nationalist politicians in Burma wanted popular backing, they had little choice but to line up with the political *pongyis*. . . . Since a monk's denunciation could ruin the standing of political aspirants, most of them sought religious support." [38]

The strong position of the political monks in the nationalist movement began to weaken following the failure of the anti-tax campaign of 1924. This agitation had led to considerable violence, at times indistinguishable from plain criminality, which had further alienated the urban nationalists. By 1925 the question of *pongyi* influence and other issues involving personal rivalries had left the GCBA fragmented into many splinter groups. Following a riot in August 1924 U Ottama had been sentenced to three years' imprisonment for sedition; this long jail term (his second) deprived the radical *pongyis* of their most able leader, and their influence declined. The first attempt to build a united nationalist movement, bridging the gap between the more westernized urban elements and the traditionalist political monks, had failed.

U Ottama was released from jail in February 1927, and the *pongyis'* political activities revived. The anti-tax campaign was taken up again, and the colonial administration had to resort to mass arrests of monks to silence the agitators.[39] A favorite tactic of the *pongyis* was to circulate rumors that the British were about to withdraw and that the revived Burmese kingdom would abolish all taxes. Several pretenders to the vacant throne at Mandalay now made their appearance in the villages and revived the old hopes of a deliverer king who would overthrow the alien ruler and restore national honor and prosperity. The most serious incident involved the savior king Bandaka in the Shwebo district of Upper Burma in 1928. Bandaka collected men and money and rose up against the British. The rising became so serious that the government had to call in troops to suppress it. Eventually Bandaka and 25 followers were rounded up, tried, and sentenced to transportation for life.[40]

In 1928 U Ottama was arrested for the third time; he eventually died in jail in 1939. The next most important leader of the political monks, U Wisara, in 1929 died after a prolonged hunger strike which he had undertaken to secure the right to wear the yellow robe during his imprisonment. Popular feeling ran high, and some 5000 Burmans participated in the cremation ceremonies for U Wisara who was regarded as Burma's *pongyi* martyr second only to U Ottama.[41] The death of U Wisara occurred while the Simon Commission was holding hearings on the future of Burma. The country's nationalists had made a futile effort to present a united front to the visiting commission. A lay-controlled group advocated separation from India, the curtailment of Indian immigration, freedom from *pongyi* domination, and the enactment of legislation designed to discipline and purify the Sangha. The *pongyis* and their lay followers, on the other hand, de-

manded a retention of the tie to India and cooperation with the
Indian National Congress. Irked at the proposals for control of
pongyis made by their rivals they formed a "Hundred Committee" and demanded obedience to the monks. It was this committee
that instigated the boycott of the Simon Commission. While the
latter attempted to find a constitutional solution to the Burmese
problem, unrest continued in the villages, and military police had
to be used to suppress political agitation against payment of the
capitation tax.[42] In the Tharrawaddy district the groundwork
was being laid for a full-scale rebellion.

THE SAYA SAN REBELLION

Saya San was a native of Upper Burma, a one-time monk, who
had settled in Belugyun in Lower Burma and earned a living as a
practitioner of indigenous medicine. He joined a radical faction
of the GCBA but in 1928 withdrew from it to form his own secret association to forcibly resist the collection of the capitation
tax. Eventually this agitation broadened into a plan to overthrow
British rule in Burma.

The upper delta district of Tharrawaddy was the center of the
planned rebellion. For years this district had been a favorite spot
for agitators, and in 1927–28 it had become notorious for a
widespread anti-tax campaign. Economic conditions were depressed, the price of paddy had fallen, and the cultivators were in
debt to moneylenders. Saya San's nationalist speeches fell upon
receptive ears. He blamed the British for the villagers' difficult
situation and exhorted the people to rise against the foreign exploiter. He reminded them of an old prophecy that a *minlaung*
(prince) would appear and free the country from British rule.[43] A
small army, albeit with few weapons, was drilled, and a "capital"
prepared in the jungle some twelve miles east of Tharrawaddy
town.

On October 28, 1930, at the auspicious moment of 11:33 P.M.
as selected by astrologers, Saya San was proclaimed King of
Burma, assuming the title *Thupannaka Galon Raja*. The galon
was a legendary bird of Hindu mythology which attacked and
destroyed the snake. In Saya San's adaptation of this fable the
snake represented the foreign ruler, and the galon thus became a
symbol of victory. In fulfillment of an ancient prophecy Saya San

next became a monk, and after a brief sojourn in a monastery he
was proclaimed king a second time. This coronation ceremony
was carried out in the traditional manner and the "Bird-King" assumed the throne with the five royal regalia: the white umbrella
(ancient Brahman symbol of divine kingship), the crown of
victory, the sacred gem-studded slippers, the victorious
sword, and the fan. A bamboo hut was built, and an inscription designated it the "Palace of the Buddhist King." [44]

On December 21 Saya San reviewed his army. As the four regiments marched past a prayer was chanted: "May Thupannaka
Galon Raja live at Aung Chan Tha, the City of Wealth and Victory, and may his contemplations be speedily successful. May
the Guardian Spirits of the Religion, the Dragons and the King
of Angels sustain him. May he become Emperor of the Four
Islands and of the thousand lesser isles adjacent to them." At
the end of the review the new king read the following proclamation:
"In the name of Our Lord and for the Church's greater glory,
I, Thupannaka Galon Raja, declare war upon the heathen English,
who have enslaved us." [45]

The deliberate use of traditionalist language, symbols, and ceremony contributed to the great emotional power of the movement. It soon became more than a peasant uprising motivated by
economic grievances, assuming the character of a quasi-millenarian rebellion propelled by militant religious ideas. "It was a
phenomenon of what anthropologists call 'nativistic' response
against overwhelming impacts of an alien civilization that had
been dissolving traditional society up to its economic foundations
and challenging the traditional conception of Burmese folk Buddhism." It was "a revolt against the new forces in the name of a
search for security in pre-colonial values, a desperate attempt to
restore the old symbols of cosmic and social harmony." In the
popular mind Saya San was identified with the *Setkya-Min*, the
ideal Buddhist ruler of the Four Island continents and a future
Buddha.[46]

On December 22, 1930 hostilities began. One of the first targets
of the rebels was the unpopular forestry service. Six officers, including one European, were killed, and some 100 forestry houses
were burned to the ground. The peasants, at first about 1500
strong, had only 30 guns, mostly homemade; the rest carried
swords. But their courage was fortified by magic and the prom-

ises of astrologers that the end of British rule in Burma was at
hand. Recruits to the rebel army were tatooed with the galon
emblem that was believed to ensure invulnerability. A magical
elixir, magical gongs, and handkerchiefs also were believed to
give them immunity from bullets or make them invisible. In some
places the galon soldiers painted white circles on their naked but-
tocks, which they exposed to their opponents, and the sight of
these weird, wriggling circles often frightened off the government's forces. The Buddha himself was too remote, but the *nats*
(spirits), who had stood by the Burmans since pre-Buddhist times
and had become absorbed in folk Buddhism, were within reach
and their help was solicited. The mixture of animism and Buddhism that inspired the rebellion can be seen from the following
oath that included this plea:

> Do away with the heathens, Oh Nats, so that our glorious Bud-
> dhist religion may prosper. . . . Hark! Ye Brahmans and Nats, King
> of Brahmas, Defender of Buddhism, and others. We swear we will
> not ill treat, nor destroy either the life or the property of the peo-
> ple who are members of the associations affiliated to the G.C.B.A.
> and the Galon Army as long as Burma does not attain freedom
> from the British yoke. . . . May we overcome the heathens speed-
> ily and may the arms and ammunition used by our heathen oppo-
> nents and their servants turn into water or air or mis-fire and
> never attain their object.[47]

From the Tharrawaddy district the rebellion spread to much of
Lower Burma and the Shan states, largely as a result of the activities of itinerant monks who worked through the local *athins*. In
the Thayetmyo district the uprising was organized by a *pongyi*
named U Arthapa, abbot of a monastery. In the Yamethin district
the revolt was led by a monk who had come from Tharrawaddy.
He succeeded in collecting 40 to 50 men; they raided two to
three villages and killed one headman and a police constable.[48]
The peak of the outbreak was reached by June 1931. Men would
advance upon machine guns holding amulets in their hands and
chanting formulas. Gradually, however, the belief of the galon
soldiers in their invulnerability was shaken by the heavy losses
they suffered in engagements with the police and troops. Still, the
Burmese police were unable to master the situation. Almost two
divisions had to be sent from India to help fight the rebels and
even then it took one and one-half years to suppress the uprising.

According to figures collected by the British, 300 rebels were killed and wounded, and 8300 were captured or arrested. Of the government forces 50 were killed and 88 wounded. Many village headmen and several forestry officers were also murdered, and general destruction of property was extensive.[49]

Toward the end the rebellion degenerated into general disorder with attacks upon Indians and Chinese; criminals took advantage of the breakdown of law and order to terrorize the villages.[50] Even the "true rebels" committed atrocities against those who refused to supply them with food or money. There were reports of villagers being roasted alive and their children killed as a reprisal for cooperating with the police. About 1000 of the captured galon soldiers received sentences of imprisonment, and 128 were hanged; the heavier sentences were not for rebellion but for the deliberate murder of inoffensive citizens.[51] Saya San himself was captured, convicted of seditious treason, and, after a series of unsuccessful appeals, executed on November 28, 1937.

A noted Burmese scholar has called the Saya San rebellion appropriately "a strange blend of faith and superstition, nationalism and madness, of courage and folly." [52] It was not a mass rising comparable to the troubles of 1886–87, but it did represent an expression of traditional Burmese nationalism. The galon revolt thrived on ignorance and superstition, and the more westernized nationalist leaders not only were not involved in the rebellion but considered many of its features repulsive and degrading.[53] Still, the uprising caught the popular imagination, and it gave heart to all parts of the nationalist movement. Cady concludes that "the perpetrators of the uprising breathed new vitality into Burmese nationalism simply by demonstrating the courage of their political commitment against impossible odds. The heat of their frenzied resistance welded a connecting bond, between the culturally disparate *pongyi*-led masses and the Westernized elite. Although the uprising did not reconcile political differences, it undoubtedly constituted an important landmark in the development of Burmese nationalism." [54]

THE EMERGENCE OF SECULAR NATIONALISM

Following the suppression of the Saya San rebellion more and more political monks lost their position of prominence in the nationalist movement, and leadership and initiative passed into the hands of secular politicians. Such a trend, as we have seen, had begun in the late 1920's, and it was essentially completed by the end of the 1930's. We will here sketch these developments in brief outline only.

The *pongyis* did not suddenly disappear from the political scene, nor could the urban politicians now afford to dispense with the support of the political monks. "Even the more sophisticated younger men," notes Cady, "who discounted the superstitious lore of religious leaders, dared not leave to their rivals the exclusive exploitation of magic and omens." [55] But as the struggle for independence shifted into constitutional channels, the influence of the *pongyis* weakened. The main force for secularism was the Dobama Asiayone (We Burmans Society), formed in 1935 by the amalgamation of two student nationalist groups. The members addressed each other as *Thakin*, the word for "lord" or "master" customarily used in Upper Burma for addressing Englishmen, and the organization soon became known as the Thakin party. It included in its ranks such young nationalist leaders as Nu, Aung San, Ohn Khin, and Ba Swe, all of whom later played a leading role in the final fight for freedom during World War II. The Thakins were not hostile to religion, but they rejected the narrow conception of nationalism along religious or racial lines and stressed national unity. Their secular nationalism was reinforced by the influence of Marxism which made itself felt within Thakin ranks.[56]

There were other factors tending to undermine the strength of traditional *pongyi*-led nationalism. The Government of Burma Act, passed in 1935, came into operation on April 1, 1937, and at last Burma enjoyed a political identity separate from India. The new constitution provided "a liberal dose of democracy," [57] and since all political factions now participated in the political process there no longer remained a boycott party to which the Sangha could belong; the monks regarded direct participation in politics and electioneering as against the Vinaya rules.[58] Finally, secularist ideas were spreading under the impact of Western education, as a result of the increasing sophistication of lay politicians, within the growing Burmese middle class resentful of *pongyi* dictation.

The political monks found an outlet for their frustrations in the series of racial explosions that plagued Burma in the 1930's. The peasants resented the Indian moneylenders and usurious Chinese shopkeepers; in the cities friction grew between Burman and Indian laborers. A first clash in Rangoon in May 1930 left 300 to 500 killed; outbreaks continued into 1931.[59] The *pongyis* played a more direct role in the anti-Indian riots of July 1938. The immediate cause was the publication in 1937 of a book authored by a Muslim which was critical of the Buddhist religion. It had first appeared in 1931 and gone almost unnoticed, but the new edition was exploited by elements of the vernacular press hostile to the government and by the Sangha. On July 26 a mass meeting was called in Rangoon by the All Burma Council of Young *Pongyis* Association which demanded that the government ban the book. A protest demonstration organized by the monks turned into a riot against Indian Muslims that lasted for several days and spread to other parts of the country. Verified casualties caused by the rioters included 192 Indians killed and 878 injured.[60] The official inquiry committee after a careful investigation found that monks had everywhere played a leading role in instigating and directing the riots. The report noted:

It is distressing to have to record that in the majority of cases which have been specifically brought to our notice *pongyis* either have been present among the mobs of looters with *dahs* [knives] and other weapons in their hands or that, worse still, *pongyis* themselves were responsible for maiming and killing defenceless Indians.[61]

Unrest continued into 1939. A series of school strikes began in December 1938 in which the young Thakins had an important part. As in similar strikes in 1936, the students quit their classes "to lend support to the nationalist movement, and partly to evade their on-coming examinations." [62] The strikes were actively supported by the Young Sangha Associations, and, on February 10, 1939, a huge demonstration of students and monks in Mandalay, held in defiance of a ban imposed by the government, was fired upon by police. Fourteen demonstrators, including seven *pongyis*, were killed. The funeral of the martyrs was a highly emotional affair and led to sympathy demonstrations in Rangoon.

But the alliance between the political monks and the Thakins did not last. In World War II the monks actively assisted the Japanese invaders, assuming that Japan, being a Buddhist country, would restore religion to its rightful place. During the Japanese occupation the *pongyis* were ardent collaborators. When the Japanese-sponsored "independence" resulted in growing disillusionment, the monks emerged discredited. They took no part in ousting the Japanese, and they got no sympathy from the student-dominated Anti-Fascist Peoples Freedom League (AFPFL) which assumed power at the end of the war. Aung San and the other leaders of the AFPFL were Western-oriented and committed to the idea of a secular state. "When independence was achieved in 1948," writes Smith, "the Thakin-Aung San nationalist tradition was so completely dominant that there was little awareness of the other Buddhist-oriented nationalism." [63]

The role played by Buddhism in independent Burma forms a separate subject and does not concern us here.[64] We will only note that Buddhism has continued to play a role in post-independence nationalism. Religion has been enlisted to help achieve a sense of national identity and restore national pride. The appeal to Buddhism and the support of the monks at times has been used for personal political advantage; U Nu's victory in 1960 is attributed in large measure to his promise to make Buddhism the state religion and to the forceful campaigning of the monks on his behalf.[65] But the very success of this appeal is an indication of the strength of the Buddhist ethos among the Burmese masses; even among some of the urban elite, a sense of religious commitment is said to be gaining. "These Burmese who had been 'culturally disinherited by colonial acculturation,' who had succumbed to Western values and ways of life, found in the reassertion of their Burmese Buddhist identity a truly galvanic experience." [66] A similar resurgence of religion has been observed in other newly independent nations—the case of Islam in North Africa is the most prominent example—and these often contradictory trends constitute a warning against hasty generalizations about the complete triumph of secularism.

Once again Buddhism functioned as an integrative force binding together the diverse ethnic groups of the country. The fact that many of the non-Buddhists in Burma are aliens tended to reinforce the traditional view that "To be a Burman is to be a Buddhist." [67] However, this conception of national identity also created serious tensions between the Buddhist majority and the religious minorities, especially the Kachins. The adoption of Buddhism as the state religion during U Nu's rule in 1961, in particular, jeopardized national unity, and the coup of General Ne Win in March 1962 was precipitated in part by the army's fear of a threatening disintegration of the state.[68] The revolutionary regime has pursued an essentially secular course, and relations with the Sangha at times have been strained. In many ways the Ne Win government is again encouraging the kind of secular Burmese nationalism first promoted by the Thakins and Aung San. It remains to be seen whether Burma is ready for the stage of modernity when nationalism has become secular.

PART IV

Church and Revolution

CHAPTER 15

The Catholic Church and the French Revolution

THE FALL OF THE OLD REGIME

Toward the end of the eighteenth century the church in France was as much in need of reform as were the other major institutions of the Old Regime. The church was wealthy: it owned at least 10 per cent of France, and its income from estates and tithes equaled the total direct tax yield of the French state.[1] Exempt from taxation, the church paid a voluntary *Don Gratuit* every five years which, however, amounted to less than 3 per cent of the crown's fiscal revenues. At a time of rising financial woes for the French state, the wealth and the privileged position of the church were frequently attacked.

The worldliness of the upper clergy did not add to the church's reputation. Between 1774 and 1790, 173 of the 192 French bishops belonged to the nobility.[2] About one-half of the episcopate lived in Paris and enjoyed the splendor of the French capital. Cardinal Polignac died in 1741 without ever having visited the archdiocese to which he had been nominated fifteen years earlier.[3] A growing spirit of laxness also afflicted the monasteries many of which were very rich. Some abbeys and cathedral chapters were headed by appointees of the crown, who were not even clerics; for them these establishments represented well-paying sinecures.

The wealth enjoyed by most bishops, canons, and abbots contrasted sharply with the economic distress of the lower clergy, especially pronounced among the parish priests or curés. Around the year 1750 the average annual income of the bishops was estimated at about 37,500 livres, whereas that of the curés was about

300 livres or less than 1 per cent of the income of the bishops.[4] Small wonder that the members of this clerical proletariat developed a growing hostility toward the episcopate and their allies among the rich canons and abbots. In many dioceses the lower clergy had created their own organizations to improve their meager living standard and to achieve a voice in the diocesan bureaux, the governing organs dominated by the bishops. This "revolt of the curés," as it became known, drew strength from the ideas of the French theologian Edmond Richer (1560–1631) who had taught that the curés were the successors of the seventy-two early followers of Jesus (Luke 10:1) and that their office was a divine institution. He had insisted that the curés not be subject to the absolute control of the bishops and had defended the dignity of the lower clergy. During the eighteenth century the Richerists tended to merge with the Jansenists. Since most of the French bishops sided with Rome against the Augustinian and ascetic ideas of Cornelius Jansen (1585–1638), which were eventually declared heretical by several successive popes, the followers of the pious Jansen were thrown into an alliance with the lower clergy and their more militant spokesmen.[5]

Representing the interests of an exploited group, the curé movement stood for greater justice in society, but its major goals were the curtailment of episcopal despotism and the purification of the church. This explains the affinity of the curés for Jansenism just as it foreshadows the later split in the ranks of the clergy over the anticlerical legislation of the French Revolution. Some leaders of the curés—men like Sieyès, Guilbert, and Grégoire —were strongly influenced by the intellectual currents of the Enlightenment, but most of the curés disagreed with the *philosophes* and secularists on such questions as religious toleration, censorship, and clerical property.[6] The stirrings of common interest and resentment on the part of the curés, writes an observer of the scene in Angers, "were really more of an ecclesiastical phenomenon than a social and economic one. It was less a question of hatred of privilege on logical and egalitarian grounds, than of a pride in their own office, and a desire to rescue its rightful dignity from eclipse or belittlement." [7]

On July 5, 1788, Louis XVI, driven by fears of total bankruptcy, agreed to convene the Estates-General for May 1789. Necker's voting law helped the lower clergy, who were able to elect 208 curés to the First Estate, giving them a clear majority in a body of

296 (the remaining 88 clerical deputies divided as follows: 47 bishops, 23 abbots, 12 canons, 6 vicars general).[8] The consequences of this predominance of the curés were far-reaching. When the Third Estate boycotted the organization of the Estates-General in the traditional form of three separate chambers and insisted that all the deputies sit as a single body a majority of the clergy threw in their lot with the revolutionary cause. On June 13, 1789, amid great applause, three parish priests joined the Third Estate. On the following day, six more priests appeared, and on June 19 a narrow majority of the First Estate voted for union with the *Tiers* which had declared itself the "National Assembly." Of the 149 clerical deputies thus willing to defy the king, 131 were curés; among the 18 members of the upper clergy also voting in favor of joining the National Assembly were two archbishops —Georges LeFranc de Pompignan of Vienne and Champion de Cicé of Bordeaux.[9]

The great majority of the upper clergy had opposed this revolutionary step, but the bishops' threats and exhortations to obedience failed to hold most of the curés in line. Pastor Jallet, one of the leaders of the curé party, defiantly told his episcopal superiors: "We dare say that we are your equals; we are citizens like you; we are deputies of the nation like you. Your rights are not more extensive than ours, and to hold an opposing opinion from yours is not to lift the standard of rebellion." [10] Another militant defender of the rights of the curés, who was soon to become a prominent leader of the Left in the National Assembly, was a parish priest from Embermésil (Lorraine), the Abbé Grégoire. In his famous picture of the Tennis Court Oath the painter David with justification depicted Grégoire in the forefront of those swearing that they would not disband until they had drafted a constitution for France.[11] The former court preacher, Claude Fauchet, is said to have participated, sword in hand, in the storming of the Bastille on July 14. Most of the curés, on the other hand, favored an alliance with the Third Estate not so much because of an ideological commitment to the cause of popular sovereignty and still less out of hostility toward the monarchy but mainly in the hope of achieving much needed economic and social improvements in their status.

The first decrees of the National Assembly (now called the Constituent Assembly because it was preparing a constitution) were applauded by the lower clergy. The measures voted in Au-

gust 1789, in response to the uprising of the peasantry, included a
suppression of the privileges of bishops, archbishops, and chapters, an order forbidding the holding of benefices in plurality if
over the value of 3000 francs, a ban on the payment of annates or
other dues to Rome, and several regulations improving the economic lot of the curés. The tithes were abolished, but it was
voted to continue to collect them provisionally until the Assembly should decide upon "some other means of providing for the
expenses of Divine Worship, for the sustenance of the ministers
of the altar, the relief of the poor, the repairs and rebuilding of
churches and presbyteries, and of all establishments, seminaries,
schools, colleges, hospitals and communities to which they are
now appropriated." [12] The bishops were less than happy with
these measures, but in view of the general libertarian fervor they
decided not to oppose them.

Even as the Assembly passed these "anti feudal" decrees, it
went out of its way to show its deference to the Catholic religion. During the famous all-night sitting of August 4 it was
voted that a *Te Deum* be sung "by way of thanksgiving in all the
parishes and churches of the kingdom," and a medal was ordered
struck for the same purpose. None thought as yet of a separation
of church and state. The Declaration of the Rights of Man and
Citizen, issued on August 26, affirmed the principle of religious
toleration rather than that of religious liberty. Article 10 stated:
"No one is to be molested for his opinions, even his religious
opinions, provided that their manifestation does not disturb public order established by the law." Though this provision enabled
the Protestants to achieve their long-sought public exercise of
worship, it did not proclaim that liberty of conscience which the
church had always condemned. The pre-eminent place of the
Catholic religion remained unchallenged. The enemy of the men
of the Constituent Assembly was not the church, but despotism.
Anticlericalism, while not entirely absent, was still subdued and
anti-Christian voices were not yet to be heard.

THE BEGINNING OF THE ERA OF RELIGIOUS
WARFARE

Spurred on by a deepening financial crisis, the Assembly on November 2, 1789 declared that all church property was at the dis-

posal of the state, and on December 19 it ordered the sale of 400 million francs of church goods (and royal domains). These measures and the conflict between church and state that developed in their wake have been viewed by many historians as unavoidable. Lefebvre considered the seizure of church property a measure imposed by serious financial trouble, and Aulard refers to the decree of November 2 as an act of "self-defense." [13] It probably is more accurate to say that the deficit in the treasury provided the Assembly with the opportunity to bring the church into line with the new political order which it was trying to realize.[14] The sovereign power of the nation, it was felt by many deputies, should not have to end outside the doors of the church. The confiscation of the goods of the church thus was less a hostile act than an assertion of sovereignty in an hour of financial stress. Several offers of help from the hierarchy were turned down precisely for this reason: the sovereign people should not have to depend on charity; the civil power was supreme and could take what it needed.

The Assembly, when putting the property of the church at the disposal of the state, added that of course it "would provide in a fitting manner for the expenses of public worship, the maintenance of the ministers and the relief of the poor." [15] No curé, it was decided at the same time, was to receive less than 1200 francs a year. This provision meant a great improvement for the impoverished curés, though the upper clergy viewed it as a serious attack upon their well-being and prestige.

Several other measures of the Assembly similarly made religious organization a matter of public policy and raised serious apprehensions among the episcopate. In February 1790 it was voted to suspend the religious vows taken by the regular clergy, enabling them to leave the monasteries or religious houses. Moreover, no new vows were to be taken, and all orders and congregations were to be dissolved. The action was defended as necessary in order to prevent the mixing of secular and spiritual powers, but the intent of overcoming long-standing abuses was obvious. Despite the fact that a similar action had been taken by the crown in 1768, and, even though the Assembly provided a pension for the ex-religious, many in the regular clergy were alienated by this measure. When in April 1790 the Assembly put aside a resolution that would have made Catholicism the official religion of the nation the supporters of secularism scored another victory. "A part of the Gallican Church was beginning to call itself persecuted, not only because the nation was seizing its goods, but because its character as the State religion—the sole religion enjoying the privilege of public worship—was contested." [16]

Meanwhile a comprehensive plan for reform of the entire manner of operation of the French church, drawn up by the Assembly's Committee on Ecclesiastical Affairs, was nearing completion. In May 1790 this so-called "Civil Constitution of the Clergy" was put on the agenda of the National Assembly, and a vigorous weeks-long debate ensued. On July 12 the Civil Constitution was adopted. The main features of this legislation [17] were as follows:

1. The 139 dioceses, which were very unequal in size, were reduced to 83, one for each department. Thus the territorial divisions of the French church were made to correspond to the new civil divisions.
2. Priests and bishops were to be elected by all registered voters. An amendment by the Abbé Grégoire that only Catholics were to vote was rejected. The voting was to take place on Sunday "at the close of the parochial Mass which all the electors will be bound to attend." Every Frenchman was thus assumed to be a Catholic.
3. The state was to pay fixed stipends for the clergy. Bishops were to receive from 12,000 to 20,000 francs; parish priests from 1,200 to 6,000 francs. For the lower clergy this meant a comfortable living; the upper clergy was also well paid.
4. The number of parish priests was considerably reduced.
5. Bishops were to receive canonical institution not from the pope but from the six metropolitans of France (archbishops presiding over a church province). A newly elected bishop, though not allowed to apply to the pope for confirmation, was to write to him "as the visible head of the Universal Church to show the unity of the faith and the communion which he ought to maintain with him." [18]

Some writers have regarded these sweeping changes in the organization and structure of the French church as merely another manifestation of that Gallicanism which had characterized the "oldest daughter of the Church" for several centuries. As early as

1438, in the Pragmatic Sanction of Bourges, the French (Gallican) church had declared its administrative independence from
the Holy See and had limited the rights of the papacy in the appointment of French prelates. The Concordat of 1516 gave the
French king the power to appoint bishops and abbots. In 1682
the Gallican Liberties had been reaffirmed; Louis XV had felt
free to suppress monasteries and ignore the pope. "It was a point
of honour with the constituents," writes one historian, "to be as
disobliging in the name of the nation as absolute monarchs had
been in their name. From the writings of the *philosophes* a similar
policy of cynical and enlightened Erastianism could be
deduced." [19] In many ways, therefore, the Constituent Assembly
was only continuing an enterprise begun by earlier kings and
churchmen. The Gallican spirit was strong especially among the
deputies from the lower clergy. To the Jansenists the new law
commended itself as a return to the simplicity of the early
church.

And yet, the Civil Constitution of the Clergy went beyond
Gallicanism as well as beyond the spirit of the early church. It
not only freed the French church from foreign control but thoroughly subordinated it to the state. The lower clergy, imbued
with Richerism, had wanted a reformed church ruled by synods
of priests. But Rousseau had defeated Richer—the rights of the
clergy were swallowed up in the rights of the nation at large.
Gatherings of laymen took the place of congregations in electing
men to ecclesiastical office. The Civil Constitution, in effect,
made the church a state agency and its officials civil servants.

Many of the bishops, imbued with the Gallican spirit, were
willing to lend their support to a reform of the church, but in
their view such reforms, to be legally binding, required the assent
of the church. M. de Boisgelin, archbishop of Aix and spokesman
of the bishops in the Assembly, argued that this assent could be
obtained either by applying to the head of the church in Rome
or by calling a national council of the French episcopate. As a
moderate and a Gallican, Boisgelin probably favored the latter
method, but the Assembly was unwilling to consent to either
proposal. Rome was once again expected to yield under pressure;
the idea of convening a national council was unacceptable to the
radical majority of the Assembly for it revived fears of the clergy
as an order or class in a sovereign state that was to recognize no

such independent force, least of all a group of aristocratic bishops. Yet, by refusing the calling of a French national council, the Assembly perhaps unnecessarily alienated many members of the clergy. "Political Gallicanism had thrown away its most useful ally, ecclesiastical Gallicanism." [20]

The defenders of the Civil Constitution, both clerical and non-clerical, admitted that the state had no right to infringe upon the spiritual domain. But the new legislation in their eyes did not interfere with Catholic faith or doctrine. It merely fixed the church's external relations with the political order and brought it into conformity with the principles governing the new state. In a constitution based on equality, justice, and the common good, they argued, it was impossible to tolerate a parasitic establishment; it was necessary to establish the free election of priests so as to open the public service to every man whose merits had been recognized by his fellow citizens. To critics of the Civil Constitution, on the other hand, even moderates like Archbishop Boisgelin, some of the reform proposals infringed upon the essential jurisdiction of the church. The sovereign state could revise political boundaries but the readjustment of dioceses, involving the resignation of bishops, could only be sanctioned by the episcopate. "The temporal power," declared the bishop of Nancy, M. de la Fare, "not having conferred or being able to confer spiritual jurisdiction to priests, does not have the power to revoke it." [21] In no Catholic country were parish priests not appointed by diocesan bishops, let alone elected not only by Catholics but by Protestants or atheists. The Civil Constitution in its present form was unacceptable and opened the door to schism.

The achievement of a compromise solution, which the moderate Gallicans among the episcopate might have been willing to accept, was made more difficult by the conduct of the church's more reactionary elements. Some bishops had already emigrated; other churchmen appeared as champions of the Right in the National Assembly and thus helped create an image of the church as the enemy of the Revolution. Typical of these conservatives were the Abbé Maury and the Jesuit, Augustin de Barruel. Jean Sifrein Maury, the son of a shoemaker, who was later to become a cardinal, was an outstanding orator. In his speeches, many of which were published as pamphlets, Maury did not defend the discredited absolutism of the Old Regime but neither did he accept the principle of unlimited popular sovereignty. Democracy, he argued, was the worst form of government, and popular sovereignty, advocated by regicides like Buchanan, Ireton, Milton, and Junius Brutus, was an "anarchical doctrine." [22] Thus though seemingly accepting the Revolution, in effect, by denying the omnipotence of the National Assembly, Maury denied the Revolution. His position amounted to "an admirable springboard for counterrevolution as long as the Assembly refused to return to June 1789." [23] Barruel similarly defended the prerogatives of the king whose authority he saw deriving from God. By abandoning the true religion, he declared in 1790, and by accepting the philosophies of Voltaire, Rousseau, and Helvétius, the Revolution had brought the nation to the brink of ruin and anarchy.[24] The Revolution was the result of a plot by the *philosophes*, while at the same time it represented God's punishment for France's intellectual and moral decline in the eighteenth century.[25]

By the end of the summer of 1790 some bishops' pastoral letters were fulminating threats of resistance. But even without such explicit calls for opposition, the sharpening of the religious struggle helped the beleaguered aristocrats. "Monarchial sentiment," notes Mathiez, "had so far been powerless to provide them with a means of retaliation, and now Heaven had come to their assistance! Religious sentiment was the great lever which they used to set in motion the counter-revolution." [26] In August 1790 the count of Artois attempted to stir up a revolt in the southeast, and, with the help of priests and nobles, he summoned the National Guards to the Château of Jalès. Twenty thousand guards appeared at the meeting place, bearing the cross as their standard. A central committee was formed, and a manifesto published in which they promised "that they would not lay down their arms till they had reinstated the King in all his glory, the clergy in their property, the nobles in their honors, and the parlements in their ancient functions." [27] The alliance between some elements of the church and the counterrevolution had begun.

The weak Louis XVI sanctioned the Civil Constitution of the Clergy on July 22, 1790; the decrees were promulgated on August 24. In October an "Exposition of Principles," composed by Archbishop Boisgelin and eventually subscribed to by all but three members of the episcopate, once again offered concessions and suggestions for bringing the legislation into line with the law of the church.[28] But the National Assembly was in no mood to yield and, with reports of passive resistance to the implementation of the law coming in from all parts of the country, on November 27, 1790 the Assembly ruled that the entire clergy be required to take the civic oath of loyalty to the constitution of the kingdom (which, of course, included the Civil Constitution) or lose their posts. The king's consent to this decree was obtained on December 26, and the long-delayed showdown, an open break between church and state, had arrived.

THE SPLIT IN THE CHURCH

The religious legislation of the Constituent Assembly, and in particular the Civil Constitution, by now had alienated many earlier supporters of the revolutionary cause. Even the Abbé Grégoire had certain reservations about this latest and most radical reform, but in the interest of preserving the unity between the Revolution and the church, and believing in a "holy alliance of Christianity and Freedom," he publicly defended the Civil Constitution and the oath. The National Assembly, he declared in a speech on December 27, has proved its respect for the Catholic religion. The new law does not touch the spiritual concerns of the church; the new diocesan boundaries merely aim to provide "political forms more advantageous for the faithful and for the state." [29] Affirming his unshaken attachment to the laws of religion as well as to those of the state, Grégoire then took the oath. The Civil Constitution for him essentially was an attempt to restore Gallicanism. He was deeply attached to the Revolution because he wanted both church and state to follow the model of representative government favored by the conciliar movement and early Gallicanism. The papal power, as well as the royal power, was to be limited by a constitution emanating from general consent. In short, as a recent writer notes, "Grégoire was a democrat out of religious conviction. His political ideas, thus, are an exact mirror image of his concepts of the inner structure of the church. A democratic church, for him, was not a demand arising only from national tradition . . . but in his view corresponded to the laws of early Christianity, to the spirit of brotherly love that had been resurrected by the revolution." [30]

Grégoire was followed by 62 other clerical deputies, but even among those who in June 1789 had defied the king and had voted to join the Third Estate many now refused to take the oath of loyalty to the revolutionary government. Of the original 149 clerics who had voted for union with the *Tiers* (all but 18 of them being curés), 130 clerics were still in the Assembly. From among these, between December 27, 1790 and January 4, 1791, 71 clerics took the oath, 59 did not.[31] Altogether about 43 clerical deputies in the Assembly made their submission, among them 2 bishops (Talleyrand and Gobel). Complete statistics are not available for the country as a whole; moreover, there were frequent changes and retractions. It is estimated that parish priests were divided half and half between so-called jurors and nonjurors, though the proportion varied greatly from region to region. In Paris, for example, 426 secular clerics took the oath, 292 refused.[32] Among the regular clergy the percentage of jurors apparently was subtantially lower.[33] Only 7 bishops agreed to the oath; of the 133 bishops in office only 4 bishops accepted the Civil Constitution.[34]

From this point on, the French church was split. The jurors became known as the Constitutional church, the nonjurors were called refractories. A careful sociological analysis that would account for this division has so far been undertaken for few locales. Charles Tilly's study of the west, the Vendée, is a pioneer work, and we will return to it later. Since the vast majority of the clergy were parish priests and since the curés, as mentioned, divided about equally between jurors and nonjurors, it certainly is impossible to explain the split simply in terms of class differences. Apart from regional variations—jurors outnumbered nonjurors by far in the southwest and southeast, and only a few priests took the oath in western France, a traditionally "clerical" area—Lefebvre notes that "the number seems also to have depended upon an individual bishop's popularity and the attitude within his seminary, upon the remaining strength of quarrels among Gallicans, Jansenists, and Ultramontanes, and upon the lingering tradition of *richérisme*."[35] Many priests undoubtedly took the oath because it was the easiest thing to do, and not because they were committed to the goals of the Revolution. Others submitted to prevent schism and dechristianization. The Constitutional clergy in large measure was Jansenist, though not all Jansenists became jurors.[36] Some of the bishops undoubtedly would have resigned themselves to the revolutionary regime had it not attacked what they considered to be their spiritual dignity and jurisdiction; others were aristocrats and opposed the Civil Constitution out of the same class motives that made them sworn enemies of the other social and political reforms of the Revolution. On the whole, as we shall soon see in more detail, those areas with a high proportion of nonjurors also became centers of counterrevolutionary activity.

Throughout the first months of the growing conflict between church and state in France, Pope Pius VI had maintained a discreet silence. On March 29, 1970, the pope had denounced the ecclesiastical policy of the Constituent Assembly in a secret consistory. The revolutionary regime and the Declaration of Rights, he had added, represented a monstrous perversion of true order; the revolutionaries had been "miserably seduced by an empty phantom of liberty and enslaved by a band of philosophers who contradict and abuse each other." [37] But this speech was little known in France, and, officially, the pope had not yet commented.

Pius VI remained silent for another full year. Mathiez has suggested that the pope delayed a public denunciation of the Civil Constitution in the hope of inducing the Assembly to guarantee the Holy See's sovereignty over the papal possessions of Avignon and the Comtat Venaissin which formed an enclave in France and whose subjects were clamoring for union with France.[38] Such temporal considerations need not be ruled out, but perhaps a more important reason for the pope's policy of cautious waiting was his fear of offending the French clergy's Gallican sentiments by an aggressive intervention in French affairs. Pius VI acted only after almost all the French episcopate had rejected the Civil Constitution and after a substantial number of French clerics had demonstrated their support of their bishops by refusing to take the Civic Oath. As we have seen, the Assembly's refusal to call a national council of bishops to discuss and sanction the Civil Constitution weakened Gallicanism and thus played into the hands of the pope. By the time Pius VI finally spoke out the French clergy's attitude had been clarified, and the pope no longer risked becoming a shepherd without a flock.

The Constitutional church had taken shape with the election of 83 bishops during the early months of 1791. Among the 55 curés elevated to high ecclesiastical office was the Abbé Grégoire who was chosen as bishop of the departement Loir-et-Cher.[39] The new bishops were consecreated by Talleyrand and Gobel who, as duly appointed members of the episcopate, were entitled to perform the rite of consecration. In a brief of March 10, 1791, addressed to the signatories of the "Exposition of Principles" of October 1790, the pope threatened to excommunicate Talleyrand and all who had followed him. In a lengthy disquisition he "condemned the breach of the concordat, the seizure of the church goods and the suppression of the religious orders, also the definitions issued in connection with the rights of man regarding the unlimited liberty of belief and the press and human equality, for they contradicted the principles of the Church." The Civil Constitution, Pius VI warned, violated unalterable dogma; the oath imposed by the Assembly, far from demanding merely civil and secular loyalty, "really contained the destruction of papal authority." [40]

On April 13, 1791, another brief addressed to the entire French clergy and laity repeated the condemnation of the Civil Constitution. All those who had taken the oath and did not retract within forty days were threatened with suspension. The elections of the Constitutional bishops were declared null and void and the parish priests installed by them also incurred suspension. All those who remained obdurate would be excommunicated.[41] Following the issuance of these two condemnatory documents diplomatic relations between Rome and Paris broke down; the schism in the French church was complete.

Thirty of the Constitutional bishops, who were members of the Constituent Assembly, defended their participation in the work of the Assembly in a letter to Pius VI of May 3, 1791. The principles of equality and political liberty recognized by the new constitutional monarchy, they argued, were not in violation of Catholic dogma; they belonged to that domain which God had assigned to the jurisdiction of the temporal government. The new bishops offered to resign if the pope were willing to confirm the Constitutional espicopate.[42] Needless to say, Pius VI had no intention of complying with this suggestion.

Similar sentiments were voiced by other Constitutional bishops in pastoral letters to their diocesans. The nation, declared the new bishop of Strasbourg, François-Antoine Brendel, has the inalienable right to choose that form of government most appropriate for the common good. The Scriptures enjoined obedience to law and civil authority; those who rejected this basic "evangelic truth" were rebels and the enemies of God. The refractory churchmen who resisted the "general will" were no longer legitimate clergy.[43] For Louis Charrier de la Roche, bishop of Rouen, the changing of diocesan boundaries was merely an exercise of the ancient power of the sovereign over the external forms of the church for which there were many historical precedents as far back as Charlemagne and the Roman emperors. The purpose of the civic oath was to aid in the reform of the church for the good of the people. The priests of God had to obey the laws of the state.[44]

The nonjuring clergymen also sought to justify their stand, but in many places local officials ousted them from their posts. Here and there mob violence against nonjurors took place, and many nonjurors left the country. On May 7, 1791 a decree of the Assembly reaffirmed liberty of worship and granted nonjuring priests the right to say mass, but the suspicion and hostility toward the refractories frequently interfered with the implementation of this law. The nonjuring church increasingly was identified with the aristocrats and especially with those nobles conspiring with the foreign enemies of the Revolution. The fact that many of the old bishops were themselves nobles and had become emigrés did not help. At the same time, many of the Constitutionalists, fearful of their precarious position, moved toward the Jacobins and encouraged the persecution of the refractories.

Just as it is wrong, in the manner of some Catholic historians, to describe the entire Constitutional church as a group of decadent careerists it would be a mistake to equate all nonjurors with the counterrevolutionaries. At the same time, as we will soon see, not all of the charges against the refractories were imaginary, and many of them did indeed engage in plotting against the Revolution. This fact strengthened the hand of the secularists in the Assembly. On November 29, 1791, a decree deprived the nonjurors of the right to conduct services, took away their pensions, and provided for their expulsion from communes where disturbances had taken place. After the Assembly in April of 1792 had declared France to be in a state of war with the King of Hungary and Bohemia, and with the fear of invasion growing, the legislature on May 27, 1792 passed an even more severe measure: "Seeing that the constant attempts of the non-juring clergy to overthrow the Constitution forbid us to think that they wish to join in the social pact, and seeing that the public safety would be endangered by regarding as members of society persons who are only anxious to destroy it," the Legislative Assembly decreed that any nonjuror denounced by twenty citizens could be banished.[45] Louis XVI refused to sanction this first general law of proscription and thus hastened his downfall. In early July Prussia entered the war. On August 10, 1792, the beginning of the "second" French Revolution, the king was imprisoned. The most radical phase of the Revolution had begun and for the nonjuring church this meant new and still more serious tribulations.

On August 14, the Assembly, following the urging of the revolutionary "Commune" of Paris, imposed a new oath upon all civil servants, including the clergy. The oath did not refer explicitly to the Civil Constitution and merely demanded a declaration of allegiance to the ideas of liberty and equality. But since the pope had condemned both of these principles as equivalent to license and heresy, and, with the monarchy now under attack, many churchmen found it impossible to take the new oath. Those like M. Emery, superior of the Society of Saint Sulpice, who were in favor of compromise, defended compliance with the oath. In a letter to Maury, by now in Rome, Emery argued that the present troubles and the split in the church were due more to the exaggerated zeal of the nonjurors than to the Constitutionalists. If all the priests were to take the oath, the revolutionary government would no longer be able to call the churchmen defenders of despotism and enemies of France and would have no reason to persecute them.[46] But Emery's center position was rapidly being eroded by the extremists on both sides—those who were unable to divorce the church from the monarchy and the anticlerical elements among the Jacobins and Girondists. The latter succeeded in pushing through the Assembly a series of new decrees. On August 17, the evacuation of all convents by October 1 was ordered. On August 18 all secular congregations were abolished, and the wearing of religious garb was prohibited. On August 26 all nonjuring priests, except the sick and those over sixty, were commanded to leave France within a fortnight or face deportation to the penal colony of Guiana.

On September 1 Paris received word of the fall of Verdun, the last fortress between the capital and the advancing Prussian infantry. Among the victims of the "September massacres" that began the following day were over two hundred refractory priests. The insurrectionary soldiers who dragged their victims from the prisons of Paris and killed them after drumhead trials were motivated less by hatred of religion than by the desire to dispose of those they regarded as the internal enemy before fighting the invaders on the frontiers.[47] Still, the killing of the priests was symptomatic of the increasingly fierce hostility toward refractories. They were denounced, hunted, imprisoned, deported, or put to death as public enemies, and the fact that all this could be done with impunity eventually began to damage the standing of the Catholic religion itself. Writes Aulard: "The sight of priests scouted and persecuted paved the way for the sight of religion scouted and persecuted." [48]

The Constitutional church, for the time being, was still an ally of the Revolution. The last act of the Legislative Assembly on September 20, the entrusting of the registration of births, marriages, and deaths to municipal officers and the legalization of divorce, offended many of the Constitutional priests, but as yet there was no serious crisis. It was Bishop Grégoire, a deputy in the newly elected National Convention, who on September 21 moved to abolish the monarchy. "Kings," he said, "are in the moral order what monsters are in the physical order." [49] Other members of the Constitutional episcopate termed the defense of the Revolution a holy war, and they celebrated the victories of the revolutionary armies. Among the 749 deputies of the Convention who on January 15, 1793 unanimously found Louis XVI guilty of treason, there were 48 Constitutional priests, including 17 bishops. Some of these votes turned the scales in favor of the death penalty for the deposed king.[50]

Not all the Constitutional bishops were as closely identified with the revolutionary cause as was Grégoire. A man of the Enlightenment and a passionate republican, Grégoire fused love of country and religious duty. Moreover, even though some 30,000 to 40,000 Constitutional priests preached complete submission to the Republic, for both Jacobins and Girondists the Constitutional church became expendable in the measure that this new church failed to win over the rural masses. Last, the Constitutional church itself became increasingly suspect as segments of the church openly allied themselves with the counterrevolution. The strengthening of the anticlerical group in the Convention, which was opposed to Christianity itself, was a natural outcome of the fact that both juring and nonjuring priests after all preached the same religion.[51] The most serious setback to the Constitutional church, in this connection, was the part taken by the nonjuring priests in the greatest of all the counterrevolutionary insurrections, the Vendée.

THE COUNTERREVOLUTION

Some refractory priests had been active in preaching opposition to the policies of the revolutionary government from the time of the split in the church, and as the Revolution progressed, political and religious opposition became increasingly allied. " 'The confessionals are schools in which rebellion is taught and commanded,' wrote the directory of Morbihan to the Minister of the Interior on June 9, 1791. Reubell, a deputy for Alsace, exclaimed during the session of July 17, 1791 that there was not a single refractory priest in the departments of Haut- and Bas-Rhin who would not be convicted of being in insurrection." [52] Exaggerated as these claims may have been, there can be no doubt that many nonjurors gradually drifted into the camp of the counterrevolution.

Some nonjuring bishops emigrated, and others went into hiding and continued to direct their dioceses in secret. As the conflict between church and state inside France intensified, the emigré bishops became more emphatic in expressing their belief that only the re-establishment of a strong monarchy could protect the interests of the church. Three prelates in particular—Archbishop Talleyrand-Périgord of Reims, Bishop De la Fare of Nancy, and Bishop Asseline of Boulogne—functioned as advisors to the late king's brother, the count of Provence, who was a known reactionary. He had left France in June 1791 and worked energetically for the return of the Old Regime; [53] in June 1795, after the death of the Dauphin, counted as Louis XVII, the count assumed the title Louis XVIII. Bishop Asseline, because of his learned reputation, was the most influential of the exiled bishops.[54]

Another churchman functioning as confidential advisor to

Louis XVIII and as diplomatic agent of the pope was the Abbé
Maury. After Maury's escape from France Pius VI had made the
ambitious churchman a cardinal, and in June 1792 he sent him to
Germany as a special legate to the new German emperor, Francis
II. There he was to enlighten the emperor on the threats to royalty everywhere posed by the events in France as well as to warn
him of what the French seizure of Avignon meant for all rulers.
However, the volatile Maury proved an indiscreet diplomat and
openly campaigned for an allied invasion of France. Visiting the
military camp at Mainz he told the emigré Prince de Condé, who
had asked him when the pope would excommunicate the constitutional clergy: "The bull will be published when they [the al-
lies] have defeated and scattered the [revolutionary] army; the
Pope has need of their swords to sharpen his pen." [55]

During the course of the year 1792 the pope also pleaded directly with the European sovereigns to help recover Avignon and
the Comtat. The spirit of impiety, he wrote the Emperor Leopold
on March 3, 1792, that afflicted the unfortunate French kingdom,
threatened to extend its ravages over all other states as well. It
menaced "the rights of religion, of thrones and of society." Pius
asked Leopold to organize a coalition that could defend "the
cause of God." [56] Similar letters were directed to Catherine II of
Russia and the king of England. The government in Paris was
well informed of the diplomatic moves in the enemy's camp;
Maury's mission and the Holy See's support of the First Coalition
undoubtedly hardened the attitude of the revolutionary leaders
toward the refractory clergy and provided an excuse for stepping
up the persecution of the nonjurors.[57]

After the execution of Louis XVI the pope, in a secret consistory on June 17, 1793, praised the heroism of the martyred
French king. The illegitimate French government first had abolished the monarchy, a form of rule preferable to all others, and
then had committed this new crime. The king had died a victim
of the Calvinists and the "perverted *philosophes*," among whom
Voltaire should shoulder most of the blame.[58] The revolutionary regime had proclaimed the false slogans of "Liberty" and
"Equality" and enacted liberty of worship as if one could get
to heaven by all sorts of routes. Only the true religion, the pope
declared, was the real guarantee of the safety and stability of
states. The declared enemies of monarchy, therefore, were intent

upon destroying the Catholic religion. By murdering Louis XVI France had incurred "the horror, indignation and vengeance of all the powers of the earth." [59]

It was in the great uprising of the West in 1793, the Vendée, that the church loyal to Rome became most directly involved in the counterrevolution. In the rural areas south of the Loire opposition to the Revolution had grown steadily after the first year of the new regime. The religious policies of the Constituent Assembly had alienated a large number of the curés, many of whom had lost income as a result of being put on fixed salaries and all of whom had been deprived of their previously dominant position in the community. In the territory of the insurrection, an area of uneven and often turbulent social change, practically all of the parish clergy were nonjurors,[60] and a great majority of their intensely religious parishioners stood with them. Refractory priests threatened the supporters of the revolutionary cause with excommunication, and they denounced the purchasers of church properties. These actions further endeared the parish clergy "to those members of the community who were unable to acquire land, who were devoted to the curé, and who had their own reasons for unease at the commanding position of the local bourgeoisie." [61] Meetings, processions, armed attacks were symptoms of the growing restiveness; most of this unrest was to prevent the removal of refractory priests—the *bon prêtres*—or to frustrate the imposition of a new and alien clergy. Still, there was neither a plot nor central direction to the disturbances. The refractory clergy contributed to the general unrest, but it did not organize a general uprising. The uprising, when it finally came, was spontaneous and without a comprehensive plan.[62]

The spark that touched off the uprising was the conscription law of February 24, 1793 that was to raise an army of 300,000 men. "An unpopular government which had deprived the peasants of their 'good priests' and their inoffensive King was proposing to march away their sons to distant battlefields." [63] After the publication of the call to arms in early March, demonstrations and rioting broke out almost simultaneously in several parts of the area between Nantes, La Rochelle, Poitiers, and Angers. Armed bands formed and within days had moved into all the important towns of the region. The first leaders were simple people; the nobles joined in later.

From the beginning the goals and ideology of the uprising were primarily religious. Almost immediately the insurgents adopted as their badge the Sacred Heart, cut out of cloth. "The peasant revolt," writes Mathiez, "assumed the appearance of a crusade." [64] Large numbers of refractory priests had been hiding out in the countryside; these men now joined the roving bands, kindled their zeal, and presided over the first massacres of republicans.[65] Three priests were involved in the attack on Palluan. They rebaptized the town church, and told the peasants that bullets and cannons would not harm them.[66]

By June the insurgents had made impressive gains. Saumur and Angers were in their hands. Four armies were now in the field, led by royalist nobles. The latter, until then far from religious, had discovered the usefulness of religion and affected an exalted piety. A declaration issued in May by the "Catholic and Royal Army" stated that they had taken up arms "to sustain the religion of their fathers and to ensure for their august and legitimate sovereign, Louis XVII, the glory and stability of his throne and his crown." [67] An ecclesiastical council was established at Châtillon by the Abbé Bernier, an able churchman from Angers, and given jurisdiction over all religious matters in the region of the uprising. Bernier shared his authority with an adventurer, Guillot de Folleville, who successfully passed himself off as the bishop of Agra, *in partibus infidelium*, and claimed to be apostolic delegate to the Vendée. In the liberated areas tithes were reinstituted, confiscated goods were returned to the church, and Constitutional clerics were imprisoned or killed. The strong religious passions that characterized the rebellion often led to great cruelties.

Tilly estimates that under one-half of the men participating in the Vendée were peasants, just over two-fifths were artisans—the rebels thus represented roughly a cross section of the rural population of the region.[68] Altogether, from 60,000 to 120,000 men probably took part in the uprising of 1793, but even though at times the chiefs of the armies planned their actions jointly, "more often, jealousy, cross-purposes, rivalries stifled their cooperation." [69] On June 29, the Vendéans suffered an important defeat at Nantes, by October 1793 the threat to the revolutionary government was checked. But the end was yet to come. In 1794 the insurgents patched together a new army and this "second war" did not end before February 1795 when the rebels were granted freedom from conscription and the unhindered exercise of their religion.[70] A new outbreak, encouraged by promises of help from the British and the emigrés, was defeated by March 1796, and pacification was finally more or less complete. Of the 800,000 inhabitants of the Vendée, 159,000 are estimated to have perished during the prolonged struggle.[71]

In the provinces north of the Loire, especially in Brittany, intermittent guerilla fighting continued for almost ten years; it has entered history as the *Chouannerie* after Jean Chouan, one of the partisan leaders. Here, too, refractory priests supported and encouraged the fighting.[72] The bishop of Dol-de-Bretagne, Urbain René de Hercé, in exile in London, on January 1, 1795 issued a pastoral letter in which he praised those fighting for religion and throne against the tyrants ruling France, and he expressed the hope that God would bless the cause of the Catholic and Royal Army.[73] The letter was distributed in northern France by the rebel leaders and when in June 1795 a British fleet landed a force of 4500 emigrés at Quiberon, sixty miles north of Nantes, M. de Hercé accompanied the invasion force. Thousands of Breton guerillas met the well-equipped emigrés, but rivalry among the commanders and friction between the returning nobles and the peasant partisans seriously hampered operations of the combined force. On July 20, a strong republican army attacked the beach-head and decisively defeated the invaders and their Chouan allies. The bishop of Dol was among the captives and was shot, together with the commander of the royalists and nine other priests, on July 22, 1795.[74] This landing marks the height of the menace of the *Chouannerie* as well as the beginning of its decline.

The struggle for and against the Revolution was fought not only with arms. Both jurors and nonjurors regularly pressed into service elaborate theological arguments that sought to buttress their respective political stands. An examination of some of the pastoral letters and other pronouncements by Constitutional and refractory clergy reveals the ease with which Catholic theology lent itself to such ideological use.

During the first years of the Revolution the clergy loyal to Rome had never tired of emphasizing the duty of obeying civil authority, i.e. the king, and they had stressed the sinfulness of rebellion. One day of insurrection, Maury told the National Assembly in 1790, equals one day of anarchy, and one single day of an-

archy is "far more disastrous than a state that governs in the most
tyrannical fashion." [75] The alleged right of rebellion against
tyranny involves all the horrors of anarchy and must be rejected
by all Christians. The Jesuit, Barruel, another of the polemicists
defending the Roman church, similarly denied the right of revolt,
and he rejected the view that an established government could be
changed by its subjects. To resist the authorities created by God
was a crime, he declared in 1791. The new constitution was illegitimate for the fundamental laws of the old regime could have
been changed only by unanimous consent of the royal sovereign
and all individuals in the nation. [76] The Catholic religion, Barruel
wrote in early 1793, rejects the principles of rebellion; "it teaches
its followers to consider as a heinous crime every violation of the
laws, every violence offered to the authorities established for the
government of empires." [77]

The doctrine that the Christian must always obey the civil authority equates might and right and means, essentially, that all rebellions are wrong—until they succeed. A consistent application of this view to the French Revolution should have led the
clergymen in question to accept the revolutionary regime once it
was firmly established in power; such recognition of *de facto*
governments has indeed been counseled by many Catholic theologians before and after the French Revolution. [78] But for the
royalist clergymen the logic of this position was unacceptable.
Monarchy and religion in their eyes were inseparable. The revolutionary regime, no matter how old, was plainly illegitimate,
and the rightful sovereign was still the king—Louis XVI, then
Louis XVII, and last Louis XVIII. As long as there was a claimant for the Bourbon throne, they were willing to honor this claim
even if its enforcement meant supporting insurrection, counterrevolution, and foreign intervention.

Thus the same Barruel who had castigated the National Assembly for engaging in rebellion soon appealed for outside help
against the revolutionary government and called for a crusade
against the new France. The cause of royalty, he warned in 1792,
was expiring amidst the convulsions of revolt and anarchy. The
doctrine of popular sovereignty was leading France to ruin. All
sovereigns and men of good will everywhere, therefore, were to
unite against this "political pest." "Never was a crusade more
necessary, more expedient and more reasonble than that which

ought to be organized against the mad agitators of France. It alone could save Europe." [79] The bishop of Rennes (Brittany), François Bareau de Girac, in a pastoral letter issued from exile in Germany in January 1795, expressed his confidence that the sacrifice of the nobility would save France. God would direct and protect the Christian army and enable it to defeat the enemies of the Lord.[80] As late as 1798, the vicar general of Laon, the future bishop of Nantes, Jean-Baptiste Duvoisin, who had left France for England in 1792, refused to regard the French government as legitimate. "Born in revolt and established through violence," he wrote in a work published in London, "it exists only through usurpation and injustice." It was a tyrannical regime in terms of its origin and its exercise of power. The right of revolt against oppression, proclaimed by the Declaration of the Rights of Man and Citizen, Duvoisin maintained, was incompatible with the maintenance of social order. But it must be remembered that "if the revolt against legitimate authority is a crime against God and society, an insurrection against usurpers covered with the blood of their king is the holiest of duties." [81] It should be noted that this defense of the rightfulness of revolt against the republican government of France was issued two years after Pope Pius VI had called on all French Catholics to submit to the republican regime and to obey the existing government with all possible zeal and willingness. We will return to this papal brief later.

Using the same theoretical foundation the Constitutional clergy found it possible to defend a diametrically opposite political stand. Supporting the existing regime, they invoked the duty of obedience which the Christian owes civil authority. No matter how political power has been acquired, or how it is exercised, declared an anonymous pamphlet by a juring clergyman in 1797, since political authority has its origin in God it demands the respect of the Christian. To rebel against authority, no matter how abused, is to rebel against God. "It is sufficient for us to know that it is Providence which disposes of the supreme power, which entrusts it to whom it will, and how it will. What more is necessary to command homage toward the public power?" [82] In everything that does not violate religion or justice, the Christian owes perfect obedience. No matter how bad a government, the individual has no right to rebel. His only recourse is God. The example of the early Christians should be followed. They obeyed a state that was far worse than the government currently in power.[83]

Claude le Coz, Constitutional bishop of Ile-et-Villaine (Brittany), in a work published around 1794, stressed the same doctrinal points. The spiritual concerns of Christianity are compatible with republics as well as monarchies. Not the form of government but man's faith was crucial. Following Christ's example, his disciples should obey the state. "They are sent not to raise thrones or break sceptres, but to preach obedience to the already constituted authorities; not to govern nations, or to give them or hinder them from receiving new laws, but to brighten their spirits, to sanctify their hearts, to bring all peoples to the knowledge of the true religion." [84] God, he argued, makes a ruler's authority legitimate, but the public will is the interpreter of the divine will and people can change the form of government. One could protest or perhaps even use passive resistance against bad laws, but individual revolt or violence was never allowed. A society could not be bettered through civil war.[85]

Only Grégoire, it appears, was willing to develop a somewhat more radical position that openly acknowledged the right of revolt against tyranny. God, he told the Jacobin club in September 1791, has created tigers but he has not created despots. Christianity commands obedience to legitimate powers, but "it is to alter Christian morality and to outrage its author to attempt to make of it a support of arbitrary power." [86] Both Grégoire and the previously quoted royalist clergyman, Jean-Baptiste Duvoisin, thus agreed on the right of revolt against despotic government. The theologico-moral principle was the same; they differed in what in practice they regarded as legitimate or usurped power. For Grégoire the monarchy was a clear example of such arbitrary authority. For Duvoisin royal power, no matter how once acquired, was legitimate and it could not lose this legitimacy as long as there was a claimant to the throne; it was the Republic that was guilty of usurpation.

DECHRISTIANIZATION

Large segments of the Catholic church were allied with the counterrevolution; Pius VI not entirely unjustly was regarded as the soul of the coalition against France. In these circumstances the Constitutional church, which recognized the pope as the visible head of the church, quite naturally increasingly fell into official disfavor. Without the Vendée and its clerical support in particular, Aulard believes, the attempt to dechristianize France would never have been undertaken.[87] After the downfall of the Girondists in May 1793, the fact that many jurors had made common cause with the Girondists and Federalists also helped discredit the Catholic religion in the eyes of the militant patriots. Marat called the Constitutional clergy the "mortal enemy" of the Jacobins, and he accused them of seeking to "establish their sacerdotal throne on the ruins of liberty."[88] Responding to the growth of anticlerical sentiments, in October 1793 the Convention passed a law that provided the death penalty for priests communicating with the enemy, whether at home or abroad. It also enjoined the transportation of all clerics, even if they were jurors, who should be denounced for want of patriotism by six citizens of their canton, this denunciation having been upheld by the Directory of the department involved. All of the Catholic clergy, jurors as well as nonjurors, thus were now placed under legal suspicion.

Until 1793 the distinction between good and bad priests had been maintained. In the changed climate of opinion those who all along had harbored hostile attitudes toward Christianity were now free to follow their atheistic or deistic impulses. In October 1793 a republican calendar was adopted that was to do away with the Christian Sunday, saints' days, and other religious holidays. Churches were closed and reopened as Temples of Reason. In the Cathedral of Notre Dame a statue of Liberty replaced that of the Virgin Mary. Festivals were held to celebrate the victory of philosophy over fanaticism.

According to Aulard, dechristianization was mainly an expedient of national defense; he points out that it was most violent in areas such as Strasbourg that were threatened by the intrigues of the clergy and close to the foreign enemy.[89] The fact that the Constitutional church failed to become a national church, functioning as a civic religion, also undoubtedly turned many in the Convention against the Christian religion. But beyond these explanations one should not lose sight of the religious messianism and fanaticism that pervaded the thinking of many of the revolutionaries and made them intent on breaking radically with the past. "Like the execution of the King," McManners notes, "sacrilege was to be a gesture of defiance, a symbol of the determination to destroy the old world, a deliberate decision to press on beyond the point of no return, a final commitment to the oath to 'live free or die.' " [90] Philosophy, they believed, rather than Christianity would redeem mankind.

On November 6, Gobel, the Constitutional bishop of Paris, was forced to resign, and on the following day he and eleven of his vicars appeared before the Convention. Taking off his cross and ring, Gobel renounced his ministry and put on a red cap. Many priests were forced to leave the church; others were exiled or executed. Among those falling victim to the terror was Claude Fauchet, the Constitutional bishop of Caen, who had opposed the death penalty for the king and who was executed together with other Girondists on October 31, 1793.

Grégoire was one of the few ecclesiastical members of the Convention who refused to yield to the pressure of dechristianization. Following the resignation of Gobel, Grégoire addressed the Convention and, invoking the principle of freedom of worship, he defied his opponents to take the office of bishop away from him. It is possible that Grégoire was emboldened to take this courageous stand by the knowledge that Robespierre strongly disapproved of dechristianization, fearing that dechristianization would alienate the masses, undermine the national defense, and give further scandal to a hostile Europe. "The man who wishes to prevent the saying of Mass," Robespierre told the Jacobins, "is a greater fanatic than he who says it." [91] Following his lead, on May 7, 1794, the Convention passed a decree establishing the Worship of the Supreme Being. Robespierre was a great admirer of Rousseau, and the new religious scheme in his eyes was a way of inspiring the nation with patriotism and dedication to the reign of virtue. The decree stated that the French people recognized the existence of the Supreme Being and the immortality of the soul. "They declare that the best service of the Supreme Being is the practice of the duties of man" such as "hatred of treachery and tyranny, the punishment of tyrants and traitors, succor of the unfortunate, respect for the weak, defense of the oppressed, doing all the good one can and not being unjust to anyone." [92]

This modified deism was defended with great ruthlessness against both Christians and atheists, and freedom of thought on religious issues was now even more difficult. Among those executed on charges of atheism was the former Constitutional bishop of Paris, Gobel. Opposition from the freethinkers was one of the factors in the downfall of Robespierre who was outlawed on 9 Thermidor (July 27, 1794) and guillotined the following day. But for the Catholic priests, jurors or nonjurors, the fall of Robespierre did not mean an immediate end to persecution. On September 18, 1794, the Thermidorean politicians stopped the payment of salaries to the clergy, and in November the Convention voted for the secularization of elementary education. Still, the new regime gradually moved toward a form of neutrality in regard to Christianity. On December 21 Grégoire, appearing in sacerdotal garb, made a long speech in which he condemned the intolerance of the Convention. Liberty of worship, he told his hostile listeners, exists in Turkey and under despotic governments but not in republican France. "Persecution is always abominable, whether it be perpetrated in the name of religion or in the name of philosophy." Grégoire praised the separation of church and state existing in the United States of America; the attachment of the American and Swiss Catholics to their republics demonstrated that there was no incompatibility between Catholicism and republicanism.[93]

Grégoire's speech made a great impression, and in many places religion came out of hiding. If the Convention on February 21, 1795 finally enacted the official separation of church and state it did so for political reasons not because it agreed with the liberal ideas of Grégoire. The Convention was anxious not to jeopardize its foreign relations by seeming to be atheistic or irreligious; at home the offer of freedom of worship, as we have mentioned earlier, was to bring final pacification to the west of France. The new law proclaimed religious liberty and the right to the free exercise of public worship. The state was prohibited from paying priests or providing buildings for worship. The enactment of this measure was followed by the reappearance of Catholicism practically everywhere. From 30,000 to 40,000 priests had emigrated during the years of persecution, finding a refuge in England, Spain, Switzerland, Germany, and the Papal States.[94] Many of these nonjurors now began to return to France to resume their clerical duties.

The Constitutional church, too, had suffered greatly, and its

revival proved slow. Of the 85 Constitutional bishops who had
been in office in October 1793, by the spring of 1795, 6 had been
executed, 23 had become apostates (9 had married), 24 had resigned or fled, 7 were in hiding, and 24 bishops had been imprisoned for various lengths of time.[95] Some 20,000 priests had ab-
jured their vocation, the vast majority of these clerical
"abdications" having taken place under pressure.[96]

Grégoire was the first to openly resume his episcopal functions.
In a pastoral letter of March 12, 1795, issued in Paris, Grégoire
announced and celebrated the reconciliation of Revolution and
Christianity. The opponents of the Christian religion had tried to
link the church to the enemies of the Revolution and the detested
monarchy; they had subjected the church to the most terrible
tribulations. But all this was now over, and freedom of worship
was restored. The regime recognized that religion was the most
solid guarantee of the social order and that it provided for security as no atheistic society could. The Gospel consecrated the
principles of equality and liberty. Hence "he who does not love
the Republic is a bad citizen and consequently a bad
Christian." [97] The natural alliance between democracy and Christianity from now on would be indissoluble. "God and fatherland:
this is our motto." [98]

Three days later several Constitutional bishops met in Paris and
issued a collective letter to the other bishops and the vacant
churches. They announced the reorganization of the Gallican
church and arranged for the election of new bishops. The government of the church, the letter said, is entirely spiritual; the
Christian has the duty to obey civil authority, i.e., to submit to
the laws of the Republic. Indeed, the bishops should pray for the
Republic, promote her prosperity, and inspire the faithful with
the same sentiments.[99]

A decree of May 30, 1795 restored the churches for the use of
religion on condition that the ministers make a declaration of
submission to the laws of the Republic. Shortly thereafter it was
announced that this declaration was not retroactive and that the
Civil Constitution of the Clergy was no longer in effect. On September 29 the Convention amalgamated the various regulations
into one comprehensive law. The principles of liberty of worship
and the separation of church and state were proclaimed anew; severe penalties were provided for priests inciting the re-establish-

ment of the monarchy or other anti-revolutionary acts. The formula of submission to the Republic was fixed as follows: "I recognize the supremacy of the body of French citizens and I promise submission and obedience to the laws of the Republic." [100] The Constitution of the Year III, which went into effect at the end of 1795, restated these provisions which remained in effect until the coming into force of the Concordat in 1802.

The revival of the Catholic religion proceeded in full force; emigrant priests returned in large numbers and, especially in the countryside, the old clergy were welcomed with joy. Some of the former refractory priests were willing to accept the declaration of submission to the Republic. They justified their stand by pointing out that the republican regime was firmly established and therefore in possession of sovereignty. Even a usurping power, they argued, had to be recognized when it had assumed full *de facto* control over a country. The new oath did not touch the religious sphere and therefore did not violate their rights of conscience. To act otherwise would once again abandon the faithful and leave them without priests. This was the position, among others, of M. Emery and M. de Bausset, the bishop of Alais, neither of whom had left France.[101]

However, many other priests, who had remained loyal to Rome, found the new declaration no less painful than the earlier oaths. Monarchical sentiments remained strong; the fact that the Republic had been born amidst a bloody persecution of the church was not easily forgotten. Most of the bishops, in particular those who had actively allied themselves with the royalist counterrevolution and had supported the aspirations of Louis XVIII, found it impossible to change sides and to accept the new regime as a *fait accompli*. Bishop Asseline of Boulogne warned that by recognizing the Republic priests became accomplices of rebels, who had overthrown the throne and resisted the order established by God. "While these usurpers and rebels demand that one declare submission to their pretended laws, the king, our legitimate sovereign, to whom his birth gives an incontestable and divinely consecrated right to the throne which his ancestors have occupied during so many centuries, protests resolutely against this usurpation and revolt and calls upon all of his subjects to render him the obedience to which he is entitled." [102]

Pope Pius VI had a more realistic sense of the chances of restoring the Old Regime. In the spring of 1796, the revolutionary army, led by General Napoleon Bonaparte, had made its way into Austrian Milan, and the Papal States now lay practically defenseless before him. The fact that both Prussia and Spain had deserted the anti-French coalition and had made a separate peace with France contributed to the pope's anxieties. On June 23 an armistice was signed at Bologna, one provision of which obligated the pope to send a plenipotentiary to Paris to conclude a formal peace. The papal legate had with him a brief, dated July 5, in which Pius VI called upon the French Catholics to submit to the republican regime. The pope's pleading in the brief *Pastoralis Sollicitudo* was emphatic. Reminding the faithful that in the teachings of the Catholic religion all authority is seen as derived from God and that to oppose civil authority is to oppose God, Pius declared: "Your disobedience would be a crime that would be punished severely not only by the authorities on earth but, what is worse, by God himself who threatens eternal damnation to those who resist political authority." The pope asked the French Catholics to demonstrate their submission and thus to convince the government that the true religion was not subversive of the civil laws.[103]

We do not know for sure at whose initiative the pope had prepared this brief. It may have been Bonaparte's.[104] In any event, the negotiations in Paris were not successful, and the brief therefore was never published. The French negotiators, at the urging of Bishop Grégoire, insisted that the pope withdraw all statements critical of the Revolution, including the condemnation of the Civil Constitution of the Clergy. This Pius VI refused to do and his legate left Paris. Meanwhile the brief had become known, and it caused lively arguments among the French clergy. The Constitutional priests and bishops were jubilant at what they regarded as a papal confirmation of the position they had held all along; the brief also pleased adherents of the centrist position like M. Emery.[105] The diehards among the former refractories, on the other hand, were greatly taken aback and several emigré bishops called the brief a forgery.[106]

After Napoleon had defeated the Austrians in February 1797 his army resumed the advance on Rome. On February 19 the pope signed a peace treaty in which he officially recognized the French Republic, agreed to the cession to France of Avignon and the Comtat Venaissin, and accepted various other onerous conditions. In France, too, developments took a turn for the worse. The Directory that assumed power in the *coup d'état* of September 4, 1797, fearful of the growing power of organized religion, adopted a more hostile attitude toward the Catholic church. The laws of banishment were reactivated, and a new "Oath of Hatred against the Monarchy and Anarchy" was imposed on the clergy. Once again, priests, many of whom had just recently returned, began to leave France; others went into hiding, and large numbers were deported.

Those opposed to the new oath argued that they could not swear to hate a form of government of which the Scriptures spoke so highly. Several bishops, unwilling to give up the newly achieved liberty of worship, argued that the oath meant no more than a promise not to harm the Republic. Others engaged in similar exercises in casuistry in order to find an acceptable formula for taking the oath.[107] Particularly striking was the about-face of M. de Mercy, the former bishop of Luçon, who earlier had been one of the most intransigent royalists. He now maintained that the Christian religion "was compatible with all forms of government" and that it was not up to the faithful to question why the kings of France had lost favor in God's eyes. The republican government of France was here to stay, he argued with cold realism, and the church had to accept this fact.[108] Despite the opposition of several emigré bishops, large numbers of priests took the oath. In Paris a majority of the former nonjurors this time decided to swear. Even in the Vendée about 20 per cent of the refractory clergy decided that it was their duty to stay with their parishes, and they submitted to the law.[109]

The Constitutional clergy by and large took the oath without hesitation. The Directory protected the Constitutional church which was allowed to hold a national council in Paris from August 15 to November 12, 1797. A proposal of that council to seek reconciliation with the pope was ignored by the latter. But when the Directory sought to enforce the strict observance of the republican calendar, including the cessation of work on the tenth day (*decadi*) instead of on Sunday, relations between the state and the Constitutional church cooled markedly. The religious policy of the Directorate, it should be noted, was rather doctrinaire and shortsighted. The government managed to alienate both

factions of the Catholic church while its own religion of patriotism, a pale reflection of the Cult of the Supreme Being, was not
popular.[110] Guerilla warfare flared up again in the Vendée, and
several royalist insurrections, supported by refractory priests,
plagued the country.

The Directory's policy toward the pope was also guided primarily by ideological considerations. The pontiff for them was a
"Prince of Darkness" and the Papal States a "scourge in the
hands of fanaticism" that had to be destroyed. There was also the
never-fulfilled task of avenging Hugo de Bassoille, the unofficial
ambassador of the French Revolution, who in January 1793 had
been killed by a Roman mob for sporting tricolor cockades and
waving republican flags. When in December 1797 another prominent Frenchman, General Duphot, was shot to death by papal
police in the streets of Rome, Paris had the excuse it had been
looking for to overthrow the papal government. On February 15,
1798 French troops entered Rome, with the help of Roman Jacobins the pope was declared deposed as temporal sovereign, and
a republican regime was set up. Pius VI was told that he would
have to leave within three days, and on February 20 he was sent
off to Sienna.[111]

Once again the pope turned for help to the Catholic courts of
Europe. In a letter of March 29 to the Tsar, Pius VI pressed for
the return of his French possessions and argued that the actions
of the French endangered all sovereigns. The most recent oath of
hatred of the monarchy was evidence of this.[112] The contents of
this letter reached the French and, needless to say, did not create
friendly feelings toward the head of the church. He was moved
several more times, finally to die at Valence on August 29, 1799.

In France the Directory proceeded with its plan, half secret
and half avowed, of destroying the Catholic religion. Help for
the latter was to come from an unexpected source.

THE CONCORDAT

On 18 Brumaire of the Year VIII (November 9, 1799), Napoleon
Bonaparte overthrew the Directory and proclaimed a new form
of republic, the Consulate, headed by himself as the First Consul.
The Constitutional church welcomed the *coup d'état*. The ambitious young general still had the reputation of being a loyal re-

publican, and men like Grégoire were on good terms with him. Napoleon shared the conviction of the Constitutionalists that religion was a necessary foundation of morality and social stability. The Constitutional church had tirelessly advanced this argument in its long conflict with the freethinkers, though often to no avail.[113] But Napoleon was not all that enthusiastic over the Constitutionalists' Christian republicanism nor was he convinced that the struggling Constitutional church could successfully play the role of a civil religion. He had even less sympathy for the emigré bishops, who continued to inspire counterrevolutionary intrigues, and he therefore finally decided upon a strategy that would get rid of both of the quarreling factions and restore religious peace to France.

A decree of December 28, 1799 had substituted for the old oath of the clergy a simple promise of loyalty to the constitution. A majority of the priests took the promise, but many of the papists, now returning to France in large numbers, refused. Once again complicated doctrinal disputes on the legitimacy of the promise of fidelity took place, and in many dioceses anarchical conditions threatened. At this point Napoleon resolved to seek the help of the new pope, Pius VII, to reorganize the French church. As a realist he recognized the continuing strength of the Catholic religion in France, and he was prepared to grant it a minimum of autonomy to further his political aims. Explaining his policy to the Council of State on August 18, 1800, Napoleon declared: "By becoming Catholic I ended the war in the Vendée, by becoming a Muslim I established myself in Egypt, and by becoming an ultramontane I won the support of Italy. If I had to govern a people consisting of Jews I would restore the temple of Solomon." [114] Rarely has the political use of religion, its treatment in terms of *raison d'état*, been stated more frankly.

We can pass over the details of the complicated negotiations for a concordat. There was opposition not only among some of the cardinals in Rome who were absolutely opposed to any compromise with revolutionary France, but also in France among the freethinkers and the Constitutional bishops, including the foreign minister, Talleyrand, who had since married and was worried over his position. The royalists among the clergy were equally hostile, and many of the old bishops went so far as to refuse to resign their sees as required by the papal brief of August 15, 1801 implementing the Concordat. Adopting the extreme Gallican position that the jurisdiction of the bishops was given to them directly by God, 36 bishops, most of them residing in England, denied the right of the pope to depose them and condemned him "as a heretic, a Jew, a pagan, and a publican."[115] They saw themselves as the first gentlemen of their native land, honorbound to remain loyal to their liege lord, Louis XVIII, and these political ties proved stronger than their priestly aspirations. Their enmity to the republican regime in France had been deepened by eleven years of persecution and exile.[116] The die-hard royalists were in no position to prevent the Concordat from coming into being, but their exhortations to the refractory clergy in France helped encourage the formation of the schismatic *petite église* which survived even its denunciation by the restored Louis XVIII after 1814. It showed strength especially among the royalist population of the Vendée.[117]

The Concordat was signed on July 15, 1801 and ratified by both sides by September 10 of the same year. However, its proclamation was delayed by Napoleon for seven months. When the Concordat was finally published at Easter 1802, it had as a lengthy appendix the famous seventy-seven "Organic Articles" which were designed to disarm the Gallican opposition to the reconciliation with Rome. In these added provisions the French government assumed a veto power over the publication of any briefs, bulls, etc. emanating from Rome, no papal envoy could exercise jurisdiction in France without the government's permission, no seminaries could be established without the First Consul's permission and their professors had to subscribe to the Gallican Liberties of 1682 asserting the superiority of a general council to the pope, the civil contract would take precedence over the religious in marriage, and so on. By unilateral action the French state had acquired just those powers over the church which the papal negotiators had been at such pains, over a year of negotiation, not to concede.[118]

With the addition of these provisions the original seventeen articles of the Concordat were even more of a triumph for the French state. Most of them were deliberately vague—bishops were given the right to found seminaries and cathedral chapters but no provision was made for endowing them, bishops were to appoint their priests "with the agreement of the government," the

public practice of the Catholic religion was to be subject to police regulations judged necessary for public tranquility, etc. The
concessions of the papacy, on the other hand, were clear and unambiguous. The Holy See agreed not to raise at any time in the
future the question of the former tithes and church lands, the
issue of the former papal enclaves in France was closed, and the
pope explicitly recognized the legitimacy of the French Republic.[119] The counterrevolution thus was deprived of one of its
trump cards, the French Republic was no longer godless.

In its long-run effects the Concordat proved no more than an
armistice in the struggle, begun by the Enlightenment and continued by the French Revolution, between church and state.[120]
Napoleon was soon again at odds with the papacy. With the restoration of the Bourbon monarchy in 1814, the league between
throne and altar was renewed, and ultramontanism became the
dominant outlook of the French clergy. These developments are
not our concern here. The Concordat of 1802 marks a convenient
cut-off point for our account of the relationship of the Catholic
church and the French Revolution, though in the history of
French Catholicism it represents merely one of many important
milestones in a bitter conflict that was to last for another one
hundred years.

The theoretical implications of the historical episode we have
outlined in this chapter will occupy us later. One point perhaps
should be made here. The split in the French church during the
Revolution and, even more important, the nature of this split
make it impossible to see the struggle between the church and the
Revolution as simply a battle between reaction and progress. Altogether, we should beware of accepting the historicist categories
of much contemporary modernization theorizing and assume that
history must always move "forward."

To see the French Revolution primarily as an agent of modernization, one of the first such radical upheavals, unduly simplifies a
more complex historical reality.[121] Revolutionary movements
seeking a total reorganization of society make their appearance
even within traditional societies and before the onset of the modern age. The French Revolution, on the other hand, as Cobban
has suggested, in some fundamental respects "may not have been
a step forward at all, but rather one backwards . . . instead of ac-
celerating the growth of a modern capitalist economy in France,

the revolution may have retarded it." [122] The victories, glories and conquests of the Revolution and Empire, notes D. W. Brogan, cost 2 million lives and caused "unknown and inculculable economic losses that may have kept France at least a generation behind in economic progress, a handicap that she has never overcome." [123] Certainly as far as French church-state relations are concerned, the Revolution left wounds that made the solution of this problem in "modern" terms more rather than less difficult.

CHAPTER 16

The Cristero Revolt in Mexico

THE MEXICAN REVOLUTION AND THE CHURCH

The term "Mexican Revolution" refers both to the events of 1910–17, during which the long dictatorship of Porfirio Díaz was finally overthrown, and to the new political and social order that claims lineal descent from that insurrection. However we use the term, the struggle between church and state forms an important part of that revolution. Opinions may differ whether this conflict should be seen as one of the "by-products of the general liquidation of the Spanish conquest" [1] or be regarded as a manifestation of anticlericalism, positivist liberalism, or atheism. The fact of the long history of this quarrel is undisputed. Indeed, the assault upon the Catholic church was close to one hundred years old when it reached its climax in a civil war known as the revolt of the Cristeros during the late 1920's—the subject of this chapter.

The movement for Mexican independence during the first two decades of the nineteenth century counted among its leaders numerous members of the clergy, both secular and regular. The instigator of the struggle for independence from Spain was a Catholic priest, Father Hidalgo, whom Mexicans honor as the Father of Mexican Independence. On the other hand, the pope in Rome and practically the entire episcopate condemned the patriots. The hypocritical ease with which the upper clergy turned into ardent supporters of independence, after the successful conclusion of the revolutionary war, was all too apparent and helped create the image of the church as a special interest group that could not be trusted.

The courageous and heroic role of many priests in the wars of independence could not prevent the church from acquiring the reputation of an exploiter. The church was rich in lands and buildings, estimated by some to include more than one-half the real property of the nation. "Church income," writes a modern historian, "was estimated to be well over 100 million pesos annually, five times that of the government. In any case it was frequently assumed, correctly or incorrectly, that the church in Mexico commanded greater economic resources and greater annual income than did the state." [2] The wealth and pomp of the church contrasted with the poverty of the population, especially in the countryside. The great majority of the clergy stayed in the urban centers; most of those ministering to the needs of the rural parishes were poorly trained, charged exorbitant fees for the administration of the sacraments, and were generally licentious in their conduct. Many priests undoubtedly were sincere and devoted men, but those who were not were regarded as typical of the entire clerical estate.

There thus developed a profound distrust of the clergy that was shared by many good Catholics. The fact that the church and all its personnel successfully claimed immunity from the laws of the land and that its special privileges or *fueros* in effect existed as a state within the state further outraged the liberal middle class. In the face of a regime "that had been shaped under the impact of a struggle against absolute monarchy and foreign dominion," Tannenbaum notes, "and in control of people who had been influenced by ideas emanating from the French Revolution, the position of the Church was difficult indeed." [3]

Anticlerical laws were enacted by Mexican regimes from the provisional government of 1821 on, but the first thorough attempt to curb the temporal power of the church came in the constitution of 1857. [4] The church was prohibited from owning or administering any real property not actually used for public worship; ecclesiastics could not serve as deputies or presidents; freedom of education was affirmed; a civil registry was provided for births, deaths, and marriages; special *fueros* were abolished. Perhaps most important, the constitution, by not declaring the Catholic religion the officially recognized religion, opened the door to religious toleration. In the eyes of the clericals this omission was "equivalent to national apostasy" and "a horrible crime." [5]

A few priests spoke in favor of the new constitution, but the great majority of the clergy vigorously opposed it. Their objections were not limited to those provisions dealing with the church specifically but often included the proclaimed political freedoms. The weapons used by the church included denial of the sacraments of confession, absolution, and burial and occasionally support of outright rebellion. A brutal and exhausting civil war that led to even harsher anticlerical measures, like the suppression of all monasteries, culminated in foreign intervention. Peace finally returned in 1867 after the execution of the Archduke Maximilian of Austria whom the French had set up as emperor. The support provided by the church for the conservative forces proved catastrophic—"thereafter it was impossible to blot out the stain of collaboration with the reactionaries and with the traitors who assisted the intervention of the French and the imposition of a foreign monarchy." [6]

During the dictatorship of Porfirio Díaz after 1876, the anticlerical laws were rarely enforced, and church and state lived in relative peace. When Díaz was at last toppled the church once again found herself unpopular. She made common cause with those opposed to the social program of the revolution—the large landowners, who were frequently Spaniards, and the powerful foreign investors. In a collective pastoral letter of January 13, 1913, the Mexican hierarchy came out against the "socialistic" threat the revolution offered to "religion and authority." [7] In the destructive period of strife that lasted from 1911 to 1916, during which various factions disputed the control of the country, many of the clergy, including most prelates, were driven into exile. Some of these emigrés called upon the United States to intervene in Mexico. By late 1915 Carranza and his Constitutionalists had emerged as victors, and in early 1917 at the Constituent Congress of Querétaro a new constitution was adopted to replace the charter of 1857. In this instrument the church was made to pay for the fact that she had stood aligned with those elements opposed to the goals of social justice and nationalism.

The anticlerical provisions of the Constitution of 1917 were harsher than those of 1857. Henceforth all primary education was to be secular, and parochial schools at the lower levels were not permitted; foreign priests were denied the right to say mass and hear confession, monastic vows were outlawed, priests were prohibited from appearing in public in clerical garb, and no religious

ceremonies were to be held outside the churches; religious political parties were banned, and churchmen were forbidden to participate in politics; national ownership of church lands was
confirmed, and state legislatures were granted the right to limit
the number of priests to the "needs of the people." A great dis-
proportion had always existed between the number of churches
and priests and the size of the population of various communities,
and the religious needs of many communities had been neglected.
Thus it could be claimed that the new provision represented an
attempt to remedy an old abuse. However, in point of fact, this
and the other provisions in articles 3, 5, 27, and 130 regulating
church affairs were enacted by men who were without any interest in organized religion, and the majority of them were hostile to
the church. Still more stringent inroads upon the spiritual domain
such as a ban on heard confessions were narrowly defeated.

The Mexican episcopate responded with a collective letter protesting these provisions of the new constitution which, in effect,
put the church under the domination of the state. However, relations between church and state soon improved, for the first two
presidents of revolutionary Mexico made little or no attempt to
enforce the constitutional articles in question. Some state governments enacted anticlerical legislation, but both Carranza and Obregón, preoccupied with consolidating their political positions
and busy with reconstructing the country after years of civil
war, refrained from stirring up additional opposition by enforcing
the constitutional provisions regarding the church. The precarious relations with the United States, strained by repeated American interventions in Mexican affairs, also dictated caution. Hence,
"for nearly eight years, so far as interference with the Church
was concerned, the new Constitution might as well have been
nonexistent." [8]

During the presidency of Obregón (1920–24), in particular,
the church recaptured much of its former strength. Religious
schools were able to function, monasteries and nunneries continued in existence, the church's program of Social Action flourished, exiled prelates and churchmen gradually returned and
wore their garb in public, the foreign clergy was not bothered,
and the provisions against public religious ceremonials were violated with impunity. Several open-air ceremonies that were particularly large and flamboyant were criticized by the government

as inflammatory (the apostolic delegate was expelled in January 1923 after one such procession), and the increased public activity of the Catholics began to cause some apprehension. But it was some time after President Calles had taken control of the government that regulatory laws enforcing the religious provisions of the Constitution of 1917 were introduced and enacted.

Plutarco Elías Calles assumed the presidency on December 1, 1924, and very soon a new tension in church-state relations began to become apparent. Early in 1925 an Orthodox Catholic Apostolic Mexican church, headed by a self-styled Mexican patriarch sympathetic to the Revolution's nationalism, was organized. When the archbishop of Mexico excommunicated the rival movement, and loyal Catholics clashed with the schismatics, President Calles ordered police protection for them and gave the impression of supporting the schismatic church. More basically, Calles felt that the growing influence of the church and its open flaunting of the constitution sooner or later would have to be checked. A confident church feeling steadily stronger had finally encountered an equally uncompromising and principled opponent. As one historian has put it: "The conflict came in 1926 not because the Church wished to mix in politics, or because the revolutionary leaders were Bolsheviks (as some Catholics charged), but because the Church and State both wanted control of Mexican society, and neither was willing to share that control. It was a clash of incompatible and mutually exclusive ideologies, not of politicians." [9] The fact that intransigent personalities headed both camps deepened this ideological conflict and made the resultant uprising all but inevitable.

TOWARD REVOLT

In 1917 a group of laymen, led by a Catholic youth leader, Miguel Palomar y Vizcarra, had attempted to organize a league of civic action to protest the new constitution and to protect religious freedom. At the time church leaders had discouraged the plan fearing that it would exacerbate the controversy with the government. In March 1925 militant lay Catholics decided to dust off the old plan, and they founded the National Religious Defense League to "reconquer religious liberty." [10] The League disclaimed any intention of functioning as a political party and

asserted its independence from the hierarchy.[11] Palomar y Vizcarra went to Rome and, according to his account, obtained the
Vatican's approval for the new organization. He also asserts that
his representation made Pius XI issue an apostolic letter to the
Mexican hierarchy.[12] In this letter, *Paterna sane*, dated February
2 and released April 19, 1926, the pope expressed his solicitude
for the "afflictions" besetting the Mexican church which "certainly bring shame to a people almost totally Catholic." He encouraged laity and clergy to develop "Catholic action" for defense against unreasonable laws that did not merit the name of
law, but he forbade the formation of a Catholic party. All the
faithful should "exercise these civic rights and duties which they
have in common with all other citizens." [13] Pius' letter could indeed be considered an expression of support for the aims and
methods of the National Religious Defense League.

In Mexico, meanwhile, a series of, in part, fortuitous events
were leading to a showdown. On January 27, 1926, the leading
Mexican newspaper, *El Universal*, had published the collective
pastoral letter of the Mexican hierarchy of February 1917, avow-
ing strong opposition to the anticlerical provisions of the 1917
constitution, under a 1926 dateline. An enterprising reporter, it
appears, looking for a sensational story, had decided to publish
this pronouncement on the eve of the ninth anniversary of the
proclamation of the constitution, and he had changed the date to
make the episcopate's protest appear current. An investigation
prompted by a complaint of the primate of Mexico, Archbishop
Mora y del Río, found the reporter guilty of violating professional ethics. The latter, to save his job, pressed the archbishop to
issue a clarification that would state whether the 1917 protest was
still in force,[14] and on February 4 *El Universal* published the following statement allegedly made by the archbishop to the reporter. It read in part:

> The doctrine of the Church is unvariable, because it is the divinely
> revealed truth. The protest which we Mexican prelates formulated
> against the Constitution of 1917 respecting the articles which are
> opposed to religious liberty and dogmas is maintained firmly. . . .
> The Episcopacy, clergy and Catholics do not recognize and com-
> bat Articles 3, 5, 27 and 130 of the existing constitution.[15]

The secretary of the interior labeled this statement "seditious"
and asked the attorney general to investigate. At a hearing the at-

torney for the archbishop denied that the prelate had been quoted correctly, and the government indicated a willingness to dismiss charges. But at this point the militant League put pressure on the episcopate not to retreat; an open letter to the archbishop declared the sympathy and solidarity of 4000 priests and 14 million faithful.[16] On February 8 the Mexican hierarchy, endorsing the position taken by the primate, formally reissued the collective protest of 1917.[17] *El Universal* printed this document the same day.[18] The reopening of old wounds was no longer a matter of an accident.

Clerical writers have argued that the episcopate's action represented an attempt to forestall and respond to the plans of the Calles administration for strict enforcement of the provisions of the 1917 constitution. Word about this allegedly had leaked in January.[19] President Calles, on the other hand, insisted that the campaign of rigid enforcement was decided upon after "bad Mexican and foreign clergy" had publicly displayed their disobedience of the law of the land.[20] The government was in the midst of delicate negotiations with the United States over provisions of the constitution bearing upon the claims of American oil companies. Calles may have felt that if domestic unrest leading to foreign intervention was to be avoided, a show of force was essential.[21]

Whatever Calles' motives, within a few days of the episcopate's declaration the government acted. The arrest and deportation of foreign priests began on February 10, and by September 1926, 183 foreign-born clerics, most of them Spaniards, had been expelled. On February 11 the attorney general announced the nationalization of all church property not already in possession of the nation. On February 12 all schools, asylums, and convents where religious instruction was given were ordered closed; by September 1926, 73 convents, 129 schools attached to convents, and 118 asylums under religious control had been closed. On February 13 the minister of interior telegraphed all the state governors asking them to submit with the least possible delay legislation to the state legislatures that would enforce articles 3, 5, 130 of the federal constitution. On February 26 the secretary of public instruction directed all private schools to register with the Ministry of Public Instruction. Religious instruction and the service of priests as teachers were forbidden. Finally, on July 21, 1926 President Calles issued a decree, to become effective July 31, that required the registration of all ministers of any religious creed with the civil authorities, and he detailed the penalties for violations of the religious clauses of the constitution. Most of the states by this time had established quotas for ministers which in effect were legislating the church out of existence. One state, Campeche, allowed five priests for the entire state.[22]

The reaction of the Mexican hierarchy to this campaign of harassment was swift. In a pastoral letter of March 1, 1926, Bishop José de Jesús Manríquez y Zárate of Juejutla condemned the crimes committed by the Mexican government against the church and he denounced "the so-called Constitution of Querétaro" and "each and every precept, issued in violation of the law of God, the rights of man, or the teachings of Holy Church." [23] He was arrested soon thereafter. The bishop of Tacámbaro, Leopoldo Ruiz y Flores, in a pastoral letter of March 26 rejected rebellion and armed revolution, but he asserted that God rather than man was to be obeyed, and he argued for the defense of the rights of the superior authority which is that of God.[24] He, too, was arrested. Finally, on April 21 the Mexican episcopate issued a joint pastoral letter in which they called upon the faithful "to enlist in organizations which teach the people theoretically and practically their rights and duties as citizens and organize the nation for the defense of religious liberty, always remaining, however, outside any party and above any party." Such conduct, the bishops continued, "is not rebellion because the Constitution itself establishes its amendability and opens the way for reforms, and because it is a just devotion to mandates superior to human law and to the just defense of legitimate interests." The church did not seek conflicts, but, in order not to disappear in fact, it had to defend itself "legally but vigorously." [25]

Despite this seeming show of unanimity the bishops in fact were by no means in full agreement on what concrete steps to take. The Vatican, it is said, advised a temporizing policy; some bishops counseled rebellion, others favored passive resistance.[26] An Episcopal Committee was therefore formed to recommend policy and to represent the hierarchy in negotiations with the government. The archbishop of Mexico City, José Mora y del Río, was elected president and the bishop of Tabasco, Pascual Díaz, became the secretary of the committee. At a meeting of the Episcopal Committee on July 11 the more intransigent bishops prevailed, and some days later the momentous decision was made to refuse clerical registration and to suspend all religious services as of August 1. The Holy See was informed of this move by telegram, and on July 23 a return cable was received stating the approval of the Vatican.[27] A joint pastoral letter, made public on July 25, announced the suspension of worship. It once again asked the Catholics of Mexico to use all legal and peaceful means to obtain the repeal of the anti-religious laws.[28]

The hierarchy had ordered all priests to withdraw from the churches though the edifices were to remain open and entrusted to the care of the faithful. But the bishops' expectation that the withdrawal of the clergy could be a powerful weapon seriously misjudged the strength of the church as a religious institution. Except in a few major cities Mexican Catholicism has always been based upon local custom—a mixture of native tradition and Catholic ritual. The invocation of saints in the home or the pilgrimage to favorite local shrines have always been more important than the mass and the sacraments administered by the few priests to be found in the rural areas. These rural districts contained about two-thirds of the population but only one-fourth of the priests.[29] The vigorous religious life of these people thus had functioned quite well without the services of a priest, and the decision to withdraw the clergy from the churches had little impact. "The Church lost the great 'strike' of 1926–29 precisely because the majority of the Mexicans did not care whether Masses were said or not and whether the bishops remained in their episcopal palaces or went into exile."[30]

Another tactic of passive resistance, decided upon by the National Religious Defense League, also met with little success. In early July the League announced an economic boycott during which Catholics were to purchase only necessities, abstain from the use of motor vehicles and electricity, and stop attendance at all amusements and at lay schools. The avowed aim of the boycott was "to paralyze the social and economic life of the nation," and in this way to "bring to an end the situation of legal oppression" of the church. The Episcopal Committee endorsed the boycott and recommended to clergy and laity "the most effective participation possible in so laudable an enterprise."[31] But here again the action did not constitute a serious blow to the government though a government spokesman denounced the boycott as "seditious." Amid reports of minor disturbances coming in from the provinces and rumors of a large-scale rebellion, President Calles termed the episcopate's renunciation of important provisions of the constitution an unacceptable challenge to the authority of the government, a serious disturbance of the public order, and he accused the bishops of inciting rebellion. The president denied any intention of limiting religious liberty.[32]

On August 19, Archbishop Leopoldo Ruiz and Bishop Díaz, acting for the Episcopal Committee, petitioned President Calles to grant the Mexican Catholics freedom of conscience, thought, worship, instruction, association, and press—"liberties to which we have the right as Christians, as citizens of a cultured nation, and as men." The bishops denied having sought revolt through the suspension of worship. "Not to exercise an act penalized by a law is not rebellion." [33] In his reply Calles acknowledged the propriety of the petition, but he argued that the liberties sought were safeguarded by the constitution and were not infringed. The constitutional provisions regulating the activities of the church, on the other hand, Calles declared, were in perfect accord with his own "philosophical and political convictions," and he therefore was not the right person to work for their reform or repeal.[34]

On August 21, through the mediation of a prominent layman, Eduardo Mestre, President Calles met with the two churchmen. In the course of a lengthy conversation that touched upon many issues, the prelates again denied any desire for armed revolt or foreign intervention. Calles termed the registration of clerics an administrative measure and disclaimed any intention to interfere in either church organization or dogma. Both sides thus were in a conciliatory mood, and the Episcopal Committee decided that the president's assurances justified the resumption of worship. A statement to this effect was prepared for release to the press, but a clause added by Bishop Díaz caused Calles to repudiate the understanding. In this clause the resumption of worship was made dependent upon the fulfillment of certain unnamed demands of the church. The president replied that he had made no promises whatever and that the clergy would have to abide by the law. According to another source, the Holy See objected to the agreement and the bishops were ordered to rescind their decision.[35] Negotiations collapsed at this point.

Early in September the bishops submitted a petition to the Federal Congress in which they demanded "in the name of the Catholic Mexican people, the repeal of some of the articles of the present constitution, and the reform of others, with the patriotic purpose of putting an end to the religious conflict." [36] The deputies by a vote of 171 to 1 rejected the petition on the grounds that the bishops by their public declarations not to observe the constitution had lost their citizenship and thus had forfeited the legal right of petition. This vote took place on September 23, 1926 and for a time marked the end of any attempt to find a peaceful solution to the church-state conflict.

REBELLION

The first armed skirmish involving the National Religious Defense League occurred August 15 in Chalchihuites, Zacatecas, when a Catholic merchant named Pedro Quintanar and 45 followers clashed with a military detachment. With reports of similar local and largely spontaneous disturbances coming into Mexico City, the League decided to build these small actions into a general campaign of guerrilla warfare to regain religious liberty. According to Palomar y Vizcarra, then vice-president of the League, the goal of this movement was not to overthrow the government but to win recognition of the "essential religious liberties." [37]

The Catholic rebels adopted the name "Cristeros" and chose as their motto the old clerical slogan *Viva Cristo Rey* ("Long live Christ the King"). The struggle was centered in the western states—Jalisco, Michoacán, and Colima—where the League and the equally militant Catholic Association of Young Mexicans (ACJM) were strong. By the middle of January 1927 the Cristero groups in Jalisco had grown from 40 to 2000 men; among the leaders were several priests.[38] In early 1927 some 8000 men were said to have been involved in armed clashes in different parts of the country. Many were students; among the leaders were seminarians and persons holding positions in various local and regional Catholic organizations. Few were military men.[39]

Throughout the first half of 1927 the movement gained strength and despite great difficulties in procuring arms it scored numerous small victories. On the other hand, many of the young students and members of the ACJM quickly tired of the strenuous life of a guerrilla and deserted. Their places were taken by peasants, rural laborers disillusioned with government land policies, landowners seeking to defend their properties, bandits who lived in the area of the conflict, military men discharged for misconduct in the army, defeated politicians who wished to return to power, and, more generally, devout men who considered it their duty to defend religious liberty.[40] The federal government became increasingly alarmed, and military outposts were reinforced.

As in most civil wars, especially those with a religious basis, fanaticism and vicious cruelty were rampant among both rebel and government forces. "The rebels burned schools and public buildings, assassinated teachers and public officials, executed labor leaders who supported the government, executed prisoners, and generally wreaked havoc where they could. The government executed prisoners, hanged some priests, took hostages, drove entire villages from their lands, and in a thousand ways mistreated men identified as sympathetic to the rebel cause." [41] Atrocities were committed by both sides. Among the best known of these is the attack by some 400 Cristeros on the Guadalajara-Mexico City train on April 20, 1927. The train carried an armed guard and a payroll, but among the victims of the assault were many passengers, including women and children. The attackers poured kerosene on the cars and ignited them, and many wounded travelers were burned to death. According to some survivors, three priests, in clerical garb, directed the attack. Church leaders acknowledged their presence but insisted that they had been chaplains rather than combatants.[42]

By the summer of 1927 the rebellion, poorly organized and lacking adequate military leadership in the field, had lost momentum in all areas save parts of Jalisco and Michoacán. Here, writes Cumberland, "the rapacity of the federal commanders rather than the fanaticism of the peasants kept it alive; some evidence suggests that the major factor in driving the Jalisco peasants to arms initially was rooted in hatred for the local military officials, and that the religious issue was distinctly secondary." [43] The poor, with no money to pay off generals and politicians, suffered most intensely at the hands of roving bands and plundering soldiers. In the towns, an American writer residing in Mexico recalls, "it became good sport to arrest Catholics on suspicion, holding them in jail without preferring charges until they paid thousands of pesos for release and promised to keep their mouths shut." [44] The government's edict ordering the confiscation of rebel property was extended to civilians, but very little loot found its way into the public treasury. In the wake of this protracted disorder, aggravated by greed and personal feuds, Jalisco, the richest agricultural state of Mexico, was left utterly prostrate. [45]

In August 1927 the rebels appointed an able professional soldier, Enrique Gorostieta, as chief of operations in Jalisco; later in 1928 he became supreme commander of the Cristero army. The military exploits of the Cristeros now became somewhat more successful, and broad regions of Jalisco came under their control. At the end of the year 1927 the Cristero army, according to. League archives, numbered 25,000 men of whom 18,000 were well armed. It was said to be active in 18 states. [46] According to another report by Miguel Palomar y Vizcarra, dated December 29, 1927, the Cristeros then numbered 20,000 well-armed men and 10,000 others less well equipped. [47] Cristero strength was highest in early 1928; thereafter it decreased. An American diplomat estimated total Cristero strength in June 1928 as a mere 5000 armed men. [48] More efficient government operations and less severe punishment meted out to captured rebels had begun to attract the peasants way from the movement, while the rebels were encountering more and more difficulties in procuring arms and other supplies.

Cristero leaders maintain to this day that they could have won the struggle and that they were "stabbed in the back" by the episcopate's willingness in 1929 to make peace with the government. They argue that discipline and organization came to the Cristeros late, that toward the end of the campaign morale was high among the troops, and that given more time they could eventually have defeated the government forces. [49] Be that as it may, there is no doubt that the negotiations that eventually got under way between the bishops and the government affected the Cristeros' fighting spirit severely and undermined popular support for them. Rumors in 1929 of an early settlement produced a notable slackening of recruitment into the Cristero army. [50] Desertions increased, and some priests were now saying that it was a mortal sin for the peasants to give food and aid to the Cristeros. [51] The loss of General Gorostieta, who was killed on June 2, 1929, just days before the *modus vivendi*, was the final blow to the movement. Some 14,000 Cristeros eventually surrendered; it is estimated that total deaths in the almost three years of revolt may have reached 24,000 to 30,000, about half of these casualties being suffered by the Cristeros.[52]

Aid provided by American Catholics probably helped the Cristeros to hold out as long as they did. However, the rebels' hope that American Catholics would convince the American government to intervene in the Mexican civil war was disappointed. The Catholic episcopate and Catholic organizations like the Knights of Columbus repeatedly asked the American government to protest the denial of religious liberty in Mexico, and they urged the withdrawal of diplomatic recognition. Their efforts failed. Relations between the two countries in 1926 and 1927 were tense because of the new Mexican oil legislation, but the American government refused to be drawn into yet another controversy and limited its diplomatic moves to appeals for the protection of American citizens in Mexico. Mexican religious strife, the government held, was a purely domestic matter.[53]

The League's efforts to obtain American help, meanwhile, were hampered by the dispatch of several unsatisfactory and unreliable representatives and by squabbles between the different envoys. Two men, René Capistran Garza and José Gandara, were at first active on behalf of the League. Gandara had some success in buying arms and ammunition. Capistran Garza, on the other hand, knew neither the English language nor was he familiar with American politics and customs, and thus he proved rather ineffective. Before long the two men were fighting each other, and at the same time relations with leading American Catholics ran into difficulties. The latter were willing to support a movement in defense of religious freedom, but the bishops, in particular, shied away from endorsing an insurrection and "holy war."[54] They also questioned the wisdom of seeking the establishment of a purely Catholic regime, a goal that jeopardized any chance of obtaining the support of the American government. Matters were further complicated by the divisions in the ranks of the Mexican episcopate many of whom soon developed doubts about the prudence of supporting the League and its actions. This lack of unanimous and strong backing by the Mexican bishops—a subject to which we will return—undoubtedly weakened the League's position in the United States. Capistran Garza's attempts to obtain large sums of money from several rich American Catholics, including a Señor Buckley, did not succeed and led to angry charges by Capistran against Bishop Díaz who was accused of having sabotaged the scheme. In his reports to the Cristero command in Mexico, on the other hand, Capistran Garza consistently exaggerated the help promised to him by American Catholics and the State Department. Indeed, some Mexican writers think that the Cristeros might not have launched their revolt but for the assurances of Capistran Garza in the fall of 1926 that American Catholics would provide substantial help in the struggle.[55]

Throughout the months of bloody conflict the Mexican government blamed the Mexican hierarchy for the revolt of the Cristeros, while the bishops in turn steadfastly denied ever having sanctioned armed rebellion. The truth is a bit more complicated and must take into account the divisions in the ranks of the episcopate. On November 26, 1926 the League presented a memorial to the hierarchy in which they asked the bishops to approve (or at least not condemn) armed defense of religious liberty and to allow priests to participate in such a fight. The leaders of the Episcopal Committee, Archbishop Mora y del Río and Bishop Díaz, replied orally that since all legal and peaceful means for obtaining the most essential liberties of civilized life had been tried in vain, in the view of the episcopate, the society's right of legitimate defense was indisputable. They added that it would not be right to embark upon an armed uprising unless there was a probability of success, and they insisted that priests not function as fighting men but only as military chaplains.[56]

The response of the Mexican episcopate thus was cautious. The Catholic militants could interpret this oral pronouncement as an endorsement of their plans for armed revolt; they maintain to this day that the Cristero revolt was begun with the express approval of the entire hierarchy.[57] Publicly the bishops could go on asserting that the church did not sanction rebellion against legitimate authority. In view of the fact that the bishops in many of their pronouncements had challenged the legitimacy of the 1917 constitution, this public position, of course, did not amount to a repudiation of the rightfulness of armed defense against this constitution on the part of the laity. Bishop Díaz subsequently

maintained "that though the Episcopate did not stop the movement, neither did it give its approval to the war." Díaz noted that
"the hierarchy had no reason to interfere in the League's affairs
since it was free to defend its rights in its own manner." [58]

The leaders of the Cristeros with considerable justice have rejected this attempt of the bishops to renege on their earlier announced approval. As Palomar y Vizcarra has put it: "If the
Episcopate did not feel that it could interfere with the com-
mencement of a war, why did it sign a truce with the government to end the war on June 21, 1929? If it were not the province of the hierarchy to sanction the League's struggle, why did
it step in and cut the ideological ground from under the League
after over two years of bloody struggle?" [59] It would appear that
the Mexican episcopate in late 1926 shared the optimism of the
leaders of the League and therefore guardedly endorsed the plans
for revolt. A statement by a highly placed churchman commenting on the American role confirms this appraisal: "A benevolent
neutrality would be enough in order for the faith to triumph; if
arms and ammunition were allowed to enter without discrimination, if money were loaned, the triumph would be rapid." [60]
However, when the expected quick victory of the Cristeros failed
to materialize, many of the bishops gradually withdrew their support, and the episcopate finally signed an agreement with the
government. Had the movement shown more definite signs of
succeeding the bishops probably would have endorsed it more
openly as a majority of the Spanish hierarchy was to do in the
next decade in the case of General Franco's uprising in Spain. In
the less certain situation in Mexico the hierarchy opted for a
more cautious course—a strategy that eventually paid political
dividends though it left many of the faithful bewildered and
angry. "To this day," an American Jesuit deeply involved in the
Mexican struggle wrote in 1936, "there exists a deep-seated ran-
cor in the hearts of many Mexican Catholics whom I know because, with one exception, the Bishop of Huejutla, the Hierarchy
would not speak the word to go out and fight." [61]

Even if we assume that the position of the episcopate was more
or less unanimous in 1926, we know that this unanimity soon was
to crumble. Bishop Díaz, for example, who was deported from
Mexico on January 12, 1927, was quoted in an Associated Press
story from Guatemala a few days later as having condemned re-

volt for whatever cause—both as bishop and as citizen.[62] This and other similar statements made by Díaz greatly disturbed the more militant members of the hierarchy, among them Archbishop José María González y Valencia of Durango who headed a committee of liaison at the Vatican. The bishops in Rome, it appears, accepted at face value the optimistic reports about the progress of the revolt sent by René Capistran Garza in the United States, a version of the state of affairs that was wishful thinking. On February 11, 1927 González y Valencia issued a pastoral letter in Rome addressed to those who find themselves "on the field of battle front to front with the enemies of Christ." Having been asked for his opinion it was his pastoral duty, the archbishop continued, "to face the issue squarely" and he therefore declared:

> We never provoked this armed movement. But once that, all pacific means exhausted, this movement exists: To our Catholic sons risen in arms for the defense of their social and religious rights, after having thought at great length before God and having consulted the sagest theologians of the city of Rome, we should say to you: Be tranquil in your consciences and receive our benedictions.[63]

Reporting on his meeting with the pope, the archbishop said:

> What great consolation filled our prelate's heart hearing with our own ears the words of holy praise, blessing, and most especial love which you have merited from the supreme head of the church. We have seen him moved on hearing the story of your struggle, we have seen him bless your admirable resistance, approve all your acts, and admire all your heroisms.[64]

The pastoral letter concluded with further words of encouragement for those defending the cause of Christ the King:

> For Him we fight, for Him we are disposed to die, for Him we shall never tolerate that Mexico be deprived of its eternal treasures, for Him we repudiate the anti-Christian arrangements called laws, and for Him we shall continue resisting all iniquitous efforts until we may guarantee through justice and charity an era of true Christian liberty and a happy republic.[65]

According to Palomar y Vizcarra, in early 1927 Pius XI fully approved of the Cristero uprising and only later was the pope mislead into accepting a settlement and defeat. A rich documentation is said to exist to back up this assertion.[66] Other sources maintain that Pius XI never sanctioned armed rebellion in Mexico.[67] We do know that apart from the sentiments expressed to Archbishop González y Valencia, Pius XI neither approved nor disapproved of the Cristeros' actions publicly. He, too, may have at first chosen to await the progress and outcome of the revolt before committing the prestige of his office one way or the other.

Following the attack on the Guadalajara train on April 20, 1927 the government again accused the Mexican episcopate of fomenting revolt. Several bishops promptly denied any responsibility for this cruel assault, but they did not disown the Cristeros. Archbishop Mora y del Río of Mexico City told the minister of the interior, Tejeda, when arraigned before him on charges of revolt:

> We have aided no revolution. We have plotted no revolution, but we do claim that the Catholics of Mexico have the right to fight for their rights by peaceful means first and with arms in an extremity.[68]

When Minister Tejeda called this statement a defense of rebellion against the government and ordered the deportation of the prelate, Archbishop Mora y del Río was quoted to have replied: "The present government is not a legal government. The world knows how it came to power and history will tell the story of its fall." [69] After his arrival in the United States Mora y del Río and the other five expelled bishops again denied the charge of rebellion and declared that "the episcopate has limited itself to stating that the Catholics are in their right to defend themselves against the tyranny that oppressed them." [70]

In June 1927 the League petitioned the episcopate to release the jewels and sacred vessels remaining in the churches so that they could be sold to finance the purchase of arms and ammunition. The financial help expected from the American Catholics had not materialized, the petition pointed out, and the situation now was critical. Unless the bishops provided this desperately needed support the cause of religion in Mexico was doomed. At the very least, the episcopate should guarantee a loan. Despite the urgent tone of this request the Episcopal Committee turned it down. The value of the jewels and chalices, even if they could be sold, the interim secretary of the Episcopal Committee in San

Antonio, Texas, Bishop Gerardo Anaya, maintained, was not enough to finance the armed struggle of the League. Moreover, the bishops had no right to dispose of them. All Mexican revolutions supported by the United States had succeeded, but the American government would never support a purely religious movement. The struggle in Mexico would be regarded as just such a religious one if the bishops became the agents and financial backers of the Cristeros.[71]

After this rebuff the League turned to its trusted friend in Rome, Archbishop González y Valencia. He was asked to persuade the Holy See to require the Mexican bishops to turn over the jewels and sacred vessels. Archbishop González replied that the Holy See could not permit the transfer of church property for the purpose of financing the purchase of arms.[72] Apparently neither the Mexican bishops nor the Holy See were willing to make so far-reaching a commitment to the cause of the Cristeros.

In September 1927 President Coolidge appointed Dwight W. Morrow the new American ambassador to Mexico, and he thereby indicated his intention of ending the drift toward American intervention. The temporary settlement of the oil controversy that followed relieved the Mexican government of the haunting fear of intervention just as it compelled most of the opponents of the Calles regime to resign themselves to the fact that they could not count on outside assistance. As Walter Lippmann correctly notes, "the removal of the interventionist threat cut the ground from under the intransigents in both camps." [73] The foundation for a settlement of the religious issue had thus been laid.

Ambassador Morrow asked two officials of the National Catholic Welfare Conference (the coordinating body of the American Roman Catholic church), Father John C. Burke and Mr. William F. Montavon, to act as mediators. The terms for a settlement suggested by Father Burke to President Calles were strikingly similar to the abortive understanding reached between the Episcopal Committee and Calles in 1926. The president of Mexico was to declare publicly that it was not the purpose of the constitution and laws of the country to destroy the identity of the church and that the government stood ready to confer with the authorized head of the church "to avoid unreasonable applications" of these legal provisions. Such a declaration would enable the Mexican clergy to resume public worship, and in the ensuing atmosphere of good will both sides might later consider changes in the laws.[74] Calles and Burke met on April 28, 1928 in Veracruz and in a letter of the same day Calles accepted the terms proposed by Burke. It was "not the purpose of the Constitution nor of the laws, nor my own purpose, to destroy the identity of any church, nor to interfere, in any form, in its spiritual functions." The president added that he would gladly listen to any complaints "regarding injustices that may be committed through excess of application of the laws." [75] A public statement to the same effect had been made by the minister of education in the presence of Calles some days earlier.

On April 23, 1928, Archbishop Mora y del Río, the primate of Mexico, died in exile in San Antonio, Texas, and Archbishop Ruiz y Flores, a man of more conciliatory views, succeeded him. Calles and Ruiz met several times in May in Mexico City, and further progress toward a settlement was made. However, at this point the League and those bishops who were in favor of continuing the rebellion until a change in the laws had been secured redoubled their efforts. Archbishop Ruiz was called to Rome; the Holy See's quick approval of the projected agreement, which the heads of the Episcopal Committee, Ruiz and Díaz, had expected was held up. It appears that the influence of the more bellicose Mexican bishops residing in Rome was still considerable. Among these intransigents were Archbishop González y Valencia and Bishop Leopoldo Lara y Torres. The latter has since published his correspondence with the leaders of the rebellion, and we find therein numerous letters, especially to Palomar y Vizcarra, in which Lara y Torres encouraged continuation of the struggle and assured the Cristeros that they were acting in line with the views of the Holy See.[76]

While the final outcome of the peace efforts was still pending a supporter of the Cristeros assassinated the Mexican president-elect, Álvaro Obregón, on July 17, 1928, and the carefully nurtured spirit of conciliation and mutual confidence once again gave way to sharp recrimination. The government immediately accused the church; the official Vatican paper, *Osservatore Romano*, charged President Calles with the murder of his friend. But with the intervention of Ambassador Morrow and Father Burke calmer voices soon prevailed. The captured assassin, José de León

Toral, who had been active in the ACJM and the League, was not shot summarily but put on trial. The legal proceedings brought out that Toral had executed his deed at the instigation of a nun, Mother Conchita, who was in charge of a clandestine convent and who was the pivot of numerous Catholic plots. He also had been under the strong influence of his father confessor who had preached the elimination of Obregón and Calles as a deed pleasing to God. After the failure of two earlier attempts on Obregón's life organized by the League and the subsequent summary executions of the assassins and alleged conspirators whom he had known personally, Toral accepted the deadly assignment in order to serve his church.[77] He was condemned to death and executed.

The tensions generated by the assassination of Obregón and by the trial, execution, and burial of Toral delayed but did not destroy the mediation efforts of Morrow and Burke. Another crisis was created by the outbreak of a military rebellion in March 1929, led by three generals who were political opponents of Calles and who aimed to wrest the presidency from his control. The military insurgents sought and obtained the support of the Cristeros,[78] and for a few weeks this rebellion posed a serious threat to the interim-president, Portes Gil. But the new revolt was suppressed; the American government had made clear its displeasure at the coup, and American Catholic authorities had pointed out that the rebels were military adventurers implicated in serious attacks upon the Mexican clergy. Thus, as Lippmann notes, "the tragedy of the rebellion proved to be a blessing in disguise for it demonstrated to the government that the clergy would not capitalize the hazards of counter-revolution, and it impelled the government to make friendly statements. The clergy, for their part, began to issue condemnations of violence." [79]

In early June 1929 negotiations resumed. Several conferences took place between the newly inaugurated president, Emilio Portes Gil, and the heads of the Episcopal Committee, Archbishop Ruiz and Bishop Díaz. Morrow, Burke, and several other non-Mexican Catholics again assisted as mediators. Portes Gil was no friend of the church, but with a special presidential election scheduled for November 1929 in which he faced strong opposition, Portes Gil was determined to play down the religious problem.[80] On June 15 the Vatican was informed of the terms of the settlement in the making, and the Holy See this time swiftly gave its approval. Pressure against an agreement from diehards in both camps proved ineffective, and on June 21, 1929 the settlement was made official.

The *modus vivendi* reached took the form of two public statements released on the same day, one by the president and the other by the primate of Mexico. These statements essentially embodied the assurances first obtained from Calles in August 1926 and restated in the Veracruz conference of April 1928. The statement of President Portes Gil took note of the fears of the Mexican bishops that the constitution and implementing legislation, especially the provisions requiring the registration of clergymen, gave the state control of the church's spiritual offices. He also noted the assurances of the bishops that they "are animated by a sincere patriotism and that they desire to resume public worship if this can be done if the Church could enjoy freedom within the law to live and exercise its spiritual offices." Portes Gil went on: "I am glad to take advantage of this opportunity to declare publicly and very clearly that it is not the purpose of the Constitution, nor of the laws, nor of the Government of the Republic to destroy the identity of the Catholic Church or of any other, or to interfere in any way with its spiritual functions." This general declaration of intent was followed by three more specific promises: (1) The government would not register ministers not "named by the hierarchical superior of the religious creed in question." (2) Though there could be no religious instruction in schools, whether public or private, clergymen could impart religious doctrines "within church confines." (3) The right of petition was available to all residents of the republic and members of any church could, therefore, "apply to the appropriate authorities for the amendment, repeal or passage of any law." [81]

Archbishop Ruiz in his brief statement confirmed that the conversations with the president of the Republic had "been marked by a spirit of mutual good will and respect. As a consequence of the said statement made by the president, the Mexican clergy will resume religious services pursuant to the laws in force." He expressed the hope that this resumption of worship would lead the Mexican people to cooperate "for the benefit of all the people of our Fatherland." [82]

The agreement negotiated by the two church moderates, Ruiz

and Díaz, thus did not give the church anything that she could not have obtained in 1926. To be sure, the government recognized more explicitly the right of the church to choose her priests, and the president apparently promised informally not to apply the existing laws in a sectarian spirit. But no promise was made of a change in the laws, and the church in effect now accepted the legitimacy of the Constitution of 1917 and of the revolutionary government. After three years of conflict, and exposure to new and more liberal ideas during exile in the United States, most members of the Mexican hierarchy had come to accept the Mexican Revolution as an accomplished fact. In the words of Walter Lippmann, they had come to realize "that a restoration of the old social order was impossible, that American intervention was no solution, that the new regime, regardless of palace rebellions and military revolts, was likely to endure." [83] This was the significance of the settlement of 1929.

The agreement between Portes Gil and the Episcopal Committee provided for an amnesty for imprisoned Cristeros and those in the field who would surrender their arms. But the Cristeros had fought for a change in constitutional provisions, and they did not regard the words of a president known for his anti-Catholic views a guarantee of religious liberty. They felt that the agreement to which the bishops had consented was thus a sham and that they had been betrayed. Nevertheless, Cristero strength was waning, and the new head of the Cristero army, Jesús Degollado Guizar, realizing the futility of further fighting, gave orders to demobilize and surrender. In a message to his troops Degollado Guizar commended them for their heroic struggle, but he pointed out that they now had to obey the supreme authority of the church, the pope, who had sanctioned the settlement.[84]

The leaders of the League did not give up so easily. They assailed the settlement by means of leaflets and newspaper articles, and, as late as September 10, 1930, Palomar y Vizcarra appealed to the pope to nullify the truce.[85] Reprisals against the surrendering Cristero troops that cost many lives added to the bitterness and encouraged recriminations against the hierarchy. At the end of September 1930, Pascual Díaz, now archbishop, formally declared that in view of the pope's approval the *modus vivendi* of 1929 was no longer a debatable issue, and he called for an end to the scandalous and discordant efforts to renew trouble.[86] This appeal was less than effective. The rebellion had failed, and the League eventually was forced to change its name, but divisions within the church continued.

MODUS VIVENDI

On June 27, 1929 masses were celebrated in Mexico for the first time since July 1926, and during the next two years the church staged a strong comeback. But the religious issue was far from settled, and tensions soon re-emerged. For ambitious politicians anticlericalism could serve as a useful political weapon, while some prominent members of the League were still dreaming of victory through the use of force. A new clandestine organization called "Justice and Action" pledged itself to use any and all means in the fight against tyranny [87]; in Veracruz an attempt was made to assassinate the anticlerical governor, Adalberto Tejeda, who had been Calles' minister of interior at the outbreak of the Cristero rebellion. Following the settlement of 1929 Tejeda had denounced Portes Gil as a "coward and traitor"; the assassination attempts and a series of other violent incidents now provided the excuse for renewing the attack upon the church. On June 18, 1931 Tejeda decreed that the maximum number of priests permitted to serve in Veracruz state would be one for each one hundred thousand inhabitants. This meant that of the nearly two hundred priests officiating only thirteen could continue in office.[88] Other states followed suit. Chiapas and Yucatan restricted the clergy to nine. Tabasco prohibited the leading of religious ceremonies by priests.[89]

The giant public celebration of the four-hundredth anniversary of the appearance of the Virgin of Guadalupe on December 12, 1931 did little to calm the aroused spirits; it further irritated the intransigent anticlericals who considered the mammoth ceremony, attended by over half a million people, a deliberate affront. The government of Jalisco exiled the archbishop of Guadalajara, and the national government limited the number of priests in the federal district to twenty-five. In the course of the year 1932 eight other states again seized church buildings, severely cut the number of priests allowed to officiate, and otherwise harassed both clergy and communicants. By 1934 thirteen of the states had closed most churches on one pretext or another ("sanitary laws" were a favorite gambit), in the states of Veracruz and Chiapas religious services were suspended altogether, and in a few states not a single priest remained.[90]

On October 10, 1934 the Mexican Congress adopted a revised constitutional article 3 that introduced a new kind of education: "The education imparted by the state shall be socialistic and, in addition to excluding all religious doctrine, shall combat fanaticism and prejudices by . . . the creation in youth of an exact and rational concept of the universe and of social life." Primary, secondary, and normal education were to be the monopoly of the state.[91] This attack upon the religious world view and the teaching role of the church was followed in 1935 by a series of decrees that provided for the nationalization of any church property or private home used for the propagation of a religious cult. Publications containing religious information were denied the use of the mails.[92]

Despite these severe restrictions again imposed upon the church, the hierarchy, profiting from the experience of the 1920's, reacted with great moderation and repeatedly warned against recourse to armed resistance. Many of the bishops issued pastoral letters protesting the injustice of the new laws, but at the same time they insisted upon peaceful measures such as petitions to the courts and other legal remedies. The idea of again suspending church services or renewing armed resistance, coming from many quarters, was turned down also by the Holy See. In his encyclical *Acerba animi* of September 29, 1932, directed to the Mexican episcopate, Pope Pius XI criticized the non-fulfillment of the 1929 agreement, but he insisted on legal protests only.[93] Archbishop Díaz, explaining the encyclical to the faithful in a pastoral letter of October 7, 1932, pointed out that the Mexican bishops and the Holy Father had now made known their stand and that it was wrong even to think of violent measures.[94] When Archbishop Ruiz y Flores defended the pope against the charge of inciting the Mexican Catholics to rebellion he was deported and remained in exile in San Antonio, Texas, until his death in 1942.

But in 1934, with the controversy over the introduction of "socialist education," some of the exiled bishops again began to flirt with the idea of armed resistance. Ruiz y Flores, writing to Díaz from the United States in September 1934, pointed out the ex-

treme delicacy of this problem and suggested the old posture of
neutrality: "Your Grace might perhaps say something to the effect that it is not our task either to approve or to disapprove.
That belongs to the politicians." [95] At about the same time, José
de Jesús Manríquez y Zárate, the exiled bishop of Juejutla, exhorted the Mexican Catholics to oppose the Judaical-Masonic
plans of the government "by all means in their power." In order
to save their children from the "Bolshevik monster" the bishop of
Juejutla advised Catholic parents to "go to any length that may
be necessary." [96] The government responded by indicting both
prelates for having incited rebellion against the government and
ordered their arrest if they should return to Mexico.

On November 20, 1934 an insurrection was proclaimed in the
state of Veracruz. The so-called "Popular Liberation Army" justified the uprising on the grounds that "since violence and brute
force are the only title that supports the tyrant and his court in
power, force and violence at the service of the law must be the
most effective means of causing such inequities to pass into
history." [97] The revolt spread to rural areas in a number of states,
but it never became a serious threat to the government. Many of
the insurgents were former Cristeros, though the last chief of the
Cristero army, Degollado Guizar, declined participation. He told
the rebels that their efforts would fail because of a lack of unity,
inadequate plans, and the ignorance of the Catholic people.[98]
Guerilla operations continued for some time; by 1937 the movement had been completely suppressed.[99]

As far as is known, the Mexican hierarchy stayed aloof from
this new armed movement. Only one prelate, Juan María Navarrette, bishop of Sonora, in a letter dated December 18, 1934 and
written in reply to an inquiry from a group of Sonora Catholics
about the permissibility of armed resistance, endorsed such a form
of struggle. Bishop Navarrette expressed the view that under the
prevailing conditions of persecution "Catholics must at least undertake a firm and organized campaign of passive resistance. . . .
If in addition to this there are those who wish to resist in another
fashion, as long as such resistance is in accord with natural law
and offers solid probability of success, I judge that such action
would be nothing more than the exercise of their natural, inalienable rights." [100] The recipient of this advice subsequently
launched an uprising in Sonora and was killed in combat a year
later. Whether he ever believed that his movement had a "solid

probability of success" is not known. The fact that the rest of the Mexican episcopate were unwilling to endorse the renewal of fighting probably doomed the uprising from the start. Lay Catholics, too, by now had learned the futility of armed struggle against the Mexican Revolution. The quasi-fascist Sinarquista movement, which grew from a mere handful in 1937 to more than 500,000 in 1940, was characterized by strong religious fervor and sought to save Mexico by making her again a truly Catholic state. Yet the Sinarquistas refused to carry arms and exalted martyrdom and passive resistance. Rural priests helped the movement with advice, but the church hierarchy dissociated itself from it.[101]

Faced with the threats of communism and fascism as well as pressing economic problems, President Lázaro Cárdenas from about 1936 on began to pursue a more conciliatory policy toward the church. The duty of his administration, Cárdenas declared in March 1936, was to foster the social and economic program of the Revolution and not to promote anti-religious campaigns. The state governments fell into line by gradually modifying their restrictive legislation. Church-state relations were improved further when on February 20, 1937, Luis María Martínez succeeded the deceased Díaz as archbishop of Mexico. Martínez was a realist with a gift for diplomacy who for years had headed the liberal faction of the church. He became known as the "peacemaking archbishop." [102]

One month after the appointment of the moderate Martínez, Pope Pius XI on March 28, 1937, issued an encyclical concerning Mexico. The encyclical *Nos es muy*, unlike previous statements from Rome, contained no harsh words for the Revolution and urged the church, primarily through "Catholic Action," "to help and protect the classes of the humble and needy, the workers, agricultural labourers and emigrants"—thus disproving the charge of reaction.[103] Pius XI once again affirmed the legitimacy of armed self-defense though he condemned "violence against the properly constituted civil power." [104] Since the Mexican hierarchy had by now fully accepted the legitimacy of the Mexican revolutionary regime the pope's remarks about just and unjust rebellions may have been meant more for the Spanish church, divided in its reaction to Franco's revolt, than for the finally tranquil Mexico.

Between 1938 and 1940 Mexico slowly returned to the

religious practices of the past. A further milestone was reached when Cárdenas' successor, President Ávila Camacho, declared publicly in 1940: "I am a believer." New church construction was authorized, and in 1946 article 3 of the constitution was amended to remove the controversial endorsement of "socialistic education." The other legal provisions governing the church remain essentially unaltered to this day, but they are not enforced. The resurgence of the church has been striking. Catholic schools are flourishing. Whereas in 1934 fewer than 500 priests were exercising their ministry, by 1940 the number was 3863; by 1967 there were 7922 priests though the rapid growth of Mexico's population has minimized the impact of these gains.[105] Anticlericalism has not disappeared, but both parties seem to have learned the lessons of the 1920's and 1930's. The remarks of a historian of the 1960's remain pertinent. The truce between church and state could be broken, Robert E. Quirk wrote in 1964, if priests and prelates should actively oppose the government, but this was not likely. "There is no real reason in the 1960's why the situation should worsen—or improve. And, after all, in this imperfect world, perhaps the best solution to all human conflicts is a *modus vivendi*."[106]

CHAPTER 17

The Spanish Civil War

On July 17, 1936 a group of high-ranking Spanish officers in Morocco rose up against the Spanish Republic. Following a plan worked out several months earlier, garrisons in Navarre, Aragon, Old Castile, and southern Andalusia quickly gained control of these areas. After four days the insurgents had captured about one-third of Spain, but the major cities remained in the hands of the Madrid government. Instead of an easy and swift victory the rebelling generals faced the prospect of a civil war the outcome of which could not readily be predicted.

The position in the Civil War taken by the Catholic church was dictated, at least in part, by the revolutionary violence that swept Republican Spain immediately after the rising of the generals. The enormous tension that had been building up since the victory of the Popular Front in the elections of February 1936 now spent itself in a wave of assassinations and destruction, and the church was one of the main targets. Churches and monasteries were burned and despoiled; during the first three months of the war between 5000 and 6000 priests, monks, and nuns were murdered by gangs of released political prisoners, anarchists, or common criminals.[1] Faced with this persecution in the Republican zone on the one hand, and the benevolence shown the church by the insurgents on the other, it is a small wonder that most of the clergy sided with the generals.

And yet, the church's attitude toward the rebellion also had deeper roots. Both the violence directed against the church as well as her cooperation with the military uprising formed but a chapter in a long history of anticlericalism and estrangement

from most Spaniards. It is with a consideration of these historical
factors consequently that any attempt to understand the actions
of the Spanish church in the Civil War must begin. Also, it is this
alienation of the church from the large majority of the Spanish
people that makes it legitimate when referring to the church in
this essay to mean primarily the clergy.

A HERITAGE OF ANTICLERICALISM

When in the summer of 1936 churches and monasteries went up
in flames, and priests and religious were killed, many saw in these
brutal acts the hand of Moscow. But such an interpretation revealed an ignorance of Spanish history, for Spain had witnessed
many such outbursts over the preceding one hundred years. The
church had incurred the enmity of the liberals by her staunch
opposition to the influx of modern ideas; as late as 1827 a deist
schoolmaster was tried for heresy by the archbishop of Valencia
and sentenced to be burned alive (a sentence that was changed at
the last moment to hanging).[2] The lower classes had come to resent the richness and pomp of the life of the clergy which contrasted so sharply with the harsh lives they themselves were
forced to lead. The clergy, in their eyes, served the rich. "A people, hard and terrible, more than other naturally akin to violence
and death, which they neither fear nor respect," Jacques Maritain
observed, "had thus the feeling of having been abandoned to their
terrestrial damnation, and at some times a bitter hatred, at others
a mortal indifference, awoke in them in regard to the representatives of a truth from which they ought to have been willing to
expect everything and where they saw nothing but imposture."[3]
Every time, therefore, that the guns guarding both monarchy and
church were removed, there followed an outbreak of violence
with mobs burning convents and massacring priests and nuns.
This is what happened in 1808, forty years before the publication
of the *Communist Manifesto*, and at intervals thereafter.

By 1870 the great majority of the working people of Spain had
become estranged from their traditional faith. Even though they
were nominally Catholics they had come to regard the church as
a self-seeking institution which ignored their interests and grievances and made common cause with their exploiters and oppres-

sors. At the turn of the century, it has been estimated, the number of practicing Catholics in the rural areas numbered less than 10 per cent; Marxism and anarcho-syndicalism were making steady headway among the urban workers in the large industrial centers and the rural workers of Andalusia and the Levant coast. The church, instead of trying to arrest the dechristianization of the working classes by persuasion and the espousal of social reform, relied upon the support of the privileged and most reactionary groups of society and tried to secure governments that would suppress her enemies by force. The inevitable result was that the church drew upon herself the hostility of every progressive force in the country. "Always on the side of the powerful, the rich, the oppressive authority," writes Salvador de Madariaga, "the priest had to become the object of general aversion."[4] Hence in April 1931, when the last of the Bourbon kings fled into exile and Spain was proclaimed a republic, both the socialists and the liberals, who had plotted the overthrow of the monarchy, were vigorously, if not fanatically, anticlerical, and the religious issue assumed an urgency quite out of proportion to its real importance.

The fact that the church had been a strong supporter of the bankrupt monarchy strengthened anti-church feelings. In the municipal elections of April 12, 1931, just before the abdication of Alfonso XIII, most members of the episcopate had opposed the republican reform movement; Bishop Mateo Múgica had stated in a pastoral letter that a vote for the republicans was a mortal sin.[5] This lack of political acumen was compounded by the action of Pedro Cardinal Segura, archbishop of Toledo and primate of Spain, who in a pastoral letter published on May 7 eulogized the king, expressed regret over the passing of the monarchy, and asked all Catholics to close ranks against the forces of anarchy menacing Spain and the church. The letter ended with these threatening words:

If we remain "quiet and idle," if we allow ourselves to give way to "apathy and timidity," if we leave open the way to those who are attempting to destroy religion or if we expect the benevolence of our enemies to secure the triumph of our ideals, we shall have no right to lament when bitter reality shows us that we had victory in our hands, yet knew not how to fight like intrepid warriors prepared to succumb gloriously.[6]

This attack upon the young Republic, "the first shot in the
contest which was to continue until the Civil War," [7] was followed a few days later by new anticlerical violence. Some two
dozen churches and convents in Madrid and in a number of
southern cities were attacked and burned; in the capital the security forces, firemen, and crowds watched passively without any
attempt to stop the arsonists. "Clearly," a recent historian notes,
"in the Spanish urban public there was a large measure of tolerance, more, of secret pleasure, in seeing the Church attacked." [8]
The embarrassed government blamed Cardinal Segura for provoking the violence and asked him to leave the country. After
the recalcitrant churchman had secretly returned to Spain and
been expelled once more, the Vatican was formally asked to remove Segura from the archbishopric of Toledo. Rome, not unhappy to have the inflexible primate out of the way, pressed Segura to resign. [9] He was succeeded in April 1932 by the scholarly
and less temperamental Isidro Gomá y Tomás, bishop of Tara-
zona.

The new republican government, composed for the most part
of men who regarded anticlericalism as the "ideological keystone
of politics," [10] meanwhile began to revamp relations between
church and state. A decree of May 22 proclaimed religious freedom. The bishops promptly protested this measure as a violation
of the Concordat of 1851, which had recognized Roman Catholicism as the state religion, but article 3 of the draft constitution affirmed the separation of church and state. Still more far-reaching
in its implications was article 26 provoking a spirited debate in
the Constituent Cortes which was hammering out the new constitution. The controversial article, as finally approved, abolished
clerical salaries within two years, required the religious orders to
register their property, and barred them from engaging in commerce and non-confessional teaching. Further laic legislation was
passed over the following three years. Spain received its first divorce law, cemeteries were secularized, the Society of Jesus was
dissolved and its property confiscated, secondary and primary
schools run by the religious orders were ordered closed. Not all
of these measures could be effectively implemented and enforced,
but they nevertheless gave rise to tension, alienated many middle-
class Catholics, and deprived the fragile Republic of much needed
support.

Despite the harassment of the church the bishops in their pronouncements exhorted the faithful to obey the constituted authorities. A collective declaration dated December 20, 1931,
insisted that "it is not by seditions and violent actions that Christians conquer the evils which afflict them." [11] Cardinal Gomá's
first pastoral letter, published in July 1933, again counseled submission to the civil power. But these statements did not mean that
the church had accepted the Republic for reasons other than ex-
pedience. For a majority of the bishops, a recent historian concludes, "Catholicism in Spain was . . . consubstantial with the
Monarchy. A republic was by definition the child of the impious
French Revolution, surreptitiously imposed upon Catholic Spain
by the Masons." [12] A popular exposition of the catechism called
the liberal principles of freedom of conscience, freedom of worship, and freedom of the press "false and pernicious forms of
freedom" [13]; another catechism pointed out that these "anti-
Christian" principles may be tolerated only "for as long and in so
far as they cannot be opposed without creating a worse evil." [14]

The same attitude of reserve toward the Republic was held by
José Maria Gil Robles, the leader of the Spanish Confederation of
Autonomous Rightists (CEDA). This political coalition had been
formed in the spring of 1933 with the avowed purpose of defending Catholic interests, and, benefiting from mass abstention of the
Anarchists and the electoral law, it emerged from the elections of
November 1933, the strongest single party in the Cortes. Gil Robles was no fascist, and he was out of sympathy with the newly
founded Falange Española, but neither was he prepared to do
more than insist on his respect for constituted authority. Motivated in part by the wish not to antagonize his monarchist backers, Gil Robles refused to affirm his loyalty to the Republic. At a
moment in history when the Catholic Center party in Germany
had just voted dictatorial powers to Hitler, and the Catholic
prime minister of Austria, Engelbert Dollfuss, had drowned the
socialist protest against the suspension of Parliament in blood, the
cautious maneuvering of the leader of the Catholic party of Spain
seemed to confirm the accusation of the liberals and the Left that
the CEDA had subversive designs against the Republic.[15] The
widespread fear that participation of the CEDA in the government was tantamount to fascism led to the abortive uprising of
October 1934 in Catalonia and Asturia. If Spanish Catholics had

accepted the Republic without mental reservations, Luigi Sturzo ventured to speculate in 1937, the "revolts of 1934 and 1936 and the consequent civil war might have been avoided." [16]

Spanish political life was rapidly becoming polarized. The bloody repression of the revolt of the Asturian miners, the appeasement of the church carried out by the government of Alejandro Lerroux, and the failure to undertake an effective agrarian reform program pushed the Socialists and Anarchists into an increasingly hostile posture toward the Republic.[17] The Monarchists and Fascists, in turn, criticized the center-right government as too weak and called for still more rigorous measures against the Left. When the elections held in February 1936 resulted in the victory of the Popular Front, a coalition of the Republican Left, Socialists, and Communists, the rightists panicked and began to plan an armed uprising. The claims of later writers, defending the military rebellion, that the elections of 1936 had actually given a popular majority to the Right and that the government formed therefore was illegitimate have no basis in fact. At the time all parties, the provincial governors, and the military praised the orderly character of the elections and acknowledged the victory of the Left.[18] It should be noted that the government of 1936 contained neither Socialists nor Communists until several months after the military revolt had broken out. Equally untenable is another attempt to find a justification for the uprising of the generals, the story of a Communist plot to set up a Soviet regime in the summer of 1936. The evidence for this allegation does not stand up under examination, and a consideration of Russian policy at the time also reveals the implausibility of such a plan.[19]

It is true, nevertheless, that Spain, on the eve of the Civil War, was in the grip of a severe social and political crisis. Armed bands of the Right and Left roamed the streets and fought each other; accounts were settled by way of assassination. In the rural areas peasants seized land and clashed with the police. The left wing of the Socialists, led by Largo Caballero, called for a proletarian revolution; the Fascists, too, proclaimed their faith in force. The government of Left Republicans valiantly tried to maintain order, but, under attack from both Left and Right, it had limited success. There were those who exaggerated the disorders to further their own designs, the American ambassador in Spain recalled later.[20] On June 16 Gil Robles charged in the Cortes that since

February 170 churches had been destroyed by fire, a figure that cannot be accepted. Yet, the fact of the matter was that the disorders were real enough, and they lent credence to those who argued that the country was rapidly approaching a state of anarchy from which only the military could rescue it.

Both the church and the government were intent upon preventing violent anticlerical outbursts. Many churches were guarded by police, and the hierarchy refrained from issuing political statements that could inflame the passions of the church's enemies. But the crucial decisions were being made elsewhere. Monarchists and other right-wing officers were well along in their plans for a military uprising, a rebellion which was to bring in its wake a prolonged and bloody civil war and cost Spain as well as the church many thousands of lives.

THE CRUSADE

Given the conservative, if not reactionary, political predilections of the Spanish church in 1936, her adherence to the military revolt was hardly surprising; it had been counted upon by the plotters. The situation in the Basque country, the one exception, will be discussed later. What sealed the alliance between the generals (the Nationalists, as they became known) and the church was the burning of the churches and the massacre of priests and religious in Republican-controlled territory.

Except in the Carlist country, a stronghold of monarchist sentiment and religious fanaticism with a long tradition of clerical participation in wars against liberals and atheists, neither the church, nor, with few exceptions, the clergy had been involved in plans for the uprising. Yet on July 18 when rumors swept Spain that priests were firing at the people from church towers they were widely believed, and these rumors provided the spark for one of the most violent outbursts of anticlericalism Spain had ever witnessed. All over the country, wherever the insurgents were defeated, hundreds of churches, chapels, monasteries, and convents were burned or desecrated. Those not completely gutted were turned into markets, schools, or hospitals. Gangs of self-styled revolutionaries went from place to place and killed all the priests they could find. It is estimated that in the first three months of the war some 5000 to 6000 members of the secular and regular clergy were murdered, sometimes under circumstances of extreme cruelty.[21]

In a number of cases, with or without the connivance of the clergy, arms had been stored in monasteries and churches; [22] other churches, like the Carmelite church in Barcelona, were used by rebel soldiers as fortresses. But by and large, the violence against the church was unprovoked by any immediate action of the clergy and derived from the same resentments that had led to anticlerical outbursts in 1835, 1868, 1873, 1909, and 1931. "The Spanish working class attacked churchmen," writes a British historian, "because they thought them hypocrites and because they seemed to give a false spiritual front to middle-class or upper-class tyranny." [23] Much of the violence was carried out by Anarchists, at times joined by young hoodlums. The other parties, especially the Communists, and the government were outspoken in their condemnation of these acts, but in the first weeks of the war they were unable to control lawless elements. Several thousand clergy, nevertheless, through the help of government officials, were able to leave the country. Frequently, churches were ordered closed as the only way of protecting them from a worse fate, and they remained closed for the same reason. That the violence against the church was caused primarily by anticlericalism rather than hatred of religion as such can be seen from the fact that Protestant chapels in Madrid, Valencia, and other cities were not touched. A mob that had set fire to a Protestant church in Barcelona helped put out the fire as soon as they realized their mistake.[24]

The members of the church hierarchy reacted to this persecution by throwing themselves even more wholeheartedly into the arms of the rebels. "They believed," the president of the Basque Republic recalled in his memoirs, "that the insurrection would triumph in fifteen days and never imagined that it would result in such a terrible and bloody war. The Basque Bishop Múgica confessed as much to me and confided that that had also been the opinion of the Primate of the Spanish Church [Cardinal Gomá]." [25] Gomá had left Toledo a few days before the outbreak of the insurrection and gone to Navarre, ostensibly for his health. He made his first public pronouncement of the war in a radio address from Pamplona on September 28, 1936, in which he celebrated the relief of the Alcázar, a stone fortress overlooking

Toledo in which some 1000 rebel soldiers had withstood a ten-week siege. The day has come, Gomá declared, "on which Jews and Masons . . . threaten the national soul with absurd doctrines, with Tartar and Mongol ideas" and with a political and social system "manipulated by the Semitic International." [26]

Cardinal Gomá issued his first pastoral letter entitled "The Case of Spain" on December 8, 1936. The present conflict, the primate of Spain explained, appeared to be merely a civil war, but "in substance we must recognize in it the spirit of a veritable crusade on behalf of the Catholic religion." The war would have been lost by the insurgents without "the divine encouragement which excites the soul of a Christian people." [27] Other members of the hierarchy sounded a similar note. Enrique Plá y Deniel, bishop of Salamanca, in a pastoral letter of September 30, 1936 entitled "The Two Cities," called the rebellion "a crusade for religion, the fatherland, and civilization." The generals had risen to defend the country against communism and barbarism; such a rebellion aiming at the defense of the common good was permissible according to the teachings of St. Thomas Aquinas, St. Bellarmine, and Suarez. When tyranny had become firmly entrenched, and no superior authority could be called upon for help, the recourse to arms was inescapable and legitimate.[28]

The Madrid government was reorganized on July 19, but, like that government formed in February 1936, it included neither Socialists nor Communists. After a reshuffling in early September the cabinet consisted of six Socialists, four Republicans, two Communists, and one representative each of the Catalan Republicans and the Basque Nationalists. Communist influence was substantial, especially after the arrival of Russian help, but it was exerted in the direction of ending "the Libertarian and Socialist revolutions started by the Anarchists and Socialists." [29] In this endeavor they were largely successful, and the excesses of the first three months were being brought under control. Still, the church persisted in regarding the civil war as a conflict between the forces of good and evil, between civilization and communist barbarism. The lower clergy in Nationalist territory, in particular, were instrumental in sowing hatred against the Republican side. "It is a regrettable fact," Monsignor Arthur H. Ryan, a defender of Franco, wrote in 1948, "that during the heat of the struggle, some Catholics, both inside and outside Spain, showed little Christian spirit in calling down fire and brimstone on the Reds. . . . No Christian should ever allow himself to speak of the enemies of the Church, however inveterate and ferocious, as if they were vermin to be exterminated." [30] Unfortunately many in the Nationalist clergy, determined to avenge their brethren on the other side, encouraged just such a war of extermination and warned against conciliation and the giving of quarter.[31]

There were instances of churchmen condemning the many thousands of summary executions carried out by the Nationalists, but the effect of preaching a crusade and holy war could only be to further inflame the fratricidal passion. Whereas in the Republican zone the unauthorized terrorism carried out by Anarchists and others had come under some control by the end of the year 1936, in Nationalist territory the physical liquidation of the enemy continued throughout the war. The reign of terror, the French Catholic writer Georges Bernanos concluded in 1938, after watching the Nationalists on Majorca, "would long since have burnt itself out, were it not that the more or less open, more or less conscious endorsement of priests and churchgoers had finally succeeded in endowing it with a religious aspect." [32]

In the early days of the war captured Communists and Anarchists were shot immediately; in many places anyone in overalls or with a black and blue mark on his shoulder (from a rifle butt) was shot without trial. Moors brought to Spain from North Africa, in particular, distinguished themselves by their savagery, often castrating the corpses of their victims in accordance with an old Moorish battle-rite. Towns taken over by the Nationalists would see mass arrests of anyone suspected of sympathy with the Republicans and the nightly shooting of prisoners who would often be left on the highways to intimidate the rest of the population. The clergy served as confessors for the prisoners and condemned. "Occasional parish priests," writes Gabriel Jackson, "pleaded for the lives of particular individuals under sentence of death, but none questioned the principle and the general extent of the purge itself." [33] Georges Bernanos was especially upset over the fact that the mass killings of innocents on Majorca were publicly approved by the great majority of secular priests, monks, and nuns.[34] Cardinal Gomá, recalls the president of the Basque Republic, was horrorstricken at the number of murders committed by the Carlists as well as by the passion and fury displayed

by them, and he decided to intervene with the Nationalist authorities.[35] This intervention does not seem to have been successful; publicly the hierarchy continued to bless the crusade.

As the insurgents gradually conquered more and more territory, the mass executions repeated themselves with deadening
regularity; this, in part, accounts for the far larger number killed
in Nationalist territory than in the Republican zone.[36] The viru-
lence of the purge carried out by the Nationalists can only be explained by the religious fervor and zeal with which the insurgents defended the traditional privileges of the army, the church,
and the propertied classes. The majority of these men were not
bloodthirsty killers but believed ". . . from the depths of their
being that they had a duty to extirpate the unclean heresies of
liberalism, socialism, communism, and anarchism. For they believed, before God, that these ideas were destroying their own
beautiful and timeless Spain." [37] The church's preaching of a crusade reinforced this sense of mission and the resulting fanaticism,
violence, and cruelty.

Outside Spain itself, meanwhile, the claim that Franco and his
Moorish, Nazi, and Fascist allies were soldiers of Christ waging a
holy war was drawing the criticism of some prominent Catholics.
Early in 1937 a "French Committee for Civil and Religious Peace
in Spain" was organized by François Mauriac, Georges Bernanos,
Yves Simon, and other leading Catholic figures in France. Similar
committees came into being in England and Switzerland; a Spanish committee was headed by the well-known liberal Catholic professors Madariaga and Mendizabal. These organizations sought to
promote a peace by mediation and conciliation. Jacques Maritain,
the president of the French committee, vigorously rejected the
tendency of most Catholics to put all the blame upon the Reds
and insisted that Christians were honor-bound to protest crimes
from whichever side they were committed.

It is horrible sacrilege to massacre priests—be they "Fascists,"
they are still ministers of Christ—out of hatred of religion; and it
is another sacrilege, horrible also, to massacre people—be they
"Marxists," they are still the people of Christ—in the name of religion. It is obvious sacrilege to burn churches and holy pictures,
sometimes in blind fury, sometimes, as in Barcelona, by cold anarchist methods and in a systematic fury. It is still another sacrilege
—religious in form—to deck Mohammedan soldiers with pic-

tures of the Sacred Heart so that they may kill the children of Christians in a holy fashion, and to claim to enlist God in the passions of a conflict where the adversary is looked upon as unworthy of respect and pity.[38]

Wars in today's profane civilization, Maritain argued, could be just but no longer holy. Religious motives were not sufficient to transform the struggle waged by the Nationalists into a war consecrated by God. The liberal Italian Catholic, Luigi Sturzo, similarly opposed the thesis pronounced by the Spanish church that on the one side there was nothing but good (Catholicism and patriotism) and on the other nothing but evil (Communism). "For us it is absurd," Sturzo said, "to call the war of the Spanish generals a war of ideals, a crusade, a holy war." [39]

The destruction of the Basque town of Guernica by German planes in April 1937 increased the unfavorable publicity that the Nationalists were receiving abroad and strenthened the position of those whom the right-wing French Catholic press called the "Red Christians." In May 1937, it appears, Franco thereupon proposed to Cardinal Gomá that the Spanish bishops issue a joint pastoral letter in which they would authoritatively restate and explain their espousal of the Nationalist cause.[40] The result was the "Joint Letter of the Spanish Bishops to the Bishops of the Whole World," published on July 1, 1937. The pastoral was drafted by Gomá and signed by all members of the hierarchy except the archbishop of Tarragona and the bishop of Vitoria, both of whom had reservations about the church's close involvement with Franco.

The truth of what was happening in Spain, the pastoral letter declared, had been obscured and distorted by forces "shielding themselves behind the name of Catholics." This fact had impelled the Spanish episcopate to address itself to its brethren in the world so that the truth might shine forth. At stake was nothing less than "the actual providential foundations of social life, religion, justice, authority, and the liberty of the citizens." [41]

The church, the bishops explained, had not wished for or provoked this war. "Since its beginning we have had our hands raised to heaven that it might cease." Efforts had been made to lessen its ravages, and charity and love had been expressed for the church's persecutors. "It is true that thousands of her sons, obeying the promptings of their conscience and of their patriotism, and under their own responsibility, revolted in arms in order to safeguard the principles of religion and Christian justice which have for ages formed the nation's life." In the face of a grave threat to the maintenance of the Catholic religion in Spain the bishops had not been able to "remain silent without abandoning the interests of our Lord Jesus Christ." Still, the church had not tied herself to anybody—"persons, powers, or institutions"— though "we are ready to collaborate, as Bishops and as Spaniards, with those who are making efforts to restore in Spain a regime of peace and justice." [42]

The Civil War had been "occasioned by the rashness, the mistakes, perhaps the malice and the cowardice of those who could have avoided it by governing the nation with justice." The constitution (of 1931) and secularist laws had abolished the rights of God. The elections of 1936 had resulted in an illegitimate parliament for "the votes of whole provinces had been cancelled at will." Spain had been drifting into anarchy with a revolution being prepared by Russia and the Spanish Communists. At that moment, when the actual existence of the common good was gravely compromised, the better elements of the nation had taken recourse to "the rights of defensive resistance by force," recognized by St. Thomas Aquinas. The severe threat to religion, justice, and peace and the leadership of "the entirety of the social authorities and of prudent men" satisfied two conditions for the exercise of this right. Concerning the probability of success, the third condition required by St. Thomas, "we leave it to the judgment of history; the facts up to the present are not contrary to it." [43]

It was not true, the bishops insisted, that without the outbreak of the rebellion the lives of many of the clery would have been saved. On the contrary, it was proved "by actual documents" that the Marxist revolution that was nipped in the bud by the civil-military movement had prepared for the extermination of all of the clergy. All legal means having been exhausted, the national conscience had had no choice but resort to force in order to escape "the definite assault of destructive communism." The present war was "like an armed plebiscite" with the people voting for order, peace, and religion or materialism and "the ultra-new 'civilization' of the Russian Soviets." [44]

The church, the pastoral letter continued, "has not been able to identify herself with conduct, tendencies, or intentions which at the present time or in the future might be able to distort the character of the Nationalist Movement, its origins, manifestations, and ends." The bishops hoped that the leaders of the government in Nationalist Spain would not build up an autocratic state, derived from foreign models. "We would be the first to regret that the irresponsible autocracy of a parliament should be replaced by the yet more terrible one of a dictatorship without roots in the nation." Still, given the savagery of "the Spanish Communist Revolution"—the letter here described the plundering of churches, the murder of priests, the acts of torture—there was no hope for justice and peace without the victory of the Nationalist movement. "Every war has its excesses, the Nationalist Movement doubtless may have had them also." But there existed an enormous difference between the conduct of the two sides. The pastoral ended by calling on the bishops of the world to disseminate the truth: "Help us to make known the contents of this letter, watching over the Catholic press and propaganda, rectifying the mistakes of that which is indifferent or adverse." [45]

The joint pastoral letter of the Spanish hierarchy, addressed to a world-wide audience, was as significant for what it included as for what it failed to say. In an obvious attempt to meet foreign criticism of the church's close identification with Franco's cause, the bishops warned against dictatorial tendencies. Having been accused of inflaming the passions of war and being indifferent to the massacres carried out by the Nationalist troops, the episcopate protested its commitment to charity and love of the enemy and took note of excesses in the Nationalist camp. The pastoral letter did not characterize the conflict as a crusade and holy war. But this attempt at impartiality and a more sober approach to the conflict was weakened by the uncritical acceptance of the Nationalist propaganda on a number of important points. The pastoral letter supported the allegation of the illegitimate character of the Republican government of 1936, and it repeated the story of an imminent Communist plot forestalled by the military rebellion. The bishops vigorously condemned the Red atrocities, in large measure carried out by mobs and gangs taking advantage of the temporary breakdown of order, but considered the atrocities of the Nationalists, ordered and approved by the military authorities, unavoidable excesses of war.

Whereas this pastoral letter directed to the outside world was basically subdued in tone, the church's pronouncements inside Spain continued at the same pitch of high emotion. Sermons were still full of vituperation against the godless enemy; a typical one is reported by a former high official in the Nationalist administration to have been preached at Badajoz on August 14, 1937, at a solemn mass commemorating the liberation of the town.

> All, as one, must exterminate the enemies of God, who are the enemies of the fatherland. It is a year ago today that our troops entered in triumph to free us of Marxism. The blood generously shed by our heroes and our dead demand it of us.[46]

In some parishes, writes Jackson, "lifelong Catholics ceased going to mass because they could not stand the weekly fulminations from the pulpit against the 'reds.' "[47]

Pastoral letters of bishops and books and pamphlets published in the Nationalist zone by other clerics continued to refer to the war as a crusade and argued that the uprising had been not only justified but was a positive duty. In 1938 Aniceto de Castro Albarrán, a canon of Salamanca, published a book with the title *Holy War*, which carried a foreword by Cardinal Gomá, dated December 12, 1937, praising the work. The present conflict, the churchman insisted again, was not a civil war, but a religious war, a holy war, a crusade blessed by God and his church.[48] The Nationalist-Fascist movement represented the reassertion of "the principle of authority against republican anarchy, of the hierarchical and efficient state against the bankruptcy and sterility of the democracies," but above all it was a movement of national reconstruction and religion, inspired by the "eternal principles of morality and justice."[49] The Republican government was illegitimate: the abdication of King Alfonso had been the result of coercion, the elections of 1931 and 1936 had been fraudulent. The Madrid government represented a regime of oppression and extermination and "against this tyranny and these tyrants Spain had not only the right but the duty to rise up in arms."[50] Such a tyrannical government lost its legitimacy and, according to Catholic doctrine, could be resisted. The papacy had blessed the defenders of the church; the Spanish war was therefore "officially a crusade, a holy war."[51]

Similar ideas were propounded by other clerics. The Jesuit

Juan de Rey Carrera called Franco "the builder of the New Spain, the Elected of God to lead our people in the attainment of that glorious destiny which providence has reserved for it." [52] The theological journals ran articles to prove the permissibility of resistance to tyrannical authority and the compatibility of war with Christian charity.[53] Since 1939 books have continued to appear which refer to the civil war as a crusade. The national conscience, wrote Canon Castro Albarrán in 1941, was enlightened by the immortal doctrines of the church, the nation had fought a crusade against tyranny, and God had blessed "its heroism and sacrifice with victory." [54]

The doctrinal legitimation of the conflict provided by the church made the church an important bulwark of Nationalist Spain, bolstering the morale of its fighting men. The generals, many of whom had not been very pious before, fully understood the importance of the religious factor. In October 1936, Franco called the uprising "a war in defense of Christian civilization. . . . We are defenders of faith and spirituality against Red materialism." [55] Attendance at religious services at the front was obligatory, religious instruction in both primary and secondary schools was required, and images of the Virgin and crucifixes were put into the classrooms. In 1938 the Society of Jesus was re-established in Spain, and diplomatic relations with the Vatican were renewed. Nationalist soldiers, including the Moors, wore upon their chests religious medals, sacred hearts, scapulars, and crucifixes. It is "a topsy-turvy world," wrote an Irish war correspondent, "where a Mohammedan kills a Christian because the Christian does not exhibit the sign of the cross." [56] Even the Falangists, in earlier years not noted for their piety, began to show religious fervor, attended mass, confessed, and took communion. "Propagandists represented the ideal Falangist as half Monk and half warrior. The ideal female Falangist was described as a combination of Saint Teresa and Isabella the Catholic." [57]

The church, nevertheless, distrusted the Falange's newly discovered zeal for religion and resented the latter's demand for the separation of church and state. In a pastoral letter entitled "What We Owe the Pope" of January 28, 1938, Cardinal Gomá protested against the Falangists' campaign on the theme "Catholics, yes! Vaticanists, no!" [58] Cardinal Segura, back in Spain as archbishop of Seville, late in 1938 denounced the irreligiousness of the

Falangists and the growing influence of the anti-Catholic Nazis in Spain.[59] Reacting to a book that called for the resurrection of Spain's greatness without the Catholic church, on February 5, 1939, Gomá issued a pastoral letter under the title "Catholicism and Country." He warned against exaggerated reactions to liberalism and democracy, which led to an absorption of all social activity by the state, and against endeavors to ignore the country's Catholicism: "Even though our war, in some of its aspects, has all the characteristics of a Crusade, at least as much as some religious wars of history . . . an attempt is made to separate the fact of the war and its consequences from the nation's Catholicism." [60]

But the fears of the hierarchy proved groundless. The tendency toward a pagan nationalism was checked; in November 1939, following Franco's victory, the financial support of the church was restored amid recognition of her important role in the Civil War: "The Spanish state, aware that its unity and greatness proceed from the Catholic faith . . . proposes by this law to render the tribute due to our self-sacrificing Spanish clergy, most efficient collaborators in our victorious Crusade." [61]

Friction between church and state has developed from time to time since 1939, and today there are indications that the forces of *aggiornamento* are not bypassing the church in Spain. In early 1965 the British historian Hugh Thomas published an article with the challenging title "The Spanish Church as a Power for Progress," [62] describing a development few would have predicted even ten years earlier. In September 1971 an assembly of bishops and priests, presided over by the cardinal primate of Spain, Enrique Tarancon, archbishop of Toledo, adopted a resolution that decried "the insufficient scope given human rights and the persistence of grave economic and social inequalities" among Spanish Christians. Another even more significant resolution apologized for the role of the church in the Civil War: "We humbly recognize, and ask pardon for it, that we failed at the proper time to be ministers of reconciliation in the midst of our people, divided by a war between brothers." [63] Still, as Hugh Thomas has noted, "the spectre of 13 bishops, 4000 priests, 2360 monks, 280 nuns, believed now to have been murdered in the civil war, contemporaries of many who still live, exerts a powerful force for restraint." [64]

THE BASQUES

Whereas most of the Spanish clergy, as we have seen, aligned themselves with Franco's rebellion from the very beginning, the Basque Catholics, including their priests, refused to follow the leadership of the hierarchy and preferred to fight on the side of the "Reds" against the "soldiers of Christ." This split in the ranks of the church put a severe strain upon the image of unity which the hierarchy attempted to project to the outside world. The fact that a people almost 100 per cent Catholic decided to oppose the alleged savior of Christianity cast doubt upon the idea of a holy war. The defection of the Basques also helps explain the temporizing and restrained attitude assumed by the Holy See toward the Civl War, a subject to which we will return.

The Basque provinces of Guipúzcoa and Vizcaya have always been considered the most European as well as the most Catholic areas of Spain. Their industry and commerce had early given them strong links with Western Europe; with nearly half the peasants owning their houses and farmlands, the Basques had no agrarian problem, and illiteracy was scarcely known. Their Catholicism, too, was modern. The clergy had always lived close to the people; priests had organized Catholic trade unions; anticlericalism was practically non-existent.

The Basques took pride in a long tradition of self-government which they had enjoyed until the Spanish monarchy abolished it in 1839. The restoration of home rule became one of the major demands of the Basque Nationalist party which appeared after 1900. The Basque Nationalists resented being governed by Castilian soldiers and landowners, whom they considered backward. Intensely religious, they also "wished to remove their country from the corrosive influence of Spanish anticlericalism and to govern it in accordance with the encyclicals of Leo XIII." [65] During the last years of the monarchy advocates of the Basque nationality were persecuted and the use of Euzkadi, the native language of the Basques with pre-Indo-European roots, was forbidden. But the Republic also failed at first to fulfill their expectations. The anticlerical Left looked upon them with suspicion because of their Catholicism; the Right resented their separatism and progressive social and political orientation. In the elections of February 1936, the Basque Nationalists ran an independent slate, but they looked with hope toward the Popular Front which promised them the long-sought autonomy statute. Following the victory of the Popular Front the Republican government indeed restored the Basque municipal governments, suspended in 1934, to their functions, and the final text of a Basque statute was ready for adoption when the military rebellion broke out.

The Basques rallied to the side of the Republic from the first day of the insurrection. The question whether they would have done so even if the Popular Front had not promised them the restoration of home rule will never be answered with finality. However, the charge later made by the insurgents and the hierarchy that the Basques had sold themselves to the Republicans in return for the granting of autonomy oversimplifies a complicated situation. It ignores the democratic leanings of the Basques and their resentment of domination by Castilian reactionaries, factors influencing their decision to remain loyal to the Madrid government.

Unlike the rest of Republican Spain, the two Basque provinces experienced neither a social revolution nor anticlerical violence. With the exception of two churches burnt by Anarchists in San Sebastian in the very first days of the uprising, churches were not destroyed, priests were not abused, and religious services were allowed to continue freely. The two Basque bishops, Mateo Múgica of Vitoria and Marcelino Olaechea of Pamplona, were caught by the insurrection in Carlist-dominated territory, and it was there that Cardinal Gomá contacted them and urged them to issue a pastoral letter condemning the Basque Nationalists' cooperation with the Republicans. A draft composed by Gomá drew reservations from both bishops, but before the latter could make changes, the pastoral, as drafted by the primate, was read over the Vitoria radio on August 6. "It is not permissible," the pastoral letter purporting to come from the two Basque bishops declared, "in any way or on any grounds and still less through the cruel means of war . . . to divide the Catholic forces in front of a common enemy." It is still less permissible to enter into a union with the enemy, and this "forbidden union becomes monstrous when the enemy is this modern monster of Marxism and Communism, the seven-headed hydra, the synthesis of all heresies, diametrically opposed to Christianity in religious, political, social, and economic doctrine." [66] Some days later the pastoral was printed in the diocesan gazette of Vitoria.

The Basque leaders in Bilbao challenged the authenticity and obligatory character of the pastoral letter. Information on how the letter had come into being had filtered through; a hastily convened commission of theologians agreed that no proof of the authentic nature of the letter, of which no copy had been received, was available, that it was based on faulty premises since no pact with the Communists had in fact been entered, and that it imposed no canonical obligation since it had been written in enemy territory. Moreover, any change in the position chosen by the Basque Nationalists, the commission suggested, would bring untold misery upon the church.[67]

The Basques adhered to their stand even after Bishop Múgica, speaking over the radio and in a letter of September 8, had objected to the commission's conclusions and accused them of defying their pastor.[68] Despite these statements the Burgos government considered him unreliable and wanted to expel him. Appearances were preserved when Cardinal Gomá announced the departure of Múgica for Rome in connection with a missionary congress. In exile Múgica explained that he had urged support of Franco in the belief that the military would triumph easily and that it would prevent bloodshed. He again denied that his signature to the pastoral letter of August 1936 had been coerced.[69] The Basques in exile to this day maintain that the sympathies of Múgica after the first few weeks of the war had actually been with them.

On September 4, 1936, José Antonio Aguirre, the leader of the Basque Nationalist party, joined the first Caballero government. On October 1, the rump Cortes in Madrid finally approved the long-pending Basque autonomy statute, and a second Basque, Manuel de Irujo, entered the cabinet. Speaking in the Cortes on the same day Aguirre explained why the Basques were supporting the Republican cause: "We are opposed to this subversive movement which is directed against the legitimate authority and the will of the people because we are led to do so by our principles which are sincerely and profoundly Christian." Christ had not ordered "the use of bayonet, bomb, and explosive for the conquest of heads and minds, but love"; the Basques, moreover, had no objection to social aims based "on a debt of justice and a necessity." The Basques, Aguirre continued, would feel free to voice their objections to certain policies if their Catholic convictions demanded it. Thus they condemned the firing of the churches, the executions carried out for no other reason but the character and opinions of the victims, and they hoped that such deeds would not be repeated. Still, Aguirre concluded, "until fascism is conquered, the Basque people will stand firm at their posts." [70]

On October 7, Aguirre was elected provisional president of the autonomous Republic of Euzkadi. He formed a cabinet which included three Socialists and one Communist (the latter was soon expelled from the Communist party since he chose to follow the Basque national policy and refused to submit to the orders of his party).[71] Twice under provocation of air raids, mobs broke into jails and murdered prisoners, but by and large the authority of the Basque government was secure, and the Anarchists were held in check. Religious life continued normally, the churches were filled with worshippers, and priests walked the streets in their ecclesiastical garb; the Basque army had one hundred priests serving as military chaplains.[72]

The Nationalist forces, slowly advancing into Basque territory, executed hundreds of Basques and arrested many priests as politically unreliable, of whom at least sixteen were shot without trial in October 1936. Among the victims was Father Aristumuño, a distinguished writer on Basque culture.[73] Cardinal Gomá protested the execution of Basque priests to Franco who ordered them halted. Several hundred priests, however, remained imprisoned or were exiled to other parts of Spain. Priests were not allowed to use the Basque tongue in their sermons.

In a speech broadcast over Radio Euzkadi on December 22, 1936, President Aguirre asked why the Spanish hierarchy remained silent on the crimes committed by the insurgents:

> When numerous Catholics, citizens of the Spanish Republic, have asked whether a Catholic is under the obligation to defend the legitimately constituted regime why does the Hierarchy not speak? When our young Basques, faithfully interpreting the classic Christian doctrine of the right of self-defense, even by force of arms against unjust aggression, and when the greater part of these young people are Christians, and would like to hear from the seat of justice a voice approving their conduct . . . why does the Hierarchy remain silent? [74]

Aguirre again denied that the conflict raging in Spain was a religious war; it was a war waged by the conservative classes to defend their archaic privileges. The church had always insisted on obedience to constituted authority; Christ's teaching should not "be brandished like a weapon, when it seems good to do so, and then trampled underfoot when that seems to be more advantageous." [75]

Cardinal Gomá accepted the challenge and answered in an open letter to President Aguirre, published also as a pastoral letter to his archdiocese. The Basque president, Gomá granted, spoke with the voice of a convinced Catholic, but he was mistaken. "This war is at bottom one of love or of hatred towards religion. It is the love of the God of our fathers that has armed one half of Spain, even if it should be granted that less spiritual motives are operating in this war; it is hatred that has ranged the other half against God." [76] The executions of Basque priests, Gomá insisted, should not "be imputed either to a movement, whose mainspring is the Christian faith" nor to the episcopate which had deplored them and acted to have them stopped. Why had Aguirre and his supporters, the primate asked now in turn, been silent in the face of the murder of thousands of priests and religious in Red Spain? The alignment of the Basques on the side of the forces of communism was a folly and an injustice. The regional characteristics of the Basques could be preserved without breaking up the unity of the fatherland. Gomá ended by asking Aguirre to reconsider: "Who knows, whether with the advent of peace and other things in addition to peace, the legitimate aspirations of the noble Basque people might not be realized." [77]

President Aguirre replied to Cardinal Gomá's open letter in private. "I am a man," he wrote the primate of Spain, "who sincerely professes the Catholic faith and would not publicly engage in a discussion with a Cardinal of the Holy Church." [78] Still, the Basque leader stressed, a reply was necessary. It is "my duty as a Christian to declare loyally and bluntly that one of the causes why the people are losing their religious faith is that they see a large number of churchmen thinking and acting in accord with a political attitude and ideas which are neither more nor less than the extermination of other ideologies." [79] The fact that the episcopate had sided with the Nationalists during the first hours of the rebellion, when the masses alienated from their religious faith had attacked the churches, was understandable. But the continued cooperation of the church with a dictatorial movement against the people and could only have disastrous effects. Aguirre mentioned in closing that he was forwarding Gomá's letter as well as his own to the pope.

Already in October 1936, Aguirre had sent a special emissary, Canon Alberto Onaindia, to Rome to explain the Basques's position. Monsignor Pizzardo, papal under-secretary of state, was said to have assured the envoy: "Morally, the Basques are above reproach." Another Vatican official had added: "Morally, it is correct that the Basques cannot be reproached, but politically you are mistaken since you have chosen the path of those who are going to lose." [80] Following the bombing of Guernica in April 1937, which killed 1654 people and wounded 889, twenty Basque priests, nine of whom were eye-witnesses of the bombing, wrote the pope in order to refute the version put out by the Nationalists that the town had been destroyed by the Basques themselves. Two Basque priests went to Rome with a copy of the letter, but despite the intervention of Bishop Múgica, Secretary of State Pacelli at first refused to see them. When he finally did consent to see them he coldly remarked, "The Church is persecuted in Barcelona," and showed them the door.[81] Obviously the recalcitrant Basques did not please the Holy See.

The military fortunes of the Basques, meanwhile, were rapidly deteriorating. The lack of confidence between the Catholic Basques and their allies, the revolutionary Asturian miners, coupled with the lack of heavy military equipment and airplanes, led to a fairly hopeless situation by May 1937. A proposal of a separate peace, suggested through the good offices of Cardinal Gomá, the papal nuncio in Paris and others, came to naught when Franco turned down the demand of the Basque leaders that the terms of the agreement be guaranteed by a foreign power.[82] By the middle of June military resistance in the Basque provinces had collapsed. On June 24, the Franco government abolished the autonomy statute and deprived the Basques of all their former privileges regarding taxation and local government. A large-scale purge was instituted among the clergy. Some of the priests arrested were still in jail in the late 1940's.[83]

The Basque leaders now moved to Barcelona where they set up a government in exile. By special permission they were allowed to hold services in a chapel reserved for their use exclusively; in the rest of Republican Spain all churches remained closed. Repeated attempts by Manuel de Irujo, the Basque representative in the Republican government, to obtain a reopening of the churches remained unsuccessful. In August 1937, the government decreed the right of private worship, but this merely legalized a situation that had existed for some time.[84] During 1938 soldiers on the Madrid and Ebro front were reported to be attending masses; [85] more than two thousand priests had returned to Barcelona. Further efforts at the normalization of religious life, pushed especially by the Communists, were said to have failed in part because the Vatican feared a resultant weakening of Franco's crusade for Christianity.[86] The Anarchists, too, remained adamant in objecting to a re-establishment of Catholic public worship. There can be little doubt that the handling of the religious issue by the Republican government cost the latter many would-be friends both inside and outside Spain.

THE ROLE OF THE HOLY SEE

As we have seen, both the Spanish hierarchy and the Basques invoked traditional Catholic teaching on the problem of resistance to constituted authority to bolster their respective causes. A majority of the episcopate argued that the Republican government was illegitimate, unjust, and tyrannical and that armed resistance to it was not only allowable but actually a moral duty. The uprising of the generals was dubbed a crusade and holy war. The Basques, on the other hand, insisted on the legitimate character of the Madrid government and denied that armed rebellion was the answer to anticlerical outbursts. The conditions for the rightfulness of resistance stipulated by the medieval scholastics and later theologians, they argued, were not present; a rebellion carried out by a totalitarian movement and supported by Moors and Nazis could not be considered a crusade. The two positions thus clashed head on; the one authority which could have adjudicated the doctrinal dispute, the papacy, failed to shoulder this task.

Throughout the Civil War both Catholic factions claimed to have the implicit if not explicit backing of the Holy See. But in reality the Holy See pursued a rather cautious policy. Two months after the start of the insurrection, on September 14, 1936, Pope Pius XI delivered an address to six hundred Spanish refugees—bishops, priests, and laymen—whom he received in audience at Castel Gandolfo. After expressing his deep sorrow over the "fratricidal carnage" which had cost so many Christian lives and the "savage persecution of the Church," the Pontiff went on to say:

> Our benediction, above any mundane consideration, goes out in a special manner to all those who have assumed the difficult and dangerous task of defending and restoring the rights and honor of God and of religion, which is to say the right and dignity of conscience. . . . This task, We have said, is both difficult and dangerous, for it is only too easy for the very ardor and difficulty of defense to go to an excess which is not wholly warranted. And further, intentions less pure, selfish interests, and mere party feeling may easily enter into, cloud and change the morality and responsibility of what is done.[87]

After these words of blessing as well as warning addressed to the Nationalists the pope expressed his continuing concern with the Catholics on the other side:

> And what of the others? What is to be said of all those others who also are and never cease to be Our sons, in spite of the deeds and methods of persecution so odious and so cruel against persons and things to Us so dear and sacred? . . . We cannot and could not for one moment doubt as to what is left for Us to do—to love them and to love them with a special love born of mercy and compassion; to love them and, since We can do nothing else, to pray for them; to pray that the serene vision of truth will illuminate their minds and will reopen their hearts to the desire and fraternal quest for the real common good.[88]

Pope Pius in this address had given his blessing to those who were "defending and restoring the rights and honor of God and of religion," but he had not endorsed the idea of a crusade or holy war, and he had warned against excessive zeal and the intrusion of selfish intentions. Those Catholics aligning themselves with the Republican government had not been condemned. One month later, as already mentioned, the papal undersecretary of state had assured a Basque emissary that the Basques's stand was above reproach, and this position was never formally repudiated. The Holy See thus had endorsed the Spanish hierarchy's support of Franco to secure the freedom of the church from persecution, but the Vatican had cautiously diassociated itself from the power politics of Franco's German and Italian backers and had not repudiated the Basques.

The Nationalists, as was to be expected, were far from pleased with the Holy See's course. On December 27, 1936, a German official in Spain reported to his government that Franco had complained strongly about the pope's attitude toward his government. "The diplomatic representative of the Nationalist government had suggested to the Pope that he publicly take a stand against cooperation of the Catholic Basque Nationalists with the Reds, in order to contribute toward a Basque withdrawal from the fighting, which Franco is hoping for. The Pope had refused." He had expressed strong disapproval of the execution of Basque priests; it was suspected that Pius XI had come under the influence of the Basque bishop of Vitoria. Franco, therefore, intended to send two bishops sympathetic to him to Rome "for the purpose of enlightening the Vatican." [89]

We do not know whether Cardinal Gomá's visit in Rome in December 1936 was in implementation of this plan of Franco. Gomá, according to the editor of a volume of the primate's pastoral letters, was able to convince the Vatican of the justice of Franco's cause and returned to Spain as the official representative of the pope at the Nationalist government in Burgos.[90] In his encyclical against Communist atheism of March 19, 1937, Pius XI once again sharply condemned Communist atrocities in Spain. He denied that these were "sporadic outbursts of violence such as every war entails"; rather they were the natural outcome of Communist propaganda and "of a system constitutionally devoid of any principle of restraint." The pope warned against cooperating with Communists "in any enterprise whatever." [91] A few days later, Pius XI in an encyclical letter addressed to the Mexican hierarchy distinguished between just and unjust rebellions. In cases "where the civil power should so trample on justice and truth as to destroy even the very foundations of authority, there would appear no reason to condemn citizens for uniting to defend the nation and themselves by lawful and appropriate means against those who make use of the power of the state to drag the nation to ruin." [92] No explicit reference had been made to the Spanish Civil War, and some of the conditions added by the pope clearly had not been fulfilled, but the cumulative effect of these various pronouncements was to strengthen the hand of those siding with the Nationalists.

As Franco's military fortunes improved, and the chance of his eventual victory became more and more certain, the Holy See took another step in the direction of coordinating its stand with that of the Spanish episcopate. The response of world Catholicism to the collective letter of the Spanish bishops of July 1937 had been gratifying. Military resistance in the two Basque provinces had come to an end. On August 28, 1937, consequently, the Vatican formally recognized the Burgos government as the *de jure* government of Spain and dispatched a nuncio. From time to time the Vatican is said to have urged upon the Nationalists a more humane conduct of the war, but by and large relations were now improved and the Holy See was clearly aligned with the Nationalists. "In perfect harmony," noted an American journalist in Rome, "*L'Osservatore Romano* and the fascist press vied with each other in publishing harrowing tales of loyalist persecutions of the clergy and faithful." [93] It was largely as a result of Catholic pressure, carefully nourished by a powerful propaganda campaign waged from pulpits and in the Catholic press, that the United States government kept its embargo on arms deliveries to Republican Spain, an important factor in Franco's ultimate victory.[94] On March 31, 1939, the new pope, Pius XII, sent a telegram to General Franco congratulating him on his triumph: "Lifting up our heart to God, we give sincere thanks with Your Excellency for Spain's Catholic Victory." [95] About two weeks later Pius XII broadcast another message to the Catholics of Spain "to express our fatherly congratulations for the gift of peace and victory with which God has deigned to crown the Christian heroism of your faith and charity, proved through such great and generous sufferings." [96]

For the journal of the Spanish Jesuits, *Razón y Fe*, this message of Pius XII represented "the unassailable justification of our redeeming movement, the canonization of the character of our crusade." [97] The conservative secretary of the Sacred Congregation of the Holy Office, Cardinal Alfredo Ottaviani, visiting Madrid in 1961 also praised those who had expelled from Spanish soil "the hordes set on ruining the name of Christians and all human dignity and freedom" and he confirmed that "yours was a

Holy Crusade in the West which stemmed the violent assault of Marxism, the enemy of the Cross of Christ." [98] But in point of fact the Holy See had never described the Civil War in these words. Rome had never formally and explicitly condemned the Basques, and thus the doctrinal questions posed by the rebellion and the resultant split in the ranks of Spanish Catholicism remain unanswered. Who conducted himself in conformity with Catholic teaching—those bishops and their clergy who saw in the conflict a holy war, thus, as Luigi Sturzo put it, "arousing in the name of religion the worst instincts of slaughter and extermination," [99] or the Basques and men like Jacques Maritain who objected to identifying the church with Franco's anticommunist crusade?

Despite the fact that Catholic teachings on the justification of resistance to tyrannical political authority today are as ambiguous as ever, facilitating their adjustment to considerations of *raison d'église*, the Spanish church since the late 1960's has definitely moved to new political ground. Except for a relatively small conservative faction, a majority of the clergy appears to have come to regret the church's role in the Civil War. The long history of estrangement between the church and the majority of the Spanish people may finally be coming to an end.

PART V

Religion and the Legitimation of Revolutionary Change

CHAPTER 18

Nasserism and Islam: A Revolution in Search of Ideology

At the time of their seizure of power in July 1952, the "Free Officers," led by Nasser, were virtually without a program that could provide direction to the tasks of government. The general vision of the group was expressed in "Six Principles" which were intimated in a manifesto circulated secretly and privately by the officers before the coup. The "Six Principles" were incorporated into the platform of the Liberation Rally in January 1953, and they were formulated more clearly in the preamble of the Constitution of 1956: "The eradication of all aspects of imperialism; the extinction of feudalism; the eradication of monopolies and the control of capitalistic influence over the system of government; the establishment of a strong national army; the establishment of social justice; and the establishment of a sound democratic society." [1] Out of these general principles there emerged an ideology often called Nasserism—a mixture of the old and the new that reflects the attempts of the Islamic intelligentsia to achieve modernization without being swallowed up by the West. The uneasy balance of traditional and revolutionary elements can be seen in two key planks of Nasserism—Arab nationalism and Arab socialism. Both have survived the death of Nasser on September 28, 1970 and continue, as of this writing, to function as the ideology behind Egyptian political life.

ARAB NATIONALISM

Before the Egyptian revolution of 1952, the ideological center of Arab nationalism—a synthesis between pan-Islamism and the local nationalism of the petty Arab states that emerged from the ruins of the Ottoman empire after the First World War—was in Syria and Lebanon.[2] Egypt had had an important role in the shaping of the cultural aspect of Arab consciousness by being the seat of several pan-Arab societies, but it was not until the 1930's that an interest in the cause of Arab unity developed in Egypt. To many Egyptians, aware of the rich Egyptian heritage of the Nile civilization that predated both the emergence of the Arabs and Islam, the term "Arab" was a synonym of backwardness.[3] By the 1940's, the pan-Arab idea had made headway; Egypt took an active role in the establishment of the Arab League in 1945. But the defeat of the Arabs in the Arab-Israeli war of 1948 strengthened Egyptian isolationism. Inter-Arab cooperation had failed a vital test, and the feeling that Egypt should concentrate on its own affairs and the promotion of Egyptian nationalism was widespread among opinion makers.[4] The Free Officers who seized power in 1952, in line with the political temper of the time, were preoccupied with solving internal problems. Relations with other Arab states for them were primarily a matter of foreign policy not ideology.[5] In Nasser's *Philosophy of the Revolution*, published in 1955, the term, Arab nationalism, does not appear. Nasser spoke of three circles within which Egypt was located and which determined its life—the Arab, the African, and the Islamic spheres:

> It is not without significance that our country is situated west of Asia, in contiguity with the Arab states with whose existence our own is interwoven. It is not without significance, too, that our country lies in northeast Africa, overlooking the Dark Continent, wherein rages a most tumultous struggle between white colonizers and black inhabitants for control of its unlimited resources. Nor is it without significance that, when the Mongols swept away the ancient capitals of Islam, Islamic civilization and the Islamic heritage fell back on Egypt and took shelter there. Egypt protected them and saved them, while checking the onslaught of the Mongols at 'Ain Jalut. All these are fundamental realities with deep roots in our lives which we cannot—even if we try—escape or forget.[6]

The Arab circle, Nasser maintained, was the most important, for Egypt was linked to the Arab world not only by the facts of geography and history, but also by a common religion. Still, the interests of Egypt clearly ranked first. Nasser spoke of "the tremendous possibilities" to be realized through the cooperation of the many millions of Muslims in the world, but, perhaps to differentiate his priorities from those of the Muslim Brotherhood, he added that such cooperation was not to go "beyond the bounds of their natural loyalty to their own countries." [7]

If Nasser thus was espousing an essentially secular nationalism in 1955, emphasizing primary allegiance to country before allegiance to ethnic groups or religion, he was soon to discover that the Egyptian masses could be reached and mobilized only by associating nationalism with Islam. For the urban Egyptian, in particular, the laborers and semi-educated who had made up the rank and file of the fundamentalist Muslim Brotherhood whose support Nasser was seeking, the emotional sustenance for the spirit of nationalism derived from an Islamic universalism. For these men to attain national dignity meant to resume the mission which Mohammed had inaugurated, it meant to reconstitute the Muslim community advocated in the Prophet's teachings and achieved by his first followers, the Arabs. Nationalism, in short, meant Arab nationalism built upon a religious foundation. Since nationalism is a force that draws on the achievements of the past, and, since the only glory the Arabs ever knew was achieved under the banner of Islam, it was natural that Arab nationalists should lean on the heritage of Islam and "find its intellectual stimulus in the great Arab-Islamic culture of the past—a culture which was made possible by Islam." [8]

Sunni Islam recognizes neither geographical nor ethnic boundaries and only distinguishes between the community of faith, the *umma*, and the outside world of unbelievers. Upon this concept of *umma* Arab nationalists grafted the idea of nationhood, and this transformation of a religious community into a political one was by and large accepted by the Muslims. [9] The masses could be enlisted through the appeal to the spirit of Islam; the intellectuals rallied to the standard of Arab unity in part because it could counteract a growing Westernization. The idea of an Arab nation thus merged with the Islamic concept of *umma*, and in this manner Arab nationalism achieved a spiritual ethos and mass support. Blurring the theoretical distinction between the Islamic community and the Arab nation, "nationalism has been able to evolve as a modern expression of traditional Muslim sentiments regarding the unity, dignity, and historic destiny of the Community rather than flying in the face of such sentiments." [10] Arab nationalism has emerged as something close to a "political religion," it functions as a "Sorelian myth." [11]

The islamization of nationalism has had many advantages. Islam provided a sense of history, identity, and solidarity, to build a heritage that was distinct from both Western liberalism and communism. Rather than fighting the tide of Muslim militancy, manifested in the popularity of the Brotherhood, Nasser's regime was able to swim with it.

At the same time, this Arab nationalism with Islamic overtones not infrequently created problems for Nasser—in domestic affairs as well as in foreign relations. For Egypt's Christian minority, the Copts, the failure to separate nationalism from religion has meant emotional and other more tangible hardships. During the short-lived union of Egypt and Syria, the latter with a well-educated and politically active Christian minority (14 per cent of the population), the Islamic aspects of Arab nationalism had to be downgraded, especially since Christian Arabs have had a leading role in its formulation and have tended to stress its secular components. The vague nature of Arab nationalism, based upon dreams of empire and a desire for a restored Muslim community, has given an appearance of unity where none exists. Beneath the commitment to Arab unity lie sharp disagreements over the content and means of achieving unity.[12] The record of Nasser's relations with the rest of the Arab world bears witness to the difficulty of linking a coherent and rational foreign policy to as emotional and undefined a principle as Arab nationalism.

Until 1955 Nasser concentrated on Egyptian affairs and was content with being *one* of the leaders of the Arab world. From 1955 on he began to pursue an increasingly assertive foreign policy and to assume the role of spokesman for the Arab people. A number of factors were involved in this reorientation. Iraq's alignment with the West in the Baghdad Pact of 1955 threatened the political and military isolation of Egypt; Nasser reacted by actively promoting Arab solidarity and unity—a policy he continued to pursue until his death. Domestically the new emphasis on Arab nationalism and the fight against imperialism diverted attention from the difficulties involved in social and economic reform. The milestones in this nationalistic and pan-Arab course are well known: In late 1955, following a major Israeli attack on the Egyptian-held Gaza strip that exposed Egypt's military weakness, Nasser concluded a barter agreement for arms with Czechoslovakia; in 1956 he nationalized the Suez Canal; and in 1957 Nasser emerged from the Suez War as the hero who had defeated two major powers, Britain and France. In February 1958, Syria and Egypt agreed to form the United Arab Republic. Nasser was at the pinnacle of his prestige. He had successfully defied the Western powers, and he had made a major advance along the road to Arab unity. For the Arab masses all over the Middle East Nasser was the new Saladin who was to fulfill their longings and hopes.

But Arab unity was not to be that easily achieved. The introduction in Syria of economic and administrative reforms based upon Egyptian rather than Syrian needs alienated wide segments of Syrian society and ultimately led to the secession of Syria.[13] "The Charter of National Action," a lengthy programmatic document adopted by the Nasser regime in June 1962, proclaimed a new formula: Arab unity to succeed presupposed the radical and revolutionary transformation of society in a socialist direction. However, the merger of states with deeply contrasting socioeconomic and political structures could not lead to real and lasting unity. Steps must be taken "to fill the economic and social gaps occurring between various Arab states as a result of imperialist-inspired differences in stages of development," [14] and it was the duty of the United Arab Republic to support all popular progressive movements in the Arab world that sought to close these gaps.

The proclamation of the Charter restored some of Nasser's popularity, but the new tactic could no more nullify and overcome the diversities of environment, language, political experience, and abilities that stood in the way of Arab unity than the earlier more direct approach. Egypt no longer was the leading power in an Arab world that now had several competing revolutionary centers—Syria, Iraq, and Algeria as well as the United Arab Republic. All the existing Arab nation-states, despite their somewhat arbitrary borders, had local ruling groups for whom the survival of these states was a matter of compelling self-interest. Israel as the common enemy is one of the few continuing unifying forces in the Arab world. In the wake of the Six Day War of 1967 several Arab countries not directly involved in the fighting agreed to provide financial aid to the United Arab Republic and Jordan, and a series of conferences have since taken place to coordinate strategy against Israel. It is too early to tell whether the new federation of the Arab Republic of Egypt, Libya, and Syria will be effective.

The acceptance of Islam by most Arabs is, of course, another reason for unification. But even Islam failed to unify the Arab world as was demonstrated in the controversy over the so-called "Islamic Pact" in early 1966. When King Faisal of Saudi Arabia proposed the idea of an "Islamic conference" of heads of Muslim states in Mecca, Nasser interpreted this proposal as an attempt to build a coalition of conservative states that would isolate revolutionary regimes like the United Arab Republic. Faisal's insistence that he had sought neither an alliance nor an anti-Egyptian campaign apparently was not mere rhetoric.[15] Nevertheless, Nasser reacted with a vigor that indicated that an exposed nerve had been touched. The idea of an Islamic conference, Nasser reminded the Arab world, had been proposed by him as early as 1954, but the Baghdad Pact of 1955 prevented the conference from convening. Real Islamic solidarity, he insisted, "is the solidarity of the Islamic peoples struggling against imperialism, not the solidarity between reactionary governments which are imperialist agents exploiting and falsifying Islam; reactionary governments that want to stop the march of history and the march of progress."[16] The Islamic Pact was an attempt to use the sacred principles of religion for reactionary ends, it was a forgery of religion aiming to attack and destroy the idea of Arab nationalism, "to stop the progressive Arab revolutionary tide in the Arab countries."[17] Nasser was apparently unwilling to let his political opponents wear the mantle of Islam. Islam was neither a factor upon which to build a viable pan-Arab unity nor yet an ideology to be discarded.

ARAB SOCIALISM

If the appeal to Islam was useful in popularizing certain goals of Nasser's foreign policy, it was equally useful in effecting the regime's social and economic program. Again, the impetus and the initial shaping of policy were not derived from Islamic principles, though Islamic loyalties could be enlisted to marshal support once these policies were adopted.[18]

The Free Officers, upon seizing power in 1952, were distressed by Egypt's gross inequality and poverty, a distress that found its expression in one of the "Six Principles"—the demand for the "establishment of social justice." But the change and the transition from this statement of a general goal to the formulation of a socialist doctrine and a program of action was gradual, pragmatic, and slow. During the early years, in fact, the new regime went out of its way to allay suspicion that it was left-wing in character. "We are not Socialists," insisted Gamal Salem, minister of national guidance, in early 1954, "I think our economy can only prosper under free enterprise." [19] Businessmen participated actively in the formulation of a program of development; incentives and private investments were encouraged to spur growth. The ranks of the Free Officers were purged of leftist elements, and most of Egypt's Communists were imprisoned. The ringleaders of a strike at a textile plant in August 1952 that had led to the seizure of the factory were summarily tried and hanged. Only the agrarian reform law of September 1952, which limited land ownership to a maximum of 200 *feddans* (about 200 acres), struck a somewhat different note.[20]

During the years 1952–56 the Egyptian economy experienced a firm government, and the state moved gradually away from a *laissez-faire* approach. Still, economic and social policy essentially continued to follow the lines initiated before the 1952 coup, and the period has been described as the "free-enterprise phase of the Egyptian revolution." [21] Perceptible changes took place after the Suez War of 1956. Realizing that Egypt's economic problems were far more serious than they had thought, the officers were gradually driven to more drastic measures. Certain foreign and, later, Egyptian establishments were nationalized, a program of central planning and intensified industrialization was initiated, and taxation of income in the higher brackets was increased sharply. These measures, extending state control over private enterprise, "were accompanied by a swift break-away from the West in both political alignment and ideological approach and by an increasing use in public pronouncements and the press, of pseudo-Marxist and class-war slogans." [22] The term "controlled capitalist economy," employed by Nasser in 1958, accurately describes this phase of the Revolution.

Egypt's first Five-Year Plan, formulated in 1959–60, involved a mixed economy and close cooperation between the public and private sectors of the economy. But the planners soon found that private enterprise was slow to achieve the targets set for production, investment, and saving. When exhortations and incentives failed to achieve the goals of the central plan, the regime inaugurated what is now referred to in Egypt as the "Social Revolution." In July 1961, the ninth anniversary of the revolution, a large share of Egypt's industrial and commercial property was nationalized. A new land reform law prohibited any individual from owning more than 100 and any family more than 300 *feddans* of agricultural land.[23] Following the secession of Syria in September of the same year, and in the face of a decline in the internal economy caused by floods and damage by parasites to the cotton crop, the property of some 850 persons was confiscated. A vigorous press campaign was launched against "reactionary, feudalist, and capitalist elements," and over 7000 persons, affected by the expropriation laws, were deprived of their political rights.[24] In August 1969 the scope of land reform was extended by a new law which stipulated that no person could own more than 50 *feddans* and no family more than 100 *feddans*.[25]

The ideological justification of the "Social Revolution" by way of a theory of Arab socialism came after the event. Egypt's economic and social system, developed piecemeal and by trial and error rather than according to a predetermined plan, now was given an ideology: the blueprint of a socialist society was laid out. The socialist revolution, Nasser explained in August 1961, was succeeding in "eradicating feudalism, in destroying the dictatorship of capital, and in establishing social justice, entirely by peaceful means." [26] The goal was the elimination of class distinctions. It was due to the particular circumstances of the Egyptian Revolution, Nasser admitted in November 1961, "that the revolutionary application, our revolutionary application, may be prior to the theory. Then what is the theory? The theory is the evidence of the action." [27]

The official formulation of "Arab socialism" was presented to the Egyptian people in the Charter of May 1962. This lengthy document described the various reforms promulgated since 1961 and outlined a program for future action. Socialism, according to the Charter, "is the way to social freedom; social freedom means equal opportunity to every citizen to obtain a fair share of the national wealth." [28] However, the national wealth must not only be redistributed, it must also be expanded. The national income should double every ten years, and this could only be achieved through scientific planning. An efficient public sector was to provide leadership—with heavy industry and financial institutions owned by the state. In light and medium industry and external trade mixed ownership could prevail. "In the agricultural sector, Arab socialism does not believe in the nationalization of land but in individual ownership within limits that prevent feudalism." [29]

Arab socialism continued to dominate the ideology of the Nasser regime. The struggle for socialism became the theme to mobilize the country to achieve economic growth. "The Revolution of July 23," Nasser stated in November 1964, "was but an introduction to the Revolution." [30] The achievement of a socialist society, he warned, would be far more difficult than the fight against the external enemy. The gains chalked up by the "Social Revolution" support Nasser's realistic appraisal. Socialist planning, now in its twelfth year, has not yet brought about the desired economic development, though the standard of living has improved somewhat. The extension of public ownership in itself cannot work wonders.

In 1952 about 0.5 per cent of all proprietors owned 34.2 per cent of the land, and 5.2 per cent owned another 30.5 per cent of all landed property.[31] Agrarian reform has broken the power of the landlords, but most rural families have not benefited much from the redistribution of land; they remain either landless or have just enough land for a meager subsistence. The law has brought no relief to the still landless laborers who in 1958 made up 73 per cent of the rural population [32]; their number was said to be three million in 1971.[33] Inequality of wealth and income has been reduced through a series of nationalizations, confiscations, the fixing of maximum salaries, and the extension of social services. But those who have gained most, concludes one observer, "seem to have been middling peasants, the employees of corporate industry and commerce, and middle-class tenants of rented accommodations, three groups who altogether form no more than a small and privileged minority of the population." [34] For the masses of the Egyptian people a marked improvement in their lot will depend upon the achievement of a rate of economic expansion sufficient to outpace the increase in population, which at an explosive growth rate of 2.7 per cent a year (compare 1.2 per cent in the United States) threatens to nullify the benefits of even as spectacular a development project as the Aswan dam.

Egypt's Social Revolution has thus not been as far-reaching as official statements have depicted it. Still, for Egypt's tradition-bound masses the changes have been revolutionary enough to require an elaborate program of ideological justification that seeks to prove the compatibility of Arab socialism with Islam. Nasser himself took the lead in 1961 when he distinguished Arab socialism and Marxian socialism and insisted that the former not only was not opposed to Islam but actually was derived from it. We have said, he explained, that "our religion is a socialist one and that in the middle ages Islam had successfully applied the first socialist experiment in the world." Reactionaries like King Hussein, Nasser continued, allege "that socialism is against Islam. Islam in his conception implies Harems and palaces, usurping the people's money and leaving them poor and naked." That was wrong. "Islam implies equity and justice. The Arab people will never be deceived." [35]

In the years that followed, Nasser time and again returned to this central theme. A few passages, taken from a collection of Nasser's speeches published in 1964, will suffice as a sampling: "Islam is the first religion to call for socialism, the first religion to call for equality and the first to call for an end to domination and inequality." "Mohammed, God's blessing be on him, gave us the example of social justice, progress and development, and thus Islam was able in these early days to defeat the strongest nations . . . and spread to all corners of the earth because it was the religion of righteousness, freedom, justice and equality." Our enemies "say that socialism is infidelity. But is socialism really what they describe by this term? What they describe applies to raising slaves, hoarding money and usurping the people's wealth. This is infidelity and this is against religion and Islam. What we apply in our country is the law of justice and the law of God." [36]

Since 1961 the regime has sponsored a large amount of scholarly and popular writing propounding the unity of Arab socialism and Islam. A formal legal opinion (fatwa), issued by a canon lawyer (mufti) in 1962, dealt with the question whether the socialist laws of 1961 violated the spirit of Islam. The Muslim expert, citing the Koran and the traditions, concluded that these laws were sanctioned by Islamic jurisprudence. "Private ownership is legitimate in the eyes of Islamic jurisprudence as long as the owner observes the ordinances of Allah concerning his wealth. But if he does not abide by them, the ruler is entitled to devise the laws and regulations which force him to adhere to the commandments of God." [37] The law of agrarian reform and the restriction of land ownership aimed at realizing the public good and social justice: "The distribution of wealth between the poor and the rich so that it may not be circulated among the rich only, is a procedure approved of by Islamic jurisprudence." [38] Islam prohibited the monopoly of food and similar resources, and "thus we can sanction the nationalization of public institutions indispensable to everyday life such as the institution established to secure water, electricity and easy transport." [39]

Other writers have argued that "Arab socialism is the only road to human freedom, it is the only way to social freedom as Islam calls for . . . our socialist revolution aims with all its strength at building a society of justice and equality, thus receiving its principles and inspiration from the pillars of Islam." [40] "Arab socialism is the system that can implement the Islamic concept of requiring the individual to fulfill his duties. In preparing him to fulfill the cooperative duties in which he is a supervisor and a partner at the same time, and in requiring him to consider the interest of the group . . . it thus reflects the Islamic ideal which requires a righteous individual and a cooperative society." [41] Socialism based upon Islam did not deny the interests of the individual, though it does oppose the struggle between classes that results in enmity and hate. "Thus it has made work the basis of distributing wealth and reward, and it forbade excessive wealth and the exploitation of others." [42] Islam did not allow unlimited freedom of ownership but insisted on conditions that would guarantee justice and equality. "Islam allowed the ruler to strike those who do not observe these conditions and allowed him to take property and redistribute it to the people in accordance with the general and public good." [43]

The practical effect of such pronouncements by religious leaders is probably less than the regime might wish. Muslim religious teachers (*ulama*) originally lived from their own resources and when eventually a class of paid religious officeholders emerged they came to be seen by the Muslim public as "venal men, prepared when necessary to twist the Law to suit the desires of their masters." To this day, therefore, the legal pronouncements of the *ulama* are received "with a good deal of cynicism." [44] Moreover, in the Arab tradition everything touched by government is suspect, and therefore the more Islam is used for propaganda purposes the less useful it becomes.[45]

As far as the soundness of the theological exegesis is concerned, the attempt to reconcile socialism and Islam raises the same problems as did the attempt to establish a synthesis between nationalism and Islam. The political, economic, and social principles evolved by a society in the seventh and eighth centuries can hardly be expected to fit the complexities of life in the twentieth century. Ideas like justice and equality are vague enough to accommodate a great variety of concrete programs. It is not difficult for modernists to go back to the Koran and the traditions and to find there permission for whatever social reform they wish to promote and uphold. "Just as in the second century of Islam the fabrication of *hadiths* and the elaboration of a system of deductive legal reasoning had sanctified the assimilation of existing local customs and precedents into a unified Islamic system of law, so today the modernist principles may be said to have performed an assimilative function." [46] And yet, this search for the endorsement of Islam by way of a highly selective reading and quoting of holy writ has to some extent the same quality of "pious fraud" which Ignaz Goldziher had attributed to the outright forgery of many of the early traditions.[47] Such a romanticizing of the Muslim past can foster national pride, and it can help justify and legitimize the contemporary state's actions; it cannot, however, define objectives or provide guidance in solving the practical problems of modernization. Writing in 1945, Sir Hamilton Gibb expressed the hope that Muslim intellectuals would turn to creative thinking, "removed from the intellectual confusions and the paralyzing romanticism which cloud the minds of the modernists of today." [48] This expectation, it appears, has been fulfilled only in part.

The idea of Arab socialism, as Malcom Kerr has noted, fulfills some of the nationalist and religious desires of the masses. "It offers advancement, social harmony, equality, public morality, collective self-respect. It responds to the populism of the nationalist, and to the believing Muslim's desire for a straight path to follow amid the uncertainties of modern life . . . the *umma* has taken its affairs in hand, in an assertion of collective will that appeals to nationalists, and simultaneously in a spirit of welcoming of communal duty and a striving for the Right that are the essence of *jihad*." [49] At the same time, the Islamic component of socialism, no matter how it has been modified, may in time create difficulties. Arab socialism, unlike communism, as the government emphasizes, rejects class violence and does not attack the institution of private property as such. In the future this conservative element, implying reconciliation rather than a class struggle, could inhibit the forward march of the social revolution. Last, Islam is a religion in which precedent and tradition carry great weight: it "tends to place on innovators and individualists the burden of proof of the moral acceptability of their actions." Religion thus may reinforce the bureaucratic mentality, the attachment to routine and thus counteract "the mixture of scientism, experimentalism, Marxism-Leninism, activism, and self-assertiveness from which so far the revolution has acquired much of its momentum." [50] For the time being these doctrines coexist in the official ideology; eventually their coexistence may end.

ISLAM AND THE PURSUIT OF LEGITIMACY

The leaders of many developing nations live in two worlds simultaneously. In order to raise their countries from poverty they seek to modernize and to acquire for their societies the education and the advanced technical know-how of the West. At the same time, to maintain rapport with their tradition-bound people, they must appeal to native pride and communal and ethnic sentiments as well as religion. What makes the resulting identity and ideological crisis more severe is the fact that these leaders themselves have often been unable to clarify their attitude to tradition and religion. Thus a policy toward religion which on the surface may look like a Machiavellian manipulation of religious sentiments is what it is sometimes not only because it is a necessary expedient but also because its originators are genuinely uncertain and ambivalent.

The majority of the officers ruling Egypt, including the late Nasser, fit this description of a leader. Well-informed observers of the Egyptian scene continue to report that most of the leaders of the revolution are practicing Muslims. "Of modest country stock, they have been unaffected by the wave of modernist scepticism and demoralization which has been sweeping over the Egyptian upper classes for over half a century." [51] "Abdel Nasser's belief in Islam," noted another writer, "appears genuine. He personally follows the rituals of his religion—not just for public display —and he takes part in the community prayer on Friday." [52] Nasser's successor, Anwar Sadat, is considered to be a deeply religious person. To be sure when Anwar Sadat in 1953 and Nasser at the height of the Suez crisis in 1956 took to the pulpits to address worshippers, they clearly were motivated not only by religious sentiments. Similarly, the attendance of Nasser with visiting Muslim dignitaries at Mosque services obviously served a ceremonial as well as a religious purpose. Nevertheless, the appeal to religion is more than just propaganda. Nasser declared in 1963:

> We boast that we stick to religion, each one of us according to his religion. The Muslim upholds his religion and the Christian upholds his, because religion represents the right and sound way. If we listen to them today telling us from Damascus that they consider our adherence to religion tantamount to our adherence to rotten religious ideas, we pride ourselves on that. We pride ourselves on the fact that since the first day of our Revolution we have adhered to religion. Not only the Revolution leaders, but the people as well. It is the great secret behind the success of this Revolution: the adherence to religion.[53]

Nasser's conception of Islam, as we have seen, was reformist and modernistic. He sought to fit Islam to modern life. In the manner of Mohammed Abduh, Nasser held an optimistic outlook upon life, and he emphasized the need for action. Aspirations and hopes cannot be realized, he told his followers in March 1965, by merely relying upon God's help. Sacrifices and persistence are essential. Islam is a religion of struggle. "It is only the way of effort, only the way of work, which is the way for the realization of our hopes and aspirations, it is only the way of construction which is the way of salvation." [54] Nasser in his political activism was opposed to the thinking of Muslim apologists who spoke of the inherent superiority of Islam and thus encouraged a spirit of complacency.

And, yet, here again lies a dilemma. Modernists like Nasser feel constrained to point out past errors and outmoded elements in their own culture and to keep the door to the West open. They reject a mere romanticizing of the Islamic past, and they stress the need of accepting many Western ideas and techniques. At the same time they often seek to hide the extent of their borrowing by asserting that the borrowed elements are actually Muslim in origin or at least a logical development of Muslim elements correctly interpreted. They strive to preserve self-respect when confronted with the power of the West by praising the accomplishments of their native civilization. They encourage pride in the Islamic past which sometimes has become a warranty of a glorious future. The result of this dualistic orientation is intellectual confusion and strain that affects Arab attitudes toward the West as well as their own history. The decay of the once flourishing Muslim civilization and the weaknesses of today's Muslim world must be admitted, but, as Professor von Grunebaum phrases the problem, on whom is the blame for the present predicament to be placed:

> Was it the theologians of the Middle Ages whose distortion of the Prophetic message caused the drying up of the Islamic inspiration? Was it the Mamluks whose ruthless rule sapped the strength of Egypt beyond recovery? Or was it Muhammad 'Ali whose precipitate steps toward Europeanization did more harm than good by creating that psychological confusion that still lies at the bottom of the incessant political unrest of the country? There is no end of questions of this order and they are becoming more burning as it is less possible to brush them aside by pointing to colonialism as the root of all evil. And even if colonialism is impugned with the problem is only pushed back one step, for it would be difficult not to ask further: What was it that weakened the Muslim world to such an extent that it no longer could or would resist the intruder? [55]

These questions are raised, but the answers given often involve considerable self-deception. We Muslims, notes Anwar Sadat, "inherited a glorious torch that could have guided us to the road to justice, knowledge and peace. Why then did we become hungry, ignorant, sick and slaves?" Because Western colonialists, in alliance with reactionary rulers and an ignorant priesthood, stole and hid the torch of the true religion which exists to improve human life.[56] This tendency to blame outsiders for present difficulties and past failures is seen in many countries undergoing modernization.

Of course, obstacles on the course of modernization are created not only by the lack of intellectual incisiveness on the part of the ruling elite, but, at least as importantly, by the continuing strength shown by the traditional Islamic ethos among the masses of the people. The very fact, notes one observer, that those in power feel the need to invoke for the justification of both Arab nationalism and Arab socialism Islamic ideas "indicates the extent to which their assessment of popular opinion has led them to conclude that the Arab Islamic past is far from having spent its force." [57] Among the poorer classes, in particular, religious elements quietly endure. The *fellahin*, the rural proletariat of Egypt who constitute about two-thirds of the total population, still live a life of isolation; reform measures bringing health centers and schools have not yet been able to change traditional behavior. In 1966, 70 per cent of the Egyptian population was illiterate.[58] Interviews conducted in 1957 among rural families who had benefited from land reform revealed that 86 per cent were illiterate, 63 per cent preferred large families, and 83 per cent had never even heard of birth control; 98 per cent of the men insisted on their religious and legal right to unilaterally divorce a wife.[59] The passions and emotional needs of the masses of the population are still tied to Islam. Unlike the guilds, the Sufi orders, though weakened, have not yet disappeared. Offering spiritual and material brotherhood and security in their ranks, they continue to appeal to men who crave a dynamic alternative to the formality of Islamic orthodoxy and to the official trade unions or the Arab Socialist Union.[60] The same factors account for the survival of the Muslim Brotherhood.

Following the attempted assassination of President Nasser on October 26, 1954 the Brotherhood was outlawed and its leaders imprisoned or executed. Many of the rank and file were jailed without trial.[61] By 1961 many of these men had completed their sentences or had been released as a result of amnesties, and the secret apparatus of the Brotherhood was reassembling. Money, it appears, was being supplied from branches of the Brotherhood in Syria, the Sudan, and other Arab countries. In August 1965 a new plot against Nasser was uncovered, and more than a thousand Brethren were arrested. Among the accused ringleaders was Sayyid Qutb, a prolific author often regarded as the theoretician and philosopher of the Brotherhood, who had called in his writings for the establishment of a truly Islamic society. The prob-

lems created by modernization, Qutb had written in 1962, were
the result of deviating from Islam. What was needed were not
more books, films, and lectures on Islam but the desire to take
Islam as charter and law.[62] He was accused of conspiring to seize
power in order to implement these ideas.

In late August 1966 sentences were passed upon the accused
plotters. Hodeiby, the former Supreme Guide of the Brotherhood, and other leaders released during earlier amnesties were
once more given prison terms ranging from three years to life.
Seven members of the so-called Sayyid Qutb group were condemned to death. The death sentences of three men were com-
muted by Nasser to life imprisonment; four men, including Qutb,
were executed on August 29, 1966.[63] By November 1967 the regime felt secure enough to release 1000 imprisoned Brethren,[64]
but members of the Brotherhood living abroad concede only the
loss of a battle and not of the war. Said Ramadan, director of the
Islamic Center in Geneva (Switzerland) and editor of a monthly
journal, al-Muslimun, told a correspondent of Die Weltwoche of
Zurich that the Brotherhood still had two million secret members
in Egypt. "Colonel Nasser is secularizing Egypt and thereby
opening the doors wide to atheism and Communism. He is perse-
cuting religion, killing our brothers." Eventually Nasser will fall.
"Tomorrow, the day after tomorrow whenever it pleases
God." [65]

Nasser has died, but unless the Muslim Brotherhood can regain
its influence in the armed forces it seems unlikely that they can
overthrow the government. Islam, even for westernized intellectuals, is part of the national heritage, and the ruling officers cher-
ish this heritage. Religious instruction is mandatory in all schools.
Radio and television schedule several daily readings from the
Koran and broadcast discussions of contemporary religious problems. A well-funded government agency, the Supreme Council
for Islamic Affairs, publishes and distributes a large number of
journals, pamphlets, and books which propagate a rejuvenated
Islam open to social change. The Muslim religion serves as the
basis for minimum agreement between the members of the political community, and it will continue to serve in this capacity until
a new and secular formula for legitimacy can evolve and find acceptance.[66] Meanwhile, a confusion of norms prevails. The task
of building a nation within the framework of Islam will be diffi-

cult for Muslims have never developed a realistic theory of the state. The original Muslim state under the so-called "Rightly guided Caliphs" cannot be resurrected nor would the system fit the Arab nation states of the twentieth century. During the thirteen hundred years of Islamic civilization there was loyalty to family and religious community, to profession or trade, but only rarely to the political unit of city or state.[67] A sense of citizenship never developed, and the emergence of a modern state today is handicapped by the suspicion with which any central authority has always been viewed. Even though the *fellah* is more truly Egyptian than many political leaders, "he is still not conscious of belonging to a nation." [68] These words of Father Ayrout were written in 1938, and change is slow in coming. The new political structures introduced by Nasser, such as the Arab Socialist Union or the village councils, a student of rural politics in Egypt concludes, "have generally failed to generate a strong commitment or a sense of loyalty among the rural peasants." [69]

The mobilization of mass support for the regime's goal of modernization and rapid social change as well as the search for a new source of legitimacy thus take place in an environment that is conducive to neither. The ruling officers are faced with a paradox: "the need to appeal to the 'Islamic Myth' of communal and cultural identity in order to work for the achievement of a new formula to supersede it." [70] Hence, the tie between modernization and legitimacy is cultivated as crucial for bridging the gap between reality and aspiration. A strong leader, endowed with charismatic qualities, becomes the focus of loyalty and inspires his followers with an enthusiastic picture of the nation's future. David Apter calls the fully developed form of such a system "mobilization regime." It relies on a "political religion" to bolster the legitimacy of the leadership. Such a regime, he says, "represents the new puritanism. Progress is its faith. Industrialization is its vision. Harmony is its goal." [71]

The disruption of traditional patterns at a time when no new integrating force has yet emerged can be hazardous. The resolution of rival and divergent views of the world is unlikely to be accomplished on the theoretical level, and the adaptation of Islam to modernity will continue to defy consistency and philosophical neatness. A new kind of Islam, radically different from anything history has known so far, will probably be defined by practice and in the heat of action. It would be presumptuous to maintain that such a religion should no longer be called Islamic. "Throughout its history," notes John S. Badeau, "Islam has been in constant interplay with the processes of society and the result has been a working compromise between Muslim and non-Muslim elements that reflects the conditions of each era. To say that Islam is changing its role today is not necessarily to say that it is on the verge of disappearing—only that once more compromise is taking place, the final form of which cannot yet be determined." [72]

CHAPTER 19

The Sinhalese Buddhist Revolution of Ceylon

HISTORICAL SETTING

Buddhism came to Ceylon in the mid-third century before the Christian era. It was said to have been introduced by Mahinda, the son of the Indian Buddhist emperor, Asoka, though the conversion of the Sinhalese people populating the island probably was a gradual process. Until the downfall of its last independent monarch in 1815, Buddhism was the state religion in Ceylon. Only a Buddhist could be ruler, and the king was not only head of state but head of the religious establishment. He made key appointments in the Sangha, he supervised the lay trustees of temple property, and he was custodian of the two national shrines where the bowl and tooth relics of the Buddha were the object of veneration. The king functioned as defender of the faith by maintaining the purity of the order through disciplinary action against derelict monks and by suppressing heresy. The intervention of the king in doctrinal quarrels sometimes created friction between crown and Sangha, but by and large relations between church and state were smooth.

The kings of Ceylon built temples and dedicated land to the Sangha in part for spiritual reasons—to attain merit. But as an historian of early Buddhism notes, "the major results were reaped immediately—in this world. The monasteries formed the centres of national culture, and bhikkhus were the teachers of the whole nation—from prince to peasant. They helped the king to rule the country in peace." [1] The king and the Buddhist hierarchy both benefited from their close association. The Sangha gained affluence and prestige, the monarchy a powerful supporter who had great influence with the people and who promoted political stability and discouraged innovations. The chronicles tell of monks serving as court advisors; they also tell of kings who claimed to be *bodhisattvas*, beings destined to become Buddhas, and of *bhikkhus* who sanctified kings on ceremonial occasions. In the absence of a clear tradition of hereditary kingship the concept of the sanctity of the person of the monarch helped establish legitimacy. Buddhism, fortified by brahmanic elements, thus played a key role in supporting the established political and social order.[2]

The Buddhist religion was of importance also in the emergence of Sinhalese nationalism. In fighting Indian invaders, who were Hindus, the king Duttha-Gamini (161–137 B.C.) rallied his troops with the war cry "Not for kingdom, but for Buddhism," and the monks accompanying his army celebrated this victory as bringing glory to the doctrine of the Buddha. When the king expressed regret over the large number of enemy soldiers killed, the monks are reported to have comforted him with the argument that the killed were "unbelievers and men of evil life . . . not more to be esteemed than beasts."[3] The chronicle relating these events was written by priests, and it tells the history of Ceylon as the history of a Buddhist people. The tie between the Buddhist religion and the Sinhalese national consciousness thus established has continued to this day.[4]

Though Buddhism usually supported the absolutist claims of the monarch and legitimized the rule of many a despot, at times it also encouraged rebellion against kings who were felt to rule tyrannically and in violation of the Buddhist precepts of mercy and mildness. Popular uprisings availed themselves of Buddhist ideas to express their social aspirations, and even the Sangha occasionally lent its support to attempts to dethrone "unrighteous kings."[5]

During Ceylon's colonial era monks are known to have participated in national uprisings. The Portuguese, in particular, who ruled sections of the island from 1505 to 1658, thoroughly alienated the Sangha by confiscating land belonging to the temples and by relentless proselytizing. During the Dutch occupation, which lasted until the arrival of the British in 1796, Buddhist public worship was forbidden, and even in the Kandyan Kingdom, the mountainous center region of Ceylon that was able to maintain its formal independence until 1815, the Sangha suffered from the turmoil brought on by a series of wars with the British. The Convention of 1815, which ended Sinhalese sovereignty in Ceylon, declared Buddhism inviolable and promised the maintenance and protection of its rites, priests, and places of worship.[6] But the patronage of the Christian government could not substitute for that of a Buddhist king, and the monks were active in organizing the "Great Rebellion" of 1817–18.

The dissatisfaction of the Sangha with British rule grew as a result of the favored position of Protestant Christians and the adoption of English as the language of administration, a measure which removed the Sinhalese-speaking monks from their traditional and esteemed position as teachers. As a result of pressure exerted by Christian missionaries and their influential friends in England the colonial administration gradually disengaged itself from its role as the patron of Buddhism, and this separation between church and state further weakened the Sangha, its property, and its status in the life of the country. The priests were without power to compel the performance of services owed them by temple tenants just as they could not enforce the disrobing of monks for offences against the rules of the Sangha. The Buddhist Temporalities Act of 1889 established a system of elected lay trustees to manage the property of the temples, but the provisions of the ordinance were often disregarded, and instances of corruption and misappropriation of funds were frequent.[7] Small wonder that to this day the Buddhists of Ceylon regard the colonial era as a period of deprivation during which Buddhism suffered and the Sangha deteriorated. The roots of the political involvement of the monks, and their role as exponents of nationalism, can be found here. There were influential monks in the Sangha who were no longer content to be part of a mere meditative order; they set themselves the goal of regaining that position of influence and prestige which the order had held during earlier centuries and to which they felt entitled as custodians of the country's majority religion.

THE EMERGENCE OF BUDDHIST MODERNISM

Ceylonese Buddhism, handicapped by the colonial government's policy and under attack by foreign missionaries, entered a period of renaissance during the last three decades of the nineteenth century. In large measure this revival was the result of Western interest in Buddhism, particularly on the part of Theosophists like the American Colonel H. S. Olcott and the English Annie Besant. While in Ceylon, Olcott organized Buddhist lay organizations and schools, and his work was ably continued by Anagarika Dharmapala, the son of a wealthy Sinhalese, who founded the Maha Bodhi Society. Ceylon celebrates him "as a great patriot and nationalist, a devoted Buddhist and religious leader." [8] Dharmapala not only crusaded for cultural emancipation and formulated a clear link between Buddhism and nationalism, he also was one of the first Buddhist intellectuals to stress the need for social reform. In an open letter of 1899 addressed to India, but of equal importance to Ceylon, Dharmapala wrote:

> Open your eyes and see, listen to the cries of distress of the 141 millions of people, and let their tears cool your dry hearts. Don't imagine that "Providence" will take care of you: for the "Almighty" does not calculate time by your watches. "A thousand years is one hour" for him, and it is foolish for you to wait with folded hands. Wake up, my brothers, for life in this world is short. Give up your dreamy philosophies and sensualizing ceremonies. Millions are daily suffering the pangs of hunger; drinking the water that animals in the forest would not drink, sleeping and living in houses, inhaling poison day after day. There is wealth in India enough to feed all. But the abominations of caste, creed and sect are making the millions suffer.[9]

Dharmapala himself opposed political activity by monks, but this view was not shared by all Buddhists. In the late 1930's we encounter what appears to have been the first political organization of monks, the Samasta Lanka Bhiksu Sammelanaya or All-Ceylon Monks' Congress. Like subsequent *bhikkhu* organizations, this association was composed primarily of young monks, many of them connected with the *pirivena* (training college for monks) of Kelaniya and other temples of the western low-country. Most of the monasteries of this region, which was the first region to be colonized and which therefore was more westernized, belong to the Amarapura and Ramanya sects of the Ceylonese Sangha. These two sects together comprise about 35 per cent of the 15,-000 to 18,000 monks on the island; founded in the nineteenth century in protest against the caste-consciousness of the majority Siamese sect, which restricts membership to the "cultivating caste," these sects are relatively poor.[10] Leading figures of the Siamese powerful high-caste sect, centered in the up-country of Kandy and traditionally more conservative, strongly opposed the political involvement of the low-country monks from the start without, however, being able to prevent the phenomenon. Many of the younger monks in the Siamese sect, too, shared, and have continued to show sympathy with, the reformist outlook. Membership in a *Nikaya* (sect) no more determines the political outlook of its members than it indicates a doctrinal distinctiveness. The split of the Sangha into three sects is primarily a caste phenomenon drawing strength from the caste distinctions and discriminations practiced by the local community in which the temples of a sect or sub-sect are located.

The political activity of the monks was publicized by the so-called "Declaration of the Vidyalankara Pirivena," issued on February 13, 1946 and entitled "Monks and Politics." It was drafted by the head of Vidyalankara Pirivena at Kelaniya, Yakkaduve Sri Pragnarama Thero, a monk whose great scholarly ability was matched by his political acumen. The declaration, issued in the name of the entire faculty, called upon the Sangha to work for the social and political progress of the people. The history of Ceylon, it said, demonstrated the close link between the well-being of Buddhism and the fate of the country. Political action on the part of the monks, therefore, was to be welcomed.[11]

The declaration created an uproar and drew spirited attack as well as defense. The expression "political *bhikkhu*" began to gain currency. Several "political monks," among them the scholarly Walpola Rahula, went so far as to identify themselves with the Marxist parties, calling the older high priests who opposed their work for the welfare of the oppressed classes "tools of the capitalists."[12] The political involvement of these monks reached its first peak on January 6, 1947 with the publication of the "Kelaniya Declaration of Independence." This statement called for an end to Ceylon's dominion status and demanded complete national independence as the historic right of the Sinhalese nation. Following the issuance of the manifesto the activity of the political monks lessened somewhat. Few Buddhist laymen approved of the monks' agitation; independence came to Ceylon on February 3, 1948 without the turmoil that had preceded the attainment of political sovereignty in India and it was the achievement of a relatively secular national movement led by Western-educated Ceylonese of various religious affiliations. During the first years of independence the religious issue seemed dormant.

Still, the intellectual re-evaluation of Ceylon's Buddhist heritage continued. Ceylon, now politically emancipated, sought a tradition on which it could build a national culture and this sense of national distinctiveness was identified with a rejuvenated Buddhism. In 1943 an astute Christian missionary noted the emergence of a new kind of Buddhism which emphasized the here-and-now of this world rather than the spirit of abnegation, which sought to find a positive meaning in human existence and encouraged Buddhists to obtain rather than to renounce.[13] This new activist Buddhism found its most systematic expression in a book entitled *The Revolt in the Temple*, published in 1953, which for many years continued to have a significant impact on the thinking of Ceylon's Buddhist intellectuals.[14]

Buddhism, the author argued, had deteriorated under the influence of Hinduism. Its doctrine "which had been designed to be a way of living the good life soon became a religion full of rituals, cults and superstitious beliefs and practices." [15] To be true to the intent of its founder "Buddhism ought to mean, not the building of temples for the housing of images of the Buddha, but leading a life in accordance with the principles of His teachings." [16] The Buddha's message aimed at the perfection of man so that he could lead a happy life in this world. "It is not, as in the case of some other religions, to prepare him to meet his Maker in another world." [17] The pursuit of *nibbana* did not involve escapism and retreat from the conflicts of life. "Far from teaching quietism, the Buddha's discourses, parables, and aphorisms abound in exhortations to indefatigable and energetic activity." [18] *Nibbana* meant mental tranquility stemming from nonattachment to wealth, fame, and social position. It was achieved not as a result of self-abnegation but as a consequence "of a power to live 'more abundantly' because all the powers of human nature have been made free to go into discernment." [19]

The Revolt in the Temple accused the Sangha of subverting the teachings of the Buddha through their selfishness. Over the centuries the monks had been taught to seek their own personal salvation through self-control and meditation. They had failed to fulfill "the equally important duty of teaching and helping others." [20] The Ceylonese Sangha had deteriorated because of the monks' "self-interest, greed and ignorance." [21] The order should be reformed so that "theirs will not be a selfish existence, pursuing their own salvation, whilst living on the charity of others, but an existence full of service and self-sacrifice." [22] The monks should be trained in some form of social service so that they could act, as in olden times, as "religious as well as social guides of the Sinhalese." [23]

For more than four centuries, the author complained, alien rule had repressed the Sinhalese and thwarted their national aspirations. But with Buddhism as an ideology the nation could be rebuilt and inspired to action. Religion and the state were to cooperate in order "to make the subject better spiritually and morally, in addition to making him happier materially." [24] They should implement the task which the Buddha had left to his followers, to wit "to create on earth a polity ordered in accordance with his teaching; a polity based, that is, on the infinite duty of each to himself and to his fellow-men." [25]

The Revolt in the Temple was none too specific in spelling out the concrete meaning of a Buddhist polity. Buddhism, the author insisted, was again to be the state religion. Arguing that nearly three-fourths of the population of Ceylon were Buddhists, he saw nothing objectionable in such a proposal. The idea of granting the Tamil minority, who were concentrated on the northern and eastern coasts of the island and who spoke their own language and professed the Hindu religion, autonomy within the framework of a federal system was rejected as impractical on a small island constituting a single geographical unit. Ceylon was to be "a state which should be Sinhalese, reared up by Sinhalese hands, and breathing a Sinhalese atmosphere in the land of Sinhalese tradition." [26] The standards of education, the arts, music, and literature should be raised so as to develop the nation's intellectual and religious qualities. Sharing the anticapitalistic sentiments of many Ceylonese nationalists, who associated capitalism with foreign capital and British-controlled enterprises that were blamed for the exploitation and poverty of the masses, the author of *The Revolt in the Temple* advocated a system of democratic socialism with public ownership of the means of production. Soviet style communism or any other appeals to violence were rejected. "The fundamental doctrine of the Buddha is the sacredness of all life." [27] National freedom and social uplift should and could be achieved by way of a new type of peaceful revolution, the instrument of which was universal suffrage.

The Revolt in the Temple was an attempt to adapt the Buddhist heritage to the tasks and requirements of social reform. The scriptures were not altered, and no new doctrines were added. The author, like intellectuals in developing countries of other religious traditions, merely stressed those elements in the religion's teaching that appeared most suitable for his objective of developing a spirit of nationalism and social reconstruction. Doctrinal aspects deemed irrelevant to this aim were relegated to the background. The traditional distinction was weakened between the monk, on the one hand, who withdraws from involvement with this world and pursues *nibbana,* and the Buddhist layman, on the other, who has no real hope of attaining *nibbana* and concentrates on good deeds in his lifetime hoping for rebirth on a higher level in the future. Both Sangha and laymen were to concentrate on the here-and-now and to be less concerned with either *nibbana* or the round of rebirths. The monk was expected to function as a kind of social worker, a way of life more similar to that of the secular clergy of Christianity than to the contemplative ideal of monasticism.

To be sure, the practice of Theravada Buddhism had never been entirely other-worldly, and Ceylonese monarchs, following the social ethos laid down by the pious Asoka, had always had a commitment to the welfare of their subjects. They had built not only monasteries but also elaborate irrigation works to ensure economic conditions that would enable both monks and laymen to pursue the Eightfold or Middle Path leading to the attainment of *nibbana.* By thus contributing to the material well-being of their people they had thought to acquire merit, for the dams, tanks, and canals created a social order in which every subject could spend at least some part of his life, no matter how short, in meditation.[28] Buddhist modernists, who argued that a filled stomach was the precondition of observing moral precepts, thus were not really such innovators. Similarly, the insistence on an active life can be supported by traditional Buddhist ethics. "All through the Buddha's teaching," notes a Burmese Buddhist scholar, "repeated stress is laid on self-reliance and resolution. Buddhism makes man stand on his own feet, it arouses his self-confidence and energy. The Buddha again and again reminded his followers that there is no one, either in heaven or on earth, who can help them or free them from the result of their past evil deeds." [29] The doctrine of *kamma*, it is true, emphasizes personal morality and concern with one's own destiny rather than with that of society at large, but the Buddhist spirit of self-reliance can undoubtedly be enlisted for the cultivation of social ethics and public service as well. The attack of modernism upon ritual and magic can facilitate the more rational facing of the strains and problems of life and encourage social reform.

This kind of reinterpretation of doctrine at times leads to inconsistencies and wishful thinking. *The Revolt in the Temple* in one chapter argues that the suffering of the people is due to bad social conditions, but in another chapter the author accepts the principle of *kamma* according to which human life is what it is due to man's actions in earlier existences. In an attempt to link Buddhism and democracy Buddha is called "a staunch democrat," [30] an instance of the loose use of terminology at best.

More programmatic in nature is another document of Buddhist modernism and Sinhalese nationalism, the 1956 report of a committee of inquiry set up by the All-Ceylon Buddhist Congress, entitled *The Betrayal of Buddhism*.[31] In 1951 the Buddhist Congress, essentially a lay organization, had requested the government to appoint a commission that would inquire into the condition of Buddhism. When Prime Minister D. S. Senanayake, a Western-educated and secularly oriented man, turned down the request, the Buddhist Congress set up its own committee composed of seven highly placed elders of the Sangha and seven laymen, one of the latter being D. C. Wijewardene, the author of *The Revolt in the Temple*. The "Buddhist Commission," as it came to be known popularly, traveled the length and breadth of the island holding hearings and taking testimony from hundreds of monks and laymen. The final report was submitted to the Buddhist Congress in February 1956, just before the election of 1956 upon which it had considerable impact.

Ceylon, the report noted, had achieved political independence, but the fate of Buddhism had not improved. The Christian churches were still rich and powerful; they controlled the press and public opinion, and unless checked, "the conquest of Ceylon by these religious bodies will soon be an accomplished fact." [32]

Christian dominance, the report complained, was especially pronounced in education. The Commission, therefore, recommended that, by January 1, 1958, all state-aided denominational schools, the majority of which were run by Christian bodies, be taken over by the state. Religious education would be compulsory in all schools.

The Buddhist Commission was bitter about the failure of the country's government, dominated by a Western-educated elite, to provide adequate support for Buddhism and to live up to its teachings. "The leaders of our country have forsaken those Buddhist ideals which for centuries were the keystone of the country's greatness, and have embraced a shallow and ephemeral materialism." [33] Ceylon was suffering from an extremely high crime rate precisely because these materialistic values had displaced the Buddha Dhamma (Doctrine of the Buddha). The report recommended that the importation and publication of obscene books, magazines, and films be prohibited, that the production and sale of intoxicants be outlawed, and that racing be banned by January 1, 1957. The well-to-do should curtail their extravagant style of living so as to make money available for capital investment and raise the country's scandalously low standard of living. "It is futile to preach mental liberation to a starving man; the first necessity is to see that he is fed." [34]

The Commission took note of the fact that Ceylon had a government and legislature in which true Buddhists were by no means the decisive element, and it, therefore, did not demand that Buddhism be treated as an established church. A secular government, they said, could and should not maintain the purity and strength of Buddhism. Hence the report recommended that the functions of the Sinhalese monarch and the prerogatives assumed by the British Crown in 1815 be vested in a Buddha Sasana Council (freely translated "Council of the Buddhist Religion," a supreme body to govern the church that was no church). After the government had passed legislation establishing this council, to consist of representatives of the Sangha and laity, and after taking "other steps necessary to rehabilitate the Buddhist religion, it must in our view sever all connections with Buddhism." [35]

The Betrayal of Buddhism included many additional recommendations such as that Ceylon become a republic. Like *The Revolt in the Temple*, the report of the Buddhist Commission was

characterized by a markedly modernistic and nationalistic interpretation of the Buddha's gospel. The tribulations of Buddhism
were attributed not to bad *kamma*, to punishment for the mis-
deeds of the Ceylonese in earlier lives, but to the betrayal of Buddhism by the British as well as by the secular native elite who
had governed the country since independence. Since it was the
result of certain restrictive policies, the decline of Buddhism
could be halted and reversed by other policies. Again, instead of
stressing the vanity of worldly life and suggesting withdrawal
from it, the report recommended concerted action to transform
the country's political, economic, and social systems.

Some elements of the Sangha were not entirely happy over the
recommendations for Sasana reform, but by and large the report
had a tremendous audience. "Its importance," noted one historian
at the time of the report's publication, "lies not so much in the
correctness of the diagnosis, the remedies suggested or the methods proposed for the restoration of Buddhism, as in the fact that
it has appealed to the sentiments of a large section of the Buddhists and captured their imagination." [36] The recommendations of
the Buddhist Commission put forward a program of action which
in the election of 1956 was largely adopted by the opposition and
which helped carry it to an overwhelming victory. *The Betrayal
of Buddhism* in effect became one of the main ideological supports for the Sinhalese Revolution that began in April 1956.

THE REVOLUTION OF 1956–59

S.W.R.D. Bandaranaike, the leader of the victorious coalition in
the General Election of April 1956, later called the elections to
Ceylon's Third Parliament a "peaceful revolution." It overthrew,
he said, a social system which under the guise of freedom had
continued colonialism.[37] Scholarly observers of the Ceylonese
scene tend to agree with the late prime minister. According to
W. Howard Wriggins, the General Election of 1956 "resulted in
a marked transfer of political power from one segment of the
population to another." [38] Donald E. Smith speaks of the "Sinhalese Buddhist Revolution," a "social revolution" ushered in by
the "dramatic revolution at the polls in 1956." [39]

The first two general elections following independence had resulted in the victory of the United National party (UNP) led by

westernized politicians who had a largely secular outlook and who had played an important role in the achievement of independence. The UNP stood for religious freedom but otherwise largely ignored the religious issue. Buddhist elements increasingly came to feel that their special grievances were being ignored, and these interests found an eloquent spokesman in S.W.R.D. Bandaranaike, the founder and leader of the Sri Lanka Freedom party * (SLFP). Bandaranaike was a member of a prominent Christian Sinhalese family; he had studied in England and there had become a Buddhist. Soon after his return to Ceylon in the early 1930's the young Bandaranaike joined the independence movement, though for ideological as well as for reasons of family rivalry he built his own organization within the Ceylon National Congress and the UNP succeeding it in 1945; this was the Sinhala Maha Sabha (Great Sinhalese Assembly).[40] Dissatisfied with the leadership and the policies of D. S. Senanayake, the country's first prime minister, in 1951 Bandaranaike and his followers left the UNP and founded the SLFP. On February 21, 1956, a few days after the dissolution of Parliament, the SLFP entered into an alliance with the VLSSP, the more extreme of Ceylon's two Trotskyite parties, and two smaller opposition groups. This coalition assumed the name Mahajana Eksath Peramuna (MEP)— People's United Front. Helped by a no-contest agreement with the other parties of the Left, the MEP in April 1956 swept to an overwhelming victory capturing 48 of the 56 seats previously held by the UNP in the House of Representatives.

The smashing victory of the MEP was due to a number of factors. The UNP government, plagued by several petty scandals, seemed to project a tired, irresolute image. The price of food, especially rice, had been allowed to rise sharply, and unemployment was spreading. The MEP's demand for the nationalization of foreign-owned estates and Bandaranaike's own rather vague socialism therefore had their appeal.[41] One of the most important issues hurting the party in power was that of national culture, especially the question of language. Strong communal and religious feelings here combined to give the MEP a decisive political advantage.

Ceylon had always been a pluralistic society, divided along re-

* Sri Lanka is the Sinhalese name for Ceylon.

ligious and ethnic lines. About 65 per cent of the population are
Buddhists, almost all of them of Sinhalese background; a little
over 20 per cent are Hindus, most of them Tamils ethnically, and
their language is that of South India, a fact never forgotten by
the Ceylonese apprehensive about their big neighbor to the north.
But it was only fairly recently that communal self-consciousness
had developed to the point of becoming a political issue. As late
as 1950, an astute observer like Sir W. I. Jennings thought that
the struggle of the nationalists for the use of the native languages
was a losing battle and that English, the language of government,
which was understood by less than 10 per cent of the Ceylonese,
would triumph.[42] This expectation was soon proved wrong. The
achievement of independence brought in its wake a revival of native culture; in their search for an idiom different from that of
the West the people of Ceylon found no common tradition, only
distinct Sinhalese and Tamil traditions.[43]

From the demand for the use of the vernacular tongues and the
exclusion of English it was a small step to communal rivalry.
"Powerful group loyalties in a pluralistic society, functioning in
the context of an economy of scarcity," notes Donald E. Smith,
"lead almost inevitably to inter-group rivalry and conflict." [44]
The Sinhalese who were in the majority, competing with the
Tamils for scarce jobs in the civil service and in other fields of
employment where education was important, developed an increasing race awareness, while economic distress fed communal
resentments. The Sinhalese demanded that their language be
given a preferred place, and by 1955 the cry "Sinhala Only" had
become a political slogan that seemed irresistible. The Buddhist
monks, in particular, supported the idea of Sinhalese as the official language of the country. Sinhalese is the lineal descendant of
Pali, the language of Buddhism, and the *bhikkhus*, expecting a
gain for the religious culture, consequently took a prominent role
in the "Sinhala Only" movement, speaking at mass meetings all
over the country. Realizing the strength of the movement, the
main competing forces in the 1956 election subscribed to the demand to adopt Sinhalese as the sole official language, but once the
communal issue had been injected into the political sphere Bandaranaike's MEP quickly gained a lead. The UNP, led by En-
glish-speaking intellectuals, could not match the nationalistic
ardor of the MEP, whose electioneering made extensive use of
traditional allegories and religious allusions. Most of the UNP

candidates, a pro-MEP journal charged during the election campaign, don't know a word of Sinhalese. "They are experts at ballroom dancing and practiced in cocktail parties; they don't care a dime for religion or morals." [45]

The MEP further benefited from the religious enthusiasm generated by the approaching celebration of Buddha Jayanti in 1956–57, the year marking the 2500th anniversary of the death of the Buddha and considered the apogee of Buddhism. The government's preparations for this event, to begin in May 1956, had been underway since 1954, and this contributed to the sense of a Buddhist revival. The flattering attention paid the Sangha and devout Buddhist laymen encouraged in these two groups an awareness of their political importance. "As they grew in political consciousness," writes Wriggins, "they articulated more precisely a sense of their own difficulties and grievances." [46] *The Betrayal of Buddhism*, the report of the Buddhist Commission, as we have noted earlier, was completed at this time, it was rushed into print to be available as an election issue, and the Sinhalese edition found its way into every Buddhist temple. Several thousand monks walked from door to door reading excerpts from the report and denouncing the UNP. For the first time in the modern history of Ceylon the Sangha assumed a decisive political role.

The MEP made its most extensive gains in the rural areas, where more than 70 per cent of Ceylon's population live. This was the section of the country most susceptible to the influence of the vernacular-educated lower middle class who felt threatened by modernization—the local official, the Sinhalese school teacher, the practitioner of *ayurvedic* (traditional) medicine and the village monk. The latter, in particular, played an important role in the rural social structure. Village Buddhism is far from pure; it is intertwined with animism, and the typical villager believes in numerous gods, demons, and ghosts. Still, the Buddhist monk is a highly esteemed figure. The island has more than 5000 temples and 15,000 to 18,000 monks. With the exception of a few big establishments in Kandy and Colombo, most monasteries have but a few monks who take charge of a temple and administer to the spiritual needs of the people. The local priest often also functions as an adviser on domestic affairs and a teacher, and his influence with the villagers is considerable.[47] As the election of 1956 approached the Sangha became increasingly politicized.

In the elections of 1947 and 1952 the Buddhist monks had been

divided, defending as well as attacking the UNP-run government.[48] In the election of 1956, on the other hand, political
monks were a well-knit pressure group, and they had a crucial
part in the MEP victory. The organization of the monks, largely
dormant since the first brief flurry of activity in 1946–47, had
been revitalized by the preparations for the Buddha Jayanti celebrations. As early as 1953, Buddhist laymen had become active in
organizing *bhikkhu* associations (*Sangha Sabhas*) most of whom
soon combined into one congress, the Sri Lanka Maha Sangha
Sabha (Ceylonese People's Monks' Association). At first this organization's main task was the nonpolitical one of Buddhist renewal,
preparing local Buddha Jayanti celebrations, but it was soon
drawn into politics, especially in connection with the work of the
Buddhist Commission.[49] As already indicated, concern for the
welfare of Buddhism necessarily focused attention upon the deteriorated position of the Sangha. Donald E. Smith sums up the
reasons for the profound feeling of alienation that was building
up in the order:

> From a place of honor under the Sinhalese kings the monks had
> become an anachronism in the modern westernized society devel-
> oping around them. Their traditional educational functions had
> been usurped by government and missionary schools, and their ig-
> norance of the English language kept them from effective commu-
> nication with those who wielded power. To the monks, the idea of
> radical political change had a powerful appeal.[50]

Another organization of political monks reappearing at this
time was the All-Ceylon Congress of *Bhikkhu* Societies which
had formed around 1940 making its first appearance before the
public in 1946. By now the Monks' Congress, as many called it,
had largely abandoned its pro-Marxist leanings and had assumed a
radical nationalistic stance. The joint secretaries were two monks,
Talpawila Seelawansa Thero and Mapitigama Buddharakkhita,
long-time members of Bandaranaike's SLFP and frequent speakers
at meetings of the "Sinhala Only" movement. The report of the
Buddhist Commission was released on February 4, 1956. A few
days later representatives of these two groups of political monks
met in Colombo to form an alliance, taking the name Eksath
Bhikkhu Peramuna (EBP)—United Monks' Front.[51] The new
organization was supposed to have over 75 regional units. It

claimed a membership of 12,000 monks, most of them belonging to the Amarapura and Ramanya sects.[52]

After the dissolution of Parliament on February 18, the EBP at first protested the timing of the election arguing that it would disturb the spiritual atmosphere being generated in the country by the preparations for the Buddha Jayanti celebrations. Groups of monks staged fasts and satyagraha (nonviolent direct action) demonstrations in various parts of the country. On February 25 about 250 monks fasted on the steps of the House of Representatives in Colombo and then marched in protest through parts of the city.[53] But the EBP soon abandoned this negative position and began to campaign forcefully for the MEP. In view of the disservice the UNP was doing to the religion of the country by holding the election during the period of the Jayanti, a monk declared at a meeting in Kandy, Buddhist monks had no alternative but to see that the UNP was defeated and that a party genuinely devoted to the cause of Buddhism was voted into power.[54]

On March 3 the EBP held a mass meeting attended by over 3000 monks from all parts of the island at which it announced a program of Ten Basic Principles. These included a call for the implementation of the Buddhist Commission report, the promotion of the national arts, crafts, and *ayurvedic* medicine, the granting of complete freedom of religion but with Buddhism placed "in a position due . . . it as the religion of the majority." With equal vagueness the program called for a fairer distribution of wealth, a program of action to protect the country against fascism and communism and "to remove the anti-democratic acts and institutions of the U.N.P. government." The principle of nonviolence was to govern all actions.[55] The leaders of the MEP were present at this gathering and, kneeling before the assembled monks, accepted the Ten Basic Principles on behalf of their party. "The meeting," comments Smith, "dramatized the fact that here was a political party which respected traditional Buddhist ways, which showed proper deference to the Sangha and was desirous of following its guidance." [56]

The campaign of the EBP stressed three issues. First, the monks popularized the arguments of the report of the Buddhist Commission, especially those directed against the Catholic church. The UNP government, they charged, had appointed Christians to key offices, Christian schools received more aid than Buddhist *piriv-*

enas, church property was left untaxed with precious revenue being lost which could have been used to lower the price of rice. Second, the leaders of the UNP, it was alleged, were ignorant of Ceylon's history and Buddhism. Their concern for Buddhism was mere pretense, for political reasons, and in reality the party served as a front for the Catholic church, the most powerful political body in Ceylon. Sir John Kotelawala, the leader of the UNP and prime minister, was attacked as a playboy who undermined the honor of the country by importing half-nude foreign women. Chapters of his memoirs, published just before the start of the campaign, were read by priests at evening temple services to prove that he was unfit to be the ruler of Buddhist Ceylon. Third, the EBP charged the party in power with selling the country to the Americans. In return for American aid the UNP would allow the Americans to establish a Christian dictatorship as they had done in South Korea and South Vietnam.[57] The regional monks' associations labored hard to carry these arguments into every Buddhist household. Monks, clad in their yellow robes, attended or spoke at election meetings, published and distributed campaign literature, and read excerpts from the Buddhist Commission report.

A key organizer of the EBP campaign was the chief priest of the temple at Kelaniya, Mapitigama Buddharakkhita, one of the three secretaries of the United Monks' Front. Buddharakkhita, then thirty-five years old, proved himself an indefatigable campaigner and speaker. He owned a chauffeur-driven car, and he was able to draw on the considerable wealth of the Kelaniya temple, an important shrine in the Sinhalese Buddhist tradition: he later claimed to have spent the equivalent of about $21,000 on the EBP campaign.[58] In view of Buddharakkhita's rather unprincipled way of life, to which we will have occasion to return, and his obvious political ambitions, some writers have tended to characterize all the political monks as a group primarily motivated by a desire for power. This view, while probably largely correct in the case of leaders like Buddharakkhita, fails to do justice to the ideology of the monks' movement. Whereas all the monks sought a return to the elevated status of the Sangha that had prevailed in earlier centuries, many of them at the same time undoubtedly joined and remained members of the monks' associations making up the EBP for strictly religious reasons, and especially the spiritual renewal of Buddhism. The search for a greater political voice for the Sangha and the religious sentiment underlying Buddhist modernism went hand in hand and cannot easily be separated one from the other.

The EBP drew its support primarily from the ranks of the younger monks. Bandaranaike, the leader of the MEP, claimed during the campaign that 12,000 *bhikkhus* actively supported him and his coalition, but estimates made after the election put that figure nearer to 3000, i.e. about 15 to 20 per cent of the Sangha.[59] Several important figures in the Sangha supported the UNP, defending the party in power from the charge of hostility to Buddhism. They pointed out that the government had spent large sums of money for the forthcoming Buddha Jayanti celebrations, and they accused the EBP of misleading the people. The prime minister himself reacted with considerable bitterness to the sharp attacks upon him. "I am a Buddhist and my forefathers were Buddhists," Kotelawala told a rally three weeks before the election. "I shall protect the Sasana as long as I live, but in the interests of this same Sasana political bhikkhus must be brought to book." Many of the monks working against the government, he maintained, were not ordained *bhikkhus* but "convicted criminals shielding under the yellow robe." [60]

Yet these counterattacks largely failed. For one thing, it was obviously unfair to attack as political monks those *bhikkhus* who opposed the UNP and to welcome the support of other *bhikkhus*. Toward the close of the campaign the prime minister was able to persuade the heads (*Mahanayake Theros*) of the Malwatte and Asgiriya chapters of the Siamese sect in Kandy, considered the highest Ceylonese Buddhist dignitaries, to issue a statement asking for political neutrality of the monks. The political involvement of the *bhikkhus*, these two conservative figures declared, increased the disunity of the Sangha and lowered its prestige. "Therefore we request all the monks in our sects to abstain from any political campaigning or aligning themselves with any party and adopt a neutral attitude." [61] Two days later this call for the neutrality of the Sangha was joined by the acting head of the Ramanya sect and by the principals of the most important *pirivenas*.[62] Still, large numbers of rank and file monks disregarded these exhortations of their spiritual superiors and continued to work for the victory of the MEP.

The elections to Ceylon's Third Parliament took place on April 5–7, 1956. When the votes had been counted it became apparent that Ceylon had undergone a fundamental political upheaval. The UNP, which had governed the country since independence, was decisively defeated. In 1952 Bandaranaike's SLFP had obtained 9 seats and the UNP 54. In 1956 the UNP won only 8 seats and Bandaranaike's coalition 51 seats. A new political force had emerged, the vernacular-educated middle class in the forefront of the ongoing cultural and religious revival, and careful wooing of these heretofore underprivileged social groups had carried the MEP to victory. "The U.N.P.," writes a well-informed student of Ceylonese politics, "under-estimated the strength of the Buddhist demands and failed to keep the support of the active Buddhist Clergy. It failed to assess the economic forces behind the language movement and the cultural revival. . . . Like many western observers, the U.N.P. failed to realise that the Independence movement was only a precursor to the national movement and not the movement itself. The latter began where the former left off. One major cause of the U.N.P. defeat can be attributed to its inability and failure to give leadership to this movement." [63]

Before the new Parliament convened Bandaranaike, his cabinet, and his supporters in Parliament visited the shrine at Kelaniya. In a ceremony organized by the EBP, the prime minister and his cabinet received the blessings of the Sangha. Buddharakkhita, in an address, expressed his satisfaction that the new government, after four and one-half centuries of darkness, was again acting in a manner in keeping with the national culture. The recommendations of *The Revolt in the Temple* should be followed, for they represented the thinking of the progressive monks. The son of the author presented a copy of this book to each of the assembled MEP legislators, and he expressed his satisfaction that *The Revolt in the Temple* had effected a "Revolt in the Country." Bandaranaike thanked the Sangha for helping to put the MEP government in power: their support, he said, had been "the principal factor" behind his victory. Another monk declared that the new government would have to do what the people wished "otherwise the fate of the UNP would overtake it." Not leaving any room for ambiguity, one of the joint secretaries of the EBP noted that whereas the *bhikkhus* "would not forcibly influence the affairs of the State," the administration should seek the advice of the

Sangha.[64] The political monks thus served notice that they expected to be listened to and that they would use their political influence, demonstrated during the election, to make the government adhere to their program.

Following a request of the EBP,[65] all members of the new party in power appeared at the opening of Parliament clad in Sinhalese national dress. Traditional Sinhalese music was played instead of a Western fanfare. But Bandaranaike also used the opportunity to make it clear that he was not an extremist in communal matters. The speech from the throne, delivered by the governor-general, reassured the religious and social minorities, promising to carry out the government's program without injustice and discrimination. "My Government will ensure to all citizens the rights, privileges and freedoms to which they are entitled in a democratic State." [66] The stage was thus set for a tug of war between the new prime minister and his extremist backers that was to last for the duration of Bandaranaike's rule.

The MEP election manifesto had contained a pledge to make Sinhalese the sole official language of the country. A little stressed and hardly noticed proviso had added: "This will not involve the suppression of such a minority language as Tamil whose reasonable use will receive due recognition." [67] The draft bill prepared by a subcommittee of the parliamentary party contained several clauses designed to implement both of these promises, but pressure emanating from the political monks and other communal extremists forced a change. Threatening statements issued by the EBP and a rally of monks on the steps of Parliament made the drafting committee eliminate the concessions made to the Tamil minority. The bill as finally reported out and voted into law, though making Sinhalese the official language, gave the government discretionary authority to postpone the implementation of the Language Act until December 31, 1960. By that time, it was hoped, communal passions inflamed by the electoral campaign would have subsided.[68]

Events were to take a somewhat different course. Responding to the preparation of the "Sinhala Only" bill, the Federal party, representing the majority of the Tamils, announced that it would organize satyagraha demonstrations in the Tamil-speaking areas and in front of the parliament building. L. H. Mettananda, a Sinhalese extremist, threatened counter-demonstrations, and a monk declared at a mass meeting held in Colombo that the Sinhalese had fought the Tamils for 2000 years and that they would not give way on the language issue. "If the Tamils forced them to fight they were prepared to do so." [69] Despite exhortations to peace by both the prime minister and several Buddhist elders, communal passions finally exploded. On June 6, 1956, the day the language bill was submitted to Parliament, riots broke out in Colombo and soon spread to the eastern province. The number of killed was estimated at over 100—the first serious outbreak of communal violence in the modern history of Ceylon. Bandaranaike, writes Wriggins, "had assumed that communal antagonism could be turned up for tactical purposes and then turned down when the political need was gone." [70] But this proved impossible. The riots of 1956 indicated the depth of the communal feeling and hatred that had been generated; belatedly the prime minister made an attempt to steer a more moderate course.

Bandaranaike's goal of establishing his independence from the Buddhist extremists, who had ensured his victory at the polls, proved difficult to attain. Many of his erstwhile supporters accused him of undue temporizing. At the end of July 1956, Mettananda issued an open letter, addressed to the prime minister, in which he took him to task for not implementing the recommendations of the Buddhist Commission. The events of "the first three months of your regime have only provided the people with sufficient indications that a second and a more shameful betrayal of Buddhism is gradually taking place under your Government." [71] The EBP, too, kept up a steady pressure. Through speeches, press releases, and visits to ministers and civil servants the monks' organization reminded the MEP government of its pledges to the Buddhists. Buddharakkhita, in particular, the secretary of the EBP and a vice-president of the SLFP, continued his energetic political activity. He had a direct phone link to Colombo, and in his air-conditioned apartment behind the temple at Kelaniya he held court with members of parliament, with local and party officials coming and going for advice and favors. Donald E. Smith has compared Buddharakkhita to Richelieu and Rasputin.[72] A local commentator called the EBP "a supra Cabinet." [73]

Many Buddhist laymen, though sympathetic to the objectives of the EBP, became concerned with the growing political involvement of the monks, an involvement that seemed far removed from the traditional contemplative life of the Sangha. The conservative leaders of the Siamese sect also repeatedly expressed their opposition to the worldly ways of Buddharakkhita and his followers. But the political monks denied any wrongdoing. The *bhikkhus* have the duty of working for the national, religious, and social improvement of the state, declared the joint secretaries of the All-Ceylon Monks' Congress and the Sri Lanka Maha Sangha Sabha in a statement released in July 1956. Now that Ceylon had a socialist government the monks had to work unitedly, disregarding sect differences, in order "to prevent setbacks to the country and the religion from traitors and non-Buddhists." In a separate statement Buddharakkhita sharply attacked the Siamese elders and defended "the progressive bhikkhus who are engaged in the public service" and exert themselves "in the interests of the country, the religion and the people." [74]

Bandaranaike continued to follow an uneasy path of compromise, pursuing policies intended to pacify all the rival factions. Under pressure for implementing the report of the Buddhist Commission, the government in October 1956 announced that it would appoint an official commission to examine and recommend ways of restoring Buddhism to its rightful place in the country. This plan drew vigorous protest from the heads of the Siamese sect who feared for their temporalities and who were especially distrustful of the idea of a Buddha Sasana Council, a supreme governing council for the Buddhist religious establishment of Ceylon consisting of members of the Sangha and laymen. Still, in early February 1957 the commission was formally launched. It was made up of ten monks and five laymen, five of these fifteen had served on the Buddhist Committee of Inquiry (the first Buddhist Commission). It is significant that the EBP was not consulted on the make-up of the new commission.

To the radical Buddhists the establishment of still another commission meant more delay if not outright betrayal. A pact between the prime minister and S.J.V. Chelvanayakam, the leader of the Tamil Federal party, in July 1957 antagonized them further. The Federal party had threatened a satyagraha campaign, to start in August 1957, unless the government granted their demand for a federal union by then. Prolonged negotiations between Bandaranaike and the Federalist leaders finally resulted in an agreement that was announced on July 26, 1957. The government promised to introduce legislation that would recognize Tamil as the "language of a national minority in Ceylon"; it promised that the administration in the Tamil areas was to be in Tamil and that regional councils were to have a degree of autonomy without representing a federal constitution, an idea abhorred by the Sinhalese. The proposed councils also were to take part in the selection of colonists for the government-sponsored settlements in the northern dry zone.[75]

The Bandaranaike-Chelvanayakam pact succeeded in preventing the satyagraha campaign as planned by the Tamils, but it solidified the opposition of the Buddhist elements to the MEP government. Radical monks and other extremist groups threatened their own satyagraha campaign unless the pact was renounced; Buddhist monks organized a boycott of Tamil stores in central Ceylon. "If the Prime Minister does not abrogate this agreement," a monk declared at a protest meeting, "the same hands that overthrew the UNP Government will overthrow the MEP Government." [76]

The UNP, trying to cash in on the government's difficulties, called the pact a "betrayal of Sinhalese" [77]; in early October 1957 the UNP organized a protest march from Kandy to Colombo, including a large contingent of monks, which was finally dispersed by the police after it had led to clashes between onlookers, counter-marchers, and the UNP demonstrators.[78] Communal tension was increased further by a tar-brush campaign undertaken by the Federalists in Jaffna against new buses with Sinhalese lettering which led to retaliatory damage of Tamil stores in the south. On April 9, 1958 some 200 monks and 300 laymen staged a sit-down demonstration against the pact in front of the prime minister's residence. Bandaranaike finally gave in and announced the abrogation of the agreement. According to the prime minister the annulment of the pact had become necessary because of Federalist activities in Jaffna and had been decided upon before the appearance of the monks.[79] To the opposition the prime minister's action was but another abject surrender to the pressure tactics of the political monks.

In May 1958 communal acrimony exploded in violence on a scale that modern Ceylon had not known before. The immediate occasion for the outburst that killed an estimated 300 to 400 persons, led to over 2000 incidents of arson and looting, and left 12,000 Ceylonese homeless as refugees [80] was an attack on May 22 upon a train presumed to be carrying Tamil delegates to the annual meeting of the Federalist party. But this incident was merely the match setting fire to the powder keg. For weeks Sinhalese extremists, some of them members of a new communal party, Jatika Vimukti Peramuna (National Liberation Front), led by the former cabinet minister K.M.P. Rajaratna, had distributed letters threatening the lives of those Tamils who did not voluntarily leave for the northern provinces. "Our sacred cities of Anuradhapura and Polonnaruwa and our capital cities of Colombo, Kandy and Galle," demanded one such leaflet, "must be made a hundred per cent Sinhala without any foreigners or non-Buddhists allowed to live in our midst and to corrupt us." [81] The extremists were encouraged by militant monks belonging to the EBP who organized a boycott of Tamil stores and made speeches to arouse the passions of the people. A monastery in Colombo was said to have been used to store weapons and explosives.[82]

Once violence had started it spread swiftly to most provinces. Rumors of acts of brutality led to further outrages. All over the island killings, looting, and savagery multiplied. "In the Colombo area," writes the best-informed observer of the riots, "the number of atrocities swiftly piled up. The atmosphere was thick with hate and fear. The thugs ran amok burning houses and shops, beating up pedestrians, holding-up vehicles and terrorizing the entire city and the suburbs." In some places, according to police reports, rioters masqueraded as monks. "These phoney priests went about whipping up race-hatred, spreading false stories and taking part in the lucrative side of this game—robbery and looting." [83] Members of other religious and ethnic communities also became the target of the xenophobes. A leaflet distributed to Christians, Muslims, and Burghers (people of Portuguese and Dutch descent) warned them to leave the country by December 31, 1958: "Otherwise you will be wiped out, as we have done with the Tamils. Shri Lanka is only for Buddhists." [84]

The prime minister hesitated for several days, but when the police, demoralized by political interference and official condonement of earlier violence, proved incapable of bringing the riots under control, on May 27 he asked the governor-general to proclaim a state of emergency. Army units and reservists eventually

re-established order; a curfew and strict censorship of the press
were imposed; the Federal party and the National Liberation
Front, at the two extremes of the communal conflict, were proscribed, and their leaders were put under house arrest. The prime
minister later talked of a coup, presumably organized by the Federalists, that had been put down,[85] but law enforcement agencies
failed to verify these allegations. Dr. N. M. Perera—head of the
NLSSP, the more moderate of Ceylon's two Trotskyite parties,*
and leader of the opposition in parliament—came closer to the
truth when in the course of a debate in the House of Representatives he drew attention to the language issue as the main cause of
the disorders. Emphasis on communal factors during the last election campaign and the adoption of the "Sinhala Only" Act in
1956, he argued, had heightened communal passions. Turning to
Bandaranaike, Perera declared: "I remember we pointed out that
you were, in June 1956, really sowing dragon's teeth and that
you would harvest a monster that would try to swallow you up
in the end." [86]

The prime minister realized that the use of force alone could
not safeguard communal peace. Taking advantage of the shock
which the country had experienced he now prepared legislation
concerning the "reasonable use of Tamil" which contained many
of the provisions promised earlier to the Federalist leaders. Thus
the Tamils were assured the right of education and of correspondence with government agencies in their own language. Before
introducing the bill in Parliament Bandaranaike conferred with
prominent representatives of the Sangha and obtained their advice
and agreement on the main features of the proposed language
bill.[87] The EBP, on the other hand, remained adamantly opposed to
any concessions to the Tamils. Militant monks, the government
learned, were discussing plans for direct action on August 5, the
day on which the bill was to be voted on, including a storming
of the Parliament building.[88]

On August 5 the House of Parliament was put under police
protection. Asking for moderation, Bandaranaike appealed for
support of the bill: "I am satisfied that extremism in this country
consists of the activities of a small minority, whether they are

* As the larger of the two Trotskyite parties, the NLSSP often is also referred to as the LSSP, the name of the original Bolshevik-Leninist party
founded in 1935.

Sinhalese or Tamil, but that the vast majority of the people are reasonable and moderate and only wish to live together with mutual respect." [89] The opposition argued that this bill should not be voted on while the Tamil leaders were still under arrest and unable to participate in the debate and vote, and all but two of their number left the chamber. The bill thereupon passed by a 46 to 3 vote. Had such legislation been enacted earlier, Wriggins observes, both the 1956 and 1958 riots might have been avoided.[90]

With the passage of the second Language Act Bandaranaike had scored an important victory, though his estrangement from the radical political monks was now all but complete. The militants had lost prestige and supporters as a result of the bloody events of May 1958, and a new organization of moderate monks, the Lanka Sangha Sabha, was gaining ground at their expense. Many monks joined the committees of peace that were being formed in many places.[91] By October the situation had improved to such an extent that the ban on the Federal party and the National Liberation Front was lifted.

The prime minister now felt secure enough to sponsor a section in a bill regulating parliamentary elections that was directly aimed at the political activity of the monks. A clause in this proposed legislation made it an offense for a person to utter "at any religious assembly any words influencing the result of such election or for the purpose of inducing any elector to vote or refrain from voting for any candidate at such election." Election meetings at places of worship were also prohibited. Bandaranaike defended the amendment by pointing out that it was meant to prevent the misuse of religion and religious worship for political ends. "This difficulty existed earlier and we are providing for it in this Clause." [92] The clause was approved by the House on March 12, 1959, and it became law in November of that year, two months after Bandaranaike had been gunned down by one of the political monks whose interference in politics this legislation curbed.

Despite some loss of support in the Sangha and the country at large, the radical monks still were a power to be reckoned with. In December 1958 they tried to influence the passage of legislation that provided for the transformation of two *pirivenas* into Buddhist universities. While the bill was being debated a leading figure in the EBP threatened: "Retribution will surely come upon those sophisticated anti-swabhasa [vernacular] elements in the Senate for attempting to delay the Pirivena Universities Bill." [93] After this legislation passed, the monks posed new demands. "The education of the country should be taken over by bhikkhus," claimed a Buddhist elder, chief inspector of *pirivenas*. And "if the Government failed to hand over education to bhikkhus they were prepared to get it by force. For over 2000 years education had been imparted to the Sinhalese by bhikkhus. Even political instructions to kings were given by them." [94] When Bandaranaike dismissed the inspector-general of the Ceylonese police force, a Buddhist, on grounds of incompetence, the militant monks accused him of being anti-Buddhist.

Bandaranaike also faced problems in his own party, the SLFP, where the right wing, supported by Buddharakkhita, was gaining ground. For a year now the powerful monk from Kelaniya had been feuding with Philip Gunawardena, leader of the Trotskyite VLSSP and minister of agriculture and food in the MEP coalition cabinet. On March 6, 1958 Gunawardena had attacked Buddharakkhita in a speech in Parliament accusing him of associating with black marketeers. "If there is a Government contract going, one finds Buddharakkita and his agents hovering about like hungry jackals." Gunawardena also had alluded to Buddharakkhita's intimate relationship with Mrs. Vimala Wijewardene, minister of health, when he castigated the taking of the yellow robe by "brawny men, somewhat sexy in their appearance . . . who make an appeal to elegant ladies who have long passed even the soaring forties." [95] Charges and countercharges were traded throughout the year 1958. Buddharakkhita and the EBP blamed the Marxists in the MEP coalition for fighting the influence of the Sangha and demanded their exclusion from the MEP coalition, while Gunawardena pressured the prime minister to dismiss reactionary ministers from the cabinet. At the meeting of the SLFP executive committee in February 1959, the right wing of the party, over the opposition of Bandaranaike, elected a Roman Catholic to the post of general secretary. Buddharakkhita had emphasized the need of a man who would not bow to the Marxists and his influence had prevailed.[96] It was at this time, as the court proceedings against Buddharakkhita later brought out, that the chairman of a shipping company in which Buddharakkhita and his brother had an interest applied for a remunerative government contract. After the refusal of this bid by the prime minister, transmitted in August 1959, Buddharakkhita and his accomplices began to plan Bandaranaike's murder.[97]

In May 1959, the Marxist members left the cabinet, and the VLSSP combined with an extremist Sinhalese group, led by L. H. Mettananda, to form a new party which took the name of the coalition the two VLSSP ministers had broken up—People's United Front (MEP). The combination of Trotskyites and communalists in the new MEP was indicative of the political opportunism that has always characterized Ceylonese politics. Bandaranaike now was becoming increasingly isolated. The secretary of the MEP, the new left-communalist coalition, called his government "a fascist government manned by a reactionary group"[98]; the radical monks missed no opportunity to attack the prime minister as a renegade from Buddhism. In June 1959 the executive committee of the EBP started to consider the possibility of starting a new political party.[99] The breach between the EBP and SLFP as political partners, on one hand, and, on a more personal level, between Buddharakkhita and Bandaranaike, on the other, was complete.

On September 25, 1959, the monk Talduwe Somarama Thero appeared on the porch of the prime minister's residence among a group of petitioners. When Bandaranaike came out of the house to pay obeisance to one of the monks Somarama took out a revolver and shot the prime minister. Following the prime minister into the house he fired three more shots. The gravely injured Bandaranaike was rushed to a hospital from which, prior to an operation, he issued a message to the nation. "A foolish man dressed in the robes of a bhikkhu" had shot him. "I appeal to all concerned to show compassion to this man and not try to wreak vengeance on him."[100] Bandaranaike died the following morning.

After a lengthy investigation, conducted by the Ceylon police with the assistance of Britain's Scotland Yard, six persons in addition to the assassin were charged with conspiracy to murder the prime minister. Among them was Mapitigama Buddharakkhita, H. P. Jayawardene, a close business associate of Buddharakkhita in the unsuccessful shipping venture, and Mrs. Vimala Wijewardene, minister of health in Bandaranike's cabinet and, as a commission of inquiry later put it, "in a more than usually intimate personal relationship" with the monk-politician-businessman from

Kelaniya. The investigation revealed that Buddharakkhita had begun to conspire against the life of the prime minister as far back as September 1958, a conspiracy motivated in part by political reasons. Personal hatred caused by Bandaranaike's failure to start legal action against the scurrilous pamphlets circulating about Buddharakkhita and Mrs. Wijewardene had also played a role. More definite plans had been made by Buddharakkhita and Jayawardene after Bandaranaike had refused their bid for the shipping contract in August 1959. They had then begun to prod the monk Somarama, a competent *ayurvedic* eye physician in his early forties, but also a drug addict, to carry out the murder, Buddharakkhita time and again telling him that "there is no future for the Sinhalese or the language if things go on like that." Somarama finally accepted the assignment and, using a revolver supplied by Buddharakkhita and under the influence of drugs, shot the prime minister. He had done so, he confessed, "for the sake of my country and my religion and race." [101]

Two of the seven defendants, including Mrs. Wijewardene, were freed before formal indictments were handed down in October 1960. On May 12, 1961, after a trial of three months, the two monks, Somarama and Buddharakkhita, as well as Jayawardene were convicted and sentenced to death by hanging. The two remaining defendants were freed.[102] Several months later the Court of Criminal Appeal reduced the death sentence passed on Jayawardene and Buddharakkhita to rigorous life imprisonment; the latter died in prison of a heart attack in May 1967. Persistent rumors about the involvement of additional persons led to the appointment of a Commission of Inquiry in 1963 composed of three high-ranking jurists, two of them non-Ceylonese. Their report, issued in 1965, confirmed that the plot had been confined to the individuals named in the indictment and cleared the EBP and SLFP qua organizations of any involvement in the assassination plot.[103]

Some students of Ceylonese politics, like Donald E. Smith, have concluded that Bandaranaike "fell victim to the extremist forces of resurgent Buddhism which he himself had helped to set in motion." [104] Heinz Bechert, on the other hand, argues that Bandaranaike died as a result of "a feud of primarily private character." [105] This writer would prefer to subscribe to a modified form of both hypotheses. There can be little doubt that Buddharakkhita was a power-hungry politician whose interest in truly religious matters was minimal. But it is also true that Buddharakkhita owed much of his political influence to the movement of monks he was leading, and it was only in the setting of a worldly and highly politicized Sangha that he could have achieved the position of eminence and riches that eventually brought him on a collision course with Bandaranaike. Many *bhikkhus* supported the cause of modernist Buddhism out of sincerely felt religious convictions; the person chosen by Buddharakkhita to carry out his murderous plot, the monk Somarama, was typical of those monks who had helped Bandaranaike attain political power and who later came to oppose him vigorously because of his relatively moderate communal policies. Had it not been for this keenly felt disappointment and the conviction that he was serving the cause of Buddhism and his nation, the monk Somarama probably would have refused to fire the fatal shots. It thus would seem correct to conclude that Bandaranaike fell victim both to a personal feud and to the forces of extremist communalism whose hopes he had kindled but not fulfilled.

The balance sheet of Bandaranaike's three and one-half years in office is a mixture of accomplishments and failures. To many of his countrymen he is the creator of a new Ceylon, they call him *bodhisattva*, one destined to become a Buddha, and his grave is a shrine for pilgrimages. Bandaranaike's victory at the polls in 1956 marked the transfer of power from the hands of the wealthy gentry and westernized politicians to the lower, Sinhalese-educated middle class, and this revolutionary shift is unlikely to be reversed, no matter which party wins in future elections. Moreover, the coalition government Bandaranaike headed introduced far-reaching changes in Ceylon's social life. Because of its language policy, its reorganization of the educational system, its establishment of temple associations, and its general upgrading of Buddhist values it seems right to speak of a Sinhalese revolution.

It is also undeniable that Buddhist rights were reasserted at the price of dividing the nation and of repeated violent communal strife. Bandaranaike proved unable to control the Sinhalese extremists who had helped him achieve political power, and he was pushed into policies which, though not far-reaching enough for his militant Buddhist backers, were sufficiently radical to alienate the Tamil minority. His period in office was one of unrest and turmoil which he himself accepted as unavoidable in a period of transition and change. But, as one recent observer has argued, it is questionable whether Bandaranaike always understood the direction in which the country was changing. "Bandaranaike was excellent at destroying the old order with its inequalities and vested interests. But he was less successful in the more formidable task of setting up a meaningful structure in its place, at giving concrete shape to the ideals of democratic nationalism and social equality that he had so eloquently held up before his supporters." [106]

Bandaranaike had injected a sense of vigor into Ceylon's political and social development. His program of social reform included the nationalization of bus transportation and the port of Colombo, the development of agricultural cooperatives, and the beginnings of a land reform. None of these programs decisively changed the island's economic life. During his three years in office yearly per capita income rose from $118 to $124—not quite 5 per cent. That is slight progress in a poor country. But Bandaranaike was able to create the feeling that things were on the move and that the government cared for the common man. The ideological underpinning of the Sinhalese revolution, clumsily and shakily led by the MEP coalition, was an imperfect mixture of traditional ideas, glorification if not outright mythology concerning the pre-colonial period, and socialist thinking of the kind taught by Harold Laski. None of this was fully grasped by the rural population, but it did inspire an active minority, and it gave the villager a new sense of importance and self-esteem.[107] If it is true that the desire to help oneself and the dream of a new and better life are at least as important for economic development as elaborate programs of planning, then Bandaranaike's contribution to Ceylon's future was indeed decisive.

EPILOGUE: THE ENTRENCHMENT OF POLITICAL BUDDHISM

The fact that the assassin of Prime Minister Bandaranaike had been a monk brought down upon the Sangha a wave of hostility that had no precedent in Ceylon's history. *Bhikkhus* were stoned in the streets, and the widow of the late prime minister had to appeal to the people to allow the Buddhist clergy to attend the funeral.[108] A state of emergency was declared immediately, public meetings and demonstrations were banned, and on October 6 press censorship was imposed. The English language press, in particular, had been vociferous in its criticism of the political monks, arguing that without the corruption that had crept into certain sections of the Sangha the assassination of the prime minister would not have taken place. For a certain type of monk, wrote the *Ceylon Daily News*, the yellow robe had become a shield and "an instrument which helped him to fulfill with the greatest of ease his desires and ambitions—to satisfy the most depraved bodily appetites, to amass wealth by crooked and dishonourable means and to gather political power into his hands by intimidation and thuggery." [109] The authorities now forbade any discussion of the Sangha and its possible role in the assassination plot; rumor had it that censorship had been introduced to silence this public outcry and to prevent violence against the political monks.[110]

The opposition in Parliament vigorously protested the state of emergency and especially the imposition of censorship, arguing that it was to protect those involved in the plot. The press censorship consequently was lifted on October 20, and there now appeared a flood of articles demanding the reform of the Sangha and in particular the prohibition of any political activity on the part of the monks. In early November 1959 the government released the report of the Buddha Sasana Commission which, as will be recalled, had been appointed in March 1957 and which had completed its assignment shortly before Bandaranaike's assassination. The report recommended the establishment of a Buddha Sasana Council as a supreme governing body to deal with matters affecting the Sangha as well as the entire Buddhist community, the creation of ecclesiastical tribunals to take charge of minor offenses involving monks and of a new government department under a commissioner of temple lands who would administer temple properties in the place of separate trustees in each temple. The report also suggested a more efficient system for the registration of monks and recommended that the consent of the Buddha Sasana Council be required before monks could accept remuneration for services rendered in teaching and similar assignments. Monks were told to regard social work in hospitals, prisons, and homes for children and the aged as their chief task, and they were to shun party politics.[111] It was this last recommendation which seemed to many to be the most timely and urgent inasmuch as the political involvement of the Sangha was blamed for the act of political assassination carried out by the monk Somarama on September 25, 1959.

Since the riots of 1958 the demand to prohibit Sangha involvement in politics had been heard with increasing frequency. A typical, though particularly sharp attack upon the political monks had appeared in the May 1959 issue of *The Buddhist*, an organ of Buddhist modernism: "The centre of the ill, the canker that afflicts present day Buddhism can fairly be attributed to the indolence of the bhikkus, to their reluctance to separate the chaff from the grain, myth and legend from the pure Dhamma, to their growing tendency to interfere in the political sphere and to make and unmake Governments." [112] Such voices now multiplied, and the All-Ceylon Buddhist Congress, too, aligned itself with those who welcomed the Buddha Sasana report and urged its immediate implementation. The Sangha itself was divided in its reaction. The elders of the Ramanya and Amarapura sects by and large approved of the report, whereas the heads of the Siamese sect, fearful of any outside interference and opposed to the work of the Buddha Sasana Commission since its inception, came out strongly against its recommendations. The Sangha, they argued, had faced many difficulties in the past, and it could take care of any shortcomings without calling upon laymen or the government of the country. [113]

W. Dahanayake, formerly minister of education and now, by appointment of the governor-general, prime minister, agreed with the position of the prestigious Siamese elders. During a visit to the Malwatte temple in Kandy, Dahanayake declared that the reform of the Sangha must come through the Sangha itself and if any government tried to force such reforms, it was not the Sangha that would break up but that government. The new prime minister assured the monks that he would not allow any legislation to be passed against their will. [114] The ban upon the political acitivty of monks thus became a casualty of its tie-in with other reforms of the Sangha which the influential conservative monks opposed.

Unable to control his cabinet and parliamentary majority, W. Dahanayake dissolved Parliament in December 1959 and scheduled a General Election for March 19, 1960. Unlike the election of 1956, the monks, still suffering from approbrium, were conspicu-

ously absent from the campaign. The Buddhist cause was promoted by the lay All-Ceylon Buddhist Congress which called
upon its followers to elect a truly Buddhist government that would
implement the recommendations of the Buddha Sasana Commission and grant "the Buddhists their proper place in this country."
The government of Bandaranaike had come to an untimely end
before it had had the opportunity to do very much for the welfare of the Buddhists. Now there existed the opportunity to
"bring into being a government that will hear our cries and listen
to them with sympathy." [115]

Even though the monks themselves did not participate in the
campaign, all of the parties affirmed their loyalty to the cause of
Buddhism and accused each other of slighting the interests of the
Sinhalese Buddhist religion. So entrenched had political Buddhism become in the political life of Ceylon that even in the absence of its most vigorous and important proponent, the political
monks, the power of Sinhalese and religious communalism continued. The new MEP, for example, whose co-founder, the Marxist Philip Gunawardena, harbored well-known anticlerical sentiments, promised the implementation of the recommendations of
the Buddhist Commission, the development of Buddhist cultural
centers, the establishment of a national system of education, and
the acceptance of Sinhalese as the official language of the country
and sole medium of education at the university level. Both leaders of the MEP, Gunawardena and Mettananda, participated
in pilgrimages and religious feasts and missed no opportunity to
demonstrate their Buddhist fervor.[116] Gunawardena claimed that
he was "a better Buddhist than any other political leader in the
country." [117]

The SLFP, similarly, once again exploited Buddhist grievances.
Early in the campaign the party announced that, like the other
political factions, it had decided not to invite monks to address its
election meetings though it added that the party "would accept
advice and expect their support." [118] The SLFP pledged the implementation of the Buddha Sasana Commission's recommendations and steps to make Sinhalese the official language of the
country. The last of the main contenders, the UNP, adopted a
more moderate program though that, too, was colored by the
prevailing mood. Sinhalese was to be the only official language
but it would replace English gradually. With regard to the press-

ing issue of monastic reform, the party offered to grant the sects corporate status, but this and any other reforms would be enacted only with the consent of the various branches of organized Buddhism.[119]

The results of the March 1960 election were inconclusive. The SLFP—led by C. P. de Silva, a member of a low-ranking caste —deprived of the help of the energetic young monks whose support had been so decisive in 1956, lost ground and obtained only 46 seats in a House enlarged to a total of 151 members. The MEP received 10, the Tamil Federal party 15, and the UNP 50 seats, respectively. Since no party had a clear majority, the UNP as the largest single force in the House was asked to form the government. But the UNP government was unable to obtain the support of a majority of the House, Parliament was dissolved for the second time in half a year, and new elections were scheduled for July 20, 1960. The communal problem and the future of the Tamil minority again were a key issue in the campaign. The UNP, in particular, accused the SLFP of trying to arrange a deal with the Tamil Federal party, and it was able to increase its share of the popular vote from 28 to 38 per cent. But the distribution of this vote was wasteful, netting the UNP only 30 seats, whereas the SLFP with 34 per cent of the popular vote was able to obtain 75 seats.[120] The SLFP benefited from a no-contest agreement with the Trotskyites (NLSSP) and Communists, it attracted Buddhist support by promising the establishment of a state system of education and an end to state aid for denominational schools (most of which were Christian), and it enjoyed the support of the extremist Buddhist National Liberation Front led by K.M.P. Rajaratna.

The new SLFP government was headed by the late prime minister's widow, Mrs. Sirimavo Bandaranaike, who had played a dynamic role in the campaign calling upon the people of Ceylon to support the party of her murdered husband and thus prevent a return to the old order that had prevailed before 1956. Mrs. Bandaranaike at first enjoyed the support of the Buddhist militants. Legislation passed in late 1960 and early 1961 nationalized state-aided private schools. This measure dealt a death blow to the Catholic schools and removed one of the main Buddhist grievances.[121] A Language of the Courts Act was enacted which provided for the use of Sinhalese in the courts of law. Turning aside the objections of the Federal party, the government announced on January 1, 1961 that Sinhalese, as provided in the Language Act of 1956, had now become the official language of the country. The Tamils reacted by launching a satyagraha campaign in the northern and eastern provinces, they blocked entrances to government offices, and army units had to be dispatched to re-establish the orderly processes of government. A state of emergency was declared, the Federal party was proscribed for one year, and its leaders were detained.[122] Once again communal strife had shown its ugly face.

But for the Sinhalese extremists all this was not enough. They pointed out that English was still being used in many government departments, and they denounced the government when it made known plans to solve the Tamil problem by again proposing the introduction of regional councils. Mrs. Bandaranaike now faced the hostility of Rajaratna's National Liberation Front and of a new militant Buddhist organization founded by the veteran extremist, L. H. Mettananda, the Bauddha Jatika Balavegagya (National Front for the Protection of Buddhism).[123]

Relations with large segments of the Sangha also deteriorated progressively. The government incurred the enmity of the monks in the Kandyan highlands, who owned extensive tracts of land, when temple lands bringing in a certain income were made subject to taxation. The application of the so-called Paddy Lands Act of 1958, which granted tenant cultivators security of tenure and a more advantageous division of the crops, to the property of monasteries also drew widespread opposition. In the middle of 1961 the government of Mrs. Bandaranaike began to take steps to implement the Buddha Sasana Commission report including an order that forbade the hiring of monks as teachers. Influential *bhikkhus* responded with threats to re-enter politics to fend off the dangers to "religion and nation." In vain did Mrs. Bandaranaike argue that the planned reforms were merely to preserve Buddhism and would not destroy the freedom of the Sangha. The government, she said, was proposing to act "in the same manner as was done by the Buddhist kings of old." [124] Even the leader of the militant All-Ceylon Bhikkhu Congress, Talpawila Seelawansa Thero, announced his opposition to the report and declared that the former UNP government was ten thousand times better than the regime of Mrs. Bandaranaike.[125] Faced with the growing hostility of so many sections of the Sangha, many of whom feared a loss of income or resented the ban on government service or political activity, the government retreated. In March 1962 the order barring the employment of monks was withdrawn, and the other proposals were never implemented. Once again the monks had won the day.

On January 27, 1962 an attempt to overthrow the government was foiled, and 24 army and police officers, the majority of them Roman Catholics, were subsequently charged with conspiracy to overthrow the government. The officers had planned to hand over the reins of government to the governor-general, Sir Oliver Goonetilleke, an Anglican Christian, and, even though the latter had had no knowledge of the plot, pressure was brought on him to resign, and he subsequently left the country. In his place Mr. William Gopallawa, a staunch Buddhist and a relative of Mrs. Bandaranaike, was installed as head of state on March 2, 1962. The ceremony, as the government took pains to emphasize, followed old Buddhist custom. Members of the Sangha chanted verses from Buddhist scriptures; the new governor-general, clad in the simple Sinhalese garb of white cloth, sat at the feet of a Buddhist monk and was told that though he was now the highest in the land he must himself be governed by the law of Buddha.[126]

The *coup d'état* attempt kindled anti-Catholic sentiment; the government claimed that the plot had had as its goal the end of Buddhism in Ceylon. The plot also led to the appointment of a commission to investigate the press which for a long time had drawn the ire of the Buddhists on the grounds that it was Christian-dominated, spiteful, and contemptuous of Sinhalese culture and religion. The Press Commission issued an interim report in late July 1964 recommending the nationalization of the largest press combine of Ceylon, the Associated Newspapers of Ceylon, Ltd., known as the Lake House Press, and various measures of control for the remaining newspapers. Mrs. Bandaranaike, who was known to be hostile to the press houses because of their frequent criticism of government policy, endorsed the commission's report and ordered legislation prepared to implement it. This step was to prove her greatest mistake and to lead to her political downfall.

Mrs. Bandaranaike's troubles began with the defection of several SLFP delegates in Parliament. After prolonged negotiations the political crisis was overcome by the formation of a new SLFP government on June 12, 1964 that included the moderate Trotskyite LSSP. At first, it appeared that the attempt of Mrs. Bandaranaike to present the new coalition as a "Buddhist government" would be successful in allaying the misgivings of the Buddhists—lay organizations and monks—who distrusted the formally Marxist LSSP. But very soon these suspicions prevailed, and the SLFP was accused of betraying country and Buddhism by entering into a coalition with a Marxist party hostile to religion. When the minister of finance, the leader of the LSSP, presented a budget that contained a proposal to allow and tax the tapping of toddy (a kind of liquor) from cocoanut trees, Buddhist groups promptly accused him of seeking to corrupt the people. Temperance is a Buddhist virtue, and the plan was branded as a move to wean the people away from religion. Mrs. Bandaranaike finally decided to withdraw the proposal explaining that she had done so "in deference to the wishes of the Maha Sangha." [127]

Opposition to Mrs. Bandaranaike and her coalition grew over the issue of the nationalization of the press. Even though many monks had earlier flirted with Marxist ideas they now turned sharply against the SLFP-LSSP coalition, fearing that it would lead to a restriction of their independence and political influence. The planned take-over of the press furnished them with the argument that Mrs. Bandaranaike intended to establish a dictatorship. Once again the monks entered the political arena in force, and, supported by the big press houses, previously their most bitter enemies, they succeeded in bringing down Mrs. Bandaranaike's government. Monks attended meetings and led demonstrations all over the country. By early November 1964 it had become obvious that the Sangha was heading a popular movement which was supported by every important Buddhist organization, most Buddhist dignitaries, and all opposition parties except the Communists.

The government, too, organized meetings to explain its policies with monks in a prominent role, but it soon sensed that the mood of the Buddhist majority was largely hostile. At this point, Mrs. Bandaranaike decided upon a last gamble to reassure the Buddhists. The speech from the throne of November 20 contained an announcement that in addition to earlier steps taken by the government to "give Buddhism its proper place in the country as the religion of the majority" the government "proposes to place be-

fore you legislation which will guarantee this proper place to
Buddhism." [128] It became known that the government planned to
amend the constitution and make Buddhism the state religion. But
this maneuver failed to mollify the monks and their supporters.
On November 28 they held a mass meeting in Colombo attended
by over 6000 monks and many others; Buddhist elders as well as
the leaders of several opposition parties addressed the meeting.
Among the resolutions adopted were the following:

> The Maha Sangha condemns the fraudulent attempt of the Co-
> alition Government to amend Section 29 with the promise of
> making Buddhism the State Religion.

> The only way to appease public opinion is to dissolve Parlia-
> ment and to hold immediate elections.

> On December 9—the day when the Press Grab Bills will be
> debated in Parliament—the Maha Sangha and the public
> should ring the temple bells, observe religious precepts, and fast
> in order to express their protest over these Bills. [129]

The political monks and Buddhist extremists like Mettananda
and Rajaratna were not so much opposed to the proposal to make
Buddhism the state religion as they were determined to bring
down the coalition government. They feared the use of the state's
power by a government that included elements indifferent if not
hostile to the Buddhist cause, and they correctly sensed the opportunistic purpose in the plan for constitutional reform.

On December 3 Parliament voted on amendments to the Address of Thanks on the Throne Speech. The MEP and the National Liberation Front in a joint amendment branded the
proposed constitutional reform "a shameless and cynical attempt"
to deceive the Sangha and the Buddhist public, and they demanded that Buddhism not only be made the state religion but
that legislation be enacted requiring the governor-general, the
prime minister and his cabinet, officers of the armed forces, and
heads of schools to be Buddhists. The amendment condemned the
agreement between India and Ceylon, signed on October 29, 1964
that provided for the repatriation of a portion of the Tamil estate
laborers in Ceylon, and it demanded the expulsion of all Indian
residents estimated at 1,600,000. The joint opposition amendment
stated that the government had "miserably failed to solve the
pressing problems of the people, such as unemployment, the high

cost of living and housing." It was adopted by a vote of 74 to 73 with 14 SLFP deputies joining the opposition. The prime minister dissolved Parliament and scheduled new elections for March 22, 1965.

The fall of the SLFP-LSSP coalition government was celebrated as a great victory of the Sangha. A Buddhist elder declared in a typical statement: "Salt that is made of water is destroyed by water itself. This government which came into power with the blessings of the Maha Sangha destroyed itself because it did not get the blessings of the Sangha. A government in this country needs the blessings of the Sangha. This is clearly shown from what has happened to this Government." [130] On December 20, 1964 one of the biggest coalitions of monks' organizations called upon the opposition parties to form a united front "to save the nation from the inhuman dictatorial forces rising to destroy religion, language and democracy" and declared that the monks would help plan a course of action "to wipe out the Communists and Sama Samajists in the coming elections." [131]

At the November 28 mass meeting of monks in Colombo Mr. Dudley Senanayake, leader of the UNP, praised the Sangha as once again the rescuer of the nation, and he concluded with the solemn promise: "We will here and now pledge before the Maha Sangha that we will not betray them but will follow their valuable advice and act accordingly." [132] The UNP continued wooing the monks during the election campaign and succeeded in considerable measure in mobilizing them in its support. The monks distrusted the pledge of the SLFP to guarantee the rights of Buddhism, and they were receptive to the argument of the UNP that by making Buddhism the state religion the SLFP and its Marxist allies would dominate the Sangha. The press, especially the Lake House group, once again lined up solidly with the UNP, and rumor had it that the campaign of the monks was generously financed by the press houses.[133]

In the election held on March 22, 1965 the UNP won 40 per cent of the popular vote, but, because of a more economical distribution of these votes, the party obtained 66 seats. The SLFP came in second with 41 seats. This gave the UNP a plurality, but in order to form a government it required and obtained the support of the Federal party. Anxious to prove its loyalty to the Sinhalese Buddhist cause, the new government declared in the

Throne Speech that Buddhism would be restored to "the place it occupied when Lanka was free," that Buddhist sabbath days would be made public holidays, and that, in consultation with the Sangha, it would "promulgate such measures as are necessary for the Maha Sangha to fulfill its noble mission." [134]

The new UNP government stressed national harmony and by and large succeeded in damping communal rivalry. Mrs. Bandaranaike, leader of the opposition, capitalized on this conciliatory policy and accused the English-educated Senanayake of betraying the Sinhalese Buddhists.[135] More importantly, the UNP government was hurt by a serious deterioration in Ceylon's economic situation, caused largely by a sharp drop in the price of tea the export of which accounts for two-thirds of the country's hard currency earnings. In the General Election of 1970 Mrs. Bandaranaike's SLFP, forming a coalition with the moderate Trotskyite LSSP and the Communists, defeated the UNP. Her United Front government has tried to project a secular and socialist image, though the Sinhalese Buddhist revolution that took place during Mr. Bandaranaike's rule cannot and will not be reversed.[136] The political influence of the Sinhalese-educated lower middle class, including the Sangha, is firmly established; the rural masses have been awakened politically, and their interests have to be cultivated. De facto Buddhism is Ceylon's state religion.[137]

The power of the Sangha appears secure though one can expect that modernization and social reform, encouraged by Buddhist modernism, will continue to undermine the monastic ideal of renunciation. The monks will go on functioning as teachers and professors (at the two Buddhist universities) and in other service roles. They will also continue to claim a responsibility for the fate of Buddhism, and this interest will propel them into an active political role whenever a government that threatens the status of the Sangha is in power. A prominent monk was involved in an alleged coup d'état in February 1966 the rallying point of which was said to have been the cry that Buddhism was in danger.[138]

It remains to be seen whether the Sangha can adjust to the realities of modern life without losing its own special identity. Large numbers of monks are said to be giving up their robes after obtaining university degrees, and a Buddhist dignitary noted in 1964 that in village temples there were only old monks.[139] Many

Buddhists believe that a reform of the Sangha along the lines of the Buddha Sasana Commission report is the way to rejuvenate Buddhism. The demand to get the Sangha out of politics is heard with great regularity. But this prescription is probably the wrong medicine. The Sangha is not only powerful enough to resist all attempts at government-sponsored reform successfully, but also the monks will not give up their concern with politics as long as the state functions as protector of Buddhism; the Sangha welcomes and encourages this role. The paradox of this situation was brought out in the utterance of a conservative monk, the head of the Siamese Malwatte chapter of Kandy, who called for government protection of Buddhism while strongly opposing the political activity of monks. He then added: "But if the Government should do anything against Buddhism then it was the duty of the Sangha to advise the Government." [140] Clearly, Buddhists who clamor for state assistance on one hand and who brook no interference of the monks in politics on the other ask for the impossible.

One must also reckon with the long tradition of Buddhism functioning as the state religion, with monks serving as the advisors of kings. In modified form this tradition has been accepted by Buddhist modernists who want the Sangha to play an active role as servants and teachers of their people instead of living a life of cloistered meditation. Here again, if the monks are to involve themselves in programs of social improvement they will necessarily drift into politics for in a democratic society social reform is directed through the political process.

For modern Buddhism to become unpolitical the fulfillment of two conditions would seem to be required. First, Buddhists would have to forswear all government assistance and protection, become entirely independent from the state, and again learn to rely upon the voluntarily given support of their followers. Second, Buddhists would have to renounce all interest in worldly affairs and return to their original preoccupation with individual self-discipline and the search for *nibbana*. Neither of these two developments, one should hasten to add, is very likely to take place. This probably means that in the foreseeable future the phenomenon of political Buddhism in Ceylon, since May 1972 the Independent Socialist Republic of Sri Lanka, is here to stay.

CHAPTER 20

Theology of Revolution: The Catholic Left in Latin America

THE THEOLOGY OF REVOLUTION

For much of its history the Roman Catholic church in Latin America has been a conservative, if not reactionary, force upholding an essentially feudal structure. The critical reaction of the archbishop of Santiago (Chile) to the forward-looking encyclical *Rerum novarum* issued by Pope Leo XIII in 1891 was typical of the Latin American hierarchy's attitude to social problems. The existence of social differences between men, declared the Chilean prelate, was a providential fact, and the poor had to accept it as normal, just, and unchangeable. The rich should consider the poor their brothers and support them in their need, whereas the poor in turn should practice resignation and find the means for their livelihood in honest work.[1]

Today, some eighty years later, one can undoubtedly still find some priests and even bishops holding such views, but the church has practically everywhere assumed a radically different posture. The ideological and political link between the church and the defenders of privilege is being severed, and a new social doctrine has at times given the church a decisively prophetic role. In short, the Roman Catholic church in Latin America today is a new church, which not only is no longer a bulwark of exploitation and injustice but often is actively engaged in legitimating rapid social change.

The manifestations of this "new church" vary from country to country. One can find radical lay groups, rebellious clerics, innovative centers of social research, priests who form guerilla bands, and, perhaps most importantly, frequent episcopal pronouncements, at both nation-wide and continent-wide levels, in favor of abolishing outdated and unjust social structures. In Mexico and Peru, notes one observer, members of the hierarchy "have staked out positions considerably to the left of the ruling 'revolutionary governments'." [2] There is much diversity of tactics but there is basic agreement on certain fundamentals. Thus while many spokesmen for the new church in Latin America will disagree with particular political and social views held by Ivan Illich, the head of the Intercultural Center for Documentation in Cuerna-vaca (Mexico), most of them probably will agree with the spirit at least of one of his recent calls for action: "I believe the specific task of the Church in the modern world is the Christian celebration of the experience of change." [3]

Recent years have seen an attempt on the part of Christian theologians to provide a theological basis not only for social change but also for the legitimacy of revolution. In a certain basic sense, this so-called "Theology of Revolution" is, of course, not new. Throughout the history of Christianity various heretical groups and sects have given the eschatological message of Jesus, the announcement of the coming Kingdom of God, a concrete social and political meaning. Several such millenarian movements have been discussed earlier in this study. Some parallels can also be drawn to the American Social Gospel theology, developed by Walter Rauschenbusch, which also saw the Christian church as an agent of social transformation.[4] If there is something new about the current theologizing of revolution it is the fact that we are dealing here not with mass movements of Christians, for whom this theology of revolution serves as ideological inspiration, but, for the most part, with elaborate theoretical structures that seek to present the Christian Gospel in a way that will appeal to the downtrodden masses in developing countries and to solicit the support of Western Christians to effect radical social change in the Third World. Whether the radical theologians will succeed in bringing the current political and social turmoil in the Third World under the ideological umbrella of such a new Christianity remains to be seen.

Catholic and Protestant theologians have contributed to the theology of revolution. Indeed the ecumenical spirit is so strong among some of these avant-garde thinkers that it is almost impossible to point to specific denominational elements. One of the first and still most influential thinkers in the group is a Presbyterian theologian at the Princeton Theological Seminary and missionary in Latin America, Richard Shaull. In a little noticed book published in 1955, *Encounter with Revolution*, Shaull argued that God's world is dynamic and that the Christian is called upon to participate in the inevitable process of change in obedience to God's will. "God is concerned about people in their need and suffering; he is the God of judgment and mercy who destroys unjust structures and opens new possibilities. He is at work in the historic process, leading it toward fulfillment." The Christian, Shaull acknowledged, had no special illumination or political knowledge: "He has only the perspective which Christian faith provides, which shows him the direction in which God's activity is going, and the guidance of the Holy Spirit as he strives, in the fellowship of the community of believers, to discover God's will." [5]

In many other writings published more recently, Shaull has elaborated his central theme: that Christians must constructively meet the challenge of revolution in the Third World. Christianity in an increasingly secular world has lost much of its old authority and influence, Shaull points out. But this process of secularization also sets the Church free to be a revolutionary force once again. The revolutionary character of biblical messianism and the biblical symbols and images stressing judgment, the end of the world, and the emergence of the radically new are some of the many strands of the Christian tradition that should enable the Christian to feel at home in the midst of revolution. He should focus upon what God is doing in the world to make and keep human life human:

> God has taken human form in the concreteness of historical life and has called us to follow this path if we are to be the salt of the earth and the light of the world (Matthew 5:13-14). In this context, the Christian is called to be fully involved in the revolution as it develops. It is only at its center that we can perceive what God is doing, understand how the struggle for humanization is being defined and serve as agents of reconciliation. From within this struggle we discover that we do not bear witness in revolution by preserving our purity in line with certain moral principles, but rather by freedom to be *for man* at every moment.[6]

The German theologian Johann Baptist Metz, a Catholic, has emphasized the importance of deprivatizing theology and of developing a political theology. Christian salvation, according to Metz, is intrinsically concerned with the here and now and must function "as a critically liberating force of this social world and its historical process. The eschatological powers of the biblical tradition—freedom, peace, justice, reconciliation—do not permit themselves to be privatized. They constantly compel us to social responsibility." [7] The eschatological element in Christianity not only points up the provisional character of every historical phase or mode of social organization, it also allows a critical perspective for the present. It may justify "a revolution in favor of justice and liberty for the sake of the 'least of our brothers'." [8]

The element of hope is stressed by both Protestants and Catholics. Indeed, a few years ago the new theology was called the "theology of hope." According to the German Protestant theologian Jürgen Moltmann, the eschatological symbolism of Christian hope must become a revolutionary force for transforming the world. It "dare not dream away any longer about an eternity beyond time. It must bring the hoped-for future into practical contact with the present. . . . In the expectation of divine transformation we transform ourselves and the conditions around us into the likeness of the new creation." [9] The Kingdom of God preached and practiced by Jesus, Moltmann insists, involves not only the bliss of the soul but also peace and dignity for the body, peace on earth, and liberation of the creature from poverty, hunger, and sickness.

> The social revolution of unjust conditions is the imminent reverse side of the transcendent resurrection hope. Only because the church limited itself to the soul's bliss in the heavenly beyond and became docetic did the active hope of bodily salvation wander out of the church and enter into social change utopias. In them, circumstances are represented in which those who labor and are heavily laden cease to be so, as Ernst Bloch correctly asserts with an unmistakable biblical emphasis. . . . Therefore, the church and Christians should recognize in the movement of changing social relationships a spirit which is of the Spirit of Christ. [10]

The biblical message, writes a Redemptorist father, Charles Snoeck, reveals "a movement of increasing humanization of man and of the progressive gathering together of all nations into a whole, starting with the Creation and going on until the eschatological consummation." [11] It is this faith in a transcendental future that gives all human endeavors a revolutionary dynamism and makes Christianity the religion of the "coming to be," the religion of development:

> Development, as we understand it, is therefore the actual saving, humanizing action of God, but embedded in the history of mankind. It is the same Providence of God which the Bible describes as the work of him who gives justice to the poor and scatters the proud, who puts down the mighty from their seat and exalts the humble (Luke 1:51-3). But this Providence is executed by men, by human history, in whose midst the People of God live as a sacrament of that presence, as the community of God interacting continuously with the community of men, constituting the only history of salvation. Inseparable from, but at the same time transcending this history, God judges, saves, condemns, restores, destroys so as better to build his Kingdom of justice and love, ever writing straight on man's crooked lines, ever guaranteeing the eventual success of his work.[12]

The theology of revolution has been ecumenical not only in bringing together Catholics and Protestants, but also in encouraging dialogue with Christians behind the Iron Curtain. Many of the latter have been evolving a very similar theology, thus facilitating the adjustment of these Christians to the Communist reality in which they live. For example, according to the Czech pastor, Jan Milic Lochman, a member of the Comenius Theological Faculty in Prague, the Christian should feel encouraged to declare his solidarity with the revolution for socialism by "the prophetic call to justice and solidarity with the oppressed and underprivileged *and* the apostolic message of the inalienable right of every human person in Christ. . . ." [13] Similarly, a study group of the Christian Peace Conference, based in Prague, in 1966 recommended the development of a theory of the "just revolution" that would be patterned on the scholastic theory of the "just war" and would support the right and duty of resisting oppressive governments "in every possible way." [14] Common interest in a theology of revolution has been one of the factors stimulating the Christian-Marxist dialogue that has been under way in Europe in the last few years.

The charge that the theology of revolution is serving the interests of communism far more than the interests of the Christian churches has been but one of the many criticisms leveled at those involved in this innovative theological enterprise. Why is it, asks the French Protestant theologian, Jacques Ellul, that the theologians of revolution are so selective in their love of the poor. Some of the poor—like the poor of Latin America, the Negroes in the United States and South Africa, the Palestinian Arabs, the Vietcong—are worthy of being loved whereas others seem not worth troubling about—like the Biafrans, the monarchist Yemenites, the South Sudanese, the Tibetans, the Khurds. The "interesting" poor, charges Ellul, "are those whose defense is in reality an attack against Europe, against capitalism, against the U.S.A." The "violent Christians" choose to support this or that group or movement "because it is socialist, anti-colonialist, anti-imperialist, etc.," not because of their love of the poor.[15]

More basically, Ellul argues, the theology of revolution represents conformism to the modern world, to the fashionable ideology of socialism and anti-colonialism. Eager to participate in these movements, Christians formulate a theology that will justify their political involvement. Just as a century ago nationalism was fashionable, and Christians adduced every imaginable religious motif to justify the defense of their country, so today Christians allege that the truth of Jesus is at stake in social conflict. For centuries Christian theologians maintained that the established order was the expression of God's will; today revolution is regarded as the manifestation of God's sovereignty. Both positions, maintains Ellul, are equally distortive of Christian truth. To seek conciliation with the world—whether it be that of feudalism, monarchy, or revolution—is to rob the Gospel of its radicalism. "Christians ought to understand clearly that Christianity has *nothing* to say in regard to this sort of thing."[16]

According to Ellul, violence is always evil, and any attempt to seek a "balanced" conception of violence—to reconcile love for the enemy with the legitimate use of violence—is casuistry that breaks with Christianity. The "violent Christians" have become so obsessed with the question of social justice and the problem of poverty that they have forgotten to practice justice and charity toward the powerful, the rich, the police, etc. They provide a Christian justification for violence and thus contribute to the climate of violence engulfing the world. Ellul is unimpressed by the disclaimers of the theologians of revolution that they do not want to "make an idol of revolution"[17] and that violence will only be "the last recourse in the face of a system essentially unjust and unbearable, and only upon the condition that there is sufficient certainty that a just system may be established within a short period." [18] The "violent Christians" warn against undue violence, and at the same time their apocalyptic eschatology encourages ruthlessness and brings about a crusade mentality in which the "bad" do not deserve pity.[19]

Richard Shaull's colleague at Princeton, Paul Ramsey, is equally critical of the theology of revolution. The talk about "what God is doing in the world," Ramsey says, is merely "a fig leaf to cover the unseemly parts of a disintegrated Christian understanding." The alleged prophetic response to God's will glosses over the fact that "there can be a number of versions of what God is doing in the world." [20] Ramsey is strongly opposed to Shaull's "revolutionary-Christocentric eschatologism." For the latter, at times, the criterion for testing "the truth of orthodoxy, neo-orthodoxy, and ecumenical theology [is] the question whether this any longer has appeal to some young revolutionaries he has known and admires." [21]

The fact that Shaull himself has warned against the "romantics of revolution," enamored with the "poetry of guerilla action," [22] has not prevented the critics of the theology of revolution from leveling just this charge against its proponents. Much of the Christian talk about revolution, argue the editors of a recent volume dedicated to this new theology, "is mindless and sloganizing," it minimizes "the role of reason in political evolution," and it is characterized by utopian thinking. "Many have exploited the theme of revolution in order to become relevant or to assert their virility or to satisfy egos; often there has been thoughtless chatter on the part of comfortable academics who have not counted the cost of revolution because they were located where they did not have to count that cost." [23]

In Latin America, on the other hand, the theology of revolution is no mere speculation and has become linked with revolutionary practice. The emergence of a revolutionary church in many Latin American countries has been called "one of the great religious dramas of our time"; the changes have been so swift that some observers compare them to the Protestant Reformation.[24] This new pattern can perhaps be observed best in the world's largest Catholic country, Brazil.

CATHOLIC RADICALS IN BRAZIL

As in the rest of Latin America, the Roman Catholic church in Brazil has usually played a conservative role supporting the existing social and political structure of the country. In 1890, shortly after the proclamation of the republic, a separation of church and state took place, freeing the church formally from its subordination to the interests of the state. Still, to this day the long tradition of partnership between church and state makes the advocacy of a more dynamic and independent role for the church appear to be a radical, if not subversive, idea.[25]

It was not until the 1920's and 1930's that innovative ideas like the social encyclicals of Leo XIII began to find a hearing in the Brazilian church. The pace of change accelerated after the Second World War as a result of Brazil's industrialization, the emergence of an urban proletariat, and the encounter with competing non-Catholic religious groups like Pentecostals, Spiritualists, and other Protestant denominations. Today Brazil, where there are more Catholics than in any other country in the world, is one of the main centers of the Catholic Left in America. The church in Brazil is now a deeply divided church in which, according to a recent observer, "the left and the right are quite evenly matched, if not in actual numbers of membership support, at least with regard to influence, pervasiveness, and articulateness." [26]

The origins of the Catholic Left in Brazil can be traced to the Catholic revival that began in the 1920's which was centered mainly in Catholic Action—organized groups of laymen who strive under the sponsorship of local bishops to extend the church's influence in society. Some intellectuals showed an interest in neo-Thomist thinkers like Maritain; others (among them the most radical member of the current Brazilian hierarchy, Helder Câmara) became fascinated by fascism. New social ideas were also introduced by the Brazilian Dominicans, whose orientation was French, who served as advisers to Catholic Action in key parts of the country.[27]

In the late 1940's and early 1950's Brazil's modernization advanced rapidly, and the country's social problems multiplied. In an essay entitled "The Brazilian Revolution," published in 1960, Charles Wagley concluded that "Brazil is in a frenzy of continu-

ous crisis as the traditional gives way to a new type of society." [28]
The older generation of middle-class Catholics continued to support conservative political candidates, whereas many young Catholics, distressed by Brazil's underdeveloped and dependent status,
broke with tradition. In this situation, and because of the threatened loss of relevance for the masses of the faithful, the Vatican
began to take a more active interest in the condition of the Brazilian church. The number of dioceses was expanded, younger
and more liberal priests were made bishops, and, in 1952, the National Conference of Brazilian Bishops was formed to coordinate
planning. Much of the credit for the renewal that soon got under
way must be given to Bishop Câmara, the first secretary-general
of Catholic Action, who, unafraid of innovation, appointed a new
kind of clergy to positions of leadership. Increasingly individual
bishops demanded reforms to alleviate the misery of the rural
population and urban workers. The development commission in
the northeast of Brazil, SUDENE, was suggested by a regional
bishops' conference organized by Câmara.[29]

The ideology of this new Catholic Action was a mixture of
Christian existentialism and humanism. The ideas of Emmanuel
Mounier, until his death in 1950 the editor of the French journal
Esprit, proved attractive. Mounier's emphasis on the overriding
importance of person-to-person relations, his criticism of capitalism, his flirtation with Marxism, and his rejection of a rigid anti-
communism all appealed to a generation of Catholics disturbed
by the backwardness and suffering of the Brazilian people.[30] Another important influence was the philosophy of "historical consciousness" formulated by the Jesuit Henrique de Lima Vaz,
formerly a professor at the Gregorian University in Rome. Father
Vaz stressed man's ability to shape history and to transform and
humanize the world. His philosophy of history was Christian and
resembled the continental theology of hope mentioned earlier; the
promise of a new and harmonious world to come was linked to
the realization of the Kingdom of God. Yet, this eschatological
hope was soon to be secularized, and it encouraged the Catholic
radicals' utopian faith in the possibility of actually creating a
world without domination and strife.[31]

Members of the university branch of Catholic Action, the Ju-
ventude Universitária Católica (JUC), became the most ardent
supporters of these new ideas. Many of them turned toward the

social sciences and set up various educational and organizational projects among the urban masses. By the end of the 1950's so many members of JUC had accepted the Communist position on university reform that a member of this group, João Manoel Conrado, with the support of the Communists, was elected president of the National Union of Students (UNE). Effectively infiltrated by Communists, UNE for several years had been committed to a program of economic planning and public control of the key sectors of the economy,[32] a position increasingly attractive to the rank and file of the Catholic students and to the young clergy acting as their advisors.

The Brazilian hierarchy reacted negatively to the close ties of JUC with the Communists. The conflict between the generations intensified in 1960 during a visit of the French Dominican, Thomas Cardonnel, to Brazil. Speaking to student groups and writing in their newspapers, the French friar attacked the "hypocrisy" of the Brazilian church and called for an alliance between workers, peasants, and students to fight for a better and juster Brazil. Tension between the episcopate and the JUC increased during 1961 to a point that a group of JUC militants finally decided to set up their own organization, free from ecclesiastical ties. Ação Popular (AP) or Popular Action was formally launched in June 1962, and by early 1964 it had about 3000 members—mainly students and recent graduates. A number of priests served in an advisory capacity though they did not formally belong to the organization. Among AP's sympathizers was Paulo de Tarso, a prominent Christian Democrat, twice elected a federal deputy of the party's small radical wing.[33]

In a programmatic "Basic Document" released in 1963, AP declared itself to be a movement dedicated to preparing the Brazilian people for the revolution that would lead to socialism. Cooperating with other anti-imperialist forces, AP was to mobilize the people by developing "their consciousness and their organization in the struggle against the dual domination of capitalism (international and national) and feudalism."[34] Religious and theological references were self-consciously omitted from this and other documents. Recognizing that large segments of the population were either estranged from or only nominally fulfilling the obligations of the church, AP did not want to appear as a Christian movement. It sought not a new Christendom but a new peo-

ple and a new humanized world. Yet, the link to the radical
Catholic thinking out of which the movement had developed was
there, at least implicitly, and many outsiders regarded AP as "a
kind of para-Christian organization."[35]

AP's philosophy of history was a mixture of Hegelianism,
Marxism, and the theology of hope. It contained the belief in the
evolutionary process of socialization which, borrowed from the
Jesuit Pierre Teilhard de Chardin, related to the growth of solidarity among mankind. It utilized the concept of historical consciousness and the need to transform the world as formulated by
Father Vaz. The fact that Pope John's encyclicals, *Mater et Magistra* (1961) and *Pacem in Terris* (1963), had backed away from
the wholesale condemnation of Marxism and devoted special attention to the problems of the underdeveloped nations helped legitimize the socialist and revolutionary ideas of these Catholic
radicals.

Also important in the philosophy of AP was their populist insistence that the revolution be made by the people themselves.
Paternalism or any manipulation of the masses were strongly repudiated. The eyes of the people were to be opened, their consciousness was to be stimulated through what was called *conscientização* (consciousness raising). Because of the same populism
the Catholic radicals distrusted too large a role for the state in the
process of economic planning, and they emphasized the
importance of evolving a form of society without "domination."

During the short two years of its legal existence the members
of AP sought ways of promoting *conscientização*, social change,
and development. Many of them associated themselves with the
Movement for Basic Education (MEB), an adult literacy program
established in 1961 at the suggestion of the Brazilian bishops but
financed by the government. At the peak of its activity in 1963
MEB was said to have over 7000 radio schools with an enroll-
ment of over 100,000.[36] The affiliation of many young leftists
with MEB broadened the range of MEB's activities. Broadcasts
and radio classes continued, but more and more stress was laid on
community development, the promotion of popular art and culture, and consciousness raising.[37] The teaching of reading and
writing linked to the promotion of *conscientização* expressed the
educational philosophy of Paulo Freire, a professor of education
at the University of Recife, later in exile in Chile. Reading and

writing, according to Freire, had to be taught by utilizing the actual vocabulary of the people and by pictorially presenting existential situations. In this way students not only became literate but also became aware of the environment, both as it was and as it should be.[38]

At the time of the first national meeting of MEB co-ordinators in late 1962, the radicalization of MEB had gone quite far, and the idea that education should be considered as a way of transforming the world was generally accepted. The new orientation led to the preparation in 1963 of a new primer entitled *Viver é Lutar* (To Live Means To Struggle), which mirrored the ideology of the Catholic radicals. Lesson 16, for example, declared: "The whole people must participate in government. Some men have more than enough, while many have nothing at all. Some make too much. Many work and their work is exploited by others. A lot of things are wrong in Brazil. A complete change is needed in Brazil." [39]

Also in 1963 came the entry of MEB cadres into rural trade unions. The first Catholic unions had been organized in 1960–61 in the northeast by a priest, António Melo, and a Jesuit, Paulo Crespo. Their goals included counteracting the Peasant Leagues, led since 1955 by the Recife lawyer, Francisco Julião, and keeping the rural masses in the church.[40] The priests selected and advised the lay leaders of the unions but otherwise did not participate in the actual running of the organizations. Later these Catholic *sindicatos* began to function independently, and this independence grew with the involvement of young people from JUC, MEB, and AP in *sindicalização*. For these radicalized young Catholics the creation of rural unions was more than just a way of defending the rights of rural laborers; it was to be a means toward the political mobilization of the peasants, toward the achievement of basic structural changes involving the redistribution of wealth and power in the countryside.

MEB's massive involvement with *sindicalização* resulted from the enactment of the Rural Labor Statute of March 1963. Seeking to broaden his political base in the countryside, President Goulart encouraged rural unionization, and the new statute was to safeguard the rights of such unions. Among those seeking to take advantage of the new statute were the forces supporting Goulart, the Communists, and also the Catholics. During this veritable "rush" into the countryside the populist tenets of MEB were forgotten, and *sindicatos* were set up with little regard for the peasants' capacity to run them.[41] Many of these unions were led by Catholic radicals. When in December 1963 the Catholic-led unions made common cause with unions assumed to be under Communist influence in order to elect officers for the National Confederation of Agricultural Workers, tension within the Catholic camp mounted, and the episcopate became increasingly concerned about the radical turn of events. The fact that the radicals' goal of creating a revolutionary consciousness among the masses had made only very limited headway did not alleviate the hierarchy's apprehensions.

By the time the Brazilian army had removed Goulart, and seized power in April 1964, the Brazilian church had started to dissociate itself from the leftist movement in its own ranks and was beginning to move to the right. Of course, even before the military coup of 1964 the "progressive" bishops had constituted a decided minority among the episcopate. According to one estimate they numbered fewer than forty out of a total of two hundred bishops.[42] Yet, in the climate of renewal created by the Second Vatican Council, and since they included many of the better-educated clerics, the progressive bishops had dominated the episcopate. Now, with the political swing to the right, the situation was reversed, and the conservative majority reasserted itself. On May 29, 1964, after a special meeting of the National Bishops' Conference of Brazil, twenty-five archbishops and bishops issued a declaration that warmly praised the new military rulers:

In response to the general and anxious expectations of the Brazilian people which saw the quickening pace of communism's rise to power, the Armed Forces came to the rescue in time to avoid the implantation of bolshevism in our country. . . . Immediately after the victory of the *Revolução*, a feeling of relief and hope could be discerned. This was the case especially because, in the face of the climate of insecurity and almost of despair in which various social classes or groups found themselves, Divine Protection made itself felt in a tangible and straightforward manner. . . . In offering our thanks to God, who heeded the prayers of millions of Brazilians and delivered us from the communist peril, we express our gratitude to the Military. These rose up in the name of the supreme interests of the Nation, with grave risks to their lives, and we are grateful to them for cooperating to liberate the Nation from the imminent abyss.[43]

Later that year Bishop Câmara was replaced as secretary of the National Bishops' Conference; MEB was steered into a more religious direction, and, in the areas of political tension, such as the northeast, MEB membership declined sharply. After a three months' suspension the Catholic unions were permitted to continue their activities, though here, too, the radical influence was decisively weakened.

From 1967 on, however, the Catholic Left began to reassert itself again. In part this was due to the stimulus provided by the pronouncements of Dom Câmara, since April 1964 archbishop of Olinda and Recife in Brazil's northeast, who has repeatedly castigated the dictatorial features of the military regime and has called for radical measures to help the poor and exploited, "those who are hungry, endure oppression, or are victims of injustice." [44] The underdeveloped world, this charismatic churchman whom his opponents call "the Red Archbishop of Recife" [45] declared in a typical talk given in April 1968, needs a structural revolution and it is those who stand in the way of this revolution who are really guilty of promoting violence:

> Violence exists in the underdeveloped world: The oppressed masses are abused by small groups of the privileged and powerful. It is well known that if the masses try to become human beings and make an effort at education or popular culture, if they organize themselves into syndicates or cooperatives, their leaders are described as subversives and Communists. . . . As for "law," very often it is an instrument of violence against the less powerful, or it is reduced to the platitudes in the text of declarations like the Universal Declaration of Human Rights, whose twentieth anniversary the world is about to commemorate. A good way for the United Nations to celebrate this anniversary would be to determine whether any of these rights are really respected in two-thirds of the world.[46]

Christianity all too often has appeared to be what Marx had alleged religion to be—opium of the people. To remedy this situation the Christians of Latin America "should help promote profound changes in social life, particularly in politics and in education. Politics cannot continue to be the property of the privileged classes, which impede basic reforms, distort them, or leave them only on paper."[47] We Christians, Câmara continued, "are on the side of non-violence, which is a choice neither of weakness nor of passivity." Violence cannot change mentalities and only begets bitterness and resentments. Yet, "with respect to those who, in conscience, feel obliged to opt for violence, not the easy violence of the guerillas of the living room, but the violence of those who have proved their sincerity by the sacrifice of their lives, it seems to me that the memory of Camilo Torres or of Ché Guevara merits as much respect as that of the Reverend Martin Luther King."[48] As a result of such pronouncements relations between Câmara and the local authorities became highly strained. In July 1969 a climate of terror was reported to have descended upon Recife's progressive Catholics. Threats were made on Dom Câmara's life, his residence was shot at, and one of Câmara's priests who was working with university students was murdered.[49]

Another churchman who has embraced the theology of revolution is Antonio Batista Fragoso, bishop of Crateus. In an address delivered in Belo Horizonte in January 1968 Fragoso declared that Christ stands for the complete liberation of man, not just his spiritual liberation: "Christ has come not only to liberate man from his sins. Christ has come to liberate him from the consequences of his sin . . . prostitution, racial discrimination . . . money concentrated in a few hands, land possessed by a small number."[50] The Gospel of Christ was directed against resignation, passive acceptance of injustice, and oppression by imperialism and colonialism. A situation like that prevailing in Brazil where 3 per cent of the people owned 62 per cent of the land represented gross social injustice and should be condemned.

The radical views of Bishops Câmara and Fragoso are not shared by most of the other members of the Brazilian hierarchy. In 1968 the archbishop of Diamantina accused Dom Helder of encouraging the infiltration of the church by Communists, and the movement "Family, Tradition, Property" collected 1,500,000 signatures to a petition asking the pope to purge the Brazilian church.[51] Still, the Catholic Left continues to make itself felt. Encouraged by the radical pronouncements of Câmara and other like-minded bishops, hundreds of priests, nuns, and students of theology have signed manifestos denouncing the archaic structure of the church, the social conditions of the country, and, openly or by implication, the government that allowed these conditions to exist. Late in October 1967 some 300 priests decried the church's paternalism, the priests' divorce from the people, and the lack of openness to the ideals and values of the poor. In May 1968 an open letter signed by 75 priests and 400 students of theology from São Paulo called the real agitators in the country those who hold power and ill-gotten money; another radical manifesto signed by 300 priests appeared in July 1968.[52]

Among the laity, too, the voices of protest could again be heard. In June 1968 the national council of the youth branch of the Catholic working-class movement (JOC) issued a manifesto that severely criticized the social, economic, and political situation in the country, "a society resting on violence," and demanded that "deep, radical, and urgent changes" be brought about by the poor and their organizations.[53] Similar statements appeared especially in the impoverished northeast, where the annual per capita income is $100, where 70 per cent of the 23 million inhabitants are illiterate, and where the infant mortality rate stands at 50 per cent.[54] Since December of 1968, as a result of the so-called "Fifth Institutional Act," the government has imposed a strict censorship on the publication of critical social, economic, or political views held by members of the hierarchy, the clergy, or Catholic organizations.[55]

Whereas the Brazilian government officially claims to maintain a neutral position toward the church, subordinate police and army commanders have been less than neutral. With the strongholds of Catholic radicals, AP, and the national student movement dissolved, former members of these groups have organized an underground opposition, and local law enforcement agencies have responded by arresting students, priests, and religious suspected of radical views and subversive activities.[56] Well-substantiated reports of the torture of such persons have appeared in the Western press and are currently being investigated by the Human Rights Commission of the Organization of American States.[57] Some of these radicals have broken entirely with their faith and have embraced outright Marxist, Castroite, or Maoist ideas. Others, however, still consider themselves part of the church, and such men, and women, too, have participated in acts of kidnapping and guerilla warfare. Church authorities have criti-

cized the involvement of priests in political violence and terrorism, but they have also denounced the arrests of religious and the
use of torture.

In 1970, Pope Paul was reported to have communicated his displeasure over the torture of suspects to the Brazilian authorities,
and at the same time he canceled a tentatively scheduled visit to
Brazil for the purpose of attending the National Eucharistic Congress.[58] Other unfavorable reactions had come from many different quarters in Europe and North America. In part, probably as a
result of this damaging publicity, during 1972 fewer charges of
torture were made. The armed forces appear to have been eased
out of police actions such as raids and interrogations, while the
underground guerilla organizations, plagued by splits in their
ranks, have slowly been broken up. Their four main leaders were
killed by government forces. The strength of the radical opposition has been further weakened by the spectacular economic
boom which Brazil has experienced during the last few years.
The country's gross national product which had increased by 2.9
per cent in 1964 increased by 11.3 per cent in 1971; the high rate
of inflation was reduced, and industrialization proceeded rapidly.
The military regime, headed by General Emilio Garrastazú
Médici since 1969, launched a massive campaign staffed by volunteers to eliminate adult illiteracy; several agencies were set up to
bring about land reform, especially in the poor northeast; and
new buildings were going up to house the millions flocking to
the cities. These measures will not immediately raise everyone out
of poverty. For some time to come, Brazil's impoverished masses
probably will be afflicted by underemployment, poor health, inadequate sanitation, and deficient education. Nevertheless, in the
long run, it may well be that these hopeful economic developments will prove more effective in undermining the standing of
the Catholic radicals than the government's continuing heavy-
handed political repression.

CAMILO TORRES: THE PRIEST AS REVOLUTIONARY

The most dramatic manifestation of the Catholic Left in Latin
America has been the participation of priests in guerilla warfare.
Best known among these clerical revolutionaries is the Colombian
priest, Camilo Torres, who was killed in February 1966 in a skir-

mish with security forces. This is not the first time that Catholic priests have fought in battles. In the wars of the Spaniards and Italians against Napoleon or in the war for Mexican independence clerics played a prominent and active role. Yet, those had been popular wars fought against foreign enemies. Today in Latin America, however, the priest-revolutionaries participate in the fight against their own government and therein lies the new element.

Camilo Restrepo Torres was born in 1929 into an upper-class urban family in Bogotá. He is said to have shown an interest in social problems from an early age, and this curiosity led him, after his ordination, to the study of sociology at Louvain, Belgium. Here he came under the influence of progressive Catholics like François Houtart, and, after obtaining his Master's degree, he stayed in Louvain as vice-rector of the Latin American College. In 1958 Torres returned to Colombia and was appointed lecturer in sociology at Bogotá's National University. He also engaged in research on the socioeconomic conditions of the Colombian capital for his doctoral dissertation and became one of the chaplains of the university. Torres was popular as a teacher and priest, and, together with his students, he engaged in community action. In June 1962, during a student strike at the university, Torres defended several students who had been expelled without a hearing, and the strikers elected Torres rector. As a result of this incident the archbishop of Bogotá asked Torres to resign his posts at the university, and the young priest now joined the Higher School of Public Administration as dean, a position that entitled him to sit on the governing board of the Colombian Institute of Agrarian Reform (INCORA).

Increasingly now Camilo Torres became involved in social action. He organized schools, set up training centers and peasant grievance meetings, and his thinking gradually became more radical.[59]

The Colombian church has been called one of the least "developed" in Latin America. In a comparison between the Colombian church and those of Argentina, Brazil, Chile, and Mexico, Ivan Vallier assigns the former the modernity score of 3 (as against 8 for Brazil and 11 for Chile).[60] Since the reign of Pope John XXIII, as a result of prodding from the Vatican and the fact that fewer sons of the upper classes are entering the priesthood, the church has begun to adopt a somewhat more open attitude toward social change. Since 1949 a network of radio schools, run by priests organized in Acción Cultural Popular, and known as Radio Sutatenza, has taught reading and writing and improved agricultural techniques, though this instruction is obviously designed to extend not only modernization but also the church's influence.[61] The church has supported the agrarian reform legislation enacted by the National Front government, and generally, as one observer puts it, "there is impressive evidence that the Colombian Church is no longer content to defend the status quo." [62] In the eyes of Torres, on the other hand, this commitment to gradual change was completely inadequate. Colombia, he insisted, needed a sweeping political and social transformation, a revolution. The hierarchy, in turn, accused Torres of advocating violence.

Back in Europe in the fall of 1964, Torres defended his Christian advocacy of revolution. In a paper read at the Second International Congress of Pro Mundi Vita in Louvain, Torres argued that the Christian apostolate in the underdeveloped countries had to have as its principal objective the practice of good works, to provide "food, drink, lodging, clothing, refuge and welcome to our brothers." [63] The solution to the problem of poverty required economic planning and basic structural change in property relations, income, investments, and education, and in political organization as well. Ideally such a revolution should be peaceful, but such a decision could only be in the hands of the ruling class. Most likely, Torres told a trade union meeting in Bavaria a little later, the minority ruling class would oppose the just reforms demanded by the majority and react violently. "If they are going to profane democracy by violence, it is important that they know we are ready to meet force with force." [64]

Returning to Colombia, Torres threw himself more and more into direct political action. He met with leading politicians of the Left, organized a "United Front of the People," and this new political alliance commissioned him to draft a platform which became public in March 1965. According to Torres, this program was for "a type of socialist state of liberation of Colombia from North American imperialism" that could be accepted by all progressive forces, including the Christian Democrats, the Communists, and "especially by the revolutionary elements not aligned in these groups." [65] The coming revolution, he told a conference at the Universidad Grancolombiano on June 15, 1965, consists of a change of structures that implies violence for those who now hold power. But such violence, which once and for all will eliminate the serious evils under which the people suffer, Torres insisted, was not excluded from the Christian ethic.[66]

On June 18, Cardinal Concha, archbishop of Bogotá, issued a statement in which he concluded that "Father Camilo Torres has consciously separated himself from the doctrines and directions of the Church" and he stated that "the activities of Father Camilo Torres are incompatible with the very ecclesiastical habit he wears." [67] Torres responded on June 24 with a request to be reduced to lay status which was granted without delay. In a statement issued a day later to the press, the radical priest explained his new position:

Ever since I became a priest I have tried all means possible to get laymen, Catholics and non-Catholics, to join the revolutionary struggle. In the absence of a massive response from the people to the action of the laymen, I have resolved to dedicate myself, fulfilling in this way part of my task of leading men through mutual love, to the love of God. I consider this an essential duty of my Christian and priestly life as a Colombian, notwithstanding that it is a task which at the present conflicts with the discipline of the Church today.

I do not wish to be unfaithful to this discipline, nor do I wish to betray my conscience. For this reason I have asked the Cardinal to free me from the clerical obligations so that I may serve the people in the secular world. I sacrifice one of the rights which I love most dearly—to be able to celebrate the eternal rite of the Church as a priest—in order to create the conditions that make the cult more authentic.[68]

In a pastoral letter issued on August 15, Cardinal Concha, without naming Torres, further criticized the advocates of revolution. Scripture, the natural law, and the teachings of the popes condemn the overthrow of legitimate authority. Even when the early Christians were victims of atrocities and bloody persecution by the Roman emperors they never attempted rebellion against the tyrannical rulers under whom they suffered so much. The cardinal went on:

It is undeniable that every nation must have changes in its institutions, in accord with the circumstances of the times. But it is equally undeniable that, under pain of falling into chaos and anarchy, these changes must be verified in a regular and legal way and never in a violent way. Certainly there are many evils which must be cured among us, as happens everywhere, and it is undeniable that every effort must be made to remedy them. The use of violence for this reason would only bring greater evils and would not correct the existing ones.[69]

Torres meanwhile was busy editing a new weekly paper, *Frente Unido*, the first issue of which appeared on August 26, 1965. In a series of editorials he argued for the revolutionary course he had chosen. All authority is from God, Torres conceded in a "Message to the Christians," but, as St. Thomas Aquinas had taught, the people appointed that authority. "When an authority is against the people, that authority is not legitimate and is called tyranny. The present government is tyrannical because only twenty percent of the electorate supports it and because its decisions come from the privileged minority." To take power from that privileged minority was the essence of the revolution, and this revolution is "not only permitted but is obligatory for Christians who must see in it the only effective and complete way to achieve love for all." [70]

In another editorial, "Message to the Communists," of September 2, Torres sought to clarify his relationship to the Communist party, a participant in the United Front. I am a revolutionary, Torres declared, and because "the Communist Party has elements that are authentically revolutionary . . . I cannot, either as a Colombian, or as a socialist, or as a Christian, or as a priest, be anti-Communist." I will not join their ranks, but "I am ready to fight alongside them for common goals: opposing the oligarchy and the domination of the United States, in order to take power for the popular class." Pope John had authorized such collaboration, and "the example of Poland shows us that Socialism can be built without destroying the essentials of Christianity." [71]

Many of the earlier supporters of the Frente Unido del Pueblo (FUP), on the other hand, soon began to condemn the alliance with the Communists. The Christian Democrats and Catholic trade unionists, therefore, pulled out of the revolutionary alliance which they saw as coming under the increasing influence of the extreme Left. With the new movement he had helped found falling apart, the disillusioned Torres in October 1965 left for the mountains and joined the guerilla forces of the Army of National Liberation (ELN), an amalgam of Communists and young radicals of varied political outlooks that had been operating in eastern Colombia since 1963.

Torres' last message reached the press in early January 1966. The people realize, he declared, the futility of elections, "that legal avenues are exhausted and that only the way of force is left." Every sincere revolutionary had to recognize this fact, and all Colombian patriots should now join the prolonged struggle that lay ahead. "I have involved myself in the armed battle. From the mountains I will continue the fight with arms in hand until power is conquered for the people. . . . Not one step back! Freedom or death!" [72] On February 15, 1966, Camilo Torres was killed, gun in hand, during an ambush of an army patrol in the mountains of northeastern Colombia. The charismatic priest, turned guerilla fighter, was 37 years old at the time of his death.

For some Colombian Catholics Torres was a martyr, and they have attempted to continue his struggle against the National Front and the clerical establishment. The leadership for this small radical Catholic movement has come from the so-called Golconda Group which was organized during the summer of 1968 by fifty priests, including Monsignor Gerardo Valencia Cano, the young bishop of Buenaventura. A programmatic statement of this group, issued in December 1968, called for "an increase in revolutionary action against imperialism and the neo-colonial bourgoisie" and for the establishment of a socialist society in Colombia.[73] The government retaliated by arresting several of the priests and by deporting four Spanish priests and an American nun allegedly involved with the Golconda Group. On February 17, 1970, *Le Monde* published an open letter from Father Domingo Lain, one of the deported Spaniards, in which he announced that he had returned to Colombia and had joined the Army of National Liberation:

> I have chosen the path of the armed struggle because of the reactionary and oppressive violence of the established systems in Colombia and Latin America, there is no other solution but a liberating and revolutionary violence. . . . I believe that, only now, my true pastoral consecration, which demands total self-sacrifice that all men may live, begins.[74]

The chances that the revolutionary Catholics of Colombia will find wider popular support are slight. The memory of the virtual civil war that ravaged the Colombian countryside between 1948 and 1964, which the Colombians call *la violencia* and which took between 100,000 and 200,000 lives,[75] is still fresh and works against any group that preaches the dreaded political strategy of violence. By identifying themselves with the phenomenon of violence, the Christian revolutionaries undercut their potential legitimation and repel many of the Catholic progressives who are ready to help promote social change.[76] By 1972 the Golconda Group had all but disappeared for lack of leadership. The three guerilla groups operating in Colombia are said to have a combined membership of less than 500 men, including two Catholic priests.[77] The guerillas operate in the rural northeast and despite occasional forays into towns have no links with urban protest.[78]

Colombia is not the only Latin American country in which priests have opted for violent struggle. In early 1968 three former American Maryknoll priests and a nun were expelled from Guatemala for having assisted Castroite guerillas. In a statement issued after their arrival in the United States, one of the group, Thomas Melville, defended revolution as the only recourse of the people of Guatemala: "If the government and the oligarchy are using arms to maintain them in their position of misery, they have the obligation to take up arms and defend their God-given rights to be men." [79] In Argentina 283 priests belonging to a group called "Priests of the Third World" have asserted a similar position and a well-known Uruguayan priest, Juan Carlos Zaffaroni, since 1968 has been with the urban guerillas operating in his country.[80]

The total number of priests actually fighting with Latin American guerilla groups is undoubtedly very small, though their conduct is admired by many in the Catholic Left. In May 1972 more than 400 self-proclaimed "Christians for Socialism," the majority of them Catholic priests, met in Santiago, Chile, and called for a strategic alliance between revolutionary Christians and Marxists to liberate the Latin American continent. The meeting castigated the distortion of the Gospel by the institutional church by which the "institutionalized violence" of the system is covered up "and the appeal to violence to fight against the dominant class and for the revolutionary struggle is held back." [81] Latin American revolutionaries themselves, however, are often wary of their Christian allies. Ché Guevara warned Christian would-be-revolutionaries against attempting to evangelize the Marxists, and more recently a European leftist rejected the theology of revolution as "a religiously embellished ideology of late capitalism" which had the purpose of splitting the anti-imperialist movement and sought to prevent the masses from joining the struggle against imperialism.[82] The Christian revolutionaries, it would appear, find it hard to please their secular friends.

THE ROLE OF THE LATIN AMERICAN EPISCOPATE

The Catholic Left represents only a small segment of Latin America's Catholics. Yet, it includes many of the continent's more sensitive, articulate, and better-educated men and women; some of the positions taken by the radical Catholics— nationalism, a modified Marxism, the call for economic development, solidarity with the Third World—have wide support among many levels of society. In these circumstances the Latin American episcopate cannot but address itself to the problems raised and dramatized by the Catholic Left. The episcopal posture has also, of course, been affected by the spirit of *aggiornamento* introduced by Pope John XXIII (1958–63) and the Second Vatican Council. Today, therefore, the Latin American bishops are no longer conservative defenders of the status quo, but, in varying degrees, they use their position of leadership to call for and to sanction social change.

The situation is in many ways similar to that prevailing around the turn of the nineteenth century. After Archbishop Gibbons of Baltimore, during a visit to Rome in 1887, had made an impassioned appeal to the papacy concerning the threatened loss to the church of the common people in America, and in the face of the rapid growth of Marxist parties in all of Central and Western Europe, Pope Leo XIII issued a number of encyclicals which were not only aimed at preserving the loyalty of the workers but were also designed as part of a more basic comprehensive program to enable the church to deal with the major economic and social problems of the day.[83] Today another such crucial turning point in the history of the Catholic church has been reached. Individual bishops, national episcopates, and continental bishops' conferences have begun to engage the church in the process of social change. What matters here is not so much whether these pronouncements represent sound and prudent counsel; on that issue opinions can differ. What is important is that the hierarchy has in principle accepted the need for structural social change and thus has created a climate of innovation and inspiration for Catholics to fight injustice and poverty. As Mark G. McGrath, archbishop of Panama, has put it: The church cannot itself create a new temporal order, but it can provide "a kind of moral umbrella" to those who are engaged in the task of trying to solve burning social problems and thus protect them against "politicians or vested interests who try to stop social reform actions." [84]

In Brazil the bishops of the northeast, acting individually or in concert, have for many years condemned injustice and demanded radical social change. As early as 1950 the Franciscan bishop of Campanha in East Brazil reminded his diocesans in a pastoral letter that the church in nineteenth-century Europe had "lost" the urban workers and that a similar danger threatened the Brazilian church with regard to the country's rural workers whose "situation is sub-human." [85] Other such pastoral letters from bishops in "development areas" made their appearance in the following years, and in May 1956 the bishops of the northeast met for the first time as a group and, with the help of lay experts, discussed the region's problems. The bishops' declaration concluded that "in the present socio-economic structures which constitute our political organization and the system of our private economy there are tremendous injustices," and they called for a comprehensive plan of development for the area. "The Church," they went on to say, "places itself on the side of those unjustly treated, so that it may co-operate with them in the task of recuperation and redemption." [86]

On the occasion of Pope John's encyclical *Pacem in Terris*, a pronouncement in the name of the entire episcopate also came out for basic social change. Entitled *"Pacem in Terris and the Brazilian Reality"* and issued at Easter 1963 by the Central Commission of the Brazilian Bishops' Conference, the declaration was considered so radical by the large conservative newspapers that they refused to publish it, and the bishops had to pay regular advertising fees in order to bring their statement before the public. Brazilian life was severely criticized:

No one can believe that the social order in which we live [the situation in Brazil] is the one proposed by the new encyclical as the unshakable foundation of peace. Our social order is still burdened by the heavy weight of a capitalist tradition which has dominated the West these past centuries. It is an order in which money and economic power are the underlying determinants in all economic, political, and social decisions. It is an order in which a minority has access to culture, a high standard of living, health, comfort and luxury, and in which the majority, having no way of obtaining these goods, are by that very fact deprived from exercising many of man's basic and natural rights, as enunciated in *Pacem in Terris:* the right to existence, the right to a decent standard of living, the respect of his dignity and freedom, the right to participate in the benefits of culture, finally, the right relative to his life in society.[87]

After denouncing the negative attitudes of the rich "who do all in their power to maintain the status quo," the opportunist reformers, and the totalitarian extremists, the document called for agrarian reform in order to help those "millions of our brothers who live in the country, unable to participate in the benefits of our development, in conditions of utter poverty which are an insult to human dignity." In such a situation "expropriation in the interest of society contains nothing contrary to the social doctrine of the Church." [88] Several bishops publicly dissociated themselves from this document which had broken with the sanctity of private property.

As mentioned earlier, during the first years of the military regime the Brazilian hierarchy exercised maximum restraint. But as incidents involving the arrest of clerics multiplied, and the government seemingly preferred the rights of property to the aspirations of the poor, the bishops in February 1969 once again sounded the call for reform and "change in the archaic structures that are flagrant obstacles to development." Such reforms, the declaration of the Central Commission of the Brazilian episcopate stated, need not accept Marxist or communist postulates "but neither can they consist in the defense and incidental improvement of a status quo in which profit is the supreme value of economic progress, competition the sole law of the economy, and private ownership of the goods of production an absolute right." [89] The church is against subversive movements that produce disorder and anarchy. "However, we also think that it is subversive of the social order to abuse one's political and economic power for one's personal benefit." [90] The statement ended by calling for an early

"re-democratization" of public life and castigated the suppression
of basic civil liberties imposed in December of 1968:

> The present situation, given institutional form last December, is an
> open invitation to arbitrary action and the violation of fundamental
> rights, such as the right of defense and the right to legitimate ex-
> pression of thought and information. It threatens human dignity
> both physically and morally. Power has been established in a way
> that makes it very difficult to have an authentic dialogue between
> governors and governed and leads many Brazilians to dangerous
> underground activity.[91]

Since then the Brazilian hierarchy, while expressing its satisfaction with the economic progress of the last few years, individually and collectively has continued to admonish the government
not to ignore the interests of the millions of poverty-stricken Indians and rural squatters in the rush for economic development.
The moderate and progressive elements now once again make the
major decisions.[92]

Seven Brazilian bishops, led by Câmara, were the moving spirit
behind a pastoral letter issued in August 1967 by "16 Bishops of
the Third World." This statement fully embraced the theology
of revolution. The signers agreed that not all revolutions were
good, but they maintained that "some revolutions have been necessary" and that "Christians and their pastors should know how
to recognize the hand of the Almighty in those events that from
time to time put down the mighty from their thrones and raise
up the humble, send away the rich empty-handed, and fill the
hungry with good things." [93] The church for centuries had tolerated capitalism even though "the Gospel has always been the
most potent ferment of deep social change." The bishops urged
that Christians utilize these currents of moral strength and brotherhood and gladly embrace true socialism "as a form of social life
better adapted to our times, more in keeping with the spirit of the
Gospel. In this way we shall stop people confusing God and religion and the oppressors of the poor and of the workers, which is
what the feudal, capitalist, and imperialist systems are." [94]

Last, one must mention in this context the pronouncements of
the Second General Conference of the Bishops of Latin America
(*Conferencia Episcopado Latin Americano*—CELAM) held at
Medellín, Colombia, after the conclusion of the Eucharistic Con-

gress attended by Pope Paul. Some 750 bishops participated in
sessions that lasted from August 24 through September 6, 1968
and adopted several documents affirming the need for radical social change in Latin America. In these pronouncements, entitled
"The Church in the Actual Transformation of Latin America in
the Light of the Council," the process of social and economic development and the emergence of a new civilization are given theological recognition and meaning. "We cannot fail to interpret
this gigantic effort for a rapid transformation and development as
an evident sign of the presence of the Spirit which conducts the
history of men and people. . . . We cannot fail to discover in this
will . . . the vestiges of the image of God in man as a potent
dynamism." [95] The existing order is criticized as unjust, and the
fatalistic interpretation of poverty as the result of the will of God
is rejected. The absence of disorder alone does not signify genuine peace. "Peace is, above all, a work of justice (*Gaudium et
Spes,* # 78). It presupposes and requires the establishment of a just
order (*Pacem in Terris,* # 167; *Popularum Progressio,* # 76). . . .
The oppression of the power groups may give the impression of
maintaining peace and order, but in truth it is nothing but the
'continuous and inevitable seed of rebellion and war.' (Message of
Paul VI, Jan. 1, 1968)." [96]

The Christian man, the bishops declare, is a man of peace. Yet,
in the face of "a situation of injustice that can be called institutionalized violence" [97] it is not surprising that the temptation to
use violence appears in Latin America. The elites of the continent, therefore, are urged not to obstruct "the profound transfor-
mations that are so necessary. If they jealously retain their privileges and defend them with force they are responsible to history
for provoking 'explosive revolutions of despair' (Speech by Paul
VI in Bogotá, in the Eucharistic Celebration of the Day of Development, August 23, 1968)." [98]

In his encyclical *Populorum Progressio* of 1967 Pope Paul rejected violent revolution "except where there is manifest, long
standing tyranny that would do great damage to fundamental
personal rights and dangerous harm to the common good of the
country" (section 31).[99] Catholic radicals welcomed this sentence
and other passages calling for profound changes as providing a
justification of their revolutionary strategy, and a manifesto
signed by 920 priests addressed to the CELAM meeting had asked

that the bishops fully endorse the "just violence of the oppressed."[100] It is probable that the pope emphasized patience and moderation in his address at the Eucharistic Congress in Bogotá in order to dampen the aroused spirits and expectations; the Medellín documents, too, sought to modify the impact of the controversial phrases. Even if it is true, as Pope Paul had stated, that revolutionary insurrection can be legitimate in the case of evident and prolonged tyranny that violates basic personal rights and undermines the common good of the country, "it is also certain that violence or armed revolution most often 'generates new injustices, introduces new imbalances and causes new disasters' *(Populorum Progressio, #31)*. One cannot combat a real evil at the price of a greater evil."[101] The revolutionary alternative was thus further discouraged. Indeed, even the earlier emphasis on the importance of social change was weakened when the bishops later warned against confusing such temporal progress with the Kingdom of Christ. "The uniqueness of the Christian message does not so much consist in the affirmation of the necessity of structural change as in the insistence we ought to feel about changing men's hearts. We will not have a new continent without new and reformed structures, but above all, not without new men, who know how to be truly free and responsible in the light of the Gospel."[102]

Despite this reminder to the Christians of Latin America that the message of Christ transcends the affairs of this earth and the achievements of any temporal reform or revolution, the overall thrust of the Medellín documents is clearly in the direction of legitimizing radical social change. The church expresses a commitment to the poor and underprivileged and seeks to forge a new relationship with the masses. Not surprisingly, in Paraguay the Medellín declarations were condemned as subversive by that country's right-wing government.[103] In the words of one interpreter:

> The bishops made a remarkable effort to criticize and analyze the structures of society. The philosophical orientation of the documents in itself constitutes a victory over the old triumphal and anti-historical heritage of the Church. They openly and concretely affirm the world and their commitment to it, while trying to educate people to the radical awareness that the situation is not an inevitable condition because *Dios lo quiere* (God wills it so). The

transition from fatalism to conscious agents of change marks the beginning of an authentic revolution.[104]

Not all members of the Latin American hierarchy share the spirit of the Medellín documents. A majority of the Colombian bishops are said to have rejected the final pronouncement and to have published their own report.[105] However, the fact that this lengthy statement was issued in the name of the continental episcopate cannot but further encourage the more progressive elements of the church in Latin America. The words of the hierarchy will legitimize their aspirations and activities, and this will also benefit the Catholic Left.

CONCLUSION

The Catholic Left in Latin America emerged during the period of *aggiornamento* ushered in by the Second Vatican Council (1963–65). Whereas in earlier times Christians turned radicals usually left the church, many of the new militants have a sense of loyalty to the Christian heritage and justify their radicalism by references to the revolutionary dynamic they see inherent in the Christian message. Christianity, writes Guzman, is founded in charity: "If charity is the service of men; if the majority of men is seen to be mired in subhuman conditions, the Christian must be a revolutionary." [106] Encouraged by the changes that have taken place in the church as a whole, the Catholic Left sees a future for the Christian faith, albeit one renewed and redirected.

Though in the past the church was seen and often indeed functioned as a bulwark of the status quo, there now exists a commitment to social reform. Less frequently are the poor taught to accept their lowly condition with resignation; fewer priests still teach that the meek will inherit the earth. The widespread desire for change in Latin America is thus reinforced, and progressive Catholics like Chile's Christian Democrats have benefited from the new image projected by the church. In turn, the strength displayed by progressive Catholics has influenced the thinking of church leaders all the way up to the pope in Rome.

And yet, the very success of gradualist social reform raises expectations which are not always easy to satisfy. The accomplishments of the Frei administration in Chile, for example, were substantial. During Frei's six years in office from 1964 to 1970, the Chilean economy made impressive gains,[107] and it may well be that had Chilean law not prevented Frei from running again, the Christian Democrats would have been returned to office. Yet the defeat of the Christian Democrats in the 1970 election by Allende's Popular Unity coalition, notes one observer, "also indicated that the Frei administration had raised reformist hopes to a level that even its solid performance could not justify." [108]

In the same way, the church's new posture against social injustice and in favor of basic social change may not only legitimize reform but may strengthen the advocates of revolutionary and violent change. Moreover, as a result of gains made by the Left, Latin American society may become more polarized and conservatives, too, may feel justified in recourse to violence. Thus, for example, Carlos Lacerda, the former governor of Guanabara, supported the take-over by the Brazilian military in 1964 and defended its violence by asserting that "to be a Catholic is to be a fighter. It is to fight with enthusiasm and valor, even using violence if necessary, in order to preserve all that is sacred and all that flows from sacred doctrine, the true Christian Doctrine." [109]

Whereas the climate of renewal in the post-Vatican church has benefited the Catholic Left, the utopian and doctrinaire thinking often found in the radical Catholic camp stand in the way of its future growth. There often prevails a highly utopian view of the future course of history which is seen to lead to a world of perfect happiness without domination and conflict. The Catholic Left's philosophy of history, like that of Marxism, is quasi-millenarian in its expectations and involves an all-or-nothing approach to human affairs. The radical commitment to social justice is usually not matched by a pragmatic understanding of economic realities. There is a tendency to blame the backwardness and failures of Latin American society exclusively on exploitative capitalism or North American imperialism; all too often there is a preoccupation with how the pie is to be divided rather than how it is to be made larger.

Whether a controlled capitalism committed to rapid economic growth and development, as it exists now in Brazil, for example, will be able to meet the continent's aroused expectations remains to be seen. But the conclusion of the Catholic radicals that only a massive revolution can solve Latin America's problems, and that such a revolution is around the corner, seems premature. Ché Guevara's call for many Vietnams in Latin America has not met with much success; the guerilla movement is not about to win popular backing. It may well be, therefore, that the radical Catholics supporting violent revolution have come too late and have hitched their carriage to a waning star. Over the past two centuries, writes Jacques Ellul, Christian intellectuals have made it a practice in political, social, and economic spheres of arriving on the stroke of midnight; they "specialize in joining struggles that are virtually over." [110] The support of revolution by the Catholic Left in time may turn out to be another example of Ellul's generalization.

So far the Catholic Left has indeed remained isolated from the main body of Catholicism, and it has, as Paul Sanders notes, "an almost sectarian quality." [111] It has no clear view of what should happen to the more conventional Catholics who prefer a less demanding religion, and its political and social programs are usually equally indefinite. There is a commitment to some sort of socialism though the concrete form of such a socialist society is left vague, and the actual experience of different socialist countries is neglected. The state-run economies of the Third World have produced disappointing rates of economic growth, and many Marxist-inspired regimes in Eastern Europe are beginning to discard the idea of central planning and reinstate various market mechanisms and types of private property. Still, the Christians for Socialism organized in 1972, for example, call for "the social ownership of the means of production and financing" and "rational, universal economic planning." [112]

The Catholic Left's emphasis on changing the structure of society, while drawing much of its impetus from a radical Christian message, logically leads to a secular outlook on politics. Instead of promoting change through clerical or lay groups that are consciously Christian, the Catholic Left works in and through secular organizations and seeks a genuinely humanistic society rather than a revived "Christian civilization." This secular orientation facilitates cooperation with the Communists and other forces of the Left. It is no accident that some Catholic radical organizations, like the Brazilian Ação Popular, have largely abandoned their Catholic character, have absorbed a Marxist ideology, and have practically merged with the secular Left. On the other hand, there are many progressive priests and laymen who are determined to stay within the church and who have misgivings about a violent strategy and an alliance with Communists or other even more radical groups. The prominent Brazilian Christian Democrat, Paulo de Tarso, at one time close to the revolutionary Left, is thus oriented.[113] Disagreements over tactics further weaken the numerically small Catholic Left. Whether Catholic radicals can overcome these difficulties and challenges to their existence and growth only the future will tell.

PART VI

Religion and Revolution: Theoretical Perspectives

CHAPTER 21

The State of the Question

The revolutions examined in the preceding chapters reveal the several ways religion is manifested politically. The phenomena of revolutionary millenarianism, as the struggle for an earthly paradise, and of religious nationalism, as anti-colonial strife, show how religious ideas can function as a revolutionary ideology to inspire revolutionary action. The collision between the Catholic church and modern revolutions of essentially secular origin points up the ambiguous political role played by a highly structured ecclesiastical institution. Last, religion is enlisted by political as well as religious leaders in several countries of the Third World to legitimate radical political and social change. Before undertaking our own analysis of this complex and varied relationship of religion and revolution we must briefly discuss the state of this question in the theoretical literature.

Revolutionary upheavals have occurred less frequently and have occupied far less time in the history of mankind than have periods of relative tranquility; in part, at least, this is undoubtedly the result of the tendency to obey authority found in all societies and at all times. Men obey because they are social beings, because the social order requires and inculcates the habit of obedience. The propensity to obey superiors, a psychiatrist has suggested, may also be a biologically rooted trait which was originally adaptive because it favored the survival of the small tribal group, the social unit of primitive man led by one or a few strong individuals.[1] Even in more complex societies obedience continues to be adaptive, and such positive attitudes toward authority, commonly implanted in childhood as part of early socialization, are eradicated only with difficulty.[2]

The relative infrequency of revolution, whatever its causes, may be one of the reasons why most students of religion and politics have emphasized primarily the integrative role of religion. Of course, the fact that religion often functions as a source of social solidarity, to weld a society together, is undoubtedly related to the very essence of religion which provides a set of basic values for the regulation of man's life on earth and guidance in his search for meaning and salvation. In tracing the development of this function it will be well to remember that in all traditional societies both nature and society were regarded as part of the same cosmic universe controlled by gods or spirits; a religious legitimation of the social order therefore developed as a matter of course.

The integrative role of religion has been known for a very long time. The eighteenth-century rationalist, Voltaire, assured his noble pupil, Frederick the Great, that a "wise and courageous prince, with money, troops and laws, can perfectly well govern men without the aid of religion," [3] but most rulers of mankind and the wise men counseling them have preferred not to take any chances on the firmness and sway of political authority. Concerning the rites and ceremonies (*li*) of the Chinese cult of ancestors, it is written in the *Book of Rites* (*Li Chi*), the ancient classic: "Of all the ways of keeping men in good order, there is none more important than sacrifice." [4] And a commentary to the *Book of Change* (*I Ching*), attributed to Confucius, put the same point more bluntly: "The sage devised guidance by way of the gods and [the people of] the land became obedient." [5] The Greek historian of Rome, Polybius, observed that "a scrupulous fear of the gods is the very thing which keeps the Roman commonwealth together." Since the common people are "fickle, and full of lawless desires," the only way to check the multitude is through "mysterious terrors and scenic effects of this sort." [6] In his *Discourses* Machiavelli called religion "the most necessary and assured support of any civil society," and he exhorted princes and heads of republics "to uphold the foundations of the religion of their countries, for then it is easy to keep their people religious, and consequently well conducted and united." [7] The length of empires, argued the French conservative, Joseph de Maistre, "has always been proportionate to the influence that the religious principle has acquired in the political system. The towns and nations most devoted to a cult of divinity have always been the most durable . . .' (Xenophon)." [8] The emphasis on the importance to society of a sense of shared values endeared de Maistre to his fellow-countryman, the sociologist Emile Durkheim, probably the best-known modern spokesman for the view that the primary function of religion is the preservation of social unity.[9]

Many of the philosophers who considered religion a source of social integration made it appear as if religious faith was deliberately manipulated by rulers to keep their subjects obedient and submissive. Polybius and Machiavelli, quoted above, indeed recommend the employment of religion for this very purpose. The inconstant mob, prone to superstititon, writes Spinoza, "is easily led, on the plea of religion, at one moment to adore its kings as gods, and anon to execrate and abjure them as humanity's common bane. Immense pains have therefore been taken to counteract this evil by investing religion, whether true or false, with such pomp and ceremony that it may rise superior to every shock, and be always observed with studious reverence by the whole people." In a despotic state in particular, "the supreme and essential mystery" is "to hoodwink the subjects, and to mask the fear, which keeps them down, with the specious garb of religion. . . . " [10] Typical of the condescending and patronizing opinion of the man in the street that characterizes many of these writers, and probably the best known, is Gibbon's comment on the different modes of worship prevailing in the Roman world during the age of the Antonines—they "were all considered by the people as equally true; by the philosopher as equally false; and by the magistrate as equally useful." [11]

The political exploitation of religion has undoubtedly taken place many times. Jacques Necker, the French minister of finance on the eve of the French Revolution, is supposed to have argued that when taxes are increased it is necessary to increase religious instruction.[12] Similar occurrences have been mentioned in earlier chapters of this study. And yet, this interpretation of religion as a means of social control, emphasizing the manipulative use of religion by the dominant forces in society, fails to explain why the masses willingly accept these ideas. Marxism addresses itself to this question.

For Marx and Engels "the religious world is but the reflex of the real world." [13] Religious ideas, as are juridical or philosophical constructs generally, "are the more or less remote offshoots of the economical relations prevailing in a given society." [14] Since all hitherto existing historical societies have been class societies, based on the exploitation of man by man, religion has reflected this condition of human subjugation and misery. Religion, writes Engels, "is nothing but the fantastic reflection in men's minds of those external forces which control their daily life, a reflection in which the terrestrial forces assume the form of supernatural forces." [15] Thus Christianity, for example, declares "all vile acts of the oppressors against the oppressed to be either the just punishment of original sin and other sins or trials that the Lord in his infinite wisdom imposes on those redeemed." [16] Religion functions to make an oppressed and alienated mankind see the unhappy reality of class society as a manifestation of divine providence and offers solace by promising rewards in the heavenly beyond.[17] Religion exists and survives because it provides for the consolation and illusory happiness of people. Or as Marx put it succinctly in an often-quoted remark: "Religion is the sigh of the oppressed creature . . . it is the opium of the people." [18]

But Marxism also recognizes another side of religion. Engels sympathetically described "theological heresies" during the Middle Ages that mounted a revolutionary attack upon feudalism and, going beyond the "equality of the children of God," demanded "civil equality, and partly even equality of property." He praised the sixteenth-century Christian theologian, Thomas Müntzer, whose religious and political doctrine "went beyond the directly prevailing social and political conditions." [19] Following Engels a host of Marxist scholars have discovered revolutionary themes in the ideologies of various pre-modern religious movements; we have had occasion to discuss the adequacy of these interpretations of religious dissent as premature expressions of revolutionary class consciousness in earlier chapters. None of these writers, it should be noted, has explained satisfactorily how, from the point of view of dialectical materialism, individual religious figures could successfully transcend "prevailing social and political conditions." Be that as it may, the fact remains that for Marxists religion is not only a sort of "spiritual booze," as Lenin once called it,[20] but also, at least potentially, a revolutionary force.

The Marxist view of the hold religious ideas have had upon men at all times is that religion is a spiritual reflection of class conflict, exploitation, and wretchedness. However, a more complete explanation of the universality of religion must go beyond such social and economic factors and must acknowledge that religion indeed meets far more basic needs of both the individual and society. Most non-Marxist scholars today probably agree with Edmund Burke's observation that "man is by his constitution a religious animal." [21] Religion persists, in large measure, because it is a response to certain primary psychological and moral needs of man. Religion helps individuals face anxiety, death, disease, loneliness, frustration, guilt, failure, and injustice—the human condition. It is similarly clear that every society needs some integrating rules, customs, and beliefs and that religion, whatever else it may do, often helps create and maintain this basic consensus of values by providing a system of social norms buttressed by rewards and punishments. Religion supports social solidarity and cohesion, though religion is not the only force working in this direction, and it often leads to conflict as well.

It is important not to confuse a condition of social integration with what is desirable or valuable. Many religious ideas damage the viability of a society or group. The belief that certain rituals can convert bullets into water may increase the willingness of a millenarian cult to attack the machine gun positions of the enemy, but these rituals are not only ineffective and fail their avowed purpose as do other innocuous superstititons such as rain dances, but they also are clearly dysfunctional for the survival of the group. Similarly, when religion promotes a state of social cohesion such a condition is not for that reason automatically good. A sociologist of religion, J. Milton Yinger observes: "A religion may give support to a society based on principles that one considers bad, such as the acceptance of slavery; the rites it employs may, from the value stand of the outsider, seem barbarous, as, for example, the custom of human sacrifice. . . . On another level, in connection with the relations between societies that have a different kind of religious integration, strong barriers to intersociety cooperation and accommodation may be erected." [22] In other words, order and integration may be good or bad, depending on one's moral point of view and taking into account to whom the benefits of such a state of stability accrue. The fact that the institution of sacred kingship helped numerous peoples to endure despotic rule and poverty for thousands of years does not

necessarily recommend this religious idea to us today. Despotic regimes, as Eugene Walter has argued, can be stabilized for decades
and centuries, but their longevity does not constitute proof of
moral excellence.[23]

A similar warning must be issued against one-sided praise of
the liberating role of religion. Just as a state of social integration
cannot automatically be considered good, so the nonconformist
thrust of religion should not automatically be equated with
progress or moral excellence. The prophetic spirit of religion has
been a source of moral protest and renewal, but it has also led to
self-righteousness, intolerance, fanaticism, and the creation of
dangerously unrealistic expectations. The prophetic denunciation
of man's moral imperfections is rarely very helpful in the plod-
ding, day-to-day effort to improve the life of the human race.
The utopian character of revolutionary millenarianism, seeking to
solve the human condition once and for all, and the Manichean
division of mankind into good and evil camps accompanying such a
Millennium, account for much of its ruthlessness and cruelty.

When evaluating the political and social role of religion we
should consider the range of alternatives. Writes Yinger:

> It is unwise to complain that an escapist religion rigidifies the status
> pattern, if the only other adjustments available to individuals are
> utter demoralization and mental illness. But it is equally unwise to
> say that religion helps a group to bear the enormous burdens of
> low status, if that very religion obscures real possibilities of other
> kinds of action that might reduce those burdens. It is unwise to re-
> gret that an aggressive sect converts mundane issues into religious
> questions, incapable of rational examination, if society furnishes few
> secular means for the resolution of those issues. A severe religion
> may be the only way to save the selves of those who have escaped
> serfdom, have had their hopes mightily raised, only to run into in-
> superable barriers. Yet it is unwise to applaud an aggressive sect
> that polarizes a society and converts the pursuit of its goals into a
> sacred battle—when it has quite effective secular means and
> many potential allies to help in their attainment.[24]

The degree to which a specific religion does, in fact, contribute
to the integration of a particular society is an empirical question
—difficult as it may be to find an answer. The functional analysis of religion has often disregarded this basic insight and instead has embraced a dogmatic assumption of functional unity. In

nonliterate societies or in modern societies with only one religion
a common set of religious values may indeed be an important
force for social integration. But in pluralistic societies where more
than one religion is practiced or where secular ideologies under-
mind the appeal of traditional belief systems or where the legitimacy of existing political and social arrangements depends less on
religious values than on their effectiveness in securing high levels
of consumption [25] the integrative or functional role of religion
will be weak. In these situations a postulate of functional unity,
ignoring the divisive and dysfunctional consequences of religion
for individuals, subgroups, or entire societies, is questionable. The
unity of the total society, Merton has stressed, cannot be usefully
posited in advance of observation. "It is a question of fact, and
not a matter of opinion." [26]

The functional approach raises other problems. It ignores the
not infrequent occasion when religious ideas are imposed by foreign conquerors, which means, of course, that they cannot be regarded as emanations of the subjugated societies.[27] It overstates
the element of intention and design in history and human culture.
Social cohesion in some situations may be a function of religion,
but this more often than not is an unintended consequence of religion. The religious minister preaching love of our fellow man is
not doing so to promote social stability, though the internaliza-
tion of this ethical principle by large numbers of people may indeed effect reconciliation. An increase in social concord may be a
latent function of the cleric's activity. In order to convert the
functional relationship into a causal explanation we would have
to show that religion is the necessary condition of social integration,[28] but this cannot be done, for the integration of society can
be promoted by other, secular, means of social support. Leni Rie-
fenstahl's famous documentary film, "Triumph of the Will," or
the Nazis' Nuremberg gatherings themselves, are good examples
of such secular rituals [29] and so is the inauguration of an American president or the commemoration of Memorial Day and
Thanksgiving Day—parts of what Robert Bellah has called
America's "civil religion," the celebration of the American experience and an important source of national solidarity.[30] As long as
institutionalized religion, tied to a supernatural referent, is neither
the necessary nor the sufficient condition of social integration, it
cannot be its cause.

Most importantly, a functionalism that stresses the interdependence of the various elements in a culture and aims at explaining the functions requisite to the maintenance of an integrated system often exaggerates the integrative role of religion and slights its innovative and revolutionary role. That religion has frequently spurred revolt, providing the ideology and social cohesion for rebellion against the existing political and social order, can undoubtedly be fitted into a functionalist framework. Social scientists like Harry Eckstein and Chalmers Johnson have analyzed the phenomenon of revolution in functionalist terms. And yet, the contribution of this approach toward a theoretical understanding of revolutionary change appears to be limited. One can call the religious ideas of a revolutionary millenarian sect functional for the members of this group and dysfunctional for the larger society against which the sectarians scheme, but such labels add little to an explanation of the origins of these ideas or how and why this sect came into being. New religious ideas do not arise only in situations where the established religion has failed to fulfill expectations. A charismatic leader with innovative ideas can change the expectations of his followers and thus establish a basis for criticism and eventually change of the old order. "Why people should be prepared to have their expectations changed," writes the philosopher-anthropologist Jarvie, "may be due not only to inadequacy in the establishment, but to the unleashed power of novel ideas." [31] The bases for social change cannot all be understood in terms of dysfunctions, quite apart from the fact that the question of whether the activity of, say, a millenarian group is indeed seen as dysfunctional from the point of view of the stability of society as a whole and thus a factor making for revolutionary unrest can often be answered only by hindsight. The study of social processes through time, therefore, is one of the crucial necessary supplementary tools of functionalist analysis as indeed of any study of revolutionary change.[32]

All students of revolution recognize the important role played by revolutionary ideologies, including religious beliefs that a radical transformation of society is necessary. Crane Brinton talks of "foundations of the revolutionary myth" or the "better world of the ideal." [33] Neil Smelser speaks of "value-oriented beliefs" involving a basic reconstitution of society.[34] Chalmers Johnson invokes revolutionary ideologies replacing the old value structure of society.[35] Ted Gurr sees the need for ideas promising a new way of life or "ideologies depicting a golden millennium."[36] Lyford Edwards argues the importance of the "social myth" (a term borrowed from Georges Sorel), a "super-rational 'theological' dynamic" which gives hope for "a new heaven and a new earth."[37] What these and other theorists dealing with the phenomenon of revolution have by and large not done is probe the conditions under which religious ideas function as agents of revolutionary mobilization and determine what kinds of religious beliefs can and in fact do operate as the spiritual dynamic of revolution.

In the five chapters that follow we will develop our examination of the multifarious political role of religion. Drawing upon the historical materials introduced in the preceding chapters, we will build our analysis around four main variables—religious doctrine, ecclesiastical organization, leadership, and the role of situational factors—all of which have political importance and political consequences.

CHAPTER 22

Religious Doctrine

Why has religion sometimes acted as a force for social integration, if not political quietism, whereas at other times it has led to rebellion? To find an answer to this question, the main theme of this book, it seems logical to begin by looking at religious doctrine. Do the teachings of the major religions on the subject of political obedience lead to certain observable political results? Do some religious ideas function as the "opium of the people," while others spur revolt?

Certain religious conceptions of rulership do appear to have entailed a pattern of subservience. The institution of sacred kingship, to be found in most pre-modern societies, upheld above all else the virtues of obedience and submissiveness. The god-kings of Egypt and Mesopotamia, the Son of the Sun ruling the Incas of Peru, the divine kings of ancient India, the king-god of old Scandinavia, the divine ruler of the Ashanti on the African Gold Coast—these and many other divine rulers of whom we have knowledge [1] usually governed a docile society in which attempts to overthrow and change the existing order were practically unknown. There arose conflicts among the ruling family or families, motivated by personal ambition, but the divine ruler's authority was beyond dispute. As a sacred figure he had no superior to whom mere men could appeal.

In India political quietism is supported by the caste system fortified by the religious doctrine of Hinduism. According to the principle of *karma*, the law of action and retribution, membership in a caste was determined by the virtues or sins of a previous existence, and misfortune or distress was considered the result of one's own doing. As Max Weber has pointed out,

. . . any possible improvement in one's chances in subsequent incarnations depended on the faithful execution in the present lifetime of the vocation assigned him by virtue of his caste status. Any
effort to emerge from one's caste, and especially to intrude into the
sphere of activities appropriate to other and higher castes, was expected to result in evil magic and entailed the likelihood of unfavorable incarnation hereafter. This explains why, according to numerous observations on affairs in India, it is precisely the lowest
classes, who would naturally be most desirous of improving their
status in subsequent incarnations, that cling most steadfastly to
their caste obligations, never thinking of toppling the caste system
through social revolutions or reforms.[2]

Moreover, Hinduism deprecated the importance of earthly sat-
isfactions and instead stressed the value of spiritual tranquility. In
the classical Hindu view the ultimate ideal was "to realize the
identity with Brahman, to enter Nirvana, or to attain to the Supreme Being, to abnegate all actions and desires and to feel oneself as a constituent of the Supreme." [3] Until the encounter with
the European style of life in the eighteenth and nineteenth centuries, at least, such an ethic naturally encouraged resignation to
suffering and oppression. The highest goal for man in history was
"not deliverance from evil but escape from the unending wheels
of history." [4]

The conception of sacred kingship and the Hindu law of
karma have had rather clear-cut political implications. Logically
and empirically, that is, on the level of ideas as well as in terms of
actual results, these religious doctrines can be said to constitute a
powerful force for political quietism. We can make this observation without regarding these religious ideas as deliberate inventions of certain dominant groups or classes. The precise origins of
the notion of sacred kingship and of the law of karma cannot be
ascertained, though most likely both arose in response to certain
basic human needs and not through manipulation by cynical
seekers of power. At a certain stage of the political and intellectual development of man sacred kingship may have emerged as a
ritual institution concerned with the maintenance of an adequate
food supply and the integration of large and often heterogeneous
empires.[5] The deification of the king brought him into contact
with the invisible and celestial forces regarded as the true powers
of the universe, establishing a harmony on which the prosperity
and welfare of human society were seen to depend. The doctrine

of *karma*, too, not only justified the manifest social inequalities of
the Aryan community but provided a credible explanation of the
mystery of human suffering. To see poverty, oppression, and
human misery generally as a result of bad *karma*, i.e., sinful action in an earlier state of existence, is clearly easier on one's self-
image than to attribute these to personal failure in this life. "To
the ordinary man," writes A. L. Basham, "such a doctrine might
not appear distasteful, and the fact that it quickly obtained almost
universal acceptance shows that it met in great measure ancient
India's spiritual needs." [6] It would indeed seem difficult to consider a religious belief shared by all classes of a society a class ideology.[7] Max Weber's linkage of the key tenets of Hinduism (as
those of all the great historical religions) to particular class interests or "carrying" classes remains unconvincing for that same reason.[8]

Most religious views of rulership have not had such unequivocal political consequences. The ancient Chinese doctrine of the
"Mandate of Heaven," for example, legitimized the rule of the
emperor, the Son of Heaven, who traced his title to deified ancestors upon whom Heaven, the supreme deity, had conferred the
right to rule. And yet, the Mandate of Heaven was not seen as
granted in perpetuity or unconditionally. Heaven demanded
righteousness and good government and deposed rulers who
abused their exalted office. Hence just as the concept had apparently come into being to justify the seizure of power by the
Chou dynasty (around 1028 B.C.), who claimed a divine mandate
for overthrowing the Shang, so the Mandate of Heaven could
later be invoked by new aspirants to the supreme rulership. Indeed, in Chinese a revolution is called *ke ming*—"breaking of
the mandate." According to Mencius (born 390 B.C.), the acceptance of a king by the people indicated that Heaven approved of
him and that he enjoyed the divine mandate. On the other hand,
if the people rallied to the cause of an insurgent who deposed
the king this, too, was an expression of the will of Heaven and
demonstrated that the earlier ruler had lost his mandate. Heaven
indicated its wishes through the actions of the people. The approval of order and the acceptance of power as an accomplished
fact were summed up in the popular saying: "If you succeed you
are king, if you fail you are a bandit." [9]

The doctrine of *karma* in Theravada Buddhism has had very

similar effects. Unlike Hinduism, where compliance with the norms of one's caste is a strict requirement of moral conduct, the Buddhist view of *karma* accepts mobility, both upward and downward, depending on one's past conduct and the accumulation of merit. Hence though *karma* supports the legitimacy of those in power it also provides justification for the usurpation of power. In the words of a recent student of Burmese Buddhism: "Specifically, a successful seizure of power must mean that the karmic fruit of the former ruler's merit has dried up and the karmic seeds of the usurper have come into fruition." [10] *Karma* thus confers legitimacy on any regime in power, and many Burmese kings acceded to the throne through violent usurpation, an evil action for which they later tried to compensate by lavish patronage of Buddhism.

The Christian ideas of divine providence and of the divine origin and sanction of rulership also have had diverse results: they have helped shore up and sanctify political authority, but they also have been used to justify rebellion. In the deterministic world view of St. Augustine nothing could exist without divine approval. Divine providence has arranged things in such a way that every evil in the world is directed to some good. God appoints rulers according to the merits of the people, and, in view of his omnipotence and justice, tyrants must be considered God's retribution for the perversity of the people. Both just kings and cruel tyrants reign by God's providence; none may be resisted.[11] This gospel of submissiveness, a justification for a theologian desirous of obtaining secular support for the suppression of heresy or for a Martin Luther in need of assistance from the princes of the Empire, was a burdensome handicap for Christians anxious to fight the pretensions of absolute temporal power. Hence, in the later sixteenth century, in particular, the doctrine of divine providence was reinterpreted so as to make possible certain political actions. The witticism of Walter Kaufman that "theology is the finding of dubious reasons for what the theologian has believed all along" [12] probably is an overstatement, but, as a historian of sixteenth-century theories of legitimate resistance to power has observed, "the development of the whole controversy is one of the most striking examples of the way in which men adjust their theories at once to their desires and to circumstances." [13]

The Calvinist Theodore Beza conceded that nothing can exist

without divine approval and that God uses the evil deeds of sinners to punish other sinners, but, he asked, why could it not be God's will that tyrants be punished by the people rather than people by tyrants? [14] During the Puritan Revolution the Christian humanist, John Milton, rejected the suggestion that God had put the English nation in slavery to Charles Stuart and that only God, therefore, could be relied upon to release it. If God can be said to give a people into slavery whenever a tyrant prevails over a people, he asked, why ought God not as well be said to set them free whenever people prevail over a tyrant? [15] This kind of politically useful theological reasoning was not devised by either Beza or Milton. Around 1110 Hugh of Fleury had taught in his *De regia potestate* that God punishes bad princes by the insubordination of their people,[16] and the same idea is found in Eastern Christendom. The Kievan chronicler considered a revolt of the citizens against their prince an act of God's will, punishing the prince for his misconduct.[17] More recently a pastoral letter issued by "16 Bishops of the Third World" declared that "Christians and their pastors should know how to recognize the hand of the Almighty in those events that from time to time put down the mighty from their thrones and raise up the humble." [18] Needless to say, the impressment of God for the cause of rebellion today is no monopoly of the Left. After the military coup of 1964 in Brazil, a group of Brazilian archbishops and bishops thanked God for having listened to their prayers for deliverance from the Communist peril. Divine providence, they said, had made itself felt in a tangible manner.

Christian teaching has always insisted that "every person be subject to the governing authorities. For there is no authority except from God, and those that exist have been instituted by God" (Rom. 13:1). More than 1800 years after Paul had written these words the innovative pope, Leo XIII, re-emphasized the divine origin of the authority of the ruling powers whom he described as "invested with a sacredness more than human": Obedience to them is not "the servitude of man to man, but submission to the will of God." [19] And yet, the obligation of the Christian to obey constituted authority has never been absolute. He must render to Caesar the things that are Caesar's, but to God the things that are God's, and in case of a conflict he may have to "obey God rather than men" (Acts 5:29). During medieval times such conflicts of duty arose as a result of clashes of temporal interests between church and state and also because of genuine differences over questions of morality or religion. Disobedience, if not resistance, to secular rulers was now further justified by distinguishing between the office and the person of the king. The office of kingship required observance of moral standards, defined by tradition as well as the church, and not every individual king was unquestionably entitled to the loyalty of his subjects. According to the twelfth-century theologian, Peter Abélard, princes receive their power to rule justly from God but act cruelly out of their own evil nature. Hence "it is one thing to resist the tyranny of an evil ruler, another to resist his just power which he has received from God. For when he plunges into violence as does not pertain to his power and the terms of his office, and we resist him in this, we oppose his tyranny rather than his power, man rather than God, since he presumes thus to act on his own and not according to the will of God." [20]

Other contradictory consequences of the doctrine of divine providence, to be found in all major religions, must be noted. The acceptance of the omnipotent role of the deity can lead to fatalism and inaction, but it can also spur people to mighty effort because of the conviction that God is on their side. Thus the early Jewish apocalyptic writers counseled complete reliance upon God's direct intervention, which would redeem Israel, whereas the later Zealots, engaged in eschatological war against Rome, believed that God would usher in the new age of freedom and justice only if pious Jewish warriors actively participated in the realization of the divine plan. Here strong faith in the certainty of divine assistance acted to inspire superior exertion and fortitude and gave the struggle against Rome the character of a holy war. Revolutionary action merged with messianic utopianism and led to an utter disregard of Rome's overwhelming might which if viewed rationally should have discouraged any hope of success.

A similar attempt to use belief in divine providence to encourage militant struggle was undertaken by the so-called Hindu Extremists around the turn of the twentieth century. The Bengali philosopher, Aurobindo Ghose, assured his followers that God was behind Indian nationalism and would see to it that it attained its goal. In a famous speech in 1909 he related how no less a deity

than Sri Krishna had told him that He was working on the side
of the national uprising and was manifesting Himself in those fighting for liberty. India's liberation, insisted another activist-scholar,
Bal Gangadhar Tilak, will be achieved by the grace of God, but it
will not do to sit idle. God only helps those who help themselves;
He becomes incarnate only for industrious people who are self-
assertive and self-reliant. Islamic modernism, too, tries to overcome the traditional acceptance of whatever is as part of God's
will and teaches the importance of human action. Aspirations and
hopes, Nasser stressed in 1965, cannot be realized by merely relying upon God's help; strong effort and persistent struggle are essential.

The ease with which religious doctrine at all times has been
subjected to the most varied interpretations is, of course, well
known, and the earlier chapters of this study have provided many
illustrations of this. Speaking of the Bible, the Westminster Confession of 1647 admitted with considerable understatement: "All
things in scripture are not alike plain in themselves, nor alike
clear unto all." [21] Small wonder that the Bible has been invoked
by some in support of the institutions of slavery, serfdom, capitalism, and the demand for strict obedience to civil authority,
whereas others have seen it as a clarion call for equality, social
justice, and even revolution. During the French Revolution the
teachings of the medieval scholastics and of sixteenth-century
neo-scholasticism on the right of rebellion against tyranny were
appealed to by both royalists and republicans; this happened
again during the Spanish Civil War of 1936–39. The *Bhagavad
Gita* has been used to support the doctrines of the Bengali terrorists fighting British colonial rule in the early years of this century
and Gandhi's doctrine of nonviolence. The Buddhist doctrine of
nirvana traditionally has symbolized the transcendence and renunciation of earthly life; for the Buddhist modernists the attainment of mental tranquility presupposes a material abundance that
alone can enable man to achieve the higher spiritual values. Orthodox Sunni Islam knows neither geographical nor ethnic
boundaries and merely distinguishes between the community of
faith, the *umma*, and the world of unbelievers. Contemporary Arab
nationalists have grafted upon this concept of *umma* the idea of
nationhood, and they have transformed a religious community
into a political one. The popularity in the developing nations of

the Third World of some form of socialism has led to the discovery of socialist precepts in the holy books of Hinduism, Buddhism, and Islam and the emergence of full-fledged doctrines of Hindu, Buddhist, and Islamic socialism.

The root of such divergent interpretations is often found in the conflict of social and political interests. Social class clearly was a factor in the split in the clergy during the French Revolution, and it appears to be important in the doctrinal disputes in the ranks of the modern Ceylonese Sangha. Discussing the way religious ideas in the Third World are often enlisted to further political aims, Donald E. Smith writes: "Politicians, clerical and lay, are engaged in manipulating religious symbols as one technique in the struggle for power, sometimes cynically but more often through the same process of rationalization by which interests become disguised as principles in politics everywhere." [22] The extent to which the adjustment of religious doctrine actually assumes a manipulative character must be determined in each specific instance; the observable participation of political rulers in such changes and the suddenness and sharpness of a doctrinal reversal may indicate the presence of outright political manipulation. We will have occasion to examine the relationship of religion to political and institutional interests in more detail in the next chapter.

In some cases, we can trace the emergence, spread, and acceptance of certain religious ideas to their political utility. St. Augustine's espousal of political quietism was probably not unrelated to his desire to enlist the temporal power in the defense of orthodoxy against the Donatist heresy. Frequent warnings against the threat of political anarchy by Islamic religious leaders were influenced by chronic political instability in the early Arab empire, a result of the uneasy coexistence of many different ethnic and cultural groups, of the strength shown by tribal kinship groups, and of the proliferation of possible male heirs in the polygamous families of the ruling dynasty.

The phenomenon of conflicting exegeses of religious doctrine at bottom probably derives from the fact that the moral codes of all religious systems are inherently vague and ambiguous. Religiously based moral principles, as indeed all moral principles, appear to be elastic for two reasons. First, principles that always apply are elastic in interpretation; we cannot easily know what we must do to conform to them. For example, no specific course of conduct is suggested by the command "love thy neighbor" without considerable elaboration as to who my neighbor is and what it means to love him. Second, those principles that are more or less unambiguous in their meaning come to be treated as elastic in application. For instance, we are not prepared to apply the maxim "do not lie" in all conceivable circumstances.[23]

The Buddhist Five Precepts are characterized by the first type of elasticity. They are formulated in the original Pali texts in such general and imprecise language that it would be humanly impossible to fulfill any precept "to the letter." Irrespective of whether this was a matter of intent or not, as a recent interpreter of Buddhism has observed, this lack of a precise formulation has had the advantage that the Five Precepts "can be accommodated to the morality of different village communities, and of different caste and class groupings, or even to quite individualistic interpretations which depend on the ethical sophistication and awareness of a particular individual. Historically, this flexibility of the precepts has facilitated the spread of Buddhism into countries with different social systems and codes of morality." [24] Hinduism, similarly, represents a great reservoir of beliefs and practices from which different sects at different times have drawn different practices; it contains its own built-in mechanisms for change, allowing the adaptation of traditional doctrines to new needs and circumstances.[25] Again, the principles of the Christian natural law are so abstract and indeterminate that they can support opposite courses of political conduct. In many past wars, which pitted Catholics against Catholics, believers on both sides were assured that they were fighting a just war. The German Catholics in 1937 were told that resistance to the Nazi state was sinful; Spanish Catholics at the same time were urged to support the rebellion of General Franco against the Second Spanish Republic. The natural law ethic, on which these teachings were based, is essentially a shell, which can offer a great variety of moral and political positions; it is in a process of constant change which is not so much a sign of corruption as a consequence of its inherent flexibility and adaptability.

The imprecision and vagueness of most moral codes may be necessary for their usefulness and survival just as the open-ended character of constitutional provisions is an essential condition for the adaptability of a political order to changing circumstances. The same point is made by the anthropologist studying village life in Burma who writes: "The inherent ambiguity of a set of cultural norms is a testament to their vitality and to their applicability to ordinary life." [26] Religion contributes to the regulation of social life by supplying a set of basic values for *all* members of society, and, in fulfilling this important function, religious ideas necessarily must operate at a high level of generality. This means, of course, that the holder of a particular political position usually will have little difficulty in finding appropriate supporting evidence in holy writ or other authoritative sources of religious dogma. Doctrine thus frequently serves as a rationalization for what religious leaders want to do in the first place, it serves to justify rather than determine their politics.

The fact that most religious doctrines are protean in character and are open to different readings does not mean that the doctrinal content of a religion is entirely irrelevant to politics. Though all religions have both quietistic and revolutionary potentials the proportions in which these different political implications are present vary. Considering the phenomenon of revolutionary millenarianism, for example, as we have noted in an earlier chapter, we see that certain religious traditions are more conducive to such expectations of a coming age of bliss than others. The cyclical view of history in Hinduism and Buddhism, providing for a perpetual flux and endless repetition of the cosmic drama, appears to discourage millenarian ideas, just as the linear theory of history and the expectation of a final salvation of mankind in Judaism, Christianity, and Islam provide inspiration for the messianic dream of eternal terrestrial redemption.

Conceptions of time and history have political implications and, to a lesser extent, so have conceptions of space. Most of the historical religions share a spatial symbolism which divides the world into the abode of members of the faith and those outside it. This division can be utilized as an ideological justification of aggressive action against non-believers, and at times it has inspired a militant nationalism even though the geographical entity did not involve a modern nation state. The best example of such a view probably is the Islamic notion of a *dar al-Islam* (the realm of Islam) and a *dar al-Harb* (the realm of war), the latter being the non-Islamic world against which a holy war could be launched in order to include it in the community of the true faith. The fact that Muslim theologians, unlike their Christian counterparts, have never regarded power as inherently sinful, and in need of justification, has often added further thrust to the utilization of ruthless power for religious purposes. Confucianism and Christianity have shared similar conceptions of space.[27]

The influence of abstract ideas on human affairs should, of course, not be overstated. Human longing for a state of paradise on earth at times has developed even in the midst of inhospitable religious settings. Millenarian ideas, it will be recalled, have appeared in Mahayana Buddhism and even in Theravada Buddhism at times. Despite the emphasis on personal virtue rather than on the improvement of society as a whole and in defiance of cosmic cycles that know no end to history, Buddhist societies have experienced revolutionary millenarian movements. The incredible length of the cycles of Buddhist cosmology has not prevented hope for a final liberation; conditions of severe decline have given rise to expectations of a better future to come similar to the Jewish conception of the messianic woes in which extreme suffering is seen to indicate the nearness of redemption.[28] These seemingly paradoxical phenomena are a testament not only to the all but universal desire for an improvement of life on earth but are proof of the malleability and richness of religious doctrines which have been able to accommodate a great many political ideologies. Max Weber notes that the religions of mankind "have been historical rather than logical or even psychological constructions without contradiction. Often they have borne within themselves a series of motives, each of which, if separately and consistently followed through, would have stood in the way of others or run against them head-on. In religious matters 'consistency' has been the exception and not the rule." [29] Weber himself did not always heed his own findings. It has been shown that his assertion that Hinduism stood in the way of modernization and the development of an industrial economy in India, was "based more on a narrow interpretation of selected scriptural texts than on observed facts of individual behavior in specific social and cultural contexts." [30]

The link between religious doctrine and politics is often tenuous, and the causal role of religion in politics appears doubtful for yet another reason. The history of British Methodism in the late eighteenth and early nineteenth centuries well illustrates the

difficulty of explaining actual political conduct by way of doctrinal formulas, and it deserves some examination and comment
here. According to the well-known thesis of the French historian,
Elie Halévy, it was Methodism that saved England from revolution during the turbulent years 1790 to 1815. England alone of all
the major European countries was able to avoid the violent crises
that rocked the continent during the age of the French Revolution, and this "miracle of modern England" Halévy traced to the
religious revival achieved by the evangelical activity of Methodism which imbued the elite of the working class "with a spirit
from which the established order had nothing to fear." [31]

John Wesley and his fellow preachers indeed were pronounced
individualists and staunch Tories whose teachings emphasized
submissiveness and unquestioning obedience to the Crown. Impressed more by the vices of the poor than by the poor conditions under which they were forced to live, the early Methodists
attributed economic distress to individual failings and regarded
their gospel of salvation through faith and individual effort as the
only way of improving society. Methodist prayer meetings were
highly emotional affairs which provided an escape from the drug-
eries of a hard life.[32] And yet, all this does not establish the correctness of Halévy's thesis. First, it has been questioned whether a
body of some 150,000 sectarians out of about ten million English
and Welsh in 1811 could have decisively affected the political situation of the day.[33] Second, and more importantly, though it is
probably true that as a result of Methodist preaching many of the
laboring poor were reconciled to their lowly condition and
stayed away from radical politics, many others were not thus influenced and in fact took part in radical activities. There were
some Methodist Jacobins, more Methodist Luddites, still more
Methodists who participated in the demonstrations and radical
agitation that followed the close of the Napoleonic wars, and numerous Methodist Chartists. In other words, the conservative orthodox Methodist preachers were not able to control the political
thoughts and actions of their congregations, and, occasionally,
even some Methodist ministers used their oratorical skill to promote radical causes. The government and Anglican church reacted with fear and suspicion to a sectarian movement that was
spreading rapidly among the mining communities, in the new industrial towns, and even in the countryside. The Methodist lead-

ers responded by denying any subversive designs and by claiming credit for averting serious social unrest. It appears that Halévy accepted the Methodists' claims of having contributed to the stability of society in a revolutionary age at face value.[34]

Much of the impact which Methodism did have on the English working class came not as a result of deliberate action on the part of Methodist ministers but as an indirect consequence of Methodist teachings and methods of organization. Methodist theology was egalitarian and thus democratic in its implications. Christian experience was open to all men and came not through birth or intellect but through a change of heart. The scope of this message of spiritual egalitarianism, as Luther had had to learn some 250 years earlier, could easily be extended and related to temporal affairs, and such reinterpretation indeed appears to have eased the entry of many Methodists into radical politics. The Bible, usually their only source of education, had taught these simple people compassion which led to the desire to fight injustice. The Methodist chapel provided men of humble origins experience in public speaking and in the conduct of meetings, and by generating a sense of community it gave them self-confidence in their ability to organize.[35] The fact that Wesley and other orthodox Methodist ministers had preached a religion of submissiveness and political quietism thus did not stand in the way of other unintended and quite different political consequences.

Basically, the political potential of a religious world view will depend on the existence and strength of transcendental standards with which a political and social order can be judged. The Jewish prophetic tradition, for example, insists that the poor and oppressed be treated justly. "Give justice to the weak and the fatherless," the psalmist makes the God of the Hebrews exhort. "Maintain the right of the afflicted and the destitute. Rescue the weak and the needy; deliver them from the hand of the wicked." [36] Similarly, Christianity has a tradition of natural law, a rule of justice, that stands above human law. Any human legislation that "deflects from the law of nature," St. Thomas Aquinas declared, "is no longer a law but a perversion of law." [37] Both traditions provide moral yardsticks which can be used to critically measure the workings of society and its government.

Such transcendent norms are seen in the Eastern religions, too. In the Hindu doctrine of kingship the ruler had duties and responsibilities under the sacred law (*dharma*), and a king who violated the sacred tradition and failed to fulfill the obligations of his office could be resisted by the people or punished by the gods. Confucianism demanded that a king respect the institution of the family and uphold the spirit of harmony that had characterized the way of the ancestors. A ruler who did not live up to tradition, of which the Confucian scholars as the interpreters of the ancient texts were the arbiters, was seen to have forfeited his divine mandate. Thus religious values helped create a vision of the good and just society and furnished criteria for political and social criticism. It does not matter whether these images of a new and better world involved progress toward an ideal future or a return to a Golden Age of the past. Such dreams must be judged by the existing situation, and then, as Lawrence Stone has pointed out, it makes no difference whether the idealized Golden Age is in the past or in the future.[38]

Of course, the setting of moral standards, no matter how demanding, does not ensure that these standards will be invoked or enforced. As we shall see in more detail in the next chapter, there must be an organized religious institution that can guard its values. The Christian church in medieval times had the power and prestige to condemn a prince who violated Christian standards of rulership. In Islamic society, on the other hand, no independent, well-organized religious establishment developed to successfully challenge the state. Thus though both Christianity and Islam set moral standards for the ruler, in the case of the latter these standards have not been followed, and despotism has been the normal pattern.

The interaction of the various parts of a certain religious world view is also important. Medieval Christianity and Hinduism both subordinated the authority of the king to a divinely sanctioned code of conduct and law, yet in India the political significance of this idea was neutralized by the doctrine of *karma*, and the general spirit was one of resignation to an imperfect world. Christianity, too, is contradictory; along with a prophetic dimension we find doctrines that encourage meek acceptance of one's lot and offer the consolation of spiritual salvation in the afterlife. Clearly, the individual parts of a religion can predispose to but seldom will provide a decisive political determinant.

It should be noted finally that at times the political effect of a certain religious doctrine has depended less on its own positive characteristics than on the reaction of the political authorities. Thus even the advocacy of withdrawal from the wicked world of power and selfishness by entirely apolitical religious groups has occasionally led to political conflict. Though such an attitude of non-participation in the affairs of society has deflected potential social and political protest, it has also deprived rulers of the active support that they demanded and needed.[39] In medieval and early modern Europe, for example, when the state was seen as a Christian state, the denial of the Christian character of public authority by completely peaceful groups like the Waldensians or the early Anabaptists could not but create an image of disrespect and rebelliousness. Such a withdrawal of the religious sanction of authority brought about persecution and ultimately open warfare between the religious sect and the state.

In summary, a few religious doctrines, like the idea of sacred kingship, are definitely conducive to political quietism and enhance subservience to rulers. Most religious views of rulership, on the other hand, are ambivalent and in fact have both encouraged as well as discouraged revolt. This dual effect has come about because of the different ways in which these doctrines can and have been interpreted, applied, and acted upon in concrete situations. In each case one must also determine the extent to which religious ideas have had an effect upon the members of a religious group. Sometimes religion dominates the political behavior of people; at other times the impact of dogma will be slight. As the case of English Methodism shows, it is never enough to merely point to certain dogmatic formulations and deduce actual political consequences from them.

In some instances it is possible to determine whether religious ideas are being used to manipulate popular opinion; in other instances it can be seen that a particular interpretation is politically or economically advantageous to a certain group. However, most traditions in most religions cannot be attributed to the desire for political or material gain. The evidence examined in this study supports the warnings of Ernst Troeltsch and Max Weber against the one-sided materialistic reductionism practiced, in particular, by many Marxist writers. Religious ideas are not simply "the product of class struggles and of economic factors." As this and other research reveals, "to some extent at least, religious thought is independent; it has its own inner dialectic and its own power of development." [40] Or as Max Weber put it:

It is not our thesis that the specific nature of a religion is a simple "function" of the social situation of the stratum which appears as its characteristic bearer, or that it represents the stratum's "ideology" or that it is a "reflection" of a stratum's material or ideal interest-situation . . . . However incisive the social influences, economically and politically determined, may have been upon a religious ethic in a particular case, it receives its stamp primarily from religious sources, and, first of all, from the content of its annunciation and its promise.[41]

Weber used the example of the Buddhist ethic of indifference to worldly affairs to show that such creeds of salvation sometimes derive primarily from "intellectualism as such, more particularly the metaphysical needs of the human mind as it is driven to reflect on ethical and religious questions, driven not by material needs but by an inner compulsion to understand the world as a meaningful cosmos and to take up a position toward it." [42] Even as political a creed as revolutionary millenarianism has at times drawn sustenance from such purely spiritual drives. The radical Anabaptists of the sixteenth century, for example, were motivated to a high degree by the search for more immediate and authentic methods of redemption than the hierarchical churches, Catholic or Protestant, were able to offer. As we have seen, similar motives are involved in twentieth-century African messianic movements.

The all-important fact that religious ideas have been subject to many different interpretations leads to a number of additional levels of analysis such as the impact of institutional interests or the influence of individual leaders. An examination of these factors will be our next task.

CHAPTER 23

Ecclesiastical Organization

The nature of ecclesiastical organization and the relationship of the religious institution to the state are significant variables affecting the political role of religion. Thus modern Hinduism, for example, lacks a distinct Hindu clergy. Clerical functions are performed by a wide variety of temple priests and holy men who do not always have much prestige. There is no congregational worship as in Christianity and Islam. The fact that Hinduism has demonstrated hardly any capacity for organization, concludes one writer, militates "against the assumption of an effective prophetic role as a proclaimer of a social gospel, as critic of government and society." [1] As a result whatever political impact Hinduism has had has been expressed through laymen who lack the authority and high repute that goes with a well-trained and disciplined clergy, and these leaders have had to forge their own organizational structure. The Bengali terrorists at the turn of the century invoked and relied upon Hinduism as a source of inspiration and cohesion, but they did not have the benefit of organizational support. Gandhi derived much of his influence over the Indian masses from his role as a Hindu holy man, but he had to function through the organization of the Indian National Congress. Hinduism with its emphasis on personal virtue, renunciation, and self-control may facilitate the appearance of charismatic leadership, but the leader has to create his own mass base.

Buddhism, on the other hand, has a relatively well-developed ecclesiastical organization, and this helps and encourages political involvement. The monastic structure of the Sangha, which at least in the urban centers brings together a considerable number

Ecclesiastical Organization

of monks, allows the quick political mobilization of these men; in Burma, Ceylon, and Vietnam the political power of the monks has been repeatedly demonstrated.

The Roman Catholic church, too, has an elaborate organization. A quasi-monarchical head is assisted by a bureaucracy in Rome and archbishops and bishops in the field, as well as by a large corps of regular and secular clergy. This extensive apparatus, made necessary by the importance of the confessional and the sacraments as the road to salvation, provides the church with a network of communications through which its social and political message can be sent to every town and village. The pastoral letters of bishops, papal encyclicals, and doctrinal pronouncements by church councils and national bishops' conferences have an extensive audience and often significantly influence the political thinking of the laity. The centralized structure of the church, manifested in the pope's power of appointment of his bishops, ensures that its national components will usually operate in ways considered advantageous by the papacy. During the nineteenth century this meant that national churches in the politically and socially more advanced countries of Europe were held back in their adjustment to the prevailing trends of secularization and democratization. In the period since the Second Vatican Council (1963–65), on the other hand, the church's belated acceptance of the various facets of modern industrial society has had a revolutionizing effect upon the Latin American church in particular. In socially underdeveloped countries like Paraguay, the new role of the church legitimates a way of life that does not yet exist to any meaningful degree, and the political orientation of most of the bishops is well ahead that of their peasant constituencies.[2] More importantly, the hierarchically and supra-nationally organized church is in a position to confront the state when she so desires. The political strength of pope and episcopate will depend in part upon the hold they exercise over their parishioners, but when rapport between clergy and laity is close the power of the church can be considerable. In medieval times the pope was able to depose secular rulers, and in the Catholic countries of Latin America the episcopate to this day is an important political force.

Islam has a clerical class, the *ulama*, but it is poorly organized and lacks the hierarchical structure of the Roman Catholic church. Islam has moral norms, against which the performance of the state could be measured, but there exist no institutions to enforce these norms. Without control over sacraments the Muslim preachers and teachers are not mediators of divine grace, and they cannot impose penalties like excommunication. Short of joining a political revolution, they are not in a position to oppose the authority of the state.[3] Islam began as a religion that was spread by force, and secular rulers have retained control over the priesthood to this day. The *ulama* originally lived from their own private resources. When they later emerged as a class of religious officeholders their prestige declined sharply, and they came to be seen as "venal men, prepared when necessary to twist the Law to suit the desires of their masters."[4] For centuries the caliph was merely a figurehead; the fusion of church and state was complete. If we add the fact that Islam emphasizes the external aspects of religion, makes few ethical demands of its followers, and does not expect any individual to challenge the state on religious grounds as long as government maintains a framework in which Muslim worship can take place, it is easy to understand why Islam has only rarely posed a challenge to the state. Similar factors were at work in the case of Confucianism which never developed a priesthood independent of the state. The men officiating in the sacrifices of the cult of Confucius and his disciples were state officials. Confucianism was part of the established political and moral order and thus ill-prepared to defend a rival value system.

Of course, a strong organizational base does not necessarily mean that the religious institution will use its power for innovative or revolutionary ends. Indeed, the contrary will often be the case. A religion with a highly developed institutional structure generates institutional interests; like every other organization it seeks to preserve itself, and it will usually follow that course of political action most likely to protect and enhance its power. The Catholic church, Max Weber has noted, seeks "to salvage its ecclesiastical power interests, which have increasingly become objectified into a doctrine of the fundamental interests of the church, by the employment of the same modern instruments of power employed by secular institutions."[5] Given the broad formulation of Catholic doctrine, this also means that the gap between abstract principle and concrete case will usually be closed by answers tied to and almost predetermined by the interests of the church as an institution. Individual Catholics turning to their church for moral guidance in such matters as the legitimacy of resistance to political authority will receive replies that derive not from the unequivocal commands of natural law, but from the exigencies of church tactics in a particular situation. In most cases institutional interests will make the men charged with defending the interests of religion defend the social and political *status quo*, though in Spain, in 1936, such conservative leanings led to the support of a revolt that sought to restore the *status quo ante*, to nullify the victory of the Republic and its anticlerical policies. The Latin American hierarchy, operating in an increasingly secular world beset with severe social problems and acting in large measure out of motives of organizational survival, now gives its blessings to programs of fundamental social change.

Institutional interests lead to political involvement. The religious institution cannot be indifferent to the way taxes are collected, to the role of the state in education, and to other issues of public policy. The necessity of taking an active part in politics or at least of supporting certain political parties will be intensified when the religious institution owns land or other property or when it is dependent upon the financial support of the state, whether through direct grants or tax exemption. Until the most recent past, the active political role of the Catholic church in Spain was directly related to these institutional concerns, and a very similar situation exists in Buddhist Ceylon. There the Sangha owns extensive tracts of rich land donated by Buddhist laymen and especially by kings desirous of earning "merit." The monastic landlords of central Ceylon are allied with the Kandyan aristocracy, and to this day they have successfully resisted land reform as well as much needed changes in the structure and organization of the Sangha.[6]

When the religious institution is also a secular power, there is an even greater tendency to follow a course of expediency. The medieval papacy much of the time conducted itself like any other political entity, seeking to preserve and enlarge its extensive temporal possessions. The highly centralized form of organization of the Catholic church further reinforced her authoritarian leanings, and the church for centuries defended monarchy as the best form of government. "It is not surprising," writes a Catholic historian, "that it was only after the temporal power of the Popes had been lost that Leo XIII felt able to give clear expression to the principle that Rome was indifferent to forms of government, urging the French to rally to their new republic."[7] Until that time the commitment of the church to the principles of legitimacy and monarchical rule had been so strong that she vehemently opposed any revolutionary movement even when rebellions were not at all anti-religious. Thus Pope Gregory XVI strongly condemned the Belgian and Polish uprisings of 1830, and he identified the interests of the church with absolute monarchy even though "in Gregory's time the monarchical system meant an anti-Catholic Tsar, an anti-Catholic King of Prussia, an anti-Catholic King of England, a free-thinking King of France, and a Josephist Emperor of Austria."[8] The way in which institutional interests can develop a momentum of their own to produce rigidity and cultural lag can hardly be revealed more clearly.

Institutional interests may influence religious doctrine and political thinking and conduct without necessarily involving any conscious bending of principle. The separation, so readily made by outsiders, between the interests of religion and the interests of the religious institution is hardly perceived by those strongly committed to a religion. Thus during the Counterreformation the Jesuits advocated popular sovereignty and the right of revolution against heretical (i.e., Protestant) rulers not just to enhance the power of the church and the pope in Rome. To most of these men, a dichotomy of interests between people, religion, and pope would have been quite unintelligible. Similarly, Pope Gregory's defense of the principle of legitimacy in the first half of the nineteenth century was not tactical; he never doubted the complete identity of the concerns of throne and altar. The Spanish bishops who in 1936 sided with Franco to defend the interests of the church undoubtedly regarded the continued existence of the religious institution as an essential prerequisite for the fulfillment of the church's sacramental mission. For much the same reason most German bishops did their best to work for a *modus vivendi* with the Nazi regime.[9]

In some instances, however, religious aims or attitudes may depend upon certain economic interests. The Byzantine monks were economically involved in the worship of icons, and the manufacture of alcoholic beverages in some Catholic monasteries certainly rules out a flat opposition to the consumption of alcohol.[10] The Sinhalese Buddhist, operating in the context of an economy of scarcity and a shortage of jobs, who argues "that Buddhism must be restored to its rightful place in Ceylon is saying, in part, that his community must enjoy unrivaled dominance in the fields of education and government service and that the influence of Christians and Hindus must be limited." [11] But most of the time, the conscious linking of self-serving policies and religious doctrines does not occur.

The characteristics of an institutionalized religion may have unintended effects. For example, the hierarchical and authoritarian plan of organization of the Roman Catholic church, headed by a pope proclaiming infallible truth in matters of dogma, has had as its by-product the fostering of authoritarian thinking in other spheres of life as well. In Latin America Catholic religious authoritarianism has undoubtedly contributed to the acceptance of authoritarian governments by *caudillos* or oligarchies.[12] Conversely, the gradual, if hesitant, democratization of the church that began with Pope John XXIII (1958–63) has weakened the hold of ideas justifying inequality and subservience to natural superiors. Paradoxically, the sheer extent, spread, and complexity of some diocesan organizations now often create obstacles to change, for an innovative bishop may find it difficult to control his far-flung diocese.[13]

We have noted earlier that Christian religious doctrine, like that of most religions, is highly indecisive, if not equivocal, in its moral demands, and this facilitates ideological change just as in past years the protean character of its dogma has helped the church to be selective in the interpretation of this doctrine. Thus when the egalitarian implications of its teaching seemed inexpedient, a Christian theologian has written, the church "discovered convenient ambiguities in the letter of the Gospels." Adapting herself to institutional imperatives, the church found "that it was easier to give to Caesar the things belonging to Caesar if the examination of what might belong to God were not too closely pressed." [14]

This type of ecclesiastical organization, which is an integral part of the existing social order and which attains her ends by a process of adaptation and compromise, Ernst Troeltsch in a well-known formulation called a "church," and he distinguished such a religious institution from a "sect," which stands in radical opposition to the world, its institutions, and its values.[15] Sectarian

groups have made their appearance in practically all formally organized religions, and, unencumbered by a large organizational
apparatus with its own institutional imperatives, they have often
provided outlets for political and social grievances. Yet, though
all sects reject the established religiosity, the unmet religious
needs which often lead to the formation of sects are not necessarily related to lack of political power or poverty. Most medieval Christian sectarian movements arose as a result of the increased and deepened piety that was behind so many other events
of that period.[16] Many modern sects, like the early Methodists,
were strongly identified with their society's political and social
institutions. In today's developed Western countries, characterized by the existence of secular opposition movements, radical
political and social protest will usually find secular outlets, and
the protesting and alienated will not necessarily be the poor.
Sects now are often rooted in the middle class. Christian Science,
for example, represents a reaction to the failure of the established
churches to deal satisfactorily with feelings of pain and inadequacy. Other sects cater to unabsorbed ethnic or immigrant
groups for whom they provide emotional security, a sense of
community, and a feeling of religious status. In the countries of
the Third World sects and cults will more often represent movements of political and social protest, though even there, as we
saw in our analysis of African independent churches, spiritual deprivation often plays an important role.

    In other words, not all sects are politically revolutionary, and
neither are all churches bulwarks of the *status quo*. We have
noted how important segments of the Catholic church in France,
Spain, and Mexico have sided with and participated in major revolutionary outbursts. In other situations powerful religious institutions lend their organization, doctrine, and prestige to the legitimation of revolutionary change. In today's world the
church-sect typology appears to only partly explain the political
role of religious organizations, and the political posture of a religious group will be only marginally affected by factors related
to this organizational dichotomy.

    Even the class membership of clergy and laity is no longer of
decisive importance. The split in the Catholic clergy during the
early stages of the French Revolution was largely class based.
The great majority of the French bishops belonged to the nobil-

ity and enjoyed a life of wealth and splendor, whereas the parish priests or curés were truly a clerical proletariat. Not surprisingly most of the curés in 1789 voted with the Third Estate, and practically all of the clerical deputies belonging to the upper clergy sided with the king. Today in a less stratified society, with considerable social mobility and an egalitarian ethos, the leaders of a religious group are no longer exclusively part of the upper class, or their thinking at least is no longer confined within narrow class horizons. The majority of the Latin American episcopate, despite the upper-class background of many of them, is committed to a program of social change and espouses programs of political and social reform an earlier generation of churchmen would have considered decidedly radical. Here the hierarchical organization of the Catholic church has helped propagate and spread a message of social criticism. Religious modernism has had a similar effect in many Buddhist and Muslim countries.

In summary, the organizational factor may condition the political posture of a religion. A well-developed ecclesiastical organization enables a religious group to articulate its own system of values and to confront the state with its demands. On the other hand, an elaborate organization often develops institutional liabilities, and, instead of being the salt of the earth, the religious institution may become a prop of the established political and social order. Whether the religious institution will be a critic or supporter of the *status quo* does not appear to depend on the type of ecclesiastical organization involved. Thus in the final analysis, the formal pattern of organization of a religious group, in and by itself, would seem to be of relatively minor political importance as compared to other variables.

CHAPTER 24

Leadership

The leadership of religious organizations or movements is often of considerable importance in determining that group's political posture. The impact of individual men will be smallest in the context of an elaborately structured religious institution relying upon collective leadership or when events pose a fundamental challenge to the survival of such an organization, thus causing it to close ranks and narrowing the range of alternatives. For example, in 1936 the reaction of the Spanish episcopate organized in the Spanish Bishops' Conference to Franco's rebellion was practically unanimous. A dissenting voice, no matter how articulate and persuasive, would have had little chance of swaying that group. The severe persecution of the church in republican territory, coupled with the known friendliness of the generals toward the Catholic cause, practically ensured the church's alignment on the side of Franco.

On the other hand, inspired and energetic leaders or prophets have been decisive in the origins as well as in the success or failure of millenarian movements. In certain historical watershed situations, or in a severe societal crisis, the presence or absence of a forceful leader may be crucial. The shooting of Hasan al-Banna, the founder and Supreme Guide of the Muslim Brotherhood, by the Egyptian political police in 1949 deprived that movement of a charismatic leader for whom no substitute seemed available. The demise of the Brotherhood in the years that followed and the comparative ease with which the Nasser regime was able to eliminate the Brotherhood from Egyptian public life are clearly related to this lack of forceful leadership. The independence of

India undoubtedly would have been achieved even if Gandhi had never appeared on the scene, but it might have come at a different time and in a different form. At least in part as a result of the Hindu mystic's dominant position in the Indian National Congress the Congress increasingly took on a Hindu complexion and gradually alienated its Muslim members. A secular leadership, paying heed to Muslim sensitivities, might have been able to undercut Hindu-Muslim antagonism and thus have avoided the ultimate partition of India.

Leadership always involves a process of interaction between a leader and his followers, between a leader's personality and the setting in which he operates. Charismatic leadership, in particular, as we have noted in an earlier chapter, depends upon the recognition by a group of followers of such a leader's powers and qualities as outstanding and awe inspiring. Once accepted, the charismatic figure is a powerful force—either for innovation or for maintenance of the *status quo*. A divine king will use his influence to bolster the existing social and political structure. Other charismatic figures will be dramatic innovators. Such a great leader, in the words of Erik H. Erikson, "creates for himself and for many others new choices and new cares. These he derives from a mighty drivenness, an intense yet flexible energy, a shocking originality, and a capacity to impose on his time what most concerns him—which he does so convincingly that his time believes this concern to have emanated 'naturally' from ripe necessities." [1] The charismatic leader of millenarian movements, in particular, is a potent agent of radical change. As the bearer of chiliastic prophecy, he is not just a champion of felt needs or a catalyst but also a cause of the movement he is heading. The millenarian prophet's ambitious and challenging vision of what the world ought to be increases the expectations and dissatisfactions which can lead to a revolutionary situation. The limited success of *conscientização*, the raising of the consciousness of the subservient peasant population of South America, by various radical groups shows that this enterprise encounters serious difficulties when entrusted to persons of ordinary and secular cast.

The appearance of an outstanding and charismatic leader cannot be predicted, though certain conditions may make his appearance more likely. It may prove possible to ascertain some of the psychological mechanisms that facilitate the transformation of some children into leaders of men. A particular kind of relationship with parental authority, specifically with the father, has been singled out as a necessary condition for the emergence of the revolutionary leader.[2] Whether such findings can be corroborated in a larger sample remains to be seen, but in any event even confirmation of such a hypothesis would not eliminate all elements of indeterminacy. Psychic configurations may figure in the production of the revolutionary personality, but we know that many individuals who live through the same traumatic experiences as a revolutionary are able to work out the resulting problems without becoming revolutionaries. "Childhood sets the stage for what happens later," writes the psychologist Keniston, but "it does not rigidly determine it. . . . The legacy of childhood sets outer limits and establishes enduring sensitivities for later development, but does not dictate it." [3] Even if we knew what causes certain people to become leaders, we could not foresee the choices they would make in certain critical situations. Thus it is impossible to know how the decisions of such a figure would affect a crisis because we cannot foresee the nature of his response.

Social conditions may or may not facilitate the emergence of a strong leader. Uncertainty and upheaval often favor the appearance and acceptance of charismatic leadership.[4] In some regions and in certain situations millenarianism is an endemic force, and when it reaches a flash point it may seize upon any available figure.[5] The fact that in such a milieu charismatic leadership is often transferred with considerable ease from one person to another indicates the strong demand for charisma under certain conditions. In circumstances where men of strong character and ambition are excluded from political participation such men may become religious leaders. The independent churches in America and Africa and the secret societies in China have often served as outlets for the drive of men and women barred from other avenues of social advancement. Also, objective circumstances will always circumscribe in broad terms the potential influence of a leader. A militant atheist, no matter how able and how strongly driven by ambition, is unlikely to be accepted as a leader in a Catholic country. Again, one important reason for the failure of the Taiping Rebellion was the Christian component of the Taipings' ideology which created the image of an alien creed. "Revolutionary personalities" are probably present in most societies at most times, but whether these would-be revolutionaries will find a following and be able to build a revolutionary movement will depend less on their personality traits than on the objective situation.[6]

Of course, the significance of the political and social environment should not be overstated. The assertion, for example, that great men appear when needed is surely pushing the environmental factor too far; it is neither self-evident nor can historical evidence be used to corroborate or refute it. However much a crisis may seem to require the appearance of such a man, his failure to appear can always be explained away by the assertion that a great man was not really necessary.[7]

The factor of leadership thus challenges the social scientist, presenting a problem he is not likely to solve in the foreseeable future. Given the present state of our knowledge and theoretical understanding of the dynamics of the human personality we cannot hope to determine why exceptional men do the unprecedented things they do. Factors of geography, climate, race, epoch, family background, economic conditions, or class will not explain the differences between Luther and Müntzer, Cromwell and Harrison, Gandhi and Nehru. Any attempt to describe the important disparities of character and personality of these individuals in the form of universal categories would surely miss the unique elements that made these outstanding men outstanding. Generalizations about leadership are possible, but a considerable element of uniqueness that defies explanation, not to mention prediction, will remain. Some religiously inspired individuals will become leaders of mass movements, others will retreat from society or engage in acts of senseless violence. The "inner light" or God's guidance motivated Gandhi to attempt to lead India to self-rule; the Australian Denis Michael Rohan believed himself chosen by God to build a temple to Jesus in Jerusalem, where the destroyed Jewish temple had stood, and for that reason on August 21, 1970 he set fire to the al-Aqsa Mosque which today occupies the same site. The fact that Thailand had a string of able leaders, who were able to protect and ensure the independence of their country, had important consequences for the political role of Thai Buddhism, yet no general explanation of this phenomenon seems possible.

The interaction between leaders, the ideology spread by them, and the objective circumstances surrounding them has been compared to the relationship between the sower, the seed, and the soil. This analogy, imperfect as all analogies are, is illuminating and can serve as a summary statement:

> Many sowers sow but their seeds wither; the seeds adapted to the soil on which they fall flourish, and their sowers become famous; on the other hand, there might be soils which are potentially receptive to a kind of seed which nobody throws on it. In other words, social circumstances might be potentially very propitious for the spread of some possible ideological concoction, but nobody propagates it. Although what is created in this field is obviously conditioned by social circumstances, pullulation of ideologues dubbed as cranks proves that the determination of ideological production by general social circumstances is only partial. Environment limits what can be imagined, but the limits are fairly wide.[8]

CHAPTER 25

Situational Factors

The variables examined so far—religious doctrine, organization, and leadership—to varying degrees are elements of and form an integral part of religion itself. We now turn to factors unrelated to religion per se, external causes, as it were, which can affect the politics of religion.

First to be noted are the basic facts of geography, for religious ideas have often spread to other societies. The acceptance or rejection of a new religion often bears some relation to the needs of the society in question, but the availability of such ideas is essentially independent of the inner structure of a society. "The fact that China is next to India, whence it could borrow Buddhism," observes a student of comparative sociology, "and not to Europe, from which Christianity might have been introduced, cannot be conceived as being dependent on the character of Chinese society and culture." [1] Similarly, the spread of Islam into North Africa was obviously related to the geographical proximity of the African continent to the Arab peninsula, the original home of Islam.

Religious diffusion, the result of conquest, missionary activity, or migration caused by religious persecution, has often created religious minorities in neighboring societies, and such minority status has frequently driven religious groups to militancy. Especially where state and church were closely linked, and religious toleration unknown, religious minorities have had to fight for their existence, in the process often repudiating those aspects of their own teaching inimical to such resistance. Thus French Protestantism, opting for survival in the face of severe persecution during the second half of the sixteenth century, abandoned Calvin's doctrine of nonresistance to civil authority and engaged in a vigorous military struggle with France's Catholic rulers. The contribution of English Puritanism to the development of liberalism may have been related more to the Puritan minority's conflict with the Anglican Stuart kings than to any tenets of Puritanism per se. The militancy of Chinese Buddhist sects and secret societies was often the result of persecution by the Confucian state, and, in colonial Africa, independent churches have frequently been driven into armed insurrection by the actions of colonial authorities who regarded any independent African activity as dangerous and subversive. Conversely, majority status, and especially the absence of competition for religious allegiance, often leads to close ties between religious and political institutions. In countries like France, Spain, and Mexico, for example, all strongholds of Catholicism, political and social change has been late in coming. The conservative influence of the church here led to anticlericalism and to revolutionary upheavals in which the church suffered grievous damage. The history of this collision between church and revolution is covered in Section IV of this study.

The patterns of Western imperialist expansion are, to some degree at least, historical accidents, related to wind and currents, the navigability of certain oceans and straits, and the interests and fortunes of individual explorers. Yet, colonial rule has had a great effect on the politics of religion. Colonials were usually of another faith, and in the face of economic exploitation, discrimination, and cultural disruption the conquered people soon fell back upon the one factor that could unite them and form a basis for an awakening national consciousness—their native religion. In the recent history of India, Burma, and Egypt Hinduism, Buddhism, and Islam, respectively, helped create an awareness of religious distinctiveness which in turn contributed decisively to the growth of the nationalist movement in these countries. In Burma, national and religious identity were so closely interwoven that the defeat and deposition of the king—the Defender of the Faith—by the British in 1885 left many of the people thinking that not only had their national independence been destroyed but their common religion had also been severely undermined. In such a situation religion readily became a symbol of self-assertion against the colonial regime, and even though Buddhism rejects violence the deprivation experienced was strong enough to overcome the Buddhas' message of peace and to fan the flames of armed rebellion.

When the native religious faith is an ethnic religion, linked and limited to a particular ethnic group, the development of this kind of religious nationalism is most easily achieved. Hinduism is the religion of the Hindus (the Persian word for Indians), and the transformation of religious consciousness into a spirit of militant nationalism, overcoming differences of social status and language, was natural and relatively swift. But even when the religions of the subjugated people were universalistic and cosmopolitan in character, as with Islam and Buddhism, the union of religion and nationalism eventually emerged triumphant, and religious identification became a focal point of national consciousness, part of the colonized people's expression of dislike for the economic dominance and political hegemony imposed by European Christian rulers.[2]

In the absence of colonial intrusion, there is usually no politicization of religion. In Thailand, for example, writes Donald E. Smith, "the traditional pattern of subservience of Sangha to king was never disrupted by foreign rule, nor was the association of monks with anti-imperialist nationalism ever necessary."[3] Hence Thailand, unlike Burma and Ceylon, does not know the phenomenon of political monks. The explanation for this divergent development is neither that monks in Thailand have a different psychological make-up nor that there are religious differences. The great majority of the people of these three countries are believers in Theravada Buddhism, and the organization of the Sangha is essentially similar. Yet, in the absence of the need to rid the country of a non-Buddhist or anti-Buddhist power, the Sangha so far has remained essentially nonpolitical.[4] Since 1964 large numbers of missionary-monks have gone to the hills and to the politically sensitive and economically least developed border regions of Thailand, and these monks preach the Buddhist *dhamma* as well as loyalty to king and nation. This so-called *dhammathud* program, originally sponsored by the Department of Religious Affairs but now under the supervision of the Supreme Ecclesiastical Council of the Sangha, not only helps satisfy the desire of the monks to be socially useful but also may in time politicize the Thai Sangha. As in the past the monks are firmly controlled by the political authority of the country and are friendly toward it, but this situation could change.[5]

After the achievement of independence religion, which earlier played an integrative and unifying role, may prove a divisive force and undermine national unity. During the struggle for independence religious consciousness increases and upon the successful conclusion of this phase those who practice the majority religion may strive to complete the national victory by making their own creed the state religion. This is what happened in both Burma and Ceylon, and in such situations intergroup conflicts will be exacerbated by religious identification. In the case of Ceylon the striving for religious and cultural exclusiveness at first provided the motive force for a decisive political upset staged by militant Buddhists over the Anglicized elite that had achieved independence, but it later led to violent communal clashes with the Tamil (Hindu) minority. In Burma, the coup of General Ne Win in March 1962 was precipitated in part by the army's fear of a threatening disintegration of the state—the result of serious tensions created by U Nu's adoption of Buddhism as the state religion. In Egypt the seizure of power by Nasser in 1952 probably forestalled a victory of the Muslim Brotherhood which would have pursued a militant and intolerant religious policy. In South Vietnam, the political militancy of Buddhism was clearly related to religious competition and other social problems created by the influx of about a million Catholic refugees from the north.[6] Under such conditions, it has been observed, "religion may become the object of loyalties which impede the development of new identities more appropriate to the new situations in which people find themselves. Religious identification may prove divisive to societies. Moreover, by sacralizing the identity it provides, it may worsen and in fact embitter conflict, and build deeply into the personality structures of people a recalcitrance to come to terms with an opponent." [7] This is what happens in communal conflicts, in religious wars as well as in civil conflicts having a religious dimension. During the Spanish Civil War, for example, the clergy's preaching of a crusade and holy war further inflamed the fires of fratricidal passion.

Another objective factor that has a bearing upon the political behavior of revolutionary groups is the strength and self-confidence of the governing authorities and the perception on the part of revolutionaries of the chances of success for a revolt. A strong correlation appears to exist between readiness to revolt against the state and the belief that the use of violence by dissident groups in the past has helped their cause.[8] The attitude of religious leaders to such outbursts or movements is often affected by very similar considerations. The Spanish hierarchy supported the rebellion of the generals in 1936 because they thought that Franco would triumph easily. On the other hand, an important reason for the rise to power of Gandhi in the Indian National Congress was the fact that the terrorists had failed to score any decisive success, and the Indian nationalist movement, therefore, was receptive to the tactic of nonviolence. To be sure, Gandhi himself always denied that he had chosen satyagraha as a result of India's weakness, and, given a choice of cowardice and violence, he advised violence. But there is no doubt that the idea of nonviolence caught the imagination of India's nationalist leaders because this tactic seemed the only realistic one under the circumstances. The perception of the strength of the existing social or political order is thus a significant variable in shaping the political tactics of both revolutionary and religious groups. "If the existing social order is perceived by the radicals as so strong that they cannot survive and flourish by the use of radical methods," a recent writer has suggested, "the process of deradicalization will set in." [9] In the case of a revolutionary movement, imbued with strong religious zeal, fanatic dedication for a while may triumph over adverse odds, but in the long run the reality principle will assert itself. Even a revolutionary millenarian group will not indefinitely count on divine assistance; repeated and decisive defeat will eventually lead to a collapse of morale.

If the strength of a regime is a factor discouraging revolt, weakness and disorder, on the other hand, are conducive to the development of revolutionary sentiments. The ineffectiveness of a government, Edward Shils has noted, is a stimulus to aggressiveness against it. "Where authority abdicates through failure, ineptitude, and weakened self-confidence, it invites aggression against itself." [10] As we have seen in Chapter 11 in more detail, one of the crucial factors in revolutionary millenarianism is the existence of a severe crisis, linked to social, economic, or religious distress. A student of Chinese religion concludes "that no major politico-religious upheaval in Chinese history was without some form of extensive agricultural crisis as a background." [11] Whereas the impact of a crisis always depends upon subjective factors, such as feelings of relative deprivation, objective elements obviously play an important role.

In conclusion, in addition to variables involving internal factors such as the nature of religious doctrine, organization, and leadership, the political role of religion is also determined by situational factors not directly related to its innate characteristics. Among such external causes are the presence or absence of foreign rule and the strength or weakness of political regimes. These factors involve existing political and social situations or perceptions of situations, and though they are not always the result of historical accidents, their roots are traceable neither to the nature of religion as such nor to human intentions. They are variables intruding from the outside, so to speak, factors that are part of what Karl Popper has called "the situational logic" of events. [12]

CHAPTER 26

Conclusion

Critics of organized religion have often exaggerated its integrating role and minimized its revolutionary potential. "There are liberating movements that sail under religious flags," concedes Peter Berger. "Yet there can be little doubt about the overwhelmingly conservative and inhibitory effect of religion in most periods of history." [1] Berger is probably correct, if only because revolutionary episodes have occurred less frequently than periods of relative political tranquility. On the other hand, the verification of this impressionistic conclusion, that is, the drawing up of a balance sheet to determine what has been the preponderant political tendency of religion in general, involves formidable and perhaps insoluble problems. As we have seen, the religious factor is one among many factors in human affairs, and it is frequently difficult to determine the importance of one factor. The fact that a religious institution often simultaneously exerts its influence in both an integrating and revolutionary direction further complicates the picture. The social theorist, therefore, will be well advised to avoid such global and necessarily highly speculative appraisals. Our conclusion here will have to be more modest.

Religion integrates and also disrupts society; it is truly Janus-faced. It may provide legitimation for the existing order, give emotional support to the fundamental values of a society, soften the impact of conflict by emphasizing values such as salvation which are common to all, and lessen social tension by stressing supramundane values. [2] But religion also involves transcendent moral standards which define an ideal against which human performance can be measured. Hence those who are dissatisfied—politically, economically, socially, or spiritually —may find in religion strong support for their attack upon the *status quo*. Religion can be a powerful agent pushing the thoughts of men beyond tradition, it may become the spiritual dynamic of revolution which Sorel called the "social myth." As the judicious Hooker observed in the sixteenth century, during a period of great religious and social upheaval, when the minds of men are once "persuaded that it is the will of God to have those things done which they fancy, their opinions are as thorns in their sides, never suffering them to take rest till they have brought their speculations into practice." [3] Religion can provide man with the zeal of the true believer who knows that he is right and who acts with fortitude since he carries out God's will and counts on God's helping hand.

The dual nature of religion is demonstrated in charisma. The charismatic figure can use the aura of the sacred that surrounds him to sanctify the existing political and social order just as he can use his exceptional powers to convince his followers of the truth of his chiliastic prophecy which promises a "new heaven and new earth." Small wonder that, as Christopher Dawson has observed, "the adoration of transcendent power embodied in a human person and in social institutions is morally ambivalent and is associated with all that is highest and lowest in human nature. On the one hand it has led to monstrous and inhuman developments like . . . human sacrifices . . . and the deification of tyrants and madmen. . . . But on the other hand it has inspired the hope of the kingdom of righteousness and the advent of a divine Saviour." [4]

The paradox we posed at the beginning of this study can thus be resolved. Religion can be both a prop for the established institutions of society and a revolutionary force, since it includes elements for integration as well as radical change. Religion can defuse social conflict by devaluing earthly concerns and emphasizing happiness in the world beyond, but its promise of divine intervention in human affairs can also strengthen the hope that a better life is possible here on earth. The answers to the questions of ultimate meaning religion supplies—questions on man's nature, purpose, or fate—will be relevant both to the privileged and the weak, to the happy and the discontented, though different aspects of these answers will appeal to different groups. In fact, many of these answers are sufficiently protean to speak to all. Hence many times different groups within one religion will line up on opposite sides of the barricades. God's will, seen through the spectacles of human desires and interests, can be, and in fact usually is, read in several different ways. The essence and real meaning of God's commands and intentions, which man searches for with so much fervor, remain shrouded in mystery or, better put, remain a postulate of man's yearning for a teleological explanation of the cosmic process.

Whether religion will bar or promote political change will depend on the variables we examined in the previous four chapters. All religions known to us can assume both roles, though the intellectual and organizational baggage they carry will incline some more in one direction than in the other. Situational factors such as the chance for the success of a revolt and the impact of individual leaders will also be important. In our study we have examined four ways in which religion can assume a revolutionary posture, and it may be useful to summarize them:

1. *Millenarian revolts* occur (a) when situations of distress or disorientation develop, and the causes are not clearly perceived or appear insoluble by ordinary and available remedies, (b) when a society or group is deeply attached to religious ways of thinking about the world and when the religion of that society attaches importance to millenarian ideas, and (c) when an individual or a group of individuals obsessed with salvationist phantasies succeeds in establishing charismatic leadership over a social movement.

2. *Militant religious nationalism* arises among colonized people in situations of awakening national consciousness. Religion supplies a sense of national identity; it becomes a symbol of self-assertion against the colonial regime which is usually indifferent, if not hostile, to the native creed.

3. *The leaders of religious bodies with a developed ecclesiastical organization support a revolutionary upheaval* because they are sympathetic to the aims of this revolution, or because they are protecting the interests of the religious institution. These interests can be temporal or spiritual or both. They can involve the defense of worldly possessions or the protection of the mission of the religious institution as the channel of divine grace to man.

4. *Individual theologians or laymen support a revolutionary*

movement to give a concrete social and political meaning to
the transcendent elements of their faith as in the Christian
"Theology of Revolution." Such religious revolutionaries
often work in concert with secular revolutionary movements
and many lose their identity in them.

These four types of revolutionary change are not always mutually exclusive. A revolutionary episode like the Saya San Rebellion in modern Burma included elements of millenarianism but
was also an expression of militant Buddhist nationalism. Anti-colonial rebellions are often linked to revolts against an internal ruling class which has made peace with the foreign conqueror. Individual believers may in time extend their influence and capture
segments of their religious organization as happened during the
French Revolution with the formation of the Constitutional
church. To some extent all four categories of radical change are
fueled by the prophetic dimension of religion—they look forward to a better world than the one that is being challenged,
though the role of religious ideas is obviously stronger in the case
of revolutionary millenarianism than in cases when religious arguments are used in a civil war of essentially secular origins.

The specific explanations for each of these four manifestations
of the revolutionary role of religion differ, and, in view of the
heterogeneous character of the phenomena involved, this is indeed what we must expect. Just as the physician cannot give us
the cause of disease in general though he may be able to explain
the etiology of specific diseases, so the social theorist cannot supply us with the cause of religiously inspired or legitimated revolutionary upheaval though he can suggest particular explanations
for particular revolts in which religion plays a part. He can also
point to multiple and interacting causes common to the different
types such as strain, revolutionary ideas, and leadership or indicate
conditions that increase or weaken the impact of religion upon
politics. However, it must be remembered that it is only probable
that the properties stated in such explanations and propositions,
derived from comparative analysis, will apply to a single
instance—the regularities described are not without exceptions.
More accurately, we should refer to these propositions as tendency statements for when we conclude, for example, that revolutionary millenarianism is a rare phenomenon in an increasingly

secular society we assert a general tendency rather than a numerical class ratio of probability.[5] We cannot specify how secular a
society must be in order to discourage the development of revolutionary millenarianism or how few cases amount to "a rare phenomenon," and yet the proposition is useful. We can increase the
usefulness of this single tendency statement by supplementing it
with others that introduce additional factors. We have found that
revolutionary millenarianism will tend to emerge in situations of
political, social, or religious stress, which appear insoluble by ordinary remedies, and when a charismatic figure appears as the
prophet of the "new heaven and new earth." Other such generalizations have been stated in earlier chapters. In none of these cases
can we go beyond tendency statements, to wit, the statement of
conditions that make a certain result more or less likely.

One conceptual scheme that tries to reduce the element of indeterminacy between determinants and outcomes in the analysis
of collective behavior is Neil J. Smelser's "value-added" approach. According to this scheme, any event or situation, to become a determinant of a collective episode, must operate within
the limits established by other determinants, and these determinants must combine and become activated in a definite pattern.[6]
The determinants of collective behavior singled out by Smelser
—structural conduciveness, structural strain, growth and spread
of a generalized belief, precipitating factors, mobilization of participants for action, and the operation of social control—
broadly resemble the factors we have discussed under the head-
ings of religious doctrine, organization, situational factors, and
leadership. As the necessary determinants combine, Smelser
argues, the explanation of an episode becomes increasingly more
determinate, and alternative outcomes are ruled out.

Smelser's model is helpful in drawing attention to explanatory
hypotheses, but two limitations are apparent. First, as Smelser
himself admits, the accumulation of necessary conditions must be
seen as an analytic, not a temporal process. For example, a charismatic leader normally will not become a leader until certain conditions are present, but he sometimes will contribute to establishing these conditions—he may put forth ideas that will make
people more aware of social strain. It was the Hindu mystic,
Gandhi, who taught his people how exploited and oppressed they
were. Using the example of Javanese rural religion, Clifford

Geertz has shown how certain religious rituals can themselves be the source of social stress instead of being merely the reflection of stress elsewhere in the society,[7] and our analysis of revolutionary millenarianism has revealed a very similar pattern. Many social elements or institutions do not arise linearly, which would make it possible to indicate which precedes the other, but rather coexist and continually modify each other. In the case of ignorance and poverty, for example, one may be said to be the cause of the other and vice versa.[8] Religious ideas are often so deeply embedded in a particular social and cultural setting that it is quite impossible to determine what is cause and what effect. This means, of course, that the sequence in which the various determinants of interest to us combine is not always specifiable or predictable, and the absence of a definite causal sequence reintroduces a considerable element of indeterminacy.

Second, and more importantly, the actions of leaders and the impact of these often cannot be foreseen. In a situation of crisis one act may or may not make a difference. History is full of contingencies and the unintended consequences of human actions; it includes events which happened but did not have to happen or which might have happened differently. If Oliver Cromwell had followed his inclination in the early 1630's to emigrate to America or if Hung Hsiu-ch'üan had passed his examinations the course of two important millenarian movements most likely would have been radically different, or the movements might never even have come into existence. Though everything that happens in history is caused, the fragmentary evidence at our disposal, our less than perfect understanding of human behavior, the irrational conduct of many men, and the impact of random events severely limits our ability to ascertain a cause with any degree of precision and to find a uniform pattern or law. "Different causal sequences," Charles Frankel writes, "cross and crisscross and tangle one another up. Bad weather puts off a battle and gives an enemy time to recoup; societies are overwhelmed by greater force and die through no fault of their own; fools are born as kings, and anonymous Miltons die mute and inglorious." [9] Whether chance is merely another word for complexity, hiding our ignorance, as the great French physicist, Henri Poincaré, is supposed to have said, or whether there are true accidents in this world is a question I will not pursue here.

In view of the difficulties enumerated, Smelser's hope of speci-
fying not only the necessary but also the sufficient conditions of
collective behavior seems quite unrealizable. Our generalizations
about the causes of important historical events will still be limited
to the enumeration of necessary rather than sufficient causes—
they tell us when a revolution might happen but not when it
will happen, they help us understand why a particular revolution
could occur rather than why it *had* to occur. As Harry Eckstein
realistically and candidly noted in regard to the precipitating factors of internal wars, the determinants involved may be so various
as to defy theoretical treatment, and they may have to be left to
the historian.[10] It is the historian who can explain a specific episode by telling us how it happened, though his explanation is not
a deductive one.[11] That explanations of certain phenomena in the
natural sciences are equally difficult may be a consolation though
it does not alleviate the problem.

Without deductive explanations there can be no prediction, although the value of a theory does not depend, of course, upon
this. In the physical sciences, too, it is often possible to explain
without being able to predict or to predict without being able to
explain. The multi-factor explanation we have advanced concerning the relationship of religion and revolution appears to be the
best our conceptual tools and the data at hand enable us to develop at this time. We can point to ways in which the various
factors interact and combine as when we examine the impact of
charismatic leadership upon the perception of deprivation, but
the precise role of these interdependent variables cannot be as-
sessed with exactness or expressed in quantitative terms. In the
words of Abraham Kaplan: "In a sense, we know too much to be
able to unify it in a single theory, and we do not know any of it
with sufficient sureness." [12] Whether the study of human affairs
will ever yield more precise explanations is an open question. In
any event, as a student of the theory of political analysis has recently reminded us, though precision and rigor are extremely important, "we cannot stop working and await the methodological
millennium. Any attempt to tailor a discipline to the Procrustean
bed of a particular epistemic requirement may prove fatal to the
patient." [13]

Robert E. Park, a pioneering student of collective behavior, has
noted that "nothing in ordinary human experience has so in-

flamed the imagination of men, encouraged so many romantic illusions, or broken so completely with the ordinary routine of existence, as has been true of revolution"—nothing, he added,
except religion (in addition to war and romantic love).[14] Expressing an attitude common to many of his contemporaries, Tom
Paine in 1791 celebrated the American and French revolutions as
"a renovation of the natural order of things, a system of principles as universal as truth and the existence of man," [15] and ever
since revolution has occupied an extraordinary and seductive
place in modern man's life. Today revolution is often equated
with liberation, modernization, and progress, and in many parts
of the world religion has become the handmaiden of revolution.
The cross of Christianity, the crescent of Islam, and even the
peaceful prayer wheel of Buddhism have been enlisted to shore
up revolutionary movements and regimes just as in earlier times
religion was often used to support the *status quo*.

Whether this new positive relationship of religion and revolution will indeed promote human liberty and happiness is, of
course, a question nobody can as yet answer, and the currently
fashionable romanticizing of revolution is undoubtedly premature. Religion has a share in this celebration of heroic ruthlessness
and violence. It continues to inspire killing in Northern Ireland
as much as on the Indian subcontinent and the Philippines, demonstrating once again that religious zeal can be a powerful force
for love but also an important force for hate and man's inhuman-
ity to man. The various theologies of revolution in vogue today
make men slight the cruelties and hatreds that commonly accompany revolutionary upheavals, they obscure the fact that especially those revolutions that are long-drawn-out and really violent "give magnificent opportunities to knaves, fools and
monsters." [16] What the theologizing of revolution cannot do is to
establish the progressive character of such revolts. That judgment
is reserved to future generations who will have an opportunity to
live with their consequences. Whereas some revolutions in history have led their people to a better life, others have merely substituted a new despotism for old oppressions. The new is not necessarily preferable to the old just because it is different. The
ultimate test, surely, is not prophetic indignation at injustice or
good intentions but performance and results.

NOTES

CHAPTER 1

1. Cf. Melford E. Spiro, "Religion: Problems of Definition and Explanation," in Michael Banton, ed., *Anthropological Approaches to the Study of Religion* (London, 1966); Charles Y. Glock and Rodney Stark, *Religion and Society in Tension* (Chicago, 1965), pp. 4–5.
2. The distinction between great and little traditions has been stressed in the writings of Robert Redfield. See also the discussion by Clifford C. Geertz in Robert N. Bellah, ed., *Religion and Progress in Modern Asia* (New York, 1865) p. 151.
3. Peter L. Berger, *The Sacred Canopy: Elements of a Sociological Theory of Religion* (New York, 1967), p. 181.
4. For a survey of the different meanings of "revolution" see Arthur Hatto, "Revolution: An Enquiry into the Usefulness of an Historical Term," *Mind* LVIII (1949): 498–508.
5. Chalmers Johnson, *Revolutionary Change* (Boston, 1966), p. 7.
6. Manfred Halpern, "The Revolution of Modernization in National and International Society," in Carl J. Friedrich, ed., *Nomos VIII: Revolution* (New York, 1966), p. 187.
7. Cf. Charles Anderson et al., *Issues of Political Development* (Englewood Cliffs, N.J., 1967), pp. 149–50.
8. *The Politics of Aristotle*, trans. Ernest Barker (New York, 1958), Bk. v, ch. 1, p. 204.
9. Cf. Eugene Kamenka, "The Concept of Political Revolution," in *Nomos VIII*, p. 124.
10. Cf. Henry Ashby Turner, Jr., "Fascism and Modernization," *World Politics* XXIV (1972): 550.
11. Crane Brinton, *The Anatomy of Revolution*, rev. ed. (New York, 1952), pp. 25–26.
12. Lawrence Stone, "The English Revolution," in Robert Forster and Jack P. Greene, eds., *Preconditions of Revolution in Early Modern Europe* (Baltimore, 1970), p. 60.

13. Hannah Arendt, *On Revolution* (New York, 1965), is one of many recent writers who restricts the phenomenon and the very idea of revolution to modern times. In her view, the notion "that an entirely new story, a story never known or told before, is about to unfold, was unknown prior to the two great revolutions of the eighteenth century" (p. 21). We regard this observation as empirically false and concur with D. W. Brogan's observation in *The Price of Revolution* (New York, 1966) that "as a concept, as a reality, revolution is one of the oldest political institutions of our western civilization" (p. 1). Indeed, as we will show in more detail in Chapter 11, the eighteenth-century concepts of progress and revolution involved a secularization of the ancient millenarian dream.
14. Stanislav Andreski, *The Uses of Comparative Sociology* (Berkeley, Calif., 1965), p. 83.
15. Some of the theoretical problems involved in explaining historical events are dealt with in my essay, "Historical Data in Comparative Political Analysis: A Note on Some Problems of Theory," *Comparative Politics* I (1968): 103–10.
16. Max Weber, *The Methodology of the Social Sciences*, trans. and ed. by Edward A. Shils and Henry A. Finch (Glencoe, Ill., 1949), pp. 90–97.
17. Karl Popper, *The Logic of Scientific Discovery* (New York, 1965), p. 280.
18. Unpublished letter of 1877 to a Russian journal in Geneva, cited by Shlomo Avineri, *The Social and Political Thought of Karl Marx* (Cambridge, 1970), p. 152.
19. Robert A. Nisbet, *Social Change and History: Aspects of the Western Theory of Development* (New York, 1970), p. 304.

CHAPTER 2

1. Charles Drekmeier, *Kingship and Community in Early India* (Stanford, Calif., 1962), pp. 116–17. The animist ingredient of Hinduism, contributed by the tribal aborigines of India, is stressed by Henry H. Presler, "Indian Aborigine Contributions to Hindu Ideas of Mukti Liberation," in R. J. Zwi Werblowsky and C. Jouco Bleeker, eds., *Types of Redemption* (Leiden, 1970), pp. 144–67.
2. Drekmeier, *op. cit.*, p. 22. See also A. S. Altekar, *State and Government in Ancient India*, 4th rev. ed. (Delhi, 1962), pp. 98–99.
3. Max Weber, *The Religion of India: The Sociology of Hinduism and Buddhism*, trans. Hans H. Gerth and Don Martindale (Glencoe, Ill., 1958), p. 144.
4. Drekmeier, *op. cit.*, p. 33.
5. Emil Abegg, *Der Messiasglaube in Indien und Iran* (Berlin, 1928), p. 22.
6. *Ibid.*, pp. 143–44. See also A. L. Basham, *The Wonder That Was*

India (New York, 1959), p. 307; M. Monier-Williams, *Brahmanism and Hinduism*, 4th rev. ed. (New York, 1891), p. 114.

7. Cf. A. L. Basham, "Some Fundamental Political Ideas of Ancient India," in C. H. Philips, ed., *Politics and Society in India* (New York, 1962), p. 12.

8. Drekmeier, *op. cit.*, p. 298.

9. *Ibid.*, p. 252.

10. Jan Gonda, *Ancient Indian Kingship from the Religious Point of View* (Leiden, 1966), p. 7.

11. *The Mahabharata*, xiii. 61, 32–33, ed. M. N. Dutt (Calcutta, 1905), p. 142.

12. Cf. John W. Spellman, *Political Theory of Ancient India: A Study of Kingship from the Earliest Times to Circa* A.D. *300* (Oxford, 1964), p. 232.

13. Drekmeier, *op. cit.*, p. 249.

14. Basham, in *Politics and Society in India*, p. 21.

15. C. K. Yang, *Religion in Chinese Society* (Berkeley, Calif., 1961), p. 107.

16. Cf. D. Howard Smith, *Chinese Religions* (London, 1968), p. 14.

17. *The Shu Ching* (Book of History), trans. James Legge (The Chinese Classics, IV), cited by H. G. Creel, *Chinese Thought from Confucius to Mao Tsë-tung* (London, 1954), p. 31.

18. Cf. Arthur Waley, *The Analects of Confucius* (New York, n.d.), p. 16.

19. This is the conclusion of D. Howard Smith, *op. cit.*, p. 33, and it fits the definition of religion used in this study.

20. Waley, *op. cit.*, pp. 14–18; H. G. Creel, *Confucius and the Chinese Way* (New York, 1960), p. 13.

21. Fung Yu-Lan, *Short History of Chinese Philosophy* (New York, 1966), p. 159.

22. Derk Bodde, "Harmony and Conflict in Chinese Thought," in Arthur F. Wright, ed., *Studies in Chinese Thought* (Chicago, 1953), p. 27.

23. *Mencius* 5A.5, trans. W.A.C.H. Dobson (Toronto, 1963), p. 65.

24. *Ibid.*, 1B.8, p. 5.

25. Cf. Otto Franke, *Studien zur Geschichte des Konfuzianischen Dogmas und der chinesischen Staatsreligion* (Hamburg, 1920), p. 247.

26. Yang, *op. cit.*, p. 139.

27. Cf. Wolfram Eberhard, "The Political Function of Astronomy and Astronomers in Han China," in John K. Fairbank, ed., *Chinese Thought and Institutions* (Chicago, 1967), pp. 33–70; Herbert Franke, "Some Remarks on the Interpretation of Chinese Dynastic Histories," *Oriens* III (1950): 117–118.

28. Max Weber, *The Religion of China*, trans. Hans H. Gerth (Glencoe, Ill., 1951), p. 31.

29. Cf. Yuji Muramatsu, "Some Themes in Chinese Rebel Ideologies,"

in Arthur F. Wright, ed., *The Confucian Persuasion* (Stanford, Calif., 1960), p. 252.

30. E. R. and K. Hughes, *Religion in China* (London, 1950), p. 43.
31. Cf. Etienne Balazs, *Chinese Civilization and Bureaucracy*, trans. H. M. Wright (New Haven, 1964), p. 155.
32. Cf. Charles O. Hucker, *The Traditional State in Ming Times (1368–1644)* (Tucson, 1964), p. 62.
33. For a detailed description of these rites see J. J. M. de Groot, *Universimus: Die Grundlagen der Religion, Ethik, des Staatswesens und der Wissenschaften Chinas* (Berlin, 1918).
34. Cf. Yang, *op. cit.*, pp. 183–84.
35. J. J. M. de Groot, *The Religion of the Chinese* (New York, 1912), pp. 120–21.
36. William Theodore de Bary, ed., *Sources of Chinese Tradition* (New York, 1966), p. 631.
37. Cf. Franklin W. Houn, "The Communist Monolith versus the Chinese Tradition," *Orbis* VII (1965): 921.
38. Edward Gibbon, *The History of the Decline and Fall of the Roman Empire* (London, 1903), I: 165.
39. Yang, *op. cit.*, p. 109.
40. John K. Shryock, *The Origin and Development of the State Cult of Confucius* (New York, 1966), p. 105.
41. *Ibid.*, p. 137.
42. Yang, *op. cit.*, p. 128.
43. *Ibid.*, p. 132.
44. Quoted in *ibid.*, p. 145.
45. Joseph M. Kitagawa, "Buddhism and Asian Politics," *Asian Survey* II, no. 5 (July 1962): 1.
46. *The Questions of King Milinda*, Part I, trans. T. W. Rhys Davids, Sacred Books of the East, vol. XXXV (Delhi, 1965), pp. 100–101.
47. Cf. Winston Lee King, *In the Hope of Nibbana: An Essay on Theravada Buddhist Ethics* (LaSalle, Ill., 1964), p. 185.
48. *Digha Nikaya*, 3.84 (A Book of Genesis), *Dialogues of the Buddha*, trans. T. W. and C. A. F. Rhys Davids (London, 1921), p. 80. See also the Sutta on "War, Wickedness and Wealth" which tells of the king who became sovereign of the earth "not by the scourge, not by the sword, but by righteousness" (3.59, p. 60).
49. U. N. Ghoshal, *A History of Indian Political Ideas* (Bombay, 1959), p. 536.
50. King, *op. cit.*, p. 124.
51. Kitagawa, *op. cit.*, p. 4.
52. Reginald Stephen Copleston, *Buddhism: Primitive and Present in Magadha and Ceylon* (London, 1892), p. 480.
53. Cf. Emil Abegg, *Der Buddha Maitreya* (St. Gallen, 1948).
54. Cf. Kitsiri Malalgoda, "Millennialism in Relation to Buddhism," *Comparative Studies in Society and History* XII (1970): 430. See

also Charles F. Keyes, "Millennialism, Theravada Buddhism, and Thai Society" (Paper delivered at the 24th annual meeting of the Association for Asian Studies in New York, March 29, 1972). The value of these essays is impaired by the fact that both Malalgoda and Keyes at times use the category "millenarianism" in an imprecise manner.

55. Drekmeier, *op. cit.*, p. 113.
56. E. Sarkisyanz, *Buddhist Backgrounds of the Burmese Revolution* (The Hague, 1965), p. 56.
57. Max Weber, *The Sociology of Religion*, trans. Ephraim Fischoff (Boston, 1964), p. 169.
58. Donald E. Smith, "The Politics of Buddhism," *Worldview* XVI, no. 1 (January 1973): 16.
59. Kenneth K. S. Ch'en, *Buddhism in China: A Historical Survey* (Princeton, 1964), pp. 48–49.
60. Yang, *op. cit.*, p. 116.
61. Ch'en, *op. cit.*, pp. 207–208.
62. *Ibid.*, pp. 204–205.
63. Cf. Wolfram Eberhard, *Das Toba-Reich Nordchinas* (Leiden, 1949), pp. 229–35.
64. Yang, *op. cit.*, p. 125.
65. Cf. A. F. Wright, *Buddhism in Chinese History* (New York, 1967), pp. 92–93.
66. Passage from the County Gazetteer of Anking, Anhwei, quoted in *ibid.*, p. 101.
67. Yang, *op. cit.*, pp. 121–23.
68. Ch'en, *op. cit.*, pp. 469 and 485.
69. R. H. Charles, *Eschatology* (New York, 1963), p. 9.
70. John Bright, *A History of Israel* (Philadelphia, 1959), p. 136.
71. For the supporting references see Joseph Klausner, *The Messianic Idea in Israel* (London, 1956), p. 17.
72. See Bertil Albrektson, *History and the Gods* (Lund, 1967) and the impressive evidence marshaled in that careful study.
73. R. H. Charles, ed., *Apocrypha and Pseudepigrapha of the Old Testament* (Oxford, 1963), II: 171.
74. Sigmund Mowinckel, *He That Cometh*, trans. G. W. Anderson (New York, 1954), p. 152.
75. Bright, *op. cit.*, p. 206.
76. For a defense of this view see the writings of Ivan Engnell, Aage Bentzen, and Geo Widengren, often also referred to as the Uppsala school. A number of shorter essays on this theme can be found in the volume edited by S. H. Hooke, *Myth, Ritual and Kingship* (Oxford, 1958).
77. Cf. Henri Frankfort, *Kingship and the Gods* (Chicago, 1948), p. 341; Roland de Vaux, *Ancient Israel* (New York, 1961), p. 112.
78. Martin Noth, *The Laws in the Pentateuch and other Studies*, trans. D. R. Ap-Thomas (Philadelphia, 1966), pp. 174–75.

79. Klausner, *op. cit.*, p. 241.
80. Mowinckel, *op. cit.*, p. 131.
81. *Iblid.*, p. 149.
82. De Vaux, *op. cit.*, p. 98.
83. 3:25–27.
84. A more guarded conclusion regarding Zoroastrian influence is reached by Franz König, *Zarathustras Jenseitsvorstellungen und das Alte Testament* (Vienna, 1964), pp. 283–85.
85. George Foot Moore, *Judaism in the First Centuries of the Christian Era* (Cambridge, Mass., 1962), II: 312.
86. Mowinckel, *op. cit.*, p. 280.
87. Oscar Cullmann, *The State in the New Testament*, rev. ed. (London, 1963), p. 16.
88. Cf. S. G. F. Brandon, *The Fall of Jerusalem and the Christian Church* (London, 1951), p. 198.
89. S. G. F. Brandon, *Jesus and the Zealots* (Manchester, 1967), p. 355.
90. See, for example, Mark 8:31 and 9:1. For a careful discussion of Jesus' eschatological message and the literature on this theme see Richard H. Hiers, *The Kingdom of God in the Synoptic Tradition* (Gainesville, Fla., 1970).
91. I Th. 4:13–17.
92. Cf. Shirley Jackson Case, *The Millennial Hope* (Chicago, 1918), p. 143.
93. On the origin of this idea see Alfred Wikenhauser, "Die Herkunft der Idee des tausendjährigen Reiches in der Johannes-Apokalypse," *Römische Quartalschrift* XLV (1937): 1–24.
94. Gal. 3:28.
95. Karl Löwith, *Meaning in History* (Chicago, 1964), pp. 4–5; Frederick Watkins, *The Political Tradition of the West* (Cambridge, Mass., 1957), p. 42.
96. Norman Cohn, *The Pursuit of the Millennium* (London, 1957), p. 307.
97. See the discussion in Case, *op. cit.*, pp. 156–71.
98. *Ibid.*, p. 155.
99. St. Augustine, *The City of God*, Bk. xx, ch. 9, trans. Marcus Dods (New York, 1948), II: 365.
100. *Ibid.*, Bk. v, chs. 19 and 21.
101. The best single source on the subject remains Fritz Kern, *Kingship and Law in the Middle Ages*, trans. S. B. Chrimes (Oxford, 1948).
102. St. Thomas Aquinas, *Summa Theologica*, IIa, IIae, qu. 42, art 2, *Selected Political Writings*, ed. A. P. D'Entrèves (Oxford, 1948), p. 161.
103. Cf. Guenter Lewy, *Constitutionalism and Statecraft during the Golden Age of Spain: A Study of the Political Philosophy of Juan de Mariana, S.J.* (Geneva, 1960), p. 76 and the literature cited there.

104. *Ibid.*, p. 77.
105. Encyclical *Quod Apostolici Muneris*, December 28, 1878, in Joseph Husslein, S.J., *Social Wellsprings* (Milwaukee, 1942), I: 19.
106. Cf. Luigi Sturzo, "The Right of Resistance to the State: Echoes of a Discussion in France," *Contemporary Review* CXXXIV (1928): 312.
107. Encyclical *Firmissimam Constantiam*, March 28, 1937, in Sydney Z. Ehler and John B. Morrall, *Church and State Through the Centuries* (London, 1954), p. 590. Cf. Luigi Sturzo, "The Right to Rebel," *The Dublin Review* CCI (1937): 35–36.
108. Louis Gardet, *La cité Musulmane: Vie sociale et politique*, 2nd rev. ed. (Paris, 1961), p. 31.
109. Gustave E. von Grunebaum, *Medieval Islam: A Study in Cultural Orientation* (Chicago, 1961), pp. 155–156. For a discussion of ancient oriental theories of political rule see Frankfort, *op. cit.*
110. Thomas W. Arnold, *The Caliphate* (Oxford, 1924), p. 11. See also Anwar G. Chejne, *Succession to the Rule in Islam* (Lahore, 1960), ch. 4.
111. Notably 4:62.
112. H. A. R. Gibb, *Mohammedanism: An Historical Survey*, 2nd ed. (New York, 1962), p. 75.
113. Ignaz Goldziher, *Vorlesungen über den Islam* (Heidelberg, 1910), p. 48.
114. Quoted in Arnold, *op. cit.*, p. 48.
115. Abu Yusuf, *Kibab el-Harac*, p. 11, quoted in H. A. R. Gibb and Harold Bowen, *Islamic Society and the West*, vol. I: *Islamic Society in the Eighteenth Century* (London, 1957), p. 28.
116. Reuben Levy, *The Social Structure of Islam* (Cambridge, 1962), p. 190.
117. *Kitab al-Iqtisad* (Cairo A. H. 1320), p. 107, cited and translated by David de Santillana, "Law and Society," in Thomas Arnold and Alfred Guillaume, eds., *The Legacy of Islam* (London, 1943), p. 302.
118. Cf. Leonard Binder, "Al-Ghazali's Theory of Islamic Government," *Muslim World* VL (1955): 229–41.
119. Cited (no source) by Santillana, *op. cit.*, pp. 302–303.
120. Von Grunebaum, *op. cit.*, p. 169.
121. Elie Adib Salem, *Political Theory and Institutions of the Khawarij* (Baltimore, 1956), p. 28.
122. Cf. my article "Some Theology About Tyranny," *Smith College Studies in History* XLIV (1964): 86–87.
123. Al-Shahrastani, *Religionsparteien und Philosophen-Schulen* (German trans. of *Al-Milal wa-'l Nihal* by Theodor Haarbrücker) (Halle, 1850), pp. 144–45.
124. Ignaz Goldziher, *Mohammed and Islam*, trans. Kate Chambers Seelye (New Haven, 1917), pp. 103–104.
125. H. A. R. Gibb, "Constitutional Organization," in Majid Khad-

duri and Herbert J. Liebesny, eds., *Law in the Middle East*, vol.
I (Washington, D.C., 1955), p. 15.
126. Bernard Lewis, "Some Observations on the Significance of Heresy in the History of Islam," *Studia Islamica* I (1953): 47.
127. D. S. Margoliouth, "Mahdi," *Encyclopaedia of Religion and Ethics* VIII (1915): 336.
128. P. M. Holt, *The Mahdist State in the Sudan 1881–1898*, 2nd rev. ed. (Oxford, 1970), pp. 28–29.
129. *Ibid.*, p. 29.
130. D. S. Margoliouth, "On Mahdis and Mahdiism," *Proceedings of the British Academy* VII (1916): 223.
131. C. Snouck Hurgronje, "Der Mahdi," *Verspreide Geschriften* (Bonn, 1923), I: 166–67.
132. Ibn Khaldun critically reviews these traditions in vol. II, ch. 3, sect. 51 of his *Muqaddimah*. See the English translation by Franz Rosenthal (New York, 1958), II: 156–84.
133. Holt, *op. cit.*, p. 25.
134. Cf. Sartono Kartodirdjo, *The Peasants' Revolt of Banten in 1888: Its Conditions, Course and Sequel* (The Hague, 1966).
135. Quoted in Bernard Lewis, *The Origins of Isma'ilism* (Cambridge, 1940), p. 83.
136. Marshall G. S. Hodgson, *The Order of Assassins* (The Hague, 1955), p. 83.
137. Louis Massignon, "Guilds (Islamic)," *Encyclopaedia of the Social Sciences* (New York, 1935), VII: 216; Bernard Lewis, "The Islamic Guilds," *Economic History Review* VIII (1937): 20–37.
138. Charles-André Julien, *Histoire de l'Afrique du Nord* (Paris, 1952), II: 292, cited by Manfred Halpern, *The Politics of Social Change in the Middle East and North Africa* (Princeton, 1963), pp. 20–21.
139. Halpern, *op. cit.*, p. 10.

CHAPTER 3

1. Holmes Welch, *Taoism: The Parting of the Way*, rev. ed. (Boston, 1966), p. 12.
2. Fung Yu-Lan, *Short History of Chinese Philosophy* (New York, 1966), p. 102.
3. C. K. Yang, *Religion in Chinese Society* (Berkeley, Calif., 1961), p. 113.
4. Welch, *op. cit.*, p. 141.
5. Cf. Yuji Muramatsu, "Some Themes in Chinese Rebel Ideologies," in Arthur F. Wright, ed., *The Confucian Persuasion* (Stanford, Calif., 1960), p. 245.
6. William Theodore de Bary, ed., *Sources of Chinese Tradition* (New York, 1966), p. 310.
7. Kenneth K. S. Ch'en, *Buddhism in China: A Historical Survey* (Princeton, 1964), p. 427.

8. Yang, *op. cit.*, p. 223.
9. *Ibid.*, p. 205.
10. Quoted in J. J. M. de Groot, *Sectarianism and Religious Persecution in China* (Taipei, 1963), pp. 372 and 379.
11. Cf. Paul Michaud, "The Yellow Turbans," *Monumenta Serica* XVII (1958): 49–53. The factor of agrarian distress is emphasized by Howard S. Levy, "Yellow Turban Religion and Rebellion at the End of Han," *Journal of the American Oriental Society* LXXVI (1956): 214. For a more general discussion of political conditions see Etienne Balazs, "Political Philosophy and Social Crisis at the End of Han," *Chinese Civilization and Bureaucracy*, trans. H. M. Wright (New Haven, 1964), pp. 187–225.
12. Michaud, *op. cit.*, p. 54.
13. See, for example, Werner Eichhorn, "Description of the Rebellion of Sun En and Earlier Taoist Rebellions," *Mitteilungen des Instituts für Orientforschung* II (1954): 325–52.
14. Michaud, *op. cit.*, p. 92.
15. Vincent Y. C Shih, "Some Chinese Rebel Ideologies," *T'oung-Pao* XLIV (1956): 170.
16. Levy, *op. cit.*, pp. 217–19.
17. See the discussion by R. A. Stein, "Remarques sur les mouvements du Taoisme politico-religieux au IIe siècle ap. J.-C.," *Toung-Pao* L (1963): 1–78. Henri Maspero, *Mélanges posthumes sur les religions et l'historie de la Chine* (Paris, 1967), II: 152, regards the movements essentially identical in organization and doctrine.
18. Michaud, *op. cit.*, pp. 80–81.
19. From the *Tung-yüan shen-chou ching*, cited by Anna K. Seidel, "The Image of the Perfect Ruler in Early Taoist Messianism: Lao Tzu and Li Hung," *History of Religions* IX (1969–70): 239.
20. *Ibid.*, 246–47.
21. Daniel L. Overmyer, "Folk Buddhist Religion: Creation and Eschatology in Medieval China," *History of Religions* XII (1972): 68.
22. From a fourteenth-century document quoted in Vincent Y. C. Shih, *The Taiping Ideology* (Seattle, 1967), p. 359.
23. Ch'en, *op. cit.*, pp. 427–28.
24. Yang, *op. cit.*, p. 122.
25. Muramatsu, *op. cit.*, p. 246; see also Wolfram Eberhard, *Das Toba-Reich Nordchinas* (Leiden, 1949), pp. 248–64.
26. Yung-deh Richard Chu, "An Introductory Study of the White Lotus Sect in Chinese History with Special Reference to Peasant Movements" (Ph.D. dissertation, Columbia University, 1967), pp. 25–35, 47–55.
27. John W. Dardess, "The Transformation of Messianic Revolt and the Founding of the Ming Dynasty," *Journal of Asian Studies* XXIX (1970): 546.

28. Ch'en, *op. cit.*, pp. 430–35.
29. Groot, *op. cit.*, pp. 166–69.
30. Muramatsu, *op. cit.*, p. 247. See also Victor Purcell, *The Boxer Uprising: A Background Study* (London, 1963), ch. vii.
31. Cf. S. Y. Teng, "A Political Interpretation of Chinese Rebellions and Revolutions," *Tsing-Hua Journal of Chinese Studies*, N.S. I (1958): 106.
32. Yang, *op. cit.*, p. 219.
33. *Ibid.*, p. 233.
34. Quoted in *ibid.*, p. 237.
35. Wolfram Eberhard, *Conquerors and Rulers: Social Forces in Medieval China*, 2nd rev. ed. (Leiden, 1965), p. 105.
36. Balazs, *Chinese Civilization*, p. 158.
37. Muramatsu, *op. cit.*, pp. 256–58.
38. Cf. Shih Shao-pin, ed., *Chung-kuo Feng-chien She-hui Nung-min Chan-cheng Wen-ti T'ao-lun Chi* (Collected Articles on the Problem of Peasant Wars in Chinese Feudal Society) (Peking, 1962), pp. 511–13. See also Li Kuang-pi and Lai Hsin-hsia, eds., *Chung-kuo Nung-min Ch'i-yi Lun-chi* (Collected Discussions on the Chinese Peasant Uprisings) (Peking, 1958). For a Western analysis of these and other studies see James P. Harrison, *The Communists and the Chinese Peasant Rebellions* (New York, 1968).
39. The importance of political corruption as a crucial factor in the inability or unwillingness of governments to overcome economic and other difficulties is stressed by Teng, *op. cit.*, p. 91.
40. Yang, *op. cit.*, p. 240.
41. *Ibid.*, p. 242.
42. *Ibid.*, p. 225.
43. Shih, *Taiping Ideology*, p. 361.
44. Max Weber, *The Religion of China*, trans. Hans H. Gerth (Glencoe, Ill., 1951), p. 224.
45. Eichhorn, *op. cit.*, p. 338.
46. Muramatsu, *op. cit.*, p. 259.
47. *Ibid.*, pp. 263–64.

CHAPTER 4

1. Elias Bickermann, *The Maccabees*, trans. Moses Hadas (New York, 1947), pp. 28–29.
2. This thesis is stated most emphatically by Elias Bickermann, *Der Gott der Makkabäer* (Berlin, 1937), p. 137.
3. Victor Tcherikover, *Hellenistic Civilization and the Jews*, trans. S. Applebaum (Philadelphia, 1961), p. 197.
4. *Ibid.*, p. 198.
5. Solomon Zeitlin, *The Rise and Fall of the Judaean State* (Philadelphia, 1964), I: 99.
6. Martin Hengel, *Judentum und Hellenismus* (Tübingen, 1969), p. 321.

7. For a discussion of the roots of this conception in oriental mythology see Sigmund Mowinckel, *He That Cometh*, trans. G. W. Anderson (New York, 1954), pp. 420–37.
8. Joseph Klausner, *The Messianic Idea in Israel* (London, 1956), pp. 235–36.
9. Bickermann, *Maccabees*, p. 117.
10. H. H. Rowley, *The Relevance of Apocalyptic*, 3rd rev. ed. (New York, 1964), p. 22.
11. R. H. Charles, *Eschatology* (New York, 1963), pp. 126–27.
12. R. H. Charles, ed., *Apocrypha and Pseudepigrapha of the Old Testament* (Oxford, 1963), ix (hereafter cited as Charles, *Apocrypha*).
13. Klausner, *op. cit.*, p. 273.
14. Otto Plöger, *Theocracy and Eschatology*, trans. S. Rudman (Richmond, Va., 1968), p. 51.
15. I Macc. 14:4–15; Mowinckel, *op. cit.*, p. 284. Ethelbert Stauffer, *Jerusalem und Rom im Zeitalter Jesu Christi* (Bern, 1957), appropriately speaks of the "hasmonean court theologians" (p. 77).
16. George Foot Moore, *Judaism in the First Centuries of the Christian Era* (Cambridge, Mass., 1962), II: 328.
17. Bickermann, *Maccabees*, p. 112.
18. Moore, *op. cit.*, I: 77.
19. Klausner, *op. cit.*, p. 385.
20. Charles, *Apocrypha*, II: 647 and 651.
21. Jacob Licht, "Taxo or the Apocalyptic Doctrine of Vengeance," *Journal of Jewish Studies* XII (1961): 97.
22. Charles, *Eschatology*, p. 329.
23. Morton Smith, in "Zealots and Sicarii: Their Origins and Relation," *Harvard Theological Review* LXIV (1971): 1–19, maintains that there existed no resistance party by that name before A.D. 67–68, only individual zealots. Smith's argument appears strained. The fact that it is accompanied by much personal abuse heaped on the holders of rival interpretations, unfortunately a not uncommon phenomenon in scholarly disputations about this period, does not make it any more convincing.
24. William Ruben Farmer, *Maccabees, Zealots and Josephus* (New York, 1956), p. 175; see also the excellent discussion in Martin Hengel, *Die Zeloten* (Leiden, 1961), pp. 151–81.
25. S. G. F. Brandon, *Jesus and the Zealots* (Manchester, 1967), p. 48 (hereafter cited as Brandon, *Jesus*).
26. *Ibid.*, p. 51.
27. Abba Hillel Silver, *A History of Messianic Speculation in Israel* (New York, 1927), p. 5.
28. *Jewish Antiquities* xciii: 5, cited by Robert Eisler, *The Messiah Jesus and John the Baptist*, trans. A. H. Krappe (London, 1931), p. 255.
29. Hengel, *Zeloten*, p. 132.
30. Acts 6:37.

31. Hengel, *Zeloten*, pp. 358–59.
32. Heinrich Graetz, *Geschichte der Juden* (Leipzig, 1905–06), III: 432.
33. *The Jewish War*, ii. 13.3, cited by Emil Schürer, *A History of the Jewish People in the Time of Jesus*, ed. Nahum N. Glatzer (New York, 1963), p. 230.
34. Schürer, *op. cit.*, p. 225.
35. *Ibid.*, p. 231.
36. *Ibid.*, pp. 170–71.
37. Eisler, *op. cit.*, p. 264. See also Jakob Taubes, *Abendländische Eschatologie* (Bern, 1947), p. 45.
38. *The Code of Maimonides*, trans. Abraham M. Hershman, Book 14, treatise V, ch. 2 (New Haven, 1949), p. xxiii.
39. Cf. Millar Burrows, *More Light on the Dead Sea Scrolls* (New York, 1958), pp. 75–76.
40. Other significant differences between the covenanters and the Essenes are elaborated upon by G. R. Driver, *The Judaean Scrolls* (Oxford, 1965), pp. 110–21.
41. The citations are from the text in Millar Burrows, *The Dead Sea Scrolls* (New York, 1955), pp. 397 and 395 (hereafter cited as Burrows, *Scrolls*).
42. Cecil Roth, *The Dead Sea Scrolls: A New Historical Approach* (New York, 1965), p. 50 (hereafter cited as Roth, *Dead Sea Scrolls*).
43. *Ibid.*, p. 27.
44. Roland de Vaux, *Ancient Israel* (New York, 1961), p. 267.
45. Hengel, *Zeloten*, p. 284, n. 1.
46. Burrows, *Scrolls*, p. 295.
47. Aboth iii: 2. the translation is from *Sayings of the Jewish Fathers*, ed. Charles Taylor (Cambridge, 1897), p. 43.
48. Cf. Hengel, *Zeloten*, p. 300.
49. Roth, *Dead Sea Scrolls*, p. 73; Driver, *op. cit.*, pp. 266–69.
50. Roth, *Dead Sea Scrolls*, p. 66.
51. Cecil Roth, "The Zealots in the War of 66–73," *Journal of Semitic Studies* IV (1959): 342.
52. *The Jewish War* vi: 312–13, cited by Brandon, *Jesus*, p. 59.
53. Hengel, *Zeloten*, p. 253.
54. Roth, *Dead Sea Scrolls*, pp. 5–6.
55. *Jewish Antiquities* xviii: 23–25, cited by Brandon, *Jesus*, p. 34.
56. Hengel, *Zeloten*, p. 249; Silver, *op. cit.*, p. 12.
57. Yigael Yadin, *Masada*, trans. Moshe Pearlman (New York, 1966), p. 174.
58. Solomon Zeitlin, "The Sicarii and Masada," *Jewish Quarterly Review* LVII (1967): 255.
59. Report on a paper delivered at the annual meeting of the American Academy of Religion, Newton, Mass., *New York Times*, October 26, 1969, p. 13.
60. Gerson D. Cohen, "The Talmudic Age," in Leo Schwarz, ed.,

Great Ages and Ideas of the Jewish People (New York, 1956), p. 202.

61. Louis Finkelstein, *Akiba* (New York, 1936), p. 60.
62. *Ibid.*, p. 74.
63. *Avot de Rabbi Natan*, ch. 31, cited by Jacob Neusner, *A Life of Rabban Yohanan ben Zakkai* (Leiden, 1962), p. 134.
64. Charles, *Apocrypha*, II: 612.
65. Salo Wittmayer Baron, *A Social and Religious History of the Jews*, 2nd rev. ed. (New York, 1952), II: 121 (hereafter cited as Baron, *History of the Jews*).
66. That Hadrian's decrees constituted a reaction to rather than a cause of the Jewish revolt is a point convincingly made by Hugo Mantel, "The Causes of the Bar Kochba Revolt," *Jewish Quarterly Review* LVIII (1968): 224–42, 274–96.
67. Saul Lieberman, "The Martyrs of Caesarea," *Annuaire de l'Institut de Philologie et d'Historie Orientales et Slaves* VII (1939–1944): 425.
68. Finkelstein, *op. cit.*, pp. 260–61.
69. W. H. C. Frend, *Martyrdom and Persecution in the Early Church* (Oxford, 1965), p. 56.
70. Hans Bietenhard, "Die Freiheitskriege der Juden unter den Kaisern Trajan und Hadrian und der Messianische Tempelbau," *Judaica* IV (1948): 101.
71. Finkelstein, *op. cit.*, p. 268.
72. Moore, *op. cit.*, I: 89.
73. Cf. Yigael Yadin, *Bar-Kokhba* (New York, 1971), pp. 124–32.
74. Cf. J. T. Milik, "Une lettre de Simeon Bar Kokheba," *Revue Biblique* LX (1953): 276–94. A skeptical view concerning Bar Kochba's authorship is taken by Isaiah Sonne, "The Newly Discovered Bar Kokeba Letters," *Proceedings of the American Academy for Jewish Research* XXIII (1954): 75–108.
75. Cf. Shmuel Yeivin, *Milhemet Bar Kochba* (The War of Bar Kochba) (Jerusalem, 1946).
76. Bietenhard, *op. cit.*, pp. 102, 168–69.
77. Schürer, *op. cit.*, p. 300.
78. *Jer. Ta'anit* 68d, cited by Gedalyah Allon, "The Attitude of the Pharisees to the Roman Government and the House of Herod," *Scripta Hierosolymitana*, VII (1961): 76.
79. *Abodah Zarah* 18a, trans. A. Mishcon and A. Cohen (London, 1935), pp. 91–92.
80. Allon, *op. cit.*, p. 76; Bietenhard, *op. cit.*, p. 168. For the opposite view see Solomon Zeitlin, "The Assumption of Moses and the Revolt of Bar Kochba," *Jewish Quarterly Review* XXXVIII (1947–48): 21.
81. Baron, *History of the Jews*, II: 102.
82. Schürer, *op. cit.*, pp. 299 and 400, n. 75.
83. Cohen, *op. cit.*, p. 163.
84. Gershom Scholem, *The Messianic Idea in Judaism and other Es-*

says on Jewish Spirituality (New York, 1971), p. 57. The close to a dozen messianic movements which took place in Spain and North Africa during the five centuries before 1492 were similarly "usually undertaken without rabbinic sanction." Gerson D. Cohen, *Messianic Postures of Ashkenazim and Sephardim (Prior to Sabbethai Zevi)* (New York, 1967), p. 10.

85. Jacob Neussner, *There We Sat Down, Talmudic Judaism in the Making* (Nashville, Tenn., 1972), pp. 38–43.

86. Baron, *History of the Jews,* II: 122.

87. Midrash Ps. XXXVI. 6, cited by Nahum N. Glatzer, "The Attitude toward Rome in Third Century Judaism," in Alois Dempf et al., eds., *Politische Ordnung und Menschliche Existenz* (Munich, 1962), pp. 250–51.

88. T. B. *Sanhedrin* 97a, cited by Wilson D. Wallis, *Messiahs: Their Role in Civilization* (Washington, D.C., 1943), p. 26.

89. T. B. *Sanhedrin* 91b, quoted in *The Code of Maimonides, op. cit.,* p. 241.

90. Moore, *op. cit.,* II: 350.

91. *Ibid.,* pp. 370–71. See also Klausner, *op. cit.,* pp. 401–403, and Siegmund Hurwitz, *Die Gestalt des sterbenden Messias* (Zurich, 1958).

92. Cf. Glatzer, *op. cit.,* pp. 251–52.

93. *Midrash Song of Songs Rabbah* II: 7, trans. Maurice Simon (London, 1951), p. 114.

94. Cf. Herbert Loewe, *"Render unto Caesar": Religion and Political Loyalty in Palestine* (Cambridge, 1940), pp. 28–29.

95. Jacob Katz, *Exclusiveness and Tolerance* (London, 1961), pp. 50–51.

96. The phrase is found in many parts of the Babylonian Talmud, e.g., *Gittin* 10b, trans. Maurice Simon (London, 1936), p. 37. See also *Baba Qamma* 113b, *Baba Bathra* 54b.

97. Katz, *op. cit.,* pp. 48–49; Israel Abrahams, *Studies in Pharisaism and the Gospels,* First series (Cambridge, 1917), p. 62.

98. *Midrash Numbers Rabbah* XIV. 6, trans. Judah J. Slotki (London, 1951), II, 589.

99. *Tanhuma,* Noah No. 10 (ed. Buber, Stettin 1865), 19a. See the discussion in Moore, *op. cit.,* II, 116–117.

100. *Abodah Zarah* 27b, *op. cit.,* p. 137.

101. Max Kadushin, *Worship and Ethics: A Study in Rabbinic Judaism* (Evanston, Ill., 1964), p. 132.

102. Baron, *History of the Jews,* IV, 141.

103. *Ibid.,* p. 105.

104. Isaiah Sonne, "On Baer and his Philosophy of Jewish History," *Jewish Social Studies* IX (1947): 77–78.

105. Salo W. Baron, *History and Jewish Historians* (Philadelphia, 1964), p. 94.

106. Gershom G. Scholem, *Major Trends in Jewish Mysticism,* 3rd rev. ed. (New York, 1954), p. 88.

107. Baron, *History of the Jews*, VIII: 47.

108. C. G. Montefiore and H. Loewe, *A Rabbinic Anthology* (Philadelphia, 1963), p. 541.

109. Glatzer, *op. cit.*, p. 257. See also his earlier *Untersuchungen zur Geschichtslehre der Tannaiten* (Berlin, 1933).

110. Scholem, *op. cit.*, p. 288.

111. R. J. Zwi Werblowsky, "Crises of Messianism," *Judaism* VII (1958): 116.

112. That this heritage of submission is one of the factors that discouraged resistance is recognized by Israel Gutman, a former member of the Jewish underground: "Well-known historians who had to their credit long and faithful service pointed out that the Jewish people had been through this sort of thing before, and that just as in the past this ancient people had often had to pay a heavy toll in blood to Moloch in order to save part of the nation, so now the imperative of history demanded acceptance of the inevitable so as to ensure the survival of part of the people." "Youth Movements in the Underground and the Ghetto Revolts," in Yad Vashem, *Jewish Resistance during the Holocaust* (Jerusalem, 1971), p. 271.

113. Alexander Donat, *The Holocaust Kingdom: A Memoir* (New York, 1965), p. 101.

114. Celia Stopnicka Rosenthal, "How the Polish Jew Saw His World: A Study of a Small-Town Community before 1939," *Commentary* XVIII (1954): 75.

115. Nachman Blumenthal, "Accepted Ideas and Active Resistance to the Nazi Regime," *Yad Wa-Shem Bulletin* no. 12 (December 1962): 43.

116. Philip Friedman, ed., *Martyrs and Fighters* (New York, 1954), p. 86.

117. Chaim Kaplan, *Scroll of Agony*, trans. Abraham Katch (New York, 1965), p. 166.

118. Leon Poliakov, Letter to the Editor, *Commentary* XXXV (1963): 253–54.

119. The phrase occurs in a pamphlet of the Wilno underground, dated January 1, 1942, and is cited by Gideon Hausner, *Justice in Jerusalem* (New York, 1966), p. 216.

120. World Hashomer Hatzair, *The Massacre of European Jewry* (Kibbutz Merchavia, 1963), pp. 224–25.

121. Rabbi Friedman in Warsaw is reported to have issued such a *Cherem* (ban), interview of Fred Lazin (research assistant) with Samuel Gringauz, July 24, 1968. See also Leo Schwartz, ed., *The Root and the Bough* (New York, 1949), p. 228.

122. Albert Nirenstein, ed., *A Tower from the Enemy: Contributions to a History of Jewish Resistance in Poland* (New York, 1954), p. 84.

123. J. L. Talmon, *The Unique and the Universal* (London, 1965), p. 84.

CHAPTER 5

1. Norman Cohn, *The Pursuit of the Millennium* (London, 1957), pp. 14–15 (hereafter cited as Cohn, *Millennium*).
2. *Ibid.*, p. 21.
3. Cf. Henry Focillon, *The Year 1000*, trans. Fred D. Wieck (New York, 1969).
4. The literature on Joachim of Fiore is extensive. For a good, brief treatment see Henry Bett, *Joachim of Flora* (London, 1931).
5. *Ibid.*, pp. 108–14.
6. For a summary of this influence see Frank E. Manuel, *Shapes of Philosophical History* (Stanford, Calif., 1965), pp. 41–45. The definitive work on the subject is Marjorie Reeves, *The Influence of Prophecy in the Later Middle Ages: A Study of Joachimism* (Oxford, 1969).
7. Gordon Leff, *Heresy in the Later Middle Ages* (New York, 1967), I: 5–6.
8. See Ernst Werner, "Messianische Bewegungen im Mittelalter," *Zeitschrift für Geschichtswissenschaft* X (1962): 371–96 and 598–622 and Bernhard Töpfer, *Das kommende Reich des Friedens: Zur Entwicklung chiliastischer Zukunftshoffnungen im Hochmittelalter* (Berlin, 1964).
9. H. Richard Niebuhr, *The Social Sources of Denominationalism* (New York, 1965), p. 5.
10. Werner Stark, *The Sociology of Religion: A Study of Christendom*, vol. II: *Sectarian Religion* (New York, 1967), p. 5.
11. Leff, *op. cit.*, pp. 10–11, n. 1.
12. Austin P. Evans, "Social Aspects of Medieval Heresy," in *Persecution and Liberty: Essays in Honor of George Lincoln Burr* (New York, 1931), p. 93.
13. Jeffrey Burton Russell, *Dissent and Reform in the Early Middle Ages* (Berkeley, Calif., 1965), p. 238.
14. *Ibid.*, p. 237.
15. Walter L. Wakefield and Austin P. Evans, eds., *Heresies of the High Middle Ages* (New York, 1969), pp. 7 and 25.
16. Cohn, *Millennium*, p. 24.
17. Norman Cohn, "Medieval Millenarism: Its Bearing on the Comparative Study of Millenarian Movements," in Sylvia L. Thrupp, ed., *Millennial Dreams in Action* (The Hague, 1962), pp. 35–36.
18. Russell, *op. cit.*, p. 234. See also the careful discussion by Herbert Grundmann, *Religiöse Bewegungen im Mittelalter* (Hildesheim, 1961), pp. 168–69.
19. See the detailed analysis in Cohn, *Millennium*, chs. 7 and 8. The stories of sexual debauchery are seen as entirely false by Robert E. Lerner, *The Heresy of the Free Spirit in the Later Middle Ages* (Berkeley, Calif., 1972).
20. Cohn in Thrupp, *op. cit.*, p. 37.

21. Roland A. Knox, *Enthusiasm* (New York, 1961), p. 114.
22. Grundmann, *op. cit.*, p. 38, n. 54.
23. Cohn in Thrupp, *op. cit.*, p. 38.
24. Frederick G. Heymann, *John Zizka and the Hussite Revolution* (Princeton, N.J., 1955), p. 11.
25. Leff, *op. cit.*, II: 484–85.
26. Cf. Howard Kaminsky, "Chiliasm and the Hussite Revolution," *Church History* XXVI (1957): 62; Karl Griewank, *Der Neuzeitliche Revolutionsbegriff* (Weimar, 1955), p. 64.
27. Kaminsky, *Church History* XXVI (1957): 57.
28. Excerpts from the 76 articles of the Taborites (1422) can be found in Gustav Adolf Benrath, ed., *Wegbereiter der Reformation* (Bremen, 1967), pp. 371–76.
29. Cf. Howard Kaminsky, *A History of the Hussite Revolution* (Berkeley, Calif., 1967), p. 341.
30. Cohn, *Millennium*, p. 237.
31. A. G. Dickens, *Reformation and Society in Sixteenth-Century Europe* (New York, 1966), p. 48. For a new interpretation of the sectarian ideas of Bosch see Wilhelm Fränger, *The Millennium of Hieronymus Bosch*, trans. Eithne Wilkins and Ernst Kaiser (Chicago, 1954).
32. For examples see Gerhard J. Neumann, "Eschatologische und Chiliastische Gedanken in der Reformationszeit, besonders bei den Täufern," *Die Welt als Geschichte* XIX (1959): 58–66; Ernst Staehelin, *Die Verkündigung des Reiches Gottes in der Kirche Jesu Christi*, vol. IV (Basel, 1957), chs. 15–16.
33. Cf. Eric W. Gritsch, *Reformer Without a Church: The Life and Thought of Thomas Müntzer* (Philadelphia, 1967), p. 192.
34. Stark, *op. cit.*, II: 9, who relies upon the work of Paul Honigsheim.
35. Grundmann, *op. cit.*, pp. 33–34.
36. Cohn, *Millennium*, pp. 254–55.
37. The Latin and two German versions are reprinted in Thomas Müntzer, *Schriften und Briefe: Kritische Gesamtausgabe*, ed. Günther Franz (Gütersloh, 1968), pp. 491–511. The Czech version (as well as the other three) can be found in Heinrich Boehmer and Paul Kirn, eds., *Thomas Müntzers Briefwechsel* (Leipzig, 1931), pp. 150–54.
38. Thomas Müntzer, "Hochverursachte Schutzrede," in *Politische Schriften*, ed. Carl Hinrichs (Halle, 1950), p. 95.
39. Carl Hinrichs, *Luther und Müntzer: Ihre Auseinandersetzung über Obrigkeit und Widerstandsrecht* (Berlin, 1952), p. 180.
40. "An Exposition of the Second Chapter of Daniel," in George Huntston Williams, ed., *Spiritual and Anabaptist Writers* (Philadelphia, 1957), pp. 62–63.
41. *Ibid.*, p. 65.
42. *Ibid.*, p. 66.

43. *Ibid.*, p. 68.
44. *Ibid.*, p. 69.
45. This was the thesis of Friedrich Engels in *Der Deutsche Bauern-krieg* (1850) and, following him, it has become the prevailing interpretation of contemporary Russian and East German scholars. For a survey of this literature see Abraham Friesen, "Thomas Müntzer in Marxist Thought," *Church History* XXXIV (1965): 306–27.
46. Thomas Nipperdey, "Theologie und Revolution bei Thomas Müntzer," *Archiv für Reformationsgeschichte* LIV (1963): 178.
47. Gerhard Zschäbitz, *Zur Mitteldeutschen Wiedertäuferbewegung nach dem Grossen Bauernkrieg* (Berlin [East], 1958), p. 44.
48. The best account of both the origins and course of the German Peasants' War remains Günther Franz's *Der Deutsche Bauern-krieg*, now in its 7th edition (Darmstadt, 1965).
49. *Ibid.*, p. 126. The German text of the Twelve Articles can be found in Günther Franz, ed., *Der Deutsche Bauernkrieg 1525 in Zeitgenössischen Zeugnissen* (Berlin, 1926), pp. 102–10. An English translation is given by Jacob S. Schapiro, *Social Reform and the Reformation* (New York, 1909), pp. 137–42.
50. Cohn, *Millennium*, p. 264.
51. Franz, *Bauernkrieg* (1965), p. 287.
52. Martin Luther, "An Exhortation to Peace," *Werke* XVIII (Weimar ed.): 311, 319, and 326, cited by Schapiro, *op. cit.*, p. 82.
53. Quoted in Gritsch, *op. cit.*, p. 144. The full German text of this letter can be found in Ernst Bloch, *Thomas Müntzer als Theologe der Revolution* (Berlin, 1960), pp. 59–60.
54. Franz, *Bauernkrieg* (1965), p. 269.
55. The texts of Müntzer's confession as well as recantation can be found in Böhmer and Kirn, *op. cit.*, pp. 160–67.
56. Cf. Franz Lau, "Die Prophetische Apokalyptik Thomas Müntzers und Luthers Absage an die Bauernrevolution," in Friedrich Hübner, ed., *Gedenkschrift für D. Werner Elert* (Berlin, 1955), pp. 169–70.
57. Harold Bender, "The Zwickau Prophets, Thomas Müntzer and the Anabaptists," *Mennonite Quarterly Review* XXVII (1953): 6.
58. Two letters from Grebel to Müntzer, written in 1524, are reproduced in English translation in Williams, ed., *Spiritual and Anabaptist Writers*, pp. 73–85.
59. Robert Friedman, "Thomas Müntzer's Relation to Anabaptism," *Mennonite Quarterly Review* XXXI (1957): 86.
60. For a similar conclusion see John S. Oyer, *Lutheran Reformers Against Anabaptists* (The Hague, 1964), p. 109 and Franklin H. Littell, *The Anabaptist View of the Church*, 2nd rev. ed. (Boston, 1958), pp. 28–29.
61. George H. Williams, *The Radical Reformation* (Philadelphia, 1962), p. 120 (hereafter cited as Williams, *Radical Reformation*).

62. Littell, *op. cit.*, p. 47.
63. Ernst Troeltsch, *The Social Teaching of the Christian Churches,*
    trans. Olive Wyon (London, 1931), I: 342.
64. Littell, *op. cit.*, p. 47.
65. Peter James Klassen, *The Economics of Anabaptism: 1525–1560*
    (The Hague, 1964), p. 28.
66. Cf. Claus-Peter Clasen, *Die Wiedertäufer im Herzogtum Wür-
    temberg und in den Benachbarten Herrschaften* (Stuttgart, 1965),
    p. 108.
67. See the detailed discussion in Paul Peachey, *Die Soziale Herkunft
    der Schweizer Täufer in der Reformationszeit* (Karlsruhe, 1954).
68. Clasen, *op. cit.*, p. 139.
69. Littell, *op. cit.*, p. 19.
70. Niebuhr, *op. cit.*, p. 62.
71. Williams, *Radical Reformation,* p. 124; Claus-Peter Clasen, *Ana-
    baptism: A Social History, 1525–1618* (Ithaca, N.Y., 1972), p.
    338.
72. Klassen, *op. cit.*, p. 85.
73. Cf. Wilhelm Emil Mühlmann, *Chiliasmus und Nativismus* (Berlin,
    1961), p. 350.
74. Cohn, *Millennium,* p. 275.
75. Cf. Hans Joachim Hillerbrand, *Die Politsche Ethik des Ober-
    deutschen Täufertums* (Leiden, 1962), p. 30.
76. Williams, *Radical Reformation,* pp. 163–64; Clasen, *op. cit.,* pp.
    69–70.
77. Zschäbitz, *op. cit.,* pp. 67–71.
78. Williams, *Radical Reformation,* p. 277.
79. Dickens, *op. cit.,* p. 130.
80. Williams, *Radical Reformation,* p. 343.
81. Cornelius Krahn, *Dutch Anabaptism* (The Hague, 1968), p. 255.
82. Cohn, *Millennium,* p. 281.
83. Cornelius Krahn, "Anabaptism and the Culture of the Nether-
    lands," in Guy F. Hershberger, ed., *The Recovery of the Ana-
    baptist Vision* (Scottdale, Pa., 1962), p. 228.
84. Klassen, *op. cit.,* p. 89.
85. Cf. Otthein Rammstedt, *Sekte und Soziale Bewegung: Soziolo-
    gische Analyse der Täufer in Münster (1534/35)* (Cologne, 1966),
    pp. 32–34.
86. Williams, *Radical Reformation,* p. 370.
87. Cohn, *Millennium,* p. 291.
88. Hermann Rothert, *Das Tausendjährige Reich der Wiedertäufer
    in Münster 1534–35* (Münster, 1947), pp. 5 and 28.
89. Williams, *Radical Reformation,* p. 372.
90. Rammstedt, *op. cit.,* p. 98.
91. Cohn, *Millennium,* p. 294.
92. Williams, *Radical Reformation,* p. 380.
93. James M. Stayer, "The Münsterite Rationalization of Bernhard

Rothmann," *Journal of the History of Ideas* XXVIII (1967): 180.
94. Bernhard Rothmann, *Van der Wrake* (Concerning Vengeance), in Heinold Fast, ed., *Der Linke Flügel der Reformation* (Bremen, 1962), pp. 359–60. The translation is that of Stayer, *op. cit.*, p. 192.
95. *Von Verborgenheit der Schrift*, cited by Stayer, *op. cit.*, p. 191.
96. Fritz Blanke, "Das Reich der Wiedertäufer zu Münster 1534/35," *Archiv für Reformationsgeschichte* XXXVII (1940): 36.
97. Williams, *Radical Reformation*, p. 382.
98. Cohn, *Millennium*, p. 306.
99. William Echard Keeney, *The Development of Dutch Anabaptist Thought and Practice from 1539–1564* (Nieuwkoop, 1968), p. 168.
100. Williams, *Radical Reformation*, p. 778.

CHAPTER 6

1. *Oliver Cromwell's Letters and Speeches*, ed. Thomas Carlyle (London, 1871), IV: 94.
2. Lawrence Stone, *The Causes of the English Revolution, 1529–1642* (London, 1972), p. 103.
3. Michael Fixler, *Milton and the Kingdoms of God* (London, 1964), p. 31; William M. Lamont, *Godly Rule: Politics and Religion 1603–60* (New York, 1969), p. 19.
4. Cf. William Haller, *The Rise of Puritanism: 1570–1643* (New York, 1938), p. 270.
5. Excerpts from *A Glimpse of Sion's Glory* can be found in A. S. P. Woodhouse, ed., *Puritanism and Liberty* (Chicago, 1951), pp. 233–41 (quotation p. 236).
6. Geoffrey F. Nuttall, *Visible Saints: The Congregational Way 1640–1660* (Oxford, 1957), p. 157 (hereafter cited as Nuttall, *Visible Saints*).
7. B. S. Capp, *The Fifth Monarchy Men: A Study in Seventeenth-Century English Millenarianism* (London, 1972), pp. 34–37; ch. 2 of Capp's work provides a detailed account of the popularity of millenarian ideas to 1649.
8. Alan Simpson, "Saints in Arms: English Puritanism as Political Utopianism," *Church History* XXIII (1954):121.
9. Cf. Leo F. Solt, *Saints in Arms: Puritanism and Democracy in Cromwell's Army* (Stanford, Calif., 1959), p. 73.
10. Woodhouse, *op. cit.*, p. 138.
11. Excerpts from Thomas Coolier's sermon, *A Discovery of the New Creation* are to be found in Woodhouse, *op. cit.*, pp. 390–96 (quotations pp. 390 and 394).
12. Nuttall, *Visible Saints*, p. 46.
13. *Certain Queries Humbly Presented . . .* , excerpts in Woodhouse, *op. cit.*, pp. 241–47 (quotations pp. 244–45).
14. Louise Fargo Brown, *The Political Activities of the Baptists and*

Fifth Monarchy Men in England during the Interregnum (Baltimore, 1912; reprint New York, n.d.), p. 27.

15. Capp, *op. cit.*, p. 80.
16. Edward Rogers, *Some Account of the Life and Opinions of a Fifth Monarchy Man* (London, 1867), p. 41; Capp, *op. cit.*, p. 41.
17. David W. Petegorsky, *Left Wing Democracy in the English Civil War* (London, 1940), p. 237.
18. Michael L. Walzer, "Puritanism as a Revolutionary Ideology," *History and Theory* III (1963): 88.
19. Cited by C. H. Simpkinson, *Thomas Harrison: Regicide and Major-General* (London, 1905), p. 45. See also Charles H. Firth, *The Life of Thomas Harrison* (Worcester, Mass., 1893) (hereafter cited as Firth, *Harrison*).
20. P. G. Rogers, *The Fifth Monarchy Men* (London, 1966), p. 19; Christopher Hill, *God's Englishman: Oliver Cromwell and the English Revolution* (New York, 1970), p. 139.
21. Edmund Ludlow, *Memoirs*, ed. C. H. Firth (Oxford, 1894), I: 352, cited by P. G. Rogers, *op. cit.*, p. 20.
22. John Rogers, *To His Excellency the Lord General Cromwell, A Few Proposals Relating to Civil Government*, cited by *ibid.*, p. 24.
23. *Loc. cit.*
24. Austin Woolrych, "Oliver Cromwell and the Rule of the Saints," in R. H. Parry, ed., *The English Civil War and After, 1642–1658* (London, 1970), p. 68.
25. *Cromwell's Letters and Speeches*, ed. Carlyle, III: 204.
26. *Ibid.*, pp. 218, 222, 225–26.
27. Brown, *op. cit.*, p. 33; P. G. Rogers, *op. cit.*, p. 36.
28. Cited by Brown, *op. cit.*, p. 31, n. 13.
29. *Ibid.*, p. 33.
30. Ivan Roots, *Commonwealth and Protectorate: The English Civil War and Its Aftermath* (New York, 1966), p. 152.
31. P. G. Rogers, *op. cit.*, p. 37.
32. Robert S. Paul, *The Lord Protector: Religion and Politics in the Life of Oliver Cromwell* (London, 1955), pp. 262–63.
33. P. G. Rogers, *op. cit.*, p. 41.
34. Brown, *op. cit.*, p. 45.
35. P. G. Rogers, *op. cit.*, p. 43.
36. *The Humble Representation and Vindication of . . . the Baptized Churches* (1654), cited by Fixler, *op. cit.*, pp. 197–98.
37. *Cromwell's Letters and Speeches*, ed. Carlyle, IV: 27–28.
38. Brown, *op. cit.*, pp. 54–55.
39. The title page of this sermon is reproduced by P. G. Rogers, *op. cit.*, p. 50. The original is in the Thomason collection in the British Museum Library.
40. From Thurloe's account in Firth, *Harrison*, pp. 44–45.
41. Leo F. Solt, "The Fifth Monarchy Men: Politics and the Millennium," *Church History* XXX (1961): 315.

42. Cited by P. G. Rogers, *op. cit.*, p. 26.
43. Excerpt in Edward Rogers, *op. cit.*, p. 95.
44. *The Protectorate of Oliver Cromwell*, ed. Robert Vaughan (London, 1839), I: 156, cited by Christopher Hill, *Puritanism and Revolution* (New York, 1964), p. 326 (hereafter cited as Hill, *Puritanism*).
45. Samuel Rawson Gardiner, *History of the Commonwealth and Protectorate 1649–1656* (New York, 1965), II: 269.
46. Cited by P. G. Rogers, *op. cit.*, p. 143; Perez Zagorin, *A History of Political Thought in the English Revolution* (London, 1965), pp. 102–103.
47. Capp, *op. cit.*, p. 156.
48. Zagorin, *op. cit.*, p. 103.
49. John Spittlehouse, *An Answer to one part of the Lord Protector's Speech or A Vindication of the Fifth Monarchymen* (1654), cited by Solt, *Church History* XXX (1961): 320–21.
50. William Aspinwall, *A Brief Description of the Fifth Monarchy or Kingdome That shortly is to come into the World* (1653), cited by Wilhelm Schenck, *The Concern for Social Justice in the Puritan Revolution* (London, 1948), p. 136.
51. John Rogers, *Sagrir*, pp. 138–40, cited by Gardiner, *op. cit.*, II: 315, n. 2.
52. P. G. Rogers, *op. cit.*, p. 141.
53. William Aspinwall, *The Legislative Power is Christ's Peculiar Prerogative* (1656), pp. 26, 30, cited by Schenck, *op. cit.*, p. 136.
54. Paul, *op. cit.*, p. 329.
55. *The Legislative Power*, cited by Brown, *op. cit.*, p. 104.
56. William Erbury, *An Olive Leaf* (1654), cited by Alfred Cohen, "Two Roads to the Puritan Millennium: William Erbury and Vavasor Powell," *Church History* XXXII (1963): 328.
57. Mary Cary's ideas are analyzed by Alfred Cohen, "The Fifth Monarchy Mind: Mary Cary and the Origins of Totalitarianism," *Social Research* XXI (1964): 195–213.
58. *Jegar Sahardutha* (1657), cited by Edward Rogers, *op. cit.*, pp. 297, 299, and 301.
59. Thurloe, *State Papers* IV: 191, cited by G. P. Gooch, *English Democratic Ideas in the Seventeenth Century* (New York, 1959), p. 221.
60. Brown, *op. cit.*, p. 101.
61. Thurloe, *State Papers* IV: 321, 650, cited by Charles Harding Firth, *The Last Years of the Protectorate: 1656–1658* (New York, 1964), I: 201 (hereafter cited as Firth, *Protectorate*).
62. Capp, *op. cit.*, p. 82.
63. P. G. Rogers, *op. cit.*, pp. 72–73; Firth, *Protectorate*, I: 209.
64. P. G. Rogers, *op. cit.*, pp. 78–79; Firth, *Protectorate*, I: 210.
65. Thurloe, *State Papers*, VI: 184–85, cited by P. G. Rogers, *op. cit.*, p. 82.

66. P. G. Rogers, *op. cit.*, pp. 82–84; Firth, *Protectorate*, I: 213–15.
67. P. G. Rogers, *op. cit.*, pp. 85–87.
68. Thurloe, *State Papers*, VI: 222, cited by Firth, *Protectorate*, I: 218.
69. Firth, *Protectorate*, II: 35.
70. Simpkinson, *op. cit.*, p. 233.
71. Firth, *Harrison*, p. 15.
72. Cited by P. G. Rogers, *op. cit.*, p. 111.
73. Cited by Champlin Burrage, "The Fifth Monarchy Insurrections," *English Historical Review* XXV (1910): 740.
74. P. G. Rogers, *op. cit.*, pp. 120–21.
75. C. E. Whiting, *Studies in English Puritanism from the Restoration to the Revolution, 1660–1688* (London, 1931), pp. 240–41; Capp, *op. cit.*, pp. 200–21.
76. Cobbett, *State Trials* VI: 198, cited in P. G. Rogers, *op. cit.*, p. 127. For a detailed study of Vane see Violet A. Rowe, *Sir Henry Vane the Younger* (London, 1970).
77. Geoffrey F. Nuttall, *The Holy Spirit in Puritan Faith and Experience* (Oxford, 1946), p. 111.
78. Cf. T. L. Underwood, "Early Quaker Eschatology," in Peter Toon, ed., *Puritans, the Millennium and the Future of Israel: Puritan Eschatology 1600 to 1660* (Cambridge, 1970).
79. Cf. Richard B. Schlatter, *Social Ideas of Religious Leaders 1660–1688* (London, 1940), p. 232.
80. Capp, *op. cit.*, p. 94.
81. Zagorin, *op. cit.*, p. 55.
82. Charles Wilson, *England's Apprenticeship 1603–1763* (New York, 1965), p. 108.
83. C. V. Wedgwood, *The Common Man in the Great Civil War* (Leicester, 1957), p. 8.
84. Maurice Ashley, *Financial and Commercial Policy under the Cromwellian Protectorate*, 2nd ed. (New York, 1962), p. 175.
85. Wilson, *op. cit.*, p. 133.
86. Hill, *Puritanism*, p. 336.

CHAPTER 7

1. Frederic Wakeman, *Strangers at the Gate: Social Disorder in South China 1839–1861* (Berkeley, Calif., 1966), p. 3.
2. James P. Harrison, *The Communists and the Chinese Peasant Rebellions* (New York, 1968), p. 298.
3. Thomas Taylor Meadows, *The Chinese and Their Rebellions* (London, 1856), p. 25.
4. For a summary analysis of the roots of the Taiping Rebellion see George E. Taylor, "The Taiping Rebellion; Its Economic Background and Social Theory," *Chinese Social and Political Science Review* XVI (1933): 545–614. For bibliographical leads to other

works see Ssu-yü Teng, *New Light on the History of the Tai-ping Rebellion* (Cambridge, Mass., 1950) (hereafter cited as Teng, *New Light*) and the same author's *Historiography of the Taiping Rebellion* (Cambridge, Mass., 1962) (hereafter cited as Teng, *Historiography*) as well as the critical bibliography in vol. III of Franz Michael, *The Taiping Rebellion* (Seattle, 1971), pp. 1617–771.

5. Taylor, *op. cit.*, p. 554. See also the statistics in Franz Michael, *The Taiping Rebellion* (Seattle, 1966) I: 15.

6. Lindesay Brine, *The Taiping Rebellion in China* (London, 1862), p. 8.

7. Hsia Nai, "The Land Tax in the Yangtse Province before and after the Taiping Rebellion," in E-tu Zen Sun and John de Francis, eds., *Chinese Social History: Translations of Selected Studies* (New York, 1966), p. 362.

8. Michael, *op. cit.*, I: 16.

9. C. K. Yang, *Religion in Chinese Society* (Berkeley, Calif., 1961), p. 221. See also Charles A. Curwen, "Les relations des Taipings avec les sociétés secrètes et des autres rebelles," in Jean Chesneaux et al., eds., *Movements populaires et sociétés secrètes en Chine aux XIXe et XXe siècles* (Paris, 1970).

10. Cf. Vincent Y. C. Shih, *The Taiping Ideology* (Seattle, 1967), pp. 474–77.

11. Chien Yu-wen, *T'ai-p'ing t'ien-kuo tien-chih t'ung-k'ao* (Studies on the Institutions of the Taiping Heavenly Kingdom) (Hongkong, 1958), pp. 1569–70.

12. Michael, *op. cit.*, I: 22.

13. Teng, *New Light*, p. 53.

14. Teng, *Historiography*, p. 2.

15. *Ibid.*, p. 5.

16. Theodore Hamberg, *The Visions of Hung-Siu-Tshuen and the Origin of the Kwang-si Insurrection* (Hongkong, 1854).

17. It is reprinted in Michael, *op. cit.*, II: 8–18.

18. Chien, *op. cit.*, pp. 1655–56.

19. Ssu-yü Teng in Arthur W. Hummel, ed., *Eminent Chinese of the Ch'ing Period (1644–1912)* (Washington, D.C., 1943–1944), I: 361.

20. Michael, *op. cit.*, I: 25.

21. Cf. P. M. Yap, "The Mental Illness of Hung Hsiu-ch'üan, Leader of the Taiping Rebellion," *Far Eastern Quarterly* XIII (1954): 287–304.

22. Mary C. Wright, *The Last Stand of Chinese Conservatism* (New York, 1966), p. 119, n.u.

23. Michael, *op. cit.*, I: 32.

24. *Ibid.*, p. 36.

25. Shih, *op. cit.*, pp. 327–28.

26. Michael, *op. cit.*, I: 42.

27. *Ibid.*, pp. 43–44.

28. *Ibid.*, p. 47.
29. *Ibid.*, pp. 55–60.
30. This wording is found in the proclamation of Yang from the year 1851 or 1852; Michael, *op. cit.*, II: 148.
31. Quoted in Brine, *op. cit.*, pp. 159 and 162.
32. Michael, *op. cit.*, I: 59.
33. Cf. William Theodore de Bary et al., eds., *Sources of Chinese Tradition* (New York, 1966), pp. 682–83.
34. Michael, *op. cit.*, I: 112–13.
35. For the text of this law see document 46, Michael, *op. cit.*, II: 309–20.
36. Michael, *op. cit.*, I: 84.
37. *Ibid.*, p. 85.
38. Cf. Taylor, *op. cit.*, p. 599; Shih, *op. cit.*, p. 490.
39. Michael, *op. cit.*, I: 193.
40. S. Y. Teng, *The Taiping Rebellion and the Western Powers* (Oxford, 1971), p. 101 (hereafter cited as Teng, *Taiping Rebellion*).
41. Teng, *New Light*, p. 65.
42. The poems are reproduced as document 179 in Michael, *op. cit.*, II: 586–666.
43. Cf. Brine, *op. cit.*, p. 352; Yap, *op. cit.*, p. 295.
44. Teng speaks of the "Taiping Restoration" (*Taiping Rebellion*, ch. 8). Part III of this book deals with the foreign relations of the Taiping regime, a subject beyond the scope of our study here. See also Kwan-wai So and Eugene P. Boardman, "Hung Jen-kan, Taiping Prime Minister, 1859–1864," in Chün-tu Hsüeh, ed., *Revolutionary Leaders of Modern China* (New York, 1971), pp. 55–70.
45. Cf. Chiang Siang-tseh, *The Nien Rebellion* (Seattle, 1954, pp. 10–15.
46. Eugene Boardman, "Millenary Aspects of the Taiping Rebellion (1851–64)," in Sylvia L. Thrupp, ed., *Millennial Dreams in Action* (The Hague, 1962), p. 71.
47. "Taiping Songs of World Salvation," quoted in Shih, *op. cit.*, p. 86.
48. Document 41 in Michael, *op. cit.*, II: 237.
49. These words appear, for example, in a document given to a British mission in 1853 and are cited by Shih, *op. cit.*, p. 89.
50. Cf. Eugene P. Boardman, *Christian Influence upon the Ideology of the Taiping Rebellion 1851–1864* (Madison, Wisc., 1952), p. 106 (hereafter cited as Boardman, *Christian Influence*).
51. Michael, *op. cit.*, I: 27.
52. Boardman, *Christian Influence*, p. 53.
53. *Ibid.*, p. 114.
54. Quoted in J. C. Cheng, *Chinese Sources for the Taiping Rebellion 1850–1864* (Hong Kong, 1963), p. 72.

55. Quoted in Brine, *op. cit.*, p. 281.
56. Shih, *op. cit.*, p. 240.
57. Michael, *op. cit.*, III: 872; Teng, *New Light*, p. 78.
58. Shih, *op. cit.*, p. 473.
59. *Ibid.*, p. 488.
60. William James Hail, *Tsêng Kuo-Fan and the Taiping Rebellion* (New York, 1964), p. xiv.
61. Michael, *op. cit.*, I: 174.
62. *Ibid.*, p. 173.
63. Hsia Nai, *op. cit.*, pp. 370–72.
64. Cf. Huang Da-show, "The Factors of the Collapse of the T'aiping T'ien-kuo," *China Today* XI, no. 7 (July 1968): 12.
65. Boardman, *Christian Influence*, p. 121.
66. Shih, *op. cit.*, p. 486; Michael, *op. cit.*, I: 96–101.
67. Boardman, *Christian Influence*, p. 126.
68. Yap, *op. cit.*, p. 288.
69. Cf. Harrison, *op. cit.*, pp. 157–63.
70. For a summary discussion of changing views of the significance of the Taiping Rebellion see Teng, *Historiography*, pp. 42–44.
71. J. S. Gregory, *Great Britain and the Taipings* (London, 1969), p. xiii.
72. Yang, *op. cit.*, p. 133.
73. Michael, *op. cit.*, I: 198.
74. Harrison, *op. cit.*, p. 260.
75. Teng, *Taiping Rebellion*, p. 413.

CHAPTER 8

1. John Spencer Trimingham, *Islam in the Sudan* (London, 1949), p. 149 (hereafter cited as Trimingham, *Islam*).
2. Cf. Saburi Biobaku and Muhammad al-Hajj, "The Sudanese Mahdiyya and the Niger-Chad Region," in I. M. Lewis, ed., *Islam in Tropical Africa* (London, 1966), pp. 425–38; John Spencer Trimingham, *The Influence of Islam upon Africa* (New York, 1968), p. 45 (hereafter cited as Trimingham, *Influence*).
3. L. Carl Brown, "The Sudanese Mahdia," in Robert I. Rotberg and Ali A. Mazrui, eds., *Protest and Power in Black Africa* (New York, 1970), p. 158; Richard H. Dekmejian and Margaret J. Wyszomirski, "Charismatic Leadership in Islam: The Mahdi of the Sudan," *Comparative Studies in Society and History* XIV (1972): 202.
4. P. M. Holt, *The Mahdist State in the Sudan 1881–1898*, 2nd rev. ed. (Oxford, 1970), pp. 33–40 (hereafter cited as Holt, *Mahdist State*); A. B. Theobald, *The Mahdia* (London, 1967), pp. 12–25.
5. Trimingham, *Influence*, pp. 25–26.
6. Holt, *Mahdist State*, p. 50.
7. Biobaku, *op. cit.*, p. 432.

8. Holt, *Mahdist State*, pp. 52–53.
9. *Ibid.*, p. 42.
10. Cited by P. M. Holt, "The Sudanese Mahdia and the Outside World: 1881–9," *Bulletin of the School of Oriental and African Studies* XXI (1958): 277.
11. Holt, *Mahdist State*, pp. 55–56.
12. *Ibid.*, pp. 56–57.
13. *Ibid.*, p. 112.
14. *Ibid.*, p. 117.
15. Theobald, *op. cit.*, p. 31.
16. Cited by Holt, *Mahdist State*, p. 125.
17. *Ibid.*, p. 120.
18. *Ibid.*, p. 121.
19. Nicola A. Ziadeh, *Sanusiyah: A Study of a Revivalist Movement in Islam* (Leiden, 1958), p. 52. The text of this letter can be found in F. R. Wingate, *Mahdiism and the Egyptian Sudan* (London, 1891), pp. 69–72. This book by Major Wingate, at the time assistant adjutant-general for intelligence in the Egyptian army, includes many other important Mahdist documents, though in the words of P. M. Holt, "the translation is at best clumsy, at worst erroneous and misleading." Cf. P. M. Holt, "The Source Materials of the Sudanese Mahdia," in *St. Antony's Papers: Middle Eastern Affairs*, no. 1 (London, 1958), p. 109 (hereafter cited as Holt, *Source Materials*).
20. Theobald, *op. cit.*, p. 44.
21. Cited by Holt, *Mahdist State*, p. 110.
22. *Ibid.*, pp. 133–34.
23. Byron Farwell, *Prisoners of the Mahdi* (London, 1967), p. 17.
24. After his escape in 1895, Rudolf Slatin published a book of memoirs, *Fire and Sword in the Sudan* (London, 1896). The book was edited and translated by Major Wingate and forms part of what P. M. Holt has called the "war propaganda" and "public relations literature of the Egyptian Military Intelligence, the voice of the British officer-class in Egypt" (*Source Materials*, p. 112).
25. Cited by Theobald, *op. cit.*, p. 84.
26. Holt, *Mahdist State*, p. 93.
27. Holt, *Bulletin of the School of Oriental and African Studies* XXI (1958): 281.
28. Ernst Ludwig Dietrich, "Der Mahdi Mohammed Ahmed vom Sudan nach arabischen Quellen," *Der Islam* XIV (1925): 269.
29. Wingate, *op. cit.*, p. 228.
30. Holt, *Mahdist State*, p. 104.
31. Farwell, *op. cit.*, p. 100.
32. Holt, *Bulletin of the School of Oriental and African Studies* XXI (1958): 283.
33. *Ibid.*, p. 288.
34. Theobald, *op. cit.*, pp. 163–64.

35. Holt, *Bulletin of the School of Oriental and African Studies* XXI (1958): 290.
36. Richard Hill, *Slatin Pasha* (London, 1965), p. 24.
37. Holt, *Mahdist State*, p. 265.
38. Theobald, *op. cit.*, pp. 180–81.
39. *Ibid.*, pp. 235–36.
40. Cf. Gabriel Warburg, *The Sudan under Wingate: Administration in the Anglo-Egyptian Sudan 1899–1916* (London, 1971), pp. 100–106; Muddathir 'Abd al-Rahmin, *Imperialism and Nationalism in the Sudan* (Oxford, 1969), p. 90.
41. Trimingham, *Islam*, p. 159; see also Harold MacMichael, *The Anglo-Egyptian Sudan* (London, 1934), pp. 98–99, 176–79.
42. Farwell, *op. cit.*, p. 321.
43. D. S. Margoliouth, "On Mahdis and Mahdiism," *Proceedings of the British Academy* VII (1916): 233.
44. J. Spencer Trimingham, *Islam in Ethiopia* (London, 1965), pp. 133–35.
45. Trimingham, *Islam*, pp. 159–60.
46. *New York Times*, April 2, 1970.
47. Robert O. Collins, *The Southern Sudan 1883–1898: A Struggle for Control* (New Haven, Conn., 1962), p. 177.
48. Thomas E. Nyquist, "Kampf zwischen Muslimen und Schwarzafrikanern: Der Bürgerkrieg im Sudan," *Bustan* X, no. 1 (1969): 1·1–17. The case of the Southerners is argued by Oliver Albino, *The Sudan: A Southern Viewpoint* (London, 1970).
49. *New York Times*, January 4, 1971.
50. *Ibid.*, February 28, 1972.

CHAPTER 9

1. These statistics are taken from David B. Barrett, "AD 2000: 350 Million Christians in Africa," *International Review of Missions* LIX (1970): 39–54.
2. Michael Banton, "African Prophets," *Race* V, no. 2 (1963): 51–52; James W. Fernandez, "African Religious Movements: Types and Dynamics," *Journal of Modern African Studies* II (1964): 533.
3. Hans Jochen Margull, *Aufbruch zur Zukunft* (Gütersloh, 1962), p. 85.
4. Bengt G. M. Sundkler, *Bantu Prophets in South Africa*, 2nd rev. ed. (London, 1961), pp. 38–39, 303.
5. David B. Barrett, *Schism and Renewal in Africa* (Nairobi, 1968), p. 34 (hereafter cited as Barrett, *Schism*). For a brief, if necessarily superficial, survey of African independent movements see G. C. Oosthuizen, *Post-Christianity in Africa* (London, 1968), ch. 2.
6. Ps. 68:31.
7. Thomas Hodgkin, *Nationalism in Colonial Africa* (New York, 1968), pp. 180–81.

8. David B. Barrett, "Analytical Methods of Studying Religious Expansion in Africa," *Journal of Religion in Africa* III (1970): 42.

9. Sundkler, *op. cit.*, p. 55.

10. Cf. Katesa Schlosser, *Eingeborenenkirchen in Süd- und Südwestafrika* (Kiel, 1958), p. 287 (hereafter cited as Schlosser, *Eingeborenenkirchen*).

11. M. L. Daneel, *Zionism and Faith-Healing in Rhodesia*, trans. V. A. February (The Hague, 1970), p. 12.

12. H. W. Turner, *History of an African Independent Church: The Church of the Lord (Aladura)* (Oxford, 1967), II: xvii.

13. Sundkler, *op. cit.*, p. 33.

14. Georges Balandier, *Sociologie actuelle de l'Afrique noire*, 2nd rev. ed. (Paris, 1963), p. 419 (hereafter cited as Balandier, *Sociologie actuelle*).

15. Sundkler, *op. cit.*, p. 295.

16. Geoffrey Parrinder, *Religion in an African City* (London, 1953), p. 193.

17. Cf. Katesa Schlosser, "Profane Ursachen des Anschlusses an Separatistenkirchen in Süd- und Südwestafrika," in Ernst Benz, ed., *Messianische Kirchen, Sekten und Bewegungen im heutigen Afrika* (Leiden, 1965), p. 41. See also G. C. Oosthuizen, *The Theology of a South African Messiah* (Leiden, 1967), pp. 5–6.

18. H. Richard Niebuhr, *The Social Sources of Denominationalism* (New York, 1965), pp. 62 and 262.

19. Hodgkin, *op. cit.*, p. 106.

20. Barrett, *Schism*, p. 148.

21. *Ibid.*, pp. 118–24.

22. Niebuhr, *op. cit.*, pp. 260–61.

23. E. Franklin Frazier, *The Negro Church in America* (Liverpool, 1964), p. 43.

24. Sundkler, *op. cit.*, p. 100.

25. Barrett, *Schism*, p. 247.

26. G. Yonina Talmon, "Millenarian Movements," *Archives Européennes de Sociologie*, VII (1966): 171.

27. Sundkler, *op. cit.*, pp. 295–96.

28. Georges Balandier, *Daily Life in the Kingdom of the Congo*, trans. Helen Weaver (London, 1968), pp. 257–63. For a general treatment of the movement of Antonianism see Louis Jadin, *Le Congo et la secte des Antoniens* (Brussels, 1961).

29. Barrett, *Schism*, p. 101.

30. *Ibid.*, p. 131.

31. *Ibid.*, p. 102.

32. *Ibid.*, p. 131. Barrett's causal analysis has been sharply criticized by Robert Cameron Mitchell, "Towards the Sociology of Religious Independency," *Journal of Religion in Africa* III (1970): 2–21; however, in my view, Barrett's major theses have not been discredited.

33. Barrett, *Schism*, p. 134.
34. *Ibid.*, p. 130.
35. E. A. Ayandele, *The Missionary Impact on Modern Nigeria* (London, 1966), p. 176, cited by Barrett, *Schism*, p. 127.
36. Hodgkin, *op. cit.*, p. 103.
37. Cf. F. B. Welbourn, "A Note on Types of Religious Society," in C. G. Baëta, ed., *Christianity in Tropical Africa* (London, 1968), p. 138. See also F. B. Welbourn, *East African Rebels: A Study of Some Independent Churches* (London, 1961).
38. Geoffrey Parrinder, *Religion in Africa* (Baltimore, 1969), p. 161.
39. H. W. Turner, "The Place of Independent Religious Movements in the Modernization of Africa," *Journal of Religion in Africa* II (1969): 45.
40. Schlosser, *Eingeborenenkirchen*, pp. 127–32.
41. Cf. Vittorio Lanternari, *The Religions of the Oppressed*, trans. Lisa Sergio (New York, 1965), p. 43.
42. Schlosser, *Eingeborenenkirchen*, p. 168.
43. *Ibid.*, p. 139.
44. *Ibid.*, pp. 162–67.
45. Cf. Efraim Andersson, *Messianic Popular Movements in the Lower Congo*, trans. Donald Burton et al. (Uppsala, 1958), pp. 3 and 48, n. 1. For a 133-item bibliography of Kimbanguism see Paul-Eric Chassard, "Essai de bibliographie sur le Kimbanguisme," *Archives de Sociologie des Religions* no. 31 (January–June 1971): 43–49.
46. Andersson, *op. cit.*, p. 4.
47. *Ibid.*, p. 56.
48. *Ibid.*, p. 61.
49. See *ibid.*, p. 65, for an example of such a song.
50. Roger Anstey, *King Leopold's Legacy: The Congo under Belgian Rule 1908–1960* (London, 1966), p. 142.
51. The complete text of the judgment can be found in Jules Chomé, *La passion de Simon Kimbangu: 1921–1951* (Brussels, 1959), pp. 66–71.
52. Andersson, *op. cit.*, p. 68.
53. *Ibid.*, pp. 69–70.
54. *Ibid.*, p. 75.
55. Crawford Young, *Politics in the Congo: Decolonization and Independence* (Princeton, N.J., 1965), p. 286.
56. Balandier, *Sociologie actuelle*, p. 440.
57. Cf. Banton, *op. cit.*, p. 49.
58. For the doctrines and composition of the EJCSK see Paul Raymaekers, "L'Église de Jesus Christ sur la Terre par le Prophète Simon Kimbangu (EJCSK)," *Zaire* XIII (1959): 675–756.
59. Wyatt MacGaffey, "The Beloved City: Commentary on a Kimbanguist Text," *Journal of Religion in Africa* II (1969): 131.
60. Young, *op. cit.*, pp. 391–92, n. 57.

61. Barrett, *Schism*, p. 201. In his 1969 article (*op. cit.*, p. 129) Mac-Gaffey reports that the EJCSK then claimed a membership of at least one million.
62. Albert Doutreloux, "Prophetism and Development," *Africa Quarterly* VI (1967): 335.
63. Young, *op. cit.*, p. 253.
64. Andersson, *op. cit.*, pp. 117–18 and 244.
65. For further details see the discussion in Balandier, *Sociologie actuelle*, pp. 396–416.
66. Andersson, *op. cit.*, p. 121.
67. *Ibid.*, p. 124.
68. Balandier, *Sociologie actuelle*, p. 398.
69. Andersson, *op. cit.*, p. 124.
70. Cited by Georges Balandier, *Ambiguous Africa: Cultures in Collision*, trans. Helen Weaver (London, 1966), p. 212.
71. *Ibid.*, p. 213.
72. Roger Bastide, "Messianisme et développement economique et social," *Cahiers Internationaux de Sociologie* VII, no. 31 (July–December 1961): 8.
73. George Shepperson, "Nyasaland and the Millennium," in Sylvia L. Thrupp, ed., *Millennial Dreams in Action: Essays in Comparative Study* (The Hague, 1962), p. 149.
74. Hans-Jürgen Greschat, *Kitawala* (Marburg, 1967), pp. 23–29.
75. Shepperson in Thrupp, *op. cit.*, p. 150.
76. Young, *op. cit.*, p. 287.
77. Robert Kaufman, *Millénarisme et acculturation* (Brussels, 1964), p. 87.
78. Daniel Biebuyck, "La Societé Kumu face au Kitawala," *Zaire* XI (1957): 7–40.
79. Anstey, *op. cit.*, p. 142; Kaufman, *op. cit.*, pp. 82–83.
80. Greschat, *op. cit.*, pp. 71–72.
81. *Ibid.*, pp. 79–81.
82. L. H. Gann, *A History of Northern Rhodesia* (London, 1964), p. 170.
83. Jean Pierre Paulus, "Le Kitawala au Congo Belge," *Revue de l'Institut de Sociologie Solvay* XXIX (1956): 257.
84. Gann, *op. cit.*, p. 235.
85. *New York Times*, October 21, 1972.
86. J. M. Assimeng, "Sectarian Allegiance and Political Authority: The Watch Tower Society in Zambia 1907–1935," *Journal of Modern African Studies* VIII (1970): 108.
87. James W. Fernandez, "The Lumpa Uprising: Why?" *Africa Report* IX, no. 10 (November 1964): 31.
88. Cf. Robert Rotberg, "The Lenshina Movement of Northern Rhodesia," *Rhodes-Livingstone Journal* XXIX (June 1961): 65–66.
89. Christine Heward, "The Rise of Alice Lenshina," *New Society*, August 13, 1964, p. 7.

90. John V. Taylor and Dorothea A. Lehmann, *Christians of the Copperbelt* (London, 1961), p. 252.

91. *Ibid.*, p. 257.

92. Andrew D. Roberts, "The Lumpa Church of Alice Lenshina," in Robert I. Rotberg and Ali A. Mazrui, eds., *Protest and Power in Black Africa* (New York, 1970), pp. 542–43.

93. Fernandez, *Africa Report* (November 1964): 30.

94. *Loc. cit.* For a chronological account of the disturbances from June 25 to October 15, 1964 see the *Report of the Commission of Inquiry into the Former Lumpa Church* (Lusaka, 1965). The Commission, headed by the Chief Justice of Zambia, gives the number of Lumpa killed by security forces as 472 (p. 36).

95. Fernandez, *Africa Report* (November 1964): 31; Heward, *op. cit.*, p. 7.

96. *Ibid.*, p. 8.

97. Cf. S. F. Nadel, *Nupe Religion* (Glencoe, Ill., 1954), pp. 275–78; A. M. Lugira, "Redemption in Ganda Traditional Belief," in R. J. Zwi Werblowsky and C. Jouco Bleeker, eds., *Types of Redemption* (Leiden, 1970), pp. 181–89.

98. John S. Mbiti, *New Testament Eschatology in an African Background* (Oxford, 1971), p. 25.

99. Margull, *op. cit.*, p. 33.

100. *Ibid.*, pp. 108–109; Talmon, *op. cit.*, p. 186.

101. Banton, *op. cit.*, p. 48.

102. See Katesa Schlosser, *Propheten in Afrika* (Braunschweig, 1949), and the literature cited there.

103. Talmon, *op. cit.*, p. 184.

104. Georges Balandier, "Messianismes et nationalismes en Afrique noire," *Cahiers Internationaux de Sociologie* XIV (1953): 54.

105. C. F. Audrey Wipper, "The Gusii Rebels," in Rotberg and Mazrui, *op. cit.*, pp. 377–426.

106. James W. Fernandez, "Politics and Prophecy: African Religious Movements," *Practical Anthropology* XII (1965): 75.

107. The writings of Vittorio Lanternari stress this element too emphatically. See in this connection the reviews by 15 authors of his *The Religions of the Oppressed* in *Current Anthropology* VI (1965): 447–65.

108. Cf. Lucy P. Mair, "Independent Religious Movements in Three Continents," *Comparative Studies in Society and History* I (1959): 122 and 134.

109. F. B. Welbourn and B. A. Ogot, *A Place to Feel at Home: A Study of Two Independent Churches in Western Kenya* (London, 1966), p. 145.

110. Fernandez, *Journal of Modern African Studies* II (1964): 547.

CHAPTER 10

1. The number of reported cults is very large; many probably have flourished secretly and have not come to the attention of the au-

thorities or interested scholars. For a bibliographical treatment see Ida Leeson, *Bibliography of Cargo Cults and other Nativistic Movements in the South Pacific* (South Pacific Commission Technical Paper, no. 30, Sydney, 1952) and, more recently, the sources cited by Peter Worsley, *The Trumpet Shall Sound: A Study of 'Cargo' Cults in Melanesia* (2nd rev. ed.: London, 1968), pp. 277-93.

2. *Ibid.*, pp. 75-88.

3. For a detailed discussion of the Mansren myth see F. Ch. Kamma, *Koreri: Messianic Movements in the Biak-Numfor Culture Area*, trans. M. J. van de Vathorst-Smit (The Hague, 1972), chs. 2-5.

4. Worsley, *op. cit.*, pp. 126-37.

5. For example, in the Maji-Maji rebellion of 1905-06 in Tanganyika, the Saya San rebellion of 1930-31 in Burma, and many others involving various religions. For a psychoanalytical explanation of this phenomenon see Weston La Barre, *The Ghost Dance: Origins of Religion* (Garden City, N.Y., 1970), pp. 309-10.

6. Kenelm Burridge, *Mambu: A Melanesian Millennium* (London, 1960), pp. 184-85 (hereafter cited as Burridge, *Mambu*).

7. Worsley, *op. cit.*, p. 106.

8. *Ibid.*, p. 108.

9. *Ibid.*, pp. 211-12; Peter Lawrence, *Road Belong Cargo* (Manchester, 1964), pp. 92-96 (hereafter cited as Lawrence, *Road*).

10. *Ibid.*, p. 164.

11. *Ibid.*, p. 194.

12. Peter Lawrence, "Cargo Cult and Politics," in Peter Hastings, ed., *Papua/New Guinea* (Sydney, 1971), pp. 110-20.

13. Gottfried Oosterwal, "Cargo Cults as a Missionary Challenge," *International Review of Missions* LVI (1967): 470.

14. Cf. Robert H. Lowie, "Primitive Messianism and an Ethnological Problem," *Diogenes* XIX (1957): 62-72.

15. Judy Inglis, "Cargo Cults: The Problem of Explanation," *Oceania* XXVII (1957): 263.

16. I. C. Jarvie, *The Revolution in Anthropology* (London, 1964), p. 145.

17. Cf. Efraim Andersson, *Messianic Popular Movements in the Lower Congo*, trans. Donald Burton et al. (Uppsala, 1958), pp. 228-29.

18. Cf. Hans Zinsser, *Rats, Lice and History* (Boston, 1935), p. 84.

19. Richard H. Niebuhr, *The Social Sources of Denominationalism* (New York, 1965), p. 30.

20. I. C. Jarvie, "Theories of Cargo Cults: A Critical Analysis," *Oceania* XXXIV (1963): 118. Jarvie's writings, it should be noted, are the most rigorous in a rich literature, and our analysis here largely follows his approach.

21. W. E. H. Stanner, "On the Interpretation of Cargo Cults," *Oceania* XXIX (1958): 16.

22. Burridge, *Mambu*, p. 179.
23. Lawrence, *Road*, p. 75.
24. Vittorio Lanternari, *The Religions of the Oppressed*, trans. Lisa Sergio (New York, 1965), pp. 186–87.
25. *Ibid.*, p. 167.
26. Lawrence, *Road*, p. 75.
27. Cf. Jean Guiart, "The Millenarian Aspect of Conversion to Christianity in the South Pacific," in Sylvia L. Thrupp, ed., *Millennial Dreams in Action* (The Hague, 1962), pp. 122–37.
28. *Ibid.*, p. 124.
29. Lawrence, *Road*, p. 249.
30. W. E. H. Stanner, *The South Seas in Transition* (Sydney, 1953), p. 63; Kenelm Burridge, *New Heaven, New Earth: A Study of Millenarian Activities* (Oxford, 1969), pp. 156–57.
31. This apparently was the situation on Tikopia in the Solomon Islands, as reported by Raymond Firth, "The Theory of 'Cargo' Cults: A Note on Tikopia," *Man* LV (1955): 130–32.
32. Herbert Ian Hogbin, *Social Change* (London, 1958), p. 220.
33. Worsley, *op. cit.*, p. 241.
34. Andersson, *op. cit.*, p. 226.
35. Worsley, *op. cit.*, p. 250.
36. Lowie, *op. cit.*, p. 70.
37. R. J. Z. Werblowsky, "Messianism in Primitive Societies," *The Listener* LXIV (1960): 685.
38. Burridge, *Mambu*, p. 31.
39. Lawrence, *Road*, p. 232; Kenelm Burridge, *Tangu Traditions* (Oxford, 1969), p. 32. Glynn Cochrane, *Big Men and Cargo Cults* (London, 1970), pp. 160–64.
40. Lawrence, *Road*, p. 223.
41. For an analysis of one such campaign see David G. Bettison et al., eds., *The Papua-New Guinea Elections 1964* (Canberra, 1965), ch. 10.
42. *New York Times*, April 4, 1972.
43. Worsley, *op. cit.*, p. 231.
44. Lucy P. Mair, "Independent Religious Movements in Three Continents," *Comparative Studies in Society and History* I (1959): 133.

CHAPTER 11

1. Our characterization of revolutionary millenarianism is derived from the definition of millenarian movements developed by Norman Cohn in "Medieval Millenarianism: Its Bearing on the Comparative Study of Millenarian Movements," in Sylvia L. Thrupp, ed., *Millennial Dreams in Action* (The Hague, 1962), p. 31 (hereafter cited as Cohn, "Medieval Millenarianism"). See also Yonina Talmon, "Millenarian Movements," *Archives Européennes de So-*

ciologie VII (1966): 159 (hereafter cited as Talmon, "Millenarian Movements").

2. Cf. Bryan A. Wilson, "Millennialism in Comparative Perspective," *Comparative Studies in Society and History* VI (1963): 97.

3. *From Max Weber: Essays in Sociology*, trans. H. H. Gerth and C. Wright Mills (New York, 1958), p. 295.

4. Max Weber, *The Theory of Social and Economic Organization*, trans. A. M. Henderson and Talcott Parsons (New York, 1964), pp. 358–59.

5. Talmon, "Millenarian Movements," p. 169; Wilson, *op. cit.*, p. 100. Wilhelm E. Mühlmann, *Chiliasmus und Nativismus* (Berlin, 1961), pp. 306–307; Peter Worsley, *The Trumpet Shall Sound*, 2nd ed. (London, 1968), p. 12.

6. Talmon, "Millenarian Movements," p. 170.

7. Henri Desroche, *Dieux d'hommes: Dictionnaire des messianismes et millénarismes de l'ère chrétienne* (Paris, 1969), p. 7.

8. Cf. Luigi Petrullo and Bernard M. Bass, eds., *Leadership and Interpersonal Behavior* (New York, 1961); Alvin W. Gouldner, ed., *Studies in Leadership* (New York, 1950).

9. Ann Ruth Willner and Dorothy Willner, "The Rise and Role of Charismatic Leaders," *Annals of the American Academy of Political and Social Science* CCCLVIII (March 1965): 84.

10. Ann Ruth Willner, *Charismatic Political Leadership: A Theory* (Center of International Studies Research monograph No. 32; Princeton, 1968), pp. 63–69 (hereafter cited as Willner, *Charismatic Leadership*). See also Eric Hoffer, *The True Believer* (New York, 1964), pp. 105–106.

11. Willner and Willner, *op. cit.*, p. 79; T. K. Oomen, "Charisma, Social Structure and Social Change," *Comparative Studies in Society and History* X (1967): 85. Reinhard Bendix has pointed out that the modern totalitarian dictatorship, controlling all channels of communication, can easily simulate the attributes of charismatic leadership and thus create a widespread belief in the charisma of the leader. "Reflections on Charismatic Leadership," in Bendix, ed., *State and Society: A Reader in Comparative Political Sociology* (Boston, 1968), p. 625.

12. Mühlmann, *op. cit.*, pp. 282–283; Talmon, "Millenarian Movements," pp. 174–75.

13. Cf. Hoffer, *op. cit.*, p. 94.

14. Yonina Talmon, "Pursuit of the Millennium: The Relation between Religion and Social Change," *European Journal of Sociology* III (1962): 134–35 (hereafter cited as Talmon, "Pursuit of Millennium").

15. Gershom Scholem, *The Messianic Idea in Judaism and Other Essays on Jewish Spirituality* (New York, 1971), p. 13.

16. Marjorie Reeves, *The Influence of Prophecy in the Later Middle Ages: A Study of Joachimism* (Oxford, 1969), p. 291.

17. P.-M. Yap, "Mental Diseases Peculiar to Certain Cultures: A Survey of Comparative Psychiatry," *Journal of Mental Science* XCVII (1951): 315. See also Erika Bourguignon, "Hallucination and Trance: An Anthropologist's Perspective," in Wolfram Keup, ed., *Origin and Mechanisms of Hallucinations* (New York, 1970), pp. 183–90.

18. H. Richard Niebuhr, *The Social Sources of Denominationalism* (New York, 1965), p. 30.

19. Vittorio Lanternari, *The Religions of the Oppressed: A Study of Modern Messianic Cults*, trans. Lisa Sergio (New York, 1965), p. 249.

20. Talmon, "Pursuit of Millennium," p. 147.

21. Cf. Ralph Linton, "Nativistic Movements," *American Anthropologist* XLV (1943): 230–40.

22. Norman Cohn, *The Pursuit of the Millennium*, 2nd rev. ed. (New York, 1970), p. 282 (hereafter cited as Cohn, *Pursuit of Millennium*). As medievalists like Gordon Leff and J. B. Russell have pointed out, Norman Cohn in some of his writings overstates the class factor in medieval heresy.

23. John Leddy Phelan, *The Millennial Kingdom of the Franciscans in the New World*, 2nd rev. ed. (Berkeley, Calif., 1970), p. 11.

24. The concept of relative deprivation was for the first time given a central role by S. A. Stouffer et al., *The American Soldier* (Princeton, 1949). Cf. the detailed discussion by Robert K. Merton, *Social Theory and Social Structure* (rev. ed., New York, 1957), ch. 8. See also W. G. Runciman, *Relative Deprivation and Social Justice* (London, 1966), p. 3; David F. Aberle, *The Peyote Religion among the Navaho* (Chicago, 1966), pp. 323–29; Charles Y. Glock and Rodney Stark, *Religion and Society in Tension* (Chicago, 1965), p. 246.

25. Worsley, *op. cit.*, p. 243.

26. Cf. Anthony F. C. Wallace, *Religion: An Anthropological View* (New York, 1966), pp. 157–58.

27. Michael Barkun, "Law and Social Revolution: Millenarianism and the Legal System," *Law and Society Review* VI (1971): 128.

28. Wilson D. Wallis, *Messiahs: Their Role in Civilization* (Washington, D.C. 1943), p. 187.

29. *Yasht*, XIX: 14, 89, cited by Mircea Eliade, *The Myth of the Eternal Return*, trans. Willard R. Trask (New York, 1965), p. 124. See also Gerardus van der Leeuw, "Primordial Time and Final Time," in Joseph Campbell, ed., *Man and Time* (Bollingen Series, XXX, New York, 1957), pp. 324–50.

30. For a still more cautious conclusion regarding Zoroastrian influence see Franz König, *Zarathustras Jenseitsvorstellungen und das Alte Testament* (Vienna, 1964), pp. 283–85.

31. Cohn, *Pursuit of Millennium*, p. 307.

32. For the Antonians see *supra*, ch. 9, n. 28. For a brief discussion

of the Lazzarettiani see E. J. Hobsbawm, *Primitive Rebels* (New York, 1965), pp. 68–73. A detailed treatment of the insurgency led by Antonio Conselheiro is found in the Brazilian classic of Euclides da Cunha, *Rebellion in the Backlands*, trans. Samuel Putnam (Chicago, 1944).

33. Cf. William A. Christian, Jr., "Holy People in Peasant Europe," *Comparative Studies in Society and History* XV (1973): 108.
34. Cf. *Acta Apostolicae Sedis* XXXVI (1944): 212 and for the background of this decree G. Gilleman, S.J., "Condamnation de millénarisme mitigé," *Nouvelle Revue Théologique* LXVII (1945): 847–49.
35. Kenelm Burridge, *New Heaven, New Earth: A Study of Millenarian Activities* (Oxford, 1969), p. 16.
36. Gayroud S. Wilmore, *Black Religion and Black Radicalism* (Garden City, N.Y., 1972), p. 52.
37. Emil Abegg, *Der Messiasglaube in Indien und Iran* (Berlin, 1928), pp. 143–44; Charles Eliot, *Hinduism and Buddhism: An Historical Sketch* (London, 1962), I: 46–47; Helmuth von Glasenapp, *Immortality and Salvation in Indian Religions*, trans. E. F. J. Payne (Calcutta, 1963), p. 102.
38. S. J. Samartha, *The Hindu View of History: Classical and Modern* (Bangalore, 1959), pp. 7 and 15.
39. Max Weber, *The Sociology of Religion*, trans. Ephraim Fischoff (Boston, 1964), pp. 55–56.
40. Cf. Surendra Prasad Sinha, *Life and Times of Birsa Bhagwan* (Ranchi, 1964) and Suresh Singh, *The Dust Storm and the Hanging Mist: A Study of Birsa Munda and his Movement in Chhotanagpur* (Calcutta, 1966).
41. Gananath Obeyesekere, "The Buddhist Pantheon in Ceylon and its Extensions," in Manning Nash, ed., *Anthropological Studies in Theravada Buddhism* (New Haven, 1966), p. 10.
42. Cf. E. Michael Mendelson, "A Messianic Buddhist Association in Upper Burma," *Bulletin of the School of Oriental and African Studies*, University of London, XXIV (1961): 560–80.
43. Cf. Charles F. Keyes, "Millennialism, Theravada Buddhism and Thai Society" (Paper delivered at the 24th annual meeting of the Association of Asian Studies in New York, March 29, 1972).
44. Manning Nash, "Buddhist Revitalization in the Nation State: The Burmese Experience," in Robert F. Spencer, ed., *Religion and Change in Contemporary Asia* (Minneapolis, 1971), p. 116. Melford E. Spiro reports that overtones of a millennial Buddhism—"the conjunction of the Buddhist notion of a Universal Emperor and a Future Buddha with the Burmese notions of a Future King, weikzahood [magicianship] and occult power"—continued to reverberate in Burma during his research there in 1961–62 [*Buddhism and Society* (New York, 1970), p. 172], but even he admits that membership in messianic sects involves no more than

"a tiny percentage of the population" (p. 186) and that "belief in savior gods is, for the most part, nonexistent" (p. 132).

45. William A. Smalley, "Cian: Khmu Culture Hero," in *Felicitation Volumes of Southeast-Asian Studies Presented to His Highness Prince Dhaninivat Kromamun Bidyalabh Bridhyakorn* (Bangkok, 1965), I: 41–54.
46. Weston La Barre, *The Ghost Dance: Origins of Religion* (Garden City, 1970), p. 313.
47. Cf. Alfred Metraux, "Messiahs of South America," *Inter-American Quarterly* III, no. 2 (April 1941): 53–60; Maria Isaura Pereira de Queiroz, "Indianische Messiasbewegungen in Brasilien," trans. Hans Schreen, *Staden-Jahrbuch* XI/XII (1963–64): 31–44; Mircea Eliade, "Paradise and Utopia: Mythical Geography and Eschatology," in Frank E. Manuel, ed., *Utopias and Utopian Thought* (Boston, 1966), pp. 260–80; René Ribeiro, "Brazilian Messianic Movements," in Thrupp, *op. cit.*, p. 56.
48. La Barre, *op. cit.*, p. 268.
49. Cf. Isidor Thorner, "Prophetic and Mystic Experience: Comparison and Consequences," *Journal for the Scientific Study of Religion* V (1965): 84.
50. This stress on the innovative role played by the charismatic leaders of revolutionary millenarian movements is not meant to contradict the observation of Edward Shils that "charisma not only disrupts social order, but it also maintains or conserves it." "Charisma, Order and Status," *American Sociological Review* XXX (1965): 200. We will return to this important point in Chapter 26.
51. Werner Stark, *The Sociology of Religion: A Study of Christendom* (London, 1967), II: 48.
52. This point is well made by Willner, *Charismatic Leadership*, p. 45, who uses Gandhi as an example of a leader who taught his people how depressed they were.
53. Cohn, "Medieval Millenarianism," p. 38.
54. See the suggestive article by Andrew M. Greeley, "Superstition, Ecstasy and Tribal Consciousness," *Social Research* XXXVII (1970): 203–11.
55. *From Max Weber*, p. 245.
56. Wilson, *op. cit.*, p. 103.
57. Christopher Hill, *The World Turned Upside Down: Radical Ideas During the English Revolution* (London, 1972), p. 73.
58. Willner, *Charismatic Leadership*, p. 45.
59. Reeves, *op. cit.*, p. 135.
60. Max Weber, *Ancient Judaism*, trans. Hans H. Gerth and Don Martindale (Glencoe, Ill., 1952), p. 286.
61. Carl W. Christensen, "Religious Conversion," *Archives of General Psychiatry* IX (1963): 210.

62. William James, *The Varieties of Religious Experience* (New York, 1958), p. 164.
63. Hans L. Zetterberg, "Religious Conversion as a Change of Social Roles," *Sociology and Social Research* XXXVI (1952): 166.
64. Cf. Leon Salzman, "The Psychology of Religious and Ideological Conversion," *Psychiatry* XVI (1953): 179.
65. Michael Walzer, *The Revolution of the Saints* (Cambridge, Mass., 1965), pp. 308–309; Christopher Hill, *God's Englishman: Oliver Cromwell and the English Revolution* (New York, 1970), p. 242.
66. Sante de Sanctis, *Religious Conversion: A Bio-Psychological Study*, trans. Helen Augur (London, 1927), p. 46.
67. Edward S. Ames, *The Psychology of Religious Experience* (Boston, 1910), ch. 14.
68. Christensen, *op. cit.*, p. 212. See also W. Lawson Jones, *A Psychological Study of Religious Conversion* (London, 1937), p. 227.
69. Anthony F. C. Wallace, "Mazeway Resynthesis: A Bio-Cultural Theory of Religious Inspiration," *Transactions of the New York Academy of Sciences* XVIII (1956): 635.
70. Dorothy Emmett, "Prophets and their Societies," *Journal of the Royal Anthropological Institute* LXXXVI (1956): 17.
71. Anton T. Boisen, *The Exploration of the Inner World: A Study of Mental Disorder and Religious Experience* (Chicago, 1936), p. 66.
72. Gerda E. Allison, "Psychiatric Implications of Religious Conversion," *Canadian Psychiatric Association Journal* XIII (1967): 60.
73. Cohn, *Pursuit of Millennium*, p. 85.
74. H. I. Schou, *Religion and Morbid Mental States*, trans. W. Worster (New York, 1926), pp. 87–88.
75. George Rosen, "Social Change and Psychopathology in the Emotional Climate of Millennial Movements," *American Behavioral Scientist* XVI (1972): 161.
76. Leon Festinger et al., *When Prophecy Fails* (Minneapolis, 1956), p. 28.
77. Cf. "Time of Rest and Refreshment at Hand," *Awake* LII, no. 19 (October 8, 1971): 28; Joseph F. Zygmunt, "Prophetic Failure and Chiliastic Identity: The Case of Jehovah's Witnesses," *American Journal of Sociology* LXXV (1970): 926–48.
78. Burridge, *op. cit.*, pp. 76–83. For an older and more detailed account see James Mooney, *The Ghost Dance Religion and the Sioux Outbreak of 1890*, ed. A. F. C. Wallace (Chicago, 1965).
79. See Audrey Wipper, "The Gusii Rebels," in Robert I. Rotberg and Ali A. Mazrui, eds., *Protest and Power in Black Africa* (New York, 1970), pp. 377–426.
80. Robert O. Crummey, *The Old Believers and the World of Antichrist: The Vyg Community and the Russian State 1694–1855* (Madison, Wisc., 1969), p. 220.

81. Frederick C. Conybeare, *Russian Dissenters* (Cambridge, Mass., 1921), p. 366.
82. *Ibid.*, p. 365; Albert F. Heard, *The Russian Church and Russian Dissent* (New York, 1887), p. 270.
83. Stark, *op. cit.*, p. 177.
84. See the perceptive essay of Robert C. Tucker on the deradicalization of Marxist movements in his *The Marxian Revolutionary Idea* (New York, 1969). The inverse relationship between organizational strength and the preservation of radicalism was first stressed by Robert Michels in 1911 in his classic *Political Parties*.
85. Mühlmann, *op. cit.*, pp. 275–76.
86. Niebuhr, *op. cit.*, pp. 19–20. As Bryan Wilson and others have shown, Niebuhr somewhat overstated the tendency of sects to turn into denominations and churches.
87. *Ibid.*, p. 20.
88. Hobsbawm, *op. cit.*, p. 71.
89. Tucker, *op. cit.*, p. 187.
90. Talmon, "Millenarian Movements," p. 184.
91. Guglielmo Guariglia, *Prophetismus und Heilserwartungs-Bewegungen als Völkerkundliches und Religionsgeschichtliches Problem* (Vienna, 1959), p. 268.
92. A. J. P. Köbben, "Prophetic Movements as an Expression of Social Protest," *Internationales Archiv für Ethnographie* XLIX (1960): 154.
93. Cf. Frances R. Hill, "Nationalist Millenarians and Millenarian Nationalists: Conflict or Cooperation in the New Jerusalem," *American Behavioral Scientist* XVI (1972):269–88.
94. Cf. Betty R. Scharf, *The Sociological Study of Religion* (London, 1970), p. 69.
95. Burridge, *op. cit.*, pp. 15–22.
96. Worsley, *op. cit.*, p. 232.
97. Cf. Herbert H. Stroup, *The Jehovah's Witnesses* (New York, 1945); William J. Whalen, *Armageddon Around the Corner: A Report on Jehovah's Witnesses* (New York, 1962); Alan Rogerson, *Millions Now Living Will Never Die: A Study of Jehovah's Witnesses* (London, 1969).
98. John Lofland and Rodney Stark, "Becoming a World Saver: A Theory of Conversion to a Deviant Perspective," *American Sociological Review* XXX (1965): 868. See also John Lofland, *Doomsday Cult* (Englewood Cliffs, N.J., 1966).
99. Walter J. Hollenweger, *Enthusiastisches Christentum: Die Pfingstbewegung in Geschichte und Gegenwart* (Zurich, 1969), p. 525.
100. Cf. David E. Smith, "Millenarian Scholarship in America," *American Quarterly* XVII (1965): 539.
101. Bryan Wilson, *Religious Sects: A Sociological Study* (London, 1970), p. 96.

102. Albert S. Cleage, *The Black Messiah* (New York, 1968), pp. 4 and 6.
103. *Ibid.*, p. 6. See also the same author's *Black Christian Nationalism: New Directions for the Black Church* (New York, 1972) and James H. Cone, *A Black Theology of Liberation* (Philadelphia, 1970). For a critique of black theology see William Jones, "Theodicy and Methodology in Black Theology: A Critique of Washington, Cone and Cleage," *Harvard Theological Review* LXLV (1971): 541–557.
104. Emilio Willems, *Followers of the New Faith: Culture Change and the Rise of Protestantism in Brazil and Chile* (Nashville, Tenn., 1967), p. 134.
105. Liston Pope, *Millhands and Preachers: A Study of Gastonia* (New Haven, 1942), p. 137.
106. Ernest Lee Tuveson, *Millennium and Utopia: A Study in the Background of the Idea of Progress* (New York, 1964), p. 75. See also Rosemary Radford Ruether, *The Radical Kingdom: The Western Experience of Messianic Hope* (New York, 1970), pp. 38–43.
107. Hans Kohn, "Messianism," *Encyclopaedia of the Social Sciences* (1935) X: 362.
108. Tucker, *op. cit.*, p. 183. See also Raymond Aron, *The Opium of the Intellectuals*, trans. Terence Kilmartin (London, 1957), p. 66; George Steiner, *In Bluebeard's Castle* (New Haven, 1971), p. 43.
109. Donald G. MacRae, "The Bolshevik Ideology: The Intellectual and Emotional Factors in Communist Affiliation," *Cambridge Journal* III (1954): 167. See also W. Banning, *Der Kommunismus als politisch-soziale Weltreligion* (Berlin, 1953).
110. Quoted in Franco Venturi, *The Roots of Revolution* (London, 1960), p. 383.
111. Maurice Cranston, ed., *Prophetic Politics: Critical Interpretations of the Revolutionary Impulse* (New York, 1972), p. 13.
112. Erwin Scheuch, *Wiedertäufer der Wohlstandsgesellschaft* (Cologne, 1968). The close similarity between the Radical Reformation and the New Left is argued by Arthur G. Gisch, *The New Left and Christian Radicalism* (Grand Rapids, Mich., 1970), ch. 2.
113. Cf. James Hitchcock, "The Intellectuals and the People," *Commentary* LV, no. 3 (March 1973): 69.

CHAPTER 12

1. Cf. Bruce Tiebout McCully, *English Education and the Origins of Indian Nationalism* (New York, 1940).
2. Cf. Verney Lovett, *A History of the Indian Nationalist Movement* (London, 1920), pp. 29–30.

3. Cf. Anil Seal, *The Emergence of Indian Nationalism* (Cambridge, 1968), pp. 206–207.
4. Lala Lajpat Rai, *The Arya Samaj* (London, 1915), p. 172.
5. Cf. Dennis Dalton, "The Idea of Freedom in the Political Thought of Vivekananda and Aurobindo," in S. N. Mukherjee, ed., *South Asian Affairs*, no. 2 (St. Anthony's Papers, no. 18; Oxford, 1966), pp. 38–39.
6. Stephen N. Hay in William Theodore de Bary, ed., *Sources of Indian Tradition* (New York, 1966), II: 156.
7. D. Mackenzie Brown, *The Nationalist Movement: Indian Political Thought from Ranade to Bhave* (Berkeley, Calif., 1961), p. 75.
8. Karl W. Deutsch estimates that "in India in 1931 the number of persons who were considered literate in English was about 1 per cent of the total population." *Nationalism and Social Communication* (Cambridge, Mass., 1953), p. 109.
9. Haridas and Uma Mukherjee, *India's Fight for Freedom or the Swadeshi Movement (1905–1906)* (Calcutta, 1958), p. 40. See also the same writers' *The Origins of the National Education Movement* (Calcutta, 1957).
10. Stanley A. Wolpert, *Tilak and Gokhale: Revolution and Reform in the Making of Modern India* (Berkeley, Calif., 1962), p. 102.
11. Valentine Chirol, *Indian Unrest* (London, 1910), p. 41.
12. D. Mackenzie Brown, *The White Umbrella: Indian Political Thought from Manu to Gandhi* (Berkeley, Calif., 1953), pp. 84 and 176.
13. Haridas and Uma Mukherjee, *Sri Aurobindo's Political Thought (1893–1908)* (Calcutta, 1958), p. 107 (hereafter cited as Mukherjee, *Sri Aurobindo*). The passage is from a series of articles entitled "New Lamps for Old" published in the *Indu Prakash* of Bombay in 1893.
14. Richard L. Park, "The Rise of Militant Nationalism in Bengal" (Ph.D. dissertation, Harvard University, 1950), p. 226.
15. Haridas and Uma Mukherjee, *Bipin Chandra Pal and India's Struggle for Swaraj* (Calcutta, 1958), pp. 70–71 (hereafter cited as Mukherjee, *B.C. Pal*).
16. Vishwanath Prasad Varma, *The Political Philosophy of Sri Aurobindo* (New York, 1960), p. 441.
17. *Bande Mataram*, Daily edition, October 7, 1907, in Mukherjee, *Sri Aurobindo*, pp. 146–47.
18. Tilak in 1906, *Speeches of Bal Gangadhar Tilak*, ed. R. R. Srivastava (Fyzabad, 1917), p. 56 (hereafter cited as Tilak, *Speeches*).
19. Cited by Karan Singh, *Prophet of Indian Nationalism: A Study of the Political Thought of Sri Aurobindo Ghosh 1893–1910* (London, 1963), p. 75.
20. Bipin Chandra Pal, *Swadeshi and Swaraj* (Calcutta, 1954), p. 291.
21. Tilak, *Speeches*, p. 53.
22. Aurobindo Ghose, *The Doctrine of Passive Resistance* (Calcutta,

1948), pp. 83–84 (hereafter cited as Aurobindo, *Passive Resistance*). This work was first published as a series of essays in *Bande Mataram* in April 1907.
23. Aurobindo Ghose, *Speeches*, 2nd rev. ed. (Calcutta, 1948), p. 72.
24. *Ibid.*, p. 77.
25. *Ibid.*, p. 67.
26. *Bande Mataram*, Weekly edition, June 19, 1908, in Mukherjee, *Sri Aurobindo*, pp. 94–95.
27. Pal, *op. cit.*, p. 222.
28. "New Lamps for Old" (1893), in Mukherjee, *Sri Aurobindo*, p. 71.
29. *Kesari*, February 4, 1908, p. 4, cited by Wolpert, *op. cit.*, p. 214.
30. Bal Gangadhar Tilak, *His Writings and Speeches* (Madras, 1922), p. 199.
31. D. Argov, "Moderates and Extremists: Two Attitudes towards British Rule in India," in St. Anthony's Papers, no. 18 (Oxford, 1966), pp. 23–24.
32. Pal, *op. cit.*, p. 55d.
33. Bal Gangadhar Tilak, *Srimad Bhagavadgita Rahasya*, trans. into English by B. S. Sukthankar (Poona, 1935), I: 562.
34. *Ibid.*, p. 555.
35. D. Mackenzie Brown, "The Philosophy of Bal Gangadhar Tilak: Karma vs. Jnana in the Gita Rahasya," *Journal of Asian Studies* XVII (1958): 197–206.
36. *The Bhagavad Gita*, trans. and interpreted by Franklin Edgerton (New York, 1965), preface, p. viii.
37. Franklin Edgerton, Review of Tilak's *Rahasya*, *Journal of the American Oriental Society* LVI (1936): 527.
38. Aurobindo, *Passive Resistance*, p. 81.
39. *Ibid.*, p. 29.
40. Mukherjee, *B.C. Pal*, p. 76.
41. Speech on June 25, 1907, Tilak, *Speeches*, p. 165.
42. Aurobindo, *Passive Resistance*, p. 30.
43. "New Lamps for Old" (1893), in Mukherjee, *Sri Aurobindo*, p. 84.
44. Aurobindo, *Passive Resistance*, p. 68.
45. Cited by Argov, *op. cit.*, pp. 28–29.
46. Speech on June 25, 1907, Tilak, *Speeches*, p. 170.
47. Pal, *op. cit.*, p. 63.
48. Aurobindo, *Passive Resistance*, p. 16.
49. *Sedition Committee 1918: Report* (Calcutta, 1918), p. 2. This report was prepared by a committee of six government officials, headed by Mr. Justice Rowlatt, and represents a rich source of information on the terrorist movement—albeit characterized by a hostile point of view.
50. M. N. Das, *India Under Morley and Minto: Politics Behind Revolution, Repression and Reforms* (London, 1964), pp. 115–16. See

also the discussion of the secret societies in Park, *op. cit.*, pp. 238–56.

51. *Sedition Committee Report*, p. 182; Park, *op. cit.*, p. 251.
52. A detailed listing of individuals and organizations involved in the Indian revolutionary movement during the period 1907–17 is given in James Campbell Ker, "Political Trouble in India: 1907–1917," pp. 515–50, a confidential report issued by the Government of India in 1917. The document is discussed by P. S. Sinha, "A New Source for the History of the Revolutionary Movement in India, 1907–1917," *Journal of Asian Studies* XXXI (1971): 151–56.
53. *Sedition Committee Report*, pp. 23–24; Lawrence J. L. D. Zetland, *The Heart of Aryavarta: A Study of the Psychology of Indian Unrest* (Boston, 1925), pp. 82–84.
54. Cited by Chirol, *op. cit.*, p. 94.
55. *Ibid.*, pp. 70–71.
56. Resolution of the 23rd Congress, cited by Annie Besant, *How India Wrought for Freedom* (Madras, 1915), p. 485.
57. Lajpat Rai, *op. cit.*, p. 169.
58. Lala Lajpat Rai, *Young India: An Interpretation and a History of the Nationalist Movement from Within* (New York, 1916), p. 233.
59. Das, *op. cit.*, p. 117.
60. *Kesari*, May 15, 1897, quoted in Wolpert, *op. cit.*, p. 87.
61. *Ibid.*, p. 97.
62. *Kesari*, June 2, 1908, quoted in *loc. cit.*
63. Aurobindo, *Passive Resistance*, p. 87.
64. Park, *op. cit.*, pp. 230–31.
65. Mukherjee, *Sri Aurobindo*, pp. 56–57; Singh, *op. cit.*, p. 104, calls him the "secret leader and inspirer of the violent, underground terrorist movement designed utterly to demoralize the British."
66. Cf. Amales Tripathi, *The Extremist Challenge: India Between 1890 and 1910* (Bombay, 1967), p. 135. The work in question is *Sri Aurobindo on Himself and on the Mother* (Pondicherry, 1953).
67. Baker to Minto, April 19, 1910, cited by Das, *op. cit.*, p. 145.
68. Daniel Argov, *Moderates and Extremists in the Indian Nationalist Movement: 1883–1920* (Bombay, 1967), pp. 177–78.
69. Mindo Adenwalla, "Hindu Concepts and the Gita in Early Indian National Thought," in Robert K. Sakai, ed., *Studies on Asia, 1961* (Lincoln, Nebraska, 1961), p. 23.
70. Cf. Singh, *op. cit.*, p. 77.
71. Cf. Hans Kohn, *A History of Nationalism in the East*, trans. Margaret M. Green (New York, 1929), p. 9.
72. Cf. S. N. Mukherjee, "Introduction," St. Anthony's Papers, no. 18 (Oxford, 1966), pp. 14–15.
73. Aurobindo, *Passive Resistance*, p. 3.
74. Wolpert, *op. cit.*, p. 302. See also Charles H. Heimsath, *Indian*

Nationalism and Hindu Social Reform (Princeton, N.J., 1964), pp. 163–65.

75. Louis Dumont, *Religion, Politics and History in India: Collected Papers in Indian Sociology* (The Hague, 1970), p. 103.

76. Donald E. Smith, *India as a Secular State* (Princeton, N.J., 1963), p. 455.

77. J. A. Curran, *Militant Hinduism in Indian Politics: A Study of the R.S.S.* (New York, 1951), pp. 9–10.

78. Cf. Craig Baxter, "The Jana Sangh: A Brief History," in Donald E. Smith, ed., *South Asian Politics and Religion* (Princeton, N.J., 1966), pp. 90–101, and the same author's *The Jana Sangh: A Biography of an Indian Political Party* (Philadelphia, 1969).

79. Cited by Stephen Fuchs, *Rebellious Prophets: A Study of Messianic Movements in Indian Religions* (London, 1965), p. 284.

80. Harold A. Gould, "Religion and Politics in a U.P. Constituency," in Smith, ed., *South Asian Politics and Religion*, p. 53.

CHAPTER 13

1. Joan V. Bondurant, *Conquest of Violence: The Gandhian Philosophy of Conflict*, rev. ed. (Berkeley, Calif., 1965), p. xv.

2. Mohandas K. Gandhi, *Satyagraha in South Africa*, trans. Valji Govindji Desai (Madras, 1938), p. 172, quoted *ibid.*, p. 8.

3. "The Doctrine of the Sword," *Young India*, August 11, 1920, in S. Radhakrishnan, ed. *Mahatma Gandhi: Essays and Reflections on His Life and Work*, 2nd rev. ed. (London, 1949), p. 501.

4. *Ibid.*, p. 499.

5. Mohandas K. Gandhi, *An Autobiography: The Story of My Experiments with Truth*, trans. Mahadev Desai (Boston, 1966), p. xii.

6. *Ibid.*, p. 504.

7. Mohandas K. Gandhi, *All Men Are Brothers*, ed. by Krishna Kripalani (New York, 1958), p. 120.

8. *Young India*, January 19, 1921, cited by Bondurant, *op. cit.*, p. 24.

9. *Young India*, April 1, 1926, in Mohandas K. Gandhi, *Young India: 1924–1926* (New York, 1927), p. 583.

10. *Harijan*, April 15, 1933, in Mohandas K. Gandhi, *Non-Violent Resistance (Satyagraha)* (New York, 1961), pp. 201–202.

11. Mohandas K. Gandhi, *Non-Violence in Peace and War*, 2nd ed. (Ahmedabad, 1944), p. 49, cited by Bondurant, *op. cit.*, p. 27.

12. *Young India*, April 3, 1924, in Gandhi, *Young India: 1924–1926*, p. 2.

13. Cf. Dhirendra Mohan Datta, *The Philosophy of Mahatma Gandhi* (Madison, Wisc., 1961), p. 135.

14. Gandhi, *All Men Are Brothers*, p. 141.

15. *Young India*, May 21, 1925, in Gandhi, *Young India: 1924–1926*, p. 928.

16. *Young India*, January 12, 1921, in Mohandas K. Gandhi, *Young India: 1919–1921* (Madras, 1922), p. 277.
17. *Young India*, August 2, 1928, in Gandhi, *Non-Violent Resistance*, p. 216.
18. Radhakrishnan, *Mahatma Gandhi*, pp. 140–41.
19. "The Doctrine of the Sword," in Radhakrishnan, *Mahatma Gandhi*, p. 499.
20. *Young India*, October 21, 1926, in Gandhi, *Young India: 1924–1926*, p. 969.
21. Louis Fisher, *The Life of Mahatma Gandhi* (New York, 1950), p. 491.
22. *Young India*, August 2, 1928, in Gandhi, *Non-Violent Resistance*, p. 216.
23. *Harijan*, June 24, 1939, in *ibid.*, p. 296.
24. Datta, *op. cit.*, p. 8.
25. *Ibid.*, p. 13.
26. Bondurant, *op. cit.*, p. 106.
27. *Young India*, May 12, 1920, in Gandhi, *Young India: 1919–1921*, p. 568.
28. Bondurant, *op. cit.*, pp. 111–19.
29. Gandhi, *Autobiography*, p. 158.
30. *Young India*, March 5, 1925, cited by Bondurant, *op. cit.*, p. 152.
31. Gandhi, *Autobiography*, p. 265.
32. *The Gospel of Selfless Action or The Gita According to Gandhi*, trans. Mahadev Desai (Ahmedabad, 1948), p. 130.
33. *Young India*, September 29, 1920, cited by Bondurant, *op. cit.*, p. 121. For a critical discussion of Gandhi's use of the *Gita* see Agehananda Bharati, "Gandhi's Interpretation of the Gita: An Anthropological Analysis," in Sibnarayan Ray, ed., *Gandhi, India and the World* (Philadelphia, 1970), pp. 57–70.
34. Jawaharlal Nehru, *The Discovery of India* (New York, 1946), p. 365.
35. Susanne H. Rudolph, "Self-Control and Political Potency: Gandhi's Asceticism," *American Scholar* XXXV (1966): 97.
36. Jawaharlal Nehru, *Toward Freedom: The Autobiography of Jawaharlal Nehru* (Boston, 1961), p. 190.
37. *Young India*, September 11, 1924, cited by Bondurant, *op. cit.*, p. 124.
38. Max Weber, *The Theory of Social and Economic Organization*, trans. A. M. Henderson and Talcott Parsons (New York, 1964), pp. 358–59.
39. Nehru, *Toward Freedom*, pp. 189–90.
40. Nehru, *Toward Freedom*, p. 53.
41. Nehru, *Discovery of India*, p. 367.
42. Nehru, *Toward Freedom*, p. 191.
43. *Ibid.*, p. 313.
44. R. C. Majumdar, *History of the Freedom Movement in India*,

vol. III (Calcutta, 1963), preface, in Martin D. Lewis, ed., *Gandhi: Maker of Modern India?* (Boston, 1965), p. 56 (hereafter cited as Lewis, *Gandhi*).

45. Sasadhar Sinha, *Indian Independence in Perspective* (New York, 1964), p. 7.
46. William James, *The Varieties of Religious Experience* (New York, 1958), p. 278.
47. T. Walter Wallbank, *India in the New Era* (Chicago, 1951), p. 111 (hereafter cited as Wallbank, *India*).
48. Cf. Rajani Palme Dutt, *India Today*, 2nd rev. ed. (Bombay, 1949), pp. 314–29.
49. Nehru, *Toward Freedom*, p. 66.
50. Sinha, *op. cit.*, p. 54.
51. Nehru, *Toward Freedom*, p. 73.
52. *Young India*, June 8, 1921, in Gandhi, *Young India: 1919–1921*, p. 649.
53. Nehru, *Toward Freedom*, p. 80.
54. T. Walter Wallbank, *A Short History of India and Pakistan* (New York, 1958), p. 159 (hereafter cited as Wallbank, *Short History*).
55. *Ibid.*, p. 183.
56. *Ibid.*, p. 158.
57. R. C. Majumdar, *Three Phases of India's Struggle for Freedom* (Bombay, 1961), p. 50 (hereafter cited as Majumdar, *Three Phases*).
58. Penderel Moon, *Divide and Quit* (Berkeley, Calif., 1962), pp. 270–71. The importance of Gandhi's religious style for the development of Hindu-Muslim antagonism is minimized by A. B. Shah, "Gandhi and the Hindu-Muslim Question," in Ray, *op. cit.*, pp. 188–208.
59. Nehru, *Toward Freedom*, p. 71.
60. Abdul Waheed Khan, *India Wins Freedom: The Other Side* (Karachi, 1961), p. 178.
61. Moon, *op. cit.*, p. 270.
62. According to E. Victor Wolfenstein, the author of a recent psychoanalytical interpretation of Gandhi's political career, the unconscious meaning of salt for Gandhi was human semen. "In the context of the Salt March, Gandhi's taking of salt from the British can thus be seen as reclaiming for the Indian people the manhood and potency which was properly theirs." *The Revolutionary Personality: Lenin, Trotsky, Gandhi* (Princeton, N.J. 1967), p. 221.
63. For a detailed description of the 1930–31 campaign see Gene Sharp, *Gandhi Wields the Weapon of Moral Power* (Ahmedabad, 1960), chs. 3–6.
64. Nehru, *Toward Freedom*, p. 240.
65. *Ibid.*, pp. 310–11.

66. Moon, *op. cit.*, p. 290; Nehru, *Toward Freedom*, p. 365.
67. Wallbank, *Short History*, p. 188.
68. *Ibid.*, p. 197.
69. *Ibid.*, p. 198.
70. Nirmal Kumar Bose, *Studies in Gandhism*, 2nd rev. ed. (Calcutta, 1947), p. 286.
71. Abul Kalam Azad, *Indian Wins Freedom: An Autobiographical Narrative* (New York, 1960), pp. 87–88.
72. Quoted in Subhas Chandra Bose, *The Indian Struggle: 1920–1942* (New York, 1964), p. 449.
73. Amba Prasad, *The Indian Revolt of 1942* (Delhi, 1958), p. 123.
74. *Ibid.*, p. 61.
75. Nehru, *Discovery of India*, p. 498.
76. Prasad, *op. cit.*, p. 79.
77. Cf. Phillips Talbot, "The Independence of India," *Foreign Policy Reports* XXIII (June 15, 1947): 76.
78. W. Norman Brown, *The United States and India and Pakistan*, rev. ed. (Cambridge, Mass., 1963), p. 125.
79. Cf. Sudhir Ghosh, *Gandhi's Emissary* (London, 1967), part I.
80. *Harijan*, April 20, 1940, cited by Majumdar, *Three Phases*, pp. 54–55.
81. Nehru, *Toward Freedom*, p. 82.
82. Lala Lajpat Rai, *Autobiographical Writings*, ed. V. C. Joshi (New Delhi, 1965), p. 8.
83. Majumdar, *Three Phases*, p. 54.
84. Nehru, *Toward Freedom*, p. 205.
85. Lloyd I. and Susanne Hoeber Rudolph, *The Modernity of Tradition: Political Development in India* (Chicago, 1967), p. 157.
86. Nehru, *Discovery of India*, p. 453.
87. Cf. Sinha, *op. cit.*, p. 154.
88. Wallbank, *India*, p. 135.
89. Cf. Wilhelm E. Mühlmann, *Mahatma Gandhi: Der Mann, sein Werk und seine Wirkung* (Tübingen, 1950), pp. 210–11.
90. James, *op. cit.*, p. 290.

CHAPTER 14

1. Thaung, "Burmese Kingship in Theory and Practice during the Reign of Mindon," *Journal of the Burma Research Society* XLII (1959): part 2, p. 175; John F. Cady, *A History of Modern Burma* (Ithaca, N.Y., 1958), p. 51.
2. Cf. Robert Heine-Geldern, "Conceptions of State and Kingship in Southeast Asia," *Far Eastern Quarterly* II (1942): 17–24; Emanuel Sarkisyanz, *Buddhist Backgrounds of the Burmese Revolution* (The Hague, 1965), pp. 52–53.
3. *Ibid.*, p. 71; Thaung, *op. cit.*, p. 173.
4. Cady, *op. cit.*, pp. 8–9.
5. *Ibid.*, pp. 53–55.

6. Donald E. Smith, *Religion and Politics in Burma* (Princeton, N.J., 1965) p. 32.

7. John F. Cady, "Religion and Politics in Modern Burma," *Far Eastern Quarterly* XII (1953): 151. Another historian concludes that "the majority of the kings of Burma were swarthy tyrants and relentless vandals caring but little for the religion." Niharranjan Ray, *An Introduction to the Study of Theravada Buddhism in Burma* (Calcutta, 1946), p. 257.

8. Sarkisyanz, *op. cit.*, p. 59; Heine-Geldern, *op. cit.*, p. 25.

9. Sarkisyanz, *op. cit.*, pp. 14–15.

10. Thaung, *op. cit.*, pp. 176–77.

11. G. E. Harvey, *History of Burma* (London, 1925), pp. 107 and 235.

12. D. Smeaton, *The Loyal Karens of Burma* (London, 1887), p. 4, cited by Fred R. von der Mehden, *Religion and Nationalism in Southeast Asia* (Madison, Wisc., 1963), p. 124.

13. Cady, *History of Modern Burma*, p. 170; O. H. Mootham, *Burmese Buddhist Law* (Oxford, 1939), pp. 123–24.

14. Cf. Cady, *Far Eastern Quarterly* XII (1953): 153.

15. Cf. Sarkisyanz, *op. cit.*, pp. 152–57.

16. Von der Mehden, *op. cit.*, p. 126.

17. Maung Htin Aung, *The Stricken Peacock: Anglo-Burmese Relations 1752–1948* (The Hague, 1965), p. 1.

18. Cf. Smith, *op. cit.*, pp. 81–86.

19. Cf. U Kyaw Thet, "Continuity in Burma," *The Atlantic* CCI (February 1958): 119.

20. Von der Mehden, *op. cit.*, pp. 7–8; Sarkisyanz, *op. cit.*, pp. 128–30.

21. Hting Aung, *op. cit.*, p. 102.

22. Cf. Albert D. Moscotti, "British Policy in Burma, 1917–1937" (Ph.D. dissertation, Yale University, 1950), pp. 15–16.

23. Cady, *History of Modern Burma*, p. 190.

24. *Ibid.*, p. 212.

25. *Ibid.*, pp. 217–18.

26. *Ibid.*, p. 221.

27. Von der Mehden, *op. cit.*, p. 116.

28. Smith, *op. cit.*, pp. 92–93.

29. *Rangoon Gazette Weekly Budget*, September 19, 1921, quoted in *ibid.*, p. 96.

30. Sarkisyanz, *op. cit.*, pp. 9 and 126–27.

31. Smith, *op. cit.*, p. 105.

32. Cf. Moscotti, *op. cit.*, p. 39.

33. Cf. Smith, *op. cit.*, pp. 93–94.

34. Cady, *History of Modern Burma*, p. 252.

35. Sarkisyanz, *op. cit.*, pp. 145–46.

36. Smith, *op. cit.*, pp. 101–102.

37. *Ibid.*, p. 103.

38. Cady, *History of Modern Burma*, p. 260.

39. Von der Mehden, *op. cit.*, p. 130.
40. Maung Maung, *Burma's Constitution*, 2nd rev. ed. (The Hague, 1961), p. 22; Maurice Collis, *Into Hidden Burma: An Autobiography* (London, 1953), pp. 162–63 (hereafter cited as Collis, *Hidden Burma*).
41. Cady, *History of Modern Burma*, p. 261.
42. *Ibid.*, pp. 281 and 297.
43. Ba U, *My Burma: The Autobiography of a President* (New York, 1959), pp. 104–105.
44. Smith, *op. cit.*, p. 108.
45. Maurice Collis, *Trials in Burma* (London, 1953), p. 214.
46. Sarkisyanz, *op. cit.*, pp. 161–62.
47. Quoted in Von der Mehden, *op. cit.*, p. 155.
48. Great Britain, House of Commons, Sessional Papers 1930–1931, vol. XII, "Report on the Rebellion in Burma up to 3rd May 1931" (London, 1931), pp. 6–8.
49. Great Britain, House of Commons, Sessional Papers 1931–1932, vol. XIX, "Moral and Material Progress and Condition of India during the year 1930–31" (London, 1932), p. 135. A Burmese scholar gives the number of rebels killed as 10,000. Maung Htin Aung, *A History of Burma* (New York, 1967), p. 292.
50. Moscotti, *op. cit.*, pp. 51–52.
51. G. E. Harvey, *British Rule in Burma: 1824–1942* (London, 1946), pp. 73–75.
52. Maung Maung, *op. cit.*, p. 23.
53. Lucian W. Pye, *Politics, Personality and Nation Building: Burma's Search for Identity* (New Haven, 1962), p. 259; Collis, *Hidden Burma*, p. 195.
54. Cady, *History of Modern Burma*, p. 318.
55. *Ibid.*, p. 365.
56. Smith, *op. cit.*, pp. 115–16.
57. Maung Maung, *op. cit.*, p. 30.
58. Von der Mehden, *op. cit.*, p. 148.
59. Cady, *History of Modern Burma*, pp. 305–306.
60. *Ibid.*, p. 394.
61. *Final Report of the Riot Inquiry Committee* (Rangoon, 1939), p. 38, cited by Von der Mehden, *op. cit.*, p. 132.
62. Maung Maung, *op. cit.*, p. 41.
63. Smith, *op cit.*, p. 119.
64. For a detailed discussion see Smith, *op. cit.*, chs. 5–8.
65. Cf. Richard Butwell, *U Nu of Burma* (Stanford, Calif., 1963), p. 67.
66. This observation of Smith, *op. cit.*, p. 124, is based on the study of John F. Brohm, "Burmese Religion and the Burmese Religious Revival" (Ph.D. dissertation, Cornell University, 1957). See also Marie Byles, *Journey into Burmese Silence* (London, 1962).

67. Smith, *op. cit.*, pp. 83 and 113.
68. *Ibid.*, pp. 281–82.

CHAPTER 15

1. Karl Dietrich Erdmann, *Volkssouveränität und Kirche* (Cologne, 1949), p. 65. In his introductory chapter Erdmann gives a good historiographical survey of the rich literature on the Catholic church at the time of the French Revolution, not all of which is explicitly cited in the footnotes of this study. For a concise bibliography see John McManners, *The French Revolution and the Church* (London, 1969), pp. 151–55 (hereafter cited as McManners, *Revolution and Church*), and, dealing with the problem both on the national and local plane, Georges Lefebvre, *The French Revolution: From its Origins to 1793*, trans. Elizabeth M. Evanson (New York, 1965), pp. 323–24. In addition to standard sources, I have been fortunate to be able to use the pamphlet collection of the Comte Alfred Boulay de la Meurthe, now in the possession of Widener Library, Harvard University.
2. Norman Ravitch, *Sword and Mitre: Government and Episcopate in France and England in the Age of the Aristocracy* (The Hague, 1966), p. 69.
3. Ludwig Pastor, *The History of the Popes*, trans. E. F. Peeler, (London, 1953) XL: 95, n. 1.
4. Ravitch, *op. cit.*, p. 180.
5. Cf. M. G. Hutt, "The Curés and the Third Estate: The Ideas of Reform in the Pamphlets of the French Lower Clergy in the Period 1787–1789," *Journal of Ecclesiastical History* VIII (1957): 84; E. E. Y. Hales, *Revolution and Papacy 1759–1846* (London, 1960) p. 296.
6. Hutt, *op. cit.*, pp. 91–92.
7. John McManners, *French Ecclesiastic Society under the Ancien Regime: A Study of Angers in the Eighteenth Century* (Manchester, 1960), p. 167 (hereafter cited as McManners, *French Society*).
8. Pastor, *op. cit.*, p. 111, n. 1.
9. M. G. Hutt, "The Role of the Curés in the Estates General of 1789," *Journal of Ecclesiastical History* VI (1955): 194–95.
10. Cited by Hans Maier, *Revolution and Church: The Early History of Christian Democracy 1789–1901*, trans. Emily M. Schossberger (Notre Dame, Ind., 1969), p. 90.
11. Norman Ravitch, "Liberalism, Catholicism, and the Abbé Grégoire," *Church History* XXXVI (1967): 422.
12. Alphonse Aulard, *Christianity and the French Revolution*, trans. Lady Frazer (New York, 1966), p. 50 (hereafter cited as Aulard, *Christianity*).

13. Lefebvre, *op. cit.*, p. 159; Aulard, *Christianity*, p. 52.
14. Erdmann, *op. cit.*, p. 154.
15. Aulard, *Christianity*, p. 52.
16. *Ibid.*, p. 54.
17. For the complete text of the "Constitution civile du clergé" see Augustin Theiner, *Documents inédits relatifs aux affaires réligieuses de la France: 1790 a 1800* (Paris, 1857), I: 243–63.
18. Article 20, cited by Aulard, *Christianity*, p. 62.
19. McManners, *French Society*, p. 263.
20. *Ibid.*, p. 263.
21. Anne Louis Henri de la Fare, *Quelle doit être l'influence de l'Assemblée Nationale de France sur les matières ecclésiastiques et réligieuses?* (n. p., 1790) pp. 21–22.
22. Jean Sifrein Maury, *Opinion sur la souveraineté du peuple prononceé dans l'Assemblée Nationale en 1790* (Avignon, 1852), p. 9.
23. Paul H. Beik, *The French Revolution Seen from the Right: Social Theories in Motion 1789–1799* (Philadelphia, 1956), p. 33.
24. Augustin de Barruel, *De la réligion dans les révolutions* (n. p., n. d.), p. 26.
25. Cf. Jacques Godechot, *La Contre-Révolution: Doctrine et action 1789–1804* (Paris, 1961), p. 53.
26. Albert Mathiez, *The French Revolution*, trans. Catherine Alison Phillips (New York, 1964), p. 114 (hereafter cited as Mathiez, *French Revolution*).
27. Quoted in *ibid.*, p. 74.
28. Cf. Josef Kiefer, *Die Deputierten Bischöfe der französischen Nationalversammlung und die Constitution Civile du Clergé in den Jahren 1790–1792* (Freiburg i. B., 1903), pp. 44–45.
29. Henri Grégoire, *Légitimité du serment civique exigé des fonctionnaires ecclésiastiques* (Paris, 1791), p. 2.
30. Maier, *op. cit.*, p. 112. See also Ravitch, *Church History* XXXVI (1967): 434–35.
31. Hutt, *Journal of Ecclesiastical History* VI (1955): 219.
32. H. Leclercq, *L'Église Constitutionnelle (Juillet 1790–Avril 1791)* (Paris, 1934), p. 217.
33. For Paris see the careful study of Bernard Plongeron, *Les réguliers de Paris devant le serment constitutionnel,* (Paris, 1964).
34. Paul Pisani, *Répertoire biographique de l'episcopat constitutionnel (1791–1802)* (Paris, 1907), pp. 18–19.
35. Lefebvre, *op. cit.*, p. 170. See also the careful appraisal of McManners, *Revolution and Church*, pp. 48–57.
36. Ravitch, *Church History* XXXVI (1967): 434, n. 65.
37. Cited by Hales, *op. cit.*, p. 85. The full text of the allocution is printed by Theiner, *op. cit.*, I: 1–4.
38. Mathiez, *Revolution* p. 112. See also the same author's *Rome et le clergé français sous la Constituante* (Paris, 1911).
39. The names and clerical background of all the constitutional bish-

ops are provided by Pisani, *op. cit.*, pp. 22–23. Full biographical sketches are given in the substance of this book.

40. Pastor, *op. cit.*, pp. 178–81; the full text of the brief *Quod Aliquantum* is printed in Theiner, *op. cit.*, I: 32–71.

41. *Ibid.*, I: 75–88.

42. Kiefer, *op. cit.*, pp. 83–85; Augustin Sicard, *Le clergé de France pendant la Révolution* (Paris, 1912) I: 166–67.

43. François-Antoine Brendel, *Lettre pastorale de M. L'Évêque du département du Bas-Rhin* [April 22, 1791] (n. p., n. d.), pp. 5–6.

44. Louis Charrier de la Roche, *Lettre pastorale de M. L'Evêque de Rouen* (Rouen, 1791).

45. Aulard, *Christianity*, pp. 87–88.

46. F. Uzureau, "Emery et Maury en 1793," *Revue Historique de la Révolution Française* XV (1923): 279.

47. Jean Leflon, *La crise révolutionnaire 1789–1846* (Paris, 1949), pp. 99–102.

48. Aulard, *Christianity*, p. 89.

49. *Moniteur*, XIV, 8, cited by Ravitch, *Church History* XXXVI (1967): 424.

50. Pastor, *op. cit.*, p. 201.

51. Lefebvre, *op. cit.*, p. 171.

52. Mathiez, *French Revolution*, p. 117.

53. Augustin Sicard, *L'ancien clergé de France*, vol. III: *Les évêques pendant la Révolution de l'exil au Concordat*, 2nd ed. (Paris, 1903), p. 196.

54. *Ibid.*, p. 80.

55. *Correspondance et mémoires inédits du Cardinal Maury* (Paris, 1891), I: 35, cited by Hales, *op. cit.*, p. 93.

56. *Brefs de N. S. P. le Pape Pie VI à l'Empereur des Romains et à l'Impératrice de Russie* (Paris, 1792), pp. 6–7. For the original Latin text see Louis Madelin, "Pie VI et la première coalition: A propos de quelques documents des archives du Saint-Siège," *Revue Historique* LXXXI (1903): 20–21.

57. Leflon, *op. cit.*, p. 96.

58. *Discours de . . . Pie VI. prononcé dans un consistoire secret tenu le 17 Juin 1793*, trans. Abbé de Limon (Brussels, 1793), pp. 10–12.

59. *Ibid.*, p. 23.

60. For a careful discussion of the complex factors underlying the division between jurors and nonjurors see Charles Tilly, *The Vendée* (Cambridge, Mass., 1964), pp. 238–42.

61. *Ibid.*, p. 205.

62. Cf. Godechot, *op. cit.*, pp. 219–23; Tilly, *op. cit.*, p. 318.

63. McManners, *French Society*, p. 285.

64. Mathiez, *French Revolution*, p. 309.

65. Alphonse Aulard, *The French Revolution: A Political History 1789–1804*, trans. Bernard Miall (New York, 1910), II: 307.

66. Ch.-L. Chassin, *La préparation de la guerre de Vendée, 1789-1793* (Paris, 1892), III: 427. A list of priests known to have taken an active part in the uprising is given on p. 439.
67. Cited by Aulard, *French Revolution,* II: 307.
68. Tilly, *op. cit.,* p. 327.
69. *Ibid.,* p. 335.
70. Peter Paret, *Internal War and Pacification: The Vendée, 1789-1796* (Princeton, N.J., 1961), p. 65.
71. *Ibid.,* p. 68.
72. Godechot, *op. cit.,* p. 242.
73. *Lettre pastorale de Monsigneur l'Évêque de Dol* (n. p., n. d.).
74. Louis Blanc and Jacques Crétineau-Joly, *La Contre-Révolution,* ed. Armel de Wismes (Paris, 1961), p. 240. The erroneous date of July 3, 1793 is given for the death of the Bishop of Dol by Pius Bonifacius Gams, ed., *Series Episcoporum Ecclesiae Catholicae* (Graz, 1957), p. 547.
75. Maury, *op. cit.,* p. 207.
76. Augustin de Barruel, *Question nationale sur l'autorité et sur les droits du peuple dans le gouvernement* (Paris, 1791). See also the discussion in Beik, *op. cit.,* p. 47.
77. Augustin de Barruel, *The History of the Clergy during the French Revolution* (London, 1794), part I, p. 2.
78. Cf. Leo XII's encyclical, *Au Milieu de Sollicitudes,* February 16, 1892.
79. [Augustin de Barruel] *Conjuration contre la réligion Catholique et les souverains* (Paris, 1792), p. 9.
80. *Lettre de Monsigneur l'Évêque de Rennes aux prêtres de son diocèse exilés pour a cause de la foi* (Wolfenbüttel, 1796), p. 29.
81. Jean Baptiste Duvoisin, *Défense de l'ordre social contre les principes de la Révolution Francaise* (London, 1798), pp. 132-33.
82. *Devoirs du chrétien envers la puissance publique* (Liege, 1797), p. 7.
83. *Ibid.,* p. 33.
84. Claude le Coz, *Accord de la réligion catholique avec le gouvernement républicain* (Rennes, n. d.), p. 14.
85. *Ibid.,* pp. 19-21.
86. "*Adresse aux Députés de la Seconde Législature,*" September 26, 1791, cited by Lord Ashbourne, *Grégoire and the French Revolution* (London, n. d.), p. 133.
87. Aulard, *Christianity,* p. 98.
88. André Latreille, *L'Église Catholique et la Révolution Française* (Paris, 1946), I: 147.
89. Aulard, *French Revolution,* IV: 163.
90. McManners, *Revolution and Church,* p. 88.
91. Aulard, *Christianity,* p. 113.
92. *Ibid.,* p. 127.
93. Grégoire's speech is reproduced in Augustin Gazier, *Études sur l'histoire réligieuse de la Révolution Française* (Paris, 1887), pp. 341-66 (quotation p. 355).

94. See the statistics in Hales, *op. cit.*, p. 78 and Pastor, *op. cit.*, p. 271.
95. Cf. Pisani, *op. cit.*, pp. 32–33.
96. McManners, *Revolution and Church*, pp. 108–109.
97. *Lettre pastorale de H. Grégoire, Évêque du diocèse de Loir et Cher* (Paris, 1795), p. 15.
98. *Ibid.*, p. 17. An English translation of this pastoral letter is given by Ashbourne, *op. cit.*, pp. 217–36.
99. Gazier, *op. cit.*, pp. 390–411.
100. Aulard, *Christianity*, p. 144.
101. Sicard, *op. cit.*, III: 304.
102. *Avertissement sur la soumission exigée par le décret du 30 mai 1795*, cited by *ibid.*, III: 312.
103. An extensive quote from the papal brief is given by Leflon, *op. cit.*, p. 143.
104. Pastor, *op. cit.*, p. 303.
105. Leflon, *op. cit.*, p. 144.
106. Cf. Paul Pisani, *L'Église de Paris et la Révolution* (Paris, 1910) III: 374.
107. Leflon, *op. cit.*, p. 149.
108. *Lettre inédite du 14 novembre 1797*, cited by Sicard, *op. cit.*, III: 374.
109. Aulard, *French Revolution*, IV: 90; Chassin, *op. cit.*, III: 228.
110. Aulard, *Christianity*, p. 155.
111. Hales, *op. cit.*, pp. 113–15.
112. Pastor, *op. cit.*, p. 362.
113. Jean Baptiste Flavigny, *Instructions pastorales sur l'accord de la réligion avec le gouvernement républicain* (Paris, 1799), p. 34.
114. Cited by Waldemar Gurian, *Die Politischen und sozialen Ideen des französischen Katholizismus 1789–1914* (M. Gladbach, 1929), p. 43.
115. Aulard, *French Revolution*, IV: 212.
116. Cf. Henry H. Walsh, *The Concordat of 1801* (New York, 1933), p. 120.
117. Ch.-L. Chassin, *Les pacifications de l'Ouest 1794–1801* (Paris, 1899), III: 730–34.
118. Hales, *op. cit.*, p. 147.
119. The full text of the Concordat is given by Hales, *op. cit.*, Appendix III.
120. Mathiez in *La Révolution et l'Église* (Paris, 1910) calls it "a truce" consented to by an "ambitious blunderer" (p. 299).
121. One among many political scientists adhering to this piece of conventional wisdom is Samuel P. Huntington in his otherwise thoughtful *Political Order in Changing Societies* (New Haven, 1969), pp. 264–74.
122. Alfred Cobban, *The Social Interpretation of the French Revolution* (Cambridge, 1968), p. 79.
123. D. W. Brogan, *The Price of Revolution* (New York, 1966), p. 18.

CHAPTER 16

1. Frank Tannenbaum, *Peace by Revolution: An Interpretation of Mexico* (New York, 1933), p. 34.
2. Charles C. Cumberland, *Mexico: The Struggle for Modernity* (New York, 1968), p. 177. See also Michael P. Costeloe, *Church Wealth in Mexico* (Cambridge, 1967), pp. 1-29.
3. Tannenbaum, *op. cit.*, p. 50. For a general study of this period see Wilfrid Hardy Calcott, *Church and State in Mexico: 1822-1857* (New York, 1926) and Charle A. Hale, *Mexican Liberalism in the Age of Mora, 1821-1853* (New Haven, 1968), ch. 4.
4. For a detailed study of the nationalization and sale of church property from 1822 until 1875 see Jan Bazant, *Alienation of Church Wealth in Mexico: Social and Economic Aspects of the Liberal Revolution, 1856-1875*, trans. Michael P. Costeloe (Cambridge, 1971).
5. These are the words of a cleric writing as late as 1927, quoted in Wilfrid Hardy Calcott, *Liberalism in Mexico: 1857-1929* (Stanford, Calif., 1931), p. 5.
6. Robert E. Quirk, "Religion and the Mexican Social Revolution," in William V. d'Antonio and Frederick B. Pike, eds., *Religion, Revolution and Reform* (New York, 1964), p. 64.
7. Cited by James W. Wilkie, "The Meaning of the Cristero Religious War against the Mexican Revolution," *Journal of Church and State* VIII (1966): 216.
8. J. Lloyd Mecham, *Church and State in Latin America*, rev. ed. (Chapel Hill, N.C., 1966), p. 389.
9. Quirk, *op. cit.*, p. 70.
10. These are the words of Palomar y Vizcarra in his unpublished memoirs, cited by Wilkie, *Journal of Church and State* VIII (1966): 220.
11. The program of the League is reproduced in Alicia Olivera Sedano, *Aspectos del conflicto religioso de 1926 a 1929* (Mexico, 1963), pp. 91-92.
12. Wilkie, *Journal of Church and State* VIII (1966): 221.
13. An English translation of *Paterna sane* can be found in William F. Montavon, *The Facts Concerning the Mexican Problem* (Washington, D.C., 1926), pp. 48-51.
14. This reconstruction of events by Wilkie, *Journal of Church and State* VIII (1966): 221, is based in large part on an account by Calles' minister of education at the time, J. M. Puig Casauranc; account published in 1936.
15. Mecham, *op. cit.*, p. 391.
16. Ambassador James Sheffield to the secretary of state, February 9, 1926, U.S., Department of State, *Records of the Department of State Relating to the Internal Affairs of Mexico: 1910-29* (Washington, D.C., 1959), S.D. 274, roll 144, 1049 (hereafter cited as *U.S., State Dept. Records*).

17. Mecham, *op. cit.*, p. 392.
18. An English translation of the full text, taken from *El Universal* of February 8, 1926, is given by Ernest Galarza, *The Roman Catholic Church as a Factor in the Political and Social History of Mexico* (Sacramento, Calif., 1928), pp. 152-54.
19. See, for example, Wilfrid Parsons, *Mexican Martyrdom* (New York, 1936), pp. 17-18.
20. Interview with President Calles reported in the *New York Herald Tribune*, February 24, 1926.
21. Cf. Walter Lippmann, "The Church and State in Mexico: The American Mediation," *Foreign Affairs* VIII (1930): 190.
22. Mecham, *op. cit.*, pp. 393-96.
23. Quoted in Montavon, *op. cit.*, p. 38.
24. Leopoldo Lara y Torres, *Documentos para la historia de la persecución religiosa en México* (Mexico, 1954), pp. 108-15.
25. Extensive excerpts from the joint pastoral letter of April 21, 1926 can be found in Montavon, *op. cit.*, pp. 51-58.
26. Lippmann, *op. cit.*, p. 191; Elizabeth Ann Rice, *The Diplomatic Relations between the United States and Mexico, as Affected by the Struggle for Religious Liberty in Mexico, 1925-1929* (Washington, D.C., 1959), p. 89.
27. The text of the two telegrams is given by Alberto María Carreño, *Al Arzobispo de México, Excmo. Sr. Dr. Don Pascual Díaz y el conflicto religioso*, 2nd ed. (Mexico, 1943), pp. 117-18, and by Olivera Sedano, *op. cit.*, p. 100.
28. The full text of the pastoral letter of July 25, 1926 can be found in Alfonso Toro, *La Iglesia y el estado en México* (Mexico, 1927), pp. 404-11, and in Luis C. Balderrama, *El clero y el gobierno de México* (Mexico, 1927), II: 17-21.
29. Nathan L. Whetten, *Rural Mexico* (Chicago, 1948), p. 469.
30. Quirk, *op. cit.*, p. 62.
31. Ernest Gruening, *Mexico and its Heritage* (New York, 1928), p. 277.
32. See the statements of Calles to a Hearst correspondent of July 26, 1926 and to the *New York Times* of July 27, 1926 in Balderrama, *op. cit.*, II: 11-28.
33. Full text in *ibid.*, pp. 51-52.
34. Text in *ibid.*, pp. 55-58.
35. Rice, *op. cit.*, pp. 90-91. A detailed report of the discussions held on August 21, 1926 is given by Carreño, *op. cit.*, pp. 126-35.
36. Galarza, *op. cit.*, p. 162. For the text of the petition see Balderrama, *op. cit.*, II: 149-54.
37. Wilkie, *Journal of Church and State* VIII (1966): 225; Olivera Sedano, *op. cit.*, pp. 113-14.
38. *Ibid.*, p. 143.
39. *Ibid.*, pp. 163-66.
40. *Ibid.*, pp. 200-201.

41. Cumberland, *op. cit.*, p. 280.
42. Gruening, *op. cit.*, p. 279; Olivera Sedano, *op. cit.*, p. 172.
43. Cumberland, *op. cit.*, p. 280.
44. Carleton Beals, *Mexican Maze* (New York, 1931), p. 312.
45. *Ibid.*, p. 323.
46. Olivera Sedano, *op. cit.*, p. 173.
47. Jesús Degollado Guizar, *Memorias de Jesús Degollado Guizar, ultimo general en jefe del ejercito cristero* (Mexico, 1957), p. 263.
48. Rice, *op. cit.*, p. 173.
49. Interview with Palomar y Vizcarra, April 1964, in James W. Wilkie and Edna Monzón de Wilkie, *México visto en el siglo XX: Entrevistas de historia oral* (Mexico, 1969), p. 456 (hereafter cited as Wilkie, *Historia oral*); Heriberto Navarrette, *Por Dios y por la patria: Memorias* (Mexico, 1961), p. 264.
50. Olivera Sedano, *op. cit.*, p. 225.
51. Degollado Guizar, *op. cit.*, p. 234.
52. Wilkie, *Journal of Church and State* VIII (1966): 230–31.
53. Cf. *U.S., State Dept. Records*, S.D. 274, roll 145.
54. Carreño, *op. cit.*, pp. 280–81, 302.
55. Olivera Sedano, *op. cit.*, p. 250; Carreño, *op. cit.*, p. 41.
56. Olivera Sedano, *op. cit.*, pp. 115–18; Leopoldo Ruiz y Flores, *Recuerdo de recuerdos* (Mexico, 1942), p. 85; Wilkie, *Journal of Church and State* VIII (1966): 225.
57. Interview with Palomar y Vizcarra, April 1964, Wilkie, *Historia oral*, p. 443.
58. Wilkie, *Journal of Church and State* VIII (1966): 225–26.
59. Interview with Palomar y Vizcarra, May 1, 1964, in *ibid.*, p. 226.
60. Cited by Rice, *op. cit.*, p. 120.
61. Parsons, *op. cit.*, p. 25.
62. Carreño, *op. cit.*, p. 171.
63. Cited by Gruening, *op. cit.*, p. 280 and Lippmann, *op. cit.*, p. 197.
64. *Loc. cit.*
65. Gruening, *op. cit.*, p. 280.
66. Interview with Palomar y Vizcarra, April 1964, Wilkie, *Historia oral*, pp. 445–46.
67. Rice, *op. cit.*, p. 122.
68. Cited by Mecham, *op. cit.*, p. 400 and Charles W. Hackett, "Manufacturing Ill Will between the United States and Mexico," *Current History* XXVI (1927): 472.
69. *Ibid.*, p. 473.
70. *Loc. cit.*
71. Carreño, *op. cit.*, pp. 97–105.
72. *Ibid.*, pp. 106–108.
73. Lippmann, *op. cit.*, p. 200.
74. Letter of Burke to Calles, March 29, 1928, full text in Rice, *op. cit.*, pp. 202–203.
75. Calles to Burke, April 28, 1928, *ibid.*, p. 203.

76. Lara y Torres, *op. cit.*, pp. 247–91.
77. Olivera Sedano, *op. cit.*, p. 208; Beals, *op. cit.*, pp. 328–32.
78. Olivera Sedano, *op. cit.*, pp. 216–17.
79. Lippmann, *op. cit.*, p. 203.
80. Wilkie, *Journal of Church and State* VIII (1966): 229.
81. Full text in Rice, *op. cit.*, pp. 205–206.
82. *Ibid.*, p. 206.
83. Lippmann, *op. cit.*, p. 206.
84. Message of August 1929, Degollado Guizar, *op. cit.*, pp. 270–73.
85. Wilkie, *Journal of Church and State* VIII (1966): 231.
86. *Loc. cit.*
87. Carreño, *op. cit.*, pp. 414–17.
88. Cumberland, *op. cit.*, p. 283.
89. Mecham, *op. cit.*, p. 404.
90. Cumberland, *op. cit.*, p. 283; Mecham, *op. cit.*, pp. 404–405.
91. Cumberland, *op. cit.*, p. 288.
92. Mecham, *op. cit.*, p. 408.
93. For an English translation see *Catholic Mind* XXX (November 8, 1932): 409–19.
94. Cf. Alberto María Carreño, *Pastorales, edictos y otros documentos del Excmo. y Revmo. Sr. Dr. D. Pascual Díaz, arzobispo de México* (Mexico, 1938), pp. 262–69.
95. Letter of Sept. 7, 1934, cited by Emilio Portes Gil, *The Conflict between the Civil Power and the Clergy* (Mexico, 1935), pp. 122–23. The original Spanish edition is *La Lucha entre el poder civil y el clero* (Mexico, 1934).
96. "Third Message to the Civilized World" of August 1934 in *ibid.*, pp. 114–16.
97. Joaquín Blanco Gil, *El clamor de la sangre* (Mexico, 1947), cited by Lyle C. Brown, "Mexican Church-State Relations, 1933–1940," *Journal of Church and State* VI (1964): 208.
98. Degollado Guizar, *op. cit.*, p. 277.
99. Brown, *op. cit.*, p. 208.
100. *Ibid.*, p. 209, n. 31.
101. See Albert L. Michaels, "Fascism and Sinarquismo: Popular Nationalisms Against the Mexican Revolution," *Journal of Church and State* VIII (1966): 234–50.
102. Brown, *op. cit.*, p. 219.
103. The English text of *Nos es muy* can be found in Sidney Z. Ehler and John B. Morrall, eds. *Church and State Through the Centuries* (London, 1954), pp. 582–92 (quotation p. 587).
104. *Ibid.*, p. 589.
105. James W. Wilkie, "Statistical Indicators of the Impact of the National Revolution on the Catholic Church in Mexico, 1910–1967," *Journal of Church and State* XII (1970): 97.
106. Quirk, *op. cit.*, p. 71.

CHAPTER 17

1. Gabriel Jackson, *The Spanish Republic and the Civil War: 1931–1939* (Princeton, N.J., 1965), p. 286. Similar figures are given by Hugh Thomas, *The Spanish Civil War* (New York, 1963), p. 173 (hereafter cited as Thomas, *Civil War*). More detailed statistics are to be found in the generally reliable *Historia de la persecución religiosa en España 1936–1939* (Madrid, 1961), pp. 762–64, by Antonio Montero.

2. Gerald Brenan, *The Spanish Labyrinth: An Account of the Social and Political Background of the Civil War* (Cambridge, 1943), p. 44.

3. Introduction to Alfred Mendizabal, *The Martyrdom of Spain: Origins of the Civil War*, trans. Charles Hope Lumley (London, 1938), pp. 12–13, n. 1.

4. Salvador de Madariaga, *Spain: A Modern History* (New York, 1958), p. 495.

5. José M. Sánchez, "The Second Spanish Republic and the Holy See: 1931–36," *Catholic Historical Review* XLIX (1963): 54.

6. Quoted in Edgar Allison Peers, *The Spanish Tragedy: 1930–1936* (New York, 1936), p. 53.

7. Thomas, *Civil War*, p. 29.

8. Jackson, *op. cit.*, p. 34.

9. Sánchez, *op. cit.*, pp. 55–57; Jackson, *op. cit.*, pp. 35–36, 49–50.

10. Stanley G. Payne, *The Spanish Revolution* (New York, 1970), p. 85.

11. Quoted in *Basques: Bulletin of the Basque Delegation in the U.S.A.* no. 5 (November 1943): 5.

12. Jackson, *op. cit.*, p. 106.

13. Felipe Diez Hidalgo, S.J., *El catecismo de la doctrina Cristiana* (Madrid, 1934), p. 675, quoted in Edgar Allison Peers, *Spain, the Church and the Orders* (London, 1939), p. 37.

14. From a catechism by Angel María de Arcos, S.J., quoted in John Langdon-Davies, *The Spanish Church and Politics* (London, 1937), p. 5.

15. A comprehensive study of the Spanish Right, with emphasis on the CEDA, is made by Richard A. H. Robinson, *The Origins of Franco's Spain: The Right, the Republic and Revolution, 1931–1936* (London, 1970).

16. Luigi Sturzo, "The Right to Rebel," *The Dublin Review* CCI (1937): 33.

17. For a careful examination of the agrarian problem see Edward E. Malefakis, *Agrarian Reform and Peasant Revolution in Spain: Origins of the Civil War* (New Haven, 1970).

18. For a detailed discussion of the election and its results see Jack-

son, *op. cit.*, ch. 10. For the view that the victory of the Popular Front was fraudulent see the report of a commission of jurists appointed by General Franco in 1938. *Dictamen de la comisión sobre ilegitimidad de poderes actuantes el 18 de julio de 1936* (Madrid, 1946).

19. The story of the red plot can be found in most histories of the period coming out of Franco Spain, and it has been accepted as true by practically all Catholic writers outside Spain. See, for example, Richard Pattee, *This is Spain* (Milwaukee, 1951), p. 507. Gabriel Jackson, *op. cit.*, pp. 514–17, firmly rejects the existence of such a plot, and the same conclusion is reached by David T. Cattell in his careful study, *Communism and the Spanish Civil War* (Berkeley, 1955), pp. 42–43. The British historian Hugh Thomas, *Civil War*, p. 108, accepts the documents describing the plans for a communist *coup d'état* as genuine but adds: "They do not justify the rising of the generals, because the plans for this were already far advanced before the plans of their enemies could have been prepared."

20. Claude G. Bowers, *My Mission to Spain* (New York, 1954), p. 200.

21. At the time of the Civil War reports of wholesale torture of priests were often exaggerated but that such deeds did occur cannot be doubted. "Many of these crimes," writes Hugh Thomas, "were accompanied by a partly frivolous, partly sadistic cruelty. . . . Several priests were undoubtedly burned alive" (*Civil War*, pp. 173–74).

22. The case of a tunnel between a church and a priest's home on Ibiza (one of the Balearic islands) filled with firearms is related by Elliot Paul, *The Life and Death of a Spanish Town* (New York, 1937), p. 361.

23. Thomas, *Civil War*, p. 175.

24. John David Hughey, Jr., *Religious Freedom in Spain: Its Ebb and Flow* (London, 1955), p. 133.

25. José Antonio de Aguirre, *Escape via Berlin* (New York, 1944), p. 296.

26. Isidro Gomá y Tomás, *Por Dios y por España* (Barcelona, 1940), pp. 312–13.

27. Isidro Gomá y Tomás, *Pastorales de la guerra de España* (Madrid, 1955), p. 53.

28. The full text of "Los dios Ciudades" is reproduced in Montero, *op. cit.*, pp. 688–708.

29. Cattell, *op. cit.*, p. 208; Franz Borkenau, *The Spanish Cockpit* (London, 1937), p. 289.

30. Arthur H. Ryan, *Spain and the World of Today* (New York, 1948), pp. 26–27.

31. Antonio Ruiz Vilaplana, *Burgos Justice: A Year's Experience of*

Nationalist Spain, trans. W. H. Carter (New York, 1938), p. 177; Antonio Bahamonde y Sanchez de Castro, *Memoirs of a Spanish Nationalist* (London, 1939), p. 69.

32. Georges Bernanos, *A Diary of My Times*, trans. Pamela Morris (New York, 1938), p. 94.

33. Jackson, *op. cit.*, p. 306.

34. Bernanos, *op. cit.*, p. 8.

35. Aguirre, *op. cit.*, p. 327.

36. Hugh Thomas estimates the number of persons killed by the Nationalists outside the battle zone to be about 40,000 (*Civil War*, p. 631). Gabriel Jackson gives the figures of 200,000 and concludes that "Nationalist political executions during and after the war constituted the largest single category of deaths attributable to the Civil War (*op. cit.*, p. 538).

37. Thomas, *Civil War*, p. 170.

38. Introduction to Mendizabal, *op. cit.*, pp. 34-35.

39. Luigi Sturzo, *Politics and Morality*, trans. Barbara B. Carter (London, 1938), p. 74.

40. A. de Lizarra, *Los Vascos y la república Española* (Buenos Aires, 1944), p. 215. Two recent students of the Civil War call the collective letter "designed for export." Pierre Broué and Emile Témine, *The Revolution and the Civil War in Spain*, trans. Tony White (London, 1972), p. 435.

41. *Joint Letter of the Spanish Bishops to the Bishops of the Whole World: The War in Spain* (New York, 1937), p. 2.

42. *Ibid.*, pp. 5-6.

43. *Ibid.*, pp. 7-8.

44. *Ibid.*, pp. 9-11.

45. *Ibid.*, pp. 12-17, 22-23, 25.

46. Bahamonde, *op. cit.*, p. 63.

47. Jackson, *op. cit.*, p. 307.

48. Aniceto de Castro Albarrán, *Guerra santa: El sentido Católico de la guerra Española* (Burgos, 1938), p. 73.

49. *Ibid.*, pp. 22-23, 56.

50. *Ibid.*, p. 94.

51. *Ibid.*, p. 115.

52. Juan Rey Carrera, S.J., *El resurgir de España previsto por nuestros grandes pensadores* (San Sebastian, 1938), p. 402.

53. See, e.g., F. Guerrero, "La obediencia a la autoridad," *Razón y Fe* CXIV (1938): 129-40; J. de la C. Martinez, "Es compatible la guerra Española con la caridad Cristiana?" *Razón y Fe* CXIII (1938): 302-27. In a pamphlet published in America in 1937 CEDA leader Gil Robles argued the same position: "The Spanish Rightists found themselves faced by a situation uniting all the conditions which, according to the traditional doctrine of Catholic political ethics, justified resistance to oppression, not only

passively, but actively, through the use of armed force." *Spain in Chains*, trans. Carmen de Arango (New York, 1937), pp. 15–16.

54. Aniceto Castro Albarrán, *El derecho al alzamiento* (Salamanca, 1941), p. 401. This was a revised edition of a work published in 1934 under the title *El derecho a la rebeldía*, a book that has been called "the doctrinal ancestor of the armed uprising against the Republic." Juan de Iturralde, *El Catolicismo y la crusada de Franco* (n.p., n.d.), p. 440. Iturralde's work, published in France in two volumes in 1955 and 1960, is that "of an exiled Basque priest whose pseudonym "Iturralde" means 'close to the source'" (Jackson, *op. cit.*, p. 107).

55. Charles A. Thomson, "Spain: Civil War," *Foreign Policy Reports* XII (1936–37): 260.

56. Francis McCullagh, *In Franco's Spain* (London, 1937), p. 172.

57. Thomson, *op. cit.*, p. 183.

58. Gomá, *Por Dios y por España*, pp. 146–47.

59. Arnold J. Toynbee, *Survey of International Affairs 1938* (London, 1941), I: 298; Charles Foltz, Jr., *The Masquerade in Spain* (Boston, 1948), p. 135.

60. Gomá, *Por Dios y por España*, p. 176. I have used the English translation of Rafael Calvo Serer, "The Church in Spanish Public Life since 1936," in Waldemar Gurian and M. A. Fitzsimons, eds., *The Church in World Affairs* (Notre Dame, Ind., 1954), p. 312.

61. Law of November 9, 1939 Reestablishing the Budget of the Clergy. The passage cited is from Calvo Serer, *op. cit.*, p. 312.

62. *New Society* V, no. 135 (April 29, 1965): 11–13.

63. *New York Times*, September 17, 1971, p. 3.

64. Thomas, *New Society* V, no. 135 (April 29, 1965): 12.

65. Brenan, *op. cit.*, p. 278.

66. The full text of the pastoral letter can be found in Montero, *op. cit.*, pp. 682–86 (quotation p. 684). I have used the English translation in De Azpilikoeta (pseudonym for José Antonio Aguirre, the Basque Leader), *The Basque Problem as Seen by Cardinal Gomá and President Aguirre* (New York, 1938), p. 106.

67. *Ibid.*, p. 142; J. de Hiriartia, *The Case of the Basque Catholics* (New York, 1939), p. 33.

68. The letter can be found in Montero, *op. cit.*, pp. 686–87.

69. Letter of Múgica to Victor Montserrat (pseudonym of a Catalan priest and author of a pamphlet, *Le Drame d'un peuple incompris: La Guerre au pays Basque* [Paris, 1937]) of July 25, 1937, full text in Iturralde, *op. cit.*, II: 326–28. See also J. de Bivort de la Saudée, "Les Martyrs d'Espagne et l'alliance Basco-Communiste," *Revue des Deux Mondes* LV (1940): 712; Angel de Zumeta, *La guerra civil en Euzkadi* (Paris, 1937), preface.

70. Azpilikoeta, *op. cit.*, pp. 128–29.

71. *Basques*, no. 1 (March 1943): 3.

72. The best account of life in the Basque provinces is George L. Steer's *The Tree of Guernica* (London, 1938).

73. Short biographical sketches of the killed Basque priests are given in *La clergé Basque: Rapports présentés par des prêtres Basques aux autorités ecclésiastiques* (Paris, 1938), pp. 95–107.

74. Azpilikoeta, *op. cit.*, p. 35.

75. *Ibid.*, pp. 33–34.

76. *Ibid.*, p. 98. The Spanish original of this pastoral letter can be found in Gomá, *Pastorales de la Guerra*, pp. 73–93.

77. Azpilikoeta, *op. cit.*, p. 112.

78. *Ibid.*, p. 158.

79. *Ibid.*, p. 160.

80. *Basques*, no. 5 (November 1943): 5.

81. Thomas, *Civil War*, p. 420 (based on the evidence of Fr. Onaindia).

82. Aguirre, *op. cit.*, pp. 51–54; Bivort, *op. cit.*, pp. 717–18.

83. Foltz, *op. cit.*, p. 320.

84. Lizarra, *op. cit.*, pp. 207–209; Prince Hubertus Friedrich von Loewenstein estimated in 1937 that 2000 masses were being said every day in private houses in Barcelona. *A Catholic in Republican Spain* (London, 1937), p. 31.

85. Toynbee, *op. cit.*, p. 287.

86. Thomas, *Civil War*, p. 495; Lizarra, *op. cit.*, p. 239; Herbert L. Matthews, *The Yoke and the Arrows: A Report on Spain* (New York, 1957), p. 141.

87. Pius XI, *To the Spanish Refugees* [*Discourse of September 14, 1936*] (New York, 1937), p. 20.

88. *Ibid.*, pp. 20–21.

89. U.S., Department of State, *Documents on German Foreign Policy 1918–1945*, Ser. D. vol. III (Washington, D.C., 1950), doc. 168, p. 189.

90. Preface of Constantino Bayle, S.J., to Gomá, *Por Dios y por España*, p. 8.

91. Encyclical *Divini redemptoris*, March 19, 1937, in Sidney Z. Ehler and John B. Morrall, eds., *Church and State through the Centuries* (London, 1954), pp. 553 and 570.

92. Encyclical *Nos es Muy*, March 28, 1937, *ibid.*, pp. 589–90.

93. Camille M. Cianfarra, *The Vatican and the War* (New York, 1944), p. 107.

94. For instances of Spanish Catholic pressure exerted upon American Catholic reporters in Spain see Foster Jay Taylor, *The United States and the Spanish Civil War* (New York, 1956), p. 151. See also Allen Guttmann, *The Wound in the Heart: America and the Spanish Civil War* (New York, 1962), ch. 3.

95. Cited by Thomas, *Civil War*, pp. 602–603.

96. Radio address "Con immenso gozo," April 16, 1939, *The Tablet* CLXXIII (1939): 514.

97. No. 497 (1939), p. 191, cited by Calvo Serer, *op. cit.*, p. 310.
98. *Church and State in Spain* (Madrid, 1962), pp. 39–40.
99. Luigi Sturzo, *Church and State*, trans. Barbara Barclay Carter (Notre Dame, Ind., 1962), II: 512.

CHAPTER 18

1. Quoted in Fayez Sayegh, "The Theoretical Structure of Nasser's Arab Socialism" in *St. Antony's Papers*, no. 17, Middle Eastern Affairs, no. 4 (London, 1965), p. 13.
2. Elie Salem, "Nationalism and Islam," *Muslim World* LII (1962): 277. See generally, Sylvia G. Haim, ed., *Arab Nationalism: An Anthology* (Berkeley, Calif., 1962), Introduction.
3. Cf. Anwar G. Chejne, "Egyptian Attitudes Towards Pan-Arabism," *Middle East Journal* XI (1957): 254–256.
4. *Ibid.*, pp. 260–61.
5. Cf. Leonard Binder, "Radical-Reform Nationalism in Syria and Egypt," *Muslim World* LLIX (1959): 105–106.
6. Gamal Abdul Nasser, *Egypt's Liberation: The Philosophy of the Revolution* (Washington, D.C., 1955), pp. 86–87.
7. *Ibid.*, p. 113.
8. Salem, *op. cit.*, p. 282.
9. Cf. Sylvia G. Haim, "Islam and the Theory of Arab Nationalism," in W. Z. Laqueur, ed., *The Middle East in Transition* (New York, 1958), p. 293.
10. Malcolm H. Kerr, "Islam and Arab Socialism," *Muslim World* LVI (1966): 277.
11. Richard H. Pfaff, "The Function of Arab Nationalism," *Comparative Politics* II (1970), 158.
12. Cf. Hisham B. Sharabi, *Nationalism and Revolution in the Arab World* (Princeton, N.J., 1966), p. 97.
13. Malcolm Kerr, *The Arab Cold War 1958–1967* (London, 1967), p. 31 (hereafter cited as Kerr, *Arab Cold War*). See also Monte Palmer, "The United Arab Republic: An Assessment of Its Failure," *Middle East Journal* XX (1966): 50–67.
14. *The National Charter of the United Arab Republic*, cited by Sharabi, *op. cit.*, p. 135. See also George Lenczowski, "The Objects and Methods of Nasserism," *Journal of International Affairs* XIX (1965): 69.
15. Cf. Kerr, *Arab Cold War*, p. 146.
16. Speech on February 22, 1966, in United Arab Republic, Supreme Council for Islamic Affairs, *The Islamic Pact: An Obvious Trick* (Cairo, n.d.), p. 50.
17. *Ibid.*, p. 44.
18. Cf. Malcolm H. Kerr, *Islamic Reform: The Political and Legal Theories of Muhammad Abduh and Rashid Rida* (Berkeley, Calif., 1966), p. 2 (hereafter cited as Kerr, *Islamic Reform*).

19. *Bourse égyptienne*, January 26, 1954, quoted in Patrick O'Brien, *The Revolution in Egypt's Economic System: From Private Enterprise to Socialism 1952–1965* (London, 1966), p. 68.

20. P. J. Vatikiotis, *The Egyptian Army in Politics* (Bloomington, Ind., 1961), p. 75.

21. O'Brien, *op. cit.*, p. 84.

22. Charles Issawi, *Egypt in Revolution: An Economic Analysis* (London, 1963), p. 54.

23. The July decrees are described in more detail in Malcolm Kerr, "The Emergence of a Socialist Ideology in Egypt," *Middle East Journal* XVI (1962): 128–29.

24. Issawi, *op. cit.*, pp. 61–62; O'Brien, *op. cit.*, pp. 130–31.

25. Rashed al-Barawy, *Economic Development in the United Arab Republic (Egypt)* (Cairo, 1970), p. 81.

26. Speech on August 17, 1961, quoted in Sayegh, *op. cit.*, p. 30.

27. Speech on November 25, 1961: "Battles and Achievements of the Political and Social Revolution" (Cairo, n.d.), p. 38.

28. *The Charter*, quoted in Sharabi, *op. cit.*, pp. 129–30. Further relevant excerpts from the Charter, based on a different translation, can be found in Sami A. Hanna and George H. Gardner, eds., *Arab Socialism: A Documentary Survey* (Leiden, 1969), pp. 344–72.

29. Sharabi, *op. cit.*, p. 131.

30. Gamal Abdul Nasser, *Address at the Opening Meeting of the Second Session of the National Assembly, November 12, 1964* (Cairo, n.d.), p. 36 (hereafter cited as Nasser, *Address of November 12, 1964*).

31. Anouar Abdel-Malek, *Egypte: Société militaire* (Paris, 1962), p. 64.

32. Issawi, *op. cit.*, p. 120. See also Bent Hansen and Girgis A. Marzouk, *Development and Economic Policy in the UAR* (Amsterdam, 1965), pp. 84–93.

33. R. Hrair Dekmejian, *Egypt under Nasir: A Study in Political Dynamics* (Albany, N.Y., 1971), p. 329, n. 36.

34. O'Brien, *op. cit.*, p. 313.

35. Nasser, *Address of November 12, 1964*, pp. 48 and 63.

36. Gamal Abdul Nasser, *Majmu'at Khutb wa-Tasrihat wa-Bayanat* (A Collection of Speeches, Statements, and Announcements) (Cairo, 1964), pp. 560, 407, and 210.

37. "The Mufti Answers Your Questions," *Minbar al-Islam: A Quarterly Magazine Devoted to the Cause of Islam* II, no. 3 (July 1962): 58 (hereafter cited as *Minbar al-Islam*, English ed.).

38. *Ibid.*, p. 60.

39. *Ibid.*, p. 59.

40. Husni Abdul-Majid, "Da'wat al-Mithaq al-Watani min Da'wat al-Islam (The Cause of the National Charter Is the Cause of Islam)," *Minbar al-Islam* XXIV, no. 9 (December 12, 1966): 52.

41. Mohammed Mohammed al-Madani, "Al-Ishtirakiyah al-Arabiyah fil-Mizan (Arab-Socialism in the Balance)," *Minbar al-Islam* XXIV, no. 7 (October 15, 1966): 22.

42. Hanafi Sharaf, "Al-Ishtirakiyah al-Arabiyah Ruh al-'Aqida al-Islamiyah (Arab Socialism is in the Spirit of Islamic Belief)," *Minbar al-Islam* XXV, no. 11 (February 10, 1967): 165.

43. Mohammed Mitwali al-Nizami, "Al-Ishtirakiyah fi al-Islam (Socialism in Islam)," *Minbar al-Islam* XXIV, no. 5 (August 17, 1966): 227.

44. H. A. R. Gibb, "The Heritage of Islam in the Modern World," *International Journal of Middle East Studies* II (1971): 141.

45. H. A. R. Gibb, "Religion and Politics in Christianity and Islam," in J. Harris Proctor, ed., *Islam and International Relations* (New York, 1965), p. 21.

46. Kerr, *Islamic Reform*, p. 220.

47. G. Ignaz Goldziher, *Vorlesungen über den Islam* (Heidelberg, 1910), p. 48.

48. H. A. R. Gibb, *Modern Trends in Islam* (Chicago, 1947), p. 105.

49. Kerr, *Muslim World* LVI (1966): 277–78.

50. *Ibid.*, p. 281.

51. Jean and Simonne Lacouture, *Egypt in Transition*, trans. Francis Scarfe (London, 1958), p. 440.

52. Cf. Hans E. Tütsch, *Facets of Arab Nationalism* (Detroit, 1965), p. 59.

53. Speech on July 28, 1963, in *Speeches and Press Interviews: January–December 1963* (Cairo, n.d.), p. 188.

54. Speech on March 8, 1965, *Pre-election Speeches . . . March 1965* (Cairo, n.d.), p. 13.

55. Gustave E. von Grunebaum, "Problems of Muslim Nationalism," in Richard N. Frye, ed., *Islam and the West* (The Hague, 1957), p. 27.

56. Anwar al-Sadat, *Nahwa Ba'th Hadid* (Toward a New Revival) (Cairo, n.d.), p. 14.

57. Ibrahim Abu-Lughod, "Retreat from the Secular Path? Islamic Dilemmas of Arab Politics," *Review of Politics* XXVII (1966): 467–68.

58. Tom Little, *Modern Egypt* (New York, 1967), p. 245.

59. Saad M. Gadalla, *Land Reform in Relation to Social Development in Egypt* (Columbia, Mo., 1962), pp. 83–84.

60. Cf. M. D. Gilsenan, "Some Factors in the Decline of the Sufi Orders in Modern Egypt," *Muslim World* LVII (1967): 11–18. In 1964 Morroe Berger found 64 functioning Sufi orders in Egypt that involved hundreds of thousands of primarily poor people. See his *Islam in Egypt: Social and Political Aspects of Popular Religion* (Cambridge, 1970), pp. 67–81.

61. For the history of the Brotherhood until 1960 see Richard Paul Mitchell, *The Society of Muslim Brothers* (London, 1969).

62. Sayyid Qutb, *Al-Islam wa-Mushkilat al-Hadarah* (Islam and the Problems of Civilization) (Cairo, 1962), pp. 181–84.
63. *Egyptian Gazette,* August 30, 1966.
64. *New York Times,* November 11, 1967.
65. Translated by *Atlas,* May 1966, p. 299.
66. Cf. P. J. Vatikiotis, "Dilemmas of Political Leadership in the Arab Middle East? The Case of the U.A.R.," *International Affairs* XXXVII (1961): 195.
67. Morroe Berger, *The Arab World Today* (Garden City, N.Y., 1962), p. 295.
68. Henry Habib Ayrout, *The Egyptian Peasant,* trans. John Alden Williams (Boston, 1963), p. 109.
69. James B. Mayfield, *Rural Politics in Nasser's Egypt: A Quest for Legitimacy* (Austin, Texas, 1971), p. 254.
70. Vatikiotis, *International Affairs* XXXVII (1961): 192.
71. David E. Apter, "Political Religion in the New Nations," in Clifford Geertz, ed., *Old Societies and New States* (New York, 1963), p. 78.
72. John S. Badeau, "Islam and the Modern Middle East," *Foreign Affairs* XXXVIII (1958): 61–62.

CHAPTER 19

1. Walpola Rahula, *History of Buddhism in Ceylon: The Anuradhapura Period 3rd Century* B.C.—*10th Century* A.C. (Colombo, 1956), p. 75.
2. Cf. Wilhelm Geiger, *Culture of Ceylon in Mediaeval Times* (Wiesbaden, 1960), pp. 111, 203–206; Ralph Pieris, *Sinhalese Social Organisation: The Kandyan Period* (Colombo, 1956), pp. 10–11.
3. *The Mahavamsa or the Great Chronicle of Ceylon,* trans. Wilhelm Geiger, xxv. 110–111 (Colombo, 1950), p. 178.
4. Heinz Bechert, *Buddhismus, Staat und Gesellschaft in den Ländern des Theravada—Buddhismus* (Frankfurt a. M., 1966), I: 363.
5. Richard A. Gard, "Buddhism and Political Authority," in Harold D. Lasswell and Harlan Cleveland, eds., *The Ethic of Power* (New York, 1962), p. 46.
6. Colvin R. De Silva, *Ceylon Under the British Occupation: 1795–1833* (Colombo, 1941), I: 153.
7. For this discussion of Buddhism under British rule I have relied mainly on Lennox A. Mills, *Ceylon Under British Rule: 1795–1932* (New York, 1965); G. C. Mendis, *Ceylon Under the British,* 2nd rev. ed. (Colombo, 1946); Frederic A. Hayley, *A Treatise on the Laws and Customs of the Sinhalese* (Colombo, 1923).
8. *Ceylon Today* VII, no. 10 (October 1958): 5.
9. Bhikshu Sangharakshita, "Anagarika Dharmapala: A Biographical

Sketch," *Maha Bodhi Society, Diamond Jubilee Souvenir* (Calcutta, 1952), p. 53, cited by Bechert, *op. cit.*, pp. 50-51.

10. The most careful discussion of the organizational structure of the Ceylonese Sangha is found in Bechert, *op. cit.*, pp. 210-67. The relationship of Sangha to caste is discussed by Bryce Ryan, *Caste in Modern Ceylon: The Sinhalese System in Transition* (New Brunswick, N.J., 1953), pp. 40-42.

11. Bechert, *op. cit.*, pp. 312-13.

12. *Ibid.*, p. 314.

13. Cf. Daniel T. Niles, "Resurgent Buddhism in Ceylon and the Christian Church," *International Review of Missions* XXXII (1943): 258-63.

14. The full title is *Dharma-Vijaya (Triumph of Righteousness) or The Revolt in the Temple: Composed to Commemorate 2500 Years of the Land, the Race and the Faith* (Colombo, 1953). The title page does not list an author but the latter is identified in the body of the book (p. 676) as D. C. Vijayavardhana (Wijewardene in the more Anglicized form of this name).

15. *Ibid.*, p. 568.

16. *Ibid.*, p. 550.

17. *Ibid.*, p. 547.

18. *Ibid.*, p. 363.

19. *Ibid.*, p. 377.

20. *Ibid.*, p. 583.

21. *Ibid.*, p. 585.

22. *Ibid.*, p. 586.

23. *Ibid.*, p. 17.

24. *Ibid.*, p. 554.

25. *Ibid.*, pp. 555-56.

26. *Ibid.*, p. 438.

27. *Ibid.*, p. 223.

28. Cf. W. Howard Wriggins, *Ceylon: Dilemmas of a New Nation* (Princeton, 1960), pp. 208-209. See also Hans-Dieter Evers, "Buddhistische Gesellschaftsordnung und Buddhistischer Wohlfahrtsstaat: Religionssoziologische Grundlagen des Ceylonesischen Nationalismus," *Moderne Welt* IV (1963): 274-77.

29. U Thittila, "The Fundamental Principles of Theravada Buddhism," in Kenneth W. Morgan, ed., *The Path of the Buddha* (New York, 1956), p. 76.

30. *Revolt in the Temple*, p. 595.

31. Buddhist Committee of Inquiry, *The Betrayal of Buddhism: An Abridged Version of the Report of the Buddhist Committee of Inquiry* (Balangoda, 1956).

32. *Ibid.*, p. 23.

33. *Ibid.*, p. 99.

34. *Ibid.*, p. 109.

35. *Ibid.*, p. 33.

36. Cf. G. C. Mendis, *Ceylon Today and Yesterday: Main Currents of Ceylon History* (Colombo, 1957), p. 108.
37. S. W. R. D. Bandaranaike, *The Government and the People: A Collection of Speeches* (Colombo, 1959), p. 83.
38. Wriggins, *op. cit.*, p. 327.
39. Donald E. Smith, ed., *South Asian Politics and Religion* (Princeton, 1966), pp. 453–54. This volume, edited by D. E. Smith, contains two informative essays by the latter on the politics of Buddhist resurgence in Ceylon (hereafter cited as Smith, *op. cit.*).
40. For a brief biographical sketch of Bandaranaike see D. B. Dhanapala, *Among Those Present* (Colombo, 1962), pp. 60–81; see also Wriggins *op. cit.*, pp. 110–11, 119–21 for some important additional details.
41. Cf. B. H. Farmer, "Politics in Ceylon," in Saul Rose, ed., *Politics in Southern Asia* (New York, 1963), p. 61.
42. Sir William Ivor Jennings, *Nationalism and Political Development in Ceylon* (New York, 1950), p. 14.
43. W. Howard Wriggins, "Impediments to Unity in New Nations: The Case of Ceylon," *American Political Science Review* LV (1961): 316. For a careful study of the political ramifications of the language issue see Robert N. Kearney, *Communalism and Language in the Politics of Ceylon* (Durham, N.C., 1967).
44. Smith, *op. cit.*, p. 23.
45. *Bauddha Peramuna*, March 28, 1956, cited by I. D. S. Weerawardana, *Ceylon General Election 1956* (Colombo, 1960), p. 121 (hereafter cited as Weerawardana, *Election 1956*).
46. Wriggins, *Ceylon*, p. 194.
47. For a discussion of village Buddhism and the role of the Sangha see Bryce Ryan, *Sinhalese Village* (Coral Gables, Florida, 1958), pp. 90–96; Wriggins, *Ceylon*, pp. 39–40, 182–84; Bechert, *op. cit.*, pp. 221–24.
48. I. D. S. Weerawardana, "General Elections in Ceylon, 1952," *The Ceylon Historical Journal* II (1952): 129.
49. Wriggins, *Ceylon*, pp. 342–43; Bechert, *op. cit.*, p. 321.
50. Smith, *op. cit.*, p. 490.
51. *Ceylon Daily News*, February 11, 1956, p. 1.
52. Weerawardana, *Election 1956*, p. 144; Wriggins, *Ceylon*, p. 198.
53. *Ceylon Daily News*, February 27, 1956, pp. 3 and 7.
54. *Ibid.*, February 27, 1956, p. 9.
55. Weerawardana, *Election 1956*, pp. 146–47.
56. Smith, *op. cit.*, p. 493.
57. Weerawardana, *Election 1956*, pp. 147–49.
58. Smith, *op. cit.*, pp. 494–95. Smith also gives interesting biographical details on pp. 490–92.
59. Wriggins, *Ceylon*, p. 347.
60. *Ceylon Daily News*, March 12, 1956, p. 3.
61. *Ibid.*, March 24, 1956, p. 1.

62. *Ibid.*, March 26, 1956, p. 1.
63. Weerawardana, *Election 1956*, pp. 233–34.
64. *Ceylon Daily News*, April 21, 1956, pp. 1, 6, 7.
65. *Ibid.*, April 13, 1956, p. 1.
66. *Ceylon Today* V, no. 4 (April 1956): 5.
67. Cited by Weerawardana, *Election 1956*, p. 67.
68. Wriggins, *Ceylon*, pp. 260–62.
69. *Ceylon Daily News*, June 4, 1956, p. 5.
70. Wriggins, *American Political Science Review* LV (1961): 319.
71. *Ceylon Daily News*, July 30, 1956, p. 5.
72. Smith, *op. cit.*, p. 495.
73. *Times of Ceylon*, March 24, 1957, cited by Wriggins, *Ceylon*, p. 207.
74. *Ceylon Daily News*, July 21, 1956, p. 1.
75. *Ibid.*, July 26, 1957, p. 1; Wriggins, *Ceylon*, pp. 265–66.
76. *Ceylon Daily News*, September 16, 1957, p. 3.
77. *Ibid.*, July 27, 1957, p. 5.
78. *Ibid.*, October 4, 1957, p. 1; October 5, 1957, p. 1.
79. Ceylon, House of Representatives, *Parliamentary Debates (Hansard)*, vol. XXXI (1958–59), col. 30 (hereafter cited as Ceylon, *Hansard*). See also *Ceylon Daily News*, April 10, 1958, p. 1.
80. The figures are those given by Wriggins, *Ceylon*, pp. 268–69. The government gave the figure of 159 deaths whereas the opposition alleged a far higher number of victims.
81. Cited by Bechert, *op. cit.*, p. 330.
82. *Ibid.*, p. 329.
83. Tarzie Vittachi, *Emergency '58: The Story of the Ceylon Race Riots* (London, 1958), pp. 49 and 38.
84. Ernst Benz, *Buddhism or Communism: Which Holds the Future of Asia?* trans. Richard and Clara Winston (Garden City, N.Y., 1965), p. 42.
85. Speech on September 18, 1958, Ceylon, *Hansard* XXXIII (1958–59): 274.
86. Speech on June 4, 1958, Ceylon, *Hansard* XXXI (1958–59): 27.
87. *Ceylon Daily News*, July 8, 1958, p. 1.
88. Bechert, *op. cit.*, p. 332.
89. Ceylon, *Hansard* XXXI (1958–59): 2080.
90. Wriggins, *Ceylon*, p. 269.
91. Bechert, *op. cit.*, p. 331.
92. Speech on February 27, 1959, Ceylon, *Hansard* XXXIV (1958–59): 1452.
93. Bechert, *op. cit.*, p. 335.
94. *Times of Ceylon*, February 2, 1959, cited by Bechert, *op. cit.*, p. 336.
95. Ceylon, *Hansard* XXX (1957–58): 3893–3894.
96. Smith, *op. cit.*, p. 498; Bechert, *op. cit.*, p. 336.
97. *The Queen v. Mapitigama Buddharakkhita Thera and 2 Others,*

63 *New Law Reports* (1962), 450 (hereafter cited as *The Queen v. Buddharakkhita*); see also Smith, *op. cit.*, p. 498.

98. *Ceylon Daily News*, May 20, 1959, p. 3.

99. *Ibid.*, June 9, 1959, p. 4.

100. *Ceylon Today* VIII, no. 9 (September 1959): 2.

101. *The Queen v. Buddharakkhita*, 440.

102. For a detailed account of the trial see Lucian G. Weeramantry, *Assassination of a Prime Minister: The Bandaranaike Murder Case* (Geneva, 1969).

103. *Report . . . by the Commission . . . of Inquiry . . . into . . . the Assassination of the Late Prime Minister . . . Bandaranaike* (Sessional Papers III—1965. Colombo, 1965), p. 11.

104. Smith, *op. cit.*, p. 499.

105. Bechert, *op. cit.*, p. 345.

106. Sinnappah Arasaratnam, *Ceylon* (Englewood Cliffs, N.J., 1964), p. 34.

107. This point is well made by E. F. C. Ludowyk, *The Story of Ceylon* (London, 1962), p. 309. See also the discussion in Bechert, *op. cit.*, pp. 338–41.

108. "Human Rights in Ceylon," *Bulletin of the International Commission of Jurists*, no. 10 (January 1960): 6.

109. *Ceylon Daily News*, October 3, 1959, p. 8.

110. Bechert, *op. cit.*, p. 77.

111. *Ibid.*, pp. 280–81; Smith, *op. cit.*, pp. 501–502.

112. H. A. C. Wickremaratne, "The Buddha Yayanti and Sentimentality," *The Buddhist* XXX, 1 (1959–60): Vesak 2503, p. 94, cited by Bechert, *op. cit.*, p. 70.

113. "Divergent Views on the Sasana Report," *World Buddhism* VIII, no. 6 (January 1960): 11.

114. *Loc. cit.*

115. "Congress Calls for Buddhist Government," *ibid.*, p. 12.

116. A. J. Wilson, "Buddhism in Ceylon Politics: 1960–1965" in D. E. Smith, *op. cit.*, pp. 510–11; Bechert, *op. cit.*, pp. 165–66.

117. *Ceylon Daily News*, February 5, 1960, p. 5.

118. *Ibid.*, January 23, 1960, p. 7.

119. Wilson, *op. cit.*, pp. 513–14.

120. For a careful analysis of the 1960 elections see Surindar Suri, "Umschwung in Ceylon: Die Gegenrevolution der Wahlzettel," *Politische Vierteljahrsschrift* VII (1966): 234–35. See also Calvin A. Woodward, *The Growth of a Party System in Ceylon* (Providence, R.I., 1969), pp. 140–57.

121. See the detailed discussion in Smith, *op. cit.*, pp. 482–87.

122. Cf. Robert N. Kearney, "The New Political Crises of Ceylon," *Asian Survey* II, no. 4 (June 1962): 21–22.

123. Wilson in Smith, *op. cit.*, p. 523. Bechert, *op. cit.*, p. 303, gives 1963 as the founding date of the new Mettananda organization.

124. *Ceylon Observer*, July 27, 1961, cited by Smith, *op. cit.*, p. 506.

125. *Ibid.*, p. 507.
126. Bechert, *op. cit.*, p. 350.
127. Wilson in Smith, *op. cit.*, p. 525; Bechert, *op. cit.*, pp. 354–55.
128. *Ceylon News*, November 26, 1964, p. 1, cited by Bechert, *op. cit.*, p. 299.
129. *Ceylon News*, December 3, 1964, p. 3, quoted in *ibid.*, p. 358.
130. *Ceylon News*, December 12, 1964, p. 6, quoted in *ibid.*, p. 359.
131. *Ceylon News*, December 24, 1964, p. 4 quoted in *ibid.*, p. 359.
132. *Ceylon Daily News*, November 30, 1964, cited by Wilson in Smith, *op. cit.*, p. 526.
133. *Ibid.*, pp. 246–47.
134. *Sun*, April 10, 1965, cited by Wilson in Smith, *op. cit.*, p. 530.
135. Robert N. Kearney, "Ceylon: Political Stresses and Cohesion," *Asian Survey* VIII (1968): 107.
136. A similar conclusion is reached by S. Arasaratnam, "Communalism and Nationalism in Ceylon," in Philip Mason, ed., *India and Ceylon: Unity and Diversity* (London, 1967), p. 277.
137. Cf. Suri, *op. cit.*, p. 251.
138. After a long trial that lasted from January 1968 to January 1970 all of the twenty-two accused were acquitted. Cf. *Ceylon Daily News*, January 3, 1970, p. 1.
139. "Should Buddhist Monks Participate in Politics?" *World Buddhism* XII, no. 10 (May 1964): 23.
140. *Loc. cit.*

CHAPTER 20

1. Cited by John J. Considine, *The Church in the New Latin America* (Notre Dame, Ind., 1964), p. 42.
2. Paul E. Sigmund, "Latin American Catholicism's Opening to the Left," *Review of Politics* XXXV (1973): 63.
3. The remark is reported by Norman Gall in an illuminating article, "Latin America: The Church Militant," *Commentary* XLI, no. 4 (April 1970): 37.
4. Cf. Rosemary Radford Ruether, *The Radical Kingdom: The Western Experience of Messianic Hope* (New York, 1970), pp. 86–91.
5. Richard Shaull, *Encounter with Revolution* (New York, 1955), pp. 83–85.
6. Richard Shaull, "Revolutionary Change in Theological Perspective," in John C. Bennett, ed., *Christian Social Ethics in the Changing World* (New York, 1966), p. 33 (hereafter cited as Shaull, "Revolutionary Change").
7. Johann Baptist Metz, "Church and Society in the Light of a Political Theology" (Paper delivered at the Colloquium on "Religion and the Modern World: Jewish and Christian Perspectives," St. Meinrad, Indiana, March 25–28, 1968), pp. 5–6.
8. *Ibid.*, p. 9.

9. Jürgen Moltmann, *Religion, Revolution and the Future*, trans. M. Douglas Meeks (New York, 1969), p. 139.
10. *Ibid.*, p. 104.
11. C. Jaime Snoeck, "The Third World, Revolution and Christianity," *Concilium* V, no. 2 (May 1966): 20.
12. *Ibid.*, p. 21.
13. Jan Milic Lochman, *Church in a Marxist Society: A Czechoslovak View* (New York, 1970), p. 106. See also his essay "Ecumenical Theology of Revolution," in Martin E. Marty and Dean G. Peerman, eds., *New Theology No. 6* (New York, 1969).
14. "A Theological Understanding of Revolution—Report of the Group for Theological Questions," *Christian Peace Conference* nos. 22–23 (January 1967): 52.
15. Jacques Ellul, *Violence: Reflections from a Christian Perspective*, trans. Cecelia Gaul Kings (New York, 1969), p. 67.
16. *Ibid.*, p. 147.
17. Shaull, "Revolutionary Change," p. 35.
18. Snoeck, *op. cit.*, p. 23. See also Arthur G. Gish, *The New Left and Christian Radicalism* (Grand Rapids, Mich., 1970), p. 142; Bernard Häring, *A Theology of Protest* (New York, 1970), p. 19.
19. Ellul, *op. cit.*, p. 24.
20. Paul Ramsey, *Who Speaks for the Church?* (Nashville, Tenn., 1967), pp. 20–21.
21. *Ibid.*, pp. 76–77.
22. Richard Shaull, "Christian Faith as Scandal in a Technocratic World," in Marty and Peerman, *op. cit.*, p. 126.
23. *Ibid.*, p. 9.
24. Gall, *op. cit.*, p. 25.
25. Marcio Moreira Alves, *O Cristo do povo* (Rio de Janeiro, 1968), p. 37.
26. Ivan Vallier, *Catholicism, Social Control and Modernization in Latin America* (Englewood Cliffs, N.J., 1970), p. 131.
27. Cf. Thomas G. Sanders, "Catholicism and Development: The Catholic Left in Brazil," in Kalman H. Silvert, ed., *Churches and States: The Religious Institution and Modernization* (New York, 1967), p. 86.
28. Charles Wagley, "The Brazilian Revolution: Social Changes since 1930," in Richard N. Adams et al., *Social Change in Latin America Today* (New York, 1960), p. 188.
29. Sanders, *op. cit.*, p. 88.
30. For a concise discussion of the "personalism" of Mounier see Roy Pierce, *Contemporary French Political Thought* (London, 1966), ch. 3.
31. The influence of Vaz is elucidated in Emanuel de Kadt, *Catholic Radicals in Brazil* (London, 1970), pp. 88–90.
32. Cf. Thomas E. Skidmore, *Politics in Brazil, 1930–1964* (London, 1967), pp. 279–80.

33. Sanders, *op. cit.*, p. 96.
34. Selections from the Basic Document of AP are printed in Paul E. Sigmund, ed., *Models of Political Change in Latin America* (New York, 1970), pp. 127–32 (quotation p. 132).
35. De Kadt, *op. cit.*, p. 83.
36. *Ibid.*, pp. 127 and 134.
37. The radicalizing role of MEB is stressed by Candido Mendes in his book on the Brazilian Catholic Left, *Memento dos vivos* (Rio de Janeiro, 1966).
38. De Kadt, *op. cit.*, p. 103. See also Thomas G. Sanders, "The Paulo Freire Method," *American Universities Field Staff Reports, West Coast South America Series*, vol. XV, no. 1 (1968) and the English language edition of the educator's major work, *Pedagogy of the Oppressed* (New York, 1970).
39. Cited by de Kadt, *op. cit.*, p. 159.
40. Cf. David E. Mutchler, "Roman Catholicism in Brazil: A Study of Church Behavior under Stress," *Studies in Comparative International Development* I (1965): 112. The allegation that the organization of Catholic rural unions received financial support from the U.S. Central Intelligence Agency is made by Joseph A. Page, *The Revolution that Never Was: Northeast Brazil, 1955–1964* (New York, 1972), p. 155.
41. De Kadt, *op. cit.*, pp. 113–14.
42. Gall, *op. cit.*, p. 29.
43. Cited by de Kadt, *op. cit.*, p. 191. The full text is reprinted in *Paz e Terra*, no. 6 (April 1968): 160–62.
44. These are the words of a pastoral letter issued by 13 bishops of the Second Northeast Region in July 1966, led by Bishop Câmara. Cf. "Bishops and Workers," in Richard Graham, ed., *A Century of Brazilian History since 1865* (New York, 1969), p. 194.
45. José de Broucker, *Dom Helder Câmara: The Violence of a Peacemaker*, trans. Herma Briffoult (Maryknoll, N.Y., 1970), p. 12.
46. "Violence—The Only Way?" in Sigmund, *op. cit.*, p. 147.
47. *Ibid.*, p. 147.
48. *Ibid.*, p. 148. Another translation of this talk can be found in Helder Câmara, *The Church and Colonialism: The Betrayal of the Third World*, trans. William McSweeney (Denville, N.J., 1969), pp. 101–11.
49. Joseph A. Page, "The Little Priest who stands up to Brazil's Generals," *New York Times Magazine*, May 23, 1971, p. 84.
50. Antonio Batista Fragoso, "Evangelo y justicia social," *Cuadernos de Marcha* XVII (September 1968): 14. A French translation of this statement can be found in Alain Gheerbrant, *L'Église rebelle d'Amerique latine* (Paris, 1969), pp. 155–70.
51. Broucker, *op. cit.*, p. 45.
52. De Kadt, *op. cit.*, p. 272.
53. *Ibid.*, p. 273.

666

Notes to Pages 519–526

54. These figures are given by Broucker, *op. cit.*, p. 31.
55. De Kadt, *op. cit.*, p. 274.
56. For an account of this persecution from the pen of a Brazilian journalist see the book of Mario Moreira Alves, *op. cit.*
57. Cf. the report on torture in Brazil in *The Review of the International Commission of Jurists* no. 6 (April–June 1971): 5–8.
58. Ronald M. Schneider, *The Political System of Brazil: Emergence of a "Modernizing" Authoritarian Regime, 1964–1970* (New York, 1971), pp. 315–16.
59. The above biographical sketch is based on Germán Guzman, *Camilo Torres*, trans. John D. Ring (New York, 1969) and the Introduction by John Gerassi to *Revolutionary Priest: The Complete Writings and Messages of Camilo Torres* (New York, 1971).
60. Vallier, *op. cit.*, p. 141.
61. Cf. Robert H. Dix, *Colombia: The Political Dimensions of Change* (New Haven, Conn., 1967), pp. 316–17.
62. *Ibid.*, p. 318.
63. *Revolutionary Writings*, trans. Robert Olsen and Linda Day (New York, 1969), p. 105. A compilation of the writings of Torres in Spanish was published by the Intercultural Center for Documentation (CIDOC), organized by Ivan Illich in Cuervanaca, Mexico, as no. 5 in the series *Sondeos* in 1966.
64. Quoted in Guzman, *op. cit.*, p. 68.
65. *Ibid.*, pp. 104–105.
66. *Ibid.*, p. 76.
67. Quoted in *ibid.*, p. 130.
68. *El Tiempo*, June 25, 1965, in *Revolutionary Writings*, pp. 163–64.
69. Quoted in Guzman, *op. cit.*, pp. 137–38.
70. *Ibid.*, pp. 291–92.
71. *Revolutionary Writings*, pp. 174–75.
72. Quoted in Guzman, *op. cit.*, pp. 239–42.
73. Gall, *op. cit.*, p. 34.
74. Quoted in Gerassi, *Revolutionary Priest*, p. 56.
75. Dix, *op. cit.*, p. 362.
76. Vallier, *op. cit.*, p. 125.
77. *New York Times*, January 23, 1972, p. 18.
78. Joan E. Garcés, "Structural Obstacles to the Development of Revolutionary Political Forces in Colombia," *Government and Opposition* VI (1971): 330.
79. *The National Catholic Reporter*, January 31, 1968, p. 5. See also Francis X. Gannon, "Catholicism, Revolution and Violence in Latin America: Lessons of the 1968 Guatemala Maryknoll Episode," *Orbis* XII (1969): 1204–25.
80. Quoted by Gerassi, *Revolutionary Priest*, p. 49.
81. "The Final Document of the First Encounter of Christians for

Socialism," cited by Thomas E. Quigley, "Christians for Socialism," *Worldview* XV, no. 8 (August 1972): 45.

82. Heinrich Werner, ed., *Christen und Revolution: Konvergenz und Theologie* (Cologne, 1971), p. 125.

83. Cf. R. L. Camp, *The Papal Ideology of Social Reform: A Study in Historical Development 1878–1967* (Leiden, 1969), pp. 1–13.

84. "Church Doctrine in Latin America after the Council," in Henry A. Landsberger, ed., *The Church and Social Change in Latin America* (Notre Dame, Ind., 1970), p. 110.

85. De Kadt, *op. cit.*, p. 72.

86. Quoted in *ibid.*, p. 75.

87. Quoted in François Houtart and Émile Pin, *The Church and the Latin American Revolution*, trans. Gilbert Barth (New York, 1965), pp. 216–17.

88. *Ibid.*, p. 217.

89. Quoted in Sigmund, *op. cit.*, p. 150.

90. *Ibid.*, p. 151.

91. *Ibid.*, p. 152.

92. Philip Raine, "The Catholic Church in Brazil," *Journal of Inter-American Studies and World Affairs* XIII (1971): 294; Thomas C. Bruneau, "Brazil's People of God—Prophets or Martyrs?" *America* CXXIV, no. 4 (January 30, 1971): 92.

93. "Gospel and Revolution," in Marty and Peerman, *op. cit.*, p. 248.

94. *Ibid.*, p. 249.

95. CELAM, *La Inglesia en la actual transformación de América Latina a la luz del concilio* (Bogotá, 1968). The translation is that of Thomas G. Sanders, "The Religious Legitimation of Change: The New Latin American Catholicism," in Donald E. Smith, ed., *Religion and Political Modernization* (New Haven, Yale University Press, in press).

96. Quoted in Daniel Abalos, "The Medellín Conference," *Cross Currents* XIX (1969): 125.

97. *Ibid.*, p. 126.

98. *Loc. cit.*

99. *The Pope Speaks* XI–XII (1966–67): 154.

100. The text of this letter is reprinted in Gheerbrant, *op. cit.*, pp. 139–43.

101. Abalos, *op. cit.*, p. 127.

102. *Ibid.*, p. 129.

103. Cf. Kenneth Westhues, "Radical Catholicism in a Pre-Secularized Setting" (Paper presented at the annual meeting of the Association for the Sociology of Religion, New Orleans, Louisiana, August 27, 1972).

104. Abalos, *op. cit.*, pp. 131–32.

105. David E. Mutchler, *The Church as a Political Factor in Latin America* (New York, 1971), p. 133.

106. Guzman, *op. cit.*, p. 71.
107. See the figures quoted in Frederick C. Turner, *Catholicism and Political Development in Latin America* (Chapel Hill, N.C., 1971), pp. 29–30.
108. *Ibid.*, p. 30.
109. Quoted in *ibid.*, p. 147.
110. Ellul, *op. cit.*, p. 153. See also his *Autopsy of Revolution*, trans. Patricia Wolf (New York, 1971).
111. Sanders in Smith, ed., *Religion and Political Modernization* (New Haven, Yale University Press, in press).
112. Quigley, *op. cit.*, p. 48.
113. In his book *Os Christãos e a revolução social*, published in 1963, Paulo de Tarso had justified revolution and violence under certain specified conditions. In an interview with Frederick C. Turner in August 1968, Tarso rejected a violent strategy for Brazil as impractical and counterproductive, and he argued against a Communist alliance. Cf. Turner, *op. cit.*, p. 146.

CHAPTER 21

1. Cf. Anthony Storr, *Human Destructiveness* (London, 1972), pp. 30–31.
2. Michael Barkun, "Law and Social Revolution: Millenarianism and the Legal System," *Law and Society Review* VI (1971): 125.
3. Voltaire to Frederick the Great, January 5, 1767, in *The Portable Voltaire*, ed. Ben Ray Redman (New York, 1949), p. 25.
4. Quoted in C. K. Yang, *Religion in Chinese Society* (Berkeley, Calif., 1961), p. 178.
5. *Ibid.*, p. 254.
6. Polybius, *The Histories*, Bk. vi, ch. 56, trans. Evelyn S. Shuckburgh (London, 1889), pp. 505–506.
7. Niccolo Machiavelli, *The Prince and the Discourses*, Bk. i, chs. 11–12 (New York, 1940), pp. 146 and 150.
8. Joseph de Maistre, "Essay on the Generative Principle of Political Constitutions," in *The Works of Joseph de Maistre*, trans. and ed. Jack Lively (New York, 1965), p. 163.
9. Emile Durkheim, *The Elementary Forms of the Religious Life*, trans. Joseph Ward Swain (New York, 1965), p. 432.
10. *Theologico-Political Treatise*, preface, in *The Chief Works of Benedict de Spinoza*, trans. R. H. M. Elwes (New York, 1951), p. 5.
11. Edward Gibbon, *The History of the Decline and Fall of the Roman Empire* (London, 1903), I: 165.
12. Cf. Ernest B. Koenker, *Secular Salvations: The Rites and Symbols of Political Religions* (Philadelphia, 1965), p. 13.
13. Karl Marx, *Capital: A Critical Analysis of Capitalist Production* (Moscow, 1954), I: 79.
14. Friedrich Engels, Introduction to the English edition of *Socialism:*

Utopian and Scientific, in Karl Marx and Friedrich Engels, On Religion (Moscow, 1957), pp. 310–11.
15. Friedrich Engels, Anti-Dühring, in ibid., p. 146.
16. Karl Marx, "The Communism of the Paper Rheinischer Beobachter," in ibid., pp. 82–83.
17. Cf. Hans Bosse, Marx-Weber-Troeltsch: Religionssoziologie und Marxistische Ideologiekritik (Munich, 1970), pp. 130–32.
18. Karl Marx, "Contribution to the Critique of Hegel's Philosophy of Right," in Marx and Engels, On Religion, p. 42.
19. Friedrich Engels, The Peasant War in Germany, in ibid., pp. 98, 100, and 111.
20. V. I. Lenin, "Socialism and Religion," in Collected Works (Moscow, 1962), X: 83–84.
21. Edmund Burke, Reflections on the French Revolution (London, 1910), pp. 87–88.
22. Y. Milton Yinger, The Scientific Study of Religion (New York, 1970), p. 110.
23. Cf. Eugene Victor Walter, Terror and Resistance: A Study of Political Violence (New York, 1969).
24. Yinger, op. cit., pp. 344–45.
25. Cf. Richard K. Fenn, "Towards a New Sociology of Religion," Journal for the Scientific Study of Religion XI (1972): 16–32.
26. Robert K. Merton, Social Theory and Social Structure, 2nd rev. ed. (New York, 1957), p. 30.
27. Cf. Stanislaw Andreski, The Uses of Comparative Sociology (Berkeley, Calif., 1965), pp. 180–81.
28. Robert Brown, Explanation in Social Science (London, 1963), p. 122.
29. Cf. Charles Y. Glock and Rodney Stark, Religion and Society in Tension (Chicago, 1965), p. 180.
30. Robert N. Bellah, "Civil Religion in America," Daedalus XCVI, no. 1 (Winter 1967): 1–21.
31. I. C. Jarvie, "Theories of Cargo Cults: A Critical Analysis," Oceania XXXIV (1963): 126.
32. Cf. Hugh Stretton, The Political Sciences: General Principles of Selection in Social Science and History (London, 1969), p. 178.
33. Crane Brinton, The Anatomy of Revolution, rev. ed. (New York, 1952), p. 49.
34. Neil J. Smelser, Theory of Collective Behavior (New York, 1966), p. 120.
35. Chalmers Johnson, Revolutionary Change (Boston, 1966), p. 84.
36. Ted Robert Gurr, Why Men Rebel (Princeton, N.J., 1970), p. 121.
37. Lyford P. Edwards, The Natural History of Revolution (Chicago, 1970), p. 91.

CHAPTER 22

1. See *The Sacral Kingship* (Studies in the History of Religions, Supplements to *Numen*, IV; Leiden, 1950) for a detailed survey of divine kingship in many different civilizations. The classic study of ancient Near Eastern conceptions of divine kingship remains Henri Frankfort, *Kingship and the Gods* (Chicago, 1948).
2. Max Weber, *The Sociology of Religion*, trans. Ephraim Fischoff (Boston, 1964), pp. 42–43.
3. Jan Gonda, "A note on Indian Pessimism," in *Studia Varia Carolo Guilielmo Vollgraff* (Amsterdam, 1948), p. 47.
4. S. J. Samartha, *The Hindu View of History: Classical and Modern* (Bangalore, 1959), p. 16.
5. Cf. the necessarily speculative ideas of E. O. James and Paul Radin in *The Sacral Kingship*, pp. 64 and 84. See also Herbert J. Muller, *Freedom in the Ancient World* (London, 1962), pp. 47–61.
6. A. L. Basham, *The Wonder That Was India* (London, 1956), p. 243.
7. Cf. John Plamenatz, *Ideology* (London, 1971), p. 109.
8. Cf. Carlo Antoni, *From History to Sociology*, trans. Hayden V. White (Detroit, 1959), pp. 165–68. Antoni also criticizes, correctly in my view, the static and non-historical character of this aspect of Weber's work. A similar criticism is made by Talcott Parsons in his introduction to Weber's *Sociology of Religion* (Boston, 1964), p. lxiii.
9. James P. Harrison, *The Communists and Chinese Peasant Rebellions* (New York, 1968), p. 70; C. K. Yang, *Religion in Chinese Society* (Berkeley, Calif., 1961), p. 132.
10. Melford E. Spiro, *Buddhism and Society: A Great Tradition and its Burmese Vicissitudes* (New York, 1970), p. 442.
11. St. Augustine, *The City of God*, trans. Marcus Dodd (New York, 1948), Bk. v, chs. 19 and 21.
12. Walter Kaufman, *Critique of Religion and Philosophy* (New York, 1958), p. 152.
13. J. W. Allen, *A History of Political Thought in the Sixteenth Century* (London, 1951), p. 304.
14. Theodore de Bèze, *Du droit des magistrats sur leurs sujets*, in Simon Goulart, ed., *Memoires de l'estat de France sous Charles IX* (Meidelbourg, 1578), II: 488.
15. *Defence of the People of England* in *The Works of John Milton*, ed. Frank Allen Patterson (New York, 1933), VII: 179–81.
16. Cf. Friedrich August von der Heydte, *Die Geburtsstunde des souveränen Staates* (Regensburg, 1952), p. 365, n. 89.
17. G. P. Fedotov, *The Russian Religious Mind* (Cambridge, Mass., 1966), I: 399.

18. Quoted in Martin E. Marty and Dean G. Peerman, eds., *New Theology no. 6* (New York, 1966), p. 248.
19. Encyclical *Immortale Dei*, November 1, 1885, in *The Church Speaks to the Modern World*, ed. Etienne Gilson (Garden City, N.Y., 1954), p. 169.
20. Peter Abélard, *Commentarii super S. Pauli espistolam ad Romanos libri V*, in *Opera*, ed. Victor Cousin (Paris, 1859), II: 322.
21. Cited by Iain H. Murray, *The Puritan Hope: A Study in Revival and the Interpretation of Prophecy* (London, 1971), p. xvii.
22. Donald E. Smith, *Religion and Political Development* (Boston, 1970), p. 145.
23. Cf. I. M. Crombie, "Moral Principles," in Ian T. Ramsey, ed., *Christian Ethics and Contemporary Philosophy* (New York, 1966), pp. 235–36.
24. Gananath Obeysekere, "Theodicy, Sin and Salvation in a Sociology of Buddhism," in E. R. Leach, ed., *Dialectic in Practical Religion* (Cambridge, 1968), pp. 27–28.
25. Cf. Milton Singer, *When a Great Tradition Modernizes: An Anthropological Approach to Indian Civilization* (New York, 1972), p. 404.
26. Manning Nash, *The Golden Road to Modernity: Village Life in Contemporary Burma* (New York, 1965), p. 296.
27. Cf. Robert N. Bellah, ed., *Religion and Progress in Modern Asia* (New York, 1965), editor's epilogue, p. 184.
28. Cf. E. Sarkisyanz, *Buddhist Backgrounds of the Burmese Revolution* (The Hague, 1965), pp. 9 and 151.
29. *From Max Weber*, trans. H. H. Gerth and C. Wright Mills (New York, 1958), p. 291.
30. Singer, *op. cit.*, p. 342.
31. Elie Halévy, *England in 1815*, trans. E. I. Watkin and D. A. Barker, 2nd rev. ed. (London, 1949), p. 425.
32. E. Thompson, *The Making of the English Working Class* (New York, 1964), p. 368.
33. E. J. Hobsbawm, "Methodism and the Threat of Revolution in England," *History Today* VII (1957): 120.
34. Cf. the introduction of Bernard Semmel to Elie Halévy, *The Birth of Methodism in England* (Chicago, 1971), p. 24.
35. Maldwyn Edwards, *After Wesley: A Study of the Social and Political Influence of Methodism in the Middle Period 1791–1849* (London, 1948), p. 141; Robert F. Wearmouth, *Methodism and the Working-Class Movements of England: 1800–1850* (London, 1947), p. 174; Thompson, *op. cit.*, p. 42.
36. Ps. 82:3–4.
37. *Summa Theologica*, IaIIae, qu. 95, art. 2, in Dino Bigongiari, ed., *The Political Ideas of St. Thomas Aquinas* (New York, 1953), p. 58.

38. Lawrence Stone, "The English Revolution," in Robert Forster and Jack P. Greene, eds., *Preconditions of Revolution in Early Modern Europe* (Baltimore, 1970), p. 60.
39. Cf. S. N. Eisenstadt, *The Political Systems of Empires* (New York, 1963), p. 191.
40. Ernst Troeltsch, *The Social Teachings of the Christian Churches*, trans. Olive Wyon (London, 1931), II: 1002 and I: 48.
41. *From Max Weber*, pp. 269–70.
42. Weber, *The Sociology of Religion*, p. 117.

CHAPTER 23

1. Donald E. Smith, *India as a Secular State* (Princeton, N.J., 1963), p. 332.
2. Cf. Kenneth Westhues, "Radical Catholicism in a Pre-Secularized Setting" (Paper presented at the annual meeting of the Association for the Sociology of Religion, New Orleans, Louisiana, August 27, 1972).
3. Cf. Joseph R. Strayer, "The State and Religion: An Exploratory Comparison in Different Cultures. Greece and Rome, the West and Islam," *Comparative Studies in Society and History* I (1958): 42.
4. H. A. R. Gibb, "The Heritage of Islam in the Modern World," *International Journal of Middle East Studies* II (1971): 141.
5. Max Weber, *The Sociology of Religion*, trans. Ephraim Fischoff (Boston, 1964), pp. 235–36.
6. Cf. Hans-Dieter Evers, *Monks, Priests and Peasants: A Study of Buddhism and Social Structure in Central Ceylon* (Leiden, 1972), pp. 16–22.
7. E. E. Y. Hales, *Revolution and Papacy: 1769–1846* (London, 1960), p. 294.
8. *Ibid.*, p. 282.
9. Cf. the author's *The Catholic Church and Nazi Germany* (New York, 1964).
10. Weber, *op. cit.*, pp. 218–19.
11. Donald E. Smith, "Emerging Patterns of Religion and Politics," in Donald E. Smith, ed., *South Asian Politics and Religion* (Princeton, N.J., 1966), p. 22.
12. Donald E. Smith, *Religion and Political Development* (Boston, 1970), p. 277.
13. Cf. Thomas C. Bruneau, "Obstacles to Change in the Church: Lessons from Four Brazilian Dioceses" (Paper presented at the annual meeting of the Association for the Sociology of Religion, New Orleans, Louisiana, August 27, 1972).
14. H. Richard Niebuhr, *The Social Sources of Denominationalism* (New York, 1965), p. 3.
15. Ernst Troeltsch, *The Social Teachings of the Christian Churches*, trans. Olive Wyon (New York, 1960), I: 331–43.

16. Cf. Walter L. Wakefield and Austin P. Evans, eds. *Heresies of the High Middle Ages* (New York, 1969), p. 7.

CHAPTER 24

1. Erik H. Erikson, *Gandhi's Truth: On the Origins of Militant Nonviolence* (New York, 1969), p. 395.
2. Cf. E. Victor Wolfenstein, *The Revolutionary Personality: Lenin, Trotsky, Gandhi* (Princeton, N.J., 1967).
3. Kenneth Keniston, *Young Radicals: Notes on Committed Youth* (New York, 1968), p. 76.
4. Ann Ruth and Dorothy Willner, "The Rise and Role of Charismatic Leaders," *Annals of the American Academy of Political and Social Science* CCCLVIII (1965): 81.
5. Cf. Yonina Talmon, "Pursuit of the Millennium: The Relation between Religion and Social Change," *Archives Européennes de Sociologie* III (1962): 134.
6. Ted Robert Gurr, *Why Men Rebel* (Princeton, N.J., 1970), p. 164; Bruce Mazlish, "Group Psychology and Problems of Contemporary History," *Journal of Contemporary History* III (1968): 172.
7. Patrick Gardiner, *The Nature of Historical Explanation* (London, 1952), p. 110.
8. Stanislaw Andreski, *The Uses of Comparative Sociology* (Berkeley, Calif., 1965), pp. 184-85.

CHAPTER 25

1. Stanislaw Andreski, *The Uses of Comparative Sociology* (Berkeley, Calif., 1965), p. 180.
2. Cf. Fred von der Mehden, *Religion and Nationalism in Southeast Asia* (Madison, Wisc., 1963), pp. 10-13; Donald E. Smith, *Religion and Politics in Burma* (Princeton, N.J., 1965), pp. 82-86.
3. Donald E. Smith, *Religion and Political Development* (Boston, 1970), p. 247.
4. Cf. Melford E. Spiro, *Buddhism and Society: A Great Tradition and its Burmese Vicissitudes* (New York, 1970), pp. 391-92.
5. Cf. S. J. Tambiah, "The Persistence and Transformation of Tradition in Southeast Asia, with Special Reference to Thailand," *Daedalus* CII, no. 1 (Winter 1973): 69-74. See also Charles F. Keyes, "Buddhism and National Integration in Thailand," *Journal of Asian Studies* XXX (1971): 551-67.
6. Cf. Charles Anderson et al., *Issues of Political Development* (Englewood Cliffs, N.J., 1967), p. 57.
7. Thomas O'Dea, *The Sociology of Religion* (Englewood Cliffs, N.J., 1966), p. 101.
8. Cf. Edward N. Muller, "A Test of a Partial Theory of Potential for Political Violence," *American Political Science Review* LXVI (1972): 928-59.

9. Communication of Tang Tsou in *American Political Science Review* LXI (1967): 1102–103. Tang Tsou commented on Robert C. Tucker's article, "The Deradicalization of Marxist Movements," *ibid*. LXI (1967): 343–58.
10. Edward Shils, *The Intellectuals and the Powers and Other Essays* (Chicago, 1972), p. 294.
11. C. K. Yang, *Religion in Chinese Society* (Berkeley, Calif., 1961), p. 225.
12. Karl Popper, *The Open Society and its Enemies* (Princeton, N.J., 1950), pp. 289–90. See also the more systematic exposition by I. C. Jarvie, *Concepts and Society* (London, 1972), ch. 1: The Logic of the Situation.

CHAPTER 26

1. Peter L. Berger, *The Precarious Vision: A Sociologist Looks at Social Fictions and Christian Faith* (Garden City, N.Y., 1951), p. 156.
2. Y. Milton Yinger, *The Scientific Study of Religion* (New York, 1970), p. 110.
3. Richard Hooker, *Of the Laws of Ecclesiastical Polity*, Preface (London, 1954), I: 139.
4. Christopher Dawson, *Religion and Culture* (New York, 1948), p. 126.
5. Cf. Quentin Gibson, *The Logic of Social Enquiry* (London, 1969), pp. 140–44.
6. Neil J. Smelser, *The Theory of Collective Behavior* (New York, 1963), pp. 13–19.
7. Clifford Geertz, "Ritual and Social Change: A Javanese Example," *American Anthropologist* LIX (1957): 32–55.
8. Cf. Morris R. Cohen, "Causation and its Application to History," *Journal of the History of Ideas* III (1942): 29.
9. Charles Frankel, *The Case for Modern Man* (New York, 1955), p. 192.
10. Harry Eckstein, "Toward the Theoretical Study of Internal War," in Harry Eckstein, ed., *Internal War: Problems and Approaches* (New York, 1964), p. 29.
11. Cf. Arthur C. Danto, *Analytical Philosophy of History* (London, 1965), p. 255.
12. Abraham Kaplan, *The Conduct of Inquiry: Methodology for Behavioral Science* (San Francisco, 1964), pp. 325–26.
13. Eugene J. Meehan, *The Theory and Method of Political Analysis* (Homewood, Ill., 1965), p. 185.
14. Introduction to Lyford P. Edwards, *The Natural History of Revolution* (Chicago, 1970), p. xvii.
15. *The Rights of Man* in *Selected Works of Tom Paine*, ed. Howard Fast (New York, n.d.), p. 181.
16. D. W. Brogan, *The Price of Revolution* (New York, 1966), pp. 266–67.

INDEX

Index

679

Machiavelli, Niccolò, 8, 540-41
McManners, John, 374
Madariaga, Salvador de, 415, 423
Magic: distinguished from reli-
  gion, 4; as "technology," 230
Mahabharata, 13-14, 285, 304
Maha Bodhi Society, 465
Mahajana Eksath Peramuna
  (MEP), 473, 477, 479-80, 482,
  484, 488, 492
Mahayana, 27, 31, 59, 256. See
  also Buddhism
Mahdism: concept of Mahdi, 51;
  in Indonesia, 52; in Niger-Chad
  region, 52, 176, 179, 191; in Sene-
  gal, 52; in Somaliland, 191; in
  the Sudan, 177, 191
Mahinda, 462
Maimonides (Moses ben Maimon),
  81
Maistre, Joseph de, 540-41
Maitreya. See Buddha Maitreya
Maitreya sect, 63-64
Majumdar, R. C., 308, 321
Malawi, 213. See also Nyasaland
Mambu, 225-26
Mamluk dynasty, 48
Manchus. See Ch'ing dynasty
Mandate of Heaven, 14-18, 68, 171,
  247, 550
Manicheism, 64, 243
Mansfeld miners, 112, 115
Mansren myth, 223, 256
Maoris of New Zealand, 204, 254,
  269
Mao Tse-tung, 273
Marat, Jean Paul, 373
Marcuse, Herbert, 274
Maritain, Jacques, 43, 414, 423-24,
  511
Martínez, Luis María (archbishop),
  411
Marxism, 153, 415, 431, 455; and
  the Catholic Left, 512-14, 534-
  35; conception of history, 237,
  272; and medieval heresy, 104-
  6; and religion, 541-42, 562; as
  secularized millenarianism, 237,
  272-73
Marx, Karl, 10, 272-73, 541-42

Masada, 82-86
Mater et Magistra (encyclical),
  514
Mathiez, Albert, 357, 368
Matswa, André, 209-11, 218, 239,
  241, 269
Mattathias the Hasmonean, 71,
  74, 78, 96
Mattys, John, 122-25, 250
Mauriac, François, 423
Maurras, Charles, 43
Maury, Jean Sifrein, 356-57, 366,
  369
Maximilian (archduke of Austria),
  387
Mazeway synthesis, 263
Mazzini, Giuseppe, 279, 289
Mecca, 181
Mede, Joseph, 131
Medellín conference, 530-33
Medina, 44, 180-81
Melanesia. See New Guinea; Cargo
  cults
Melchiorites, 123, 126, 128
Melo, António, 515
Melville, Thomas, 526
Menahem, 82-83
Mencius, 17-18, 171, 550
Mendizabal, Alfredo, 423
Mennonites, 117, 129, 134, 266
Mercy, Marie-Charles-Isidore de
  (bishop), 379
Merit, accumulation of, 28, 325,
  551, 567
Merton, Robert K., 545
Messiah ben Joseph, 93
Messiah, concept of: in Buddhism,
  28, 254-55; in Christianity, 38-
  39, 252-53; in Hinduism, 254;
  in Islam, 51; in Judaism, 33, 81,
  92-93; in Taoism, 256
Messianic associations (Burma),
  255-56
Messianic woes, 73, 78, 84, 103, 121,
  242, 249, 264, 558
Messianism. See Millenarianism
Mestre, Eduardo, 394
Methodism, 198, 570; and social
  unrest in England, 558-60; and
  Halévy thesis, 559